Purchasing Power Parities and the Size of World Economies

Purchasing Power Parities and the Size of World Economies

Results from the 2017 International Comparison Program

WORLD BANK GROUP

1 2 3 4 23 22 21 20

ISBN (paper): 978-1-4648-1530-0
ISBN (electronic): 978-1-4648-1531-7
DOI: 10.1596/978-1-4648-1530-0

Cover image and design: Jomo Tariku/World Bank Group

The Library of Congress Control Number has been requested.

Contents

Foreword ix

Acknowledgments xi

Abbreviations xiii

Chapter 1 **Overview of main findings** 1

- Size of economies 1
- GDP expenditure components 2
- Per capita measures 6
- Intercountry income inequality 7
- Price levels 9
- Variability across economies 11
- Comparison of 2017 results with revised 2011 results 14

Chapter 2 **ICP 2017 results** 17

- Tables of 2017 results 17
- Survey framework 19

Chapter 3 **Purchasing power parities and real expenditures** 63

- Concepts and definitions 63
- Use and applications of PPPs and real expenditures 67

Chapter 4 **Governance and organization** 73

- Governance of ICP 2017 73
- Regional and national organization 74

Chapter 5 **Methodology** 77

- Conceptual framework 78
- Expenditure data 78
- Price data 79
- PPP calculation and estimation 81

Chapter 6 **Looking forward** 87

Appendix A **History of the International Comparison Program** 89

Appendix B **The ICP's governance framework** 95

- The ICP's governance structure 95
- The roles and responsibilities of the ICP governance bodies 95

Appendix C **ICP expenditure classification** **101**

2017 ICP expenditure classification structure 101
Main aggregates 102
Deriving actual individual consumption 102
Facilitating the input price approach 103
Adjusting household expenditure to the national concept 103
Updates introduced for the 2017 ICP expenditure classification 103

Appendix D **Reference PPPs used in ICP 2017** **115**

Appendix E **Revised 2011 results and comparisons with original ICP 2011 results** **119**

Appendix F **Comparison of ICP 2017 results with World Development Indicators data** **167**

Appendix G **ICP research agenda** **179**

Appendix H **ICP data access and archive policy** **181**

Background 181
Data access objectives 182
Guiding principles 182
Procedures for archiving data 183
Procedures for accessing data 184

Appendix I **ICP revision policy** **185**

Background 185
Triggers for revising ICP indicators 185
Guidelines for revising ICP indicators 186
Timing and communication of revisions 187

Appendix J **Classification of the world's economies** **189**

Glossary **195**

References **207**

Boxes

3.1 Using market exchange rates and PPPs to convert to a common currency 64

3.2 Use of purchasing power parities 70

4.1 ICP 2017 cycle: Participating economies, by region 75

Figures

1.1 Share of global PPP-based and market exchange rate–based GDP and share of global population, by region and income group, 2017 2

1.2 PPP-based GDP and share of global PPP-based GDP, by economy, 2017 3

1.3 Share of PPP-based global actual individual consumption for the six economies with the largest shares, 2017 4

1.4 Share of global PPP-based expenditure on selected expenditure components of actual individual consumption, by region and income group, 2017 4

1.5 Nominal expenditure on selected expenditure components of actual individual consumption as a share of nominal GDP, by region and income group, 2017..... 5

1.6 Share of PPP-based global consumption expenditure by government for the six economies with the largest shares, 2017 5

1.7 Share of PPP-based global gross fixed capital formation for the six economies with the largest shares, 2017 5

1.8 Index of PPP-based GDP per capita and share of global population, by economy, 2011 and 2017........ 6

1.9 PPP-based actual individual consumption per capita and share of global population, by economy, 2017 7

1.10 PPP-based GDP per capita and actual individual consumption per capita for the 12 economies with the highest PPP-based GDP per capita, 2017............ 8

1.11 Index of PPP-based expenditure per capita for GDP and major expenditure components, by region and income group, 2017........ 8

1.12 Lorenz curves for the distributions of 2017, revised 2011, and original 2011 PPP-based GDP per capita........ 9

1.13 Lorenz curves for the distributions of 2017, revised 2011, and original 2011 PPP-based actual individual consumption per capita 9

1.14 GDP price level index versus PPP-based GDP per capita (and PPP-based GDP), by economy, 2017 and 2011........ 10

1.15 Price level indexes for GDP and major expenditure components, by region and income group, 2017........ 11

1.16 Price level indexes for GDP and 17 expenditure components, by region, 2017........ 12

1.17 Coefficients of variation: Index of PPP-based expenditure per capita and price level index for GDP and 17 expenditure components, by region, 2017.... 13

1.18 Share of global PPP-based and market exchange rate–based GDP and share of global population, by region and income group, 2011 and 2017.................. 14

1.19 Index of PPP-based expenditure per capita for GDP and major expenditure components, by region and income group, 2011 and 2017 15

1.20 Price level indexes for GDP and major expenditure components, by region and income group, 2011 and 2017........ 16

4.1 ICP governance structure........ 74

B.1 ICP governance structure........ 96

Tables

2.1 Gross domestic product (GDP): ICP 2017 results 20

2.2 Actual individual consumption (AIC): ICP 2017 results........ 26

2.3 Individual consumption expenditure by households: ICP 2017 results............. 32

2.4 Consumption expenditure by government: ICP 2017 results........ 38

2.5 Gross fixed capital formation (GFCF): ICP 2017 results........ 44

2.6 Domestic absorption: ICP 2017 results ... 50
2.7 Gross domestic product (GDP) and individual consumption expenditure by households for nonparticipating economies: ICP 2017 results ... 56
2.8 ICP 2017 Individual consumption expenditure by households, survey framework ... 57
C.1 Structure of the ICP expenditure classification, ICP 2017 ... 102
C.2 Expenditure classification, ICP 2017 ... 104
D.1 ICP 2017 Reference PPPs ... 116
E.1 Gross domestic product (GDP): Revised ICP 2011 results ... 120
E.2 Actual individual consumption (AIC): Revised ICP 2011 results ... 126
E.3 Individual consumption expenditure by households: Revised ICP 2011 results ... 132
E.4 Consumption expenditure by government: Revised ICP 2011 results ... 138
E.5 Gross fixed capital formation (GFCF): Revised ICP 2011 results ... 144
E.6 Domestic absorption: Revised ICP 2011 results ... 150
E.7 Gross domestic product (GDP) and individual consumption expenditure for nonparticipating economies: Revised ICP 2011 results ... 156
E.8 Gross domestic product: Comparison of revised ICP 2011 results with original ICP 2011 results ... 157
E.9 Individual consumption expenditure by households: Comparison of revised ICP 2011 results with original ICP 2011 results ... 162
F.1 Gross domestic product (GDP): Comparison of ICP 2017 results with data in World Development Indicators ... 168
F.2 Individual consumption expenditure by households: Comparison of ICP 2017 results with data in World Development Indicators ... 173
J.1 Economies in East Asia and Pacific, classified by ICP 2017 administrative region and World Bank fiscal year 2020 income group ... 190
J.2 Economies in Europe and Central Asia, classified by ICP 2017 administrative region and World Bank fiscal year 2020 income group ... 191
J.3 Economies in Latin America and the Caribbean, classified by ICP 2017 administrative region and World Bank fiscal year 2020 income group ... 192
J.4 Economies in Middle East and North Africa, classified by ICP 2017 administrative region and World Bank fiscal year 2020 income group ... 193
J.5 Economies in North America, classified by ICP 2017 administrative region and World Bank fiscal year 2020 income group ... 193
J.6 Economies in South Asia, classified by ICP 2017 administrative region and World Bank fiscal year 2020 income group ... 193
J.7 Economies in Sub-Saharan Africa, classified by ICP 2017 administrative region and World Bank fiscal year 2020 income group ... 194

Foreword

As this report goes to publication, our planet is in the midst of the COVID-19 pandemic, with countries facing costs to both lives and livelihoods. This report presents the latest results from the International Comparison Program's (ICP) 2017 cycle and provides a view of the global economy prior to the emergence of this pandemic. The ICP 2017 results will serve as a crucial benchmark of the pre-COVID-19 size of the world economies from which to measure the economic impact on various countries across the globe.

In 2017, the United States and China were the two largest economies in the world and together accounted for a third of the global economy. India, the third largest economy, accounted for around 7 percent of global gross domestic product (GDP). The global economy, when measured using purchasing power parities (PPPs) rather than market exchange rates, is split more or less equally between high-income and middle-income economies, with low-income economies contributing just 1 percent of global GDP. The United States remained the economy with the highest level of per capita consumption, at nearly US$45,000 in PPP terms, more than four times the world average. Cross-country inequality persisted, with around three-quarters of the world's population living in economies where the mean per capita income and consumption were below their respective global averages of US$16,596 and US$10,858.

The ICP is a global statistical initiative to collect comparative price and expenditure data and estimate PPPs for the world's economies. PPPs are used in monitoring progress toward the United Nations Sustainable Development Goals—in particular, the goals focusing on poverty and inequality, agriculture, health, education, energy and emissions, labor, and research and development. PPPs are also used in other international indicators of economies' socioeconomic development, such as the World Bank's twin goals of ending extreme poverty and promoting shared prosperity by 2030, the United Nations' human development index, the World Economic Forum's global competitiveness index, the Gates Foundation's Goalkeepers Report, and the International Labour Organization's Global Wage Report, to name a few. The International Bank for Reconstruction and Development and the International Monetary Fund both rely on the GDP in PPP terms of economies to determine their shareholding and drawing rights.

The ICP is globally one of the largest data collection exercises undertaken—176 economies participated in its 2017 cycle. At the same time, it is one of the most enduring—the program celebrated its 50th anniversary in 2018, having grown from a modest research project spearheaded by the United Nations Statistical Division and the International Comparisons Unit of the University of Pennsylvania, supported by financial contributions from the Ford Foundation and the World Bank.

Today the successful execution of the ICP is reliant on the close collaboration of national statistical offices, regional agencies, and international organizations. That partnership, together with a robust governance structure, an extensive capacity-building program, and an ambitious research agenda, ensures that the program and its results remain impactful and relevant to its constituents and users and reflect our ever-changing world and its dynamic economies.

Looking ahead, we anticipate that the ICP will evolve to meet both our users' demands and the challenges of the new decade by reflecting the rapid change in buying habits taking place across the world, not only in what we consume today but also in the outlets and platforms through which we purchase these goods and services, and by complementing traditional surveys with new data sources such as scanner data and web scraping. We also expect participation in the program to increase so that we leave no country behind. This is especially true for countries that are fragile and those that are affected by conflict and violence. We have strived to ensure that these countries partook in ICP 2017 capacity-building activities, and we hope that they will join subsequent ICP cycles.

We would like to thank the participating economies that conducted the extensive surveys and data collections that underlie the PPPs. We thank as well our partners who contributed to the success of ICP 2017—the African Development Bank, the Asian Development Bank, the International Monetary Fund, the Interstate Statistical Committee of the Commonwealth of Independent States, the Organisation for Economic Co-operation and Development, the Statistical Office of the European Union, the United Kingdom's Department for International Development, the United Nations Economic Commission for Latin America and the Caribbean, and the United Nations Economic and Social Commission for Western Asia. Although the responsibility for oversight rested with the ICP Governing Board, the program would not have been a success without the invaluable theoretical, conceptual, and methodological advice of the ICP Technical Advisory Group of renowned experts, chaired by Nobel Laureate Sir Angus Deaton.

The ICP 2017 results are based on the most comprehensive price and national accounts expenditure data available, using the best methods that have been developed to date. We trust that users of the ICP 2017 results will find this report useful and that those results will provide them with a base of crucial information for research in comparative analysis and policy making.

Over time, the ICP has evolved to become a leading "global public good" exercise through the efforts of its worldwide partnership. We are two years into the ICP's second half century, one in which the world is growing more data savvy and more data hungry, and we look forward to PPPs and ICP data entering common parlance and throwing a much-needed spotlight on the economies, big and small, that together make up our global economy.

Mari Elka Pangestu
Managing Director for Development Policy and Partnerships
The World Bank

Acknowledgments

The International Comparison Program (ICP) is one of the world's largest statistical exercises. The 2017 cycle involved a partnership of 176 economies and global, regional, and subregional agencies, working together within the program's governance structure to produce the results presented in this report. These achievements were made possible by the financial support of donors who contributed to funding this cycle. Special thanks go to the International Monetary Fund (IMF) and the United Kingdom's Department for International Development (UK DFID), which contributed to a global Multi-Donor Trust Fund, to the regional development banks and implementing agencies that contributed to funding regional programs, and to the World Bank, which contributed to funding the global program.

The program is managed by the ICP Global Office, located at the World Bank Development Data Group (DECDG), under the leadership of Nada Hamadeh, Program Manager, and the oversight of Haishan Fu, DECDG Director. As the strategic and policy-making body, the ICP Governing Board provides leadership and ensures strict adherence to the program's objectives and strategic lines. The board was co-chaired by Statistics Austria and India's Ministry of Statistics and Programme Implementation.

Thanks are extended to the institutions represented on the board: the African Development Bank (AfDB), the Asian Development Bank (ADB), the Brazilian Institute of Geography and Statistics, the National Statistical Committee of the Republic of Belarus, China's National Bureau of Statistics, the Interstate Statistical Committee of the Commonwealth of Independent States (CIS-STAT), the Statistics Department of the European Union (Eurostat), the Statistics Department of the IMF, the Fiji Bureau of Statistics, the Organisation for Economic Co-operation and Development (OECD), the Kingdom of Saudi Arabia's General Authority for Statistics, the National Agency for Statistics and Demography of Senegal, Statistics South Africa, Suriname's General Bureau of Statistics, UK DFID, the US Bureau of Labor Statistics, the United Nations Economic Commission for Latin America and the Caribbean (UN-ECLAC), the United Nations Economic and Social Commission for Western Asia (UN-ESCWA), the United Nations Statistics Division (UNSD), and the World Bank's DECDG. Thanks are also extended to previous co-chairs of the Governing Board Konrad Pesendorfer, former Director General, Statistics Austria, and T. C. A. Anant, former Chief Statistician of India and Secretary, Ministry of Statistics and Programme Implementation.

The ICP Technical Advisory Group (TAG) deserves special acknowledgment. Under the chairmanship of Nobel Laureate Sir Angus Deaton, technical issues linked to the conceptual integrity and methodological soundness of the program were addressed by the group comprising W. Erwin Diewert, Robert C. Feenstra, Alan Heston, Walter Radermacher, D. Prasada Rao, Pronab Sen, Paul Shreyer, and Xianchun Xu. Over the cycle, the TAG appointed task forces and task teams to undertake specific research topics under its research agenda. Task forces and teams comprised the following experts: Alan Heston, Bettina Aten, Luigi Biggeri, W. Erwin Diewert, Levan Gogoberishvili, Brian Graf, Robert Hill, Robert Inklaar, Massimiliano Iommi, Kaushal Joshi, Patrick Kelly, Francette Koechlin, Paul Konijn, Dilip Kumar Sinha, Vasily Kuznetsov, Gregory Max Henri Legoff, Michel Mouyelo-Katoula, Bala Bhaskar Naidu Kalimili,

Liu Nan, Niall O'Hanlon, D. Prasada Rao, David Roberts, Sergey Sergeev, Majed Skaini, Michael Smedes, and staff of the Global Office.

The results of ICP 2017 were calculated by the group of experts forming the computation task team: Yuri Dikhanov, Alan Heston, Robert Hill, Robert Inklaar, Francette Koechlin, Paul Konijn, D. Prasada Rao, Miriam Steurer, and Sergey Sergeev. Bettina Aten and Eric Figueroa advised on the process for producing the results. Our achievement was made possible by the relentless work of the regional coordinators with their supporting teams: Ben Paul Mungyereza and Gregoire Mboya De Loubassou (AfDB) for Africa; Kaushal Joshi with the support of Criselda de Dios and Stefan Schipper (ADB) for Asia and the Pacific; Andrey Kosarev and Valerica Accibas (CIS-STAT) for the Commonwealth of Independent States; Rolando Ocampo, Giovanni Savio, Bruno Lana, María Paz Collinao, and Federico Dorin (UN-ECLAC) with Philomen Harrison (CARICOM) for Latin America and the Caribbean; and Majed Skaini with the support of Sadim Sbeiti (UN-ESCWA) for Western Asia. The program also relied on close cooperation with Francette Koechlin and Sophie Bournot (OECD) and Paul Konijn and Marjanca Gasic (Eurostat), who led the Eurostat-OECD PPP Programme.

Although the Global Office and the regional coordinators play a crucial role in implementing the ICP, the cornerstone of the program consists of the national implementing agencies, which are responsible for the bulk of ICP activities, from the collection of price data to the compilation of national accounts expenditure data. The 2017 participating economies demonstrated complete commitment and dedication to the ICP. We truly owe them the utmost gratitude and appreciation for the amazing job they did in carrying out rigorous ICP activities over the last few years.

The Global Office team responsible for the day-to-day work comprised Hanan Abushanab, Shriya Chauhan, Rui Costa, Yuri Dikhanov, Nancy Kebe, Maurice Nsabimana, Christelle Signo Kouame, Elizabeth Purdie, Marko Olavi Rissanen, Inyoung Song, William Vigil Oliver, Mizuki Yamanaka, and Zhe Zhao. Several colleagues from other DECDG units provided valuable support to the Global Office, including Jomo Tariku and David Mariano.

This report was drafted by the Global Office team and presents a summary of results for 2017, alongside revised results for 2011. More detailed data for both of these reference years and data for the interim years can be accessed through icp.worldbank.org. It was edited by Elizabeth Purdie and David Roberts. Final editing was done by Elizabeth Forsyth, and proofreading was done by Alfred Imhoff. The cover was designed by Jomo Tariku.

We are grateful to all of the dedicated renowned experts and global, regional, and subregional institutions that contributed their knowledge, expertise, time, and resources to this daunting effort. We particularly recognize the major role played by the national implementing agencies in all 176 participating economies. We all share the credit for the production of this unique global public good.

Pravin Srivastava
Chief Statistician of India and Secretary,
Ministry of Statistics and Programme Implementation

Werner Holzer
Director General–Statistics,
Statistics Austria

Abbreviations

ADB	Asian Development Bank
AfDB	African Development Bank
AFRISTAT	Economic and Statistical Observatory of Sub-Saharan Africa
AIC	actual individual consumption
CAR	country approach with redistribution (procedure)
CARICOM	Caribbean Community
CEP	consumption expenditure of the population
CIS	Commonwealth of Independent States
CIS-STAT	Interstate Statistical Committee of the Commonwealth of Independent States
COFOG	Classification of the Functions of Government
COICOP	Classification of Individual Consumption According to Purpose
COMECON	Council for Mutual Economic Assistance
COMESA	Common Market for Eastern and Southern Africa
COPNI	Classification of the Purposes of Nonprofit Institutions Serving Households
CPA	Statistical Classification of Products by Activity in the European Economic Community
CPD	country product dummy (method)
CPD-W	country product dummy-weighted (method)
CPI	consumer price index
CV	coefficient of variation
DECDG	Development Data Group (World Bank)
DFID	Department for International Development (United Kingdom)
ECOSOC	United Nations Economic and Social Council
Eurostat	Statistical Office of the European Union
FISIM	financial intermediation services indirectly measured
f.o.b.	free on board
FOC	UNSC Friends of the Chair group
GCL	global core list
GDP	gross domestic product
GEKS	Gini-Éltető-Köves-Szulc (method)
GFCF	gross fixed capital formation
GNI	gross national income
IACG	Inter-Agency Coordination Group (ICP)
ICP	International Comparison Program (International Comparison Project prior to 1990)
IMF	International Monetary Fund

ISO	International Organization for Standardization
n.e.c.	not elsewhere classified
NPISHs	nonprofit institution serving households
OECD	Organisation for Economic Co-operation and Development
OEEC	Organisation for European Economic Co-operation
PLI	price level index
PPI	producer price index
PPP	purchasing power parity
SAR	special administrative region
SDGs	Sustainable Development Goals
SHA	System of Health Accounts
SNA	System of National Accounts
SPD	structured product description
TAG	Technical Advisory Group (ICP)
UNESCO	United Nations Educational, Scientific, and Cultural Organization
UNSC	United Nations Statistical Commission
UNSD	United Nations Statistics Division
UNSO	United Nations Statistics Office
UN-ECLAC	United Nations Economic Commission for Latin America and the Caribbean
UN-ESCWA	United Nations Economic and Social Commission for Western Asia
VAT	value added tax
WDI	World Development Indicators
XR	market exchange rate

All dollar amounts are US dollars unless otherwise indicated.

CHAPTER 1

Overview of main findings

Size of economies

In 2017, global output, when measured by purchasing power parities (PPPs), was $119,547 billion, compared with $79,715 billion, when measured by market exchange rates. In both cases, global output refers to the sum of gross domestic product (GDP) for all 176 economies that participated in the International Comparison Program (ICP) 2017 cycle. Figure 1.1 shows the distribution of global output by geographic region and income group and compares PPP-based shares with market exchange rate–based shares, examining these distributions against shares of the global population. It illustrates that, in PPP terms, low- and middle-income economies contributed more than half of the global economy in 2017, a significantly higher share than when measured using market exchange rates.

In 2017 lower-middle-income economies contributed around 16 percent to PPP-based global GDP, while upper-middle-income economies contributed 34 percent. At the same time, high-income economies contributed 49 percent. In terms of market exchange rates, these shares were 8 percent, 28 percent, and 64 percent, respectively. Low-income economies contributed less than 1 percent to the global economy under both measures—namely, 0.8 percent of global GDP in PPP terms and 0.5 percent in market exchange rate terms—despite accounting for nearly 8 percent of the world's population.

East Asia and Pacific accounted for the largest regional share under both measures—just under one-third of global GDP. This economic share was roughly in line with the region's population share of 32 percent. A similar consistency was also seen in Latin America and the Caribbean—the region's share of GDP in PPP terms, GDP in market exchange rate terms, and population were all around 7 to 8 percent of the global total. At the same time, both North America and Europe and Central Asia had economic shares under the two alternative economic measures that far exceeded their population shares, while the converse was true in South Asia and Sub-Saharan Africa. The consequences of these distributions are explored further in the analysis of expenditure per capita.

Figure 1.2 shows, for a given economy, its GDP in 2017 and its share of global GDP, represented by the size of the economy's respective box. Economies are grouped by geographic region, and each color-coded area represents that region's share of global GDP in PPP-based US dollars.

China's GDP stood at $19,617 billion in PPP terms in 2017, while the United States' GDP was $19,519 billion. Together they accounted for one-third of global GDP. India, at $8,051 billion, was the third-largest economy, followed by Japan, Germany, and the Russian Federation. Overall, 19 economies contributed three-quarters of global GDP; three of these economies (India, Indonesia, and the Arab Republic of Egypt) were classified as lower-middle-income economies,

Figure 1.1 Share of global PPP-based and market exchange rate–based GDP and share of global population, by region and income group, 2017

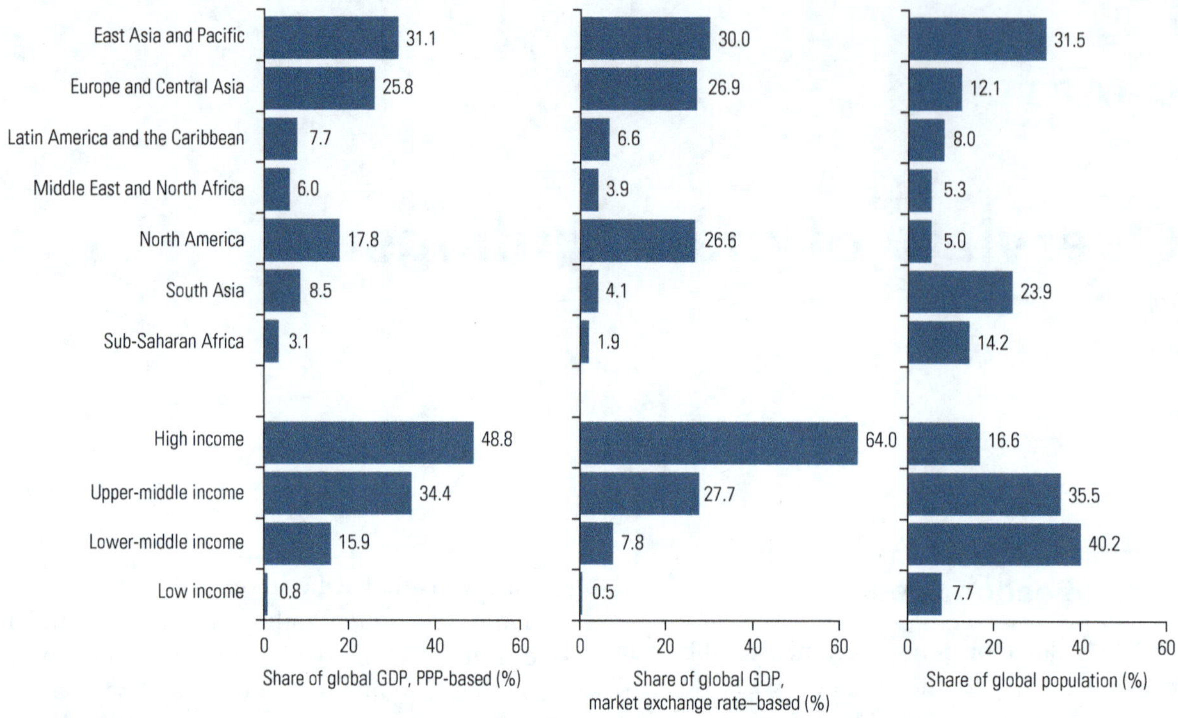

Source: ICP 2017.
Note: PPP = purchasing power parity.

and six (China, the Russian Federation, Brazil, Mexico, Turkey, and the Islamic Republic of Iran) were classified as upper-middle-income economies, with the remainder classified as high-income economies. Together, they represented nearly 64 percent of the global population.

GDP expenditure components

It is also possible to examine the global distribution of the expenditure components of GDP, such as expenditure by households, by government, and on investment.

Figure 1.3 shows the distribution of expenditure on actual individual consumption (AIC), a measure to assess average material well-being, defined as individual consumption expenditure by households, plus individual consumption expenditure by government, plus individual consumption expenditure by nonprofit institutions serving households (NPISHs). The United States accounted for just under one-fifth of AIC across the world. Overall, six economies accounted for around half of all global AIC expenditure. Figure 1.4 provides an overview of the regional and income group distribution of global expenditure for a selection of the expenditure components within AIC, while figure 1.5 shows the share of nominal GDP that is spent on these components in each income group or region.

Of note, Sub-Saharan Africa had a greater share of global expenditure on food and nonalcoholic beverages (8 percent) than its share of global health expenditure (2 percent). This outcome is explained to a large extent by these expenditure components' share of GDP in the region: food and nonalcoholic beverages accounted for nearly 30 percent of GDP, about eight times as much as was spent on health.

Despite high-income economies contributing half of global GDP, the group collectively accounted for around just one-third of global expenditure on food and nonalcoholic beverages and for just over one-third of global spending on actual education. Furthermore, this income group, representing 17 percent of the global population, accounted for more than half of global expenditure on health and allocated more than 10 percent of its collective GDP to that

Figure 1.2 PPP-based GDP and share of global PPP-based GDP, by economy, 2017

2017 PPP $ (billions), and global share (%)

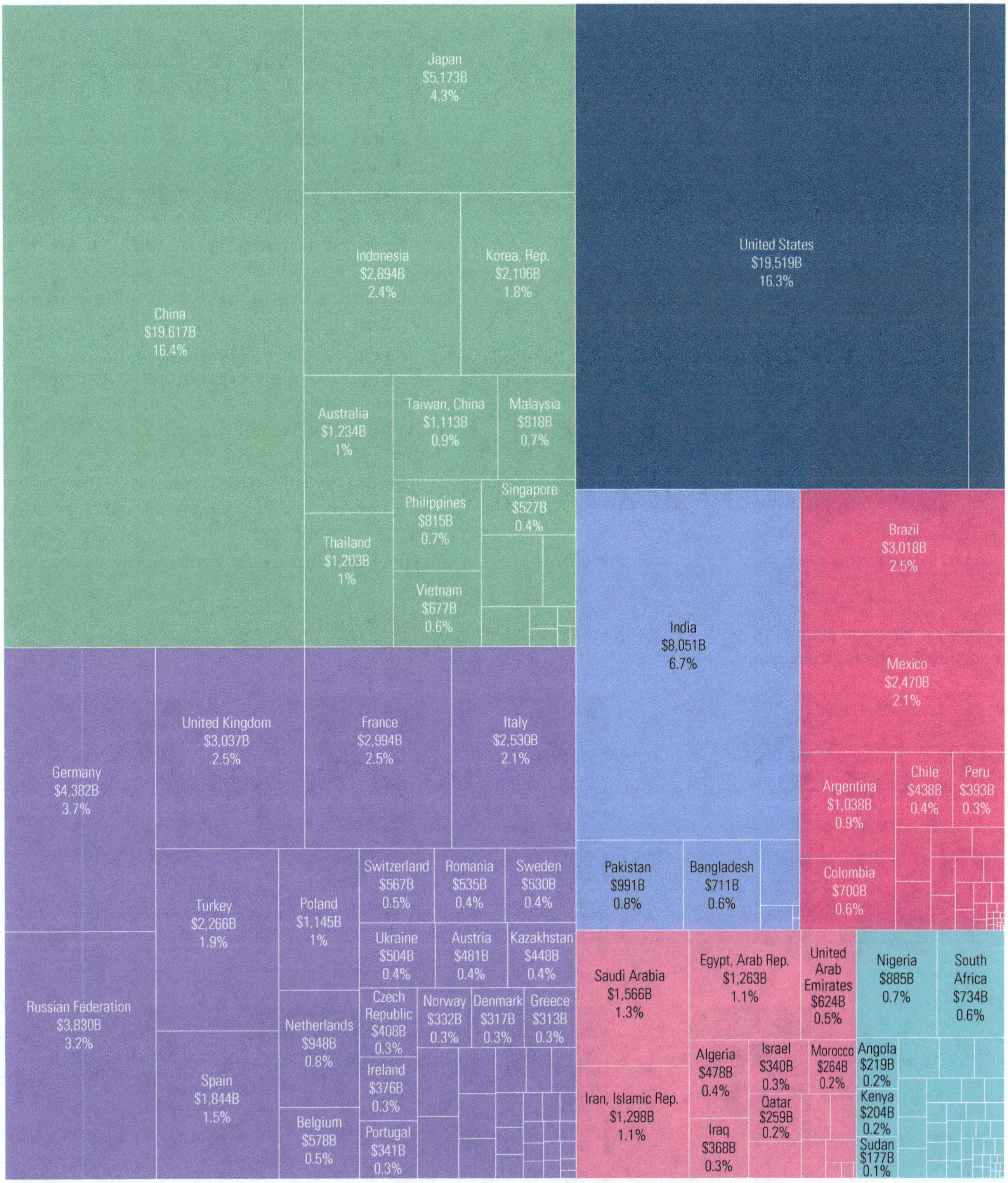

East Asia and Pacific; Europe and Central Asia; Latin America and the Caribbean; Middle East and North Africa; North America; South Asia; Sub-Saharan Africa

Source: ICP 2017.
Note: PPP = purchasing power parity.

Figure 1.3 Share of PPP-based global actual individual consumption for the six economies with the largest shares, 2017

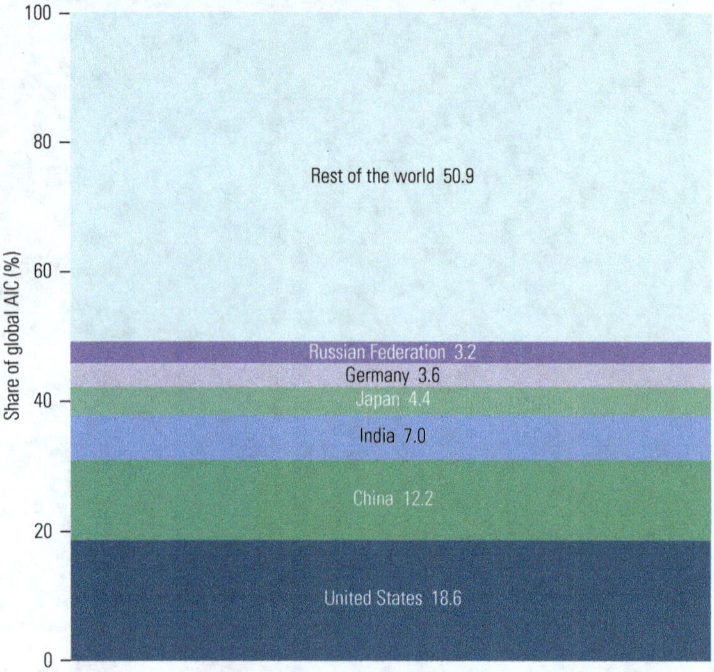

Source: ICP 2017.
Note: AIC = actual individual consumption; PPP = purchasing power parity.

component. Much of this spending was due to the large North American share of global health spending (around one-quarter) and the relatively high cost of health care in the United States (around 80 percent higher than the world average). Price levels of this and other expenditure components are examined later in this chapter.

On average, around 11 percent of GDP was spent on housing and utilities (water, electricity, gas, and other fuels), ranging from nearly 8 percent in Sub-Saharan Africa to nearly 13 percent in Europe and Central Asia and North America. Globally, around 5 percent was spent on education, and there is relatively little variation between regions and income groups for this category of spending (figure 1.5).

Figure 1.6 shows consumption expenditure by government. China had the largest share, accounting for around 14 percent of the global total.

Figure 1.7 shows expenditure on investment as defined by gross fixed capital formation (GFCF). China had by far the largest share of expenditure on investment, nearly double that

Figure 1.4 Share of global PPP-based expenditure on selected expenditure components of actual individual consumption, by region and income group, 2017

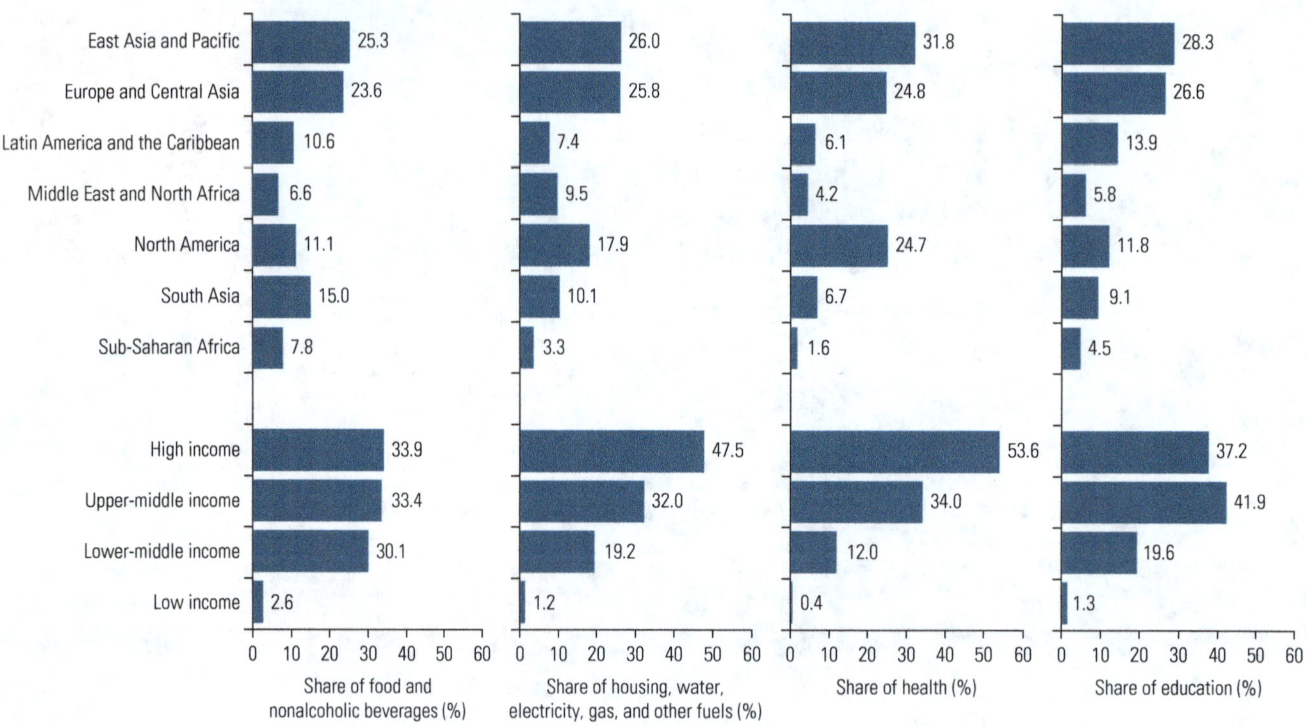

Source: ICP 2017.
Note: PPP = purchasing power parity.

Figure 1.5 Nominal expenditure on selected expenditure components of actual individual consumption as a share of nominal GDP, by region and income group, 2017

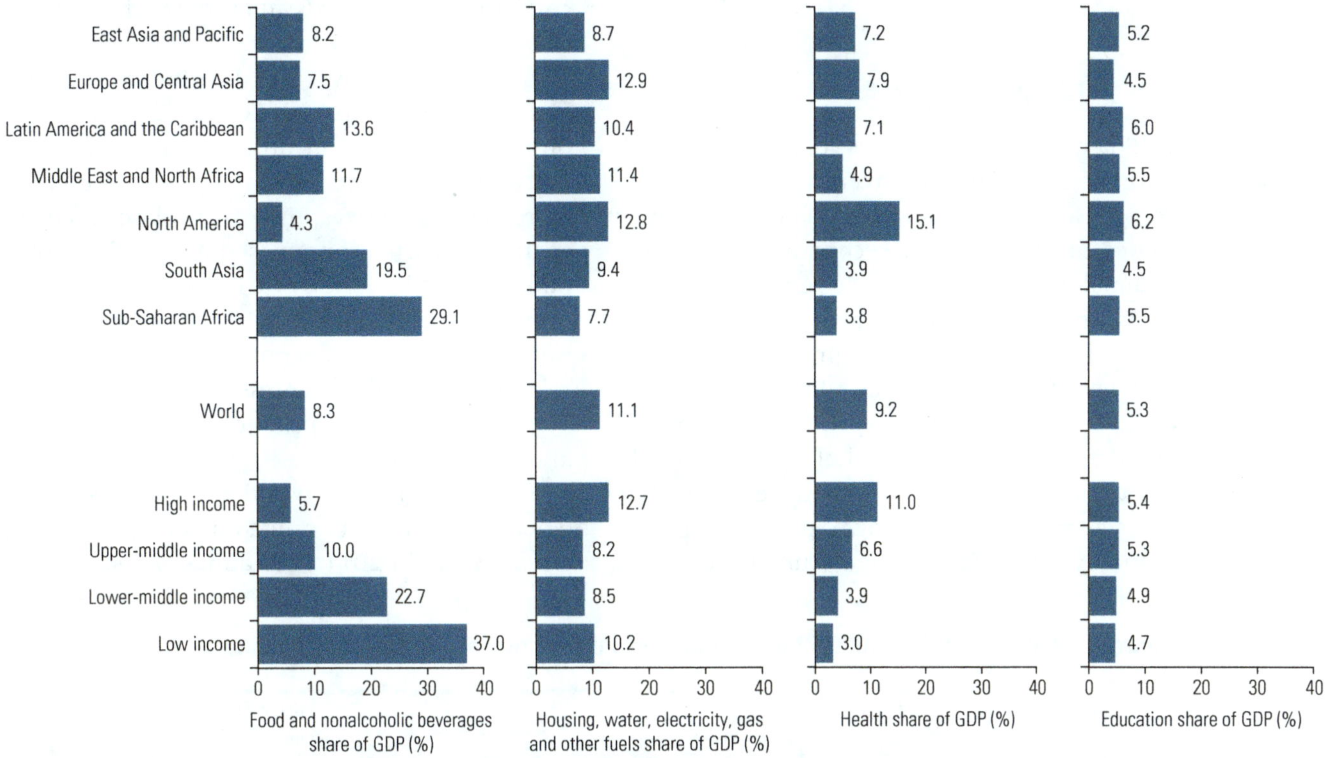

Source: ICP 2017.

Figure 1.6 Share of PPP-based global consumption expenditure by government for the six economies with the largest shares, 2017

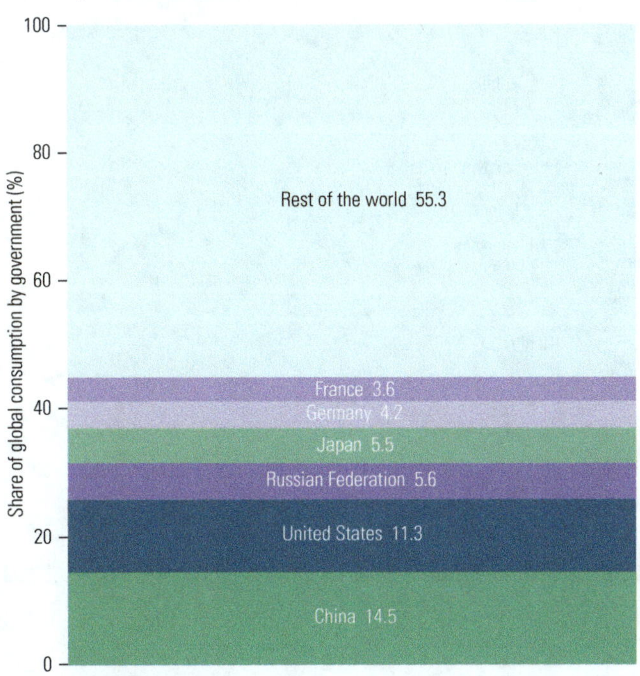

Source: ICP 2017.
Note: PPP = purchasing power parity.

Figure 1.7 Share of PPP-based global gross fixed capital formation for the six economies with the largest shares, 2017

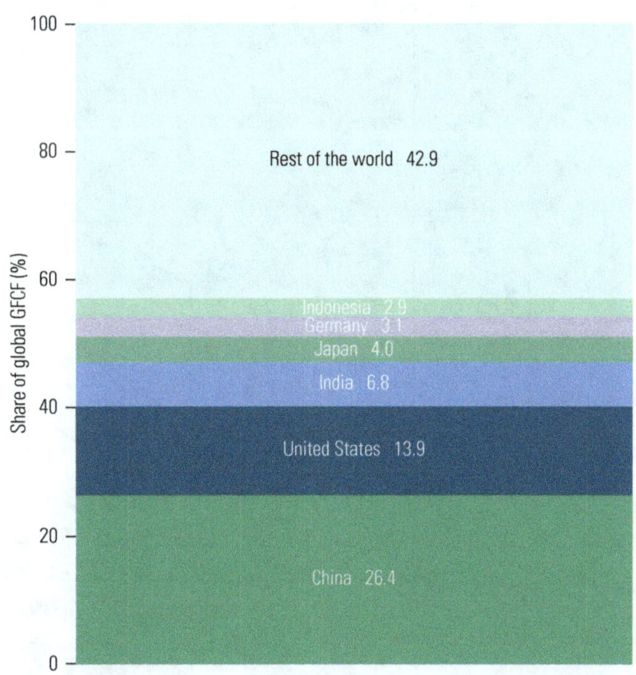

Source: ICP 2017.
Note: GFCF = global expenditure on gross fixed capital formation; PPP = purchasing power parity.

of the United States and equating to more than one-quarter of global investment.

Per capita measures

GDP per capita is sometimes considered an indicator of an economy's average material well-being. However, GDP per capita assigns high values to "income-rich" economies where the national wealth is not reflected to the same extent in the material well-being of their populations. In addition, an economy's high value of GDP per capita can at times reflect high levels of GFCF and consumption expenditure by government, as well as a high level of net exports. AIC per capita is more useful when describing the average material well-being of people within an economy. Using PPP-derived estimates of either measure is important for cross-country comparisons, as they reflect the purchasing power of a consumer for the goods and services they choose to buy.

Figure 1.8 shows the distribution of GDP across economies in both 2011 and 2017. Economies are arranged in order of increasing GDP per capita along the vertical axis and presented as rectangular boxes. The vertical scale corresponds to each economy's share of the global population. The index of GDP per capita, based on the world set equal to 100, is shown on the horizontal axis. Each economy's size in terms of relative GDP is thus represented by the area of its box, which is the product of GDP per capita and population.

The dotted lines at world = 100 represent the global mean GDP per capita for each year, which was $13,920 in 2011 PPPs and $16,596 in 2017

Figure 1.8 Index of PPP-based GDP per capita and share of global population, by economy, 2011 and 2017

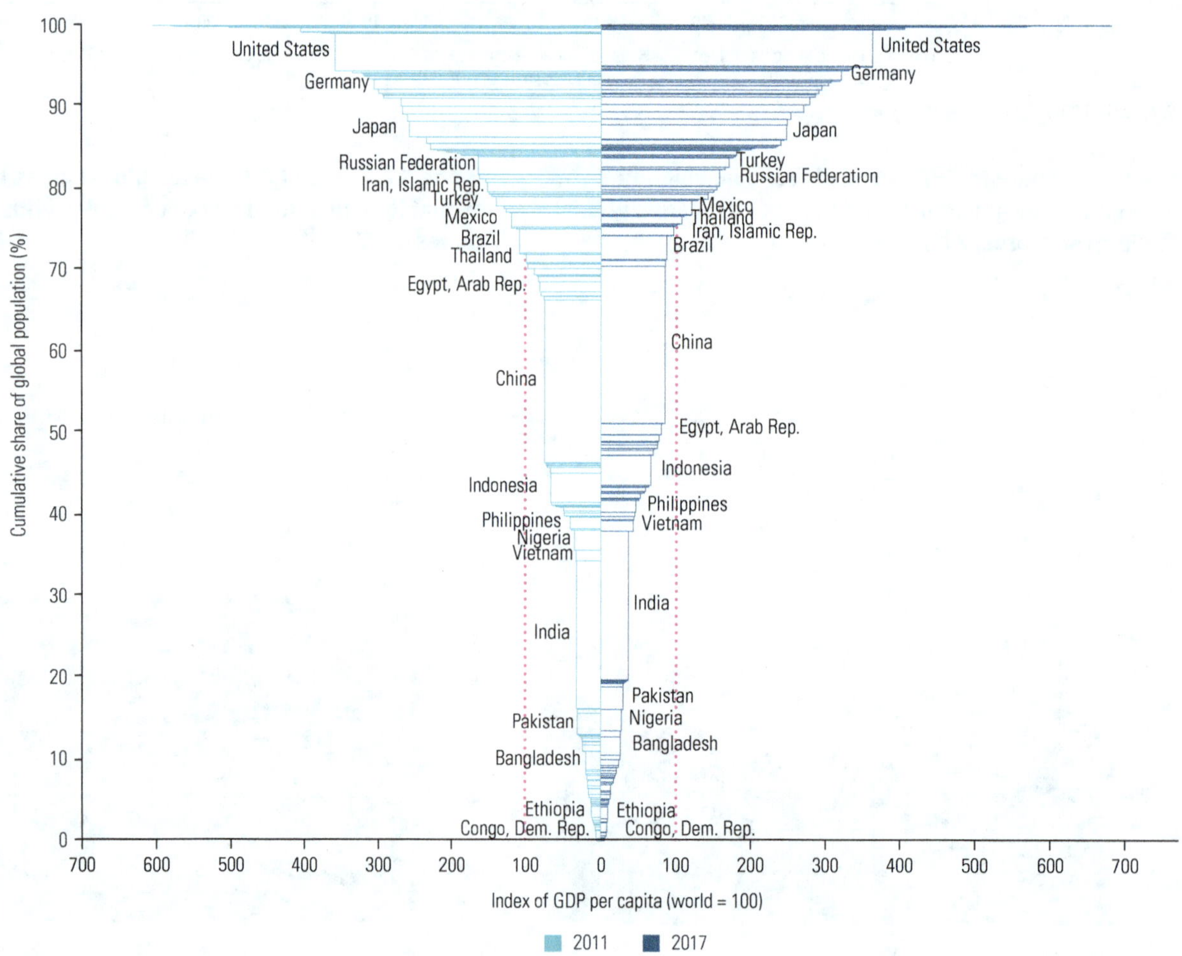

Source: ICP 2017.
Note: PPP = purchasing power parity.

PPPs. The lines' intersection with the boxes shows the disparity in GDP per capita across the globe for the two years. Comparing the two halves of the graph reveals changes in economies' standing relative to each other in the world order of GDP per capita. For example, it shows that between 2011 and 2017, China and India moved up the ladder to occupy relatively higher positions in 2017 vis-à-vis other economies than they did in 2011.

In 2017, Luxembourg had the highest GDP per capita at $112,701, or 679 percent of the world average, and Burundi had the lowest at $784, at around 5 percent.

Figure 1.9 shows the distribution of AIC in 2017. Economies are arranged in order of increasing AIC per capita along the vertical axis and presented as rectangles. Again, the vertical scale corresponds to each economy's share of the global population. AIC per capita is shown on the horizontal axis. Each economy's size in terms of AIC is thus represented by the area of its box.

The United States had the highest level of AIC per capita, at $44,620, and Niger had the lowest, at $661. The mean AIC per capita for the world was $10,858.

Figure 1.10 compares PPP-based GDP per capita with PPP-based AIC per capita for the 12 economies with the highest GDP per capita. The big disparities between GDP per capita and AIC per capita for Brunei Darussalam and Qatar are explained by the fact that these economies had AIC values that accounted for just 27 percent and 31 percent of their nominal GDP, respectively. They are therefore "income-rich" economies, where the national wealth is not reflected to the same extent in the average consumption levels of their populations.

Figure 1.11 shows the variability in the index of PPP-based per capita measures of GDP and its major expenditure components across regions and income groups based on world = 100. The high expenditure on GFCF in China was reflected in a relatively high GFCF per capita index of 131 for the East Asia and Pacific region, the only expenditure component for that region above the world average. Sub-Saharan Africa was well below the world average, with an index of 14 for GFCF per capita. North America, Europe and Central Asia, and

Figure 1.9 PPP-based actual individual consumption per capita and share of global population, by economy, 2017

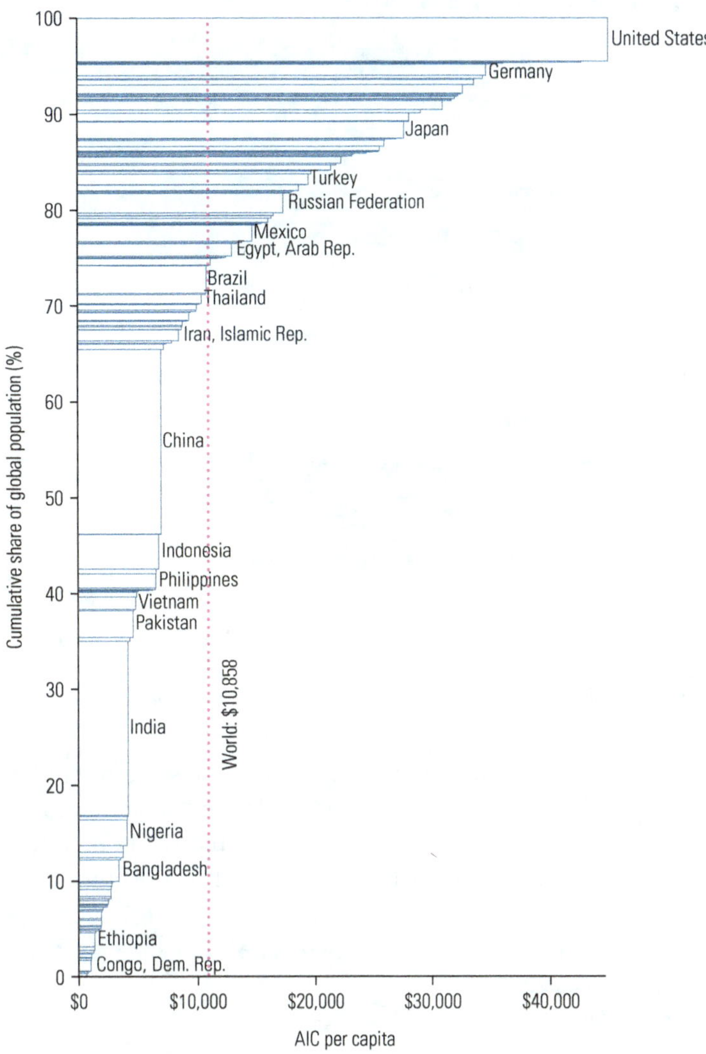

Source: ICP 2017.
Note: AIC = actual individual consumption; PPP = purchasing power parity.

the high-income group of economies all spent nearly three times as much on a per capita basis as the world average on consumption expenditure by government.

Intercountry income inequality

Intercountry income inequality can be measured by the population-weighted Gini measure of income inequality based on PPP-based GDP per capita.

Figure 1.12 compares the distribution of GDP per capita in 2017 and 2011. For 2011, both revised data and originally published data are

Figure 1.10 PPP-based GDP per capita and actual individual consumption per capita for the 12 economies with the highest PPP-based GDP per capita, 2017

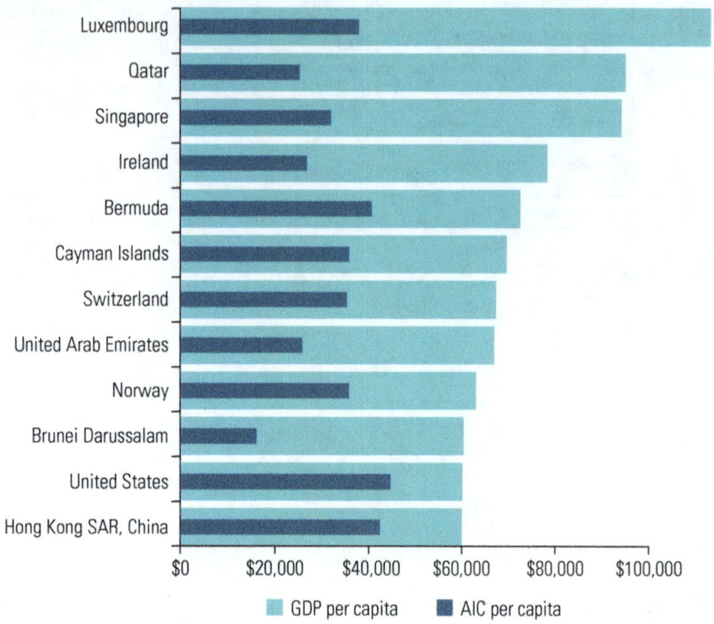

Source: ICP 2017.
Note: AIC = actual individual consumption; PPP = purchasing power parity.

presented, and the three data sets are plotted as Lorenz curves of cumulative percentages of expenditure against the cumulative population, beginning with the poorest economy. Only economies common to both the 2011 and 2017 ICP cycles are included. A 45-degree line represents perfect income equality. The Gini coefficient measures the distribution of expenditure across economies and the extent to which an economy deviates from the hypothetical distribution if all economies had the same share of global GDP as their share of global population. It reflects the area between the Lorenz curve and the line of equality, with a value of 0 reflecting perfect income equality and a value of 1 representing perfect income inequality.

While the intercountry Gini coefficient for PPP-based GDP per capita improved slightly, from 0.487 in 2011 (for both revised and original data) to 0.474 in 2017, the share of the global population living in economies where the mean GDP per capita is below the global average increased from 72.1 percent to 75.9 percent over the same time period.

The same plot can be made for PPP-based AIC per capita, and figure 1.13 shows a bigger change than that for GDP per capita, with Gini coefficients falling from 0.506 in 2011 to 0.477 in 2017. However, the share of the global population living in economies where the mean AIC per capita is below the global average increased from 69.7 percent in 2011 to 74.3 percent in 2017.

Figure 1.11 Index of PPP-based expenditure per capita for GDP and major expenditure components, by region and income group, 2017
(world = 100)

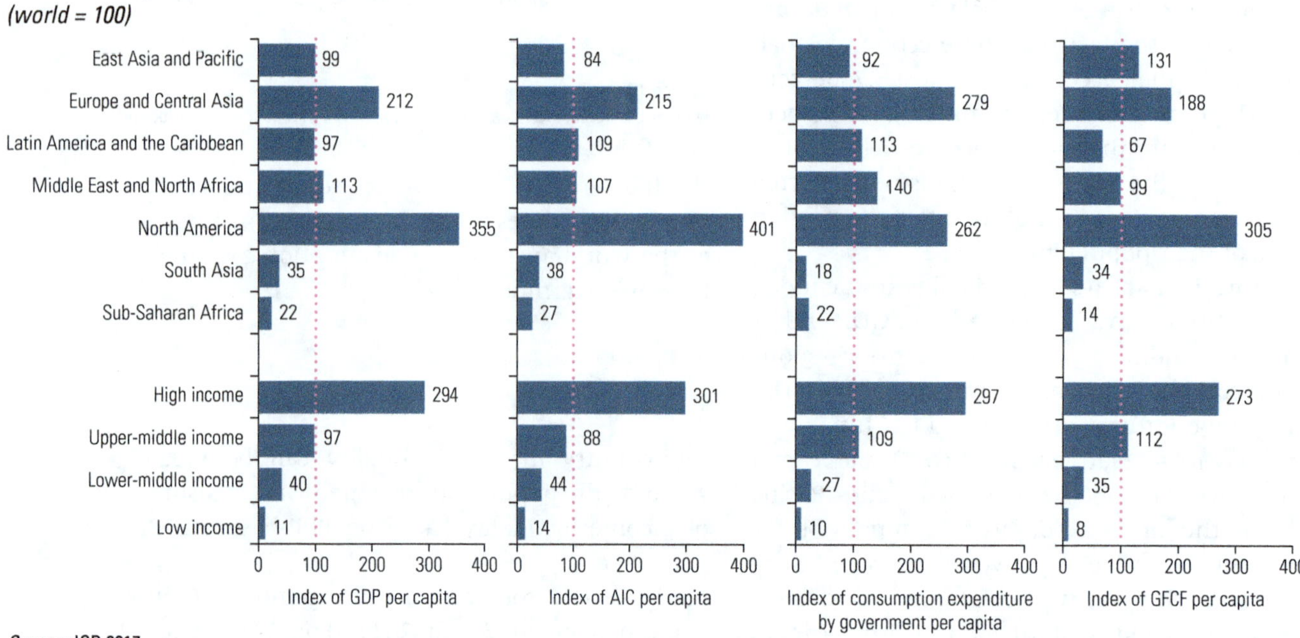

Source: ICP 2017.
Note: AIC = actual individual consumption; GFCF = gross fixed capital formation; PPP = purchasing power parity.

Price levels

The price level index (PLI)—the ratio of a PPP to its corresponding market exchange rate—is used to compare the price levels of economies. Figure 1.14 (panel a) presents a multidimensional comparison of PPP-based GDP per capita of each economy relative to its GDP PLI based on the world set equal to 100 for 2017. Each economy is represented by a circle with an area proportional to its GDP and color-coded by region. As a general observation, PLIs at the GDP level tend to be generally lower in economies with lower GDP per capita. This observation is consistent with the fact that, as an economy develops, consumers move from consuming basic goods that are also tradable to consuming more services that are not tradable. As wage rates increase, so do the costs of services, which subsequently push up the general price level.

In the case of most high-income economies, toward the right of the figure, price levels increase very sharply with relatively small changes in GDP per capita, whereas price levels for less wealthy economies increase less prominently with changes in income. Bermuda was the most expensive economy, with a PLI of 205. There are some interesting outliers: small, high-income economies within the Middle East and North Africa and the East Asia and Pacific regions had relatively low price levels, while Egypt had the lowest PLI of all economies, despite having a GDP per capita in excess of $13,000 and being one of the richest of the lower-middle-income group of economies.

Figure 1.15 charts the PLIs for major expenditure components by region and income group. It shows the high price levels prevalent in North America. It also shows both the high cost of GFCF in both Sub-Saharan Africa and the low-income economies and the low PLI for AIC in South Asia and the lower-middle-income group.

Figure 1.16 shows the PLIs for 17 expenditure components alongside the PLI for GDP for each region. Across most expenditure components, South Asia recorded the lowest PLIs, while North America recorded the highest. The difference between these two regions was most pronounced for education, ranging from a PLI of 38 in South Asia to 261 in North America.

Figure 1.12 Lorenz curves for the distributions of 2017, revised 2011, and original 2011 PPP-based GDP per capita

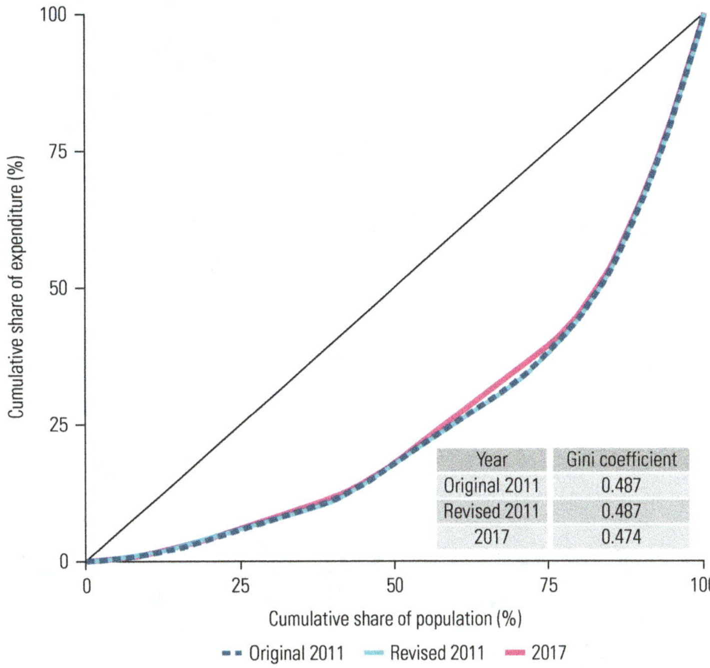

Sources: ICP 2011, 2017.
Note: Gini coefficients are population-weighted and based on the 173 economies common to both ICP 2011 and ICP 2017. PPP = purchasing power parity.

Figure 1.13 Lorenz curves for the distributions of 2017, revised 2011, and original 2011 PPP-based actual individual consumption per capita

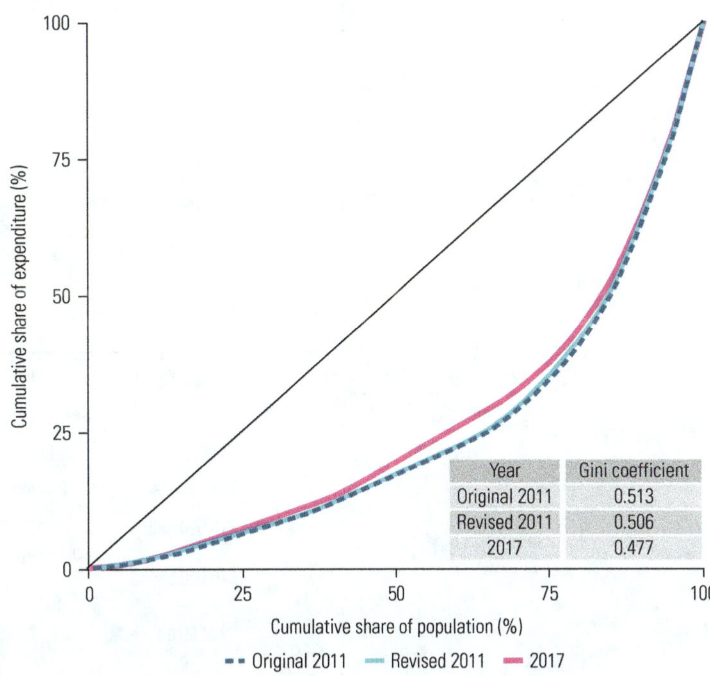

Sources: ICP 2011, 2017.
Note: Gini coefficients are population-weighted and based on the 173 economies common to both ICP 2011 and ICP 2017. PPP = purchasing power parity.

Figure 1.14 GDP price level index versus PPP-based GDP per capita (and PPP-based GDP), by economy, 2017 and 2011

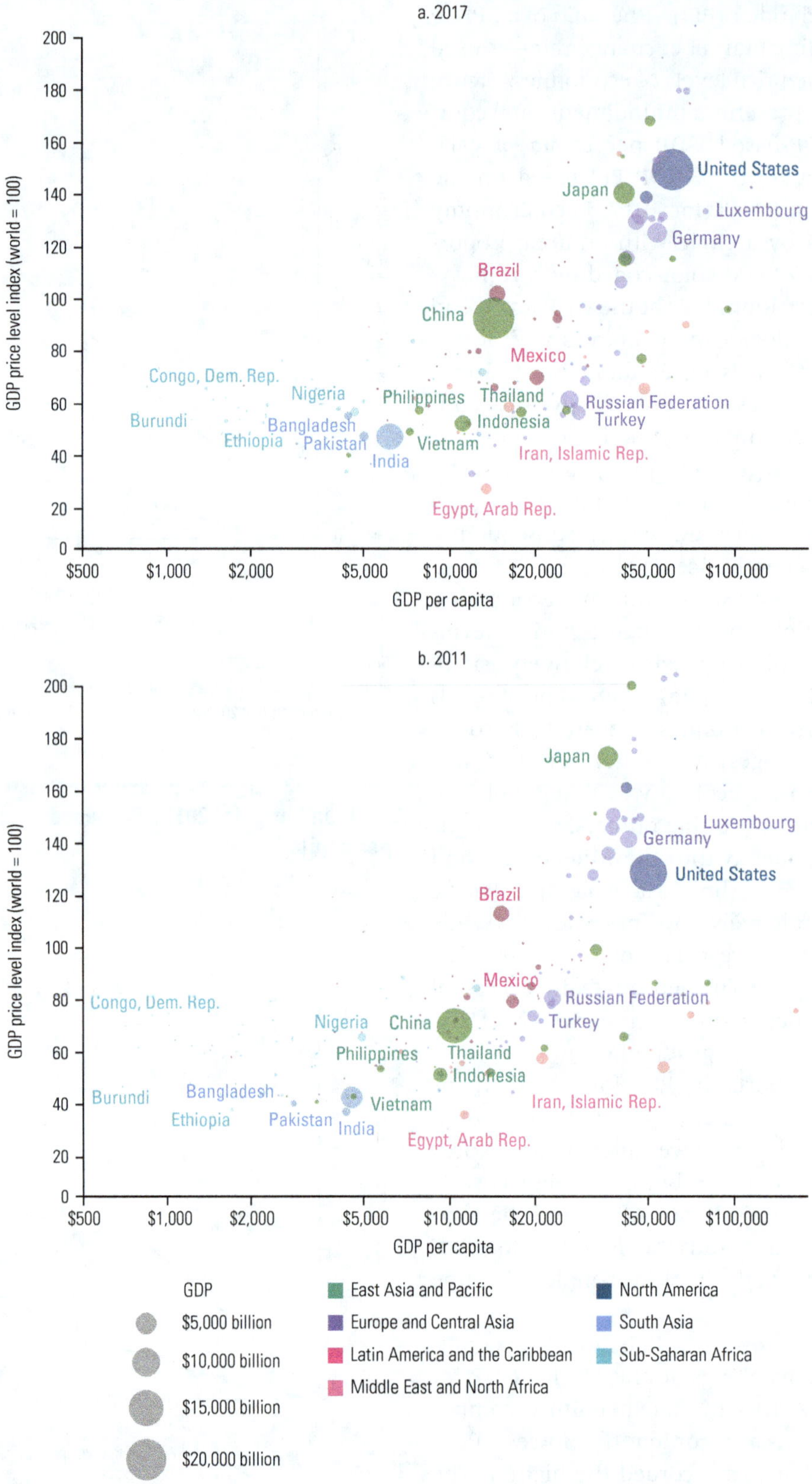

Source: ICP 2017.
Note: A logarithmic scale is used for GDP per capita. PPP = purchasing power parity.

Figure 1.15 Price level indexes for GDP and major expenditure components, by region and income group, 2017
(world = 100)

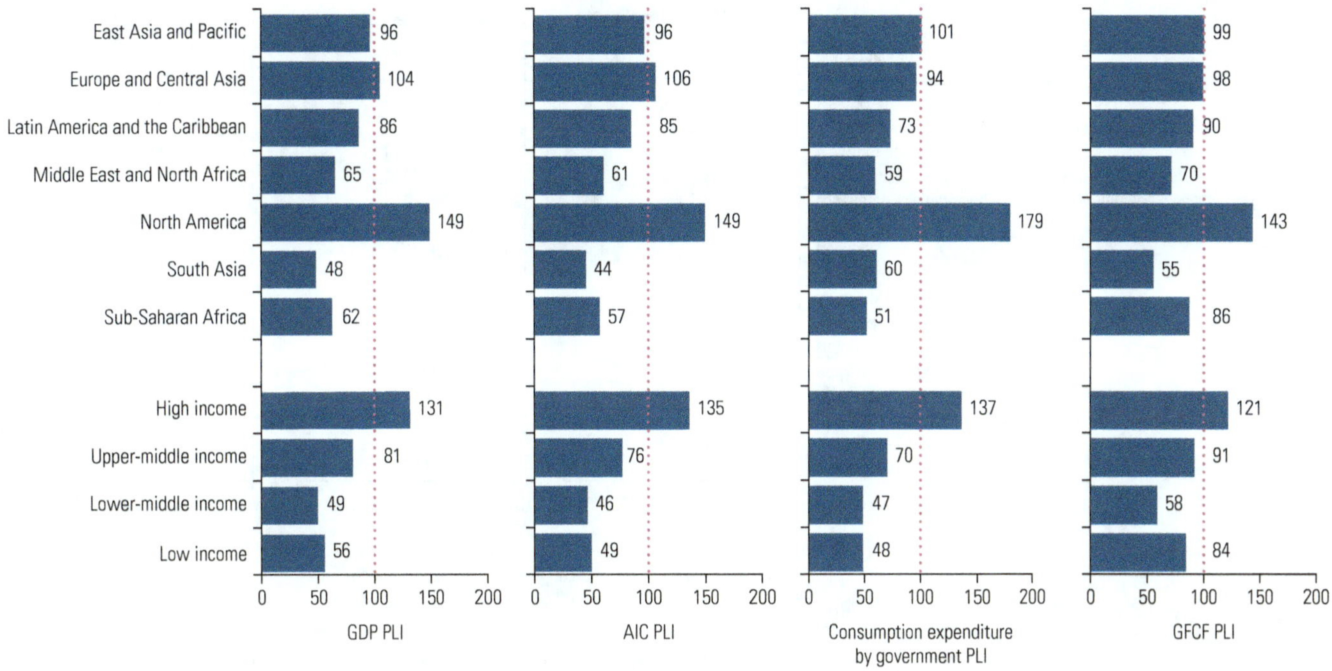

Source: ICP 2017.
Note: AIC = actual individual consumption; GFCF = gross fixed capital formation; PLI = price level index.

In Sub-Saharan Africa, PLIs for all expenditure components, except machinery and equipment, were significantly below the world average of 100. In South Asia, the lowest PLIs were recorded for health and housing, and the highest were for alcoholic beverages, narcotics, and tobacco and for machinery and equipment. Both East Asia and Pacific and Europe and Central Asia had PLIs across many expenditure components that clustered near the world average of 100. This pattern is also seen to a large extent in Latin America and the Caribbean—however, education is an outlier, with a PLI of 54. The Middle East and North Africa had PLIs below the world average, with the PLI for housing being the lowest, at 42.

Variability across economies

The global economy is very complex, with extreme differences in the overall size of economies as measured by GDP and how it is distributed across the major expenditure components. Per capita measures provide another view, as do PLIs. This section reviews the inherent variability across economies with regard to expenditure per capita and PLIs.

Across the 176 economies analyzed here, PPP-based GDP per capita ranged from $112,701 in Luxembourg to $784 in Burundi—a range of 144 based on the ratio of the maximum to minimum values. The GDP PLI across the 176 economies varied from 205 in Bermuda to 27 in Egypt—a range of 7.5—suggesting that there is much less variation in price levels than in per capita measures.

The coefficient of variation (CV) provides a measure of average variability. Figure 1.17 shows the CVs for both the index of PPP-based expenditure per capita and the PLI for expenditure components and examines the homogeneity of economies within each region and across the world. The CV for the index of expenditure per capita appears on the left-hand side of each graph, and the CV for the PLI appears on the right-hand side. The number of economies that participated in the 2017 cycle within each region differed

Figure 1.16 Price level indexes for GDP and 17 expenditure components, by region, 2017
(world = 100)

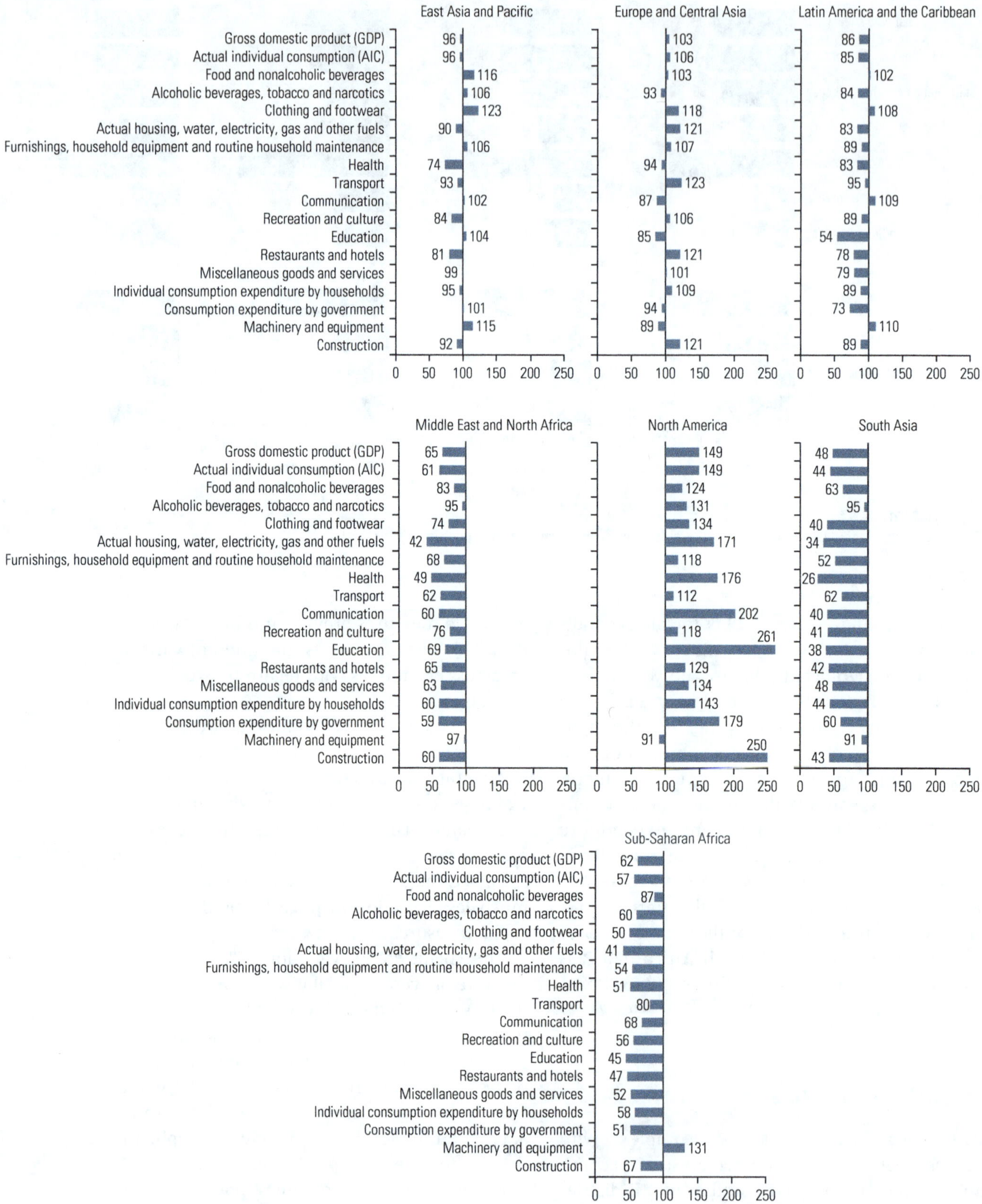

Source: ICP 2017.

Figure 1.17 Coefficients of variation: Index of PPP-based expenditure per capita and price level index for GDP and 17 expenditure components, by region, 2017

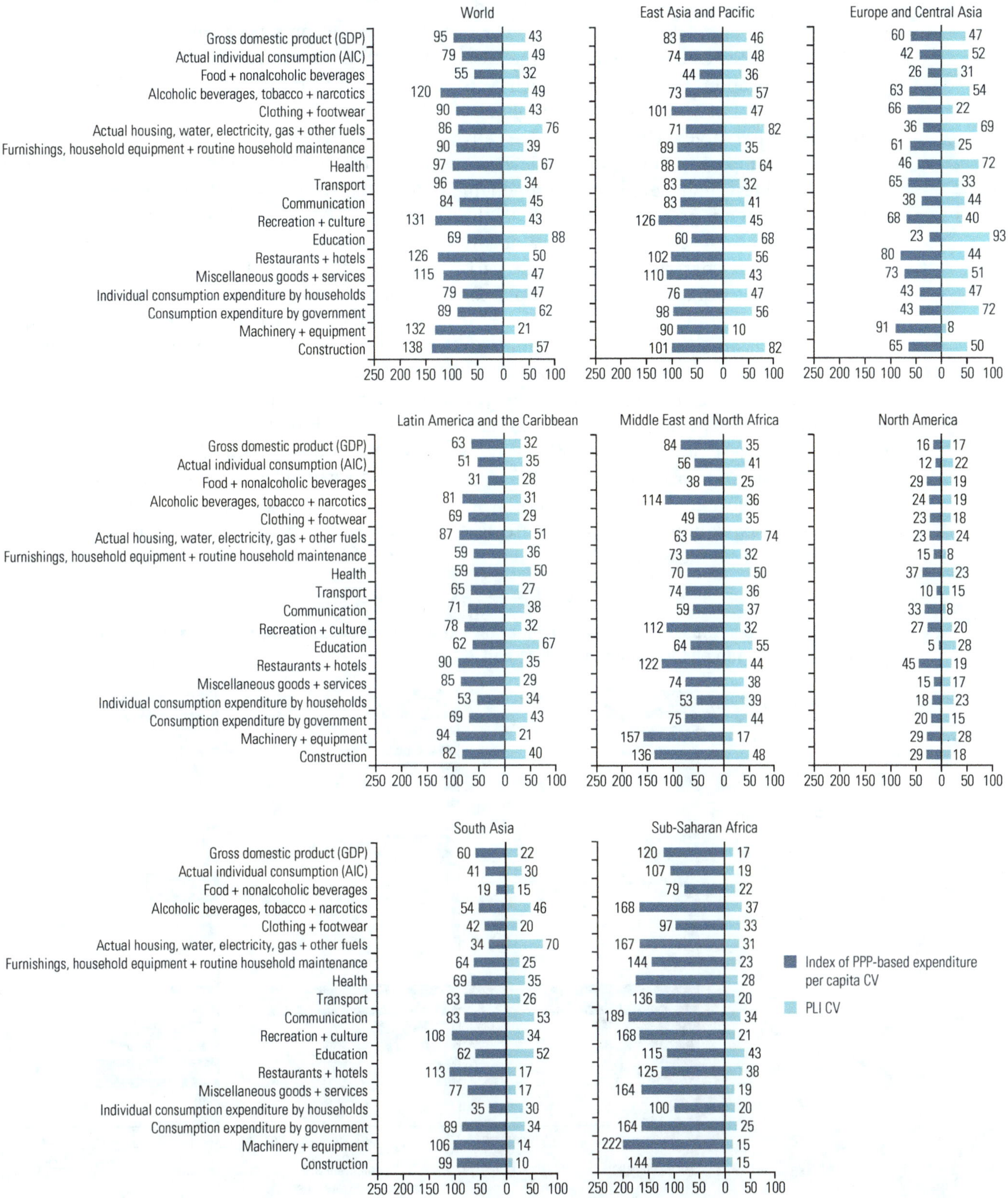

Source: ICP 2017.
Note: CV = coefficient of variation; PLI = price level index; PPP = purchasing power parity.

widely—from three economies in North America to 46 economies in Europe and Central Asia.

Generally, the variation in index of expenditure per capita was much greater than the variation in price levels. One exception was the variability of education price levels, which was driven by the CV of 93 percent for Europe and Central Asia, the largest CV for the PLI of any expenditure component at the regional level.

The machinery and equipment component exhibited the lowest price variation at both the regional and global levels, which is explained by its highly tradable character. However, the variability of the index of expenditure per capita for machinery and equipment exceeded that for most, if not all, other expenditure components across regions and for the world.

Services such as health and education, as well as consumption expenditure by government, showed the largest price level variations both across the globe and across most regions. Housing, too, had high PLI variances. It is noteworthy that these expenditure components are also the most difficult to measure.

Comparison of 2017 results with revised 2011 results

This section presents summary charts comparing 2017 results to the revised 2011 results. Revised 2011 results are provided in appendix E. The set of economies that participated in the 2017 cycle differed somewhat from the set of economies in the 2011 cycle. Thus the results from the two years can be compared with some caution. The income grouping used for both years reflects the World Bank's fiscal year 2020 classification of economies.

Figure 1.18 shows the regional and income group shares of GDP in both PPP terms and market exchange rate terms as well as their respective shares of the global population. Compared with 2017, high-income economies had a higher share of GDP both in PPP terms and in market exchange rate terms in 2011. Correspondingly, both lower-middle- and upper-middle-income economies increased their share between the two cycles. This mostly reflects the increases in the shares of East Asia and Pacific and South Asia.

Figure 1.18 Share of global PPP-based and market exchange rate–based GDP and share of global population, by region and income group, 2011 and 2017

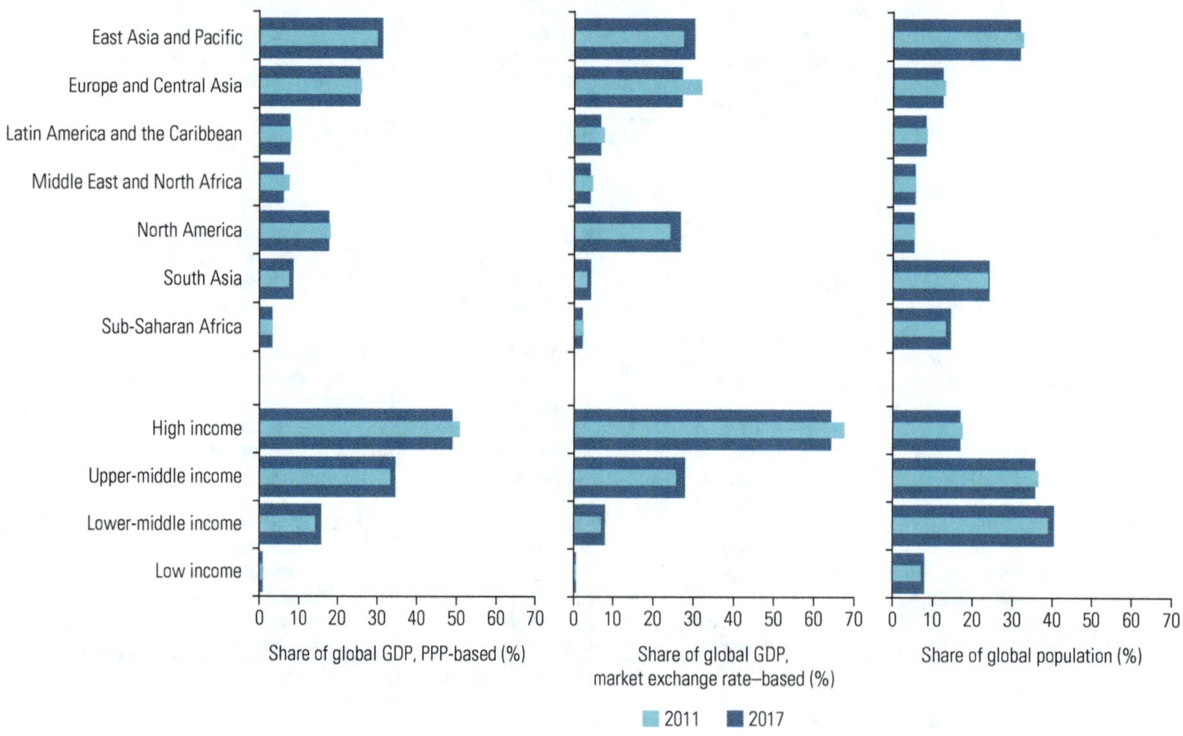

Source: ICP 2017.
Note: PPP = purchasing power parity.

Figure 1.19 Index of PPP-based expenditure per capita for GDP and major expenditure components, by region and income group, 2011 and 2017
(world = 100)

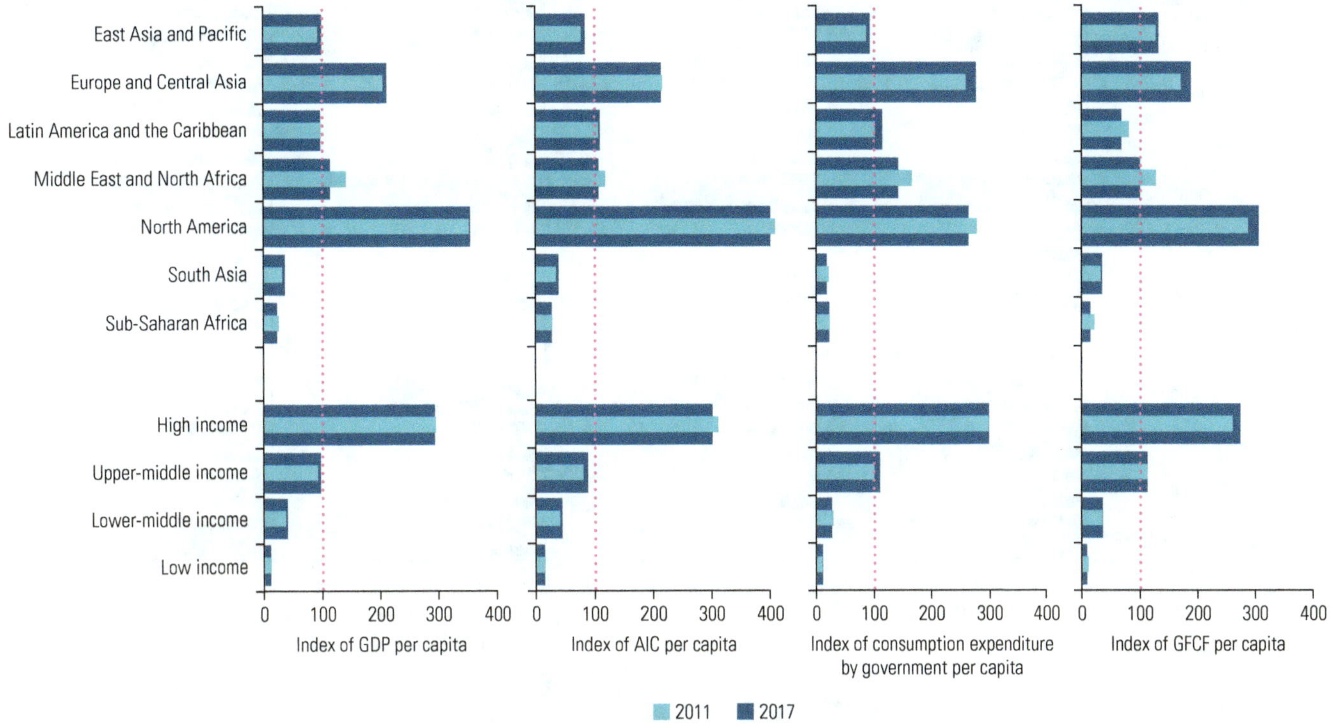

Source: ICP 2017.
Note: AIC = actual individual consumption; GFCF = gross fixed capital formation; PPP = purchasing power parity.

Comparing the index of PPP-based expenditure per capita for major expenditure components across the two years in figure 1.19 reveals that East Asia and Pacific slightly increased its index value versus the world average in all expenditure components, while the Middle East and North Africa saw a decrease. Both the upper-middle- and lower- middle-income groups saw an increase in their index of GDP per capita and AIC per capita, while the high-income group experienced a decrease in these expenditure components' indexes between 2011 and 2017.

Price levels fell between 2011 and 2017 in Europe and Central Asia and in Latin America and the Caribbean across all expenditure components. They also fell in all but GFCF in Sub-Saharan Africa (figure 1.20). PLIs increased over the period in North America and in East Asia and Pacific.

Figure 1.14 (panel b) plots GDP PLI against GDP per capita in PPP terms for each economy for 2011 and allows comparison with the same for 2017. Comparing 2017 to 2011, the most pronounced change is the drift of China and India to the right (increasing GDP per capita) and upward (increasing PLI relative to the world average).

Notes on the main findings

Analyses are limited to the economies that participated in the specific reference year, and this group differs between 2011 and 2017. Macao SAR, China; Guatemala; the República Bolivariana de Venezuela; and the Republic of Yemen participated in the 2011 cycle but not in 2017 and, thus, are included only in analyses for 2011. Conversely, Argentina and Guyana did not participate in 2011, but were part of the 2017 cycle and are included in the latter's analyses only. Uzbekistan participated in the 2017 cycle on an experimental basis, with results for actual individual consumption and individual consumption expenditure by

Figure 1.20 Price level indexes for GDP and major expenditure components, by region and income group, 2011 and 2017
(world = 100)

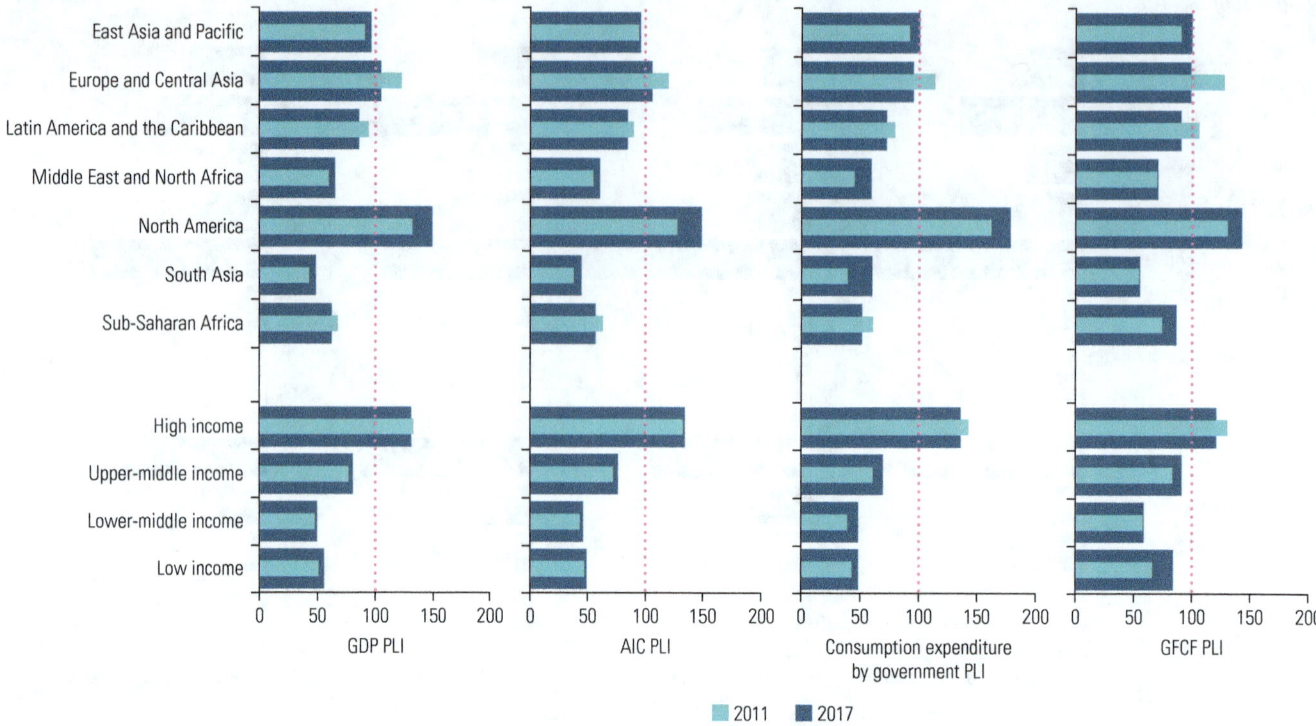

Source: ICP 2017.
Note: AIC = actual individual consumption; GFCF = gross fixed capital formation; PLI = price level index.

households only. Furthermore, Bonaire also participated at the level of individual consumption expenditure by households. As a result, data for both of these economies are excluded from analyses.

In a number of figures in this chapter, the ICP participating economies are classified by the World Bank's fiscal year 2020 income groups as of July 1, 2019. However, three economies—Anguilla, Bonaire, and Monserrat—are not included in the classification because their populations were below the World Bank's classification threshold of 30,000. Anguilla and Montserrat are excluded from these income group–based figures, as is Bonaire.

In other figures, a geographic grouping of economies, based largely on the World Bank's regions is used. This approach differs from analyses in previous ICP reports, which presented results by ICP administrative region. This geographic grouping avoids the issues of having dual-participation economies appear in more than one region and having economies appear in the same group as economies that are geographically distant, such as Organisation for Economic Co-operation and Development (OECD) economies. As the aggregate data presented for income groups and geographic regions exclude the economies that did not participate in the ICP, these totals should not be compared with data from non-ICP sources.

Appendix J of this report lists all of the economies by their ICP administrative region, by World Bank fiscal year 2020 income group, and by geographic region.

In a number of figures, results are presented for the following GDP expenditure components: (a) housing, water, electricity, gas, and other fuels; (b) health; (c) recreation and culture; (d) education; and (e) miscellaneous goods and services. These include their respective expenditures under individual consumption expenditure by households, individual consumption expenditure by nonprofit institutions serving households (NPISHs), and individual consumption expenditure by government. Appendix C provides a list of all expenditure components under the ICP expenditure classification.

CHAPTER 2

ICP 2017 results

The 2017 results presented in this report are based exclusively on the prices and national accounts expenditures provided by the economies participating in the 2017 cycle of the International Comparison Program (ICP). Purchasing power parities (PPPs) and real expenditures were compiled in accordance with the established ICP methods and procedures, as outlined in chapter 5 of this report. In addition, users should refer to the correct use and application of PPPs and real expenditures, as described in chapter 3 of this report.

In addition to the summary results presented here, more detailed data sets are available through curated online tables and databases, accessible through the ICP website[1] and through the World Bank's Databank[2] and Data Catalog.[3] In addition, researchers may request access to unpublished ICP data sets, as detailed in appendix H.

Tables of 2017 results

This report provides the main set of results for the following headings:

- Table 2.1. Gross domestic product (GDP)
- Table 2.2. Actual individual consumption (AIC)
- Table 2.3. Individual consumption expenditure by households
- Table 2.4. Consumption expenditure by government
- Table 2.5. Gross fixed capital formation (GFCF)
- Table 2.6. Domestic absorption.

In addition, supplementary table 2.7 provides a limited set of results for nonparticipating economies. The PPPs for these economies were imputed following the approach described in chapter 5.

The headings are defined as follows:

- *Gross domestic product.* Actual individual consumption at purchasers' prices *plus* collective consumption expenditure by government at purchasers' prices *plus* gross capital formation at purchasers' prices *plus* the f.o.b. (free on board) value of exports of goods and services *less* the f.o.b. value of imports of goods and services. *Code in ICP expenditure classification, appendix C: 1000000.*
- *Actual individual consumption.* The total value of the individual consumption expenditures of households, nonprofit institutions serving households (NPISHs), and government at purchasers' prices. *Code in ICP expenditure classification, appendix C: sum of 1100000 + 1200000 + 1300000.*
- *Individual consumption expenditure by households.* The total value of actual and imputed final consumption expenditures incurred by

households and NPISHs on individual goods and services. It also includes expenditures on individual goods and services sold at prices that are not economically significant. *Code in ICP expenditure classification, appendix C: sum of 1100000 + 1200000.*

- *Consumption expenditure by government.* The total value of actual and imputed final consumption expenditures incurred by government on individual goods and services and final consumption expenditure of government on collective services. *Code in ICP expenditure classification, appendix C: sum of 1300000 + 1400000.*
- *Gross fixed capital formation (GFCF).* The total value of acquisitions less disposals of fixed assets by resident institutional units during the accounting period plus additions to the value of nonproduced assets realized by the productive activity of resident institutional units. *Code in ICP expenditure classification, appendix C: 1501000.*
- *Domestic absorption.* Actual individual consumption at purchasers' prices plus collective consumption expenditure by government at purchasers' prices plus gross capital formation at purchasers' prices. *Code in ICP expenditure classification, appendix C: sum of 1100000 + 1200000 + 1300000 + 1400000 + 1500000.*

The tables of main results cover the following indicators for each heading:

- *Column (00).* Name of the economy and its International Organization for Standardization (ISO) code
- *Column (01).* Expenditure based on PPPs in US dollars[4]
- *Column (02).* Expenditure based on market exchange rates in US dollars
- *Column (03).* Expenditure per capita based on PPPs in US dollars
- *Column (04).* Expenditure per capita based on market exchange rates in US dollars
- *Column (05).* Price level index with the world equal to 100
- *Column (06).* Expenditure per capita index based on PPPs with the world equal to 100
- *Column (07).* Expenditure per capita index based on market exchange rates with the world equal to 100
- *Column (08).* Expenditure per capita index based on PPPs with the United States equal to 100
- *Column (09).* Expenditure per capita index based on market exchange rates with the United States equal to 100
- *Column (10).* Share of PPP-based world total expenditures
- *Column (11).* Share of market exchange rate–based world total expenditures
- *Column (12).* Share of world population
- *Column (13).* PPP with the US dollar[5] equal to 1
- *Column (14).* Market exchange rate with the USdollar equal to 1
- *Column (15).* Nominal expenditures in local currency unit
- *Column (16).* Resident population.

Column (01) shows the real expenditures of economies and regions in US dollars. The expenditures reflect only volume differences between economies and regions. They were obtained by dividing the nominal expenditures in column (15) by the PPPs in column (13). The expenditures per capita in column (03), the expenditures per capita indexes in columns (06) and (08), and the shares of world total expenditures in column (10) are all based on the real expenditures in column (01).

Column (02) shows the nominal expenditures of economies and regions in US dollars. The expenditures reflect both price differences and volume differences between economies and regions. They were derived by dividing the nominal expenditures in column (15) by the market exchange rates in column (14). The expenditures per capita in column (04), the expenditures per capita indexes in columns (07) and (09), and the shares of world GDP in column (11) are all based on the nominal expenditures in column (02).

Column (05) shows price level indexes relative to the world average. A value above 100 indicates that the economy's price level is higher than the world average; a value below 100 indicates that the economy's price level for the analytical category is lower than the world average. They were derived by dividing the nominal expenditures in US dollars in column (02) by the real expenditures of economies and regions in US dollars in column (01) and by subsequently normalizing the price level to the world average.

It is important to remember that market exchange rate–converted expenditures are not reliable measures of either the size of economies or the mean per capita income and consumption of their populations. They are included in the main tables and in the supplementary table for reference only.

The results for participating economies are presented following the World Bank Group geographic regions:[6]

- East Asia and Pacific: 19 economies
- Europe and Central Asia: 46 economies
- Latin America and the Caribbean: 39 economies
- Middle East and North Africa: 17 economies
- North America: 3 economies
- South Asia: 7 economies
- Sub-Saharan Africa: 45 economies
- World: 176 economies.

In addition, supplementary table 2.7 provides results for 12 nonparticipating economies.

In all tables, results are presented by economy and by region and include regional totals and averages, as well as world totals and averages. The results for the nonparticipating economies are not included in world totals.

Results presented in these tables are produced by the ICP Global Office and regional implementing agencies, based on data supplied by participating economies, and in accordance with the methodology recommended by the ICP Technical Advisory Group and approved by the ICP Governing Board. As such, these results are not produced by participating economies as part of their national official statistics.

Survey framework

Metadata on the ICP 2017 survey framework in participating economies are summarized in table 2.8. The table provides information on the geographic scope of the price surveys for individual consumption expenditure by households as well as details on the types of outlets and number of items covered.

Notes

1. See icp.worldbank.org.
2. See data.worldbank.org.
3. See datacatalog.worldbank.org.
4. Real expenditures are not additive, meaning that the real expenditures at higher levels of aggregation are not equal to the sum of the real expenditures of their components. Additivity can be considered to be an important feature of real expenditures. However, in practice it is not possible to maintain the additivity of the component aggregates within real GDP without having real expenditures for GDP that are significantly biased between low- and high-income economies (that is, the Gerschenkron effect).
5. The United States serves as the base and the US dollar as numéraire. However, PPPs are base economy–invariant, so they can be rebased on another economy or on a region by dividing them by the PPP for the economy or region selected as the new base. PPPs also maintain other key characteristics, as described in chapter 5.
6. See appendix J for details.

Table 2.1 Gross domestic product (GDP): ICP 2017 results

GROSS DOMESTIC PRODUCT		Expenditure (billion US$)		Expenditure per capita (US$)		Price level index (world = 100.0)[a]	Expenditure per capita indexes[b]				Share (world = 100%)[b]			PPPs[c] (US$ = 1.000)	Reference data		
							World = 100.0		United States = 100.0		Expenditure				Market exchange rates[c] (US$ = 1.000)	Expenditure (billion LCU)	Population (millions)
Economy		Based on PPPs	Based on XRs	Based on PPPs	Based on XRs		Based on PPPs	Based on XRs	Based on PPPs	Based on XRs	Based on PPPs	Based on XRs	Population				
(00)		(01)	(02)	(03)	(04)	(05)	(06)	(07)	(08)	(09)	(10)	(11)	(12)	(13)	(14)	(15)	(16)
East Asia and Pacific																	
Australia	AUS	1,233.9	1,386.2	50,153	56,344	168.5	302.2	509.2	83.6	93.9	1.0	1.7	0.3	1.466	1.305	1,808.6	24.60
Brunei Darussalam	BRN	25.9	12.1	60,282	28,238	70.3	363.2	255.2	100.5	47.1	0.0	0.0	0.0	0.647	1.381	16.7	0.43
Cambodia	KHM	62.9	22.2	3,968	1,399	52.9	23.9	12.6	6.6	2.3	0.1	0.0	0.2	1,428.354	4,050.580	89,830.5	15.85
China	CHN	19,617.4	12,143.6	14,150	8,759	92.8	85.3	79.2	23.6	14.6	16.4	15.2	19.2	4.184	6.759	82,075.4	1,386.40
Fiji	FJI	11.8	5.4	13,436	6,104	68.1	81.0	55.2	22.4	10.2	0.0	0.0	0.0	0.939	2.067	11.1	0.88
Hong Kong SAR, China	HKG	443.0	341.7	59,927	46,225	115.7	361.1	417.7	99.9	77.1	0.4	0.4	0.1	6.011	7.793	2,662.8	7.39
Indonesia	IDN	2,893.6	1,015.4	11,049	3,877	52.6	66.6	35.0	18.4	6.5	2.4	1.3	3.6	4,695.659	13,380.872	13,587,212.6	261.89
Japan	JPN	5,173.0	4,860.0	40,827	38,356	140.9	246.0	346.6	68.1	63.9	4.3	6.1	1.8	105.379	112.166	545,121.9	126.71
Korea, Rep.	KOR	2,105.9	1,623.9	41,001	31,617	115.6	247.1	285.7	68.4	52.7	1.8	2.0	0.7	871.696	1130.425	1,835,698.2	51.36
Lao PDR	LAO	50.4	16.8	7,310	2,441	50.1	44.0	22.1	12.2	4.1	0.0	0.0	0.1	2,789.109	8,351.526	140,697.7	6.90
Malaysia	MYS	817.9	314.7	25,540	9,828	57.7	153.9	88.8	42.6	16.4	0.7	0.4	0.4	1.655	4.300	1,353.4	32.02
Mongolia	MNG	35.2	11.4	11,186	3,628	48.6	67.4	32.8	18.6	6.0	0.0	0.0	0.0	791.436	2,439.777	27,876.3	3.15
Myanmar	MMR	234.5	63.2	4,411	1,189	40.4	26.6	10.7	7.4	2.0	0.2	0.1	0.7	366.713	1,360.359	85,980.8	53.15
New Zealand	NZL	194.5	200.9	40,261	41,577	154.9	242.6	375.7	67.1	69.3	0.2	0.3	0.1	1.453	1.407	282.7	4.83
Philippines	PHL	815.5	313.6	7,772	2,989	57.7	46.8	27.0	13.0	5.0	0.7	0.4	1.5	19.385	50.404	15,807.6	104.92
Singapore	SGP	527.4	338.4	93,981	60,297	96.2	566.3	544.9	156.7	100.5	0.4	0.4	0.1	0.886	1.381	467.3	5.61
Taiwan, China	TWN	1,112.6	574.9	47,223	24,401	77.5	284.6	220.5	78.7	40.7	0.9	0.7	0.3	15.730	30.442	17,501.2	23.56
Thailand	THA	1,203.0	455.3	17,781	6,729	56.8	107.1	60.8	29.6	11.2	1.0	0.6	0.9	12.845	33.940	15,452.0	67.65
Vietnam	VNM	676.9	223.8	7,183	2,375	49.6	43.3	21.5	12.0	4.0	0.6	0.3	1.3	7,395.338	2,2370.087	5,005,975.5	94.24
Total (19)	**EAB**	**37,235.1**	**23,923.4**	**16,392**	**10,532**	**96.4**	**98.8**	**95.2**	**27.3**	**17.6**	**31.1**	**30.0**	**31.5**	**n.a.**	**n.a**	**n.a.**	**2,271.55**
Europe and Central Asia																	
Albania	ALB	37.6	13.1	13,094	4,546	52.1	78.9	41.1	21.8	7.6	0.0	0.0	0.0	41.231	118.748	1,551.3	2.87
Armenia	ARM	35.7	11.5	11,974	3,869	48.5	72.2	35.0	20.0	6.4	0.0	0.0	0.0	155.971	482.720	5,564.5	2.98
Austria	AUT	480.7	418.3	54,653	47,563	130.5	329.3	429.8	91.1	79.3	0.4	0.5	0.1	0.770	0.885	370.3	8.80
Azerbaijan	AZE	139.2	40.9	14,296	4,198	44.0	86.1	37.9	23.8	7.0	0.1	0.1	0.1	0.505	1.721	70.3	9.73
Belarus	BLR	173.6	54.7	18,280	5,763	47.3	110.2	52.1	30.5	9.6	0.1	0.1	0.1	0.609	1.932	105.7	9.50
Belgium	BEL	577.5	504.3	50,771	44,330	130.9	305.9	400.6	84.6	73.9	0.5	0.6	0.2	0.773	0.885	446.4	11.38
Bosnia and Herzegovina	BIH	46.4	18.1	13,843	5,407	58.6	83.4	48.9	23.1	9.0	0.0	0.0	0.0	0.676	1.731	31.4	3.35
Bulgaria	BGR	151.8	59.1	21,447	8,351	58.4	129.2	75.5	35.8	13.9	0.1	0.1	0.1	0.674	1.731	102.3	7.08
Croatia	HRV	110.1	55.5	26,666	13,430	75.5	160.7	121.4	44.5	22.4	0.1	0.1	0.1	3.327	6.607	366.4	4.13
Cyprus	CYP	32.6	22.6	37,915	26,339	104.2	228.5	238.0	63.2	43.9	0.0	0.0	0.0	0.615	0.885	20.0	0.86
Czech Republic	CZE	407.8	216.6	38,507	20,453	79.7	232.0	184.8	64.2	34.1	0.3	0.3	0.1	12.378	23.304	5,047.3	10.59
Denmark	DNK	317.4	330.3	55,046	57,280	156.1	331.7	517.6	91.8	95.5	0.3	0.4	0.1	6.852	6.585	2,175.1	5.77
Estonia	EST	44.6	26.9	33,867	20,416	90.4	204.1	184.5	56.5	34.0	0.0	0.0	0.0	0.534	0.885	23.8	1.32
Finland	FIN	261.5	255.1	47,471	46,307	146.3	286.0	418.5	79.1	77.2	0.2	0.3	0.1	0.863	0.885	225.8	5.51
France	FRA	2,994.5	2,592.7	44,651	38,661	129.8	269.1	349.4	74.4	64.5	2.5	3.3	0.9	0.766	0.885	2,295.1	67.06

Table 2.1 *(Continued)*

GROSS DOMESTIC PRODUCT		Expenditure (billion US$)		Expenditure per capita (US$)		Price level index (world = 100.0)[a]	Expenditure per capita indexes[b]				Share (world = 100%)[b]			PPPs[c] (US$ = 1.000)	Reference data		
							World = 100.0		United States = 100.0		Expenditure				Market exchange rates[c] (US$ = 1.000)	Expenditure (billion LCU)	Population (millions)
Economy		Based on PPPs	Based on XRs	Based on PPPs	Based on XRs		Based on PPPs	Based on XRs	Based on PPPs	Based on XRs	Based on PPPs	Based on XRs	Population				
(00)		(01)	(02)	(03)	(04)	(05)	(06)	(07)	(08)	(09)	(10)	(11)	(12)	(13)	(14)	(15)	(16)
Georgia	GEO	50.7	16.2	13,590	4,357	48.1	81.9	39.4	22.7	7.3	0.0	0.0	0.1	0.805	2.510	40.8	3.73
Germany	DEU	4,381.8	3,665.9	53,012	44,350	125.5	319.4	400.8	88.4	73.9	3.7	4.6	1.1	0.741	0.885	3,245.0	82.66
Greece	GRC	312.8	203.6	29,089	18,931	97.6	175.3	171.1	48.5	31.6	0.3	0.3	0.1	0.576	0.885	180.2	10.75
Hungary	HUN	289.0	141.9	29,529	14,497	73.6	177.9	131.0	49.2	24.2	0.2	0.2	0.1	134.363	273.692	38,835.2	9.79
Iceland	ISL	19.1	24.5	55,492	71,313	192.7	334.4	644.4	92.5	118.9	0.0	0.0	0.0	137.122	106.701	2,613.0	0.34
Ireland	IRL	375.6	335.7	78,211	69,898	134.0	471.3	631.6	130.4	116.5	0.3	0.4	0.1	0.791	0.885	297.1	4.80
Italy	ITA	2,529.5	1,961.8	41,785	32,407	116.3	251.8	292.9	69.7	54.0	2.1	2.5	0.8	0.687	0.885	1,736.6	60.54
Kazakhstan	KAZ	448.5	166.8	24,863	9,248	55.8	149.8	83.6	41.4	15.4	0.4	0.2	0.3	121.253	326.000	54,378.9	18.04
Kyrgyz Republic	KGZ	31.3	7.7	5,263	1,298	37.0	31.7	11.7	8.8	2.2	0.0	0.0	0.1	16.959	68.769	530.5	5.94
Latvia	LVA	55.3	30.3	28,505	15,596	82.1	171.8	140.9	47.5	26.0	0.0	0.0	0.0	0.484	0.885	26.8	1.94
Lithuania	LTU	95.7	47.8	33,821	16,883	74.9	203.8	152.6	56.4	28.1	0.1	0.1	0.0	0.442	0.885	42.3	2.83
Luxembourg	LUX	67.3	64.2	112,701	107,513	143.1	679.1	971.6	187.9	179.2	0.1	0.1	0.0	0.844	0.885	56.8	0.60
Moldova	MDA	32.1	9.7	9,045	2,726	45.2	54.5	24.6	15.1	4.5	0.0	0.0	0.0	5.572	18.490	178.9	3.55
Montenegro	MNE	12.3	4.9	19,704	7,804	59.4	118.7	70.5	32.8	13.0	0.0	0.0	0.0	0.351	0.885	4.3	0.62
Netherlands	NLD	948.2	833.9	55,349	48,677	131.9	333.5	439.9	92.3	81.1	0.8	1.0	0.2	0.778	0.885	738.1	17.13
North Macedonia	MKD	32.5	11.3	15,646	5,467	52.4	94.3	49.4	26.1	9.1	0.0	0.0	0.0	19.043	54.505	618.1	2.07
Norway	NOR	332.1	399.1	62,940	75,638	180.2	379.3	683.5	104.9	126.1	0.3	0.5	0.1	9.922	8.256	3,295.4	5.28
Poland	POL	1,145.0	527.9	29,802	13,740	69.1	179.6	124.2	49.7	22.9	1.0	0.7	0.5	1.737	3.768	1,989.4	38.42
Portugal	PRT	340.8	221.4	33,086	21,491	97.4	199.4	194.2	55.2	35.8	0.3	0.3	0.1	0.575	0.885	195.9	10.30
Romania	ROU	534.7	212.1	27,293	10,827	59.5	164.5	97.8	45.5	18.1	0.4	0.3	0.3	1.604	4.044	857.9	19.59
Russian Federation	RUS	3,829.5	1,578.6	26,079	10,750	61.8	157.1	97.1	43.5	17.9	3.2	2.0	2.0	24.050	58.343	92,101.3	146.84
Serbia	SRB	116.5	44.3	16,599	6,305	57.0	100.0	57.0	27.7	10.5	0.1	0.1	0.1	40.795	107.406	4,754.4	7.02
Slovak Republic	SVK	168.1	95.5	30,911	17,556	85.2	186.3	158.7	51.5	29.3	0.1	0.1	0.1	0.503	0.885	84.5	5.44
Slovenia	SVN	75.7	48.6	36,661	23,508	96.2	220.9	212.4	61.1	39.2	0.1	0.1	0.0	0.568	0.885	43.0	2.07
Spain	ESP	1,844.0	1,312.6	39,627	28,207	106.8	238.8	254.9	66.1	47.0	1.5	1.6	0.6	0.630	0.885	1,161.9	46.53
Sweden	SWE	530.0	541.8	52,693	53,870	153.3	317.5	486.8	87.8	89.8	0.4	0.7	0.1	8.719	8.529	4,621.0	10.06
Switzerland	CHE	567.4	680.4	67,139	80,501	179.8	404.6	727.5	111.9	134.2	0.5	0.9	0.1	1.180	0.984	669.5	8.45
Tajikistan	TJK	27.4	7.2	3,105	810	39.1	18.7	7.3	5.2	1.4	0.0	0.0	0.1	2.231	8.550	61.2	8.84
Turkey	TUR	2,265.5	852.7	28,209	10,617	56.4	170.0	95.9	47.0	17.7	1.9	1.1	1.1	1.373	3.648	3,110.7	80.31
Ukraine	UKR	504.4	112.2	11,871	2,641	33.4	71.5	23.9	19.8	4.4	0.4	0.1	0.6	5.916	26.597	2,983.9	42.49
United Kingdom	GBR	3,037.0	2,669.6	45,988	40,424	131.8	277.1	365.3	76.7	67.4	2.5	3.3	0.9	0.682	0.776	2,071.7	66.04
Total (46)	**ECB**	**30,810.7**	**21,449.6**	**35,255**	**24,544**	**104.4**	**212.4**	**221.8**	**58.8**	**40.9**	**25.8**	**26.9**	**12.1**	**n.a.**	**n.a**	**n.a.**	**873.93**
Latin America and the Caribbean																	
Anguilla	AIA	0.3	0.3	22,877	19,441	127.4	137.9	175.7	38.1	32.4	0.0	0.0	0.0	2.295	2.700	0.8	0.01
Antigua and Barbuda	ATG	2.0	1.5	20,494	15,891	116.3	123.5	143.6	34.2	26.5	0.0	0.0	0.0	2.094	2.700	4.1	0.10
Argentina	ARG	1,037.8	642.7	23,621	14,627	92.9	142.3	132.2	39.4	24.4	0.9	0.8	0.6	10.257	16.563	10,644.8	43.94
Aruba	ABW	4.1	3.1	38,440	29,006	113.2	231.6	262.1	64.1	48.4	0.0	0.0	0.0	1.351	1.790	5.5	0.11

Table 2.1 *(Continued)*

GROSS DOMESTIC PRODUCT Economy		Expenditure (billion US$) Based on PPPs	Expenditure (billion US$) Based on XRs	Expenditure per capita (US$) Based on PPPs	Expenditure per capita (US$) Based on XRs	Price level index (world = 100.0)[a]	Expenditure per capita indexes[b] World = 100.0 Based on PPPs	Expenditure per capita indexes[b] World = 100.0 Based on XRs	Expenditure per capita indexes[b] United States = 100.0 Based on PPPs	Expenditure per capita indexes[b] United States = 100.0 Based on XRs	Share (world = 100%)[b] Expenditure Based on PPPs	Share (world = 100%)[b] Expenditure Based on XRs	Share (world = 100%)[b] Population	PPPs[c] (US$ = 1.000)	Reference data Market exchange rates[c] (US$ = 1.000)	Reference data Expenditure (billion LCU)	Reference data Population (millions)
(00)		(01)	(02)	(03)	(04)	(05)	(06)	(07)	(08)	(09)	(10)	(11)	(12)	(13)	(14)	(15)	(16)
Bahamas, The	BHS	13.5	12.2	35,309	31,828	135.2	212.8	287.6	58.9	53.1	0.0	0.0	0.0	0.901	1.000	12.2	0.38
Barbados	BRB	4.3	4.7	14,941	16,457	165.2	90.0	148.7	24.9	27.4	0.0	0.0	0.0	2.203	2.000	9.4	0.29
Belize	BLZ	2.7	1.9	7,210	4,957	103.1	43.4	44.8	12.0	8.3	0.0	0.0	0.0	1.375	2.000	3.7	0.38
Bolivia	BOL	94.3	37.2	8,424	3,327	59.2	50.8	30.1	14.0	5.5	0.1	0.0	0.2	2.749	6.960	259.2	11.19
Bonaire[d]	BON	...	...	...	...	...	...	...	...	...	...	...	...	...	1.000	...	0.03
Brazil	BRA	3,017.7	2,062.8	14,520	9,925	102.5	87.5	89.7	24.2	16.5	2.5	2.6	2.9	2.182	3.191	6,583.3	207.83
Cayman Islands	CYM	4.4	5.1	69,421	81,122	175.2	418.3	733.1	115.7	135.2	0.0	0.0	0.0	0.974	0.833	4.3	0.06
Chile	CHL	438.2	277.7	23,657	14,995	95.1	142.6	135.5	39.4	25.0	0.4	0.3	0.3	411.264	648.834	180,211.3	18.52
Colombia	COL	699.9	311.8	14,199	6,325	66.8	85.6	57.2	23.7	10.5	0.6	0.4	0.7	1,314.787	2,951.327	920,194.0	49.29
Costa Rica	CRI	98.0	60.6	19,823	12,254	92.7	119.4	110.7	33.0	20.4	0.1	0.1	0.1	350.817	567.513	34,386.7	4.94
Curaçao	CUW	4.1	3.1	25,183	19,234	114.5	151.7	173.8	42.0	32.1	0.0	0.0	0.0	1.367	1.790	5.6	0.16
Dominica	DMA	0.8	0.5	11,304	7,275	96.5	68.1	65.7	18.8	12.1	0.0	0.0	0.0	1.738	2.700	1.4	0.07
Dominican Republic	DOM	175.9	80.0	16,735	7,609	68.2	100.8	68.8	27.9	12.7	0.1	0.1	0.1	21.613	47.537	3,802.7	10.51
Ecuador	ECU	195.0	104.3	11,618	6,214	80.2	70.0	56.1	19.4	10.4	0.2	0.1	0.2	0.535	1.000	104.3	16.79
El Salvador	SLV	53.9	24.9	8,437	3,902	69.4	50.8	35.3	14.1	6.5	0.0	0.0	0.1	0.463	1.000	24.9	6.39
Grenada	GRD	1.8	1.1	16,235	10,164	93.9	97.8	91.8	27.1	16.9	0.0	0.0	0.0	1.690	2.700	3.0	0.11
Guyana	GUY	7.0	3.5	8,989	4,463	74.5	54.2	40.3	15.0	7.4	0.0	0.0	0.0	105.353	212.190	734.2	0.78
Haiti	HTI	20.6	9.2	1,877	840	67.1	11.3	7.6	3.1	1.4	0.0	0.0	0.2	28.498	63.687	587.5	10.98
Honduras	HND	52.4	23.0	5,562	2,443	65.9	33.5	22.1	9.3	4.1	0.0	0.0	0.1	10.362	23.588	543.4	9.43
Jamaica	JAM	28.1	14.8	9,619	5,080	79.2	58.0	45.9	16.0	8.5	0.0	0.0	0.0	67.582	127.965	1,898.8	2.92
Mexico	MEX	2,470.1	1,157.7	20,023	9,385	70.3	120.7	84.8	33.4	15.6	2.1	1.5	1.7	8.871	18.927	21,911.9	123.36
Montserrat	MSR	0.1	0.1	18,142	12,030	99.4	109.3	108.7	30.2	20.1	0.0	0.0	0.0	1.790	2.700	0.2	0.00
Nicaragua	NIC	38.5	13.8	6,029	2,168	53.9	36.3	19.6	10.1	3.6	0.0	0.0	0.1	10.807	30.051	416.0	6.38
Panama	PAN	125.2	62.3	30,486	15,166	74.6	183.7	137.1	50.8	25.3	0.1	0.1	0.1	0.497	1.000	62.3	4.11
Paraguay	PRY	86.5	39.4	12,594	5,738	68.3	75.9	51.9	21.0	9.6	0.1	0.0	0.1	2,534.377	5,562.276	219,188.4	6.87
Peru	PER	393.3	211.0	12,507	6,712	80.5	75.4	60.7	20.8	11.2	0.3	0.3	0.4	1.749	3.260	688.0	31.44
Sint Maarten	SXM	1.3	1.0	31,579	24,461	116.2	190.3	221.0	52.6	40.8	0.0	0.0	0.0	1.387	1.790	1.8	0.04
St. Kitts and Nevis	KNA	1.2	0.9	23,966	18,105	113.3	144.4	163.6	40.0	30.2	0.0	0.0	0.0	2.040	2.700	2.5	0.05
St. Lucia	LCA	2.3	1.7	12,735	9,413	110.9	76.7	85.1	21.2	15.7	0.0	0.0	0.0	1.996	2.700	4.6	0.18
St. Vincent and the Grenadines	VCT	1.4	0.8	13,075	7,702	88.3	78.8	69.6	21.8	12.8	0.0	0.0	0.0	1.590	2.700	2.3	0.11
Suriname	SUR	9.3	3.2	16,341	5,580	51.2	98.5	50.4	27.2	9.3	0.0	0.0	0.0	2.578	7.550	24.0	0.57
Trinidad and Tobago	TTO	37.1	22.8	26,806	16,458	92.1	161.5	148.7	44.7	27.4	0.0	0.0	0.0	4.162	6.780	154.4	1.38
Turks and Caicos Islands	TCA	1.0	1.0	25,982	26,447	152.7	156.6	239.0	43.3	44.1	0.0	0.0	0.0	1.018	1.000	1.0	0.04
Uruguay	URY	73.3	59.5	21,325	17,322	121.8	128.5	156.5	35.6	28.9	0.1	0.1	0.0	23.294	28.676	1,707.1	3.44
Virgin Islands, British	VGB	1.2	1.3	40,834	43,642	160.3	246.1	394.4	68.1	72.8	0.0	0.0	0.0	1.069	1.000	1.3	0.03
Total (39)	**LCB**	**9,198.6**	**5,262.8**	**16,048**	**9,181**	**85.8**	**96.7**	**83.0**	**26.8**	**15.3**	**7.7**	**6.6**	**8.0**	**n.a.**	**n.a**	**n.a.**	**573.20**

Table 2.1 *(Continued)*

GROSS DOMESTIC PRODUCT		Expenditure (billion US$)		Expenditure per capita (US$)		Price level index (world = 100.0)[a]	Expenditure per capita indexes[b]				Share (world = 100%)[b]			PPPs[c] (US$ = 1.000)	Reference data		
							World = 100.0		United States = 100.0		Expenditure				Market exchange rates[c] (US$ = 1.000)	Expenditure (billion LCU)	Population (millions)
Economy		Based on PPPs	Based on XRs	Based on PPPs	Based on XRs		Based on PPPs	Based on XRs	Based on PPPs	Based on XRs	Based on PPPs	Based on XRs	Population				
(00)		(01)	(02)	(03)	(04)	(05)	(06)	(07)	(08)	(09)	(10)	(11)	(12)	(13)	(14)	(15)	(16)
Middle East and North Africa																	
Algeria	DZA	478.5	167.5	11,561	4,048	52.5	69.7	36.6	19.3	6.7	0.4	0.2	0.6	38.856	110.973	18,591.7	41.39
Bahrain	BHR	70.9	35.3	47,256	23,517	74.6	284.8	212.5	78.8	39.2	0.1	0.0	0.0	0.187	0.376	13.3	1.50
Djibouti	DJI	4.9	2.9	5,197	3,100	89.5	31.3	28.0	8.7	5.2	0.0	0.0	0.0	106.023	177.720	520.2	0.94
Egypt, Arab Rep.	EGY	1,263.4	231.3	13,327	2,439	27.4	80.3	22.0	22.2	4.1	1.1	0.3	1.3	3.267	17.847	4,127.1	94.80
Iran, Islamic Rep.	IRN	1,298.1	510.3	16,012	6,294	59.0	96.5	56.9	26.7	10.5	1.1	0.6	1.1	13,061.295	33,226.298	16,954,811.5	81.07
Iraq	IRQ	368.3	164.4	9,917	4,427	67.0	59.8	40.0	16.5	7.4	0.3	0.2	0.5	560.761	1,256.000	206,530.1	37.14
Israel	ISR	339.5	353.3	38,983	40,558	156.0	234.9	366.5	65.0	67.6	0.3	0.4	0.1	3.745	3.600	1,271.6	8.71
Jordan	JOR	96.6	41.0	9,610	4,077	63.6	57.9	36.8	16.0	6.8	0.1	0.1	0.1	0.300	0.708	29.0	10.05
Kuwait	KWT	199.8	116.9	48,928	28,628	87.7	294.8	258.7	81.6	47.7	0.2	0.1	0.1	0.177	0.303	35.5	4.08
Malta	MLT	19.6	12.8	41,741	27,254	97.9	251.5	246.3	69.6	45.4	0.0	0.0	0.0	0.578	0.885	11.3	0.47
Morocco	MAR	264.3	109.7	7,583	3,148	62.3	45.7	28.5	12.6	5.2	0.2	0.1	0.5	4.023	9.691	1,063.4	34.85
Oman	OMN	135.7	70.6	29,758	15,482	78.0	179.3	139.9	49.6	25.8	0.1	0.1	0.1	0.200	0.385	27.1	4.56
Qatar	QAT	259.0	166.5	95,063	61,099	96.4	572.8	552.1	158.5	101.9	0.2	0.2	0.0	2.346	3.650	607.6	2.72
Saudi Arabia	SAU	1,565.9	688.6	48,015	21,114	65.9	289.3	190.8	80.0	35.2	1.3	0.9	0.5	1.649	3.750	2,582.2	32.61
Tunisia	TUN	121.6	39.9	10,638	3,492	49.2	64.1	31.6	17.7	5.8	0.1	0.1	0.2	0.794	2.419	96.6	11.43
United Arab Emirates	ARE	624.3	377.7	67,100	40,594	90.7	404.3	366.8	111.9	67.7	0.5	0.5	0.1	2.222	3.673	1,387.1	9.30
West Bank and Gaza	PSE	25.6	14.5	5,756	3,255	84.8	34.7	29.4	9.6	5.4	0.0	0.0	0.1	2.036	3.600	52.2	4.45
Total (17)	**MEB**	**7,136.1**	**3,103.1**	**18,774**	**8,164**	**65.2**	**113.1**	**73.8**	**31.3**	**13.6**	**6.0**	**3.9**	**5.3**	**n.a.**	**n.a**	**n.a.**	**380.10**
North America																	
Bermuda	BMU	4.6	6.2	72,356	98,868	204.9	436.0	893.4	120.6	164.8	0.0	0.0	0.0	1.366	1.000	6.2	0.06
Canada	CAN	1,778.0	1,650.6	48,658	45,171	139.2	293.2	408.2	81.1	75.3	1.5	2.1	0.5	1.205	1.298	2,142.0	36.54
United States	USA	19,519.4	19,519.4	59,984	59,984	150.0	361.4	542.1	100.0	100.0	16.3	24.5	4.5	1.000	1.000	19,519.4	325.41
Total (3)	**NAB**	**21,302.0**	**21,176.2**	**58,843**	**58,496**	**149.1**	**354.6**	**528.6**	**98.1**	**97.5**	**17.8**	**26.6**	**5.0**	**n.a.**	**n.a**	**n.a.**	**362.01**
South Asia																	
Bangladesh	BGD	710.6	262.7	4,392	1,624	55.4	26.5	14.7	7.3	2.7	0.6	0.3	2.2	29.738	80.438	21,131.5	161.80
Bhutan	BTN	8.6	2.5	11,787	3,477	44.2	71.0	31.4	19.6	5.8	0.0	0.0	0.0	19.208	65.122	164.6	0.73
India	IND	8,050.5	2,552.5	6,149	1,950	47.5	37.1	17.6	10.3	3.3	6.7	3.2	18.2	20.648	65.122	166,225.6	1,309.20
Maldives	MDV	9.2	4.9	18,662	9,898	79.5	112.5	89.4	31.1	16.5	0.0	0.0	0.0	8.161	15.387	74.9	0.49
Nepal	NPL	83.6	25.0	2,900	867	44.8	17.5	7.8	4.8	1.4	0.1	0.0	0.4	31.235	104.512	2,611.2	28.83
Pakistan	PAK	990.5	315.5	4,975	1,585	47.8	30.0	14.3	8.3	2.6	0.8	0.4	2.8	33.589	105.455	33,270.4	199.11
Sri Lanka	LKA	269.6	87.4	12,574	4,074	48.6	75.8	36.8	21.0	6.8	0.2	0.1	0.3	49.390	152.446	13,317.3	21.44
Total (7)	**SAB**	**10,122.6**	**3,250.5**	**5,880**	**1,888**	**48.2**	**35.4**	**17.1**	**9.8**	**3.1**	**8.5**	**4.1**	**23.9**	**n.a.**	**n.a**	**n.a.**	**1,721.60**
Sub-Saharan Africa																	
Angola	AGO	219.1	122.7	7,348	4,117	84.0	44.3	37.2	12.3	6.9	0.2	0.2	0.4	92.952	165.916	20,365.4	29.82
Benin	BEN	25.1	9.4	2,250	838	55.9	13.6	7.6	3.8	1.4	0.0	0.0	0.2	216.774	582.075	5,450.9	11.18
Botswana	BWA	38.1	17.4	17,276	7,903	68.6	104.1	71.4	28.8	13.2	0.0	0.0	0.0	4.734	10.347	180.3	2.21

Table 2.1 *(Continued)*

GROSS DOMESTIC PRODUCT		Expenditure (billion US$)		Expenditure per capita (US$)		Price level index (world = 100.0)[a]	Expenditure per capita indexes[b]				Share (world = 100%)[b]			PPPs[c] (US$ = 1.000)	Reference data		
							World = 100.0		United States = 100.0		Expenditure				Market exchange rates[c] (US$ = 1.000)	Expenditure (billion LCU)	Population (millions)
Economy		Based on PPPs	Based on XRs	Based on PPPs	Based on XRs		Based on PPPs	Based on XRs	Based on PPPs	Based on XRs	Based on PPPs	Based on XRs	Population				
(00)		(01)	(02)	(03)	(04)	(05)	(06)	(07)	(08)	(09)	(10)	(11)	(12)	(13)	(14)	(15)	(16)
Burkina Faso	BFA	34.8	12.5	1,813	650	53.8	10.9	5.9	3.0	1.1	0.0	0.0	0.3	208.757	582.075	7,263.3	19.19
Burundi	BDI	8.5	3.2	784	297	56.8	4.7	2.7	1.3	0.5	0.0	0.0	0.2	654.896	1,729.055	5,562.4	10.83
Cabo Verde	CPV	3.6	1.8	6,617	3,280	74.3	39.9	29.6	11.0	5.5	0.0	0.0	0.0	48.477	97.799	172.4	0.54
Cameroon	CMR	87.1	34.8	3,546	1,418	60.0	21.4	12.8	5.9	2.4	0.1	0.0	0.3	232.801	582.075	20,277.0	24.57
Central African Republic	CAF	4.3	2.1	937	462	73.9	5.6	4.2	1.6	0.8	0.0	0.0	0.1	286.829	582.075	1,235.2	4.60
Chad	TCD	24.4	10.2	1,622	679	62.8	9.8	6.1	2.7	1.1	0.0	0.0	0.2	243.655	582.075	5,936.3	15.02
Comoros	COM	2.5	1.1	3,101	1,350	65.3	18.7	12.2	5.2	2.3	0.0	0.0	0.0	190.126	436.571	479.8	0.81
Congo, Dem. Rep.	COD	112.2	49.4	1,378	607	66.1	8.3	5.5	2.3	1.0	0.1	0.1	1.1	645.391	1,464.418	72,390.1	81.40
Congo, Rep.	COG	26.3	13.4	5,145	2,631	76.7	31.0	23.8	8.6	4.4	0.0	0.0	0.1	297.674	582.075	7,827.5	5.11
Côte d'Ivoire	CIV	87.3	38.1	3,572	1,557	65.4	21.5	14.1	6.0	2.6	0.1	0.0	0.3	253.746	582.075	22,150.8	24.44
Equatorial Guinea	GNQ	28.7	12.3	22,771	9,738	64.1	137.2	88.0	38.0	16.2	0.0	0.0	0.0	248.934	582.075	7,153.6	1.26
Eswatini	SWZ	9.8	4.6	8,717	4,057	69.8	52.5	36.7	14.5	6.8	0.0	0.0	0.0	6.206	13.334	60.8	1.12
Ethiopia	ETH	172.0	61.4	1,617	577	53.5	9.7	5.2	2.7	1.0	0.1	0.1	1.5	8.521	23.866	1,466.0	106.40
Gabon	GAB	26.1	12.5	12,631	6,071	72.1	76.1	54.9	21.1	10.1	0.0	0.0	0.0	279.766	582.075	7,296.5	2.06
Gambia, The	GMB	4.4	1.4	1,970	646	49.2	11.9	5.8	3.3	1.1	0.0	0.0	0.0	15.286	46.608	66.7	2.21
Ghana	GHA	145.5	59.0	4,997	2,026	60.8	30.1	18.3	8.3	3.4	0.1	0.1	0.4	1.764	4.351	256.7	29.12
Guinea	GIN	34.4	12.1	2,847	1,003	52.9	17.2	9.1	4.7	1.7	0.0	0.0	0.2	3,216.035	9,125.743	110,474.2	12.07
Guinea-Bissau	GNB	3.5	1.3	1,925	737	57.4	11.6	6.7	3.2	1.2	0.0	0.0	0.0	222.749	582.075	784.0	1.83
Kenya	KEN	204.0	79.3	4,062	1,578	58.3	24.5	14.3	6.8	2.6	0.2	0.1	0.7	40.185	103.411	8,196.7	50.22
Lesotho	LSO	6.3	2.6	2,996	1,237	61.9	18.1	11.2	5.0	2.1	0.0	0.0	0.0	5.506	13.334	34.5	2.09
Liberia	LBR	6.0	2.8	1,274	588	69.1	7.7	5.3	2.1	1.0	0.0	0.0	0.1	51.957	112.707	311.4	4.70
Madagascar	MDG	39.9	13.0	1,561	508	48.8	9.4	4.6	2.6	0.8	0.0	0.0	0.4	1,013.435	3,116.110	40,445.3	25.57
Malawi	MWI	18.5	6.3	1,045	359	51.6	6.3	3.2	1.7	0.6	0.0	0.0	0.2	251.074	730.273	4,635.6	17.67
Mali	MLI	41.6	15.3	2,249	829	55.3	13.6	7.5	3.7	1.4	0.0	0.0	0.3	214.509	582.075	8,931.3	18.51
Mauritania	MRT	15.8	4.9	3,695	1,150	46.7	22.3	10.4	6.2	1.9	0.0	0.0	0.1	111.258	357.493	1,760.7	4.28
Mauritius	MUS	31.7	15.5	25,051	12,265	73.4	151.0	110.8	41.8	20.4	0.0	0.0	0.0	16.882	34.481	534.8	1.26
Mozambique	MOZ	35.2	12.7	1,229	442	53.9	7.4	4.0	2.0	0.7	0.0	0.0	0.4	22.856	63.584	804.5	28.65
Namibia	NAM	25.5	13.4	10,614	5,597	79.1	64.0	50.6	17.7	9.3	0.0	0.0	0.0	7.021	13.313	179.0	2.40
Niger	NER	18.3	8.1	847	376	66.6	5.1	3.4	1.4	0.6	0.0	0.0	0.3	258.460	582.075	4,727.1	21.60
Nigeria	NGA	884.6	335.5	4,634	1,758	56.9	27.9	15.9	7.7	2.9	0.7	0.4	2.6	115.978	305.790	102,593.5	190.87
Rwanda	RWA	21.6	8.4	1,804	705	58.6	10.9	6.4	3.0	1.2	0.0	0.0	0.2	325.126	831.531	7,025.7	11.98
São Tomé and Príncipe	STP	0.7	0.3	3,255	1,505	69.4	19.6	13.6	5.4	2.5	0.0	0.0	0.0	10.055	21.741	6.8	0.21
Senegal	SEN	49.3	20.9	3,195	1,355	63.6	19.3	12.2	5.3	2.3	0.0	0.0	0.2	246.787	582.075	12,158.0	15.42
Seychelles	SYC	2.7	1.6	27,794	16,228	87.6	167.5	146.7	46.3	27.1	0.0	0.0	0.0	7.969	13.648	21.4	0.10
Sierra Leone	SLE	12.3	3.7	1,642	499	45.6	9.9	4.5	2.7	0.8	0.0	0.0	0.1	2,244.995	7,384.432	27,610.8	7.49
South Africa	ZAF	733.7	353.6	12,870	6,203	72.3	77.5	56.1	21.5	10.3	0.6	0.4	0.8	6.427	13.334	4,715.2	57.01
Sudan	SDN	176.6	40.5	4,331	994	34.4	26.1	9.0	7.2	1.7	0.1	0.1	0.6	4.619	20.130	815.9	40.78

Table 2.1 *(Continued)*

GROSS DOMESTIC PRODUCT Economy		Expenditure (billion US$) Based on PPPs	Expenditure (billion US$) Based on XRs	Expenditure per capita (US$) Based on PPPs	Expenditure per capita (US$) Based on XRs	Price level index (world = 100.0)[a]	Expenditure per capita indexes[b] World = 100.0 Based on PPPs	Expenditure per capita indexes[b] World = 100.0 Based on XRs	Expenditure per capita indexes[b] United States = 100.0 Based on PPPs	Expenditure per capita indexes[b] United States = 100.0 Based on XRs	Share (world = 100%)[b] Expenditure Based on PPPs	Share (world = 100%)[b] Expenditure Based on XRs	Share (world = 100%)[b] Population	PPPs[c] (US$ = 1.000)	Reference data Market exchange rates[c] (US$ = 1.000)	Reference data Expenditure (billion LCU)	Reference data Population (millions)
(00)		(01)	(02)	(03)	(04)	(05)	(06)	(07)	(08)	(09)	(10)	(11)	(12)	(13)	(14)	(15)	(16)
Tanzania	TZA	125.0	49.6	2,287	908	59.6	13.8	8.2	3.8	1.5	0.1	0.1	0.8	885.083	2,228.858	110,651.1	54.66
Togo	TGO	11.2	4.6	1,457	600	61.8	8.8	5.4	2.4	1.0	0.0	0.0	0.1	239.722	582.075	2,689.4	7.70
Uganda	UGA	91.5	32.2	2,223	782	52.8	13.4	7.1	3.7	1.3	0.1	0.0	0.6	1,270.608	3,611.224	116,251.5	41.17
Zambia	ZMB	56.5	24.9	3,354	1,477	66.0	20.2	13.3	5.6	2.5	0.0	0.0	0.2	4.193	9.520	237.0	16.85
Zimbabwe	ZWE	36.4	18.6	2,560	1,309	76.7	15.4	11.8	4.3	2.2	0.0	0.0	0.2	0.511	1.000	18.6	14.24
Total (45)	**SSB**	**3,742.5**	**1,549.4**	**3,665**	**1,517**	**62.1**	**22.1**	**13.7**	**6.1**	**2.5**	**3.1**	**1.9**	**14.2**	**n.a.**	**n.a**	**n.a.**	**1,021.22**
World (176)	**WLD**	**119,547.5**	**79,715.0**	**16,596**	**11,066**	**100.0**	**100.0**	**100.0**	**27.7**	**18.4**	**100.0**	**100.0**	**100.0**	**n.a.**	**n.a.**	**n.a.**	**7,203.60**

Note: PPP = purchasing power parity; XR = market exchange rate; LCU = local currency unit; n.a. = not applicable; ... = data suppressed due to unavailability.

a. World totals used to calculate price level indexes (PLIs) in this table exclude nonparticipating economies.

b. Indexes and shares are rounded to one decimal place for presentation in this table.

c. PPPs and market exchange rates are rounded to three decimal places for presentation in this table.

d. Bonaire's results are provided only for individual consumption expenditure by households. Therefore, to ensure consistency across tables, Bonaire is not included in either the Latin America and the Caribbean or the world totals.

Table 2.2 Actual individual consumption (AIC): ICP 2017 results

ACTUAL INDIVIDUAL CONSUMPTION		Expenditure (billion US$)		Expenditure per capita (US$)		Price level index (world = 100.0)[a]	Expenditure per capita indexes[b]				Share (world = 100%)[b]			PPPs[c] (US$ = 1.000)	Reference data		
							World = 100.0		United States = 100.0		Expenditure				Market exchange rates[c] (US$ = 1.000)	Expenditure (billion LCU)	Population (millions)
Economy		Based on PPPs	Based on XRs	Based on PPPs	Based on XRs		Based on PPPs	Based on XRs	Based on PPPs	Based on XRs	Based on PPPs	Based on XRs	Population				
(00)		(01)	(02)	(03)	(04)	(05)	(06)	(07)	(08)	(09)	(10)	(11)	(12)	(13)	(14)	(15)	(16)
East Asia and Pacific																	
Australia	AUS	838.7	944.5	34,091	38,393	168.6	314.0	529.5	76.4	86.0	1.1	1.8	0.3	1.469	1.305	1,232.4	24.60
Brunei Darussalam	BRN	6.9	3.2	16,118	7,560	70.2	148.4	104.3	36.1	16.9	0.0	0.0	0.0	0.648	1.381	4.5	0.43
Cambodia	KHM	55.7	18.9	3,512	1,190	50.8	32.3	16.4	7.9	2.7	0.1	0.0	0.2	1,372.850	4,050.580	76,416.3	15.85
China	CHN	9,574.3	5,731.9	6,906	4,134	89.6	63.6	57.0	15.5	9.3	12.2	11.0	19.2	4.046	6.759	38,740.6	1,386.40
Fiji	FJI	8.7	3.9	9,967	4,451	66.9	91.8	61.4	22.3	10.0	0.0	0.0	0.0	0.923	2.067	8.1	0.88
Hong Kong SAR, China	HKG	313.2	242.2	42,371	32,760	115.8	390.2	451.8	95.0	73.4	0.4	0.5	0.1	6.026	7.793	1,887.2	7.39
Indonesia	IDN	1,755.5	617.3	6,703	2,357	52.7	61.7	32.5	15.0	5.3	2.2	1.2	3.6	4,705.548	13,380.872	8,260,567.4	261.89
Japan	JPN	3,476.7	3,282.1	27,439	25,903	141.4	252.7	357.3	61.5	58.1	4.4	6.3	1.8	105.886	112.166	368,137.8	126.71
Korea, Rep.	KOR	1,137.2	908.1	22,140	17,680	119.6	203.9	243.8	49.6	39.6	1.5	1.7	0.7	902.695	1,130.425	1,026,524.0	51.36
Lao PDR	LAO	28.7	9.6	4,158	1,387	49.9	38.3	19.1	9.3	3.1	0.0	0.0	0.1	2,785.475	8,351.526	79,927.0	6.90
Malaysia	MYS	509.4	193.2	15,908	6,032	56.8	146.5	83.2	35.7	13.5	0.7	0.4	0.4	1.631	4.300	830.7	32.02
Mongolia	MNG	21.7	6.7	6,884	2,138	46.5	63.4	29.5	15.4	4.8	0.0	0.0	0.0	757.817	2,439.777	16,427.7	3.15
Myanmar	MMR	143.5	37.6	2,700	708	39.3	24.9	9.8	6.1	1.6	0.2	0.1	0.7	356.688	1,360.359	51,180.5	53.15
New Zealand	NZL	134.6	137.0	27,860	28,353	152.4	256.6	391.0	62.4	63.5	0.2	0.3	0.1	1.432	1.407	192.8	4.83
Philippines	PHL	677.6	247.5	6,458	2,359	54.7	59.5	32.5	14.5	5.3	0.9	0.5	1.5	18.409	50.404	12,474.5	104.92
Singapore	SGP	179.4	133.8	31,966	23,836	111.7	294.4	328.7	71.6	53.4	0.2	0.3	0.1	1.030	1.381	184.7	5.61
Taiwan, China	TWN	680.0	347.4	28,863	14,746	76.5	265.8	203.4	64.7	33.0	0.9	0.7	0.3	15.553	30.442	10,575.9	23.56
Thailand	THA	697.3	253.7	10,307	3,750	54.5	94.9	51.7	23.1	8.4	0.9	0.5	0.9	12.349	33.940	8,611.0	67.65
Vietnam	VNM	452.8	143.2	4,805	1,520	47.4	44.3	21.0	10.8	3.4	0.6	0.3	1.3	7,075.976	22,370.087	3,204,308.7	94.24
Total (19)	**EAB**	**20,692.0**	**13,261.8**	**9,109**	**5,838**	**96.0**	**83.9**	**80.5**	**20.4**	**13.1**	**26.5**	**25.4**	**31.5**	**n.a.**	**n.a**	**n.a.**	**2,271.55**
Europe and Central Asia																	
Albania	ALB	31.2	11.1	10,872	3,865	53.2	100.1	53.3	24.4	8.7	0.0	0.0	0.0	42.215	118.748	1,318.8	2.87
Armenia	ARM	32.5	9.8	10,893	3,276	45.0	100.3	45.2	24.4	7.3	0.0	0.0	0.0	145.175	482.720	4,711.6	2.98
Austria	AUT	293.9	269.9	33,412	30,693	137.6	307.7	423.3	74.9	68.8	0.4	0.5	0.1	0.813	0.885	239.0	8.80
Azerbaijan	AZE	103.7	25.4	10,655	2,612	36.7	98.1	36.0	23.9	5.9	0.1	0.0	0.1	0.422	1.721	43.8	9.73
Belarus	BLR	130.1	35.3	13,697	3,714	40.6	126.2	51.2	30.7	8.3	0.2	0.1	0.1	0.524	1.932	68.1	9.50
Belgium	BEL	364.8	335.3	32,066	29,475	137.6	295.3	406.5	71.9	66.1	0.5	0.6	0.2	0.814	0.885	296.8	11.38
Bosnia and Herzegovina	BIH	40.3	16.1	12,021	4,792	59.7	110.7	66.1	26.9	10.7	0.1	0.0	0.0	0.690	1.731	27.8	3.35
Bulgaria	BGR	108.5	40.0	15,336	5,656	55.2	141.2	78.0	34.4	12.7	0.1	0.1	0.1	0.639	1.731	69.3	7.08
Croatia	HRV	73.2	37.7	17,736	9,137	77.1	163.4	126.0	39.7	20.5	0.1	0.1	0.1	3.404	6.607	249.3	4.13
Cyprus	CYP	22.7	16.6	26,378	19,280	109.5	242.9	265.9	59.1	43.2	0.0	0.0	0.0	0.647	0.885	14.7	0.86
Czech Republic	CZE	244.1	124.8	23,054	11,787	76.6	212.3	162.6	51.7	26.4	0.3	0.2	0.1	11.915	23.304	2,908.8	10.59
Denmark	DNK	186.3	211.6	32,306	36,688	170.1	297.5	506.0	72.4	82.2	0.2	0.4	0.1	7.478	6.585	1,393.2	5.77
Estonia	EST	27.0	16.5	20,554	12,506	91.1	189.3	172.5	46.1	28.0	0.0	0.0	0.0	0.539	0.885	14.6	1.32
Finland	FIN	173.7	174.2	31,526	31,632	150.2	290.4	436.3	70.7	70.9	0.2	0.3	0.1	0.888	0.885	154.2	5.51
France	FRA	2,061.5	1,802.3	30,740	26,874	130.9	283.1	370.6	68.9	60.2	2.6	3.5	0.9	0.774	0.885	1,595.4	67.06

Table 2.2 *(Continued)*

ACTUAL INDIVIDUAL CONSUMPTION		Expenditure (billion US$)		Expenditure per capita (US$)		Price level index (world = 100.0)[a]	Expenditure per capita indexes[b]				Share (world = 100%)[b]			PPPs[c] (US$ = 1.000)	Reference data		
							World = 100.0		United States = 100.0		Expenditure				Market exchange rates[c] (US$ = 1.000)	Expenditure (billion LCU)	Population (millions)
Economy		Based on PPPs	Based on XRs	Based on PPPs	Based on XRs		Based on PPPs	Based on XRs	Based on PPPs	Based on XRs	Based on PPPs	Based on XRs	Population				
(00)		(01)	(02)	(03)	(04)	(05)	(06)	(07)	(08)	(09)	(10)	(11)	(12)	(13)	(14)	(15)	(16)
Georgia	GEO	37.7	12.2	10,123	3,267	48.3	93.2	45.1	22.7	7.3	0.0	0.0	0.1	0.810	2.510	30.6	3.73
Germany	DEU	2,842.2	2,385.4	34,385	28,859	125.7	316.7	398.0	77.1	64.7	3.6	4.6	1.1	0.743	0.885	2,111.5	82.66
Greece	GRC	233.2	157.1	21,688	14,608	100.9	199.7	201.5	48.6	32.7	0.3	0.3	0.1	0.596	0.885	139.1	10.75
Hungary	HUN	174.7	84.8	17,851	8,662	72.7	164.4	119.5	40.0	19.4	0.2	0.2	0.1	132.801	273.692	23,203.5	9.79
Iceland	ISL	11.3	16.1	32,888	47,021	214.1	302.9	648.5	73.7	105.4	0.0	0.0	0.0	152.553	106.701	1,722.9	0.34
Ireland	IRL	128.4	135.3	26,744	28,169	157.7	246.3	388.5	59.9	63.1	0.2	0.3	0.1	0.932	0.885	119.7	4.80
Italy	ITA	1,687.2	1,395.8	27,870	23,057	123.9	256.7	318.0	62.5	51.7	2.2	2.7	0.8	0.732	0.885	1,235.6	60.54
Kazakhstan	KAZ	295.3	96.4	16,373	5,346	48.9	150.8	73.7	36.7	12.0	0.4	0.2	0.3	106.447	326.000	31,436.8	18.04
Kyrgyz Republic	KGZ	29.9	7.0	5,023	1,179	35.1	46.3	16.3	11.3	2.6	0.0	0.0	0.1	16.140	68.769	481.9	5.94
Latvia	LVA	37.1	20.7	19,108	10,650	83.5	176.0	146.9	42.8	23.9	0.0	0.0	0.0	0.493	0.885	18.3	1.94
Lithuania	LTU	70.0	34.2	24,753	12,084	73.1	228.0	166.7	55.5	27.1	0.1	0.1	0.0	0.432	0.885	30.3	2.83
Luxembourg	LUX	22.6	25.5	37,852	42,732	169.1	348.6	589.4	84.8	95.8	0.0	0.0	0.0	0.999	0.885	22.6	0.60
Moldova	MDA	32.6	9.2	9,177	2,601	42.4	84.5	35.9	20.6	5.8	0.0	0.0	0.0	5.240	18.490	170.7	3.55
Montenegro	MNE	9.9	4.0	15,871	6,501	61.3	146.2	89.7	35.6	14.6	0.0	0.0	0.0	0.363	0.885	3.6	0.62
Netherlands	NLD	544.3	506.4	31,775	29,559	139.3	292.7	407.7	71.2	66.2	0.7	1.0	0.2	0.823	0.885	448.2	17.13
North Macedonia	MKD	24.0	8.4	11,575	4,060	52.5	106.6	56.0	25.9	9.1	0.0	0.0	0.0	19.120	54.505	459.1	2.07
Norway	NOR	189.0	242.8	35,819	46,003	192.3	329.9	634.5	80.3	103.1	0.2	0.5	0.1	10.603	8.256	2,004.2	5.28
Poland	POL	817.0	359.0	21,265	9,344	65.8	195.8	128.9	47.7	20.9	1.0	0.7	0.5	1.656	3.768	1,352.9	38.42
Portugal	PRT	238.4	163.6	23,148	15,882	102.7	213.2	219.0	51.9	35.6	0.3	0.3	0.1	0.607	0.885	144.8	10.30
Romania	ROU	383.0	148.8	19,551	7,594	58.2	180.1	104.7	43.8	17.0	0.5	0.3	0.3	1.571	4.044	601.7	19.59
Russian Federation	RUS	2,524.0	948.5	17,188	6,459	56.3	158.3	89.1	38.5	14.5	3.2	1.8	2.0	21.924	58.343	55,336.6	146.84
Serbia	SRB	93.1	35.3	13,264	5,034	56.8	122.2	69.4	29.7	11.3	0.1	0.1	0.1	40.767	107.406	3,796.3	7.02
Slovak Republic	SVK	106.4	61.7	19,557	11,345	86.9	180.1	156.5	43.8	25.4	0.1	0.1	0.1	0.513	0.885	54.6	5.44
Slovenia	SVN	45.9	30.9	22,205	14,977	101.0	204.5	206.6	49.8	33.6	0.1	0.1	0.0	0.597	0.885	27.4	2.07
Spain	ESP	1,198.8	909.0	25,763	19,534	113.5	237.3	269.4	57.7	43.8	1.5	1.7	0.6	0.671	0.885	804.6	46.53
Sweden	SWE	317.0	346.6	31,514	34,461	163.8	290.2	475.3	70.6	77.2	0.4	0.7	0.1	9.327	8.529	2,956.1	10.06
Switzerland	CHE	298.7	406.5	35,344	48,094	203.8	325.5	663.3	79.2	107.8	0.4	0.8	0.1	1.339	0.984	400.0	8.45
Tajikistan	TJK	25.0	6.3	2,828	715	37.9	26.0	9.9	6.3	1.6	0.0	0.0	0.1	2.162	8.550	54.0	8.84
Turkey	TUR	1,551.1	583.9	19,313	7,270	56.4	177.9	100.3	43.3	16.3	2.0	1.1	1.1	1.373	3.648	2,130.2	80.31
Ukraine	UKR	420.6	88.7	9,899	2,089	31.6	91.2	28.8	22.2	4.7	0.5	0.2	0.6	5.612	26.597	2,360.0	42.49
United Kingdom	GBR	2,142.6	2,061.8	32,445	31,220	144.1	298.8	430.6	72.7	70.0	2.7	3.9	0.9	0.747	0.776	1,600.0	66.04
Total (46)	**ECB**	**20,424.5**	**14,418.5**	**23,371**	**16,499**	**105.7**	**215.2**	**227.5**	**52.4**	**37.0**	**26.1**	**27.6**	**12.1**	**n.a.**	**n.a**	**n.a.**	**873.93**
Latin America and the Caribbean																	
Anguilla	AIA	0.3	0.2	18,348	16,076	131.2	169.0	221.7	41.1	36.0	0.0	0.0	0.0	2.366	2.700	0.6	0.01
Antigua and Barbuda	ATG	0.9	0.7	9,776	7,801	119.5	90.0	107.6	21.9	17.5	0.0	0.0	0.0	2.155	2.700	2.0	0.10
Argentina	ARG	812.2	485.6	18,485	11,052	89.5	170.2	152.4	41.4	24.8	1.0	0.9	0.6	9.903	16.563	8,043.0	43.94
Aruba	ABW	2.5	1.9	23,294	17,788	114.4	214.5	245.3	52.2	39.9	0.0	0.0	0.0	1.367	1.790	3.4	0.11

Table 2.2 *(Continued)*

ACTUAL INDIVIDUAL CONSUMPTION		Expenditure (billion US$)		Expenditure per capita (US$)		Price level index (world = 100.0)[a]	Expenditure per capita indexes[b]				Share (world = 100%)[b]			PPPs[c] (US$ = 1.000)	Reference data		
							World = 100.0		United States = 100.0		Expenditure				Market exchange rates[c] (US$ = 1.000)	Expenditure (billion LCU)	Population (millions)
Economy		Based on PPPs	Based on XRs	Based on PPPs	Based on XRs		Based on PPPs	Based on XRs	Based on PPPs	Based on XRs	Based on PPPs	Based on XRs	Population				
(00)		(01)	(02)	(03)	(04)	(05)	(06)	(07)	(08)	(09)	(10)	(11)	(12)	(13)	(14)	(15)	(16)
Bahamas, The	BHS	8.2	8.3	21,562	21,762	151.1	198.6	300.1	48.3	48.8	0.0	0.0	0.0	1.009	1.000	8.3	0.38
Barbados	BRB	3.3	3.7	11,662	13,053	167.6	107.4	180.0	26.1	29.3	0.0	0.0	0.0	2.239	2.000	7.5	0.29
Belize	BLZ	2.0	1.4	5,356	3,674	102.7	49.3	50.7	12.0	8.2	0.0	0.0	0.0	1.372	2.000	2.8	0.38
Bolivia	BOL	72.0	26.0	6,436	2,318	53.9	59.3	32.0	14.4	5.2	0.1	0.0	0.2	2.507	6.960	180.6	11.19
Bonaire[d]	BON	...	...	...	...	...	...	...	...	...	...	...	...	...	1.000	...	0.03
Brazil	BRA	2,224.3	1,510.8	10,702	7,269	101.7	98.6	100.3	24.0	16.3	2.8	2.9	2.9	2.168	3.191	4,821.5	207.83
Cayman Islands	CYM	2.3	2.9	35,781	46,030	192.6	329.5	634.8	80.2	103.2	0.0	0.0	0.0	1.072	0.833	2.4	0.06
Chile	CHL	300.0	201.6	16,199	10,884	100.6	149.2	150.1	36.3	24.4	0.4	0.4	0.3	435.970	648.834	130,809.6	18.52
Colombia	COL	545.0	229.1	11,058	4,648	63.0	101.8	64.1	24.8	10.4	0.7	0.4	0.7	1,240.682	2,951.327	676,230.0	49.29
Costa Rica	CRI	74.4	46.0	15,052	9,306	92.6	138.6	128.3	33.7	20.9	0.1	0.1	0.1	350.863	567.513	26,114.6	4.94
Curaçao	CUW	2.9	2.2	18,181	13,760	113.3	167.4	189.8	40.7	30.8	0.0	0.0	0.0	1.355	1.790	4.0	0.16
Dominica	DMA	0.7	0.5	10,481	6,654	95.1	96.5	91.8	23.5	14.9	0.0	0.0	0.0	1.714	2.700	1.3	0.07
Dominican Republic	DOM	129.7	59.9	12,340	5,700	69.2	113.7	78.6	27.7	12.8	0.2	0.1	0.1	21.958	47.537	2,848.7	10.51
Ecuador	ECU	131.1	70.6	7,812	4,208	80.7	72.0	58.0	17.5	9.4	0.2	0.1	0.2	0.539	1.000	70.6	16.79
El Salvador	SLV	46.9	22.5	7,336	3,528	72.0	67.6	48.7	16.4	7.9	0.1	0.0	0.1	0.481	1.000	22.5	6.39
Grenada	GRD	1.8	1.1	15,824	9,715	91.9	145.7	134.0	35.5	21.8	0.0	0.0	0.0	1.658	2.700	2.9	0.11
Guyana	GUY	5.0	2.5	6,447	3,190	74.1	59.4	44.0	14.4	7.1	0.0	0.0	0.0	104.981	212.190	524.7	0.78
Haiti	HTI	21.6	9.7	1,968	883	67.2	18.1	12.2	4.4	2.0	0.0	0.0	0.2	28.588	63.687	617.9	10.98
Honduras	HND	43.7	19.3	4,635	2,042	66.0	42.7	28.2	10.4	4.6	0.1	0.0	0.1	10.389	23.588	454.1	9.43
Jamaica	JAM	24.9	12.6	8,525	4,317	75.8	78.5	59.5	19.1	9.7	0.0	0.0	0.0	64.797	127.965	1,613.6	2.92
Mexico	MEX	1,795.8	826.7	14,557	6,701	68.9	134.1	92.4	32.6	15.0	2.3	1.6	1.7	8.713	18.927	15,645.7	123.36
Montserrat	MSR	0.1	0.1	16,099	11,257	104.7	148.3	155.3	36.1	25.2	0.0	0.0	0.0	1.888	2.700	0.2	0.00
Nicaragua	NIC	31.4	10.8	4,924	1,697	51.6	45.3	23.4	11.0	3.8	0.0	0.0	0.1	10.355	30.051	325.5	6.38
Panama	PAN	73.9	34.5	18,004	8,405	69.9	165.8	115.9	40.4	18.8	0.1	0.1	0.1	0.467	1.000	34.5	4.11
Paraguay	PRY	64.5	27.1	9,386	3,953	63.1	86.4	54.5	21.0	8.9	0.1	0.1	0.1	2,342.430	5,562.276	150,972.8	6.87
Peru	PER	273.8	146.3	8,708	4,654	80.0	80.2	64.2	19.5	10.4	0.4	0.3	0.4	1.742	3.260	477.1	31.44
Sint Maarten	SXM	1.0	0.8	24,297	18,744	115.5	223.8	258.5	54.5	42.0	0.0	0.0	0.0	1.381	1.790	1.4	0.04
St. Kitts and Nevis	KNA	0.9	0.7	16,402	13,555	123.8	151.1	186.9	36.8	30.4	0.0	0.0	0.0	2.231	2.700	1.9	0.05
St. Lucia	LCA	0.9	0.6	5,042	3,560	105.7	46.4	49.1	11.3	8.0	0.0	0.0	0.0	1.906	2.700	1.7	0.18
St. Vincent and the Grenadines	VCT	1.1	0.7	10,345	6,354	92.0	95.3	87.6	23.2	14.2	0.0	0.0	0.0	1.658	2.700	1.9	0.11
Suriname	SUR	5.3	1.9	9,306	3,251	52.3	85.7	44.8	20.9	7.3	0.0	0.0	0.0	2.637	7.550	14.0	0.57
Trinidad and Tobago	TTO	29.2	17.2	21,101	12,432	88.2	194.3	171.5	47.3	27.9	0.0	0.0	0.0	3.994	6.780	116.6	1.38
Turks and Caicos Islands	TCA	0.4	0.4	10,146	11,640	171.8	93.4	160.5	22.7	26.1	0.0	0.0	0.0	1.147	1.000	0.4	0.04
Uruguay	URY	56.2	45.0	16,355	13,092	119.9	150.6	180.6	36.7	29.3	0.1	0.1	0.0	22.954	28.676	1,290.2	3.44
Virgin Islands, British	VGB	0.5	0.5	15,371	16,199	157.8	141.6	223.4	34.4	36.3	0.0	0.0	0.0	1.054	1.000	0.5	0.03
Total (39)	**LCB**	**6,790.9**	**3,832.5**	**11,847**	**6,686**	**84.5**	**109.1**	**92.2**	**26.6**	**15.0**	**8.7**	**7.3**	**8.0**	**n.a.**	**n.a**	**n.a.**	**573.20**

Table 2.2 *(Continued)*

ACTUAL INDIVIDUAL CONSUMPTION Economy		Expenditure (billion US$) Based on PPPs	Expenditure (billion US$) Based on XRs	Expenditure per capita (US$) Based on PPPs	Expenditure per capita (US$) Based on XRs	Price level index (world = 100.0)[a]	Expenditure per capita indexes[b] World = 100.0 Based on PPPs	Expenditure per capita indexes[b] World = 100.0 Based on XRs	Expenditure per capita indexes[b] United States = 100.0 Based on PPPs	Expenditure per capita indexes[b] United States = 100.0 Based on XRs	Share (world = 100%)[b] Expenditure Based on PPPs	Share (world = 100%)[b] Expenditure Based on XRs	Share (world = 100%)[b] Population	PPPs[c] (US$ = 1.000)	Reference data Market exchange rates[c] (US$ = 1.000)	Reference data Expenditure (billion LCU)	Reference data Population (millions)
(00)		(01)	(02)	(03)	(04)	(05)	(06)	(07)	(08)	(09)	(10)	(11)	(12)	(13)	(14)	(15)	(16)
Middle East and North Africa																	
Algeria	DZA	295.2	91.1	7,133	2,201	46.2	65.7	30.4	16.0	4.9	0.4	0.2	0.6	34.248	110.973	10,111.0	41.39
Bahrain	BHR	34.0	17.3	22,643	11,514	76.1	208.5	158.8	50.7	25.8	0.0	0.0	0.0	0.191	0.376	6.5	1.50
Djibouti	DJI	3.7	2.1	3,964	2,182	82.4	36.5	30.1	8.9	4.9	0.0	0.0	0.0	97.833	177.720	366.1	0.94
Egypt, Arab Rep.	EGY	1,218.2	212.7	12,850	2,243	26.1	118.4	30.9	28.8	5.0	1.6	0.4	1.3	3.116	17.847	3,795.3	94.80
Iran, Islamic Rep.	IRN	679.7	257.6	8,385	3,177	56.7	77.2	43.8	18.8	7.1	0.9	0.5	1.1	12,591.238	33,226.298	8,558,679.2	81.07
Iraq	IRQ	241.2	101.5	6,495	2,733	63.0	59.8	37.7	14.6	6.1	0.3	0.2	0.5	528.486	1,256.000	127,485.2	37.14
Israel	ISR	211.4	236.7	24,273	27,180	167.7	223.6	374.9	54.4	60.9	0.3	0.5	0.1	4.031	3.600	852.1	8.71
Jordan	JOR	87.2	37.1	8,673	3,690	63.7	79.9	50.9	19.4	8.3	0.1	0.1	0.1	0.301	0.708	26.3	10.05
Kuwait	KWT	103.4	63.9	25,331	15,654	92.5	233.3	215.9	56.8	35.1	0.1	0.1	0.1	0.187	0.303	19.4	4.08
Malta	MLT	10.4	7.0	22,102	14,897	100.9	203.6	205.5	49.5	33.4	0.0	0.0	0.0	0.597	0.885	6.2	0.47
Morocco	MAR	170.9	72.1	4,902	2,070	63.2	45.2	28.5	11.0	4.6	0.2	0.1	0.5	4.092	9.691	699.1	34.85
Oman	OMN	68.3	36.8	14,973	8,072	80.7	137.9	111.3	33.6	18.1	0.1	0.1	0.1	0.207	0.385	14.2	4.56
Qatar	QAT	68.8	51.8	25,247	18,997	112.7	232.5	262.0	56.6	42.6	0.1	0.1	0.0	2.746	3.650	188.9	2.72
Saudi Arabia	SAU	827.3	369.2	25,368	11,320	66.8	233.6	156.1	56.9	25.4	1.1	0.7	0.5	1.673	3.750	1,384.4	32.61
Tunisia	TUN	112.5	32.5	9,842	2,842	43.2	90.6	39.2	22.1	6.4	0.1	0.1	0.2	0.699	2.419	78.6	11.43
United Arab Emirates	ARE	240.0	177.1	25,794	19,030	110.5	237.6	262.5	57.8	42.6	0.3	0.3	0.1	2.709	3.673	650.2	9.30
West Bank and Gaza	PSE	27.7	14.6	6,226	3,279	78.9	57.3	45.2	14.0	7.3	0.0	0.0	0.1	1.896	3.600	52.6	4.45
Total (17)	**MEB**	**4,400.0**	**1,780.9**	**11,576**	**4,685**	**60.6**	**106.6**	**64.6**	**25.9**	**10.5**	**5.6**	**3.4**	**5.3**	**n.a.**	**n.a**	**n.a.**	**380.10**
North America																	
Bermuda	BMU	2.6	3.9	40,559	61,155	225.8	373.6	843.4	90.9	137.1	0.0	0.0	0.0	1.508	1.000	3.9	0.06
Canada	CAN	1,219.8	1,152.6	33,382	31,543	141.5	307.4	435.0	74.8	70.7	1.6	2.2	0.5	1.226	1.298	1,495.7	36.54
United States	USA	14,519.8	14,519.8	44,620	44,620	149.7	411.0	615.4	100.0	100.0	18.6	27.8	4.5	1.000	1.000	14,519.8	325.41
Total (3)	**NAB**	**15,742.1**	**15,676.2**	**43,485**	**43,303**	**149.1**	**400.5**	**597.2**	**97.5**	**97.0**	**20.1**	**30.0**	**5.0**	**n.a.**	**n.a**	**n.a.**	**362.01**
South Asia																	
Bangladesh	BGD	545.1	186.9	3,369	1,155	51.4	31.0	15.9	7.6	2.6	0.7	0.4	2.2	27.584	80.438	15,036.6	161.80
Bhutan	BTN	5.2	1.5	7,169	2,021	42.2	66.0	27.9	16.1	4.5	0.0	0.0	0.0	18.361	65.122	95.7	0.73
India	IND	5,457.4	1,588.8	4,169	1,214	43.6	38.4	16.7	9.3	2.7	7.0	3.0	18.2	18.959	65.122	103,467.7	1,309.20
Maldives	MDV	3.9	2.3	7,960	4,626	87.0	73.3	63.8	17.8	10.4	0.0	0.0	0.0	8.943	15.387	35.0	0.49
Nepal	NPL	72.0	19.7	2,496	683	40.9	23.0	9.4	5.6	1.5	0.1	0.0	0.4	28.577	104.512	2,056.5	28.83
Pakistan	PAK	912.0	273.5	4,580	1,374	44.9	42.2	18.9	10.3	3.1	1.2	0.5	2.8	31.623	105.455	28,840.0	199.11
Sri Lanka	LKA	184.9	57.8	8,624	2,696	46.8	79.4	37.2	19.3	6.0	0.2	0.1	0.3	47.659	152.446	8,813.7	21.44
Total (7)	**SAB**	**7,180.5**	**2,130.5**	**4,171**	**1,238**	**44.4**	**38.4**	**17.1**	**9.3**	**2.8**	**9.2**	**4.1**	**23.9**	**n.a.**	**n.a**	**n.a.**	**1,721.60**
Sub-Saharan Africa																	
Angola	AGO	128.5	74.9	4,309	2,513	87.3	39.7	34.7	9.7	5.6	0.2	0.1	0.4	96.738	165.916	12,430.4	29.82
Benin	BEN	21.4	7.4	1,917	661	51.6	17.7	9.1	4.3	1.5	0.0	0.0	0.2	200.759	582.075	4,300.8	11.18
Botswana	BWA	22.0	9.8	9,972	4,429	66.5	91.8	61.1	22.3	9.9	0.0	0.0	0.0	4.596	10.347	101.1	2.21

Table 2.2 *(Continued)*

ACTUAL INDIVIDUAL CONSUMPTION		Expenditure (billion US$)		Expenditure per capita (US$)		Price level index (world = 100.0)[a]	Expenditure per capita indexes[b]				Share (world = 100%)[b]			PPPs[c] (US$ = 1.000)	Reference data		
							World = 100.0		United States = 100.0		Expenditure				Market exchange rates[c] (US$ = 1.000)	Expenditure (billion LCU)	Population (millions)
Economy		Based on PPPs	Based on XRs	Based on PPPs	Based on XRs		Based on PPPs	Based on XRs	Based on PPPs	Based on XRs	Based on PPPs	Based on XRs	Population				
(00)		(01)	(02)	(03)	(04)	(05)	(06)	(07)	(08)	(09)	(10)	(11)	(12)	(13)	(14)	(15)	(16)
Burkina Faso	BFA	24.3	7.8	1,266	406	48.0	11.7	5.6	2.8	0.9	0.0	0.0	0.3	186.741	582.075	4,537.5	19.19
Burundi	BDI	8.6	3.0	794	274	51.7	7.3	3.8	1.8	0.6	0.0	0.0	0.2	596.887	1,729.055	5,132.9	10.83
Cabo Verde	CPV	2.9	1.3	5,396	2,415	67.0	49.7	33.3	12.1	5.4	0.0	0.0	0.0	43.767	97.799	126.9	0.54
Cameroon	CMR	68.2	25.2	2,777	1,027	55.4	25.6	14.2	6.2	2.3	0.1	0.0	0.3	215.335	582.075	14,692.0	24.57
Central African Republic	CAF	4.2	2.0	910	434	71.5	8.4	6.0	2.0	1.0	0.0	0.0	0.1	277.743	582.075	1,161.9	4.60
Chad	TCD	21.5	8.2	1,429	544	57.0	13.2	7.5	3.2	1.2	0.0	0.0	0.2	221.479	582.075	4,753.2	15.02
Comoros	COM	2.4	1.0	2,909	1,259	64.8	26.8	17.4	6.5	2.8	0.0	0.0	0.0	188.913	436.571	447.2	0.81
Congo, Dem. Rep.	COD	83.1	33.3	1,021	409	60.0	9.4	5.6	2.3	0.9	0.1	0.1	1.1	586.896	1,464.418	48,775.7	81.40
Congo, Rep.	COG	12.5	5.5	2,441	1,082	66.4	22.5	14.9	5.5	2.4	0.0	0.0	0.1	258.018	582.075	3,219.1	5.11
Côte d'Ivoire	CIV	66.8	26.9	2,732	1,100	60.3	25.2	15.2	6.1	2.5	0.1	0.1	0.3	234.310	582.075	15,643.8	24.44
Equatorial Guinea	GNQ	15.5	6.8	12,302	5,413	65.9	113.3	74.7	27.6	12.1	0.0	0.0	0.0	256.108	582.075	3,976.1	1.26
Eswatini	SWZ	8.9	3.8	7,933	3,412	64.4	73.1	47.1	17.8	7.6	0.0	0.0	0.0	5.735	13.334	51.2	1.12
Ethiopia	ETH	144.7	47.1	1,360	442	48.7	12.5	6.1	3.0	1.0	0.2	0.1	1.5	7.761	23.866	1,123.0	106.40
Gabon	GAB	12.0	5.9	5,823	2,859	73.5	53.6	39.4	13.1	6.4	0.0	0.0	0.0	285.813	582.075	3,436.6	2.06
Gambia, The	GMB	4.5	1.3	2,028	605	44.7	18.7	8.3	4.5	1.4	0.0	0.0	0.0	13.904	46.608	62.4	2.21
Ghana	GHA	119.1	43.7	4,091	1,502	55.0	37.7	20.7	9.2	3.4	0.2	0.1	0.4	1.597	4.351	190.3	29.12
Guinea	GIN	28.9	9.3	2,398	769	48.0	22.1	10.6	5.4	1.7	0.0	0.0	0.2	2,927.525	9,125.743	84,702.7	12.07
Guinea-Bissau	GNB	3.2	1.2	1,762	638	54.2	16.2	8.8	3.9	1.4	0.0	0.0	0.0	210.648	582.075	678.4	1.83
Kenya	KEN	187.6	69.4	3,735	1,382	55.4	34.4	19.1	8.4	3.1	0.2	0.1	0.7	38.262	103.411	7,177.1	50.22
Lesotho	LSO	6.3	2.4	3,019	1,133	56.2	27.8	15.6	6.8	2.5	0.0	0.0	0.0	5.003	13.334	31.6	2.09
Liberia	LBR	5.1	2.0	1,076	420	58.4	9.9	5.8	2.4	0.9	0.0	0.0	0.1	43.949	112.707	222.4	4.70
Madagascar	MDG	34.4	9.7	1,344	381	42.4	12.4	5.3	3.0	0.9	0.0	0.0	0.4	883.278	3,116.110	30,365.1	25.57
Malawi	MWI	18.7	5.7	1,059	324	45.9	9.7	4.5	2.4	0.7	0.0	0.0	0.2	223.770	730.273	4,185.6	17.67
Mali	MLI	38.2	12.5	2,063	676	49.1	19.0	9.3	4.6	1.5	0.0	0.0	0.3	190.811	582.075	7,287.4	18.51
Mauritania	MRT	9.9	3.1	2,313	729	47.2	21.3	10.1	5.2	1.6	0.0	0.0	0.1	112.644	357.493	1,115.7	4.28
Mauritius	MUS	22.9	11.1	18,105	8,759	72.5	166.7	120.8	40.6	19.6	0.0	0.0	0.0	16.683	34.481	381.9	1.26
Mozambique	MOZ	31.1	10.2	1,085	357	49.3	10.0	4.9	2.4	0.8	0.0	0.0	0.4	20.935	63.584	650.8	28.65
Namibia	NAM	21.7	10.6	9,019	4,421	73.4	83.1	61.0	20.2	9.9	0.0	0.0	0.0	6.526	13.313	141.4	2.40
Niger	NER	14.3	5.7	661	264	59.7	6.1	3.6	1.5	0.6	0.0	0.0	0.3	232.238	582.075	3,317.2	21.60
Nigeria	NGA	773.4	264.3	4,052	1,385	51.2	37.3	19.1	9.1	3.1	1.0	0.5	2.6	104.502	305.790	80,823.2	190.87
Rwanda	RWA	20.1	6.6	1,676	549	49.0	15.4	7.6	3.8	1.2	0.0	0.0	0.2	272.324	831.531	5,468.3	11.98
São Tomé and Príncipe	STP	0.7	0.3	3,552	1,579	66.5	32.7	21.8	8.0	3.5	0.0	0.0	0.0	9.662	21.741	7.1	0.21
Senegal	SEN	41.6	15.9	2,696	1,029	57.2	24.8	14.2	6.0	2.3	0.1	0.0	0.2	222.146	582.075	9,234.3	15.42
Seychelles	SYC	1.9	1.1	19,668	11,375	86.6	181.1	156.9	44.1	25.5	0.0	0.0	0.0	7.893	13.648	15.0	0.10
Sierra Leone	SLE	14.1	3.8	1,885	501	39.8	17.4	6.9	4.2	1.1	0.0	0.0	0.1	1,964.228	7,384.432	27,726.4	7.49
South Africa	ZAF	526.5	243.5	9,235	4,271	69.3	85.1	58.9	20.7	9.6	0.7	0.5	0.8	6.166	13.334	3,246.3	57.01
Sudan	SDN	151.6	36.0	3,717	883	35.6	34.2	12.2	8.3	2.0	0.2	0.1	0.6	4.780	20.130	724.7	40.78

Table 2.2 *(Continued)*

ACTUAL INDIVIDUAL CONSUMPTION Economy		Expenditure (billion US$) Based on PPPs	Expenditure (billion US$) Based on XRs	Expenditure per capita (US$) Based on PPPs	Expenditure per capita (US$) Based on XRs	Price level index (world = 100.0)[a]	Expenditure per capita indexes[b] World = 100.0 Based on PPPs	Expenditure per capita indexes[b] World = 100.0 Based on XRs	Expenditure per capita indexes[b] United States = 100.0 Based on PPPs	Expenditure per capita indexes[b] United States = 100.0 Based on XRs	Share (world = 100%)[b] Expenditure Based on PPPs	Share (world = 100%)[b] Expenditure Based on XRs	Share (world = 100%)[b] Population	PPPs[c] (US$ = 1.000)	Reference data Market exchange rates[c] (US$ = 1.000)	Reference data Expenditure (billion LCU)	Reference data Population (millions)
(00)		(01)	(02)	(03)	(04)	(05)	(06)	(07)	(08)	(09)	(10)	(11)	(12)	(13)	(14)	(15)	(16)
Tanzania	TZA	105.3	34.3	1,926	627	48.7	17.7	8.6	4.3	1.4	0.1	0.1	0.8	725.219	2,228.858	76,360.1	54.66
Togo	TGO	9.0	3.5	1,173	456	58.2	10.8	6.3	2.6	1.0	0.0	0.0	0.1	226.395	582.075	2,044.8	7.70
Uganda	UGA	78.8	24.1	1,914	586	45.9	17.6	8.1	4.3	1.3	0.1	0.0	0.6	1,106.057	3,611.224	87,153.7	41.17
Zambia	ZMB	31.6	13.0	1,872	769	61.5	17.2	10.6	4.2	1.7	0.0	0.0	0.2	3.907	9.520	123.3	16.85
Zimbabwe	ZWE	36.1	16.2	2,539	1,141	67.3	23.4	15.7	5.7	2.6	0.0	0.0	0.2	0.449	1.000	16.2	14.24
Total (45)	**SSB**	**2,984.0**	**1,130.4**	**2,922**	**1,107**	**56.7**	**26.9**	**15.3**	**6.5**	**2.5**	**3.8**	**2.2**	**14.2**	**n.a.**	**n.a**	**n.a.**	**1,021.22**
World (176)	**WLD**	**78,214.1**	**52,231.0**	**10,858**	**7,251**	**100.0**	**100.0**	**100.0**	**24.3**	**16.2**	**100.0**	**100.0**	**100.0**	**n.a.**	**n.a.**	**n.a.**	**7,203.60**

Note: PPP = purchasing power parity; XR = market exchange rate; LCU = local currency unit; n.a. = not applicable; ... = data suppressed due to unavailability.

a. World totals used to calculate price level indexes (PLIs) in this table exclude nonparticipating economies.

b. Indexes and shares are rounded to one decimal place for presentation in this table.

c. PPPs and market exchange rates are rounded to three decimal places for presentation in this table.

d. Bonaire's results are provided only for individual consumption expenditure by households. Therefore, to ensure consistency across tables, Bonaire is not included in either the Latin America and the Caribbean or the world totals.

Table 2.3 Individual consumption expenditure by households: ICP 2017 results

INDIVIDUAL CONSUMPTION EXPENDITURE BY HOUSEHOLDS		Expenditure (billion US$)		Expenditure per capita (US$)		Price level index	Expenditure per capita indexes[b] World = 100.0		Expenditure per capita indexes[b] United States = 100.0		Share (world = 100%)[b] Expenditure		Share (world = 100%)[b]	PPPs[c]	Reference data: Market exchange rates[c]	Reference data	Reference data
Economy		Based on PPPs	Based on XRs	Based on PPPs	Based on XRs	(world = 100.0)[a]	Based on PPPs	Based on XRs	Based on PPPs	Based on XRs	Based on PPPs	Based on XRs	Population	(US$ = 1.000)	(US$ = 1.000)	Expenditure (billion LCU)	Population (millions)
(00)		(01)	(02)	(03)	(04)	(05)	(06)	(07)	(08)	(09)	(10)	(11)	(12)	(13)	(14)	(15)	(16)
East Asia and Pacific																	
Australia	AUS	667.5	782.4	27,132	31,801	168.0	302.0	507.5	66.3	77.7	1.0	1.7	0.3	1.529	1.305	1,020.8	24
Brunei Darussalam	BRN	4.9	2.5	11,464	5,783	72.3	127.6	92.3	28.0	14.1	0.0	0.0	0.0	0.697	1.381	3.4	0
Cambodia	KHM	48.5	17.8	3,059	1,124	52.7	34.1	17.9	7.5	2.7	0.1	0.0	0.2	1,488.798	4,050.580	72,193.8	15
China	CHN	7,467.3	4,581.3	5,386	3,304	87.9	60.0	52.7	13.2	8.1	11.5	10.1	19.2	4.147	6.759	30,964.1	1,386
Fiji	FJI	7.6	3.6	8,636	4,120	68.4	96.1	65.7	21.1	10.1	0.0	0.0	0.0	0.986	2.067	7.5	0
Hong Kong SAR, China	HKG	286.0	229.1	38,698	30,995	114.8	430.8	494.6	94.6	75.8	0.4	0.5	0.1	6.242	7.793	1,785.5	7
Indonesia	IDN	1,530.2	582.0	5,843	2,222	54.5	65.0	35.5	14.3	5.4	2.4	1.3	3.6	5,089.686	13,380.872	7,788,168.4	261
Japan	JPN	2,676.4	2,696.8	21,123	21,284	144.4	235.1	339.6	51.6	52.0	4.1	6.0	1.8	113.023	112.166	302,490.5	126
Korea, Rep.	KOR	895.9	772.1	17,443	15,032	123.5	194.2	239.9	42.6	36.7	1.4	1.7	0.7	974.206	1,130.425	872,791.4	51
Lao PDR	LAO	24.4	9.2	3,535	1,326	53.8	39.4	21.2	8.6	3.2	0.0	0.0	0.1	3,133.812	8,351.526	76,447.5	6
Malaysia	MYS	433.6	174.1	13,541	5,438	57.6	150.7	86.8	33.1	13.3	0.7	0.4	0.4	1.727	4.300	748.9	32
Mongolia	MNG	17.1	6.1	5,425	1,942	51.3	60.4	31.0	13.3	4.7	0.0	0.0	0.0	873.542	2,439.777	14,922.2	3
Myanmar	MMR	125.6	36.0	2,363	677	41.1	26.3	10.8	5.8	1.7	0.2	0.1	0.7	389.843	1,360.359	48,963.3	53
New Zealand	NZL	103.4	115.6	21,405	23,919	160.2	238.3	381.7	52.3	58.5	0.2	0.3	0.1	1.573	1.407	162.7	4
Philippines	PHL	598.9	230.4	5,708	2,196	55.2	63.5	35.0	14.0	5.4	0.9	0.5	1.5	19.393	50.404	11,614.1	104
Singapore	SGP	155.3	121.5	27,666	21,647	112.2	308.0	345.4	67.6	52.9	0.2	0.3	0.1	1.080	1.381	167.8	5
Taiwan, China	TWN	558.2	304.3	23,693	12,918	78.2	263.8	206.1	57.9	31.6	0.9	0.7	0.3	16.598	30.442	9,265.1	23
Thailand	THA	555.3	217.4	8,208	3,213	56.1	91.4	51.3	20.1	7.9	0.9	0.5	0.9	13.287	33.940	7,378.1	67
Vietnam	VNM	378.8	132.2	4,019	1,403	50.0	44.7	22.4	9.8	3.4	0.6	0.3	1.3	7,807.612	22,370.087	2,957,279.8	94
Total (19)	**EAB**	**16,534.8**	**11,014.5**	**7,279**	**4,849**	**95.5**	**81.0**	**77.4**	**17.8**	**11.9**	**25.6**	**24.4**	**31.5**	**n.a.**	**n.a**	**n.a.**	**2,271**
Europe and Central Asia																	
Albania	ALB	24.6	10.4	8,549	3,625	60.8	95.2	57.9	20.9	8.9	0.0	0.0	0.0	50.357	118.748	1,237.1	2
Armenia	ARM	26.6	9.2	8,933	3,096	49.7	99.5	49.4	21.8	7.6	0.0	0.0	0.0	167.312	482.720	4,453.3	2
Austria	AUT	232.7	218.4	26,456	24,835	134.6	294.5	396.3	64.7	60.7	0.4	0.5	0.1	0.831	0.885	193.3	8
Azerbaijan	AZE	83.2	23.5	8,545	2,418	40.6	95.1	38.6	20.9	5.9	0.1	0.1	0.1	0.487	1.721	40.5	9
Belarus	BLR	93.4	29.8	9,834	3,138	45.7	109.5	50.1	24.0	7.7	0.1	0.1	0.1	0.617	1.932	57.6	9
Belgium	BEL	271.5	259.3	23,871	22,796	136.9	265.7	363.8	58.4	55.7	0.4	0.6	0.2	0.845	0.885	229.5	11
Bosnia and Herzegovina	BIH	31.5	14.2	9,413	4,251	64.7	104.8	67.8	23.0	10.4	0.0	0.0	0.0	0.782	1.731	24.7	3
Bulgaria	BGR	83.7	35.5	11,822	5,022	60.9	131.6	80.1	28.9	12.3	0.1	0.1	0.1	0.735	1.731	61.5	7
Croatia	HRV	55.8	32.2	13,510	7,801	82.8	150.4	124.5	33.0	19.1	0.1	0.1	0.1	3.815	6.607	212.8	4
Cyprus	CYP	19.6	14.8	22,847	17,246	108.2	254.3	275.2	55.8	42.2	0.0	0.0	0.0	0.668	0.885	13.1	0
Czech Republic	CZE	175.3	102.7	16,555	9,698	84.0	184.3	154.8	40.5	23.7	0.3	0.2	0.1	13.651	23.304	2,393.2	10
Denmark	DNK	128.3	153.7	22,240	26,653	171.8	247.6	425.3	54.4	65.2	0.2	0.3	0.1	7.891	6.585	1,012.1	5
Estonia	EST	20.1	13.5	15,240	10,269	96.6	169.7	163.9	37.3	25.1	0.0	0.0	0.0	0.596	0.885	12.0	1
Finland	FIN	128.7	135.7	23,372	24,642	151.1	260.2	393.2	57.1	60.2	0.2	0.3	0.1	0.933	0.885	120.2	5
France	FRA	1,483.8	1,400.3	22,126	20,880	135.3	246.3	333.2	54.1	51.0	2.3	3.1	0.9	0.835	0.885	1,239.5	67

Table 2.3 *(Continued)*

INDIVIDUAL CONSUMPTION EXPENDITURE BY HOUSEHOLDS		Expenditure (billion US$)		Expenditure per capita (US$)		Price level index	Expenditure per capita indexes[b]				Share (world = 100%)[b]				Reference data		
							World = 100.0		United States = 100.0		Expenditure				Market exchange rates[c]		
Economy		Based on PPPs	Based on XRs	Based on PPPs	Based on XRs	(world = 100.0)[a]	Based on PPPs	Based on XRs	Based on PPPs	Based on XRs	Based on PPPs	Based on XRs	Population	PPPs[c] (US$ = 1.000)	(US$ = 1.000)	Expenditure (billion LCU)	Population (millions)
(00)		(01)	(02)	(03)	(04)	(05)	(06)	(07)	(08)	(09)	(10)	(11)	(12)	(13)	(14)	(15)	(16)
Georgia	GEO	30.8	11.3	8,258	3,043	52.8	91.9	48.6	20.2	7.4	0.0	0.0	0.1	0.925	2.510	28.5	3.73
Germany	DEU	2,155.8	1,917.1	26,081	23,193	127.5	290.3	370.1	63.8	56.7	3.3	4.2	1.1	0.787	0.885	1,697.0	82.66
Greece	GRC	191.6	139.9	17,813	13,006	104.7	198.3	207.5	43.5	31.8	0.3	0.3	0.1	0.646	0.885	123.8	10.75
Hungary	HUN	130.5	70.3	13,333	7,179	77.2	148.4	114.6	32.6	17.5	0.2	0.2	0.1	147.377	273.692	19,232.5	9.79
Iceland	ISL	8.5	12.3	24,649	35,957	209.1	274.4	573.8	60.3	87.9	0.0	0.0	0.0	155.648	106.701	1,317.5	0.34
Ireland	IRL	98.5	108.0	20,502	22,483	157.2	228.2	358.8	50.1	55.0	0.2	0.2	0.1	0.971	0.885	95.6	4.80
Italy	ITA	1,364.5	1,182.6	22,539	19,536	124.2	250.9	311.7	55.1	47.8	2.1	2.6	0.8	0.767	0.885	1,046.8	60.54
Kazakhstan	KAZ	228.3	87.7	12,656	4,863	55.1	140.9	77.6	30.9	11.9	0.4	0.2	0.3	125.263	326.000	28,596.7	18.04
Kyrgyz Republic	KGZ	22.5	6.3	3,782	1,065	40.4	42.1	17.0	9.2	2.6	0.0	0.0	0.1	19.373	68.769	435.4	5.94
Latvia	LVA	28.9	18.1	14,912	9,329	89.7	166.0	148.9	36.5	22.8	0.0	0.0	0.0	0.554	0.885	16.0	1.94
Lithuania	LTU	53.8	29.7	19,015	10,491	79.1	211.7	167.4	46.5	25.6	0.1	0.1	0.0	0.488	0.885	26.3	2.83
Luxembourg	LUX	17.5	19.1	29,377	32,052	156.4	327.0	511.5	71.8	78.4	0.0	0.0	0.0	0.966	0.885	16.9	0.60
Moldova	MDA	24.0	8.3	6,762	2,334	49.5	75.3	37.2	16.5	5.7	0.0	0.0	0.0	6.383	18.490	153.2	3.55
Montenegro	MNE	7.7	3.6	12,338	5,837	67.8	137.4	93.1	30.2	14.3	0.0	0.0	0.0	0.419	0.885	3.2	0.62
Netherlands	NLD	385.2	369.7	22,487	21,581	137.6	250.3	344.4	55.0	52.8	0.6	0.8	0.2	0.850	0.885	327.3	17.13
North Macedonia	MKD	18.6	7.6	8,959	3,644	58.3	99.7	58.1	21.9	8.9	0.0	0.0	0.0	22.167	54.505	412.0	2.07
Norway	NOR	137.0	178.2	25,960	33,779	186.5	289.0	539.0	63.5	82.6	0.2	0.4	0.1	10.743	8.256	1,471.7	5.28
Poland	POL	629.8	307.9	16,390	8,013	70.1	182.5	127.9	40.1	19.6	1.0	0.7	0.5	1.842	3.768	1,160.2	38.42
Portugal	PRT	192.5	143.0	18,687	13,879	106.5	208.0	221.5	45.7	33.9	0.3	0.3	0.1	0.657	0.885	126.5	10.30
Romania	ROU	299.4	133.6	15,281	6,820	64.0	170.1	108.8	37.4	16.7	0.5	0.3	0.3	1.805	4.044	540.4	19.59
Russian Federation	RUS	1,923.9	831.6	13,101	5,663	62.0	145.9	90.4	32.0	13.8	3.0	1.8	2.0	25.218	58.343	48,516.2	146.84
Serbia	SRB	70.2	31.4	9,994	4,466	64.1	111.3	71.3	24.4	10.9	0.1	0.1	0.1	47.992	107.406	3,367.5	7.02
Slovak Republic	SVK	81.5	53.3	14,988	9,810	93.8	166.9	156.5	36.6	24.0	0.1	0.1	0.1	0.579	0.885	47.2	5.44
Slovenia	SVN	35.4	25.6	17,149	12,378	103.5	190.9	197.5	41.9	30.3	0.1	0.1	0.0	0.639	0.885	22.6	2.07
Spain	ESP	965.0	766.2	20,737	16,466	113.8	230.9	262.8	50.7	40.2	1.5	1.7	0.6	0.703	0.885	678.2	46.53
Sweden	SWE	225.2	243.6	22,393	24,215	155.0	249.3	386.4	54.7	59.2	0.3	0.5	0.1	9.223	8.529	2,077.2	10.06
Switzerland	CHE	264.7	365.5	31,321	43,240	197.9	348.7	690.0	76.6	105.7	0.4	0.8	0.1	1.359	0.984	359.6	8.45
Tajikistan	TJK	18.3	5.6	2,071	629	43.5	23.1	10.0	5.1	1.5	0.0	0.0	0.1	2.595	8.550	47.5	8.84
Turkey	TUR	1,115.1	503.3	13,884	6,267	64.7	154.6	100.0	33.9	15.3	1.7	1.1	1.1	1.647	3.648	1,836.2	80.31
Ukraine	UKR	285.7	75.3	6,725	1,771	37.8	74.9	28.3	16.4	4.3	0.4	0.2	0.6	7.006	26.597	2,001.5	42.49
United Kingdom	GBR	1,727.3	1,735.6	26,156	26,281	144.0	291.2	419.4	63.9	64.2	2.7	3.8	0.9	0.780	0.776	1,346.9	66.04
Total (46)	**ECB**	**15,596.2**	**11,844.6**	**17,846**	**13,553**	**108.9**	**198.7**	**216.3**	**43.6**	**33.1**	**24.1**	**26.2**	**12.1**	**n.a.**	**n.a**	**n.a.**	**873.93**
Latin America and the Caribbean																	
Anguilla	AIA	0.2	0.2	15,529	14,923	137.7	172.9	238.1	38.0	36.5	0.0	0.0	0.0	2.595	2.700	0.6	0.01
Antigua and Barbuda	ATG	0.7	0.6	7,154	6,539	131.0	79.6	104.4	17.5	16.0	0.0	0.0	0.0	2.468	2.700	1.7	0.10
Argentina	ARG	675.0	440.5	15,363	10,025	93.5	171.0	160.0	37.6	24.5	1.0	1.0	0.6	10.808	16.563	7,295.3	43.94
Aruba	ABW	2.2	1.9	21,323	17,636	118.6	237.4	281.4	52.1	43.1	0.0	0.0	0.0	1.480	1.790	3.3	0.11

Table 2.3 *(Continued)*

INDIVIDUAL CONSUMPTION EXPENDITURE BY HOUSEHOLDS		Expenditure (billion US$)		Expenditure per capita (US$)		Price level index	Expenditure per capita indexes[b]				Share (world = 100%)[b]				Reference data		
							World = 100.0		United States = 100.0		Expenditure						
Economy		Based on PPPs	Based on XRs	Based on PPPs	Based on XRs	(world = 100.0)[a]	Based on PPPs	Based on XRs	Based on PPPs	Based on XRs	Based on PPPs	Based on XRs	Population	PPPs[c] (US$ = 1.000)	Market exchange rates[c] (US$ = 1.000)	Expenditure (billion LCU)	Population (millions)
(00)		(01)	(02)	(03)	(04)	(05)	(06)	(07)	(08)	(09)	(10)	(11)	(12)	(13)	(14)	(15)	(16)
Bahamas, The	BHS	7.0	7.7	18,222	20,096	158.1	202.9	320.7	44.5	49.1	0.0	0.0	0.0	1.103	1.000	7.7	0.38
Barbados	BRB	2.8	3.4	9,918	11,755	169.9	110.4	187.6	24.2	28.7	0.0	0.0	0.0	2.371	2.000	6.7	0.29
Belize	BLZ	1.8	1.3	4,662	3,443	105.9	51.9	54.9	11.4	8.4	0.0	0.0	0.0	1.477	2.000	2.6	0.38
Bolivia	BOL	67.1	25.2	5,998	2,251	53.8	66.8	35.9	14.7	5.5	0.1	0.1	0.2	2.612	6.960	175.3	11.19
Bonaire[d]	BON	0.3	0.2	11,088	9,002	116.4	123.4	143.7	27.1	22.0	0.0	0.0	0.0	0.812	1.000	0.2	0.03
Brazil	BRA	1,824.0	1,330.2	8,776	6,400	104.5	97.7	102.1	21.5	15.6	2.8	2.9	2.9	2.327	3.191	4,245.1	207.83
Cayman Islands	CYM	2.0	2.8	31,757	43,810	197.7	353.5	699.1	77.6	107.1	0.0	0.0	0.0	1.150	0.833	2.3	0.06
Chile	CHL	237.1	175.0	12,800	9,450	105.8	142.5	150.8	31.3	23.1	0.4	0.4	0.3	478.996	648.834	113,565.7	18.52
Colombia	COL	444.4	213.7	9,016	4,336	68.9	100.4	69.2	22.0	10.6	0.7	0.5	0.7	1,419.374	2,951.327	630,818.0	49.29
Costa Rica	CRI	59.9	39.3	12,112	7,954	94.1	134.8	126.9	29.6	19.4	0.1	0.1	0.1	372.669	567.513	22,319.8	4.94
Curaçao	CUW	2.4	2.0	14,573	12,073	118.8	162.2	192.7	35.6	29.5	0.0	0.0	0.0	1.483	1.790	3.5	0.16
Dominica	DMA	0.6	0.4	8,908	6,190	99.6	99.2	98.8	21.8	15.1	0.0	0.0	0.0	1.876	2.700	1.2	0.07
Dominican Republic	DOM	108.3	55.6	10,299	5,284	73.5	114.7	84.3	25.2	12.9	0.2	0.1	0.1	24.391	47.537	2,641.0	10.51
Ecuador	ECU	108.8	62.5	6,479	3,722	82.4	72.1	59.4	15.8	9.1	0.2	0.1	0.2	0.575	1.000	62.5	16.79
El Salvador	SLV	40.5	20.8	6,335	3,263	73.8	70.5	52.1	15.5	8.0	0.1	0.0	0.1	0.515	1.000	20.8	6.39
Grenada	GRD	1.5	1.0	13,758	9,170	95.5	153.2	146.3	33.6	22.4	0.0	0.0	0.0	1.800	2.700	2.7	0.11
Guyana	GUY	4.1	2.2	5,240	2,855	78.1	58.3	45.6	12.8	7.0	0.0	0.0	0.0	115.626	212.190	469.7	0.78
Haiti	HTI	18.1	8.8	1,644	803	70.0	18.3	12.8	4.0	2.0	0.0	0.0	0.2	31.103	63.687	561.6	10.98
Honduras	HND	38.5	17.7	4,085	1,877	65.9	45.5	30.0	10.0	4.6	0.1	0.0	0.1	10.839	23.588	417.4	9.43
Jamaica	JAM	21.2	11.6	7,247	3,987	78.9	80.7	63.6	17.7	9.7	0.0	0.0	0.0	70.392	127.965	1,490.0	2.92
Mexico	MEX	1,450.2	755.6	11,756	6,125	74.7	130.9	97.7	28.7	15.0	2.2	1.7	1.7	9.861	18.927	14,301.2	123.36
Montserrat	MSR	0.1	0.0	12,382	9,712	112.4	137.8	155.0	30.3	23.7	0.0	0.0	0.0	2.118	2.700	0.1	0.00
Nicaragua	NIC	25.6	9.8	4,007	1,537	55.0	44.6	24.5	9.8	3.8	0.0	0.0	0.1	11.528	30.051	294.9	6.38
Panama	PAN	61.7	31.3	15,018	7,630	72.8	167.2	121.8	36.7	18.7	0.1	0.1	0.1	0.508	1.000	31.3	4.11
Paraguay	PRY	55.1	25.2	8,031	3,667	65.5	89.4	58.5	19.6	9.0	0.1	0.1	0.1	2,539.985	5,562.276	140,077.6	6.87
Peru	PER	233.1	135.4	7,412	4,305	83.3	82.5	68.7	18.1	10.5	0.4	0.3	0.4	1.894	3.260	441.3	31.44
Sint Maarten	SXM	0.9	0.7	21,227	17,649	119.2	236.3	281.6	51.9	43.1	0.0	0.0	0.0	1.488	1.790	1.3	0.04
St. Kitts and Nevis	KNA	0.7	0.6	13,138	12,395	135.2	146.3	197.8	32.1	30.3	0.0	0.0	0.0	2.547	2.700	1.7	0.05
St. Lucia	LCA	0.8	0.6	4,239	3,264	110.4	47.2	52.1	10.4	8.0	0.0	0.0	0.0	2.079	2.700	1.6	0.18
St. Vincent and the Grenadines	VCT	0.9	0.6	8,563	5,730	95.9	95.3	91.4	20.9	14.0	0.0	0.0	0.0	1.807	2.700	1.7	0.11
Suriname	SUR	4.2	1.6	7,434	2,889	55.7	82.8	46.1	18.2	7.1	0.0	0.0	0.0	2.934	7.550	12.4	0.57
Trinidad and Tobago	TTO	23.3	14.5	16,835	10,458	89.0	187.4	166.9	41.2	25.6	0.0	0.0	0.0	4.212	6.780	98.1	1.38
Turks and Caicos Islands	TCA	0.3	0.4	8,618	10,737	178.6	95.9	171.3	21.1	26.2	0.0	0.0	0.0	1.246	1.000	0.4	0.04
Uruguay	URY	46.2	40.0	13,432	11,642	124.2	149.5	185.8	32.8	28.5	0.1	0.1	0.0	24.854	28.676	1,147.3	3.44
Virgin Islands, British	VGB	0.4	0.5	13,979	15,319	157.1	155.6	244.5	34.2	37.4	0.0	0.0	0.0	1.096	1.000	0.5	0.03
Total (39)	**LCB**	**5,571.5**	**3,441.4**	**9,720**	**6,004**	**88.5**	**108.2**	**95.8**	**23.8**	**14.7**	**8.6**	**7.6**	**8.0**	**n.a.**	**n.a**	**n.a.**	**573.20**

Table 2.3 *(Continued)*

INDIVIDUAL CONSUMPTION EXPENDITURE BY HOUSEHOLDS		Expenditure (billion US$)		Expenditure per capita (US$)		Price level index (world = 100.0)[a]	Expenditure per capita indexes[b]				Share (world = 100%)[b]			PPPs[c] (US$ = 1.000)	Reference data		
							World = 100.0		United States = 100.0		Expenditure				Market exchange rates[c] (US$ = 1.000)		
Economy		Based on PPPs	Based on XRs	Based on PPPs	Based on XRs		Based on PPPs	Based on XRs	Based on PPPs	Based on XRs	Based on PPPs	Based on XRs	Population			Expenditure (billion LCU)	Population (millions)
(00)		(01)	(02)	(03)	(04)	(05)	(06)	(07)	(08)	(09)	(10)	(11)	(12)	(13)	(14)	(15)	(16)
Middle East and North Africa																	
Algeria	DZA	211.3	72.7	5,104	1,757	49.4	56.8	28.0	12.5	4.3	0.3	0.2	0.6	38.210	110.973	8,071.9	41.39
Bahrain	BHR	27.4	14.9	18,267	9,916	77.8	203.4	158.2	44.7	24.2	0.0	0.0	0.0	0.204	0.376	5.6	1.50
Djibouti	DJI	3.2	1.9	3,386	1,996	84.5	37.7	31.8	8.3	4.9	0.0	0.0	0.0	104.737	177.720	334.8	0.94
Egypt, Arab Rep.	EGY	1,063.3	203.0	11,216	2,142	27.4	124.9	34.2	27.4	5.2	1.6	0.4	1.3	3.408	17.847	3,623.5	94.80
Iran, Islamic Rep.	IRN	581.2	243.9	7,169	3,009	60.2	79.8	48.0	17.5	7.4	0.9	0.5	1.1	13,944.904	33,226.298	8,104,686.7	81.07
Iraq	IRQ	205.4	90.8	5,530	2,445	63.4	61.6	39.0	13.5	6.0	0.3	0.2	0.5	555.391	1,256.000	114,058.4	37.14
Israel	ISR	165.2	193.1	18,969	22,168	167.5	211.2	353.7	46.4	54.2	0.3	0.4	0.1	4.207	3.600	695.0	8.71
Jordan	JOR	75.6	35.1	7,518	3,495	66.6	83.7	55.8	18.4	8.5	0.1	0.1	0.1	0.329	0.708	24.9	10.05
Kuwait	KWT	79.8	49.3	19,541	12,074	88.6	217.5	192.7	47.8	29.5	0.1	0.1	0.1	0.187	0.303	15.0	4.08
Malta	MLT	7.9	5.6	16,957	12,031	101.7	188.8	192.0	41.5	29.4	0.0	0.0	0.0	0.628	0.885	5.0	0.47
Morocco	MAR	143.5	63.6	4,118	1,823	63.5	45.8	29.1	10.1	4.5	0.2	0.1	0.5	4.291	9.691	615.9	34.85
Oman	OMN	53.4	29.4	11,710	6,444	78.9	130.4	102.8	28.6	15.8	0.1	0.1	0.1	0.212	0.385	11.3	4.56
Qatar	QAT	51.6	40.9	18,950	15,019	113.6	211.0	239.7	46.3	36.7	0.1	0.1	0.0	2.893	3.650	149.4	2.72
Saudi Arabia	SAU	621.2	285.5	19,049	8,755	65.9	212.1	139.7	46.6	21.4	1.0	0.6	0.5	1.724	3.750	1,070.8	32.61
Tunisia	TUN	93.8	28.8	8,200	2,516	44.0	91.3	40.1	20.0	6.1	0.1	0.1	0.2	0.742	2.419	69.6	11.43
United Arab Emirates	ARE	181.1	139.8	19,464	15,025	110.6	216.7	239.8	47.6	36.7	0.3	0.3	0.1	2.835	3.673	513.4	9.30
West Bank and Gaza	PSE	22.2	12.8	4,990	2,864	82.3	55.5	45.7	12.2	7.0	0.0	0.0	0.1	2.066	3.600	45.9	4.45
Total (17)	**MEB**	**3,587.1**	**1,511.1**	**9,437**	**3,976**	**60.4**	**105.1**	**63.4**	**23.1**	**9.7**	**5.5**	**3.3**	**5.3**	**n.a.**	**n.a**	**n.a.**	**380.10**
North America																	
Bermuda	BMU	2.1	3.3	33,063	52,096	225.9	368.1	831.3	80.8	127.3	0.0	0.0	0.0	1.576	1.000	3.3	0.06
Canada	CAN	949.5	941.4	25,984	25,762	142.1	289.3	411.1	63.5	63.0	1.5	2.1	0.5	1.287	1.298	1,221.6	36.54
United States	USA	13,312.1	13,312.1	40,909	40,909	143.3	455.4	652.8	100.0	100.0	20.6	29.5	4.5	1.000	1.000	13,312.1	325.41
Total (3)	**NAB**	**14,263.6**	**14,256.7**	**39,401**	**39,382**	**143.3**	**438.6**	**628.4**	**96.3**	**96.3**	**22.0**	**31.6**	**5.0**	**n.a.**	**n.a**	**n.a.**	**362.01**
South Asia																	
Bangladesh	BGD	499.8	183.4	3,089	1,133	52.6	34.4	18.1	7.6	2.8	0.8	0.4	2.2	29.514	80.438	14,751.8	161.80
Bhutan	BTN	4.2	1.3	5,835	1,834	45.1	65.0	29.3	14.3	4.5	0.0	0.0	0.0	20.474	65.122	86.9	0.73
India	IND	5,024.0	1,502.0	3,837	1,147	42.9	42.7	18.3	9.4	2.8	7.8	3.3	18.2	19.469	65.122	97,813.2	1,309.20
Maldives	MDV	3.0	1.9	6,198	3,945	91.2	69.0	63.0	15.2	9.6	0.0	0.0	0.0	9.794	15.387	29.8	0.49
Nepal	NPL	65.6	19.2	2,277	665	41.9	25.3	10.6	5.6	1.6	0.1	0.0	0.4	30.513	104.512	2,002.9	28.83
Pakistan	PAK	822.7	259.4	4,132	1,303	45.2	46.0	20.8	10.1	3.2	1.3	0.6	2.8	33.251	105.455	27,355.3	199.11
Sri Lanka	LKA	148.9	54.2	6,943	2,528	52.2	77.3	40.3	17.0	6.2	0.2	0.1	0.3	55.501	152.446	8,262.7	21.44
Total (7)	**SAB**	**6,568.4**	**2,021.4**	**3,815**	**1,174**	**44.1**	**42.5**	**18.7**	**9.3**	**2.9**	**10.2**	**4.5**	**23.9**	**n.a.**	**n.a**	**n.a.**	**1,721.60**
Sub-Saharan Africa																	
Angola	AGO	110.9	71.7	3,720	2,405	92.7	41.4	38.4	9.1	5.9	0.2	0.2	0.4	107.270	165.916	11,898.4	29.82
Benin	BEN	18.1	6.8	1,616	609	54.0	18.0	9.7	4.0	1.5	0.0	0.0	0.2	219.476	582.075	3,964.4	11.18
Botswana	BWA	17.7	8.6	8,039	3,891	69.4	89.5	62.1	19.7	9.5	0.0	0.0	0.0	5.009	10.347	88.8	2.21

Table 2.3 *(Continued)*

INDIVIDUAL CONSUMPTION EXPENDITURE BY HOUSEHOLDS		Expenditure (billion US$)		Expenditure per capita (US$)		Price level index	Expenditure per capita indexes[b]				Share (world = 100%)[b]			PPPs[c]	Reference data		
							World = 100.0		United States = 100.0		Expenditure				Market exchange rates[c]		
Economy		Based on PPPs	Based on XRs	Based on PPPs	Based on XRs	(world = 100.0)[a]	Based on PPPs	Based on XRs	Based on PPPs	Based on XRs	Based on PPPs	Based on XRs	Population	(US$ = 1.000)	(US$ = 1.000)	Expenditure (billion LCU)	Population (millions)
(00)		(01)	(02)	(03)	(04)	(05)	(06)	(07)	(08)	(09)	(10)	(11)	(12)	(13)	(14)	(15)	(16)
Burkina Faso	BFA	20.9	7.2	1,089	374	49.2	12.1	6.0	2.7	0.9	0.0	0.0	0.3	199.741	582.075	4,173.7	19.19
Burundi	BDI	7.3	2.8	675	255	54.3	7.5	4.1	1.6	0.6	0.0	0.0	0.2	654.422	1,729.055	4,781.8	10.83
Cabo Verde	CPV	2.3	1.1	4,268	2,078	69.8	47.5	33.2	10.4	5.1	0.0	0.0	0.0	47.612	97.799	109.2	0.54
Cameroon	CMR	59.8	24.3	2,435	991	58.3	27.1	15.8	6.0	2.4	0.1	0.1	0.3	236.912	582.075	14,169.0	24.57
Central African Republic	CAF	3.6	1.9	790	416	75.6	8.8	6.6	1.9	1.0	0.0	0.0	0.1	306.808	582.075	1,113.8	4.60
Chad	TCD	18.9	7.7	1,257	513	58.5	14.0	8.2	3.1	1.3	0.0	0.0	0.2	237.656	582.075	4,484.7	15.02
Comoros	COM	2.0	1.0	2,502	1,224	70.1	27.8	19.5	6.1	3.0	0.0	0.0	0.0	213.518	436.571	434.7	0.81
Congo, Dem. Rep.	COD	73.5	31.6	902	389	61.7	10.0	6.2	2.2	0.9	0.1	0.1	1.1	630.606	1,464.418	46,322.8	81.40
Congo, Rep.	COG	10.6	5.2	2,068	1,016	70.4	23.0	16.2	5.1	2.5	0.0	0.0	0.1	285.969	582.075	3,022.7	5.11
Côte d'Ivoire	CIV	58.9	25.0	2,409	1,023	60.9	26.8	16.3	5.9	2.5	0.1	0.1	0.3	247.134	582.075	14,550.6	24.44
Equatorial Guinea	GNQ	10.9	5.7	8,663	4,529	74.9	96.4	72.3	21.2	11.1	0.0	0.0	0.0	304.287	582.075	3,326.9	1.26
Eswatini	SWZ	7.6	3.5	6,726	3,086	65.8	74.9	49.2	16.4	7.5	0.0	0.0	0.0	6.118	13.334	46.3	1.12
Ethiopia	ETH	124.5	44.3	1,170	417	51.0	13.0	6.6	2.9	1.0	0.2	0.1	1.5	8.496	23.866	1,058.1	106.40
Gabon	GAB	10.1	5.5	4,874	2,672	78.6	54.3	42.6	11.9	6.5	0.0	0.0	0.0	319.160	582.075	3,211.8	2.06
Gambia, The	GMB	4.0	1.3	1,793	582	46.5	20.0	9.3	4.4	1.4	0.0	0.0	0.0	15.114	46.608	60.0	2.21
Ghana	GHA	106.6	42.9	3,660	1,473	57.7	40.7	23.5	8.9	3.6	0.2	0.1	0.4	1.751	4.351	186.6	29.12
Guinea	GIN	25.7	9.0	2,126	749	50.5	23.7	11.9	5.2	1.8	0.0	0.0	0.2	3,213.984	9,125.743	82,442.7	12.07
Guinea-Bissau	GNB	2.8	1.1	1,543	615	57.2	17.2	9.8	3.8	1.5	0.0	0.0	0.0	232.199	582.075	654.9	1.83
Kenya	KEN	148.8	59.9	2,963	1,193	57.7	33.0	19.0	7.2	2.9	0.2	0.1	0.7	41.635	103.411	6,196.5	50.22
Lesotho	LSO	5.3	2.1	2,549	1,003	56.4	28.4	16.0	6.2	2.5	0.0	0.0	0.0	5.244	13.334	28.0	2.09
Liberia	LBR	4.0	1.7	851	362	61.0	9.5	5.8	2.1	0.9	0.0	0.0	0.1	47.996	112.707	192.1	4.70
Madagascar	MDG	30.0	9.3	1,173	363	44.3	13.1	5.8	2.9	0.9	0.0	0.0	0.4	962.960	3,116.110	28,886.2	25.57
Malawi	MWI	16.5	5.5	933	309	47.5	10.4	4.9	2.3	0.8	0.0	0.0	0.2	241.931	730.273	3,989.0	17.67
Mali	MLI	34.0	12.0	1,838	648	50.6	20.5	10.3	4.5	1.6	0.1	0.0	0.3	205.273	582.075	6,986.4	18.51
Mauritania	MRT	7.9	2.8	1,855	646	49.9	20.6	10.3	4.5	1.6	0.0	0.0	0.1	124.453	357.493	988.6	4.28
Mauritius	MUS	19.4	10.1	15,332	8,008	74.9	170.7	127.8	37.5	19.6	0.0	0.0	0.0	18.009	34.481	349.2	1.26
Mozambique	MOZ	26.0	9.0	908	314	49.6	10.1	5.0	2.2	0.8	0.0	0.0	0.4	21.988	63.584	572.3	28.65
Namibia	NAM	18.0	9.3	7,508	3,890	74.3	83.6	62.1	18.4	9.5	0.0	0.0	0.0	6.898	13.313	124.4	2.40
Niger	NER	12.8	5.4	591	249	60.4	6.6	4.0	1.4	0.6	0.0	0.0	0.3	245.160	582.075	3,129.6	21.60
Nigeria	NGA	709.2	260.0	3,716	1,362	52.5	41.4	21.7	9.1	3.3	1.1	0.6	2.6	112.098	305.790	79,505.3	190.87
Rwanda	RWA	17.7	6.2	1,476	522	50.6	16.4	8.3	3.6	1.3	0.0	0.0	0.2	293.705	831.531	5,195.5	11.98
São Tomé and Príncipe	STP	0.6	0.3	3,009	1,489	70.9	33.5	23.8	7.4	3.6	0.0	0.0	0.0	10.757	21.741	6.7	0.21
Senegal	SEN	35.8	14.7	2,324	953	58.8	25.9	15.2	5.7	2.3	0.1	0.0	0.2	238.578	582.075	8,550.5	15.42
Seychelles	SYC	1.3	0.9	13,731	9,082	94.8	152.9	144.9	33.6	22.2	0.0	0.0	0.0	9.027	13.648	12.0	0.10
Sierra Leone	SLE	12.8	3.7	1,705	491	41.3	19.0	7.8	4.2	1.2	0.0	0.0	0.1	2,128.519	7,384.432	27,172.5	7.49
South Africa	ZAF	429.4	210.9	7,533	3,700	70.4	83.9	59.0	18.4	9.0	0.7	0.5	0.8	6.549	13.334	2,812.5	57.01
Sudan	SDN	133.1	35.5	3,262	871	38.3	36.3	13.9	8.0	2.1	0.2	0.1	0.6	5.377	20.130	715.4	40.78

Table 2.3 *(Continued)*

INDIVIDUAL CONSUMPTION EXPENDITURE BY HOUSEHOLDS		Expenditure (billion US$)		Expenditure per capita (US$)		Price level index (world = 100.0)[a]	Expenditure per capita indexes[b]				Share (world = 100%)[b]			PPPs[c] (US$ = 1.000)	Reference data		
							World = 100.0		United States = 100.0		Expenditure				Market exchange rates[c] (US$ = 1.000)	Expenditure (billion LCU)	Population (millions)
Economy		Based on PPPs	Based on XRs	Based on PPPs	Based on XRs		Based on PPPs	Based on XRs	Based on PPPs	Based on XRs	Based on PPPs	Based on XRs	Population				
(00)		(01)	(02)	(03)	(04)	(05)	(06)	(07)	(08)	(09)	(10)	(11)	(12)	(13)	(14)	(15)	(16)
Tanzania	TZA	95.0	32.2	1,738	588	48.5	19.3	9.4	4.2	1.4	0.1	0.1	0.8	754.621	2,228.858	71,675.1	54.66
Togo	TGO	7.8	3.3	1,016	431	60.7	11.3	6.9	2.5	1.1	0.0	0.0	0.1	246.596	582.075	1,929.5	7.70
Uganda	UGA	67.9	23.0	1,650	558	48.5	18.4	8.9	4.0	1.4	0.1	0.1	0.6	1,221.088	3,611.224	82,956.1	41.17
Zambia	ZMB	27.4	12.2	1,625	721	63.6	18.1	11.5	4.0	1.8	0.0	0.0	0.2	4.224	9.520	115.7	16.85
Zimbabwe	ZWE	29.1	14.1	2,042	990	69.5	22.7	15.8	5.0	2.4	0.0	0.0	0.2	0.485	1.000	14.1	14.24
Total (45)	**SSB**	**2,586.6**	**1,052.4**	**2,533**	**1,030**	**58.3**	**28.2**	**16.4**	**6.2**	**2.5**	**4.0**	**2.3**	**14.2**	**n.a.**	**n.a**	**n.a.**	**1,021.22**
World (176)	**WLD**	**64,708.2**	**45,142.1**	**8,983**	**6,267**	**100.0**	**100.0**	**100.0**	**22.0**	**15.3**	**100.0**	**100.0**	**100.0**	**n.a.**	**n.a.**	**n.a.**	**7,203.60**

Note: PPP = purchasing power parity; XR = market exchange rate; LCU = local currency unit; n.a. = not applicable; ... = data suppressed due to unavailability.

a. World totals used to calculate price level indexes (PLIs) in this table exclude nonparticipating economies.

b. Indexes and shares are rounded to one decimal place for presentation in this table.

c. PPPs and market exchange rates are rounded to three decimal places for presentation in this table.

d. Bonaire's results are provided only for individual consumption expenditure by households. Therefore, to ensure consistency across tables, Bonaire is not included in either the Latin America and the Caribbean or the world totals.

Table 2.4 Consumption expenditure by government: ICP 2017 results

CONSUMPTION EXPENDITURE BY GOVERNMENT		Expenditure (billion US$)		Expenditure per capita (US$)		Price level index (world = 100.0)[a]	Expenditure per capita indexes[b]				Share (world = 100%)[b]			PPPs[c] (US$ = 1.000)	Reference data		
							World = 100.0		United States = 100.0		Expenditure				Market exchange rates[c] (US$ = 1.000)	Expenditure (billion LCU)	Popu- tion (millic
Economy		Based on PPPs	Based on XRs	Based on PPPs	Based on XRs		Based on PPPs	Based on XRs	Based on PPPs	Based on XRs	Based on PPPs	Based on XRs	Popula- tion				
(00)		(01)	(02)	(03)	(04)	(05)	(06)	(07)	(08)	(09)	(10)	(11)	(12)	(13)	(14)	(15)	(16
East Asia and Pacific																	
Australia	AUS	266.9	257.7	10,848	10,476	178.7	320.6	572.8	128.0	123.6	1.1	2.0	0.3	1.260	1.305	336.3	24
Brunei Darussalam	BRN	11.6	3.2	26,911	7,477	51.4	795.3	408.8	317.6	88.2	0.0	0.0	0.0	0.384	1.381	4.4	[illegible]
Cambodia	KHM	7.4	1.9	466	118	46.7	13.8	6.4	5.5	1.4	0.0	0.0	0.2	1,021.905	4,050.580	7,551.7	15
China	CHN	3,526.8	1,930.2	2,544	1,392	101.3	75.2	76.1	30.0	16.4	14.5	14.7	19.2	3.699	6.759	13,045.7	1,38
Fiji	FJI	2.7	0.9	3,078	1,049	63.1	91.0	57.4	36.3	12.4	0.0	0.0	0.0	0.705	2.067	1.9	[illegible]
Hong Kong SAR, China	HKG	47.0	33.6	6,362	4,539	132.0	188.0	248.2	75.1	53.6	0.2	0.3	0.1	5.560	7.793	261.5	7
Indonesia	IDN	403.1	92.3	1,539	352	42.4	45.5	19.3	18.2	4.2	1.7	0.7	3.6	3,062.762	13,380.872	1,234,554.3	261
Japan	JPN	1,340.7	956.0	10,581	7,545	131.9	312.7	412.6	124.9	89.1	5.5	7.3	1.8	79.983	112.166	107,234.8	12
Korea, Rep.	KOR	426.6	250.4	8,305	4,875	108.6	245.4	266.6	98.0	57.5	1.7	1.9	0.7	663.553	1,130.425	283,045.8	51
Lao PDR	LAO	15.9	2.5	2,303	363	29.2	68.1	19.9	27.2	4.3	0.1	0.0	0.1	1,317.505	8,351.526	20,941.2	6
Malaysia	MYS	128.1	38.3	3,999	1,196	55.3	118.2	65.4	47.2	14.1	0.5	0.3	0.4	1.286	4.300	164.7	32
Mongolia	MNG	10.4	1.5	3,312	462	25.8	97.9	25.3	39.1	5.5	0.0	0.0	0.0	340.394	2,439.777	3,550.2	3
Myanmar	MMR	67.4	11.7	1,267	220	32.1	37.4	12.0	15.0	2.6	0.3	0.1	0.7	236.340	1,360.359	15,918.2	53
New Zealand	NZL	50.2	36.1	10,399	7,467	132.9	307.3	408.3	122.7	88.1	0.2	0.3	0.1	1.011	1.407	50.8	4
Philippines	PHL	111.0	35.3	1,058	336	58.8	31.3	18.4	12.5	4.0	0.5	0.3	1.5	16.007	50.404	1,776.9	104
Singapore	SGP	66.9	35.6	11,912	6,337	98.4	352.0	346.5	140.6	74.8	0.3	0.3	0.1	0.735	1.381	49.1	5
Taiwan, China	TWN	214.2	80.9	9,093	3,432	69.8	268.7	187.7	107.3	40.5	0.9	0.6	0.3	11.491	30.442	2,461.6	23
Thailand	THA	267.4	73.0	3,953	1,080	50.5	116.8	59.0	46.7	12.7	1.1	0.6	0.9	9.270	33.940	2,479.1	67
Vietnam	VNM	141.7	25.8	1,503	274	33.7	44.4	15.0	17.7	3.2	0.6	0.2	1.3	4,078.183	22,370.087	577,719.4	94
Total (19)	**EAB**	**7,105.9**	**3,866.7**	**3,128**	**1,702**	**100.7**	**92.4**	**93.1**	**36.9**	**20.1**	**29.2**	**29.4**	**31.5**	**n.a.**	**n.a**	**n.a.**	**2,271**
Europe and Central Asia																	
Albania	ALB	10.4	1.5	3,622	521	26.6	107.0	28.5	42.7	6.2	0.0	0.0	0.0	17.086	118.748	177.8	2
Armenia	ARM	10.2	1.4	3,408	477	25.9	100.7	26.1	40.2	5.6	0.0	0.0	0.0	67.503	482.720	685.5	2
Austria	AUT	100.7	81.5	11,447	9,272	149.9	338.3	507.0	135.1	109.4	0.4	0.6	0.1	0.717	0.885	72.2	8
Azerbaijan	AZE	37.1	4.6	3,807	476	23.1	112.5	26.0	44.9	5.6	0.2	0.0	0.1	0.215	1.721	8.0	9
Belarus	BLR	61.5	8.6	6,475	902	25.8	191.3	49.3	76.4	10.6	0.3	0.1	0.1	0.269	1.932	16.6	9
Belgium	BEL	142.2	116.3	12,499	10,227	151.4	369.4	559.2	147.5	120.7	0.6	0.9	0.2	0.724	0.885	103.0	11
Bosnia and Herzegovina	BIH	15.9	3.7	4,739	1,098	42.9	140.1	60.0	55.9	13.0	0.1	0.0	0.0	0.401	1.731	6.4	3
Bulgaria	BGR	45.0	9.2	6,358	1,306	38.0	187.9	71.4	75.0	15.4	0.2	0.1	0.1	0.356	1.731	16.0	7
Croatia	HRV	34.1	10.8	8,268	2,622	58.7	244.3	143.4	97.6	30.9	0.1	0.1	0.1	2.095	6.607	71.5	4
Cyprus	CYP	5.2	3.4	6,079	3,946	120.1	179.7	215.7	71.8	46.6	0.0	0.0	0.0	0.574	0.885	3.0	[illegible]
Czech Republic	CZE	128.2	41.6	12,107	3,924	60.0	357.8	214.6	142.9	46.3	0.5	0.3	0.1	7.554	23.304	968.4	10
Denmark	DNK	88.3	81.3	15,306	14,104	170.5	452.3	771.2	180.6	166.5	0.4	0.6	0.1	6.067	6.585	535.6	5
Estonia	EST	13.5	5.3	10,267	4,056	73.1	303.4	221.8	121.2	47.9	0.1	0.0	0.0	0.350	0.885	4.7	1
Finland	FIN	72.8	58.2	13,216	10,562	147.9	390.5	577.5	156.0	124.7	0.3	0.4	0.1	0.707	0.885	51.5	5
France	FRA	870.9	614.1	12,986	9,157	130.5	383.8	500.7	153.3	108.1	3.6	4.7	0.9	0.624	0.885	543.6	67

Table 2.4 *(Continued)*

CONSUMPTION EXPENDITURE BY GOVERNMENT		Expenditure (billion US$)		Expenditure per capita (US$)		Price level index (world = 100.0)[a]	Expenditure per capita indexes[b]				Share (world = 100%)[b]			PPPs[c] (US$ = 1.000)	Reference data		
							World = 100.0		United States = 100.0		Expenditure				Market exchange rates[c] (US$ = 1.000)	Expenditure (billion LCU)	Population (millions)
Economy		Based on PPPs	Based on XRs	Based on PPPs	Based on XRs		Based on PPPs	Based on XRs	Based on PPPs	Based on XRs	Based on PPPs	Based on XRs	Population				
(00)		(01)	(02)	(03)	(04)	(05)	(06)	(07)	(08)	(09)	(10)	(11)	(12)	(13)	(14)	(15)	(16)
Georgia	GEO	14.5	2.3	3,898	604	28.7	115.2	33.0	46.0	7.1	0.1	0.0	0.1	0.389	2.510	5.6	3.73
Germany	DEU	1,027.4	727.9	12,430	8,806	131.1	367.3	481.5	146.7	103.9	4.2	5.5	1.1	0.627	0.885	644.3	82.66
Greece	GRC	81.0	40.3	7,535	3,750	92.1	222.7	205.0	88.9	44.3	0.3	0.3	0.1	0.440	0.885	35.7	10.75
Hungary	HUN	92.9	28.9	9,493	2,949	57.5	280.5	161.2	112.0	34.8	0.4	0.2	0.1	85.011	273.692	7,898.8	9.79
Iceland	ISL	4.8	5.8	13,936	16,755	222.5	411.8	916.2	164.5	197.7	0.0	0.0	0.0	128.285	106.701	613.9	0.34
Ireland	IRL	48.1	40.2	10,022	8,376	154.6	296.2	458.0	118.3	98.9	0.2	0.3	0.1	0.740	0.885	35.6	4.80
Italy	ITA	525.8	369.3	8,685	6,100	130.0	256.7	333.6	102.5	72.0	2.2	2.8	0.8	0.622	0.885	326.9	60.54
Kazakhstan	KAZ	122.1	17.6	6,767	974	26.6	200.0	53.3	79.9	11.5	0.5	0.1	0.3	46.939	326.000	5,729.3	18.04
Kyrgyz Republic	KGZ	13.1	1.3	2,200	222	18.7	65.0	12.2	26.0	2.6	0.1	0.0	0.1	6.950	68.769	90.9	5.94
Latvia	LVA	16.7	5.5	8,604	2,824	60.7	254.3	154.4	101.5	33.3	0.1	0.0	0.0	0.291	0.885	4.9	1.94
Lithuania	LTU	26.9	7.8	9,523	2,754	53.5	281.4	150.6	112.4	32.5	0.1	0.1	0.0	0.256	0.885	6.9	2.83
Luxembourg	LUX	9.2	10.5	15,481	17,662	211.1	457.5	965.8	182.7	208.4	0.0	0.1	0.0	1.010	0.885	9.3	0.60
Moldova	MDA	12.4	1.5	3,484	410	21.8	103.0	22.4	41.1	4.8	0.1	0.0	0.0	2.175	18.490	26.9	3.55
Montenegro	MNE	4.4	0.9	7,086	1,438	37.6	209.4	78.6	83.6	17.0	0.0	0.0	0.0	0.180	0.885	0.8	0.62
Netherlands	NLD	248.8	202.8	14,521	11,836	150.8	429.1	647.2	171.4	139.7	1.0	1.5	0.2	0.722	0.885	179.5	17.13
North Macedonia	MKD	9.9	1.7	4,780	816	31.6	141.2	44.6	56.4	9.6	0.0	0.0	0.0	9.301	54.505	92.2	2.07
Norway	NOR	84.5	95.8	16,020	18,158	209.7	473.4	992.9	189.1	214.3	0.3	0.7	0.1	9.358	8.256	791.1	5.28
Poland	POL	325.6	93.3	8,474	2,429	53.0	250.4	132.8	100.0	28.7	1.3	0.7	0.5	1.080	3.768	351.7	38.42
Portugal	PRT	76.7	38.0	7,444	3,693	91.8	220.0	201.9	87.9	43.6	0.3	0.3	0.1	0.439	0.885	33.7	10.30
Romania	ROU	153.9	33.3	7,857	1,701	40.1	232.2	93.0	92.7	20.1	0.6	0.3	0.3	0.875	4.044	134.8	19.59
Russian Federation	RUS	1,369.1	285.4	9,323	1,943	38.6	275.5	106.3	110.0	22.9	5.6	2.2	2.0	12.161	58.343	16,649.2	146.84
Serbia	SRB	41.6	7.2	5,928	1,020	31.8	175.2	55.7	70.0	12.0	0.2	0.1	0.1	18.473	107.406	768.8	7.02
Slovak Republic	SVK	53.1	18.1	9,757	3,320	63.0	288.3	181.5	115.2	39.2	0.2	0.1	0.1	0.301	0.885	16.0	5.44
Slovenia	SVN	18.4	9.0	8,920	4,333	89.9	263.6	236.9	105.3	51.1	0.1	0.1	0.0	0.430	0.885	7.9	2.07
Spain	ESP	406.9	244.4	8,744	5,252	111.1	258.4	287.2	103.2	62.0	1.7	1.9	0.6	0.532	0.885	216.3	46.53
Sweden	SWE	148.2	141.2	14,738	14,043	176.3	435.5	767.9	173.9	165.7	0.6	1.1	0.1	8.127	8.529	1,204.6	10.06
Switzerland	CHE	63.8	81.9	7,553	9,684	237.2	223.2	529.5	89.1	114.3	0.3	0.6	0.1	1.262	0.984	80.5	8.45
Tajikistan	TJK	10.9	1.0	1,236	118	17.7	36.5	6.5	14.6	1.4	0.0	0.0	0.1	0.819	8.550	8.9	8.84
Turkey	TUR	667.1	123.5	8,306	1,538	34.3	245.5	84.1	98.0	18.2	2.7	0.9	1.1	0.675	3.648	450.6	80.31
Ukraine	UKR	255.9	23.2	6,023	546	16.8	178.0	29.8	71.1	6.4	1.0	0.2	0.6	2.410	26.597	616.6	42.49
United Kingdom	GBR	670.3	498.3	10,150	7,545	137.5	299.9	412.6	119.8	89.0	2.7	3.8	0.9	0.577	0.776	386.7	66.04
Total (46)	**ECB**	**8,240.0**	**4,199.3**	**9,429**	**4,805**	**94.3**	**278.6**	**262.7**	**111.3**	**56.7**	**33.8**	**31.9**	**12.1**	**n.a.**	**n.a**	**n.a.**	**873.93**
Latin America and the Caribbean																	
Anguilla	AIA	0.1	0.1	8,210	3,821	86.1	242.6	208.9	96.9	45.1	0.0	0.0	0.0	1.257	2.700	0.2	0.01
Antigua and Barbuda	ATG	0.7	0.3	7,300	2,706	68.6	215.7	148.0	86.2	31.9	0.0	0.0	0.0	1.001	2.700	0.7	0.10
Argentina	ARG	313.7	115.6	7,140	2,631	68.2	211.0	143.8	84.3	31.0	1.3	0.9	0.6	6.102	16.563	1,914.3	43.94
Aruba	ABW	1.0	0.5	9,448	4,842	94.8	279.2	264.7	111.5	57.1	0.0	0.0	0.0	0.917	1.790	0.9	0.11

Table 2.4 *(Continued)*

CONSUMPTION EXPENDITURE BY GOVERNMENT		Expenditure (billion US$)		Expenditure per capita (US$)		Price level index	Expenditure per capita indexes[b]				Share (world = 100%)[b]				Reference data		
							World = 100.0		United States = 100.0		Expenditure						
Economy		Based on PPPs	Based on XRs	Based on PPPs	Based on XRs	(world = 100.0)[a]	Based on PPPs	Based on XRs	Based on PPPs	Based on XRs	Based on PPPs	Based on XRs	Population	PPPs[c] (US$ = 1.000)	Market exchange rates[c] (US$ = 1.000)	Expenditure (billion LCU)	Population (millions)
(00)		(01)	(02)	(03)	(04)	(05)	(06)	(07)	(08)	(09)	(10)	(11)	(12)	(13)	(14)	(15)	(16)
Bahamas, The	BHS	3.4	1.6	8,950	4,316	89.2	264.5	236.0	105.6	50.9	0.0	0.0	0.0	0.482	1.000	1.6	0.38
Barbados	BRB	1.0	0.9	3,636	3,112	158.4	107.4	170.2	42.9	36.7	0.0	0.0	0.0	1.712	2.000	1.8	0.29
Belize	BLZ	0.6	0.3	1,669	814	90.3	49.3	44.5	19.7	9.6	0.0	0.0	0.0	0.976	2.000	0.6	0.38
Bolivia	BOL	15.3	6.3	1,364	566	76.8	40.3	31.0	16.1	6.7	0.1	0.0	0.2	2.891	6.960	44.1	11.19
Bonaire[d]	BON	...	...	...	...	...	...	...	...	...	...	...	...	...	1.000	...	0.03
Brazil	BRA	730.6	416.0	3,515	2,002	105.4	103.9	109.5	41.5	23.6	3.0	3.2	2.9	1.817	3.191	1,327.8	207.83
Cayman Islands	CYM	0.5	0.5	8,288	7,551	168.6	244.9	412.9	97.8	89.1	0.0	0.0	0.0	0.759	0.833	0.4	0.06
Chile	CHL	93.1	38.9	5,028	2,101	77.3	148.6	114.9	59.3	24.8	0.4	0.3	0.3	271.088	648.834	25,246.3	18.52
Colombia	COL	203.1	46.5	4,121	943	42.3	121.8	51.5	48.6	11.1	0.8	0.4	0.7	675.127	2,951.327	137,133.0	49.29
Costa Rica	CRI	23.7	9.9	4,790	2,012	77.7	141.5	110.0	56.5	23.7	0.1	0.1	0.1	238.378	567.513	5,645.7	4.94
Curaçao	CUW	1.0	0.5	6,412	3,301	95.3	189.5	180.5	75.7	39.0	0.0	0.0	0.0	0.922	1.790	1.0	0.16
Dominica	DMA	0.2	0.1	3,004	1,263	77.8	88.8	69.1	35.5	14.9	0.0	0.0	0.0	1.136	2.700	0.2	0.07
Dominican Republic	DOM	35.4	8.8	3,364	832	45.8	99.4	45.5	39.7	9.8	0.1	0.1	0.1	11.763	47.537	416.0	10.51
Ecuador	ECU	36.7	15.2	2,186	905	76.6	64.6	49.5	25.8	10.7	0.2	0.1	0.2	0.414	1.000	15.2	16.79
El Salvador	SLV	12.6	4.1	1,973	635	59.5	58.3	34.7	23.3	7.5	0.1	0.0	0.1	0.322	1.000	4.1	6.39
Grenada	GRD	0.3	0.1	2,988	1,185	73.4	88.3	64.8	35.3	14.0	0.0	0.0	0.0	1.071	2.700	0.4	0.11
Guyana	GUY	2.5	0.7	3,232	877	50.2	95.5	47.9	38.1	10.3	0.0	0.0	0.0	57.542	212.190	144.2	0.78
Haiti	HTI	3.4	1.0	307	88	53.4	9.1	4.8	3.6	1.0	0.0	0.0	0.2	18.375	63.687	61.9	10.98
Honduras	HND	7.2	3.1	766	330	79.7	22.6	18.0	9.0	3.9	0.0	0.0	0.1	10.160	23.588	73.4	9.43
Jamaica	JAM	5.9	2.0	2,012	682	62.7	59.5	37.3	23.7	8.0	0.0	0.0	0.0	43.352	127.965	254.8	2.92
Mexico	MEX	556.2	134.6	4,508	1,091	44.8	133.2	59.7	53.2	12.9	2.3	1.0	1.7	4.581	18.927	2,548.0	123.36
Montserrat	MSR	0.1	0.0	18,728	6,511	64.3	553.4	356.0	221.0	76.8	0.0	0.0	0.0	0.939	2.700	0.1	0.00
Nicaragua	NIC	10.7	2.0	1,669	319	35.3	49.3	17.4	19.7	3.8	0.0	0.0	0.1	5.739	30.051	61.1	6.38
Panama	PAN	22.5	6.9	5,481	1,673	56.5	162.0	91.5	64.7	19.7	0.1	0.1	0.1	0.305	1.000	6.9	4.11
Paraguay	PRY	13.7	4.3	1,988	621	57.8	58.8	33.9	23.5	7.3	0.1	0.0	0.1	1,736.632	5,562.276	23,712.2	6.87
Peru	PER	77.2	27.9	2,454	887	66.9	72.5	48.5	29.0	10.5	0.3	0.2	0.4	1.178	3.260	90.9	31.44
Sint Maarten	SXM	0.4	0.2	9,252	4,812	96.2	273.4	263.1	109.2	56.8	0.0	0.0	0.0	0.931	1.790	0.4	0.04
St. Kitts and Nevis	KNA	0.5	0.2	9,504	3,104	60.4	280.8	169.7	112.2	36.6	0.0	0.0	0.0	0.882	2.700	0.4	0.05
St. Lucia	LCA	0.9	0.4	4,803	2,213	85.2	141.9	121.0	56.7	26.1	0.0	0.0	0.0	1.244	2.700	1.1	0.18
St. Vincent and the Grenadines	VCT	0.5	0.2	4,163	1,513	67.2	123.0	82.7	49.1	17.9	0.0	0.0	0.0	0.981	2.700	0.4	0.11
Suriname	SUR	3.2	0.5	5,696	947	30.8	168.3	51.8	67.2	11.2	0.0	0.0	0.0	1.255	7.550	4.1	0.57
Trinidad and Tobago	TTO	6.5	3.1	4,678	2,238	88.5	138.2	122.4	55.2	26.4	0.0	0.0	0.0	3.243	6.780	21.0	1.38
Turks and Caicos Islands	TCA	0.3	0.2	8,646	5,723	122.5	255.5	312.9	102.0	67.5	0.0	0.0	0.0	0.662	1.000	0.2	0.04
Uruguay	URY	15.1	8.7	4,396	2,518	106.0	129.9	137.7	51.9	29.7	0.1	0.1	0.0	16.425	28.676	248.1	3.44
Virgin Islands, British	VGB	0.1	0.1	3,401	3,701	201.4	100.5	202.4	40.1	43.7	0.0	0.0	0.0	1.088	1.000	0.1	0.03
Total (39)	**LCB**	**2,199.9**	**862.2**	**3,838**	**1,504**	**72.5**	**113.4**	**82.2**	**45.3**	**17.8**	**9.0**	**6.5**	**8.0**	**n.a.**	**n.a**	**n.a.**	**573.20**

Table 2.4 *(Continued)*

CONSUMPTION EXPENDITURE BY GOVERNMENT Economy		Expenditure (billion US$) Based on PPPs	Expenditure (billion US$) Based on XRs	Expenditure per capita (US$) Based on PPPs	Expenditure per capita (US$) Based on XRs	Price level index (world = 100.0)[a]	Expenditure per capita indexes[b] World = 100.0 Based on PPPs	Expenditure per capita indexes[b] World = 100.0 Based on XRs	Expenditure per capita indexes[b] United States = 100.0 Based on PPPs	Expenditure per capita indexes[b] United States = 100.0 Based on XRs	Share (world = 100%)[b] Expenditure Based on PPPs	Share (world = 100%)[b] Expenditure Based on XRs	Share (world = 100%)[b] Population	PPPs[c] (US$ = 1.000)	Reference data Market exchange rates[c] (US$ = 1.000)	Reference data Expenditure (billion LCU)	Reference data Population (millions)
(00)		(01)	(02)	(03)	(04)	(05)	(06)	(07)	(08)	(09)	(10)	(11)	(12)	(13)	(14)	(15)	(16)
Middle East and North Africa																	
Algeria	DZA	173.7	31.9	4,197	771	34.0	124.0	42.1	49.5	9.1	0.7	0.2	0.6	20.381	110.973	3,540.4	41.39
Bahrain	BHR	17.3	5.9	11,532	3,923	62.9	340.8	214.5	136.1	46.3	0.1	0.0	0.0	0.128	0.376	2.2	1.50
Djibouti	DJI	0.8	0.4	846	392	85.6	25.0	21.4	10.0	4.6	0.0	0.0	0.0	82.209	177.720	65.7	0.94
Egypt, Arab Rep.	EGY	182.1	20.7	1,921	218	21.0	56.8	11.9	22.7	2.6	0.7	0.2	1.3	2.024	17.847	368.6	94.80
Iran, Islamic Rep.	IRN	371.8	74.3	4,586	917	37.0	135.5	50.1	54.1	10.8	1.5	0.6	1.1	6,641.413	33,226.298	2,469,173.8	81.07
Iraq	IRQ	75.7	28.8	2,039	775	70.3	60.3	42.4	24.1	9.1	0.3	0.2	0.5	477.203	1,256.000	36,143.2	37.14
Israel	ISR	93.9	80.1	10,779	9,198	157.9	318.5	502.9	127.2	108.6	0.4	0.6	0.1	3.072	3.600	288.4	8.71
Jordan	JOR	25.4	6.2	2,523	612	44.9	74.6	33.5	29.8	7.2	0.1	0.0	0.1	0.172	0.708	4.4	10.05
Kuwait	KWT	58.6	30.0	14,356	7,360	94.9	424.2	402.4	169.4	86.9	0.2	0.2	0.1	0.156	0.303	9.1	4.08
Malta	MLT	4.0	2.0	8,616	4,189	90.0	254.6	229.1	101.7	49.4	0.0	0.0	0.0	0.430	0.885	1.7	0.47
Morocco	MAR	61.0	20.8	1,751	598	63.2	51.7	32.7	20.7	7.1	0.3	0.2	0.5	3.308	9.691	201.8	34.85
Oman	OMN	42.0	19.8	9,205	4,341	87.2	272.0	237.3	108.6	51.2	0.2	0.2	0.1	0.181	0.385	7.6	4.56
Qatar	QAT	49.8	28.3	18,286	10,392	105.2	540.4	568.3	215.8	122.7	0.2	0.2	0.0	2.074	3.650	103.3	2.72
Saudi Arabia	SAU	500.6	166.4	15,351	5,101	61.5	453.6	278.9	181.2	60.2	2.1	1.3	0.5	1.246	3.750	623.9	32.61
Tunisia	TUN	34.5	8.3	3,016	725	44.5	89.1	39.7	35.6	8.6	0.1	0.1	0.2	0.582	2.419	20.1	11.43
United Arab Emirates	ARE	103.7	52.6	11,147	5,653	93.8	329.4	309.1	131.6	66.7	0.4	0.4	0.1	1.862	3.673	193.2	9.30
West Bank and Gaza	PSE	10.2	3.8	2,296	855	68.9	67.9	46.8	27.1	10.1	0.0	0.0	0.1	1.341	3.600	13.7	4.45
Total (17)	**MEB**	**1,805.2**	**580.2**	**4,749**	**1,526**	**59.5**	**140.4**	**83.5**	**56.1**	**18.0**	**7.4**	**4.4**	**5.3**	**n.a.**	**n.a**	**n.a.**	**380.10**
North America																	
Bermuda	BMU	0.9	1.0	14,002	15,815	209.0	413.8	864.8	165.3	186.7	0.0	0.0	0.0	1.130	1.000	1.0	0.06
Canada	CAN	456.1	354.3	12,481	9,695	143.7	368.8	530.1	147.3	114.4	1.9	2.7	0.5	1.008	1.298	459.7	36.54
United States	USA	2,757.2	2,757.2	8,473	8,473	185.0	250.4	463.3	100.0	100.0	11.3	20.9	4.5	1.000	1.000	2,757.2	325.41
Total (3)	**NAB**	**3,214.2**	**3,112.5**	**8,879**	**8,598**	**179.2**	**262.4**	**470.1**	**104.8**	**101.5**	**13.2**	**23.6**	**5.0**	**n.a.**	**n.a**	**n.a.**	**362.01**
South Asia																	
Bangladesh	BGD	57.2	16.3	354	100	52.6	10.4	5.5	4.2	1.2	0.2	0.1	2.2	22.859	80.438	1,307.6	161.80
Bhutan	BTN	3.0	0.4	4,135	571	25.6	122.2	31.2	48.8	6.7	0.0	0.0	0.0	8.999	65.122	27.1	0.73
India	IND	775.6	275.0	592	210	65.6	17.5	11.5	7.0	2.5	3.2	2.1	18.2	23.094	65.122	17,911.5	1,309.20
Maldives	MDV	2.1	0.7	4,352	1,517	64.5	128.6	83.0	51.4	17.9	0.0	0.0	0.0	5.365	15.387	11.5	0.49
Nepal	NPL	10.5	2.8	366	98	49.7	10.8	5.4	4.3	1.2	0.0	0.0	0.4	28.085	104.512	296.3	28.83
Pakistan	PAK	130.7	36.3	656	182	51.4	19.4	10.0	7.7	2.2	0.5	0.3	2.8	29.283	105.455	3,826.9	199.11
Sri Lanka	LKA	62.4	7.4	2,909	346	22.0	86.0	18.9	34.3	4.1	0.3	0.1	0.3	18.124	152.446	1,130.8	21.44
Total (7)	**SAB**	**1,041.5**	**339.0**	**605**	**197**	**60.2**	**17.9**	**10.8**	**7.1**	**2.3**	**4.3**	**2.6**	**23.9**	**n.a.**	**n.a**	**n.a.**	**1,721.60**
Sub-Saharan Africa																	
Angola	AGO	62.1	15.8	2,083	530	47.1	61.6	29.0	24.6	6.3	0.3	0.1	0.4	42.195	165.916	2,621.1	29.82
Benin	BEN	7.0	1.6	630	143	42.1	18.6	7.8	7.4	1.7	0.0	0.0	0.2	132.363	582.075	932.3	11.18
Botswana	BWA	10.9	3.2	4,945	1,453	54.4	146.1	79.5	58.4	17.2	0.0	0.0	0.0	3.041	10.347	33.2	2.21

Table 2.4 *(Continued)*

CONSUMPTION EXPENDITURE BY GOVERNMENT Economy		Expenditure (billion US$) Based on PPPs	Expenditure (billion US$) Based on XRs	Expenditure per capita (US$) Based on PPPs	Expenditure per capita (US$) Based on XRs	Price level index (world = 100.0)[a]	Expenditure per capita indexes[b] World = 100.0 Based on PPPs	Expenditure per capita indexes[b] World = 100.0 Based on XRs	Expenditure per capita indexes[b] United States = 100.0 Based on PPPs	Expenditure per capita indexes[b] United States = 100.0 Based on XRs	Share (world = 100%)[b] Expenditure Based on PPPs	Share (world = 100%)[b] Expenditure Based on XRs	Share (world = 100%)[b] Population	PPPs[c] (US$ = 1.000)	Reference data Market exchange rates[c] (US$ = 1.000)	Reference data Expenditure (billion LCU)	Reference data Population (millions)
(00)		(01)	(02)	(03)	(04)	(05)	(06)	(07)	(08)	(09)	(10)	(11)	(12)	(13)	(14)	(15)	(16)
Burkina Faso	BFA	10.0	2.7	521	143	50.7	15.4	7.8	6.2	1.7	0.0	0.0	0.3	159.363	582.075	1,595.0	19.19
Burundi	BDI	2.4	0.6	218	53	45.2	6.4	2.9	2.6	0.6	0.0	0.0	0.2	422.575	1,729.055	995.4	10.83
Cabo Verde	CPV	1.2	0.4	2,262	666	54.5	66.8	36.4	26.7	7.9	0.0	0.0	0.0	28.812	97.799	35.0	0.54
Cameroon	CMR	16.5	3.9	671	158	43.7	19.8	8.7	7.9	1.9	0.1	0.0	0.3	137.467	582.075	2,264.4	24.57
Central African Republic	CAF	1.0	0.3	221	56	47.0	6.5	3.1	2.6	0.7	0.0	0.0	0.1	147.882	582.075	149.9	4.60
Chad	TCD	3.3	1.0	217	69	58.5	6.4	3.8	2.6	0.8	0.0	0.0	0.2	184.106	582.075	600.7	15.02
Comoros	COM	0.7	0.1	821	141	31.9	24.3	7.7	9.7	1.7	0.0	0.0	0.0	75.195	436.571	50.2	0.81
Congo, Dem. Rep.	COD	18.2	5.6	223	69	57.3	6.6	3.8	2.6	0.8	0.1	0.0	1.1	453.425	1,464.418	8,235.3	81.40
Congo, Rep.	COG	6.3	1.6	1,242	321	47.9	36.7	17.6	14.7	3.8	0.0	0.0	0.1	150.549	582.075	955.7	5.11
Côte d'Ivoire	CIV	15.6	5.5	640	224	64.6	18.9	12.2	7.6	2.6	0.1	0.0	0.3	203.341	582.075	3,181.2	24.44
Equatorial Guinea	GNQ	17.9	3.1	14,200	2,479	32.3	419.6	135.5	167.6	29.3	0.1	0.0	0.0	101.603	582.075	1,820.7	1.26
Eswatini	SWZ	3.2	1.1	2,853	970	62.9	84.3	53.0	33.7	11.4	0.0	0.0	0.0	4.534	13.334	14.6	1.12
Ethiopia	ETH	36.3	8.3	341	78	42.4	10.1	4.3	4.0	0.9	0.1	0.1	1.5	5.474	23.866	198.9	106.40
Gabon	GAB	12.3	2.8	5,959	1,376	42.7	176.1	75.2	70.3	16.2	0.1	0.0	0.0	134.408	582.075	1,653.8	2.06
Gambia, The	GMB	0.6	0.1	289	58	37.3	8.5	3.2	3.4	0.7	0.0	0.0	0.0	9.404	46.608	6.0	2.21
Ghana	GHA	19.0	4.6	651	157	44.5	19.2	8.6	7.7	1.8	0.1	0.0	0.4	1.047	4.351	19.8	29.12
Guinea	GIN	8.9	1.8	735	146	36.7	21.7	8.0	8.7	1.7	0.0	0.0	0.2	1,810.683	9,125.743	16,066.0	12.07
Guinea-Bissau	GNB	1.2	0.2	634	137	39.9	18.7	7.5	7.5	1.6	0.0	0.0	0.0	125.408	582.075	145.3	1.83
Kenya	KEN	59.6	16.1	1,186	321	50.1	35.1	17.6	14.0	3.8	0.2	0.1	0.7	28.023	103.411	1,669.3	50.22
Lesotho	LSO	2.6	0.9	1,222	418	63.3	36.1	22.9	14.4	4.9	0.0	0.0	0.0	4.565	13.334	11.7	2.09
Liberia	LBR	1.9	0.7	407	140	63.7	12.0	7.7	4.8	1.7	0.0	0.0	0.1	38.827	112.707	74.2	4.70
Madagascar	MDG	9.5	2.1	370	81	40.6	10.9	4.4	4.4	1.0	0.0	0.0	0.4	683.217	3,116.110	6,463.9	25.57
Malawi	MWI	2.3	0.6	132	34	47.8	3.9	1.9	1.6	0.4	0.0	0.0	0.2	188.730	730.273	439.4	17.67
Mali	MLI	8.1	2.3	439	127	53.4	13.0	6.9	5.2	1.5	0.0	0.0	0.3	168.091	582.075	1,365.4	18.51
Mauritania	MRT	6.3	1.1	1,464	255	32.2	43.3	13.9	17.3	3.0	0.0	0.0	0.1	62.288	357.493	390.5	4.28
Mauritius	MUS	6.8	1.9	5,383	1,512	52.0	159.1	82.7	63.5	17.9	0.0	0.0	0.0	9.689	34.481	65.9	1.26
Mozambique	MOZ	11.8	3.6	412	125	56.1	12.2	6.8	4.9	1.5	0.0	0.0	0.4	19.286	63.584	227.8	28.65
Namibia	NAM	8.0	3.2	3,330	1,334	74.1	98.4	72.9	39.3	15.7	0.0	0.0	0.0	5.332	13.313	42.7	2.40
Niger	NER	3.5	1.3	162	62	70.5	4.8	3.4	1.9	0.7	0.0	0.0	0.3	221.810	582.075	776.9	21.60
Nigeria	NGA	81.0	17.4	425	91	39.7	12.5	5.0	5.0	1.1	0.3	0.1	2.6	65.570	305.790	5,313.5	190.87
Rwanda	RWA	4.2	1.4	350	115	60.9	10.3	6.3	4.1	1.4	0.0	0.0	0.2	273.795	831.531	1,146.8	11.98
São Tomé and Príncipe	STP	0.2	0.1	1,134	243	39.6	33.5	13.3	13.4	2.9	0.0	0.0	0.0	4.658	21.741	1.1	0.21
Senegal	SEN	8.8	2.9	573	187	60.5	16.9	10.2	6.8	2.2	0.0	0.0	0.2	190.274	582.075	1,681.4	15.42
Seychelles	SYC	1.1	0.3	11,045	3,280	55.0	326.4	179.4	130.4	38.7	0.0	0.0	0.0	4.053	13.648	4.3	0.10
Sierra Leone	SLE	1.8	0.4	240	52	40.1	7.1	2.8	2.8	0.6	0.0	0.0	0.1	1,600.765	7,384.432	2,874.4	7.49
South Africa	ZAF	207.4	72.6	3,639	1,273	64.7	107.5	69.6	42.9	15.0	0.9	0.6	0.8	4.666	13.334	967.9	57.01
Sudan (AFR)	SDN	34.5	2.8	846	68	14.8	25.0	3.7	10.0	0.8	0.1	0.0	0.6	1.615	20.130	55.7	40.78

Table 2.4 *(Continued)*

CONSUMPTION EXPENDITURE BY GOVERNMENT		Expenditure (billion US$)		Expenditure per capita (US$)		Price level index (world = 100.0)[a]	Expenditure per capita indexes[b]				Share (world = 100%)[b]			PPPs[c] (US$ = 1.000)	Reference data		
							World = 100.0		United States = 100.0		Expenditure				Market exchange rates[c] (US$ = 1.000)		
Economy		Based on PPPs	Based on XRs	Based on PPPs	Based on XRs		Based on PPPs	Based on XRs	Based on PPPs	Based on XRs	Based on PPPs	Based on XRs	Population			Expenditure (billion LCU)	Population (millions)
(00)		(01)	(02)	(03)	(04)	(05)	(06)	(07)	(08)	(09)	(10)	(11)	(12)	(13)	(14)	(15)	(16)
Tanzania	TZA	18.5	7.1	338	130	71.2	10.0	7.1	4.0	1.5	0.1	0.1	0.8	857.419	2,228.858	15,859.2	54.66
Togo	TGO	3.4	0.9	442	112	46.7	13.1	6.1	5.2	1.3	0.0	0.0	0.1	146.888	582.075	499.7	7.70
Uganda	UGA	13.2	2.8	322	68	39.3	9.5	3.7	3.8	0.8	0.1	0.0	0.6	767.411	3,611.224	10,166.4	41.17
Zambia	ZMB	8.7	2.7	518	159	56.7	15.3	8.7	6.1	1.9	0.0	0.0	0.2	2.917	9.520	25.5	16.85
Zimbabwe	ZWE	11.9	4.8	834	334	74.2	24.6	18.3	9.8	3.9	0.0	0.0	0.2	0.401	1.000	4.8	14.24
Total (45)	**SSB**	**769.8**	**214.2**	**754**	**210**	**51.5**	**22.3**	**11.5**	**8.9**	**2.5**	**3.2**	**1.6**	**14.2**	**n.a.**	**n.a**	**n.a.**	**1,021.22**
World (176)	**WLD**	**24,376.5**	**13,174.1**	**3,384**	**1,829**	**100.0**	**100.0**	**100.0**	**39.9**	**21.6**	**100.0**	**100.0**	**100.0**	**n.a.**	**n.a.**	**n.a.**	**7,203.60**

Note: PPP = purchasing power parity; XR = market exchange rate; LCU = local currency unit; n.a. = not applicable; ... = data suppressed due to unavailability

a. World totals used to calculate price level indexes (PLIs) in this table exclude nonparticipating economies.

b. Indexes and shares are rounded to one decimal place for presentation in this table.

c. PPPs and market exchange rates are rounded to three decimal places for presentation in this table.

d. Bonaire's results are provided only for individual consumption expenditure by households. Therefore, to ensure consistency across tables, Bonaire is not included in either the Latin America and the Caribbean or the world totals.

Table 2.5 Gross fixed capital formation (GFCF): ICP 2017 results

GROSS FIXED CAPITAL FORMATION Economy		Expenditure (billion US$)		Expenditure per capita (US$)		Price level index (world = 100.0)[a]	Expenditure per capita indexes[b]				Share (world = 100%)[b]			PPPs[c] (US$ = 1.000)	Reference data		
							World = 100.0		United States = 100.0		Expenditure				Market exchange rates[c] (US$ = 1.000)	Expenditure (billion LCU)	Popu-tion (millio
		Based on PPPs	Based on XRs	Based on PPPs	Based on XRs		Based on PPPs	Based on XRs	Based on PPPs	Based on XRs	Based on PPPs	Based on XRs	Popula-tion				
(00)		(01)	(02)	(03)	(04)	(05)	(06)	(07)	(08)	(09)	(10)	(11)	(12)	(13)	(14)	(15)	(16
East Asia and Pacific																	
Australia	AUS	285.1	335.1	11,587	13,621	169.5	289.4	490.5	94.4	110.9	1.0	1.7	0.3	1.534	1.305	437.2	24
Brunei Darussalam	BRN	9.1	5.0	21,241	11,597	78.7	530.6	417.6	173.0	94.5	0.0	0.0	0.0	0.754	1.381	6.9	[illegible]
Cambodia	KHM	5.7	2.4	360	151	60.5	9.0	5.4	2.9	1.2	0.0	0.0	0.2	1,699.937	4,050.580	9,703.4	15
China	CHN	7,625.8	5,204.0	5,500	3,754	98.4	137.4	135.2	44.8	30.6	26.4	26.0	19.2	4.612	6.759	35,172.3	1,38
Fiji	FJI	1.9	1.0	2,207	1,086	70.9	55.1	39.1	18.0	8.8	0.0	0.0	0.0	1.017	2.067	2.0	[illegible]
Hong Kong SAR, China	HKG	92.6	73.9	12,529	9,999	115.0	313.0	360.1	102.0	81.4	0.3	0.4	0.1	6.219	7.793	576.0	7
Indonesia	IDN	846.3	326.6	3,232	1,247	55.6	80.7	44.9	26.3	10.2	2.9	1.6	3.6	5,164.131	13,380.872	4,370,574.8	261
Japan	JPN	1,156.5	1,158.4	9,128	9,142	144.4	228.0	329.2	74.3	74.5	4.0	5.8	1.8	112.342	112.166	129,927.9	12
Korea, Rep.	KOR	699.2	511.7	13,613	9,963	105.5	340.1	358.8	110.9	81.1	2.4	2.6	0.7	827.318	1,130.425	578,456.9	51
Lao PDR	LAO	13.4	5.6	1,936	815	60.7	48.4	29.4	15.8	6.6	0.0	0.0	0.1	3,517.220	8,351.526	46,996.3	6
Malaysia	MYS	190.7	79.4	5,955	2,480	60.0	148.8	89.3	48.5	20.2	0.7	0.4	0.4	1.791	4.300	341.5	32
Mongolia	MNG	6.6	2.8	2,101	894	61.4	52.5	32.2	17.1	7.3	0.0	0.0	0.0	1,038.379	2,439.777	6,869.3	3
Myanmar	MMR	60.0	19.5	1,130	367	46.8	28.2	13.2	9.2	3.0	0.2	0.1	0.7	442.034	1,360.359	26,540.2	53
New Zealand	NZL	39.1	46.0	8,098	9,522	169.5	202.3	342.9	66.0	77.6	0.1	0.2	0.1	1.655	1.407	64.8	4
Philippines	PHL	165.3	78.4	1,576	748	68.4	39.4	26.9	12.8	6.1	0.6	0.4	1.5	23.916	50.404	3,953.6	104
Singapore	SGP	136.7	89.3	24,360	15,920	94.2	608.5	573.3	198.4	129.7	0.5	0.4	0.1	0.902	1.381	123.4	5
Taiwan, China	TWN	197.0	117.7	8,360	4,998	86.2	208.8	180.0	68.1	40.7	0.7	0.6	0.3	18.199	30.442	3,584.4	23
Thailand	THA	241.2	103.4	3,565	1,528	61.8	89.1	55.0	29.0	12.4	0.8	0.5	0.9	14.544	33.940	3,507.9	67
Vietnam	VNM	127.8	53.2	1,356	565	60.0	33.9	20.3	11.0	4.6	0.4	0.3	1.3	9,313.698	22,370.087	1,190,474.0	94
Total (19)	**EAB**	**11,900.1**	**8,213.5**	**5,239**	**3,616**	**99.5**	**130.9**	**130.2**	**42.7**	**29.5**	**41.3**	**41.1**	**31.5**	**n.a.**	**n.a**	**n.a.**	**2,271**
Europe and Central Asia																	
Albania	ALB	7.7	3.2	2,678	1,115	60.0	66.9	40.2	21.8	9.1	0.0	0.0	0.0	49.444	118.748	380.6	2
Armenia	ARM	3.4	2.0	1,138	680	86.1	28.4	24.5	9.3	5.5	0.0	0.0	0.0	288.252	482.720	977.7	2
Austria	AUT	127.3	98.4	14,473	11,191	111.5	361.5	403.0	117.9	91.1	0.4	0.5	0.1	0.684	0.885	87.1	8
Azerbaijan	AZE	18.1	9.7	1,856	1,000	77.7	46.4	36.0	15.1	8.1	0.1	0.0	0.1	0.927	1.721	16.8	9
Belarus	BLR	26.0	14.2	2,741	1,495	78.6	68.5	53.9	22.3	12.2	0.1	0.1	0.1	1.054	1.932	27.4	9
Belgium	BEL	161.0	116.6	14,154	10,246	104.4	353.6	369.0	115.3	83.5	0.6	0.6	0.2	0.641	0.885	103.2	11
Bosnia and Herzegovina	BIH	7.2	3.3	2,155	974	65.2	53.8	35.1	17.6	7.9	0.0	0.0	0.0	0.783	1.731	5.7	3
Bulgaria	BGR	23.4	10.9	3,304	1,534	66.9	82.5	55.2	26.9	12.5	0.1	0.1	0.1	0.804	1.731	18.8	7
Croatia	HRV	22.8	11.2	5,529	2,704	70.5	138.1	97.4	45.0	22.0	0.1	0.1	0.1	3.231	6.607	73.8	4
Cyprus	CYP	8.1	4.8	9,384	5,561	85.4	234.4	200.2	76.4	45.3	0.0	0.0	0.0	0.525	0.885	4.2	0
Czech Republic	CZE	93.9	53.7	8,864	5,067	82.4	221.4	182.4	72.2	41.3	0.3	0.3	0.1	13.319	23.304	1,250.3	10
Denmark	DNK	78.8	70.0	13,670	12,138	128.0	341.5	437.1	111.3	98.9	0.3	0.3	0.1	5.847	6.585	460.9	5
Estonia	EST	10.7	6.7	8,155	5,066	89.5	203.7	182.4	66.4	41.3	0.0	0.0	0.0	0.550	0.885	5.9	1
Finland	FIN	61.8	59.3	11,226	10,765	138.2	280.4	387.6	91.4	87.7	0.2	0.3	0.1	0.849	0.885	52.5	5
France	FRA	711.4	582.8	10,608	8,691	118.1	265.0	313.0	86.4	70.8	2.5	2.9	0.9	0.725	0.885	515.9	67

Table 2.5 *(Continued)*

GROSS FIXED CAPITAL FORMATION		Expenditure (billion US$)		Expenditure per capita (US$)		Price level index (world = 100.0)[a]	Expenditure per capita indexes[b]				Share (world = 100%)[b]			PPPs[c] (US$ = 1.000)	Reference data		
							World = 100.0		United States = 100.0		Expenditure				Market exchange rates[c] (US$ = 1.000)	Expenditure (billion LCU)	Population (millions)
Economy		Based on PPPs	Based on XRs	Based on PPPs	Based on XRs		Based on PPPs	Based on XRs	Based on PPPs	Based on XRs	Based on PPPs	Based on XRs	Population				
(00)		(01)	(02)	(03)	(04)	(05)	(06)	(07)	(08)	(09)	(10)	(11)	(12)	(13)	(14)	(15)	(16)
Georgia	GEO	10.4	4.1	2,783	1,111	57.5	69.5	40.0	22.7	9.0	0.0	0.0	0.1	1.002	2.510	10.4	3.73
Germany	DEU	886.7	752.3	10,728	9,101	122.3	268.0	327.7	87.4	74.1	3.1	3.8	1.1	0.751	0.885	665.9	82.66
Greece	GRC	44.8	26.3	4,162	2,442	84.6	104.0	87.9	33.9	19.9	0.2	0.1	0.1	0.519	0.885	23.2	10.75
Hungary	HUN	61.5	31.5	6,286	3,222	73.9	157.0	116.0	51.2	26.2	0.2	0.2	0.1	140.293	273.692	8,631.6	9.79
Iceland	ISL	4.9	5.4	14,273	15,621	157.8	356.5	562.5	116.3	127.2	0.0	0.0	0.0	116.782	106.701	572.4	0.34
Ireland	IRL	145.6	105.4	30,317	21,939	104.3	757.3	790.0	246.9	178.7	0.5	0.5	0.1	0.641	0.885	93.3	4.80
Italy	ITA	554.5	341.0	9,160	5,633	88.6	228.8	202.8	74.6	45.9	1.9	1.7	0.8	0.544	0.885	301.8	60.54
Kazakhstan	KAZ	60.5	36.2	3,352	2,007	86.3	83.7	72.3	27.3	16.3	0.2	0.2	0.3	195.136	326.000	11,798.9	18.04
Kyrgyz Republic	KGZ	4.8	2.4	808	408	72.9	20.2	14.7	6.6	3.3	0.0	0.0	0.1	34.765	68.769	166.9	5.94
Latvia	LVA	11.0	6.3	5,675	3,232	82.1	141.8	116.4	46.2	26.3	0.0	0.0	0.0	0.504	0.885	5.6	1.94
Lithuania	LTU	16.7	9.5	5,898	3,375	82.5	147.3	121.5	48.0	27.5	0.1	0.0	0.0	0.507	0.885	8.4	2.83
Luxembourg	LUX	15.8	12.0	26,410	20,170	110.1	659.7	726.3	215.1	164.3	0.1	0.1	0.0	0.676	0.885	10.7	0.60
Moldova	MDA	3.7	2.2	1,035	608	84.6	25.8	21.9	8.4	4.9	0.0	0.0	0.0	10.857	18.490	39.9	3.55
Montenegro	MNE	2.7	1.3	4,366	2,101	69.4	109.1	75.7	35.6	17.1	0.0	0.0	0.0	0.426	0.885	1.2	0.62
Netherlands	NLD	215.4	168.0	12,576	9,804	112.4	314.1	353.0	102.4	79.9	0.7	0.8	0.2	0.690	0.885	148.7	17.13
North Macedonia	MKD	6.2	2.6	2,984	1,229	59.4	74.5	44.3	24.3	10.0	0.0	0.0	0.0	22.460	54.505	139.0	2.07
Norway	NOR	90.9	98.0	17,220	18,578	155.5	430.2	669.0	140.3	151.3	0.3	0.5	0.1	8.907	8.256	809.4	5.28
Poland	POL	170.6	92.5	4,439	2,409	78.2	110.9	86.7	36.2	19.6	0.6	0.5	0.5	2.045	3.768	348.7	38.42
Portugal	PRT	67.8	37.2	6,578	3,607	79.0	164.3	129.9	53.6	29.4	0.2	0.2	0.1	0.485	0.885	32.9	10.30
Romania	ROU	107.5	47.5	5,487	2,426	63.7	137.1	87.4	44.7	19.8	0.4	0.2	0.3	1.788	4.044	192.2	19.59
Russian Federation	RUS	584.4	340.8	3,979	2,321	84.1	99.4	83.6	32.4	18.9	2.0	1.7	2.0	34.025	58.343	19,882.6	146.84
Serbia	SRB	15.8	7.9	2,252	1,119	71.6	56.2	40.3	18.3	9.1	0.1	0.0	0.1	53.368	107.406	843.7	7.02
Slovak Republic	SVK	34.6	20.3	6,367	3,732	84.5	159.1	134.4	51.9	30.4	0.1	0.1	0.1	0.519	0.885	18.0	5.44
Slovenia	SVN	15.6	8.9	7,551	4,306	82.2	188.6	155.1	61.5	35.1	0.1	0.0	0.0	0.505	0.885	7.9	2.07
Spain	ESP	406.0	245.0	8,724	5,264	87.0	217.9	189.6	71.1	42.9	1.4	1.2	0.6	0.534	0.885	216.8	46.53
Sweden	SWE	142.4	136.3	14,157	13,556	138.0	353.7	488.1	115.3	110.4	0.5	0.7	0.1	8.167	8.529	1,162.8	10.06
Switzerland	CHE	168.7	166.2	19,955	19,662	142.0	498.5	708.0	162.5	160.1	0.6	0.8	0.1	0.970	0.984	163.5	8.45
Tajikistan	TJK	3.8	1.9	428	216	72.6	10.7	7.8	3.5	1.8	0.0	0.0	0.1	4.307	8.550	16.3	8.84
Turkey	TUR	648.9	256.5	8,080	3,193	57.0	201.8	115.0	65.8	26.0	2.3	1.3	1.1	1.442	3.648	935.7	80.31
Ukraine	UKR	52.2	17.7	1,228	416	48.8	30.7	15.0	10.0	3.4	0.2	0.1	0.6	9.012	26.597	470.3	42.49
United Kingdom	GBR	657.0	460.1	9,949	6,968	101.0	248.5	250.9	81.0	56.8	2.3	2.3	0.9	0.543	0.776	357.1	66.04
Total (46)	**ECB**	**6,572.8**	**4,489.8**	**7,521**	**5,138**	**98.5**	**187.9**	**185.0**	**61.3**	**41.8**	**22.8**	**22.4**	**12.1**	**n.a.**	**n.a**	**n.a.**	**873.93**
Latin America and the Caribbean																	
Anguilla	AIA	0.1	0.1	4,460	4,127	133.4	111.4	148.6	36.3	33.6	0.0	0.0	0.0	2.498	2.700	0.2	0.01
Antigua and Barbuda	ATG	0.5	0.5	5,375	5,028	134.8	134.3	181.1	43.8	41.0	0.0	0.0	0.0	2.526	2.700	1.3	0.10
Argentina	ARG	117.2	96.7	2,668	2,201	118.9	66.7	79.2	21.7	17.9	0.4	0.5	0.6	13.660	16.563	1,601.5	43.94
Aruba	ABW	0.7	0.6	7,110	5,635	114.2	177.6	202.9	57.9	45.9	0.0	0.0	0.0	1.419	1.790	1.1	0.11

Table 2.5 *(Continued)*

GROSS FIXED CAPITAL FORMATION		Expenditure (billion US$)		Expenditure per capita (US$)		Price level index (world = 100.0)[a]	Expenditure per capita indexes[b]				Share (world = 100%)[b]			PPPs[c] (US$ = 1.000)	Reference data		
							World = 100.0		United States = 100.0		Expenditure				Market exchange rates[c] (US$ = 1.000)		
Economy		Based on PPPs	Based on XRs	Based on PPPs	Based on XRs		Based on PPPs	Based on XRs	Based on PPPs	Based on XRs	Based on PPPs	Based on XRs	Population			Expenditure (billion LCU)	Population (millions)
(00)		(01)	(02)	(03)	(04)	(05)	(06)	(07)	(08)	(09)	(10)	(11)	(12)	(13)	(14)	(15)	(16)
Bahamas, The	BHS	3.9	3.2	10,088	8,425	120.4	252.0	303.4	82.2	68.6	0.0	0.0	0.0	0.835	1.000	3.2	0.38
Barbados	BRB	0.9	0.8	2,999	2,760	132.7	74.9	99.4	24.4	22.5	0.0	0.0	0.0	1.841	2.000	1.6	0.29
Belize	BLZ	0.5	0.3	1,228	914	107.2	30.7	32.9	10.0	7.4	0.0	0.0	0.0	1.488	2.000	0.7	0.38
Bolivia	BOL	15.2	7.9	1,361	708	74.9	34.0	25.5	11.1	5.8	0.1	0.0	0.2	3.617	6.960	55.1	11.19
Bonaire[d]	BON	...	...	...	...	...	...	...	...	...	...	...	...	...	1.000	...	0.03
Brazil	BRA	473.0	300.4	2,276	1,446	91.6	56.8	52.1	18.5	11.8	1.6	1.5	2.9	2.027	3.191	958.8	207.83
Cayman Islands	CYM	0.6	0.7	9,761	11,095	163.9	243.8	399.5	79.5	90.4	0.0	0.0	0.0	0.947	0.833	0.6	0.06
Chile	CHL	99.1	58.6	5,352	3,161	85.1	133.7	113.8	43.6	25.7	0.3	0.3	0.3	383.232	648.834	37,993.7	18.52
Colombia	COL	105.7	67.8	2,144	1,375	92.5	53.5	49.5	17.5	11.2	0.4	0.3	0.7	1,893.568	2,951.327	200,075.0	49.29
Costa Rica	CRI	14.8	11.1	2,991	2,241	108.0	74.7	80.7	24.4	18.3	0.1	0.1	0.1	425.207	567.513	6,288.0	4.94
Curaçao	CUW	1.0	0.9	6,420	5,409	121.5	160.4	194.8	52.3	44.1	0.0	0.0	0.0	1.508	1.790	1.6	0.16
Dominica	DMA	0.1	0.1	1,521	1,207	114.4	38.0	43.4	12.4	9.8	0.0	0.0	0.0	2.142	2.700	0.2	0.07
Dominican Republic	DOM	36.9	19.0	3,511	1,806	74.1	87.7	65.0	28.6	14.7	0.1	0.1	0.1	24.448	47.537	902.4	10.51
Ecuador	ECU	47.9	26.5	2,852	1,579	79.8	71.2	56.8	23.2	12.9	0.2	0.1	0.2	0.553	1.000	26.5	16.79
El Salvador	SLV	8.3	3.9	1,292	607	67.8	32.3	21.9	10.5	4.9	0.0	0.0	0.1	0.470	1.000	3.9	6.39
Grenada	GRD	0.3	0.3	2,675	2,304	124.2	66.8	83.0	21.8	18.8	0.0	0.0	0.0	2.326	2.700	0.7	0.11
Guyana	GUY	1.6	1.1	2,001	1,388	100.0	50.0	50.0	16.3	11.3	0.0	0.0	0.0	147.143	212.190	228.3	0.78
Haiti	HTI	4.5	2.5	408	223	78.9	10.2	8.0	3.3	1.8	0.0	0.0	0.2	34.856	63.687	156.2	10.98
Honduras	HND	11.7	5.4	1,242	575	66.7	31.0	20.7	10.1	4.7	0.0	0.0	0.1	10.922	23.588	127.9	9.43
Jamaica	JAM	4.1	3.3	1,405	1,122	115.1	35.1	40.4	11.4	9.1	0.0	0.0	0.0	102.195	127.965	419.4	2.92
Mexico	MEX	441.8	256.2	3,581	2,077	83.6	89.5	74.8	29.2	16.9	1.5	1.3	1.7	10.975	18.927	4,848.8	123.36
Montserrat	MSR	0.0	0.0	2,035	1,873	132.7	50.8	67.5	16.6	15.3	0.0	0.0	0.0	2.485	2.700	0.0	0.00
Nicaragua	NIC	6.5	3.6	1,019	564	79.7	25.5	20.3	8.3	4.6	0.0	0.0	0.1	16.621	30.051	108.2	6.38
Panama	PAN	38.4	24.7	9,344	6,020	92.9	233.4	216.8	76.1	49.0	0.1	0.1	0.1	0.644	1.000	24.7	4.11
Paraguay	PRY	11.7	7.6	1,702	1,101	93.2	42.5	39.6	13.9	9.0	0.0	0.0	0.1	3,598.079	5,562.276	42,054.5	6.87
Peru	PER	73.6	43.5	2,340	1,383	85.2	58.4	49.8	19.1	11.3	0.3	0.2	0.4	1.927	3.260	141.8	31.44
Sint Maarten	SXM	0.2	0.2	4,947	4,319	125.9	123.6	155.5	40.3	35.2	0.0	0.0	0.0	1.563	1.790	0.3	0.04
St. Kitts and Nevis	KNA	0.4	0.3	6,953	5,599	116.1	173.7	201.6	56.6	45.6	0.0	0.0	0.0	2.174	2.700	0.8	0.05
St. Lucia	LCA	0.3	0.2	1,501	1,376	132.1	37.5	49.6	12.2	11.2	0.0	0.0	0.0	2.475	2.700	0.7	0.18
St. Vincent and the Grenadines	VCT	0.3	0.2	2,757	1,851	96.8	68.9	66.7	22.5	15.1	0.0	0.0	0.0	1.813	2.700	0.5	0.11
Suriname	SUR	2.4	1.2	4,215	2,069	70.8	105.3	74.5	34.3	16.9	0.0	0.0	0.0	3.706	7.550	8.9	0.57
Trinidad and Tobago	TTO	4.0	2.8	2,886	2,033	101.6	72.1	73.2	23.5	16.6	0.0	0.0	0.0	4.776	6.780	19.1	1.38
Turks and Caicos Islands	TCA	0.2	0.2	4,958	4,273	124.2	123.8	153.9	40.4	34.8	0.0	0.0	0.0	0.862	1.000	0.2	0.04
Uruguay	URY	10.8	9.8	3,143	2,854	130.9	78.5	102.8	25.6	23.2	0.0	0.0	0.0	26.039	28.676	281.2	3.44
Virgin Islands, British	VGB	0.3	0.3	8,964	10,435	167.8	223.9	375.7	73.0	85.0	0.0	0.0	0.0	1.164	1.000	0.3	0.03
Total (39)	**LCB**	**1,539.2**	**962.2**	**2,685**	**1,679**	**90.1**	**67.1**	**60.4**	**21.9**	**13.7**	**5.3**	**4.8**	**8.0**	**n.a.**	**n.a**	**n.a.**	**573.20**

Table 2.5 *(Continued)*

GROSS FIXED CAPITAL FORMATION		Expenditure (billion US$)		Expenditure per capita (US$)		Price level index	Expenditure per capita indexes[b]				Share (world = 100%)[b]			PPPs[c]	Reference data		
							World = 100.0		United States = 100.0		Expenditure						
Economy		Based on PPPs	Based on XRs	Based on PPPs	Based on XRs	(world = 100.0)[a]	Based on PPPs	Based on XRs	Based on PPPs	Based on XRs	Based on PPPs	Based on XRs	Population	(US$ = 1.000)	Market exchange rates[c] (US$ = 1.000)	Expenditure (billion LCU)	Population (millions)
(00)		(01)	(02)	(03)	(04)	(05)	(06)	(07)	(08)	(09)	(10)	(11)	(12)	(13)	(14)	(15)	(16)
Middle East and North Africa																	
Algeria	DZA	118.3	69.3	2,858	1,674	84.5	71.4	60.3	23.3	13.6	0.4	0.3	0.6	65.019	110.973	7,691.1	41.39
Bahrain	BHR	20.5	10.1	13,680	6,727	70.9	341.7	242.2	111.4	54.8	0.1	0.1	0.0	0.185	0.376	3.8	1.50
Djibouti	DJI	1.5	1.0	1,559	1,096	101.3	38.9	39.5	12.7	8.9	0.0	0.0	0.0	124.927	177.720	183.9	0.94
Egypt, Arab Rep.	EGY	97.4	34.7	1,028	366	51.3	25.7	13.2	8.4	3.0	0.3	0.2	1.3	6.349	17.847	618.6	94.80
Iran, Islamic Rep.	IRN	187.4	91.0	2,311	1,122	70.0	57.7	40.4	18.8	9.1	0.6	0.5	1.1	16,132.669	33,226.298	3,022,951.0	81.07
Iraq	IRQ	58.0	29.1	1,563	784	72.3	39.0	28.2	12.7	6.4	0.2	0.1	0.5	630.220	1,256.000	36,582.2	37.14
Israel	ISR	79.0	73.4	9,073	8,433	134.0	226.6	303.7	73.9	68.7	0.3	0.4	0.1	3.346	3.600	264.4	8.71
Jordan	JOR	16.2	8.1	1,607	802	71.9	40.2	28.9	13.1	6.5	0.1	0.0	0.1	0.353	0.708	5.7	10.05
Kuwait	KWT	69.4	34.2	17,005	8,382	71.1	424.8	301.8	138.5	68.3	0.2	0.2	0.1	0.150	0.303	10.4	4.08
Malta	MLT	4.1	2.6	8,657	5,590	93.1	216.3	201.3	70.5	45.5	0.0	0.0	0.0	0.572	0.885	2.3	0.47
Morocco	MAR	76.8	31.4	2,202	902	59.0	55.0	32.5	17.9	7.3	0.3	0.2	0.5	3.968	9.691	304.6	34.85
Oman	OMN	44.2	19.3	9,688	4,235	63.0	242.0	152.5	78.9	34.5	0.2	0.1	0.1	0.168	0.385	7.4	4.56
Qatar	QAT	144.3	74.3	52,960	27,265	74.2	1323.0	981.8	431.3	222.1	0.5	0.4	0.0	1.879	3.650	271.1	2.72
Saudi Arabia	SAU	395.4	167.2	12,123	5,126	61.0	302.8	184.6	98.7	41.8	1.4	0.8	0.5	1.586	3.750	626.9	32.61
Tunisia	TUN	12.4	7.6	1,085	661	87.8	27.1	23.8	8.8	5.4	0.0	0.0	0.2	1.473	2.419	18.3	11.43
United Arab Emirates	ARE	179.5	81.3	19,288	8,738	65.3	481.8	314.6	157.1	71.2	0.6	0.4	0.1	1.664	3.673	298.6	9.30
West Bank and Gaza	PSE	5.3	3.3	1,190	730	88.4	29.7	26.3	9.7	5.9	0.0	0.0	0.1	2.207	3.600	11.7	4.45
Total (17)	**MEB**	**1,509.6**	**737.9**	**3,972**	**1,941**	**70.5**	**99.2**	**69.9**	**32.3**	**15.8**	**5.2**	**3.7**	**5.3**	**n.a.**	**n.a**	**n.a.**	**380.10**
North America																	
Bermuda	BMU	0.6	0.9	9,770	13,765	203.1	244.1	495.7	79.6	112.1	0.0	0.0	0.0	1.409	1.000	0.9	0.06
Canada	CAN	423.8	378.3	11,598	10,352	128.7	289.7	372.8	94.5	84.3	1.5	1.9	0.5	1.158	1.298	490.9	36.54
United States	USA	3,995.3	3,995.3	12,278	12,278	144.2	306.7	442.1	100.0	100.0	13.9	20.0	4.5	1.000	1.000	3,995.3	325.41
Total (3)	**NAB**	**4,419.7**	**4,374.4**	**12,209**	**12,084**	**142.7**	**305.0**	**435.1**	**99.4**	**98.4**	**15.3**	**21.9**	**5.0**	**n.a.**	**n.a**	**n.a.**	**362.01**
South Asia																	
Bangladesh	BGD	172.1	81.2	1,064	502	68.0	26.6	18.1	8.7	4.1	0.6	0.4	2.2	37.935	80.438	6,528.9	161.80
Bhutan	BTN	3.0	1.3	4,128	1,784	62.3	103.1	64.2	33.6	14.5	0.0	0.0	0.0	28.145	65.122	84.5	0.73
India	IND	1,965.9	724.9	1,502	554	53.2	37.5	19.9	12.2	4.5	6.8	3.6	18.2	24.012	65.122	47,205.0	1,309.20
Maldives	MDV	4.0	2.0	8,116	4,140	73.5	202.7	149.1	66.1	33.7	0.0	0.0	0.0	7.849	15.387	31.3	0.49
Nepal	NPL	18.7	7.9	648	276	61.3	16.2	9.9	5.3	2.2	0.1	0.0	0.4	44.434	104.512	830.7	28.83
Pakistan	PAK	112.2	46.9	564	235	60.2	14.1	8.5	4.6	1.9	0.4	0.2	2.8	44.052	105.455	4,942.9	199.11
Sri Lanka	LKA	52.6	23.0	2,455	1,071	62.9	61.3	38.6	20.0	8.7	0.2	0.1	0.3	66.518	152.446	3,502.1	21.44
Total (7)	**SAB**	**2,328.5**	**887.2**	**1,353**	**515**	**54.9**	**33.8**	**18.6**	**11.0**	**4.2**	**8.1**	**4.4**	**23.9**	**n.a.**	**n.a**	**n.a.**	**1,721.60**
Sub-Saharan Africa																	
Angola	AGO	52.7	37.0	1,768	1,239	101.1	44.2	44.6	14.4	10.1	0.2	0.2	0.4	116.327	165.916	6,131.1	29.82
Benin	BEN	4.3	2.5	383	220	83.1	9.6	7.9	3.1	1.8	0.0	0.0	0.2	335.364	582.075	1,433.7	11.18
Botswana	BWA	9.0	5.1	4,078	2,297	81.2	101.9	82.7	33.2	18.7	0.0	0.0	0.0	5.828	10.347	52.4	2.21

Table 2.5 *(Continued)*

GROSS FIXED CAPITAL FORMATION		Expenditure (billion US$)		Expenditure per capita (US$)		Price level index (world = 100.0)[a]	Expenditure per capita indexes[b]				Share (world = 100%)[b]			PPPs[c] (US$ = 1.000)	Reference data		
							World = 100.0		United States = 100.0		Expenditure				Market exchange rates[c] (US$ = 1.000)	Expenditure (billion LCU)	Population (millions)
Economy		Based on PPPs	Based on XRs	Based on PPPs	Based on XRs		Based on PPPs	Based on XRs	Based on PPPs	Based on XRs	Based on PPPs	Based on XRs	Population				
(00)		(01)	(02)	(03)	(04)	(05)	(06)	(07)	(08)	(09)	(10)	(11)	(12)	(13)	(14)	(15)	(16)
Burkina Faso	BFA	6.0	3.2	314	168	76.9	7.9	6.0	2.6	1.4	0.0	0.0	0.3	310.379	582.075	1,872.8	19.19
Burundi	BDI	0.7	0.4	68	41	87.3	1.7	1.5	0.6	0.3	0.0	0.0	0.2	1,047.500	1,729.055	776.9	10.83
Cabo Verde	CPV	1.0	0.7	1,864	1,290	99.7	46.6	46.4	15.2	10.5	0.0	0.0	0.0	67.662	97.799	67.8	0.54
Cameroon	CMR	13.8	8.0	563	327	83.6	14.1	11.8	4.6	2.7	0.0	0.0	0.3	337.463	582.075	4,670.1	24.57
Central African Republic	CAF	0.7	0.4	147	85	83.6	3.7	3.1	1.2	0.7	0.0	0.0	0.1	337.388	582.075	227.4	4.60
Chad	TCD	2.6	1.5	172	102	85.3	4.3	3.7	1.4	0.8	0.0	0.0	0.2	344.322	582.075	889.5	15.02
Comoros	COM	0.4	0.2	463	267	83.1	11.6	9.6	3.8	2.2	0.0	0.0	0.0	251.528	436.571	94.8	0.81
Congo, Dem. Rep.	COD	26.0	16.1	319	198	89.4	8.0	7.1	2.6	1.6	0.1	0.1	1.1	908.478	1464.418	23,608.6	81.40
Congo, Rep.	COG	6.1	5.3	1,196	1,033	124.5	29.9	37.2	9.7	8.4	0.0	0.0	0.1	502.828	582.075	3,072.4	5.11
Côte d'Ivoire	CIV	14.2	8.1	582	333	82.5	14.5	12.0	4.7	2.7	0.0	0.0	0.3	333.217	582.075	4,740.5	24.44
Equatorial Guinea	GNQ	2.6	1.5	2,071	1,218	84.8	51.7	43.8	16.9	9.9	0.0	0.0	0.0	342.274	582.075	894.5	1.26
Eswatini	SWZ	0.7	0.4	621	356	82.6	15.5	12.8	5.1	2.9	0.0	0.0	0.0	7.644	13.334	5.3	1.12
Ethiopia	ETH	36.5	20.6	343	193	81.2	8.6	7.0	2.8	1.6	0.1	0.1	1.5	13.443	23.866	490.7	106.40
Gabon	GAB	4.9	3.1	2,367	1,497	91.2	59.1	53.9	19.3	12.2	0.0	0.0	0.0	368.156	582.075	1,799.5	2.06
Gambia, The	GMB	0.5	0.3	236	144	88.1	5.9	5.2	1.9	1.2	0.0	0.0	0.0	28.475	46.608	14.9	2.21
Ghana	GHA	25.8	16.3	886	558	90.8	22.1	20.1	7.2	4.5	0.1	0.1	0.4	2.741	4.351	70.7	29.12
Guinea	GIN	2.9	1.8	240	145	87.0	6.0	5.2	2.0	1.2	0.0	0.0	0.2	5,507.752	9,125.743	15,970.1	12.07
Guinea-Bissau	GNB	0.1	0.1	80	46	82.4	2.0	1.6	0.7	0.4	0.0	0.0	0.0	332.806	582.075	48.7	1.83
Kenya	KEN	33.5	16.4	666	326	70.5	16.6	11.7	5.4	2.7	0.1	0.1	0.7	50.590	103.411	1,692.3	50.22
Lesotho	LSO	1.1	0.6	534	298	80.4	13.3	10.7	4.3	2.4	0.0	0.0	0.0	7.441	13.334	8.3	2.09
Liberia	LBR	1.7	1.1	356	236	95.5	8.9	8.5	2.9	1.9	0.0	0.0	0.1	74.705	112.707	125.2	4.70
Madagascar	MDG	3.9	2.3	154	92	85.7	3.9	3.3	1.3	0.7	0.0	0.0	0.4	1,851.792	3,116.110	7,313.8	25.57
Malawi	MWI	1.3	0.8	74	47	90.4	1.9	1.7	0.6	0.4	0.0	0.0	0.2	458.113	730.273	600.0	17.67
Mali	MLI	5.3	3.1	288	165	82.8	7.2	6.0	2.3	1.3	0.0	0.0	0.3	334.157	582.075	1,782.7	18.51
Mauritania	MRT	4.8	2.1	1,116	493	63.7	27.9	17.8	9.1	4.0	0.0	0.0	0.1	157.964	357.493	754.8	4.28
Mauritius	MUS	9.0	5.3	7,084	4,217	85.8	177.0	151.8	57.7	34.3	0.0	0.0	0.0	20.525	34.481	183.9	1.26
Mozambique	MOZ	5.8	3.0	202	104	73.9	5.0	3.7	1.6	0.8	0.0	0.0	0.4	32.589	63.584	188.6	28.65
Namibia	NAM	3.5	2.1	1,462	888	87.5	36.5	32.0	11.9	7.2	0.0	0.0	0.0	8.084	13.313	28.4	2.40
Niger	NER	4.7	2.7	219	127	83.2	5.5	4.6	1.8	1.0	0.0	0.0	0.3	335.880	582.075	1,590.9	21.60
Nigeria	NGA	82.9	55.3	435	290	96.1	10.9	10.4	3.5	2.4	0.3	0.3	2.6	203.839	305.790	16,908.1	190.87
Rwanda	RWA	3.1	2.1	262	176	96.6	6.6	6.3	2.1	1.4	0.0	0.0	0.2	557.283	831.531	1,751.4	11.98
São Tomé and Príncipe	STP	0.2	0.1	828	502	87.4	20.7	18.1	6.7	4.1	0.0	0.0	0.0	13.187	21.741	2.3	0.21
Senegal	SEN	9.1	5.4	588	348	85.2	14.7	12.5	4.8	2.8	0.0	0.0	0.2	343.977	582.075	3,119.4	15.42
Seychelles	SYC	0.9	0.6	8,918	5,895	95.3	222.8	212.3	72.6	48.0	0.0	0.0	0.0	9.022	13.648	7.8	0.10
Sierra Leone	SLE	0.8	0.6	111	79	101.9	2.8	2.8	0.9	0.6	0.0	0.0	0.1	5,222.409	7,384.432	4,354.3	7.49
South Africa	ZAF	112.1	61.4	1,966	1,076	78.9	49.1	38.8	16.0	8.8	0.4	0.3	0.8	7.299	13.334	818.1	57.01
Sudan	SDN	13.2	4.5	325	111	49.1	8.1	4.0	2.6	0.9	0.0	0.0	0.6	6.858	20.130	90.9	40.78

Table 2.5 *(Continued)*

GROSS FIXED CAPITAL FORMATION		Expenditure (billion US$)		Expenditure per capita (US$)		Price level index (world = 100.0)[a]	Expenditure per capita indexes[b]				Share (world = 100%)[b]			PPPs[c] (US$ = 1.000)	Reference data		
							World = 100.0		United States = 100.0		Expenditure				Market exchange rates[c] (US$ = 1.000)	Expenditure (billion LCU)	Population (millions)
Economy		Based on PPPs	Based on XRs	Based on PPPs	Based on XRs		Based on PPPs	Based on XRs	Based on PPPs	Based on XRs	Based on PPPs	Based on XRs	Population				
(00)		(01)	(02)	(03)	(04)	(05)	(06)	(07)	(08)	(09)	(10)	(11)	(12)	(13)	(14)	(15)	(16)
Tanzania	TZA	22.5	15.5	411	283	99.1	10.3	10.2	3.4	2.3	0.1	0.1	0.8	1,532.051	2,228.858	34,444.3	54.66
Togo	TGO	2.0	1.1	255	144	81.6	6.4	5.2	2.1	1.2	0.0	0.0	0.1	329.689	582.075	646.7	7.70
Uganda	UGA	14.2	8.9	345	215	89.9	8.6	7.7	2.8	1.8	0.0	0.0	0.6	2,252.249	3,611.224	31,966.1	41.17
Zambia	ZMB	16.7	9.9	992	588	85.4	24.8	21.2	8.1	4.8	0.1	0.0	0.2	5.643	9.520	94.4	16.85
Zimbabwe	ZWE	3.3	2.1	232	149	92.6	5.8	5.4	1.9	1.2	0.0	0.0	0.2	0.643	1.000	2.1	14.24
Total (45)	**SSB**	**567.3**	**339.5**	**555**	**332**	**86.3**	**13.9**	**12.0**	**4.5**	**2.7**	**2.0**	**1.7**	**14.2**	**n.a.**	**n.a**	**n.a.**	**1,021.22**
World (176)	**WLD**	**28,837.2**	**20,004.5**	**4,003**	**2,777**	**100.0**	**100.0**	**100.0**	**32.6**	**22.6**	**100.0**	**100.0**	**100.0**	**n.a.**	**n.a.**	**n.a.**	**7,203.60**

Note: PPP = purchasing power parity; XR = market exchange rate; LCU = local currency unit; n.a. = not applicable; ... = data suppressed due to unavailability.

a. World totals used to calculate price level indexes (PLIs) in this table exclude nonparticipating economies.

b. Indexes and shares are rounded to one decimal place for presentation in this table.

c. PPPs and market exchange rates are rounded to three decimal places for presentation in this table.

d. Bonaire's results are provided only for individual consumption expenditure by households. Therefore, to ensure consistency across tables, Bonaire is not included in either the Latin America and the Caribbean or the world totals.

Table 2.6 Domestic absorption: ICP 2017 results

DOMESTIC ABSORPTION Economy		Expenditure (billion US$) Based on PPPs	Expenditure (billion US$) Based on XRs	Expenditure per capita (US$) Based on PPPs	Expenditure per capita (US$) Based on XRs	Price level index (world = 100.0)[a]	Expenditure per capita indexes[b] World = 100.0 Based on PPPs	Expenditure per capita indexes[b] World = 100.0 Based on XRs	Expenditure per capita indexes[b] United States = 100.0 Based on PPPs	Expenditure per capita indexes[b] United States = 100.0 Based on XRs	Share (world = 100%)[b] Expenditure Based on PPPs	Share (world = 100%)[b] Expenditure Based on XRs	Share (world = 100%)[b] Population	PPPs[c] (US$ = 1.000)	Reference data Market exchange rates[c] (US$ = 1.000)	Reference data Expenditure (billion LCU)	Reference data Poputic (mill
(00)		(01)	(02)	(03)	(04)	(05)	(06)	(07)	(08)	(09)	(10)	(11)	(12)	(13)	(14)	(15)	(1
East Asia and Pacific																	
Australia	AUS	1,215.5	1,378.8	49,405	56,046	169.7	300.6	510.1	80.0	90.8	1.0	1.7	0.3	1.480	1.305	1,799.1	2
Brunei Darussalam	BRN	22.1	10.4	51,467	24,293	70.6	313.1	221.1	83.3	39.3	0.0	0.0	0.0	0.652	1.381	14.4	
Cambodia	KHM	62.8	22.2	3,960	1,401	52.9	24.1	12.7	6.4	2.3	0.1	0.0	0.2	1,432.774	4,050.580	89,927.9	1
China	CHN	19,117.4	11,932.7	13,789	8,607	93.4	83.9	78.3	22.3	13.9	16.1	15.1	19.2	4.219	6.759	80,650.5	138
Fiji	FJI	12.2	5.5	13,906	6,323	68.0	84.6	57.6	22.5	10.2	0.0	0.0	0.0	0.940	2.067	11.5	
Hong Kong SAR, China	HKG	434.3	338.0	58,753	45,724	116.4	357.4	416.2	95.1	74.0	0.4	0.4	0.1	6.065	7.793	2,633.9	
Indonesia	IDN	2,859.8	1,005.1	10,920	3,838	52.6	66.4	34.9	17.7	6.2	2.4	1.3	3.6	4,702.844	13,380.872	13,449,387.6	26
Japan	JPN	5,085.3	4,814.5	40,134	37,998	141.6	244.2	345.9	65.0	61.5	4.3	6.1	1.8	106.194	112.166	540,025.7	12
Korea, Rep.	KOR	1,993.0	1,546.8	38,804	30,116	116.1	236.1	274.1	62.8	48.8	1.7	2.0	0.7	877.332	1,130.425	1,748,548.6	5
Lao PDR	LAO	51.5	17.3	7,461	2,505	50.2	45.4	22.8	12.1	4.1	0.0	0.0	0.1	2,804.389	8,351.526	144,385.0	
Malaysia	MYS	762.2	292.9	23,803	9,145	57.5	144.8	83.2	38.5	14.8	0.6	0.4	0.4	1.652	4.300	1,259.4	3
Mongolia	MNG	34.4	11.2	10,937	3,543	48.5	66.5	32.2	17.7	5.7	0.0	0.0	0.0	790.306	2,439.777	27,216.7	
Myanmar	MMR	248.7	68.0	4,680	1,280	40.9	28.5	11.7	7.6	2.1	0.2	0.1	0.7	372.132	1,360.359	92,561.4	5
New Zealand	NZL	190.1	198.4	39,339	41,065	156.2	239.3	373.8	63.7	66.5	0.2	0.3	0.1	1.469	1.407	279.3	
Philippines	PHL	890.2	344.5	8,485	3,283	57.9	51.6	29.9	13.7	5.3	0.8	0.4	1.5	19.506	50.404	17,364.5	10
Singapore	SGP	367.5	253.1	65,480	45,099	103.0	398.4	410.5	106.0	73.0	0.3	0.3	0.1	0.951	1.381	349.5	
Taiwan, China	TWN	954.4	501.6	40,508	21,290	78.6	246.4	193.8	65.6	34.5	0.8	0.6	0.3	16.000	30.442	15,269.8	2
Thailand	THA	1,040.2	392.3	15,375	5,799	56.4	93.5	52.8	24.9	9.4	0.9	0.5	0.9	12.801	33.940	13,315.0	6
Vietnam	VNM	658.4	217.5	6,986	2,308	49.4	42.5	21.0	11.3	3.7	0.6	0.3	1.3	7,390.658	22,370.087	4,865,693.1	9
Total (19)	**EAB**	**35,999.9**	**23,351.0**	**15,848**	**10,280**	**97.0**	**96.4**	**93.6**	**25.7**	**16.6**	**30.4**	**29.5**	**31.5**	**n.a.**	**n.a**	**n.a.**	**2,27**
Europe and Central Asia																	
Albania	ALB	42.5	15.0	14,795	5,230	52.9	90.0	47.6	24.0	8.5	0.0	0.0	0.0	41.980	118.748	1,784.7	
Armenia	ARM	39.3	12.9	13,191	4,340	49.2	80.3	39.5	21.4	7.0	0.0	0.0	0.0	158.817	482.720	6,241.8	
Austria	AUT	461.7	404.5	52,500	45,993	131.1	319.4	418.6	85.0	74.5	0.4	0.5	0.1	0.775	0.885	358.1	
Azerbaijan	AZE	133.7	38.1	13,738	3,917	42.7	83.6	35.7	22.2	6.3	0.1	0.0	0.1	0.491	1.721	65.6	
Belarus	BLR	175.2	54.6	18,450	5,751	46.6	112.2	52.3	29.9	9.3	0.1	0.1	0.1	0.602	1.932	105.5	
Belgium	BEL	566.9	497.2	49,837	43,712	131.2	303.2	397.9	80.7	70.8	0.5	0.6	0.2	0.776	0.885	440.1	1
Bosnia and Herzegovina	BIH	53.2	21.1	15,877	6,291	59.3	96.6	57.3	25.7	10.2	0.0	0.0	0.0	0.686	1.731	36.5	
Bulgaria	BGR	149.8	56.5	21,164	7,989	56.5	128.8	72.7	34.3	12.9	0.1	0.1	0.1	0.654	1.731	97.9	
Croatia	HRV	111.0	55.1	26,883	13,346	74.3	163.6	121.5	43.5	21.6	0.1	0.1	0.1	3.280	6.607	364.2	
Cyprus	CYP	32.9	22.7	38,233	26,437	103.5	232.6	240.6	61.9	42.8	0.0	0.0	0.0	0.612	0.885	20.1	
Czech Republic	CZE	384.0	200.3	36,260	18,914	78.0	220.6	172.2	58.7	30.6	0.3	0.3	0.1	12.156	23.304	4,667.5	1
Denmark	DNK	287.6	307.2	49,869	53,272	159.8	303.4	484.9	80.8	86.3	0.2	0.4	0.1	7.034	6.585	2,022.9	
Estonia	EST	43.1	25.7	32,745	19,542	89.3	199.2	177.9	53.0	31.6	0.0	0.0	0.0	0.528	0.885	22.8	
Finland	FIN	259.8	254.8	47,160	46,254	146.7	286.9	421.0	76.4	74.9	0.2	0.3	0.1	0.868	0.885	225.5	
France	FRA	3,022.0	2,620.2	45,062	39,070	129.7	274.2	355.6	73.0	63.3	2.6	3.3	0.9	0.767	0.885	2,319.4	6

Table 2.6 *(Continued)*

DOMESTIC ABSORPTION		Expenditure (billion US$)		Expenditure per capita (US$)		Price level index (world = 100.0)[a]	Expenditure per capita indexes[b]				Share (world = 100%)[b]			PPPs[c] (US$ = 1.000)	Reference data		
							World = 100.0		United States = 100.0		Expenditure				Market exchange rates[c] (US$ = 1.000)	Expenditure (billion LCU)	Population (millions)
Economy		Based on PPPs	Based on XRs	Based on PPPs	Based on XRs		Based on PPPs	Based on XRs	Based on PPPs	Based on XRs	Based on PPPs	Based on XRs	Population				
(00)		(01)	(02)	(03)	(04)	(05)	(06)	(07)	(08)	(09)	(10)	(11)	(12)	(13)	(14)	(15)	(16)
Georgia	GEO	55.9	18.0	14,986	4,836	48.3	91.2	44.0	24.3	7.8	0.0	0.0	0.1	0.810	2.510	45.2	3.73
Germany	DEU	4,028.7	3,405.5	48,739	41,201	126.5	296.5	375.0	78.9	66.7	3.4	4.3	1.1	0.748	0.885	3,014.5	82.66
Greece	GRC	318.0	205.7	29,566	19,124	96.8	179.9	174.1	47.9	31.0	0.3	0.3	0.1	0.573	0.885	182.1	10.75
Hungary	HUN	274.9	131.6	28,085	13,440	71.6	170.9	122.3	45.5	21.8	0.2	0.2	0.1	130.973	273.692	36,004.6	9.79
Iceland	ISL	17.8	23.5	51,862	68,354	197.2	315.5	622.2	84.0	110.7	0.0	0.0	0.0	140.631	106.701	2,504.6	0.34
Ireland	IRL	282.8	261.5	58,883	54,460	138.4	358.2	495.7	95.4	88.2	0.2	0.3	0.1	0.819	0.885	231.5	4.80
Italy	ITA	2,451.5	1,903.4	40,496	31,442	116.2	246.4	286.2	65.6	50.9	2.1	2.4	0.8	0.687	0.885	1,684.8	60.54
Kazakhstan	KAZ	423.7	153.5	23,489	8,511	54.2	142.9	77.5	38.0	13.8	0.4	0.2	0.3	118.115	326.000	50,044.8	18.04
Kyrgyz Republic	KGZ	38.3	10.2	6,439	1,715	39.8	39.2	15.6	10.4	2.8	0.0	0.0	0.1	18.313	68.769	700.8	5.94
Latvia	LVA	55.8	30.2	28,771	15,571	81.0	175.0	141.7	46.6	25.2	0.0	0.0	0.0	0.479	0.885	26.8	1.94
Lithuania	LTU	94.9	46.6	33,555	16,481	73.5	204.1	150.0	54.3	26.7	0.1	0.1	0.0	0.435	0.885	41.3	2.83
Luxembourg	LUX	40.4	41.6	67,728	69,708	154.0	412.0	634.5	109.7	112.9	0.0	0.1	0.0	0.911	0.885	36.8	0.60
Moldova	MDA	37.9	11.9	10,678	3,365	47.1	65.0	30.6	17.3	5.4	0.0	0.0	0.0	5.827	18.490	220.8	3.55
Montenegro	MNE	14.8	6.0	23,709	9,633	60.8	144.2	87.7	38.4	15.6	0.0	0.0	0.0	0.360	0.885	5.3	0.62
Netherlands	NLD	829.9	744.2	48,444	43,442	134.2	294.7	395.4	78.4	70.3	0.7	0.9	0.2	0.794	0.885	658.8	17.13
North Macedonia	MKD	36.6	12.9	17,622	6,223	52.8	107.2	56.6	28.5	10.1	0.0	0.0	0.0	19.250	54.505	703.7	2.07
Norway	NOR	314.6	385.2	59,626	72,989	183.1	362.8	664.4	96.6	118.2	0.3	0.5	0.1	10.107	8.256	3,180.0	5.28
Poland	POL	1,123.6	505.8	29,244	13,166	67.4	177.9	119.8	47.4	21.3	0.9	0.6	0.5	1.696	3.768	1,906.2	38.42
Portugal	PRT	339.3	219.1	32,937	021,274	96.6	200.4	193.6	53.3	34.5	0.3	0.3	0.1	0.572	0.885	194.0	10.30
Romania	ROU	554.6	216.6	28,307	11,057	58.4	172.2	100.6	45.8	17.9	0.5	0.3	0.3	1.580	4.044	876.1	19.59
Russian Federation	RUS	3,688.5	1,494.3	25,119	10,176	60.6	152.8	92.6	40.7	16.5	3.1	1.9	2.0	23.635	58.343	87,180.0	146.84
Serbia	SRB	124.2	47.2	17,693	6,720	56.8	107.6	61.2	28.7	10.9	0.1	0.1	0.1	40.795	107.406	5,067.7	7.02
Slovak Republic	SVK	166.3	93.4	30,586	17,172	84.0	186.1	156.3	49.5	27.8	0.1	0.1	0.1	0.497	0.885	82.7	5.44
Slovenia	SVN	69.7	44.3	33,716	21,424	95.1	205.1	195.0	54.6	34.7	0.1	0.1	0.0	0.562	0.885	39.2	2.07
Spain	ESP	1,784.1	1,265.6	38,340	27,198	106.1	233.3	247.6	62.1	44.0	1.5	1.6	0.6	0.628	0.885	1,120.3	46.53
Sweden	SWE	505.5	524.4	50,261	52,142	155.2	305.8	474.6	81.4	84.4	0.4	0.7	0.1	8.848	8.529	4,472.8	10.06
Switzerland	CHE	488.1	608.6	57,753	72,002	186.5	351.4	655.4	93.5	116.6	0.4	0.8	0.1	1.227	0.984	598.9	8.45
Tajikistan	TJK	32.5	9.0	3,675	1,014	41.3	22.4	9.2	6.0	1.6	0.0	0.0	0.1	2.359	8.550	76.6	8.84
Turkey	TUR	2,379.4	891.1	29,627	11,096	56.0	180.2	101.0	48.0	18.0	2.0	1.1	1.1	1.366	3.648	3,251.0	80.31
Ukraine	UKR	544.2	120.8	12,809	2,844	33.2	77.9	25.9	20.7	4.6	0.5	0.2	0.6	5.905	26.597	3,213.3	42.49
United Kingdom	GBR	3,072.7	2,702.0	46,527	40,914	131.6	283.1	372.4	75.3	66.3	2.6	3.4	0.9	0.682	0.776	2,096.8	66.04
Total (46)	**ECB**	**29,951.7**	**20,719.8**	**34,273**	**23,709**	**103.5**	**208.5**	**215.8**	**55.5**	**38.4**	**25.3**	**26.2**	**12.1**	**n.a.**	**n.a**	**n.a.**	**873.93**
Latin America and Caribbean																	
Anguilla	AIA	0.4	0.3	26,804	22,607	126.2	163.1	205.8	43.4	36.6	0.0	0.0	0.0	2.277	2.700	0.9	0.01
Antigua and Barbuda	ATG	1.8	1.4	18,400	14,301	116.3	111.9	130.2	29.8	23.2	0.0	0.0	0.0	2.098	2.700	3.7	0.10
Argentina	ARG	1,066.6	660.3	24,275	15,028	92.6	147.7	136.8	39.3	24.3	0.9	0.8	0.6	10.254	16.563	10,936.2	43.94
Aruba	ABW	4.0	3.0	37,820	28,513	112.8	230.1	259.5	61.2	46.2	0.0	0.0	0.0	1.349	1.790	5.4	0.11

Table 2.6 *(Continued)*

DOMESTIC ABSORPTION Economy		Expenditure (billion US$) Based on PPPs	Expenditure (billion US$) Based on XRs	Expenditure per capita (US$) Based on PPPs	Expenditure per capita (US$) Based on XRs	Price level index (world = 100.0)[a]	Expenditure per capita indexes[b] World = 100.0 Based on PPPs	Expenditure per capita indexes[b] World = 100.0 Based on XRs	Expenditure per capita indexes[b] United States = 100.0 Based on PPPs	Expenditure per capita indexes[b] United States = 100.0 Based on XRs	Share (world = 100%)[b] Expenditure Based on PPPs	Share (world = 100%)[b] Expenditure Based on XRs	Share (world = 100%)[b] Population	PPPs[c] (US$ = 1.000)	Reference data Market exchange rates[c] (US$ = 1.000)	Reference data Expenditure (billion LCU)	Reference data Population (millions)
(00)		(01)	(02)	(03)	(04)	(05)	(06)	(07)	(08)	(09)	(10)	(11)	(12)	(13)	(14)	(15)	(16)
Bahamas, The	BHS	14.1	12.7	36,947	33,195	134.4	224.8	302.1	59.8	53.8	0.0	0.0	0.0	0.898	1.000	12.7	0.38
Barbados	BRB	4.9	5.2	17,027	18,222	160.1	103.6	165.9	27.6	29.5	0.0	0.0	0.0	2.140	2.000	10.4	0.29
Belize	BLZ	2.8	1.9	7,445	5,126	103.0	45.3	46.7	12.1	8.3	0.0	0.0	0.0	1.377	2.000	3.9	0.38
Bolivia	BOL	98.6	39.8	8,813	3,556	60.4	53.6	32.4	14.3	5.8	0.1	0.1	0.2	2.809	6.960	277.1	11.19
Bonaire[d]	BON	. . .	. . .	. . .	. . .	. . .	. . .	. . .	. . .	. . .	. . .	. . .	. . .	. . .	1.000	. . .	0.03
Brazil	BRA	2,991.1	2,048.0	14,392	9,854	102.4	87.6	89.7	23.3	16.0	2.5	2.6	2.9	2.185	3.191	6,536.0	207.83
Cayman Islands	CYM	3.2	4.0	50,619	62,528	184.8	308.0	569.1	82.0	101.3	0.0	0.0	0.0	1.029	0.833	3.3	0.06
Chile	CHL	432.1	273.9	23,330	14,788	94.8	141.9	134.6	37.8	23.9	0.4	0.3	0.3	411.271	648.834	177,722.7	18.52
Colombia	COL	731.6	327.6	14,842	6,646	67.0	90.3	60.5	24.0	10.8	0.6	0.4	0.7	1,321.594	2,951.327	966,890.0	49.29
Costa Rica	CRI	97.6	60.4	19,741	12,216	92.6	120.1	111.2	32.0	19.8	0.1	0.1	0.1	351.198	567.513	34,282.0	4.94
Curaçao	CUW	4.9	3.8	30,552	23,408	114.6	185.9	213.1	49.5	37.9	0.0	0.0	0.0	1.371	1.790	6.8	0.16
Dominica	DMA	0.9	0.6	12,840	8,356	97.4	78.1	76.1	20.8	13.5	0.0	0.0	0.0	1.757	2.700	1.6	0.07
Dominican Republic	DOM	179.1	82.3	17,034	7,827	68.7	103.6	71.2	27.6	12.7	0.2	0.1	0.1	21.842	47.537	3,911.4	10.51
Ecuador	ECU	195.5	105.1	11,644	6,260	80.4	70.8	57.0	18.9	10.1	0.2	0.1	0.2	0.538	1.000	105.1	16.79
El Salvador	SLV	61.7	29.0	9,657	4,546	70.4	58.7	41.4	15.6	7.4	0.1	0.0	0.1	0.471	1.000	29.0	6.39
Grenada	GRD	2.2	1.4	19,686	12,588	95.7	119.8	114.6	31.9	20.4	0.0	0.0	0.0	1.726	2.700	3.8	0.11
Guyana	GUY	7.7	4.0	9,981	5,120	76.7	60.7	46.6	16.2	8.3	0.0	0.0	0.0	108.840	212.190	842.1	0.78
Haiti	HTI	26.6	12.2	2,421	1,115	68.9	14.7	10.1	3.9	1.8	0.0	0.0	0.2	29.334	63.687	779.9	10.98
Honduras	HND	59.1	26.5	6,263	2,813	67.2	38.1	25.6	10.1	4.6	0.0	0.0	0.1	10.594	23.588	625.7	9.43
Jamaica	JAM	31.3	17.0	10,723	5,813	81.1	65.2	52.9	17.4	9.4	0.0	0.0	0.0	69.370	127.965	2,172.7	2.92
Mexico	MEX	2,517.1	1,178.7	20,404	9,555	70.1	124.1	87.0	33.0	15.5	2.1	1.5	1.7	8.863	18.927	22,309.5	123.36
Montserrat	MSR	0.1	0.1	26,641	18,292	102.7	162.1	166.5	43.1	29.6	0.0	0.0	0.0	1.854	2.700	0.2	0.00
Nicaragua	NIC	42.2	15.7	6,611	2,463	55.8	40.2	22.4	10.7	4.0	0.0	0.0	0.1	11.199	30.051	472.7	6.38
Panama	PAN	128.1	64.2	31,201	15,628	74.9	189.8	142.3	50.5	25.3	0.1	0.1	0.1	0.501	1.000	64.2	4.11
Paraguay	PRY	82.4	37.8	11,996	5,504	68.6	73.0	50.1	19.4	8.9	0.1	0.0	0.1	2,552.236	5,562.276	210,244.3	6.87
Peru	PER	383.6	207.0	12,199	6,582	80.7	74.2	59.9	19.8	10.7	0.3	0.3	0.4	1.759	3.260	674.7	31.44
Sint Maarten	SXM	1.4	1.1	34,548	26,780	116.0	210.2	243.8	55.9	43.4	0.0	0.0	0.0	1.388	1.790	2.0	0.04
St. Kitts and Nevis	KNA	1.4	1.1	27,849	21,100	113.4	169.4	192.1	45.1	34.2	0.0	0.0	0.0	2.046	2.700	3.0	0.05
St. Lucia	LCA	1.7	1.2	9,306	6,853	110.2	56.6	62.4	15.1	11.1	0.0	0.0	0.0	1.988	2.700	3.3	0.18
St. Vincent and the Grenadines	VCT	1.7	1.0	15,135	9,132	90.3	92.1	83.1	24.5	14.8	0.0	0.0	0.0	1.629	2.700	2.7	0.11
Suriname	SUR	9.2	3.2	16,108	5,683	52.8	98.0	51.7	26.1	9.2	0.0	0.0	0.0	2.664	7.550	24.5	0.57
Trinidad and Tobago	TTO	34.3	20.8	24,747	15,006	90.7	150.6	136.6	40.1	24.3	0.0	0.0	0.0	4.111	6.780	140.8	1.38
Turks and Caicos Islands	TCA	0.7	0.8	19,920	20,733	155.7	121.2	188.7	32.3	33.6	0.0	0.0	0.0	1.041	1.000	0.8	0.04
Uruguay	URY	70.6	57.7	20,548	16,786	122.2	125.0	152.8	33.3	27.2	0.1	0.1	0.0	23.426	28.676	1,654.3	3.44
Virgin Islands, British	VGB	0.8	0.8	25,845	28,614	165.6	157.2	260.5	41.9	46.3	0.0	0.0	0.0	1.107	1.000	0.8	0.03
Total (39)	**LCB**	**9,293.0**	**5,311.7**	**16,213**	**9,267**	**85.5**	**98.6**	**84.3**	**26.3**	**15.0**	**7.8**	**6.7**	**8.0**	**n.a.**	**n.a**	**n.a.**	**573.20**

Table 2.6 *(Continued)*

DOMESTIC ABSORPTION Economy		Expenditure (billion US$) Based on PPPs	Expenditure (billion US$) Based on XRs	Expenditure per capita (US$) Based on PPPs	Expenditure per capita (US$) Based on XRs	Price level index (world = 100.0)[a]	Expenditure per capita indexes[b] World = 100.0 Based on PPPs	Expenditure per capita indexes[b] World = 100.0 Based on XRs	Expenditure per capita indexes[b] United States = 100.0 Based on PPPs	Expenditure per capita indexes[b] United States = 100.0 Based on XRs	Share (world = 100%)[b] Expenditure Based on PPPs	Share (world = 100%)[b] Expenditure Based on XRs	Share (world = 100%)[b] Population	PPPs[c] (US$ = 1.000)	Reference data Market exchange rates[c] (US$ = 1.000)	Reference data Expenditure (billion LCU)	Reference data Population (millions)
(00)		(01)	(02)	(03)	(04)	(05)	(06)	(07)	(08)	(09)	(10)	(11)	(12)	(13)	(14)	(15)	(16)
Middle East and North Africa																	
Algeria	DZA	519.8	185.7	12,558	4,488	53.5	76.4	40.8	20.3	7.3	0.4	0.2	0.6	39.654	110.973	20,611.5	41.39
Bahrain	BHR	65.2	32.4	43,435	21,615	74.5	264.3	196.7	70.3	35.0	0.1	0.0	0.0	0.187	0.376	12.2	1.50
Djibouti	DJI	5.5	3.2	5,852	3,403	87.0	35.6	31.0	9.5	5.5	0.0	0.0	0.0	103.348	177.720	571.0	0.94
Egypt, Arab Rep.	EGY	1,318.3	259.6	13,906	2,739	29.5	84.6	24.9	22.5	4.4	1.1	0.3	1.3	3.515	17.847	4,633.2	94.80
Iran, Islamic Rep.	IRN	1,267.1	498.6	15,629	6,150	58.9	95.1	56.0	25.3	10.0	1.1	0.6	1.1	13,074.531	33,226.298	16,566,404.5	81.07
Iraq	IRQ	336.5	150.2	9,061	4,045	66.8	55.1	36.8	14.7	6.6	0.3	0.2	0.5	560.709	1,256.000	188,683.3	37.14
Israel	ISR	332.0	349.1	38,119	40,087	157.3	231.9	364.9	61.7	64.9	0.3	0.4	0.1	3.785	3.600	1,256.8	8.71
Jordan	JOR	116.7	49.7	11,610	4,939	63.6	70.6	45.0	18.8	8.0	0.1	0.1	0.1	0.301	0.708	35.2	10.05
Kuwait	KWT	195.5	114.1	47,879	27,947	87.3	291.3	254.4	77.5	45.3	0.2	0.1	0.1	0.177	0.303	34.6	4.08
Malta	MLT	15.6	10.1	33,216	21,470	96.7	202.1	195.4	53.8	34.8	0.0	0.0	0.0	0.572	0.885	8.9	0.47
Morocco	MAR	288.5	120.2	8,276	3,449	62.3	50.4	31.4	13.4	5.6	0.2	0.2	0.5	4.038	9.691	1,164.9	34.85
Oman	OMN	132.1	68.6	28,967	15,043	77.7	176.2	136.9	46.9	24.4	0.1	0.1	0.1	0.200	0.385	26.4	4.56
Qatar	QAT	219.3	143.5	80,482	52,676	97.9	489.6	479.5	130.3	85.3	0.2	0.2	0.0	2.389	3.650	523.9	2.72
Saudi Arabia	SAU	1,489.3	650.6	45,667	19,950	65.4	277.8	181.6	74.0	32.3	1.3	0.8	0.5	1.638	3.750	2,439.9	32.61
Tunisia	TUN	132.7	44.8	11,609	3,922	50.5	70.6	35.7	18.8	6.4	0.1	0.1	0.2	0.817	2.419	108.5	11.43
United Arab Emirates	ARE	453.5	284.4	48,736	30,571	93.8	296.5	278.3	78.9	49.5	0.4	0.4	0.1	2.304	3.673	1,044.6	9.30
West Bank and Gaza	PSE	36.9	19.9	8,284	4,461	80.6	50.4	40.6	13.4	7.2	0.0	0.0	0.1	1.939	3.600	71.5	4.45
Total (17)	**MEB**	**6,924.4**	**2,984.9**	**18,217**	**7,853**	**64.5**	**110.8**	**71.5**	**29.5**	**12.7**	**5.8**	**3.8**	**5.3**	**n.a.**	**n.a**	**n.a.**	**380.10**
North America																	
Bermuda	BMU	3.5	5.1	55,957	81,676	218.4	340.4	743.4	90.6	132.3	0.0	0.0	0.0	1.460	1.000	5.1	0.06
Canada	CAN	1,815.3	1,687.1	49,681	46,170	139.0	302.3	420.2	80.5	74.8	1.5	2.1	0.5	1.206	1.298	2,189.4	36.54
United States	USA	20,094.8	20,094.8	61,752	61,752	149.6	375.7	562.1	100.0	100.0	17.0	25.4	4.5	1.000	1.000	20,094.8	325.41
Total (3)	**NAB**	**21,913.6**	**21,787.0**	**60,533**	**60,183**	**148.7**	**368.3**	**547.8**	**98.0**	**97.5**	**18.5**	**27.5**	**5.0**	**n.a.**	**n.a**	**n.a.**	**362.01**
South Asia																	
Bangladesh	BGD	755.1	281.2	4,667	1,738	55.7	28.4	15.8	7.6	2.8	0.6	0.4	2.2	29.957	80.438	22,620.8	161.80
Bhutan	BTN	10.0	3.0	13,770	4,188	45.5	83.8	38.1	22.3	6.8	0.0	0.0	0.0	19.806	65.122	198.3	0.73
India	IND	8,226.3	2,626.1	6,283	2,006	47.8	38.2	18.3	10.2	3.2	6.9	3.3	18.2	20.789	65.122	171,016.7	1309.20
Maldives	MDV	9.0	4.8	18,247	9,732	79.8	111.0	88.6	29.5	15.8	0.0	0.0	0.0	8.206	15.387	73.6	0.49
Nepal	NPL	106.9	33.4	3,709	1,159	46.8	22.6	10.6	6.0	1.9	0.1	0.0	0.4	32.668	104.512	3,493.5	28.83
Pakistan	PAK	1,074.7	347.6	5,397	1,746	48.4	32.8	15.9	8.7	2.8	0.9	0.4	2.8	34.110	105.455	36,657.4	199.11
Sri Lanka	LKA	285.8	93.6	13,328	4,367	49.0	81.1	39.7	21.6	7.1	0.2	0.1	0.3	49.946	152.446	14,274.6	21.44
Total (7)	**SAB**	**10,467.8**	**3,389.8**	**6,080**	**1,969**	**48.4**	**37.0**	**17.9**	**9.8**	**3.2**	**8.8**	**4.3**	**23.9**	**n.a.**	**n.a**	**n.a.**	**1,721.60**
Sub-Saharan Africa																	
Angola	AGO	208.3	115.7	6,985	3,881	83.1	42.5	35.3	11.3	6.3	0.2	0.1	0.4	92.186	165.916	19,200.1	29.82
Benin	BEN	28.9	11.0	2,590	983	56.8	15.8	8.9	4.2	1.6	0.0	0.0	0.2	220.967	582.075	6,394.9	11.18
Botswana	BWA	36.0	16.4	16,304	7,438	68.3	99.2	67.7	26.4	12.0	0.0	0.0	0.0	4.720	10.347	169.7	2.21

Table 2.6 ***(Continued)***

DOMESTIC ABSORPTION		Expenditure (billion US$)		Expenditure per capita (US$)		Price level index (world = 100.0)[a]	Expenditure per capita indexes[b]				Share (world = 100%)[b]			PPPs[c] (US$ = 1.000)	Reference data		
							World = 100.0		United States = 100.0		Expenditure				Market exchange rates[c] (US$ = 1.000)	Expenditure (billion LCU)	Population (millions)
Economy		Based on PPPs	Based on XRs	Based on PPPs	Based on XRs		Based on PPPs	Based on XRs	Based on PPPs	Based on XRs	Based on PPPs	Based on XRs	Population				
(00)		(01)	(02)	(03)	(04)	(05)	(06)	(07)	(08)	(09)	(10)	(11)	(12)	(13)	(14)	(15)	(16)
Burkina Faso	BFA	36.2	13.2	1,888	689	54.6	11.5	6.3	3.1	1.1	0.0	0.0	0.3	212.365	582.075	7,696.2	19.19
Burundi	BDI	9.9	3.8	919	354	57.7	5.6	3.2	1.5	0.6	0.0	0.0	0.2	666.758	1,729.055	6,632.4	10.83
Cabo Verde	CPV	4.5	2.2	8,398	4,090	72.9	51.1	37.2	13.6	6.6	0.0	0.0	0.0	47.630	97.799	215.0	0.54
Cameroon	CMR	90.0	36.2	3,665	1,475	60.2	22.3	13.4	5.9	2.4	0.1	0.0	0.3	234.290	582.075	21,094.7	24.57
Central African Republic	CAF	5.3	2.6	1,162	563	72.5	7.1	5.1	1.9	0.9	0.0	0.0	0.1	282.192	582.075	1,507.5	4.60
Chad	TCD	26.0	10.9	1,730	728	62.9	10.5	6.6	2.8	1.2	0.0	0.0	0.2	244.802	582.075	6,359.4	15.02
Comoros	COM	2.9	1.3	3,601	1,570	65.2	21.9	14.3	5.8	2.5	0.0	0.0	0.0	190.290	436.571	557.8	0.81
Congo, Dem. Rep.	COD	115.4	50.9	1,418	625	66.0	8.6	5.7	2.3	1.0	0.1	0.1	1.1	645.590	1,464.418	74,500.4	81.40
Congo, Rep.	COG	22.9	11.8	4,489	2,313	77.1	27.3	21.1	7.3	3.7	0.0	0.0	0.1	299.907	582.075	6,880.4	5.11
Côte d'Ivoire	CIV	85.1	37.2	3,481	1,521	65.4	21.2	13.8	5.6	2.5	0.1	0.0	0.3	254.355	582.075	21,640.1	24.44
Equatorial Guinea	GNQ	24.2	10.2	19,199	8,053	62.8	116.8	73.3	31.1	13.0	0.0	0.0	0.0	244.161	582.075	5,915.8	1.26
Eswatini	SWZ	11.0	5.1	9,759	4,517	69.3	59.4	41.1	15.8	7.3	0.0	0.0	0.0	6.172	13.334	67.7	1.12
Ethiopia	ETH	200.9	73.6	1,888	692	54.8	11.5	6.3	3.1	1.1	0.2	0.1	1.5	8.741	23.866	1,756.4	106.40
Gabon	GAB	23.8	11.4	11,543	5,523	71.6	70.2	50.3	18.7	8.9	0.0	0.0	0.0	278.524	582.075	6,638.4	2.06
Gambia, The	GMB	5.0	1.7	2,278	775	50.9	13.9	7.1	3.7	1.3	0.0	0.0	0.0	15.849	46.608	79.9	2.21
Ghana	GHA	149.5	60.9	5,133	2,092	61.0	31.2	19.0	8.3	3.4	0.1	0.1	0.4	1.773	4.351	265.0	29.12
Guinea	GIN	34.7	12.4	2,877	1,028	53.5	17.5	9.4	4.7	1.7	0.0	0.0	0.2	3,262.076	9,125.743	113,237.6	12.07
Guinea-Bissau	GNB	3.7	1.4	2,002	773	57.8	12.2	7.0	3.2	1.3	0.0	0.0	0.0	224.831	582.075	823.1	1.83
Kenya	KEN	234.4	92.4	4,667	1,839	59.0	28.4	16.7	7.6	3.0	0.2	0.1	0.7	40.755	103.411	9,551.5	50.22
Lesotho	LSO	8.8	3.7	4,186	1,752	62.6	25.5	15.9	6.8	2.8	0.0	0.0	0.0	5.580	13.334	48.9	2.09
Liberia	LBR	7.6	3.5	1,610	739	68.7	9.8	6.7	2.6	1.2	0.0	0.0	0.1	51.726	112.707	391.6	4.70
Madagascar	MDG	40.5	13.4	1,585	526	49.6	9.6	4.8	2.6	0.9	0.0	0.0	0.4	1,033.584	3,116.110	41,898.0	25.57
Malawi	MWI	21.2	7.5	1,202	426	53.1	7.3	3.9	1.9	0.7	0.0	0.0	0.2	259.008	730.273	5,500.3	17.67
Mali	MLI	47.4	17.9	2,562	965	56.4	15.6	8.8	4.1	1.6	0.0	0.0	0.3	219.235	582.075	10,396.9	18.51
Mauritania	MRT	17.8	5.8	4,153	1,345	48.4	25.3	12.2	6.7	2.2	0.0	0.0	0.1	115.754	357.493	2,059.0	4.28
Mauritius	MUS	35.0	17.0	27,685	13,430	72.6	168.4	122.2	44.8	21.7	0.0	0.0	0.0	16.727	34.481	585.6	1.26
Mozambique	MOZ	46.7	17.4	1,629	608	55.8	9.9	5.5	2.6	1.0	0.0	0.0	0.4	23.717	63.584	1,106.7	28.65
Namibia	NAM	28.3	14.7	11,760	6,112	77.8	71.5	55.6	19.0	9.9	0.0	0.0	0.0	6.919	13.313	195.5	2.40
Niger	NER	21.3	9.4	985	437	66.4	6.0	4.0	1.6	0.7	0.0	0.0	0.3	258.494	582.075	5,499.4	21.60
Nigeria	NGA	880.2	335.5	4,612	1,758	57.0	28.1	16.0	7.5	2.8	0.7	0.4	2.6	116.558	305.790	102,598.7	190.87
Rwanda	RWA	24.6	9.8	2,055	816	59.4	12.5	7.4	3.3	1.3	0.0	0.0	0.2	330.139	831.531	8,129.6	11.98
São Tomé and Príncipe	STP	1.0	0.5	4,979	2,269	68.2	30.3	20.7	8.1	3.7	0.0	0.0	0.0	9.909	21.741	10.2	0.21
Senegal	SEN	56.0	23.8	3,629	1,545	63.7	22.1	14.1	5.9	2.5	0.0	0.0	0.2	247.845	582.075	13,869.7	15.42
Seychelles	SYC	3.1	1.7	31,888	18,138	85.1	194.0	165.1	51.6	29.4	0.0	0.0	0.0	7.763	13.648	23.9	0.10
Sierra Leone	SLE	14.6	4.7	1,950	625	47.9	11.9	5.7	3.2	1.0	0.0	0.0	0.1	2,365.205	7,384.432	34,542.3	7.49
South Africa	ZAF	727.8	349.2	12,767	6,125	71.8	77.7	55.7	20.7	9.9	0.6	0.4	0.8	6.397	13.334	4,655.6	57.01
Sudan	SDN	180.0	42.9	4,413	1,053	35.7	26.8	9.6	7.1	1.7	0.2	0.1	0.6	4.803	20.130	864.5	40.78

Table 2.6 *(Continued)*

DOMESTIC ABSORPTION		Expenditure (billion US$)		Expenditure per capita (US$)		Price level index (world = 100.0)[a]	Expenditure per capita indexes[b]				Share (world = 100%)[b]			PPPs[c] (US$ = 1.000)	Reference data		
							World = 100.0		United States = 100.0		Expenditure				Market exchange rates[c] (US$ = 1.000)	Expenditure (billion LCU)	Population (millions)
Economy		Based on PPPs	Based on XRs	Based on PPPs	Based on XRs		Based on PPPs	Based on XRs	Based on PPPs	Based on XRs	Based on PPPs	Based on XRs	Population				
(00)		(01)	(02)	(03)	(04)	(05)	(06)	(07)	(08)	(09)	(10)	(11)	(12)	(13)	(14)	(15)	(16)
Tanzania	TZA	127.6	50.9	2,334	931	59.7	14.2	8.5	3.8	1.5	0.1	0.1	0.8	888.911	2,228.858	113,405.3	54.66
Togo	TGO	13.1	5.4	1,702	706	62.1	10.4	6.4	2.8	1.1	0.0	0.0	0.1	241.413	582.075	3,163.3	7.70
Uganda	UGA	93.8	33.4	2,277	813	53.4	13.9	7.4	3.7	1.3	0.1	0.0	0.6	1,288.420	3,611.224	120,792.5	41.17
Zambia	ZMB	57.4	25.3	3,405	1,502	66.0	20.7	13.7	5.5	2.4	0.0	0.0	0.2	4.198	9.520	240.9	16.85
Zimbabwe	ZWE	41.7	21.0	2,927	1,475	75.4	17.8	13.4	4.7	2.4	0.0	0.0	0.2	0.504	1.000	21.0	14.24
Total (45)	**SSB**	**3,854.1**	**1,596.8**	**3,774**	**1,564**	**62.0**	**23.0**	**14.2**	**6.1**	**2.5**	**3.3**	**2.0**	**14.2**	**n.a.**	**n.a**	**n.a.**	**1,021.22**
World (176)	**WLD**	**118,404.6**	**79,140.9**	**16,437**	**10,986**	**100.0**	**100.0**	**100.0**	**26.6**	**17.8**	**100.0**	**100.0**	**100.0**	**n.a.**	**n.a.**	**n.a.**	**7,203.60**

Note: PPP = purchasing power parity; XR = market exchange rate; LCU = local currency unit; n.a. = not applicable; ... = data suppressed due to unavailability.

a. World totals used to calculate price level indexes (PLIs) in this table exclude nonparticipating economies.

b. Indexes and shares are rounded to one decimal place for presentation in this table.

c. PPPs and market exchange rates are rounded to three decimal places for presentation in this table.

d. Bonaire's results are provided only for individual consumption expenditure by households. Therefore, to ensure consistency across tables, Bonaire is not included in either the Latin America and the Caribbean or the world totals.

Table 2.7 Gross domestic product (GDP) and individual consumption expenditure by households for nonparticipating economies: ICP 2017 results

Economy		GROSS DOMESTIC PRODUCT						Reference data			INDIVIDUAL CONSUMPTION EXPENDITURE BY HOUSEHOLDS
		Expenditure (billion US$)		Expenditure per capita (US$)		Price level index[a] (world = 100.0)	PPPs[b] (US$ = 1.000)	Market exchange rates[b] (US$ = 1.000)	Expenditure, gross domestic product (billion LCU)	Population (millions)	PPPs[b] (US$ = 1.000)
		Based on PPPs	Based on XRs	Based on PPPs	Based on XRs						
(00)		(01)	(02)	(03)	(04)	(05)	(13)	(14)	(15)	(16)	(13)
Nonparticipating economies											
Afghanistan	AFG	79.9	20.2	2,203	557	38.0	17.206	68.027	1,375.5	36.30	17.360
Guatemala[c]	GTM	141.3	75.7	8,353	4,473	80.5	3.933	7.344	555.6	16.91	4.403
Kosovo	KSV	18.9	7.2	10,302	3,958	57.7	0.340	0.885	6.4	1.83	0.357
Lebanon	LBN	109.5	53.4	16,082	7,838	73.3	734.776	1,507.500	80,491.2	6.81	761.833
Libya	LBY	87.1	37.9	13,665	5,942	65.4	0.606	1.394	52.8	6.37	0.638
Macao SAR, China[c]	MAC	79.0	50.8	126,918	81,517	96.5	5.155	8.026	407.3	0.62	5.940
Puerto Rico	PRI	115.2	104.3	34,634	31,353	136.1	0.905	1.000	104.3	3.33	0.977
Somalia	SOM	12.7	4.5	858	306	53.5	8,229.531	23,097.987	104,148.3	14.74	7,861.360
South Sudan	SSD	9.8	3.1	898	280	47.0	35.505	113.648	347.7	10.91	34.920
Timor-Leste	TLS	3.9	1.6	3,166	1,295	61.5	0.409	1.000	1.6	1.24	0.423
Turkmenistan	TKM	81.8	37.9	14,205	6,587	69.7	1.623	3.500	132.7	5.76	1.663
Uzbekistan[d]	UZB	211.1	60.5	6,519	1,869	43.1	1,432.907	4,999.020	302,536.8	32.39	1,521.475

Note: PPP = purchasing power parity; XR = market exchange rate; LCU = local currency unit; n.a. = not applicable.

a. World totals used to calculate price level indexes (PLIs) in this table include nonparticipating economies.

b. PPPs and market exchange rates are rounded to three decimal places for presentation in this table.

c. GDP and individual consumption expenditure by households PPPs for Guatemala and Macao SAR, China are based on a time-series estimation approach.

d. Individual consumption expenditure by households PPP for Uzbekistan is based on an experimental participation approach; the ICP online database covers additional headings based on this approach.

Table 2.8 ICP 2017 Individual consumption expenditure by households, survey framework

Economy		Geographic coverage[a]	Total outlets covered	Large shops	Medium and small shops	Markets	Street outlets	Bulk and discount shops	Specialized shops	Private service providers	Public or semipublic service providers	Other kinds of trades and outlets	ICP Global Core List and regional items	ICP Global Core List items
			#	%	%	%	%	%	%	%	%	%	#	#
East Asia and Pacific														
Australia	AUS	Urban only	...	...	...	...	...	...	...	...	...	...	1,599	352
Brunei Darussalam	BRN	Urban only	213	4.69	4.23	2.35	0.00	0.00	53.05	28.64	7.04	0.00	610	307
Cambodia	KHM	Urban and Rural	1,244	3.62	21.14	45.18	5.47	0.16	0.48	21.22	2.57	0.16	590	276
China	CHN	Urban and Rural	39,587	10.35	10.79	3.03	12.29	0.41	16.34	18.29	10.84	17.65	901	437
Fiji	FJI	Urban only	878	13.44	27.33	6.83	0.11	0.23	9.45	8.09	33.71	0.80	455	227
Hong Kong SAR, China	HKG	Urban only	1,880	6.54	2.98	18.35	0.00	0.00	46.81	22.50	2.82	0.00	703	352
Indonesia	IDN	Urban and Rural	1,156	12.72	21.97	8.56	3.72	0.26	26.30	24.39	1.38	0.69	676	339
Japan	JPN	Capital-city only	...	...	...	...	...	...	...	...	...	...	1,224	278
Korea, Rep.	KOR	Urban only	...	...	...	...	...	...	...	...	...	...	1,478	318
Lao PDR	LAO	Urban and Rural	1,254	0.80	0.96	76.71	0.00	0.40	4.31	9.49	3.75	3.59	639	323
Malaysia	MYS	Urban and Rural	9,641	22.00	18.99	20.99	0.00	0.00	3.00	17.01	18.01	0.00	739	365
Mongolia	MNG	Urban and Rural	2,714	4.53	28.81	7.04	0.52	0.04	2.84	46.13	6.82	3.28	787	382
Myanmar	MMR	Urban and Rural	3,568	2.24	24.69	45.66	3.73	0.25	11.66	7.74	1.99	2.05	775	375
New Zealand	NZL	Capital-city only	...	...	...	...	...	...	...	...	...	...	1,267	276
Philippines	PHL	Urban and Rural	6,399	5.61	8.05	25.39	9.16	0.02	29.85	16.42	2.66	2.84	849	413
Singapore	SGP	Urban only	792	1.89	2.78	3.03	0.00	0.00	32.83	53.66	2.02	3.79	713	358
Taiwan, China	TWN	Urban only	596	2.52	3.36	13.26	0.00	0.00	48.83	25.67	5.03	1.34	711	345
Thailand	THA	Urban and Rural	3,534	4.90	10.16	13.92	1.50	0.96	35.51	23.66	8.89	0.51	653	321
Vietnam	VNM	Urban and Rural	983	7.32	24.31	14.65	8.34	0.20	13.33	23.80	8.04	0.00	757	369
Europe and Central Asia														
Albania	ALB	Urban only	...	34.06	0.94	0.70	0.00	0.00	45.91	16.42	0.01	1.92	1,605	347
Armenia	ARM	Urban only	955	2.62	5.13	2.30	1.36	0.00	38.74	46.07	1.88	1.88	1,548	489
Austria	AUT	Urban only	...	29.35	0.01	2.80	0.00	6.69	38.08	15.52	0.37	7.20	1,933	377
Azerbaijan	AZE	Urban only	3,347	7.59	25.90	2.42	0.00	0.00	4.72	40.39	18.97	0.00	1,460	461
Belarus	BLR	Urban only	4,484	4.82	8.65	10.97	0.83	0.76	27.54	28.68	9.14	8.61	1,473	470
Belgium	BEL	Urban only	...	61.19	1.50	0.10	0.00	2.59	19.31	12.21	0.22	2.84	1,797	349
Bosnia and Herzegovina	BIH	Urban only	...	49.94	0.86	1.90	0.00	0.00	26.52	12.41	2.26	6.09	1,566	351
Bulgaria	BGR	Capital-city only	...	39.52	0.47	1.70	0.00	0.00	38.65	11.49	0.26	7.94	1,968	397
Croatia	HRV	Urban only	...	39.42	7.75	3.80	0.00	0.52	30.15	14.79	0.76	2.76	1,967	392
Cyprus	CYP	Urban only	...	52.65	2.78	0.70	0.00	0.00	27.32	14.93	1.54	0.08	1,769	376
Czech Republic	CZE	Capital-city only	...	45.07	1.08	0.00	0.00	3.77	34.23	13.85	0.46	1.54	1,879	371
Denmark	DNK	Urban only	...	14.15	0.11	0.00	0.00	1.76	33.80	34.24	0.36	15.58	1,733	360
Estonia	EST	Urban only	...	60.07	1.31	0.50	0.00	0.03	20.25	11.69	1.67	4.47	1,752	360
Finland	FIN	Urban only	...	48.12	0.01	0.00	0.10	4.78	24.79	17.75	0.48	3.95	1,792	355
France	FRA	Capital-city only	...	51.72	3.29	2.60	0.00	4.56	20.33	14.82	0.00	2.68	1,961	383
Georgia	GEO	Capital-city only	800	2.50	2.13	4.50	0.00	0.00	35.63	52.63	1.38	1.25	1,381	324
Germany	DEU	Capital-city only	...	34.88	0.18	0.40	0.00	7.57	21.91	22.48	2.32	10.30	1,768	360
Greece	GRC	Urban only	...	45.57	0.43	3.20	0.00	3.58	32.95	14.08	0.12	0.10	1,890	386

Table 2.8 *(Continued)*

Economy		Geographic coverage[a]	Total outlets covered	Large shops	Medium and small shops	Markets	Street outlets	Bulk and discount shops	Specialized shops	Private service providers	Public or semipublic service providers	Other kinds of trades and outlets	ICP Global Core List and regional items	ICP Global Core List items
			#	%	%	%	%	%	%	%	%	%	#	#
Hungary	HUN	Capital-city only	...	27.55	13.69	2.60	0.00	5.64	29.53	17.52	0.27	3.24	1,855	369
Iceland	ISL	Urban only	...	48.76	0.38	0.00	0.00	0.05	27.80	21.61	0.18	1.22	1,638	335
Ireland	IRL	Urban only	...	49.52	2.89	0.00	0.00	4.38	24.47	17.84	0.89	0.01	1,832	365
Italy	ITA	Capital-city only	...	50.07	0.23	1.10	0.00	9.37	23.10	15.05	0.19	0.88	1,964	392
Kazakhstan	KAZ	Urban only	4,983	7.39	11.34	4.01	0.80	0.00	21.15	39.07	5.02	11.22	1,720	524
Kyrgyzstan	KGZ	Capital city only	213	4.23	0.94	4.23	0.94	0.00	18.78	58.69	3.76	8.45	1,451	467
Latvia	LVA	Urban only	...	47.08	2.31	2.30	0.00	1.00	31.51	14.13	0.73	0.92	1,835	375
Lithuania	LTU	Capital-city only	...	45.78	5.89	2.20	0.00	2.05	26.80	15.03	0.13	2.07	1,887	382
Luxembourg	LUX	Urban only	...	62.14	0.51	0.00	0.00	4.23	19.41	13.20	0.19	0.32	1,932	379
Moldova	MDA	Urban only	297	7.74	27.95	4.04	1.01	0.00	34.01	15.49	7.74	2.02	1,541	483
Montenegro	MNE	Urban only	...	44.07	3.85	0.80	0.00	8.64	28.61	13.55	0.20	0.20	1,631	363
Netherlands	NLD	Urban only	...	28.64	0.03	0.80	0.10	1.50	41.19	16.12	0.38	11.20	1,902	375
North Macedonia	MKD	Urban only	...	43.50	5.43	2.70	0.00	0.00	29.82	16.24	0.29	2.04	1,616	350
Norway	NOR	Urban only	...	30.61	4.88	0.00	0.00	26.61	21.22	10.24	0.90	5.54	1,780	349
Poland	POL	Capital-city only	...	32.14	10.89	1.10	0.10	4.22	31.91	14.87	1.42	3.37	1,937	385
Portugal	PRT	Capital-city only	...	45.42	0.67	2.50	0.00	2.55	26.95	21.03	0.24	0.62	1,896	378
Romania	ROU	Capital-city only	...	45.27	0.75	1.20	0.00	1.72	27.76	16.74	0.07	6.47	1,834	370
Russian Federation	RUS	Capital-city only	...	6.38	3.72	1.77	1.33	1.51	23.74	2.21	25.78	33.57	1,368	331
Serbia	SRB	Urban only	...	56.64	7.21	3.50	0.00	0.00	17.63	11.62	0.58	2.80	1,859	377
Slovakia	SVK	Urban only	...	51.25	1.60	1.20	0.20	0.65	29.99	13.34	0.03	1.73	1,914	382
Slovenia	SVN	Urban only	...	57.84	0.82	0.00	0.00	5.58	22.44	9.74	0.47	3.11	1,905	383
Spain	ESP	Capital-city only	...	35.76	0.71	9.10	0.10	4.97	25.68	22.63	0.41	0.56	1,932	384
Sweden	SWE	Urban only	...	83.39	0.04	0.00	0.00	0.17	9.59	5.18	0.15	1.48	1,804	356
Switzerland	CHE	Capital-city only	...	60.17	0.18	0.00	0.00	11.09	14.57	9.46	0.54	3.98	1,835	361
Tajikistan	TJK	Capital city only	59	10.17	25.42	8.47	0.00	3.39	16.95	23.73	5.08	6.78	1,381	448
Turkey	TUR	Capital-city only	...	52.66	0.03	0.10	0.00	3.02	30.59	12.05	0.61	0.93	1,869	377
Ukraine	UKR	Capital-city only	2,219	6.89	14.38	0.36	0.90	0.00	43.35	28.26	0.90	4.96	1,352	342
United Kingdom	GBR	Capital-city only	...	47.54	5.39	0.30	0.00	4.22	18.26	21.23	0.18	2.89	1,873	374
Latin America and the Caribbean														
Anguilla	AIA	Urban and Rural	...	...	...	...	...	...	...	...	...	...	406	368
Antigua and Barbuda	ATG	Urban Only	80	0.00	100.00	0.00	0.00	0.00	0.00	0.00	0.00	0.00	250	231
Argentina	ARG	Capital city only	3,988	4.29	95.71	0.00	0.00	0.00	0.00	0.00	0.00	0.00	286	268
Aruba	ABW	Urban Only	45	100.00	0.00	0.00	0.00	0.00	0.00	0.00	0.00	0.00	404	364
Bahamas, The	BHS	...	...	...	...	...	...	...	...	...	...	...	259	249
Barbados	BRB	Urban and Rural	70	0.00	100.00	0.00	0.00	0.00	0.00	0.00	0.00	0.00	279	256
Belize	BLZ	Urban only	161	0.00	100.00	0.00	0.00	0.00	0.00	0.00	0.00	0.00	261	239
Bolivia	BOL	Urban only	...	0.50	7.92	0.00	47.25	0.00	22.88	14.57	0.09	6.80	222	207
Bonaire	BON	Urban only	80	0.00	100.00	0.00	0.00	0.00	0.00	0.00	0.00	0.00	177	168

Table 2.8 *(Continued)*

Economy		Geographic coverage[a]	Total outlets covered	*Large shops*	*Medium and small shops*	*Markets*	*Street outlets*	*Bulk and discount shops*	*Specialized shops*	*Private service providers*	*Public or semipublic service providers*	*Other kinds of trades and outlets*	ICP Global Core List and regional items	ICP Global Core List items
			#	%	%	%	%	%	%	%	%	%	#	#
Brazil	BRA	Urban only	3,662	15.84	3.90	3.69	0.00	0.11	46.12	27.61	2.68	0.05	349	330
Cayman Islands	CYM	Capital city only	210	...	...	...	...	...	...	...	...	...	422	389
Chile	CHL	Urban only	...	...	...	...	...	...	...	...	...	...	1,379	337
Colombia	COL	Urban only	...	...	...	...	...	...	...	...	...	...	1,048	298
Costa Rica	CRI	Urban only	...	...	...	...	...	...	...	...	...	...	1,034	268
Curaçao	CUW	Urban and Rural	...	...	...	...	...	...	...	...	...	...	392	373
Dominica	DMA	Urban and Rural	13	...	...	...	...	...	...	...	...	...	294	269
Dominican Republic	DOM	Urban only	3,585	17.57	65.86	2.40	0.00	0.00	14.17	0.00	0.00	0.00	423	387
Ecuador	ECU	Urban only	811	4.44	5.67	1.60	1.11	0.00	49.08	35.64	2.47	0.00	285	266
El Salvador	SLV	Urban only	1,324	62.54	3.85	6.27	0.53	0.00	0.00	0.23	0.00	26.59	170	161
Grenada	GRD	Capital city only	6	...	...	...	...	...	...	...	...	...	234	214
Guyana	GUY	Capital city only	97	11.34	69.07	5.15	0.00	10.31	0.00	4.12	0.00	0.00	368	336
Haiti	HTI	...	...	...	...	...	...	...	...	...	...	...	203	195
Honduras	HND	...	...	...	...	...	...	...	...	...	...	...	241	224
Jamaica	JAM	...	...	...	...	...	...	...	...	...	...	...	174	160
Mexico	MEX	Urban only	...	...	...	...	...	...	...	...	...	...	1,481	342
Montserrat	MSR	Urban and Rural	...	...	...	...	...	...	...	...	...	...	215	196
Nicaragua	NIC	Urban only	1,086	...	...	...	...	...	...	...	...	...	255	238
Panama	PAN	Urban only	132	9.85	21.97	1.52	0.00	0.00	24.24	30.30	0.00	12.12	203	197
Paraguay	PRY	Urban only	377	7.16	12.20	1.86	1.06	0.00	32.63	38.46	5.84	0.80	273	257
Peru	PER	Capital city only	607	6.92	13.01	7.74	2.31	0.00	22.73	45.47	0.66	1.15	444	404
Sint Maarten	SXM	Urban only	155	11.61	20.65	0.00	0.00	0.65	10.97	52.26	3.87	0.00	256	249
St. Kitts and Nevis	KNA	Capital city only	69	...	...	...	...	...	...	...	...	...	402	371
St. Lucia	LCA	Urban and Rural	153	3.92	7.19	1.31	0.00	0.00	49.67	35.95	1.96	0.00	370	341
St. Vincent and the Grenadines	VCT	Urban and Rural	91	14.29	0.00	3.30	0.00	0.00	25.27	52.75	4.40	0.00	356	321
Suriname	SUR	Urban and Rural	383	26.37	8.88	1.83	2.09	0.78	26.37	30.03	3.66	0.00	414	384
Trinidad and Tobago	TTO	Urban only	532	14.10	23.87	1.32	0.75	0.19	38.53	20.68	0.56	0.00	432	398
Turks and Caicos Islands	TCA	...	...	...	...	...	...	...	...	...	...	...	325	303
Uruguay	URY	Capital city only	...	...	...	...	...	...	...	...	...	...	284	267
Virgin Islands, British	VGB	Capital city only	122	...	...	...	...	...	...	...	...	...	287	262
Middle East and North Africa														
Algeria	DZA	Urban and Rural	364	0.00	3.30	11.81	7.69	4.12	0.00	57.69	12.36	3.02	458	357
Bahrain	BHR	Urban only	287	2.44	4.18	2.09	0.00	0.35	62.02	27.53	1.39	0.00	554	392
Djibouti	DJI	Capital city only	97	5.66	28.30	1.89	3.77	0.00	28.30	28.30	3.77	0.00	451	358
Egypt, Arab Rep.	EGY	Urban and Rural	3,425	8.29	5.43	1.02	0.00	0.00	85.26	0.00	0.00	0.00	716	459
Iran, Islamic Rep.	IRN	Urban only	3,241	5.71	36.25	24.99	14.10	2.31	2.81	10.34	2.99	0.49	548	382
Iraq	IRQ	Urban only	102	6.86	24.51	0.00	0.00	0.00	0.00	19.61	24.51	24.51	648	449

Table 2.8 *(Continued)*

Economy		Geographic coverage[a]	Total outlets covered	*Large shops*	*Medium and small shops*	*Markets*	*Street outlets*	*Bulk and discount shops*	*Specialized shops*	*Private service providers*	*Public or semipublic service providers*	*Other kinds of trades and outlets*	ICP Global Core List and regional items	ICP Global Core List items
			#	%	%	%	%	%	%	%	%	%	#	#
Israel	ISR	Urban only	...	...	...	...	...	...	...	...	...	...	1,673	358
Jordan	JOR	Urban only	1,812	4.25	13.19	11.20	1.21	0.33	33.39	34.44	1.60	0.39	647	445
Kuwait	KWT	Urban only	280	9.64	8.93	12.14	5.36	0.36	31.79	15.71	16.07	0.00	627	430
Malta	MLT	Urban only	...	34.62	6.73	0.50	0.00	2.79	34.55	20.06	0.43	0.35	1,830	376
Morocco	MAR	Urban and Rural	577	2.08	5.72	4.33	1.91	0.35	48.53	34.32	2.43	0.35	842	531
Oman	OMN	Urban only	62	17.74	0.00	82.26	0.00	0.00	0.00	0.00	0.00	0.00	607	409
Qatar	QAT	Urban only	450	...	...	...	...	...	...	...	...	...	625	432
Saudi Arabia	SAU	Urban only	450	...	...	...	...	...	...	...	...	...	641	440
Tunisia	TUN	Urban and Rural	969	15.69	18.16	22.29	1.03	0.31	26.93	12.07	0.31	3.20	478	371
United Arab Emirates	ARE	Urban only	654	12.20	26.60	8.90	4.30	2.30	17.90	18.70	4.30	4.90	642	445
West Bank and Gaza	PSE	Urban only	1,899	8.43	56.19	0.00	3.11	0.42	0.21	23.64	0.74	7.27	538	377
North America														
Bermuda	BMU	Urban only	41	0.00	29.27	0.00	0.00	0.00	53.66	7.32	9.76	0.00	155	149
Canada	CAN	Urban only	...	...	...	...	...	...	...	...	...	...	1,354	318
United States	USA	Urban only	...	...	...	...	...	...	...	...	...	...	1,304	324
South Asia														
Bangladesh	BGD	Urban and Rural	720	0.00	0.00	100.00	0.00	0.00	0.00	0.00	0.00	0.00	780	365
Bhutan	BTN	Urban and Rural	482	0.41	48.76	8.09	0.00	0.00	13.07	26.97	2.70	0.00	442	219
India	IND	Urban and Rural	897	...	...	...	...	...	...	...	...	...	945	441
Maldives	MDV	Urban and Rural	241	0.41	20.75	0.41	0.00	0.00	44.40	27.80	3.32	2.90	359	182
Nepal	NPL	Urban and Rural	4,016	7.74	51.00	2.61	3.96	0.22	14.54	15.01	2.37	2.54	667	307
Pakistan	PAK	Urban and Rural	120	...	...	...	...	...	...	...	...	...	890	415
Sri Lanka	LKA	Urban and Rural	3,948	7.29	32.90	8.08	2.05	1.37	29.08	16.26	2.36	0.61	652	313
Sub-Saharan Africa														
Angola	AGO	Urban and Rural	402	7.46	21.64	8.46	0.00	0.00	31.34	29.60	1.49	0.00	217	177
Benin	BEN	Urban and Rural	1,769	5.71	8.88	12.21	16.05	6.05	37.82	11.25	1.87	0.17	547	420
Botswana	BWA	Urban and Rural	1,592	5.19	2.59	1.98	2.10	0.00	27.90	14.94	0.00	45.31	482	391
Burkina Faso	BFA	Urban and Rural	255	5.10	5.10	10.20	5.10	0.00	37.25	30.20	7.06	0.00	520	399
Burundi	BDI	Urban and Rural	185	5.41	29.73	9.19	3.24	0.00	34.59	16.76	1.08	0.00	468	359
Cabo Verde	CPV	Urban and Rural	280	5.38	8.60	10.75	3.23	0.00	45.16	21.51	5.38	0.00	489	383
Cameroon	CMR	Urban and Rural	924	21.84	10.34	5.75	4.60	0.00	25.29	29.89	2.30	0.00	548	420
Central African Republic	CAF	Urban and Rural	221	11.90	21.43	5.95	1.19	0.00	36.90	22.62	0.00	0.00	444	347
Chad	TCD	Capital city only	135	7.21	5.41	8.11	6.31	0.00	12.61	57.66	2.70	0.00	512	392
Comoros	COM	Urban only	56	7.14	25.00	7.14	3.57	0.00	17.86	35.71	3.57	0.00	388	313
Congo, Dem. Rep.	COD	Urban only	130	12.15	21.50	12.15	1.87	0.00	26.17	24.30	1.87	0.00	510	392
Congo, Rep.	COG	Urban only	602	10.53	13.16	2.63	2.63	0.00	38.16	30.26	2.63	0.00	562	428
Côte d'Ivoire	CIV	Urban and Rural	241	16.13	32.26	8.06	8.06	0.00	16.13	16.13	3.23	0.00	559	426
Equatorial Guinea	GNQ	Capital city only	81	12.20	21.95	2.44	4.88	0.00	24.39	29.27	4.88	0.00	548	418

Table 2.8 *(Continued)*

Economy		Geographic coverage[a]	Total outlets covered	Large shops	Medium and small shops	Markets	Street outlets	Bulk and discount shops	Specialized shops	Private service providers	Public or semipublic service providers	Other kinds of trades and outlets	ICP Global Core List and regional items	ICP Global Core List items
			#	%	%	%	%	%	%	%	%	%	#	#
Eswatini	SWZ	Urban only	125	37.60	0.80	5.60	7.20	0.00	48.80	0.00	0.00	0.00	483	382
Ethiopia	ETH	Urban only	453	10.68	29.13	10.68	4.85	0.00	21.36	21.36	1.94	0.00	523	405
Gabon	GAB	Urban only	313	8.95	35.46	9.58	2.24	0.00	28.75	7.03	7.99	0.00	423	332
Gambia, The	GMB	Urban and Rural	460	4.78	12.61	8.26	9.35	0.00	15.87	38.91	10.22	0.00	533	404
Ghana	GHA	Urban only	328	20.73	14.33	8.54	1.52	0.00	33.23	21.04	0.61	0.00	526	401
Guinea	GIN	Urban and Rural	210	10.87	21.74	15.22	4.35	0.00	21.74	21.74	4.35	0.00	499	382
Guinea-Bissau	GNB	Capital city only	403	7.94	14.29	4.76	1.59	0.00	11.11	57.14	3.17	0.00	544	417
Kenya	KEN	Urban and Rural	1,484	11.81	23.62	11.81	3.94	0.00	23.62	23.62	1.57	0.00	507	392
Lesotho	LSO	Urban only	474	37.97	14.35	1.69	3.38	0.00	36.08	6.54	0.00	0.00	406	340
Liberia	LBR	Capital city only	150	10.67	12.00	11.33	11.33	0.00	15.33	33.33	6.00	0.00	475	370
Madagascar	MDG	Capital city only	519	4.24	37.76	6.55	3.47	0.00	22.54	24.86	0.58	0.00	461	364
Malawi	MWI	Urban and Rural	151	15.25	25.42	23.73	3.39	0.00	15.25	11.86	5.08	0.00	516	395
Mali	MLI	Urban and Rural	466	11.36	22.73	11.36	4.55	0.00	22.73	22.73	4.55	0.00	556	422
Mauritania	MRT	Urban and Rural	2,438	4.18	15.75	33.10	0.00	0.00	23.13	5.58	18.25	0.00	453	351
Mauritius	MUS	Urban and Rural	520	4.62	31.73	2.12	0.58	0.00	46.92	10.38	3.65	0.00	502	395
Mozambique	MOZ	Urban only	706	50.82	45.90	1.64	0.00	0.00	1.64	0.00	0.00	0.00	502	385
Namibia	NAM	Urban only	242	14.46	4.96	1.24	0.00	0.00	28.10	41.32	9.92	0.00	509	406
Niger	NER	Capital city only	210	9.05	11.90	7.14	8.10	0.00	7.14	49.52	7.14	0.00	525	404
Nigeria	NGA	Urban and Rural	1,004	6.87	14.94	11.45	8.96	0.00	20.12	29.88	7.77	0.00	546	417
Rwanda	RWA	Urban and Rural	184	7.30	29.60	11.00	6.00	0.00	33.10	12.00	1.00	0.00	489	384
São Tomé and Principe	STP	Capital city only	276	3.99	11.59	3.99	2.90	0.00	51.09	21.01	5.43	0.00	366	284
Senegal	SEN	Urban and Rural	254	12.66	25.32	6.33	2.53	0.00	25.32	25.32	2.53	0.00	544	415
Seychelles	SYC	Capital city only	53	50.94	11.32	1.89	0.00	0.00	32.08	1.89	1.89	0.00	477	384
Sierra Leone	SLE	Urban only	101	8.91	10.89	12.87	6.93	0.00	10.89	47.52	1.98	0.00	515	393
South Africa	ZAF	Urban and Rural	1,016	32.09	10.33	1.28	1.57	0.00	8.66	34.94	11.12	0.00	366	313
Sudan	SDN	Urban and Rural	3,165	18.70	14.63	2.53	1.80	9.51	23.44	6.41	7.58	15.39	602	407
Tanzania	TZA	Urban and Rural	1,134	5.49	13.50	9.70	9.92	0.00	22.15	37.76	1.48	0.00	540	410
Togo	TGO	Capital city only	209	5.26	26.32	5.26	5.26	0.00	26.32	26.32	5.26	0.00	315	247
Uganda	UGA	Urban and Rural	777	10.53	21.05	10.53	2.63	0.00	26.32	26.32	2.63	0.00	543	416
Zambia	ZMB	Urban only	378	25.13	5.56	0.26	2.12	2.38	39.42	15.34	9.79	0.00	488	385
Zimbabwe	ZWE	Urban and Rural	1,040	11.92	5.38	0.67	21.15	0.00	26.06	27.88	6.92	0.00	523	405

Note: ICP = International Comparison Program; … = information not available.

a. ICP data requirements require that all average prices reported by participating economies and used in PPP calculations be nationally representative annual average prices, irrespective of the survey geographical coverage reported here.

CHAPTER 3

Purchasing power parities and real expenditures

Concepts and definitions

The ICP approach to GDP comparisons

The International Comparison Program (ICP) comparisons of gross domestic product (GDP) are based on the value of an individual item equaling the product of its price and quantity (that is, the identity: value = price × quantity). Once more than one item is involved, the identity can no longer be expressed in terms of price × quantity. Therefore, in ICP terms, it becomes value = price × volume.

GDP is a measure of production within an economy, and it is commonly estimated as the sum of the value of the outputs from production less the cost of the goods and services used in their production—the so-called production approach. It also can be estimated as the sum of the final expenditures on goods and services plus exports less imports of goods and services, which is known as the expenditure side of national accounts and is the approach used by the ICP. Yet another alternative is to estimate GDP as the sum of the incomes arising from production (wages, profits, and so forth), which is referred to as the income approach. In theory, the three approaches yield the same result. However, whereas values estimated from the production side and the expenditure side can be split into meaningful price and volume components, values estimated from the income side cannot. In other words, price and volume comparisons of GDP can be made from the production side and from the expenditure side, but not from the income side. ICP comparisons are made from the expenditure side. This approach allows comparison of the levels of the principal elements of final demand—that is, consumption and investment. It also avoids the difficulties encountered in organizing comparisons from the production side, which requires data for both intermediate consumption and gross output in order to effect double deflation. The disadvantage of the expenditure approach is that, unlike the production approach, it does not identify individual industries, and so productivity can be compared only at the level of the whole economy. On the other hand, a major advantage is that the estimates of final demand can be used in many different types of economic analysis, including forecasting and poverty analysis.

Economies estimate their expenditures on GDP at national price levels and in local currency units. But before these nominal expenditures can be used to compare the volumes of goods and services produced by economies, differences in national price levels have to be eliminated and local currency units have to be converted to a common currency. Differences in price levels between economies can be removed either by observing volumes directly as the sum of their underlying quantities or by deriving them indirectly using a measure of relative prices to place the expenditures of all economies on the same price level. Prices are easier to observe than quantities, and direct measures of relative prices usually have a smaller variability than direct measures of relative quantities. In ICP comparisons, volumes (referred to as real expenditures) are mostly estimated indirectly using direct measures of relative prices—purchasing power parities (PPPs)—to deflate nominal expenditures. In addition to being spatial price deflators, PPPs are currency converters. Thus PPP-deflated expenditures are expressed in a common currency unit and are also valued at the same price level.

Market exchange rates

Before PPPs became widely available, market exchange rates were used to make international comparisons of GDP. Market exchange rates, however, only convert GDP to a common currency. They do not provide GDP valued at a common price level because market exchange rates do not reflect the relative purchasing power of currencies in their national markets. For them to do so, all goods and services would have to be traded internationally, and the supply and demand for currencies would have to be driven predominantly, if not solely, by the currency requirements of international trade. But this is not the case. Many goods and services—such as buildings, government services, and most household market services—are not traded internationally, and the supply and demand for currencies are influenced primarily by factors such as currency speculation, interest rates, government intervention, and capital flows between economies. Consequently, as equation (B3.1.2) in box 3.1 indicates, GDP converted to a common currency using market exchange rates remains valued at national price levels. The differences between the levels of GDP in two or more economies reflect both differences in the volumes of goods and services produced by the economies and differences in the price levels of the economies. However, as equation (B3.1.4) in box 3.1 shows, GDP converted with PPPs reflect only differences in the volumes produced by the economies.

Market exchange rate–converted GDP—that is, nominal GDP converted to a common

Box 3.1 Using market exchange rates and PPPs to convert to a common currency

1. The ratio of the GDPs of two economies when both are valued at national price levels and expressed in local currency units has three component ratios:

$$\text{GDP ratio} = \text{price level ratio} \times \text{volume ratio} \times \text{currency ratio.} \quad \text{(B3.1.1)}$$

2. When converting the GDP ratio in equation (B3.1.1) to a common currency using the market exchange rate, the resulting GDP_{XR} ratio has two component ratios:

$$\text{GDP}_{XR}\text{ ratio} = \text{price level ratio} \times \text{volume ratio.} \quad \text{(B3.1.2)}$$

The GDP ratio in equation (B3.1.2) is expressed in a common currency, but it reflects both the price level differences and the volume differences between the two economies.

3. A PPP is defined as a spatial price deflator and currency converter. It is composed of two component ratios:

$$\text{PPP} = \text{price level ratio} \times \text{currency ratio.} \quad \text{(B3.1.3)}$$

4. When a PPP is used, the GDP ratio in equation (B3.1.1) is divided by equation (B3.1.3), and the resulting GDP_{PPP} ratio has only one component ratio:

$$\text{GDP}_{PPP}\text{ ratio} = \text{volume ratio.} \quad \text{(B3.1.4)}$$

The GDP ratio in equation (B3.1.4) is expressed in a common currency, is valued at a common price level, and reflects only differences in volume between the two economies.

currency using market exchange rates—can be highly misleading with regard to the relative size of economies. Price levels are normally higher in high-income economies than they are in low-income economies; as a result, differences in price levels between high-income economies and low-income economies are greater for nontraded items than they are for traded items. Before the addition of tariffs, subsidies, and trade costs, the prices of traded items are basically determined globally by the law of one price, whereas the prices of nontraded items are determined by local circumstances, in particular, by wages and salaries, which are generally higher in high-income economies. If the larger differences in price level for nontraded items are not taken into account when converting GDP to a common currency, the size of high-income economies with high price levels will be overstated and the size of low-income economies with low price levels will be understated. This is known as the Penn effect. No distinction is made between traded items and nontraded items when market exchange rates are used to convert GDP to a common currency—the rate is the same for all items. PPP-converted GDP does not have this bias because, as explained in chapter 5, PPPs are calculated first for individual items. They thus take into account the different price levels for traded items and nontraded items.

ICP PPPs are designed specifically for international comparisons of GDP. They are not designed for comparisons of monetary flows or trade flows. International comparisons of flows—such as development aid, foreign direct investment, migrants' remittances, or imports and exports of goods and services—should be made with market exchange rates, not with PPPs.

Purchasing power parities

PPPs are price relatives that show the ratio of the prices in local currency units of the same good or service in different economies. For example, if the price of a hamburger is €4.80 in France and $4.00 in the United States, the PPP for hamburgers between the two economies is $0.83 to the €1.00 from France's perspective (4.00/4.80) and €1.20 to the dollar from the United States' perspective (4.80/4.00). In other words, for every €1.00 spent on hamburgers in France, $0.83 would have to be spent in the United States to obtain the same quantity and quality—that is, the same volume—of hamburgers. Conversely, for every $1.00 spent on hamburgers in the United States, €1.20 would have to be spent in France to obtain the same volume of hamburgers. To compare the volumes of hamburgers purchased in the two economies, either the expenditure on hamburgers in France can be expressed in dollars by dividing by 1.20, or the expenditure on hamburgers in the United States can be expressed in euros by dividing by 0.83.

PPPs are calculated in stages: first for item groups, then for various aggregates, and finally for GDP. PPPs continue to be price relatives whether they refer to an item group, to an aggregate, or to GDP. As one moves up the aggregation hierarchy, the price relatives refer to increasingly complex assortments of goods and services. Therefore, if the PPP for GDP between France and the United States is €0.95 to $1.00, it can be inferred that for every $1.00 spent on GDP in the United States, €0.95 would have to be spent in France to purchase the same volume of goods and services. Purchasing the same volume of goods and services does not mean that the baskets of goods and services purchased in both economies will be identical. The composition of the baskets will vary between economies and reflect differences in taste, culture, climate, price structure, item availability, and income level, but both baskets will, in principle, provide equivalent satisfaction or utility.

Price level indexes

PPPs are spatial price indexes. They show, with reference to a base economy (or region), the price of a given basket of goods and services in each of the economies being compared. This index is similar to a temporal price index, which shows, with reference to a base period, the price of a given basket of goods and services at different points in time. However, unlike a temporal price index in which the indexes at the different points in time are expressed in the same currency unit so that changes in price over time are readily identifiable, the PPP index for each economy is expressed in the economy's local currency. It is thus not possible to say whether one economy is more expensive or less expensive than another. For this type of comparison, one would have to standardize the indexes by expressing them in a common unit of currency. The common currency used for the global comparison is the US dollar, so each economy's PPP has been standardized by dividing it by that economy's dollar market exchange rate. The standardized indexes so obtained are called price level indexes (PLIs).

Economies with PLIs greater than 100 have price levels that are higher than that of the base economy. Economies with PLIs less than 100 have price levels that are lower than that of the base economy. So, returning to the hamburger example, if the market exchange rate is $1.00 to €0.79, the PLI for a hamburger with the United States as the base economy is 152 (1.20/0.79 × 100). From this, it can be inferred that, given the relative purchasing power of the dollar and the euro, hamburgers cost 52 percent more in France than they do in the United States. In addition to items, PLIs can be calculated for GDP and its expenditure components. At the level of GDP, PLIs provide a measure of the differences in the general price levels of economies. Thus, if the PPP for GDP between France and the United States is €0.95 to $1.00, the PLI for GDP based on the United States is 120 (0.95/0.79 × 100), indicating that the general price level of France is 20 percent higher than that of the United States. The PLIs of economies can be compared directly. For example, if the PLI of one economy is 120 while that of another economy is 80 (both with the United States as base), then it is valid to infer that the price level is 50 percent (that is, 120/80) higher in the former than in the latter.

It is worth remembering that PPPs evolve slowly, whereas market exchange rates can change quickly. Sudden changes in PLIs are usually the result of fluctuations in market exchange rates. When market exchange rates change rapidly, a PLI for an economy could change rapidly as well, reflecting the fact that an economy that was relatively cheap has now become relatively expensive compared with the base economy. The volatility of market exchange rates is another reason they should not be used to compare the size of economies. Fluctuations in market exchange rates can make economies appear suddenly larger or smaller even though there has been little or no change in the relative volume of goods and services produced.

Real expenditures

Economies report aggregate and detailed nominal expenditures on GDP in local currency units. Nominal expenditures are expenditures that are valued at national price levels. They can be expressed in local currency units or, when converted with market exchange rates, in a common currency. In the latter, the converted expenditures remain nominal because, as explained earlier, market exchange rates do not correct for differences in price levels between economies, and so the expenditures are still valued at national price levels. For the ICP, economies report their nominal expenditures in local currency units.

PPPs are used to convert these nominal expenditures to real expenditures. Real expenditures are expenditures that are valued at a common price level. They reflect real or actual differences in the volumes purchased in economies and provide the measures required for international comparisons of volume: indexes of real expenditure and indexes of real expenditure per capita. It should be noted that the term "real" has a specific meaning when considering data in PPP terms and throughout this report. Confusion may arise when considering the terms "real" and "nominal" in temporal and spatial contexts. While nominal expenditures, in both contexts, refer to expenditures in current-year prices valued at national price levels and expressed in local currency units or in a common currency using market exchange rates, the term "real expenditures" can take on different meanings in spatial and temporal contexts. In the case of the former—most relevant for this text—real expenditures (or expenditures in real terms) refer to expenditures in current-year prices converted to a common currency and valued at a uniform price level with PPPs. Hence, the meaning of "real expenditures" or "real GDP" throughout this text should not be confused with its meaning in a temporal context, where it is commonly used to describe nominal expenditures or GDP adjusted for inflation.

GDP compared with gross national income

GDP measures the production by producers who reside within an economy's territory. The income generated from such production is distributed mainly to residents of the economy, but some of the income may accrue to nonresidents (such as the interest or dividends that have to be paid abroad or the cost of servicing foreign debt). Similarly, some residents may receive income from nonresidents (such as interest or dividends paid to residents from abroad). For some types of analysis, these income flows can be of interest, which leads to the concept of gross national income (GNI). GNI measures the value of the incomes received by residents. It differs from GDP by the net amount of the income flows between an economy's residents and the residents of other economies.

Actual individual consumption

One aggregate below the level of GDP that has particular significance in ICP comparisons is actual individual consumption (AIC), which measures the individual goods and services that households actually consume as opposed to what they actually purchase. AIC includes the value of what households purchase (that is, individual consumption expenditure of households) plus the value of services they receive from the government and nonprofit institutions serving households (NPISHs), such as charities and nongovernmental organizations. On a per capita basis, AIC is conceptually a better measure of average material well-being than individual consumption expenditure of households alone when material well-being is defined in terms of the goods and services consumed by households to satisfy their individual needs.

AIC is used because in some economies the government or NPISHs provide an important element of household services, such as health or education, and these expenditures are included in the individual consumption expenditure of government or NPISHs. But in other economies, these same services are purchased by households from market producers and are included in the individual consumption expenditure of households. It follows that individual consumption expenditure of households does not capture all goods and services consumed by households in all economies. However, AIC covers all such goods regardless of whether they are purchased by households themselves or are provided as social transfers in kind by the government or NPISHs.

The concept of actual individual consumption dates back to the earliest years of the ICP, when it was called the consumption expenditure of the population. Initially, the individual consumption expenditure by NPISHs was not included. Later, however, the concept was expanded to include the consumption expenditure of NPISHs, and it was adopted by national accountants in the System of National Accounts (SNA) 1993 (UNSC 1993). In the ICP 2017, a separate PPP was calculated for individual consumption expenditure by households and for actual individual consumption. In addition, PPPs belonging to the following analytical categories were calculated on the basis of actual individual consumption: health; education; housing; water, electricity, and other fuels; recreation and culture; and miscellaneous goods and services.

Use and applications of PPPs and real expenditures

Use and limitations of PPPs and real expenditures

As explained in the previous section on concepts and definitions, the major use of PPPs is in making intercountry comparisons of real GDP and its expenditure components. GDP is the aggregate used most frequently to represent the size of an economy and, on a per capita basis, the average income per person in that economy during a given year. Calculating PPPs is the first step in the process of converting the level of GDP and its major aggregates, expressed in local currencies, into a common currency to enable these comparisons to be made.

Anyone comparing economies by the size of their real GDP or their real GDP per capita should do so with caution. Such comparisons require that all of the economies employ the same definition of GDP and that their measurement of GDP be equally exhaustive. Although the first requirement is broadly met because the GDP estimates of most economies participating in ICP 2017 are compiled more or less in line with SNA 2008 (UNSC 2009), the measurement of GDP is not sufficiently uniform over all participants to satisfy the second requirement. In particular, the GDP of participants with large nonobserved economies, such as a large informal sector, could be underestimated. Bearing in mind that there may be errors in the population data in addition to errors in the price and expenditure data, small differences between real GDP and real GDP per capita should not be considered significant.

ICP 2017 includes economies ranging from city-states, such as Singapore, and small islands, such as Grenada, to large and diverse economies, such as Brazil, China, India, the Russian Federation, South Africa, and the United States. Because of wide differences in the price and economic structure of economies and inherent statistical variability in the methods used to calculate PPPs, the following guidelines are recommended for analyses using the 2017 PPPs and real expenditures.

- Comparisons between economies that are similar are more precise than comparisons between economies that are dissimilar. For example, the PPP between Nigeria and South Africa is more precise than the PPP between either economy and Liberia or Zimbabwe. Comparisons between economies in the same region are more precise than comparisons between economies in other regions. For example, the China-India comparison is more precise than the comparison of either to the United States.
- PPPs based on the prices of goods are more precise than PPPs based on the prices of services. Areas such as housing and health care will have wider measures of error than areas such as food.
- PPPs provide the overall price level of an economy, but they do not capture price differences within an economy.

Because of the sampling and statistical errors arising from the calculation methods, differences in real GDP of less than 5 percent should not be considered significant. This margin of error can rise to plus or minus 15 percent for economies that differ widely in their price and economic structures. This margin of error should be kept in mind when using, for example, the PPPs of Brazil, China, India, and the United States to compare these economies not only with each other but also with more disparate economies such as most of those in Africa.

PPPs appear in international trade theory in the context of equilibrium exchange rates (the underlying rates of exchange to which actual market exchange rates are assumed to converge in the long term). But ICP PPPs should not be interpreted as equilibrium exchange rates. They have been calculated specifically to enable international comparisons of prices and real expenditures for GDP. They refer to the entire range of goods and services that make up GDP and include many items that are not traded internationally. Moreover, except for exports and imports, they are valued at domestic market prices, and PPPs for GDP are calculated using expenditure weights that reflect domestic demand. For the same reason, ICP PPPs do not indicate whether a currency is undervalued or overvalued and should not be used for this purpose.

ICP comparisons are designed to compare the volumes of goods and services that enter GDP at specific points in time. They are not designed to measure the relative rates of growth in GDP between these points. Each ICP comparison produces indexes of real GDP that show the relative volume levels of GDP among participating economies for the reference year. When the indexes for consecutive reference years are placed side by side, they appear to provide points in a time series of relative volume levels of GDP over the intervening years. This apparent time series of volume measures is actually a time series of value indexes because the volume indexes for each reference year are calculated using the prices and expenditures for that year. Changes in the volume indexes between reference years are thus due to changes in the relative price levels as well as to changes in the relative volume levels. As a result, the rates of relative growth derived from the indexes are not consistent with those obtained from times series of GDP volumes estimated by the economies themselves. The rates of growth estimated by the economies should be used to determine relative rates of growth in GDP.

The PLIs for individual consumption expenditure by households provide a measure of differences in the cost of living between economies—that is, they indicate whether the overall price level for consumer goods and services faced by the average household in one economy is higher or lower than that faced by the average household in another economy. Even so, people considering moving from one economy to another should not use these PLIs to infer how the change of economy will affect their cost of living. For one thing, PLIs reflect the expenditure pattern of the average household, which in all likelihood is different from that of the person contemplating the move. For another, PLIs are national averages and do not reflect differences in the cost of living between specific locations within an economy.

Global poverty numbers require a large and varied set of inputs from different data sources. Five unique data sources are required for the World Bank's calculation of global poverty numbers: household income and expenditure surveys, population data, national accounts, consumer price indexes, and ICP PPPs for individual consumption expenditures by households. Each new ICP cycle brings revisions of the PPPs, and these revisions, like revisions of the other data sources, can have large effects on global, regional, and national poverty counts stemming from a common international poverty line. ICP PPPs for individual consumption expenditures by households are based on the patterns of aggregate household consumption provided by an economy's national accounts. The use of these PPPs for measuring global poverty has sometimes been criticized on the grounds that people who live at or below the global poverty line have different patterns of consumption than those provided by national accounts aggregates. In particular, they spend a much larger share of their budgets on food, and they spend very little on housing and essentially nothing at all on air travel or on financial services indirectly measured. A second common criticism is that ICP PPPs are compiled based on average prices for the economy as a whole and not on the prices faced by the poor in that economy. In response, some attempts have been made to use the consumption patterns of the poor to calculate poverty-specific PPPs. Most of these studies have concluded that these poverty-specific PPPs are not significantly different from the ICP PPPs for individual consumption expenditures by households. Regarding the prices faced by the poor, if these were systematically different from the average prices in a way that differed from one economy to another—for example, if one of the economies had extensive food subsidies so that the poor pay lower prices—then the PPPs generated by the ICP are less suitable for measuring poverty. However, this approach has not yet been explored in detail, as studying it fully would likely require a separate price collection, parallel to the ICP.

Box 3.2 summarizes the recommended uses of PPPs, the uses of PPPs with limitations, and the instances where the use of PPPs is not recommended.

Main applications of PPPs and real expenditures

PPPs, and the PLIs and real expenditures to which they give rise, are used for research and analysis, for index compilation, for policy making, and for administrative purposes at the global, regional, and national levels.

They are used across a range of themes under the economic, environmental, and social development umbrellas. Users include international bodies such as the World Bank, the International Monetary Fund (IMF), the United Nations and its affiliates, the Organisation for Economic Co-operation and Development (OECD), the European Commission, and regional organizations such as the African Development Bank (AfDB), the Asian Development Bank (ADB), and the Interstate Statistical Committee of the Commonwealth of Independent States (CIS-STAT). Additionally, there has been a rapid growth in their use by the media, with frequent articles mentioning PPPs, by the private sector, and by national governments. Universities and research institutes have long applied PPPs and ICP data in their academic analyses.

Box 3.2 Use of purchasing power parities

Recommended uses

1. To make spatial comparisons of
   - Gross domestic product (GDP): relative size of economies
   - GDP per hour worked: labor productivity
   - GDP per capita: income per capita
   - Actual individual consumption (AIC) per capita: a measure of average material well-being
2. To make spatial comparisons of price levels
3. To group economies by their
   - Volume index of GDP or AIC per capita
   - Price levels of GDP or AIC.

Recommended uses with limitations

1. To analyze changes over time in relative GDP per capita and relative prices
2. To analyze price convergence
3. To make spatial comparisons of the cost of living
4. To use PPPs calculated for GDP and its expenditure components as deflators for other values—as, for example, household income.

Uses not recommended

1. As a precise measure to establish strict rankings of economies
2. As a means of constructing national growth rates
3. As a measure to generate output and productivity comparisons by industry
4. As an indicator of the undervaluation or overvaluation of currencies
5. As an equilibrium exchange rate.

PPPs are used as inputs for economic research and policy analysis that involve comparisons of economies. In this context, PPPs are employed either to generate measures of real expenditure with which to compare the size of economies and their levels of consumption, investment, government expenditure, and overall productivity or to generate price measures with which to compare price levels, price structures, price convergence, and competitiveness.

GDP and GDP per capita measured in PPPs are used in many socioeconomic analyses covering topics such as poverty and shared prosperity, economic growth, trade and competitiveness, sustainable development, human development, health, education, labor productivity and wages, the environment, energy, climate, waste, information and communication technology, and peace and conflict. PPP-converted GDP is used to standardize other economic variables such as carbon emissions per unit of GDP, energy use per unit of GDP, GDP per employee, or GDP per hour worked. Multinational corporations, for example, use PPPs to evaluate the cost of investment in different economies.

The United Nations' 2030 Agenda for Sustainable Development covers many of the topics listed above, and the wide use of PPPs in many of the agenda's goals—the Sustainable Development Goals (SDGs)—reflects the importance and relevance of this indicator for monitoring progress. PPPs are used for monitoring how far the world has come in achieving no poverty (SDG 1); zero hunger (SDG 2); good health and well-being (SDG 3); quality education (SDG 4); affordable and clean energy (SDG 7); decent work and economic growth (SDG 8); better industry, innovation, and infrastructure (SDG 9), and reduced inequalities (SDG 10).

One major use of PPPs is for poverty assessment using the World Bank's international poverty line of $1.90 per day per person, which is used in SDG 1. National poverty assessments differ because the purchasing power of local currency units differs from one economy to another. Therefore, establishing an international poverty line requires equalizing purchasing power over economies. The current international poverty line of $1.90 per day is converted to national price levels by using the ICP 2011 PPPs for individual consumption expenditure by households. Data from household income and expenditure surveys are then used to determine the number of people whose consumption per capita is below this poverty line. The international poverty line itself has typically been calculated as the average of the PPP equivalents of the national poverty lines of some the world's poorest economies, using PPPs for individual consumption expenditure by households. The PPPs thus enter the calculation at two stages: first, in establishing the international poverty line; and second, in calculating the number of people living below it in each economy—the poverty headcount. People living below the $1.90 a day line represent the extreme poor. Other international poverty lines are based on income and consumption levels in lower-middle-income ($3.20) and upper-middle-income ($5.50) economies measured using ICP 2011 PPPs.

SDG 2 focuses on agricultural productivity. PPPs are used to define the revenue of small-scale producers as well as to measure output and individuals' income derived from farming. In SDG 3, target 3.1 seeks to reduce the proportion of mothers who die in childbirth, and the modeled indicator used to monitor this is PPP-converted GDP. Target 3.8 looks at achieving universal health coverage, and analyses exploring this use PPPs to compare out-of-pocket expenditures on health in different countries as well as the number of people pushed below the poverty line by catastrophic expenditures. SDG 4 compares expenditures by both government and households on education using PPPs. SDG 7 tracks energy efficiency by measuring the amount of energy used to produce one dollar's (in PPPs) worth of goods and services. SDG 8 uses PPP-converted GDP per person employed to monitor economic productivity. In SDG 9, target 9.4 monitors progress toward sustainable, efficient, and clean industry and measures carbon dioxide emissions per unit of PPP-converted GDP. Target 9.5 encourages scientific innovation and monitors spending on research and development using PPPs. SDG 10 monitors growth in the income of the poorest citizens and uses PPPs to compare per capita consumption and income for the poorest 40 percent against the national average.

The World Bank's twin goals of ending poverty and boosting shared prosperity mirror SDGs 1 and 10 and thus also rely on PPPs.

Beyond the SDGs, other notable uses include the United Nations Development Programme's Human Development Index, which measures average achievement in three basic dimensions of human development—a long and healthy life, knowledge, and a decent standard of living. The index uses PPPs in income, economy, poverty, and environmental composite measures.

The World Economic Forum's Global Competitiveness Index uses GDP and the value of imports measured using PPPs in its 10th pillar on market size.

The World Bank also uses PPPs to facilitate comparisons of public service pay and wage bill data across countries. Other examples of using PPPs as spatial price deflators include cross-country comparisons of the value of unpaid care work, minimum wages, user revenue for internet providers, the cost of violence and natural disasters, the cost of disease and potential savings through reduced child mortality, and better nutrition and other medical interventions.

PPPs are also used for statistical compilation. International organizations use PPPs to obtain totals and averages for a group of economies such as a region or income group. Real GDP and its components are aggregated across the economies in a group to obtain totals for the group. The shares of economies in these totals are used as weights when economic indicators, such as price indexes or growth rates, are combined to obtain averages for the group. Both the IMF and the OECD use PPP-based GDP and GDP aggregates to provide estimates of regional and world output and growth in their respective publications, *World Economic Outlook* and *Economic Outlook*.

Finally, the European Commission, the IMF, and the World Bank employ PPPs for administrative purposes. The European Commission uses the PPPs of its member states when allocating the structural funds intended to reduce economic disparities between and within member states. The principal indicator influencing the allocation is PPP-deflated intracountry regional GDP per capita. The IMF uses PPP-based GDP from the *World Economic Outlook* in its current quota formula. In the past, this measure often helped to guide increases in members' quotas. Quota subscriptions determine the maximum financial resources that member economies are obliged to provide the IMF, the amount of financing that members can obtain from the IMF, their share in a general allocation of Special Drawing Rights, and their voting power in IMF decisions. PPP-based GDP has a weight of 20 percent in the current quota formula. Similarly, the World Bank Group now incorporates PPPs into its dynamic formula for computing the shareholding rights of the International Bank for Reconstruction and Development member countries, with PPP-based GDP contributing a weight of 40 percent to the economic weight, which in turn provides a weight of 80 percent to the total, the remainder coming from a measure of contributions to the International Development Association.

In addition to these applications of PPPs and other ICP indicators, the data collected by the ICP on prices and expenditures support various analyses by policy makers and researchers from international, regional, and national agencies as well as from academic and research institutions. Examples include analysis of the cost of nutritional food and recommended diets around the world, the cost of living for foreign service staff living overseas, consumption patterns and income elasticities, the effect of prices on the share of expenditure on housing, the price of traditional goods and skill-intensive goods against GDP per capita, trade elasticity, and wage inequality indexes, to name but a few. Hence, the detailed data sets generated by the ICP make an important contribution to the overall value of the program. The ICP Global Office has established a set of rules governing access to unpublished results and underlying data. The resulting data access and archive policy (described in appendix H) meets a long-standing objective of the ICP: that data derived from the ICP should be used to the maximum extent possible for statistical, research, and analytical purposes.

The applications of PPPs and underlying data continue to expand as the limitations of the main alternative method of adjusting values to a common currency using market exchange rates become more widely recognized. As these data and indicators are produced more frequently and for an expanding number of economies, their use is likely to accelerate.

CHAPTER 4

Governance and organization

Governance of ICP 2017

The International Comparison Program (ICP) was established in the late 1960s on the recommendation of the United Nations Statistical Commission (UNSC). It began as a research project carried out jointly by the United Nations Statistical Office (UNSO) and the University of Pennsylvania. It is now a permanent element of the Global Statistical Programme, run under the auspices of the UNSC, supported by a federated governance structure, and coordinated and carried out by implementing agencies at the national, regional, and global levels. To date, nine comparisons have been conducted. The first was in 1970 (covering 10 economies), followed by 1973 (16 economies), 1975 (34 economies), 1980 (60 economies), 1985 (64 economies), 1993 (115 economies), 2005 (146 economies), 2011 (199 economies), and 2017 (176 economies). After the 1975 comparison, the ICP shifted from being a research project to being a regular operational component of the UNSO work program. It was also regionalized, whereby comparisons were organized by region and then combined to obtain a global comparison. Details of the history of the ICP are given in appendix A and on the ICP website.[1]

The UNSC commissioned a major review of the ICP in 1997, before agreeing to further cycles. This review was in response to problems with ICP 1993, in which the regional comparisons could not be combined to produce a global comparison. The findings of the review were reported to the UNSC in 1999. Among the principal shortcomings identified were the lack of a formally defined governance structure and the consequent poor coordination between regions. Methods, processes, and timetables were not uniform across regions; results were not consistent between regions; and there was no blueprint for linking the regional comparisons.

As a result of the review, the World Bank put in place in 2002 a governance structure to ensure that each region produced results consistent with the results of other regions and that each region's results could be combined with the results of other regions in a global comparison. This goal was to be achieved by coordinating the work globally, establishing a single set of standards, providing centralized technical and practical guidance, and ruling on issues that had the potential to be interpreted in different ways in the regions. The structure had several tiers: the UNSC, the Executive/Governing Board, the ICP Global Office, the Technical Advisory Group (TAG), the regional implementing agencies, and the national implementing agencies. This strengthened governance contributed significantly to the successful conclusion of the 2005 and 2011 comparisons and the timely publication of their results.

Figure 4.1 ICP governance structure

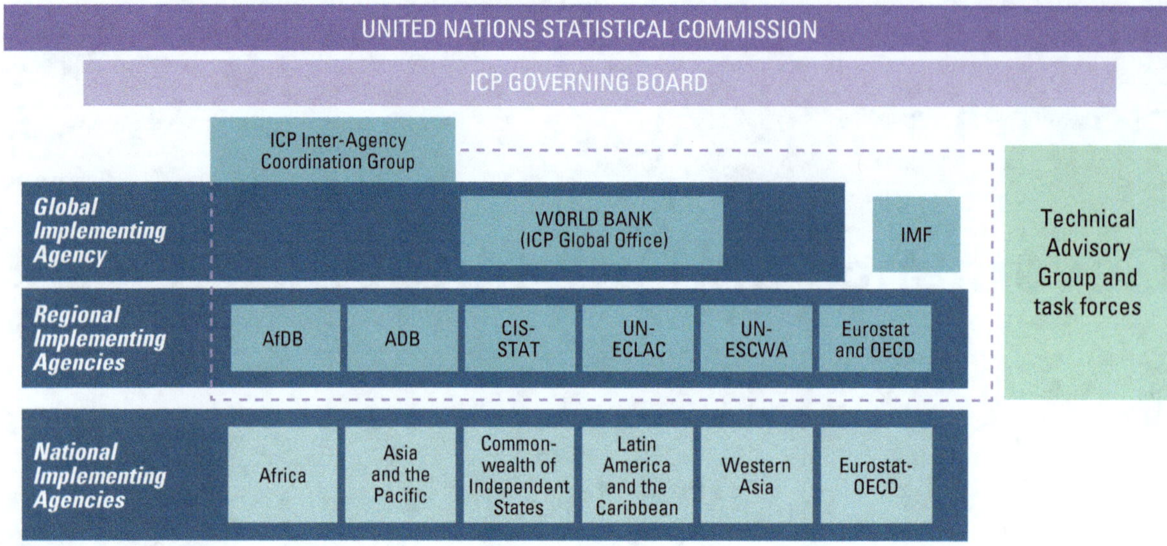

Note: AfDB = African Development Bank; ADB = Asian Development Bank; CIS-STAT = Interstate Statistical Committee of the Commonwealth of Independent States; UN-ECLAC = United Nations Economic Commission for Latin America and the Caribbean; UN-ESCWA = United Nations Economic and Social Commission for Western Asia; Eurostat = Statistical Office of the European Union; OECD = Organisation for Economic Co-operation and Development; IMF = International Monetary Fund.

In November 2016, the ICP Governing Board adopted an updated ICP governance framework. In place for the ICP 2017 cycle, this framework's overall mandate was to ensure that the global, regional, and national efforts to produce reliable purchasing power parity (PPP) estimates and related measures of real expenditures adhere to approved policies, protocols, methodologies, and quality assurance standards, and that the estimates are produced efficiently, in keeping with available resources.

The framework outlines the current governance structure and the roles and responsibilities of the governance bodies. These include the UNSC; the Governing Board; the TAG; the ICP Global Office; the Inter-Agency Coordination Group (IACG), comprising the World Bank, the regional implementing agencies, and the International Monetary Fund (IMF); and the national implementing agencies. Figure 4.1 depicts the ICP governance structure. The governance bodies meet periodically to discuss issues and move the program forward. Details of their activities are available on the ICP website.[2] More details on the governance framework and its bodies are given in appendix B.

Regional and national organization

To calculate PPPs, the ICP conducts worldwide surveys at regular intervals to collect comparable price and expenditure data for the whole range of final goods and services that make up the final expenditure on GDP: consumer goods and services, government services, and capital goods. While the ICP global comparison is coordinated through the Global Office at the World Bank, the surveys are carried out by national implementing agencies, such as the national statistical office, and overseen by a regional implementing agency. The intention is to produce regional comparisons that can be combined into a single global comparison for a given reference year.

Conducting the surveys on a regional basis ensures that the items to be priced are more homogeneous within regions, expenditure patterns are likely to be similar, and language obstacles are reduced. In addition, there are operational advantages in having the ICP carried out by regional agencies that are in relatively close proximity to the economies they are coordinating. In 2017 the six regional programs were as follows[3]: Africa region, coordinated by the African Development Bank (AfDB); Asia and the Pacific region, overseen by the Asian Development Bank (ADB); the Commonwealth of Independent States region, run by the Interstate Statistical Committee of the Commonwealth of Independent States (CIS-STAT); Latin America and the Caribbean region, overseen by the United Nations Economic Commission for Latin America and the Caribbean (UN-ECLAC) with support from the Caribbean Community (CARICOM); and Western Asia region, coordinated by the United Nations Economic and Social Commission for Western Asia (UN-ESCWA). Member states and associated economies of the European Union and the Organisation for Economic Co-operation and Development (OECD) are covered by the Eurostat-OECD PPP Programme. Georgia and Ukraine were included in the Eurostat-OECD PPP Programme as special participants. The Islamic Republic of Iran was also included as a special participant in the global exercise, linked through the Western Asia region. Uzbekistan participated on a limited and experimental basis within the Commonwealth of Independent States region. Box 4.1 lists all participating economies by region for the 2017 cycle.

Box 4.1 ICP 2017 cycle: Participating economies, by region

Africa: 50 economies
Regional implementing agency: African Development Bank (AfDB)
Algeria; Angola; Benin; Botswana; Burkina Faso; Burundi; Cameroon; Cabo Verde; Central African Republic; Chad; the Comoros; the Republic of Congo; the Democratic Republic of Congo; Côte d'Ivoire; Djibouti; Arab Republic of Egypt;[a] Equatorial Guinea; Eswatini; Ethiopia; Gabon; The Gambia; Ghana; Guinea; Guinea-Bissau; Kenya; Lesotho; Liberia; Madagascar; Malawi; Mali; Mauritania; Mauritius; Morocco;[a] Mozambique; Namibia; Niger; Nigeria; Rwanda; São Tomé and Príncipe; Senegal; the Seychelles; Sierra Leone; South Africa; Sudan;[a] Tanzania; Togo; Tunisia; Uganda; Zambia; Zimbabwe

Asia and the Pacific: 22 economies
Regional implementing agency: Asian Development Bank (ADB)
Bangladesh; Bhutan; Brunei Darussalam; Cambodia; China; Fiji; Hong Kong SAR, China; India; Indonesia; Lao People's Democratic Republic; Malaysia; the Maldives; Mongolia; Myanmar; Nepal; Pakistan; the Philippines; Singapore; Sri Lanka; Taiwan, China; Thailand; Vietnam

Commonwealth of Independent States: 8 economies
Regional implementing agency: Interstate Statistical Committee of the Commonwealth of Independent States (CIS-STAT)
Armenia; Azerbaijan; Belarus; Kazakhstan; Kyrgyz Republic; Moldova; Russian Federation;[a] Tajikistan

Latin America and the Caribbean: 36 economies
Regional implementing agency: United Nations Economic Commission for Latin America and the Caribbean (UN-ECLAC)
Argentina; Bolivia; Brazil; Dominican Republic; Ecuador; El Salvador; Guyana; Haiti; Honduras; Nicaragua; Panama; Paraguay; Peru; and Uruguay. Anguilla; Antigua and

(continued)

Box 4.1 ***(Continued)***

Barbuda; Aruba; The Bahamas; Barbados; Belize; Bermuda; Bonaire; Cayman Islands; Curaçao; Dominica; Grenada; Jamaica; Montserrat; St. Kitts and Nevis; St. Lucia; St. Vincent and the Grenadines; Sint Maarten; Suriname; Trinidad and Tobago; Turks and Caicos Islands; British Virgin Islands

Western Asia: 12 economies
Regional implementing agency: United Nations Economic and Social Commission for Western Asia (UN-ESCWA)
Bahrain; Arab Republic of Egypt;[a] Iraq; Jordan; Kuwait; Morocco;[a] Oman; Qatar; Saudi Arabia; Sudan;[a] United Arab Emirates; West Bank and Gaza

Europe and Organisation for Economic Co-operation and Development (OECD): 49 economies
Implementing agencies: Eurostat and OECD
Albania; Australia; Austria; Belgium; Bosnia and Herzegovina; Bulgaria; Canada; Chile; Colombia; Costa Rica; Croatia; Cyprus; Czech Republic; Denmark; Estonia; Finland; France; Germany; Greece; Hungary; Iceland; Ireland; Israel; Italy; Japan; the Republic of Korea; Latvia; Lithuania; Luxembourg; Malta; Mexico; Montenegro; the Netherlands; New Zealand; North Macedonia; Norway; Poland; Portugal; Romania; the Russian Federation;[a] Serbia; Slovak Republic; Slovenia; Spain; Sweden; Switzerland; Turkey; United Kingdom; United States

Special participation: 3 economies
Georgia; the Islamic Republic of Iran; Ukraine

a. Dual-participation economies.

Notes

1. See icp.worldbank.org/programs/icp#2.
2. See icp.worldbank.org/programs/icp#3.
3. See icp.worldbank.org/programs/icp#4.

CHAPTER 5

Methodology

The International Comparison Program (ICP) is a complex international statistical exercise, and its methodology has evolved over several decades.

The 2011 cycle of the ICP introduced several major methodological innovations, including a new approach for combining regional results into a global set of results, a simplified approach for comparing the construction and civil engineering component of gross domestic product (GDP), a wider application of productivity adjustment to government labor, and the implementation of enhanced data quality assurance and computation procedures. The 2017 cycle maintained the same methods and procedures applied in the 2011 cycle, further strengthened data quality assurance approaches using the latest technology, and introduced a fully documented and more transparent process for producing results.

Overall, the ICP methodology has three major components. The first is the System of National Accounts (SNA) definition of final expenditures on GDP. The second is the basket of goods and services from which items are selected for pricing: these items should be comparable across economies and should represent an important part of each economy's final purchases. The national annual average prices or related data collected for these goods and services must be consistent with the underlying values in the national accounts. The third component is the methodology used to compute purchasing power parities (PPPs), first within regions for the regional comparisons and then across regions for the global comparison.

Each ICP comparison has a reference year, such as 2005, 2011, and 2017. Each participating economy provides the following required data for the reference year: a set of prices for a selection of items chosen from a common basket of precisely defined goods and services, a detailed breakdown of the national accounts expenditures in local currency units, according to a common classification, the economy's market exchange rates, and its resident population. The prices and expenditures are used to calculate PPPs and real expenditures (or volumes—that is, PPP-converted expenditures); the market exchange rates and PPPs are used to calculate price level indexes; and the population totals and real expenditures are used to calculate real expenditures per capita. Prices and expenditures are reported by participating economies in their local currencies. Both cover the whole range of final goods and services constituting the GDP.

The ICP methodology is documented in *Measuring the Real Size of the World Economy: The Framework, Methodology, and Results of the International Comparison Program* (World Bank 2013); in *Operational Guidelines and Procedures for Measuring the Real Size of the World Economy* (World Bank 2015); and on the ICP website.[1] A brief overview of the ICP's conceptual framework, data requirements, and PPP computation methodology follows.

Conceptual framework

The conceptual framework for an ICP comparison is determined by the definition of GDP. The ICP 2017 cycle adopted the internationally agreed-on definition of GDP provided by SNA 2008 as its framework for the common ICP expenditure classification.[2] The previous 2005 and 2011 cycles used the definition of GDP provided by SNA 1993.[3]

The SNA defines GDP from the expenditure side as the sum of expenditures on final consumption, gross capital formation, and net exports. Final consumption is the total expenditure on the goods and services consumed by individual households or the community to satisfy their individual or collective needs. Gross capital formation is the total expenditure on gross fixed capital formation, changes in inventories, and acquisitions less disposals of valuables. Net exports are the difference between the value of goods and services exported and the value of goods and services imported. ICP comparisons are based largely on PPPs calculated using prices collected for the expenditure components of final consumption and gross fixed capital formation. Prices are not collected for changes in inventories, the acquisition and disposal of valuables, or net exports because they are deflated using reference PPPs.

Expenditure data

The data on national expenditures in local currency provided by the participating economies are essential to the ICP comparison. First, they are used as weights to aggregate PPPs through the various levels of aggregation up to GDP. Second, they are ultimately deflated by the PPPs and expressed as real expenditures.

Expenditure data compilation

Economies are expected to estimate their GDP for the reference year in line with SNA 2008 and to disaggregate this GDP estimate into the relevant expenditure components identified in the ICP expenditure classification.

At the lowest level of the classification, the expenditure components are termed *basic headings*. The classification breaks down the expenditure on final goods and services into 155 basic headings that comply with the functional and product classifications of SNA 2008 and are the building blocks of the ICP comparison. They are the level at which expenditures are defined and estimated, items are selected for pricing, and prices are collected. Basic headings are the level at which PPPs are first calculated.

In principle, a basic heading consists of a group of similar well-defined goods or services. In practice, a basic heading is defined by the lowest level of final expenditure for which the participating economies can estimate explicit expenditures. Consequently, basic headings can cover a broader range of goods or services than is theoretically desirable.

Expenditure data validation

National accounts data validation requires three stages: first, intracountry validation carried out by the individual participating economies; second, intercountry validation carried out at the regional level; and third, interregional validation carried out at the global level.

Before the national accounts expenditure data are sent to the regional offices, basic edits are carried out by the national implementing agencies. These include:

- Ensuring SNA compliance, including data completeness, applicability of positive and negative values, and additivity
- Ensuring the correct estimation of financial intermediation services indirectly measured (FISIM), net purchases abroad, and nonprofit institutions serving households (NPISHs).

Furthermore, an economic plausibility assessment, such as verifying per capita basic-heading expenditures and basic-heading shares of GDP, is also advised.

The validation edits carried out at the national level are repeated at the regional level. The aim of the regional validation is to compare the consistency of data from similar economies within a region. The regional implementing agency identifies clusters of economies based on their economic similarities. GDP per capita in previous years serves as a key indicator of the cluster to which an economy is allocated.

The global comparison of real expenditures (and their per capita equivalents) is achieved by linking regional results to form a global set of results. At the global level, the same intracountry validation processes as previously defined are followed. The intercountry validation process is also followed across economies and within and between regions.

Price data

Economies participating in the ICP collect prices for a selection of the goods and services that make up final consumption expenditure and gross capital formation. There are four main surveys:

- Household consumption
- Government consumption
- Machinery and equipment
- Construction and civil engineering.

The household consumption survey covers the largest expenditure share, accounting for more than 60 percent of GDP in the majority of economies. It includes a wide assortment of goods and services purchased by households for individual consumption. This survey also includes two additional surveys that are treated separately due to different data requirements; these are the private education and housing surveys.

The government consumption survey compiles administrative or survey data on the compensation of public employees in a variety of collective services, public health services, and public education services. This selection of government occupations represents the various education and skills levels that are commonly found among employees working in these three government sectors.

The machinery and equipment survey is based on a list of industrial, transportation, and electronic items commonly used in a variety of industries for the production of goods and services. The items on this list are often paired as brand specific and not brand specific—that is, generic—items with the same characteristics.

The construction and civil engineering survey is based on a list of common resources for construction work, including materials, equipment hire rates, and labor costs. In addition, respondents are required to provide information on resource mixes, typical markups, and professional fees.

For each of these surveys there is a global core list (GCL) of items, prepared in consultation with regional and national implementing agencies and based on previous ICP cycles to maintain temporal comparability. In addition, each region develops its own list of regional items for the regional comparison, which includes region-specific items representative of the consumption pattern in the region, as well as GCL items needed to facilitate linking the regional results to form a global set of results.

All prices reported are national annual average prices, in local currency, for the reference year—that is, they should be the average of the prices collected at regular intervals throughout the year. When price surveys are conducted outside the reference year, prices are retropolated or extrapolated based on consumer price index (CPI) data.

Household consumption

Household consumption survey

This main survey collects prices for a wide range of goods and services for household consumption such as food, beverages, tobacco, clothing, footwear, utilities, furniture, household appliances, pharmaceuticals, private health care services, motor vehicles, transportation services, electronic equipment, communication services, catering services, accommodation services, recreational activities, personal hygiene, and other goods and services. For this survey, each economy classifies the items priced as important or less important for the consumption patterns of its inhabitants.

Private education survey

This survey collects annual tuition prices for private education institutions at the primary, secondary, and tertiary levels as well as other education services, such as foreign language and private tutoring. The private education survey was not conducted by the Eurostat–Organisation for Economic Co-operation and Development (OECD) PPP Programme, which instead follows an output approach for total education.

Housing survey and related data

This survey collects annual rental prices or dwelling stock data for housing services. Four basic headings within the ICP expenditure classification require data on rentals:

- Actual rentals for housing
- Imputed rentals for housing
- Housing under individual consumption expenditures by NPISHs
- Housing under individual consumption expenditures by government.

Since these last two basic headings use reference PPPs derived from the first two basic headings listed, it is sufficient to focus on how to compute PPPs for actual and imputed rentals. Actual rents are the rents that tenants pay to the owner of the dwelling they are leasing. Imputed rents are estimates of the rents that owner-occupiers would have to pay for their dwelling were they renting rather than owning the dwelling. The SNA requires that households' housing expenditures include both the actual expenditure on rents and an estimate of the rent that the owners would have to pay if they were obliged to rent (imputed rents).

The PPPs for housing services can be calculated either directly, using the rental (price) approach, or indirectly, using the dwelling stock (volume) approach. The survey was designed to collect data for both approaches.

Under the rental approach, rental prices are collected for similar dwelling types in each economy. This method has been found to work well in economies in which the dwellings actually rented are representative of the stock of dwellings as a whole and where statistical agencies collect information on rents paid for the different kinds of dwellings that are rented in most parts of the economy.

Under the dwelling stock approach, it is necessary to calculate both a measure of relative quantity and a measure of relative quality of housing services. The quality measure is used to adjust the quantity measure when converting it into a real expenditure (volume) measure. Therefore, for the dwelling stock approach, the housing survey collects data on both the quantity and quality of the dwelling stock.

Government consumption

This survey collects prices for the compensation of government employees, which comprises the basic salary or wage, allowances and cash payments over and above the basic salary or wage, income in kind, and the employer's actual and imputed social security contribution. The sources of the data reported are the administrative government pay scales for each of the selected occupations or dedicated surveys on the compensation of government employees. The GCL defines these occupations using job descriptions taken from the International Labour Organization's International Standard Classification of Occupations 2008.

Gross fixed capital formation

Machinery and equipment

This survey collects prices for machinery and equipment typically used in a variety of industries. The GCL includes one item identified by brand and model and another generic item with the exact same characteristics, but not identified by brand and model. For consistency with national accounts, prices for equipment goods that are consistent with the valuation of those goods as fixed capital assets in the national accounts are required. Thus the prices must include the import duties and other taxes actually paid by the purchaser, the costs of transporting the asset to the place where it will be used, and any charges for installing the asset so that it will be ready for use in production. Deducted from the price are the discounts generally available to most purchasers.

Construction and civil engineering

This survey collects prices for inputs to construction work, including materials, equipment hire, and labor. The prices provided are those paid by construction contractors to their suppliers. For materials, these are typically the prices paid, after discounts, to manufacturers or intermediaries (agents or merchants), including all nonrecoverable taxes and excluding all recoverable taxes such as a value added tax. For equipment, prices are the rental charges paid to hire companies or internal hire rates. For labor, these reflect the cost to the contractor of employing workers. In addition, resource weights for each input component (materials, equipment hire, labor) for typical residential, nonresidential, and civil engineering projects are collected.

Price data validation

Validation procedures are an iterative process carried out at the national, regional, and global levels to ensure data quality and comparability across all participating economies.

The validation process comprises three distinct stages. The first is the intracountry or national validation stage, during which the prices collected by a single economy are edited and verified. The second is the intercountry or regional validation stage, during which the prices collected by all economies participating in a regional comparison are edited and verified. The third is the interregional, or global, validation stage, during which the prices that have been collected for global core items from the GCL and have already been edited and verified within regions during the intercountry validation are edited and verified across all economies and all regions.

This process is repeated over several rounds, since changes and revisions to price data from one economy impact the PPPs calculated for all other economies. Once errors are found and corrected, overall results need to be recalculated and a new validation round begins. The new results, once cleared of major errors, may reveal mistakes that were not previously detected. This process repeats itself until the final price data are deemed reliable.

It should be stressed that validation procedures are complementary to good survey practices. Data quality depends to a large extent on the design and management of each price survey. Price collections must be planned carefully, carried out efficiently, and supervised properly. Item specifications must be sufficiently detailed to enable price collectors to identify items unambiguously in the outlets they visit. Any difficulties arising with each price survey should be documented and reflected in the design and conduct of future surveys.

PPP calculation and estimation

In general, price relatives are first computed at the individual item level within each basic heading for each pair of economies being compared. Suppose three economies—A, B, and C—price two kinds of rice under the rice basic heading. For each kind of rice, there are three price relatives: P_B/P_A, P_C/P_A, and P_C/P_B. The basic-heading PPP for each pair of economies can be computed directly by taking the geometric mean of the price relatives between them for the two kinds of rice. This is a bilateral comparison. The PPP between economies B and A can be computed indirectly: $PPP_{C/A} \times PPP_{B/C} = PPP_{B/A}$. The use of both direct and indirect PPPs is a multilateral comparison. This means that the PPPs between any two economies are affected by their respective PPPs with other economies in the comparison. As a result, a change in the mix of economies included in the comparison will also change the PPPs between any two economies.

Different methods can be used to compute multilateral PPPs. The choice of method is based on two basic properties: transitivity and base country invariance. PPPs are transitive when the PPP between any two economies is the same whether it is computed directly or indirectly through a third economy. PPPs are base country invariant if the PPP between any two economies is the same regardless of the choice of base economy. These properties apply for every computational step: computing basic-heading PPPs between economies, aggregating basic-heading PPPs to the within-region GDP PPPs, linking PPPs across regions, and finally computing global PPPs.

Another property underlying the computational steps to obtain PPPs is that economies are treated equally regardless of the size of their GDP. Weights based on basic-heading expenditures are used in the methodology to weight a group of basic headings to an aggregate level. Therefore, PPPs are first weighted using economy A's weights (Laspeyres index) and then weighted again using economy B's weights (Paasche index). Each index provides a weighted average of the PPP between economy A and economy B. To maintain symmetry, the geometric mean is taken of the two aggregated PPPs for every pair of economies in the comparison. The result is the Fisher index. For each pair of economies, the multilateral PPP is the geometric mean of the direct and indirect Fisher indexes.

This method, however, does not satisfy the additivity requirement. Additivity occurs when the sum of the real expenditures of the basic headings constituting an aggregate equals the real expenditures based on the PPPs for the aggregate. Additive methods have the disadvantage of giving more weight to the relative prices of the larger, more developed economies. As a result, the real expenditures of poor economies become artificially larger and move closer to the real expenditures of rich economies. This is known as the Gerschenkron effect. For the uses of ICP PPPs, such as for poverty analysis, nonadditive methods that avoid the Gerschenkron effect are preferred.

Fixity is yet another concept that determines the methods used. The fixity concept means that the relative volume—the ratio of real expenditures—between any pair of economies in a region remains the same after the regional results have been combined into a set of global results including all economies.

PPP estimation at the basic-heading level

The PPP estimation process begins with the participating economies collecting prices for items chosen from a common list of precisely defined items. These common lists include both regional items, priced in a specific region, as well as global core items as set out in the GCL, priced in all ICP regions. These two sets of prices cover the whole range of final goods and services included in GDP: household consumption expenditures, government consumption expenditures, and gross capital formation expenditures.

Two basic methods are used in the ICP to calculate basic-heading PPPs. The first approach is based on the Jevons index made transitive by the Gini-Éltető-Köves-Szulc (GEKS) method, which transforms bilateral PPPs into multilateral PPPs. The other method uses a regression model known as the country product dummy (CPD) method, which directly estimates PPPs that are transitive and base-country invariant in one step. The results obtained by both methods are the same if every economy prices every item.

Both methods can be modified to include weighting at the item level. As there are no expenditure weights below the basic-heading level, participating economies are asked to use their expert judgment to determine which items would have the largest expenditure shares within each basic heading. For instance, if basmati rice is deemed to be important within the rice basic heading, then basmati rice will have a higher weight in the PPP calculation for that economy. This weighting at the item level is only applied in the household consumption survey. The modified methods are simply known as GEKS* and weighted CPD (CPD-W). However, the results provided by the two methods differ. This is because these methods provide different results in their unweighted form, and in addition the GEKS* method assigns a weight of 1 to the most important items and a weight of zero to the least important items, while the CPD-W method assigns weights of 3 and 1, respectively.

Reference PPPs

For some basic headings, expenditure data exist, but price collection is considered too expensive or time-consuming or the price data are unreliable. For these basic headings, reference PPPs are used, and they can be categorized as follows:

- Price-based reference PPPs, specific or neutral
- Market exchange rate reference PPPs.

Price-based reference PPPs form the majority of all reference PPPs used. They are based on the PPPs of other basic headings for which prices were collected. These PPPs are referred to as *specific* reference PPPs. They may be the PPPs for a single basic heading or an average of the PPPs for several basic headings. In the latter case, they will be GEKS averages of the selected PPPs weighted by expenditure shares. In other cases, reference PPPs are the PPPs of a large group of basic headings, such as all the basic headings under gross capital formation for which prices have been collected. In this case, the purpose is to ensure that the use of a reference PPP will not change the PPP for that larger group. These are referred to as *neutral* reference PPPs because the intention is for them to have no impact on the PPPs of the larger group of basic headings.

Market exchange rate reference PPPs are used for the following four basic headings: net purchases abroad, acquisitions less disposals of valuables, exports of goods and services, and imports of goods and services. For the calculation of PPPs for exports and imports, it would be prohibitively expensive to collect prices in the same manner as for other items of final expenditure, and the use of market exchange rates can be justified on practical grounds. For net purchases abroad, however, there may be better alternatives to the use of market exchange rates. A full list of reference PPPs is provided in appendix D.

PPP aggregation above the basic headings

Once PPPs are computed for each basic heading for all participating economies within a region, they are used as inputs for the higher levels of aggregation using the GEKS method. This method consists of two steps:

- *Step 1.* Aggregate the basic-heading PPPs using the national accounts expenditure structures to obtain the bilateral PPPs for each pair of economies. Usually Fisher-type PPPs will be used, which require calculating both Paasche-type and Laspeyres-type PPPs. The Fisher-type binary PPPs will simply be the geometric mean of the Laspeyres-type and Paasche-type PPPs.
- *Step 2.* Average the Fisher-type PPPs obtained to arrive at the final vector of GEKS PPPs. The GEKS calculations are performed separately for each aggregation level and for each category within a given aggregation level.

It is important to note that the GEKS method is not additive. Additivity occurs when the sum of the real expenditures of the basic headings constituting an aggregate equals the real expenditures based on the PPPs for the aggregate. While this property may be desirable for some uses, additive methods have the disadvantage of giving more weight to the relative prices of high-income economies. As a result, the real expenditures of low-income economies become artificially larger and move closer to the real expenditures of high-income economies, per the Gerschenkron effect.

Calculation of global PPPs

Standard linking approach

At the global level, regional PPPs are linked to form a global set of PPPs and measures of price and volume relatives. In order to link the regional basic-heading PPPs for each participating economy, the so-called interregional linking factors are calculated based on the prices of global items from the GCL collected in all ICP regions.

The GEKS aggregation method, with further redistribution of regional volumes in accordance with an economy's regional volume shares (known as the country aggregation with redistribution [CAR] procedure), is used to obtain real expenditures (hereafter referred to as volumes) and aggregated PPPs with regional fixity. All economies in the standard ICP regions participated simultaneously and equally in the global aggregation using the GEKS method.

Linking at the basic-heading level involves the following four steps:

- *Step A1.* Calculate the regional basic-heading PPPs based on both the regional and GCL items. The regional basic-heading PPPs must follow the ICP classification in appendix C.
- *Step A2.* Convert all GCL item prices in local currency to a common regional currency by using the regional basic-heading PPPs from step A1.
- *Step A3.* Calculate the interregional linking factors by applying the CPD-W method to the GCL item prices from step A2.[4]
- *Step A4.* Multiply each economy's regional basic-heading PPP from step 1 by the interregional linking factor resulting from step A3. The PPPs derived from this step are the global basic-heading PPPs with regional fixity.

Linking at the above, the basic-heading level involves the following six steps:

- *Step B1.* Calculate the regional PPPs by applying the GEKS aggregation to the regional basic-heading PPPs from step A1 and the national accounts basic-heading expenditures in local currency units for each level of aggregation up to GDP.

- *Step B2.* Obtain an economy's volume shares in the regional results for each level of aggregation up to GDP using data from step B1.
- *Step B3.* Calculate an economy's aggregated PPPs in the global comparison by applying the unrestricted GEKS aggregation to the global basic-heading PPPs derived from step A4 and the national accounts basic-heading expenditures in local currency for each level of aggregation up to GDP.
- *Step B4.* Obtain the regional volume totals in the global comparison by summing up the total volumes for individual economies for each region derived from step B3 for each level of aggregation up to GDP.
- *Step B5.* Distribute the regional volume totals from step B4 among the economies in the regions according to the economy shares in the regional results derived from step B2 in order to uphold regional fixity for each level of aggregation up to GDP.
- *Step B6.* Calculate the aggregated global PPPs indirectly by dividing the economies' nominal expenditures by the volumes derived from step B5 for each level of aggregation up to GDP.

The resulting linked global PPPs maintain the fixity of the regional results.

Nonstandard linking approaches

While the standard linking approach is applicable to most household consumption basic headings for all regions, other basic headings require different approaches due to the specific nature of their surveys.

Housing

All economies participating in ICP 2017 were asked to collect annual average rents for a global list of dwelling types, as well as dwelling stock data: number of dwellings, usable surface area in square meters, and information on three quality indicators—availability of electricity, water supply, and an in-house toilet. National accounts expenditure data on actual and imputed rentals were collected by means of expenditure questionnaires. However, not all economies were able to report rents and dwelling stock data, and some economies were only able to provide rents for a limited subset of dwelling types or limited dwelling stock data. Each regional coordinating agency decided on the best way to use the collected data for its region.

Rental data were used to link the Africa, Latin America and the Caribbean, and Western Asia regions. The linking factors for these three regions were calculated using the CPD method. The Asia and the Pacific and the Eurostat-OECD regions were linked to each other and to the rest of the world using the dwelling stock approach.

Government compensation

The ICP approach for estimating PPPs for government services is based on an input approach in which compensation data for selected government occupations are collected across economies. Given the differences in productivity, adjustment factors are applied to account for differences in capital per worker. These adjustment factors are based on differences in countrywide levels of capital per worker and their estimated contribution to output using the aggregate share of capital income in GDP from the Penn World Tables.[5]

Adjustments were made to the PPPs for government in the Africa, Asia and the Pacific, Latin America and the Caribbean, and Western Asia regions. No productivity adjustments were applied to the Eurostat-OECD and Commonwealth of Independent States (CIS) regions because differences in labor productivity within each of those regions were considered to be relatively low. However, productivity adjustments were made to all regions when the interregional linking factors were estimated to maintain consistency in the global comparison.

Education and health

For education and health, Eurostat-OECD followed an output approach to calculating their PPPs; thus it was necessary to link their PPPs to those of other ICP regions that follow the input approach to calculating their PPPs for health and education.

For education, since Eurostat-OECD does not collect expenditure weights at the basic-heading level, a simplified weighting system was used, based on information on education expenditure structures in the OECD–United Nations Educational, Scientific, and Cultural Organization (UNESCO) database. Data on average compensation of employees in education in Eurostat-OECD economies were used to bridge their output-based PPPs to those of other ICP regions that follow the input approach.

For health, since Eurostat-OECD does not collect expenditure weights at the basic-heading level, the System of Health Accounts (SHA) was used, as it offers a breakdown with a significant overlap with basic headings in the ICP. For comparison purposes, it was necessary to combine the basic headings for household, NPISHs, and government consumption for other ICP regions because the SHA does not distinguish between these different types of expenditures.

Construction and civil engineering

The standard regional approach for estimating construction and civil engineering PPPs covered four steps:

- Input prices collected for materials, labor, and hire of equipment were allocated to the three construction basic headings (residential buildings, nonresidential buildings, and civil engineering works).
- PPPs for the input groups (materials, equipment hire, and labor) were calculated using the CPD method, resulting in nine sets of input-group PPPs.
- The input-group PPPs were aggregated using resource mixes as weights, resulting in three sets of basic-heading PPPs.
- PPPs for the three basic headings were aggregated using national accounts expenditure data as weights, resulting in PPPs for the construction category.

The Eurostat-OECD approach to estimating construction and civil engineering PPPs differs from the ICP approach, and thus several economies in the Eurostat-OECD comparison conducted the ICP survey in tandem, which provided a link for construction between the Eurostat-OECD economies and the rest of the world. A modified approach was used for linking, in which regional PPPs were not used to convert construction item prices in local currency.

Special linking cases

In tandem with the calculation of global results, special linking cases included the linking of CIS results with Eurostat-OECD results, the linking of Caribbean economies with Latin American economies, the treatment of dual-participation economies in the Africa and Western Asia regions, and the inclusion of the special participation economies Georgia, the Islamic Republic of Iran, and Ukraine.

Linking CIS with Eurostat-OECD

The Russian Federation participates in both the CIS and the Eurostat-OECD comparison, and the CIS economies were linked with the Eurostat-OECD results using Russia's data at the basic-heading level. At the aggregated level, however, the CIS economies were linked through a multilateral procedure that used data from all participating economies to link the CIS with Eurostat-OECD.

Linking the Caribbean with Latin America

The method used to link the Caribbean economies with Latin America included three steps. First, PPPs were produced for the full set of Latin American and Caribbean economies. Second, separate subregional PPP aggregations were carried out, one for the Latin American economies and another for the Caribbean economies. As a third and final step, the PPPs in the first step were reindexed in accordance with results from the second step, in order to maintain fixity of both Latin American and Caribbean PPPs.

Linking dual-participation and single economies

The Arab Republic of Egypt, Morocco, and Sudan participated in both the Africa and Western Asia comparisons. Published global PPPs for these economies are geometric means of their respective global PPPs in the Africa and Western Asia comparisons. Russia participated in the CIS and Eurostat-OECD comparisons, but only the Eurostat-OECD results for Russia are published.

The single economies, Georgia and Ukraine, were included as guest participants in the Eurostat-OECD comparison and followed the Eurostat-OECD methodology, while the Islamic Republic of Iran was linked through the Western Asia comparison.

PPPs for nonparticipating economies

In the 2017 cycle, 176 economies participated in the ICP. Other economies did not participate in the comparison for a variety of reasons, including civil unrest, lack of resources, or lack of capacity. Although these nonparticipating economies account for a small share of the world economy and world population, it is important that they be included in any comprehensive measurement of the size of the world economy or of global poverty.

The method used for imputing PPPs for nonparticipating economies uses two regression models, one based on the price level index (PLI) for GDP and the other based on the PLI for individual consumption expenditure by households, including NPISHs. The two regressions are estimated jointly using the "seemingly unrelated regression" method. The required explanatory variables are the following: GDP per capita in US dollars based on market exchange rates, imports as a share of GDP, exports as a share of GDP, and the age dependency ratio. Dummy variables are required for the Sub-Saharan African economies, the Eurostat-OECD PPP Programme participants, island economies, and landlocked economies. Interaction terms of GDP per capita in US dollars based on market exchange rates and the dummy variables are also required.

Interpolated annual PPPs

For the years between reference years 2011 and 2017—namely, 2012 to 2016—PPPs were calculated based on an approach in which basic-heading PPPs were first interpolated between the reference years and subsequently aggregated using the standard GEKS method. In addition, regional PPPs between the reference years, where available,[6] were incorporated using the CAR procedure. The resulting annual PPPs uphold the same properties of base-country invariance and fixity as the PPPs from reference year comparisons.[7]

The data required to construct annual PPPs included global PPPs for the two reference years; regional PPPs between the reference years, where available; national accounts deflators and consumer price indexes; national accounts expenditures at current prices in local currency units; market exchange rates; and population.

Notes

1. See icp.worldbank.org/programs/icp#6.
2. See https://unstats.un.org/unsd/nationalaccount/docs/SNA2008.pdf.
3. See https://unstats.un.org/unsd/nationalaccount/docs/1993sna.pdf.
4. CPD is used for selected basic headings under household consumption (housing and education) and for all nonhousehold consumption expenditure components.
5. The Penn World Tables are a data set of National Accounts developed and maintained by the University of California, Davis, and the University of Groningen to measure GDP across economies from 1950 to 2017.
6. Regional PPPs between the reference-year comparisons were available as follows: CIS (2014), Eurostat-OECD (2012–16), and Western Asia (2012–16).
7. For further details on the approach to constructing annual PPPs, see Inklaar and Rao (2020).

CHAPTER 6

Looking forward

As we release the results of the 2017 cycle of the ICP, the world is in crisis battling the COVID-19 pandemic. In addition to its principal costs to human life and health, countries across the globe face considerable economic costs that will influence the size and distribution of the global economy in 2020 and beyond. Our response to this pandemic will transform the way we collect, process, and analyze data and information over the next decade, and timely and reliable economic data will be critical and instrumental to how policy makers, economists, statisticians, data scientists, and the wider development community come together to assess the outcomes and aftermath of this global crisis.

The International Comparison Program (ICP) will evolve and respond to this changing world as it launches its 2021 cycle.[1] This cycle will be implemented following the established ICP methodology, while incorporating updates to item lists to reflect consumption patterns in 2021.

For the ICP to accurately reflect prices and expenditures prevalent in its participating economies and to produce high-quality, timely results, the program needs to embrace the advance of new technologies, both in how the program collects its data and in what items it prices. In terms of the former, scanner data collected directly from the retailer's own records will provide point-of-sale prices and accurate metadata. Additionally, web scraping of prices will help to collect data on hard-to-price items and the latest consumer trends, such as consumer electronics, clothing, flights, hotel rates, and housing rents items. Crowdsourcing, whereby contributors provide price data via an app, could lead to more granular prices being gathered and facilitate pricing items for sale in noncentral and rural locations. Data from administrative records could be extended beyond the current collection of government compensation data to encompass the price of public utilities and public transport, among others. Machine learning could be used to analyze item specifications and item lists and to recognize, classify, and tag items through imaging.

With regard to the basket of goods and services that the ICP prices, the program will need to react quickly to changes in consumers' purchasing patterns and how these are reflected in the System of National Accounts. E-commerce and online marketplaces have enabled trade in goods that are not confined to a locality, economy, or region, disrupting the previous geographic boundaries of commerce. The sharing economy also has influenced purchasing habits and the choice of goods and services available to consumers. Both of these channels are growing in size and will continue to widen consumer choice and, in many instances, will replace traditional models of exchange and commerce.

Furthermore, as the permanent ICP transitions to being implemented on a three-year cycle, its research agenda (presented in appendix G) will continue to move forward under the guidance of the Technical Advisory Group and evolve to ensure that the program meets its users' needs and the challenges of the new decade.

Note

1. Following the three-year cycle implementation plan, ICP stakeholders had planned to conduct an ICP 2020 cycle. However, restrictions and lockdowns in response to Covid-19 halted field collection of prices in 2020 in many economies. In consideration of this setback, the ICP Governing Board decided in April 2020 to conduct an ICP 2021 cycle in lieu of an ICP 2020 cycle.

APPENDIX A

History of the International Comparison Program

This appendix summarizes the history of the International Comparison Program (ICP). The ICP website provides addtional details.[1] Statisticians have long recognized that using market exchange rates to compare levels of economic activity across economies can lead to misleading results. In particular, the differences between the size of high-income economies with high price levels and low-income economies with low price levels will appear larger than they actually are. This distortion can be avoided by using purchasing power parities (PPPs) instead of market exchange rates to undertake such comparisons.

In his study *The Conditions of Economic Progress*, the British economist Colin Clark was the first to use PPPs to estimate levels of real income. The first edition of his study was published in 1940, followed by second and third editions in 1951 and 1957 (Clark 1940, 1951, 1957). The first edition covered the United States and 52 other economies. Other economies were linked through a series of bilateral comparisons with the United States. The results were then used to quantify the intercountry spread in real income per capita and to provide an estimate of world income. Income was defined as consumer expenditure and did not include government expenditure or capital expenditure. For income per capita, total persons employed rather than total population was the denominator. PPPs were calculated using Fisher's ideal index formula.[2] Referred to as international units, they measured the purchasing power of national currencies over the period 1925–34 based on average prices for the period. In the second and third editions of his study, Clark increased the number of economies covered and refined the methodology applied.

Clark's pioneering studies stimulated further research. In the 1950s, the Organisation for European Economic Cooperation (OEEC) [3] used purchasing power equivalents to compare the national products of France, Germany, Italy, the United Kingdom, and the United States (Gilbert and Kravis 1954). The comparison was subsequently enlarged to include Belgium, Denmark, the Netherlands, and Norway (Gilbert and Associates 1958). All final expenditures, including government and capital expenditures, were covered in the comparison. In the 1960s, the Economic Commission for Latin America carried out PPP-based comparisons of real product in 19 Latin American economies; the Council for Mutual Economic Assistance (COMECON) conducted PPP-based comparisons of national income between several Central and Eastern European centrally planned economies, and the Conference of European Statisticians approved a project to undertake PPP-based comparisons of consumption levels among a small group of market economies and centrally planned economies.

In 1965 the United Nations Statistical Commission (UNSC) discussed the problems inherent in market exchange rate–based comparisons and agreed that the United Nations Statistical Office (UNSO)[4] should develop a more suitable methodology for making international comparisons of gross domestic product (GDP). In 1968 the UNSC considered a report that outlined a research project to be run from 1968 to 1971 aimed at developing PPP-based comparisons. The report proposed using a small group of economies representative of different income levels, social systems, and geographic areas to test and assess methodology. The UNSC agreed that the project should proceed, and, because the UNSO had only limited resources, asked other international organizations and United Nations member economies to assist with the project. At this stage, the research endorsed by the UNSC was to cover GDP measured from both the expenditure and production sides of national accounts. Even so, it was understood that initial efforts would concentrate on the expenditure side—it was less difficult to implement in practice because a single set of expenditures was involved rather than both outputs and inputs, which gave rise to the added complexity of double deflation.

The International Comparison Project (ICP) was launched in 1968 as a joint undertaking between the UNSO and the University of Pennsylvania, which established a special unit funded by a grant from the Ford Foundation. The World Bank became involved, providing financial assistance both directly and through a grant from the Scandinavian economies that was channeled through the World Bank. The United States Agency for International Development and the US-based Social Science Research Council assisted with monetary contributions. The United Kingdom offered in-kind statistical support for the participating economies. The UNSO director was responsible for supervising the project. An advisory board set up to provide technical advice considered detailed proposals for the project at a meeting held in October 1969.

One of the proposals discussed by the advisory board resulted in the ICP adopting a concept of consumption that summed the individual consumption expenditures of households and government to obtain an aggregate of total individual consumption called the consumption expenditure of the population (CEP). The objective in measuring the CEP was to minimize the effect on the volume comparisons of differences in institutional arrangements, particularly regarding the extent to which the government and private sectors provided health and education services in different economies. In this respect, the ICP was more than two decades ahead of the *System of National Accounts 1993,* which set out the concept of actual individual consumption (defined almost identically to the CEP) as an official national accounts measure (UNSC 1993).

Up to and including 1993, the ICP was conducted in phases. Phase I had two stages. The first stage was a pilot study based on data collected for 1967 for six economies (Hungary, India, Japan, Kenya, the United Kingdom, and the United States). The second stage was run for 1970 and included four additional economies (Colombia, France, Germany, and Italy) that had not been able to report the necessary data for 1967. The outcome consisted of different sets of estimates, including multilateral comparisons between all 10 economies for GDP and a range of expenditure components for 1970. The results of phase I were published in 1975 in *A System of International Comparisons of Gross Product and Purchasing Power* (Kravis et al. 1975). The details presented in this publication included the overall results of the multilateral comparison for 1970, a variety of bilateral comparisons for both 1967 and 1970, and the outcomes of various experiments on important issues such as rents, motor vehicle prices, and the consistency of different quantity comparisons.

Phase II included six more economies—Belgium, the Islamic Republic of Iran, the Republic of Korea, Malaysia, the Netherlands, and the Philippines—initially to enable a broader comparison for 1970, but mainly to update the PPPs and associated price and volume measures to 1973. Results for the 16 economies were published in 1978 in *International Comparisons of Real Product* (Kravis, Heston, and Summers 1978).

Thirty-four economies participated in phase III, with 1975 as the reference year. In the earlier phases, the detailed characteristics of items in the US consumer price index were used as the starting point for developing the ICP item lists. Later, they were modified in consultation with some of the participating economies, including India and the COMECON group, to make the specifications of ICP items more generally applicable—for example, by removing characteristics such as brand name that were specific to the United States. The greater diversity of economies in phase III meant that the range of items to be priced had to be expanded further so that all participating economies could price a sufficient number of items representative of their expenditures. At this point, the ICP considered the pros and cons of continuing with a single global comparison or moving to regional comparisons that would be linked to produce worldwide results. The trade-off involved in regionalizing the project was improved comparisons between economies within a region but at the expense of comparisons between economies in different regions because of the difficulties inherent in linking results between regions. In the end, however, phase III went ahead as a single global comparison, although some regional results were presented as having been calculated for the relevant economies from the globally based results. The results of this phase were published in 1982 in *World Product and Income: International Comparisons of Real Gross Product and Purchasing Power* (Kravis, Heston, and Summers 1982).

Phase IV saw some major developments in the program. The first was that the number of participating economies almost doubled, from 34 to 60. The second was that the ICP shifted from being a research project to being a regular operational part of the UNSO work program. With this development, the University of Pennsylvania's participation in the day-to-day running of the project ended, although it continued to advise on methodological issues. The third significant change was the regionalization of the organization of the program. The principal reason for regionalization was the large number of economies now involved worldwide, making it no longer feasible to organize comparisons centrally. Another factor was the decision by the Organisation for Economic Co-operation and Development (OECD) to set up a PPP program for its member economies in conjunction with the PPP program being run by the Statistical Office of the European Union (Eurostat) for economies in what is now the European Union. In addition to the Eurostat-OECD comparison, Africa, Asia, and Latin America participated in phase IV as regions. The regions were linked using the bridge economy approach, in which selected economies priced a range of item specifications from another region to provide a bridge or link between their region and the other region. The reference year for phase IV was 1980.

The reference year for phase V was 1985. It saw only a small increase in the number of participating economies, from 60 to 64, with some new economies replacing some that had been in phase IV but had then dropped out of phase V. Once again, a regional approach was adopted. The regions were Africa, Asia, and the Caribbean, alongside the Eurostat-OECD comparison. In addition, three Central and Eastern European economies were added to the Eurostat-OECD comparison, using Austria as a bridge. The bridge economy approach was used again to link the regions, but some of the links were problematic because several bridge economies encountered difficulties collecting prices for a sufficiently broad range of items from the other region.

In 1990 the exercise was renamed the International Comparison Program. Phase VI, conducted with 1993 as the reference year, was the most ambitious phase to date, covering 115 economies. From the outset, this phase was beset by difficulties. The lack of funding was the major problem, although the lack of overall coordination also led to some major deficiencies in the final outcome. Regional comparisons were undertaken for Africa, Asia, Eurostat-OECD, and Western Asia, but not for Latin America. Moreover, there was no global comparison because it proved virtually impossible to link the regions. In response to these problems, in 1997 the UNSC commissioned a major review of the ICP before further phases were attempted.

The report on the review was presented to the UNSC in 1999 (ECOSOC 1999). It concluded that PPPs and PPP-related statistics were needed, but that the ICP was not producing these data on a timely and regular basis for a sufficient number of economies, as required by potential users. Poor management and insufficient resources at all levels—central, regional, and national—were identified as the principal reasons for the difficulties. Other important contributory factors were inadequate documentation, heavy data requirements that did not take into account the circumstances of individual economies, lack of uniformity in the execution of activities across regions, lack of confidence among economies that others were following guidelines and standards consistently, and failure to involve economies in the editing and calculation stages of the exercise. The report recommended that the UNSC not sanction a new cycle until at least the management and resource issues had been resolved.

The UNSC responded by asking the World Bank to consult with other interested parties and propose a strategy to address the deficiencies identified by the review and to draw up an implementation plan for a new cycle of the ICP. The plan involved mobilizing funds from a variety of sources and establishing a governance infrastructure to provide effective management and coordination between the global center and the regions and between the regions and the participating economies. It also involved providing complete and clearly written documentation on the ICP's technical and procedural guidelines and standards. Such guidelines would allow economies to participate in a full comparison covering GDP or in a partial comparison covering actual individual consumption, using, as far as possible, regular national statistical programs to obtain price and national accounts data for the ICP and linking participation in the ICP to national statistical capacity building.

The UNSC considered the implementation plan in 2000 and again in 2001. It was reluctant to start another cycle of the ICP before adequate funding had been secured. However, after the World Bank embarked on a successful major fund-raising exercise, the UNSC agreed, at its 33rd session, to a new cycle in 2002. At the same time, the UNSC reviewed and endorsed a new strategic framework for the ICP, including an international governance arrangement and a broad implementation plan.

The new cycle was launched in 2003 and ended in 2008. The reference year was 2005. Regional comparisons were organized by the ICP regional coordinating agencies—the African Development Bank (AfDB); the Asian Development Bank (ADB), assisted by the Australian Bureau of Statistics; the Interstate Statistical Committee of the Commonwealth of Independent States (CIS-STAT), with the State Statistical Service of the Russian Federation; the United Nations Economic Commission for Latin America and the Caribbean (UN-ECLAC), with Statistics Canada; and the United Nations Economic and Social Commission for Western Asia (UN-ESCWA)—and by Eurostat and the OECD. The ICP Global Office was established at the World Bank to provide overall coordination and to ensure technical and procedural uniformity across the regions. The Global Office was also responsible for organizing the ring comparison that, by comparing a small number of economies from each region across regions, provided the means to link the regional comparisons in one global or worldwide comparison. The final results of the regional and global comparisons were published at the end of 2007 and the beginning of 2008.

A review by the UNSC's Friends of the Chair (FOC) group of the ICP 2005 cycle concluded that it was generally considered to be a success (ECOSOC 2008). It produced estimates of the relative price levels of GDP and its principal aggregates for 146 economies—including the major emerging ones such as Brazil, China, India, Indonesia, the Russian Federation, and South Africa—and its results were published on a timely basis in 2008 in *Global Purchasing Power Parities and Real Expenditures: 2005 International Comparison Program* (World Bank 2008). An important contributory factor was the governance structure that the World Bank had put in place prior to the start of the exercise to ensure that the ICP regional coordinating agencies would deliver, within a common time frame, regional results that would be consistent across regions and that could be combined in a global comparison. The governance structure was retained after ICP 2005 to commence preparations for the next cycle of the ICP proposed for 2011. The proposal was approved by the UNSC at its 39th session in 2009, and the UNSC requested that the World Bank host the Global Office and coordinate the global program for the 2011 cycle.

The ICP 2011, with its considerably expanded coverage of 199 economies, including 21 Pacific Island economies whose participation was limited to individual household consumption, brought a broader acceptance compared to earlier exercises. Furthermore, the wide availability of reliable PPPs, referenced to 2011 and published in 2014 in *Purchasing Power Parities and the Real Size of World Economies: A Comprehensive Report of the 2011 International Comparison Program* (World Bank 2014), increased their use in subject matter and across the globe. Notably, the international poverty line was updated in 2015 to $1.90 a day, reflecting PPPs for 2011. The major improvements in the program were documented by the FOC, which was asked by the UNSC at its 45th session, in March 2014, to evaluate the 2011 cycle (ECOSOC 2016). The FOC observed that the 2011 cycle had put the program on a firm methodological basis by introducing approaches such as the global core lists and applying major technical innovations. Specifically, the provision of technical assistance to countries, the broad documentation of metadata, and the further development of ICP operational guides and handbooks contributed significantly to the knowledge of staff conducting the work around the world.

The 47th session of the UNSC, held in March 2016, discussed the future of the ICP in light of the recommendations of the FOC in its evaluation of ICP 2011. As a result, the UNSC instituted the ICP as a permanent element of the global statistical work program to be conducted at more frequent intervals from the 2017 cycle onward.

At the same time, the UNSC also endorsed the strengthening of the governance structure[5] consisting of the ICP Governing Board, the Inter-Agency Coordination Group (IACG), the Technical Advisory Group (TAG), with its intermittent task forces, and implementing agencies at the national, regional, and global levels. The structure ensures efficient functioning and balanced representation of countries and coordinating agencies in the governing bodies. The Global Office was established as a permanent unit at the World Bank, responsible for global coordination, data validation, calculation of global results, and related day-to day organizational activities. With regard to the methodology of the ICP, the UNSC agreed that no major changes should be introduced and that a research agenda, to be developed by the TAG, should focus on methodological improvements to be considered for future comparison cycles.

With the launch of the United Nations 2030 Agenda for Sustainable Development,[6] the UNSC also emphasized the need to link the capacity-building activities of the ICP with efforts to enhance the statistical capacity of countries for monitoring progress toward the Sustainable Development Goals. The UNSC also suggested exploring a closer alignment of ICP price surveys with national consumer price index compilation.

Data collection for the ICP's 2017 cycle began in 2016 and continued through to the end of 2018. The number of participating economies decreased slightly, to 176, with Fiji the only representative from the Pacific Islands. Argentina and Guyana joined the Latin America and the Caribbean comparison, while Colombia and Costa Rica moved to the OECD exercise. Some other economies that participated in the 2011 cycle were affected by conflict or natural disasters and were not included in 2011. These included Guatemala and the República Bolivariana de Venezuela in Latin America and the Caribbean and the Republic of Yemen in Western Asia. The AfDB oversaw the work of the 50 economies in Africa, with the Economic and Statistical Observatory of Sub-Saharan Africa (AFRISTAT) coordinating 30 of those and the Common Market for Eastern and Southern Africa (COMESA) coordinating the remaining 20. Three economies in this region also participated in the Western Asia exercise (the Arab Republic of Egypt, Morocco, and Sudan). The ADB coordinated the work of its 22 participating economies, while CIS-STAT oversaw its eight economies and an experimental participation by Uzbekistan. UN-ECLAC coordinated the work of its 36 economies, with support from CARICOM for the 23 Caribbean islands. UN-ESCWA coordinated the 12 economies in Western Asia. Eurostat and OECD provided results for their joint total of 49 economies and assisted with the special participation of Georgia and Ukraine. The Islamic Republic of Iran participated through a special exercise linked with Western Asia. To encourage and prepare for future participation, several economies also benefited from ICP capacity-building efforts. These included Eritrea, Libya, Somalia, South Sudan, Turkmenistan, Uzbekistan, and the Republic of Yemen.

Notes

1. See icp.worldbank.org/programs/#2.
2. Fisher's ideal volume index is the geometric mean of the Laspeyres and Paasche volume indexes. See icp.worldbank.org/programs/icp#6.
3. Now called the Organisation for Economic Co-operation and Development (OECD).
4. Now called the United Nations Statistics Division (UNSD).
5. See icp.worldbank.org/programs/icp#3.
6. See https://www.un.org/sustainabledevelopment/development-agenda/.

APPENDIX B

The ICP's governance framework

This appendix presents the elements of the International Comparison Program's (ICP) governance framework, as approved by the ICP Governing Board at its first meeting in November 2016 (World Bank 2016b). It sets out the overall governance structure and the roles and responsibilities of its main bodies, based on the lessons learned from earlier ICP cycles.

The ICP's governance structure

The overall mandate of the ICP governance framework is to ensure that the global, regional, and national efforts to produce reliable purchasing power parity (PPP) estimates and related measures of real expenditures adhere to approved policies, protocols, methodologies, and quality assurance standards and that the estimates are produced efficiently, in keeping with available resources.

The ICP's governance structure, outlined in figure B.1, comprises the United Nations Statistical Commission (UNSC), the Governing Board, the Inter-Agency Coordination Group (IACG), and the Technical Advisory Group (TAG) and its task forces. Within this scheme, the global implementing agency, the regional implementing agencies, the Statistical Office of the European Union (Eurostat), the Organisation for Economic Co-operation and Development (OECD), and the national implementing agencies carry out the various activities to coordinate and implement the program.

The roles and responsibilities of the ICP governance bodies

United Nations Statistical Commission

The UNSC, the ultimate stakeholder of the ICP,

- Decides on the frequency and operational modality of the program
- Establishes the ICP Governing Board
- Ensures an adequate and balanced representation of economies and organizations
- Selects the global implementing agency
- Reviews and acts on issues raised in the annual reports to the UNSC, prepared by the global implementing agency
- Reviews the functioning of the ICP governance structure and the membership of its governing bodies after a three-year period and introduces modifications, if needed
- Considers specific issues related to the ICP governance structure or membership of its governance bodies, if raised in the annual reports to the UNSC.

Figure B.1 ICP governance structure

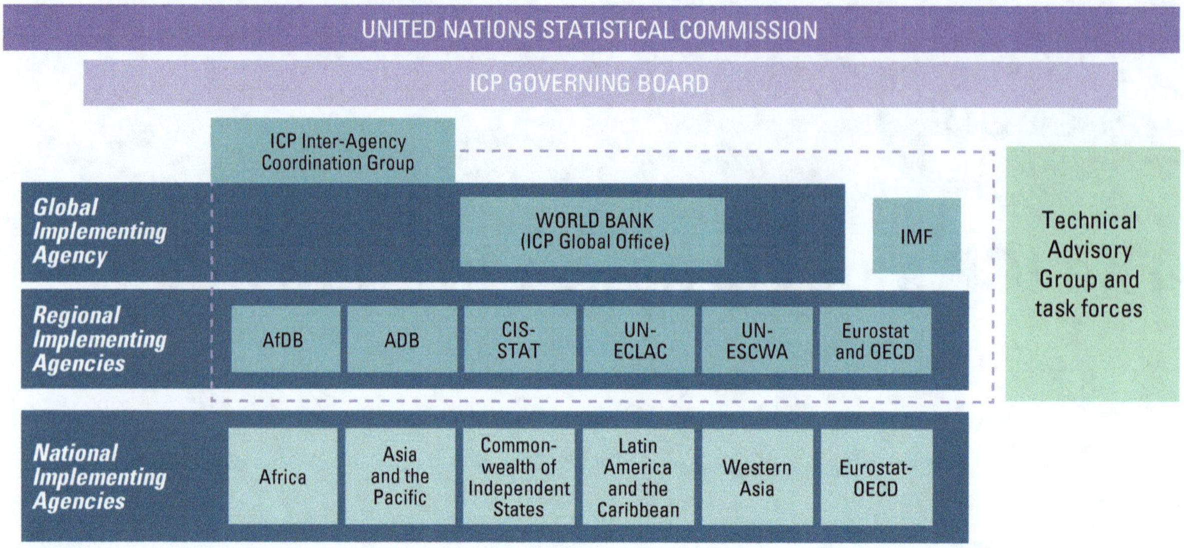

Note: AfDB = African Development Bank; ADB = Asian Development Bank; CIS-STAT = Interstate Statistical Committee of the Commonwealth of Independent States; UN-ECLAC = United Nations Economic Commission for Latin America and the Caribbean; UN-ESCWA = United Nations Economic and Social Commission for Western Asia; Eurostat = Statistical Office of the European Union; OECD = Organisation for Economic Co-operation and Development; IMF = International Monetary Fund.

The Governing Board

The Governing Board, a strategic and policy-making body,

- Puts forth the policies and protocols that govern the production of regional and global PPP estimates
- Forms the TAG
- Approves the technical research agenda, methodology for producing PPPs, and any methodological improvement thereafter
- Ensures that regional and global ICP results are produced following the agreed-on timetables and in line with the agreed-on policies, protocols, and methodology to secure the integrity of the estimates
- Sets up a sustainable funding model that corresponds to the frequency and operational modality of the program
- Reaches out and demonstrates the value of the ICP to policy makers in order to ensure that the program is included in the regular national statistical work and to increase national funding for the ICP
- Ensures that the ICP responds to user needs
- Puts forth an ICP data access and archive policy that promotes further openness with regard to access to data and metadata.

Members of the Governing Board include chief statisticians or senior-level directors of statistics from 11 national implementing agencies, representing their respective ICP regions. The 11 board members are distributed geographically as follows: Africa (two), Asia (two), Pacific Islands (one), Latin America (one), Caribbean (one), Western Asia (one), Commonwealth of Independent States (one), European Union (one), and non–European Union OECD (one). A rotation system within each ICP region ensures a broad representation of economies on the board over time. The duration of each rotation is three years.

In addition to the 11 national implementing agencies, seven international and regional organizations serve as members of the Governing Board, including the World Bank, International Monetary Fund (IMF), United Nations Statistics Division, African Development Bank (AfDB), and Asian Development Bank (ADB). The Eurostat-OECD PPP Programme is represented by a seat on the Governing Board, and Eurostat and the OECD rotate on this seat. Another board seat is assigned to the smaller regional programs, with the United Nations Economic Commission for Latin America and the Caribbean (UN-ECLAC), United Nations Economic and Social Commission for Western Asia (UN-ESCWA), and Interstate Statistical Committee of the Commonwealth of Independent States (CIS-STAT) rotating in this seat. The duration of rotation is one year. Members of the IACG not holding a seat during a given rotation period are invited to attend Governing Board meetings as observers.

Governing Board members elect a chair or co-chairs for the duration of three years. The chair or co-chairs convene meetings of the Governing Board with support from the ICP Global Office, which serves as the secretariat for the Governing Board.

The Governing Board holds regular annual meetings, around the UNSC sessions in New York, to discuss policies, protocols, and methodology governing the production of PPP estimates and ICP advocacy and funding aspects. Ad hoc meetings may be organized, if need arises.

Governing Board decisions are made by consensus. If a consensus cannot be achieved, decisions are made by majority vote.

The Technical Advisory Group and its task forces

The TAG, a technical body,

- Assures the methodological soundness and overall quality of the PPP estimates
- Ensures the transparency of the PPP estimation process
- Supports the establishment of a permanent and more frequent ICP.

The TAG, in collaboration with the IACG, sets forth a technical research agenda to inform future ICP comparisons, for the Governing Board's review and approval.

In order to ensure the comparability of PPP estimates, the short-term technical research agenda focuses on methodological aspects related to compiling annual PPPs and fine-tuning established methods and procedures to improve the quality of the estimates.

The TAG is formed by the ICP Governing Board, with the membership of prominent experts in the fields of index numbers, PPPs, price statistics, and national accounts, with knowledge of national statistical systems and capacity-building challenges across the various regions. The membership brings together a group of leading academics, practitioners, former chief statisticians, and prominent users. Members participate in their own independent capacity and do not represent any specific region or institution.

TAG members select a chair for the duration of three years. The chair convenes meetings of the group with support from the ICP Global Office, which serves as its secretariat.

The TAG holds regular annual meetings to discuss methodological improvements under the technical research agenda and to review the methodological soundness and overall quality of the PPP estimates. Ad hoc meetings are organized, if a need arises. The TAG forms task forces on specific topics and invites recognized experts on the practical application of index numbers, PPPs, price statistics, and national accounts to take part in them, as needed, to develop concrete proposals to address items on the research agenda. The task forces meet as needed, physically or virtually. They may also join IACG meetings to discuss their proposals and TAG meetings to present their findings and recommendations for consideration.

The Inter-Agency Coordination Group and its agencies

The IACG, a coordinating body,

- Collaborates on establishing timetables and work plans for data collection, validation, calculation, and dissemination
- Develops common standards and protocols to ensure comparability across regions and economies
- Provides the quality assurance standards that national and regional data and metadata must satisfy to be included in the global PPP estimates

- Develops a technical research agenda on the methodological choices and implementation arrangements, to inform future ICP comparisons, together with the TAG
- Prepares and updates operational guidelines and materials, including classifications, lists of items, and survey forms
- Promotes and supports the integration of ICP and consumer price index survey activities to decrease the burden on economies
- Takes stock of existing capacity-building activities undertaken by the various agencies in the areas of prices and national accounts and plans and implements statistical capacity-building activities related to the ICP.

The IACG comprises the World Bank as the global implementing agency, the regional implementing agencies, the OECD, Eurostat, and the IMF. It is chaired by the ICP Global Office, which also serves as its secretariat.

As the global implementing agency, the World Bank is responsible for establishing the ICP Global Office, which supports the ICP governance framework and undertakes the global coordination and implementation of the ICP. The ICP Global Office

- Carries out day-to-day management of the global program
- Serves as the secretariat of the Governing Board and TAG
- Chairs the IACG and serves as its secretariat
- Drafts and implements common policies and procedures for sharing data and metadata between economies, regions, and the ICP Global Office
- Drafts operational guidelines and materials to support the conduct of the program
- Assesses national and regional data and metadata submitted by the regions against the quality assurance standards agreed to by the IACG to determine their suitability for inclusion in the global PPP calculations
- Provides technical support to the regions on the implementation of standards, data validation, analysis, and computation of regional results
- Links the regional data and then calculates, validates, and disseminates the global ICP results as per the agreed-on timetables
- Implements the ICP results dissemination policy and manages relevant databases, ensuring that access to detailed ICP data and metadata is granted per the ICP data access and archive policy
- Prepares annual reports for submission to the UNSC.

The regional implementing agencies

- Coordinate the regional ICP comparisons and facilitate data and information flow between the ICP Global Office and participating economies
- Carry out day-to-day management of the regional programs
- Plan and implement the regional ICP activities in line with the agreed-on timetables
- Participate in the preparation of operational guidelines and materials, as IACG members
- Ensure adequate national and regional data and metadata quality as per the agreed-on standards
- Carry out regional capacity-building activities and provide technical support to the economies on data and metadata collection and validation
- Prepare and disseminate regional ICP results as per the agreed-on timetables
- Transmit national and regional data and metadata, including quality indicators, to the ICP Global Office as per the ICP data access and archive policy
- Contribute to global ICP research initiatives by identifying and undertaking research priorities relevant to their regions.

The following organizations are currently acting as the regional implementing agencies:

- AfDB for the Africa region
- ADB for the Asia and the Pacific region
- CIS-STAT for the Commonwealth of Independent States
- UN-ECLAC for the Latin America and the Caribbean region

- UN-ESCWA for the Western Asia region.

If additional organizations are selected to coordinate the program in other regional groupings, such as the Pacific Islands, these regional implementing agencies will join the IACG as members.

Reflecting existing arrangements of the long-standing Eurostat-OECD PPP Programme, Eurostat is responsible for the ICP activities for European economies and OECD is responsible for non-European OECD economies and other OECD accession economies. Eurostat and the OECD

- Coordinate and execute their own permanent comparison program, including determining the program's approaches and timetables
- Participate in the preparation of operational guidelines and materials, as members of the IACG
- Transmit national and regional data and metadata, including quality indicators, to the ICP Global Office as per the ICP data access and archive policy
- Ensure the availability of data necessary to link the Eurostat and OECD economies to the global comparison.

The IMF is one of the leading agencies that plan and deliver statistical capacity-building activities related to the consumer price index (CPI), producer price index (PPI), and national accounts. Moreover, the IMF compiles and maintains, jointly with the OECD, a database of detailed CPIs that can be used in the extrapolation and retropolation of data underlying the PPPs. In this role, the IMF

- Supports the planning and conduct of regional statistical capacity-building activities to improve the quality and availability of CPI, PPI, and national accounts expenditure data
- Advances the agenda for integrating ICP and CPI survey activities
- Contributes to formulation of the framework and approaches for assessing the quality of CPI, PPI, and national accounts expenditure data used in the calculation of the ICP results.

The IACG holds regular biannual meetings and ad hoc meetings, if need arises. The meetings mainly review the following:

- Progress of the regional and global comparisons against the agreed-on timetables
- Operational and technical challenges in implementing the ICP program in the regions and needed improvements in standards, methods, and protocols
- Operational guidelines and materials, including classifications, lists of items, and survey forms
- Prices, national accounts expenditures, and other data and metadata underlying the regional and global comparisons
- Preliminary and final regional and global PPP estimates.

The national implementing agencies

Each participating economy designates a national implementing agency, which is responsible for planning, coordinating, and implementing national ICP activities under the overall work program of the ICP region to which it belongs. National implementing agencies

- Collect and compile the data and metadata required for estimating PPPs following the agreed-on standards, protocols, and guidelines for ensuring cross-country comparability
- Ensure adequate national data and metadata quality as per the agreed-on quality assurance standards
- Facilitate the transmission of data and metadata to regional implementing agencies as per the ICP data access and archive policy
- Participate in regional workshops and activities to discuss operational guidelines and materials, data and metadata quality, and preliminary and final regional results.

APPENDIX C

ICP expenditure classification

Economies participating in the International Comparison Program (ICP) are required to provide a detailed breakdown of their national accounts expenditures for the reference year according to a common classification. The breakdown is used first in the regional comparison in which the reporting economy is engaged and then in the global comparison. The classification of gross domestic product (GDP) expenditures used by the ICP adheres to the internationally agreed-on concepts, definitions, classifications, and accounting rules of the *System of National Accounts* (SNA) *2008* (UNSC 2009). It is structured first by type of final expenditure—individual consumption expenditure, collective consumption expenditure, or capital expenditure—and then, in the case of individual consumption expenditure, by purchaser—households, nonprofit institutions serving households (NPISHs), and government.

This appendix provides an overview of the 2017 ICP expenditure classification. More details are available on the ICP website,[1] including a description of the full classification (see World Bank 2016a).

2017 ICP expenditure classification structure

GDP comprises six main aggregates, which are broken down into 28 expenditure categories, 63 expenditure groups, 126 expenditure classes, and 155 basic headings, as shown in table C.1

In the outline of the expenditure classification that appears in table C.2, main aggregates are identified by a two-digit code, categories by a four-digit code, groups by a five-digit code, classes by a six-digit code, and basic headings by a seven-digit code:

> 1100000 **INDIVIDUAL CONSUMPTION EXPENDITURE BY HOUSEHOLDS** (main aggregate)
> **11**01000 **FOOD AND NONALCOHOLIC BEVERAGES** (category)
> **1101**100 **FOOD** (group)
> **11011**10 **Bread and cereals** (class)
> **1101111** Rice (basic heading)

Of these aggregation levels, the basic-heading level is particularly important. At this level, expenditures are defined and estimated, items are selected for pricing, prices are collected and validated, and purchasing power parities (PPPs) are first calculated. In principle, a basic heading consists of a group of similar well-defined goods or services. In practice, a basic heading is defined by the lowest level of final expenditure for which explicit expenditures can be estimated by the participating economies. Consequently, basic headings can cover a broader range of goods or services than is theoretically desirable.

Table C.1 Structure of the ICP expenditure classification, ICP 2017

Main aggregates	Categories	Groups	Classes	Basic headings
11. Individual consumption expenditure by households	13	44	91	110
12. Individual consumption expenditure by nonprofit institutions serving households (NPISHs)	5	5	5	5
13. Individual consumption expenditure by government	5	7	16	21
14. Collective consumption expenditure by government	1	1	5	5
15. Gross capital formation	3	5	8	12
16. Balance of exports and imports	1	1	1	2
GDP	26	63	126	155

Source: ICP.

Main aggregates

Individual consumption by households is broken down by purpose, in line with the Classification of Individual Consumption by Purpose (COICOP) (see UNSD 2000a). Individual consumption expenditure by NPISHs is broken down by purpose, in line with the Classification of the Purposes of Non-Profit Institutions Serving Households (COPNI) (see UNSD 2000b). And consumption expenditure by government is broken down into individual consumption expenditure and collective consumption expenditure by purpose and by type of service, in line with the Classification of the Functions of Government (COFOG) (UNSD 2000c). Gross capital formation consists of three categories: gross fixed capital formation, changes in inventories, and acquisitions less disposals of valuables. Of these, gross fixed capital formation is broken down by the type of product, in line with the Statistical Classification of Products by Activity (CPA) in the European Economic Community (see Eurostat 2008). The balance of exports and imports comprises exports of goods and services and imports of goods and services.

Deriving actual individual consumption

Actual individual consumption is obtained by summing the individual consumption expenditures of households, NPISHs, and government. The individual consumption expenditures of NPISHs and government cover their expenditures on the services they provide to individual households as social transfers in kind—that is, services related to housing, health care, recreation and culture, education, and social protection. Combining these expenditures is necessary because of the various ways in which individual services are financed in different economies. If the expenditures are not combined and only the individual consumption expenditures of households are compared, households in economies in which NPISHs or government provide individual services will appear to consume a smaller volume of goods and services than households in economies in which households themselves pay directly for these services.

To effect the merger, the individual consumption expenditures of NPISHs and government are broken down so that they can be added to their counterpart expenditures under household expenditure. The breakdowns are structured so that the summation can be at the lowest level of aggregation feasible, which is generally at the level of the basic heading. Many economies are unable to break down the individual consumption expenditures of NPISHs to the required level of detail. When this is the case, the expenditures of NPISHs are reported in total. This total is subsequently distributed over the relevant basic headings under household expenditure in the same proportions as household expenditure is distributed across the basic headings.

Facilitating the input price approach

The collective and individual services produced by government are nonmarket services because they are either provided free or sold at prices that are not economically significant. In the absence of economically significant prices, national accountants obtain the expenditure on nonmarket services by summing the costs of the inputs required to produce them. To maintain consistency with the prices underlying the estimated expenditure on nonmarket services in the national accounts, the PPPs for nonmarket services are based on input prices. This is the input price approach. To enable application of the input price approach, the classification breaks down the consumption expenditure by government on the production of collective services and the principal individual services—education and health—into the following components: compensation of employees, intermediate consumption, gross operating surplus, and net taxes on production (the sum of these four components is a measure of government output). Receipts from sales (such as those from statistical publications) are deducted from output to provide the estimate of consumption expenditure by government.

A distinction is made between the government's expenditure on the health and education services it produces and the government's expenditure on the health and education services it purchases from market producers in the private sector under benefits and reimbursements. This approach ensures that the input price approach is applied only to government expenditure on government-produced services.

Adjusting household expenditure to the national concept

Expenditures on the basic headings constituting individual consumption expenditure by households are defined according to the national concept—that is, they cover only expenditures by resident households, including their expenditures abroad, and exclude the expenditures of nonresident households within the economic territory. Many economies, however, estimate the expenditures on these basic headings according to the domestic concept—that is, irrespective of whether the household making the purchase is resident or not. For these economies, the classification contains a global adjustment to rectify this difference. The adjustment is defined as the balance of the expenditures of residents abroad less the expenditures of nonresidents within the economic territory or as net purchases abroad. It is important to note that many economies base their estimates of individual consumption expenditure by households on household budget surveys, so the estimates are automatically on a national basis. For these economies, global adjustment is not required.

Updates introduced for the 2017 ICP expenditure classification

The classification of expenditure on GDP used for ICP 2005 and ICP 2011 has been updated (a) to reflect the lessons learned during the 2005 and 2011 cycles; (b) to maintain consistency with the Eurostat expenditure classification, which has recently been revised; and (c) to take account of the changes in the classification introduced by SNA 2008. *Gross capital formation* has been introduced as a main aggregate. It replaces the former main aggregates *gross fixed capital formation* and *changes in inventories and acquisitions less disposals of valuables,* which are now aggregates at the expenditure-category level. Three sets of balancing basic headings were merged to become single basic headings (net purchases abroad, changes in inventories, and acquisitions less disposals of valuables). Other changes concern *rentals for housing* and *individual consumption expenditure by NPISHs*. Previously, these were single basic headings, but the housing rentals category is now broken down into two basic headings, one for actual rentals and one for imputed rentals, while NPISHs expenditures are divided across five basic headings that cover the individual services provided by NPISHs (housing, health, recreation and culture, education, social protection, and other services). ICP basic-heading code numbers remain unchanged, except for the basic headings under gross capital formation and the newly introduced basic headings.

SNA 2008 does not differ fundamentally from SNA 1993 (UNSC 1993), and the basic structure of the classification stays the same. Within the basic structure, changes occur under *gross fixed capital formation* as a result of the changes that have been introduced in the classification of fixed assets relating to research and development, military weapons systems and ammunition, computer software and databases, land improvements, and ownership transfer costs on nonproduced assets including land.

Note

1. See icp.worldbank.org/programs/#6.

Table C.2 Expenditure classification, ICP 2017

Code	Name	Expenditure level
1000000	**GROSS DOMESTIC PRODUCT**	**GDP**
1100000	**INDIVIDUAL CONSUMPTION EXPENDITURE BY HOUSEHOLDS**	**Main aggregate**
1101000	FOOD AND NONALCOHOLIC BEVERAGES	Category
1101100	FOOD	Group
1101110	Bread and cereals	Class
1101111	Rice	Basic heading
1101112	Other cereals, flour, and other cereal products	Basic heading
1101113	Bread	Basic heading
1101114	Other bakery products	Basic heading
1101115	Pasta products and couscous	Basic heading
1101120	Meat	Class
1101121	Beef and veal	Basic heading
1101122	Pork	Basic heading
1101123	Lamb, mutton, and goat	Basic heading
1101124	Poultry	Basic heading
1101125	Other meats and meat preparations	Basic heading
1101130	Fish and seafood	Class
1101131	Fresh, chilled, or frozen fish and seafood	Basic heading
1101132	Preserved or processed fish and seafood	Basic heading
1101140	Milk, cheese, and eggs	Class
1101141	Fresh milk	Basic heading
1101142	Preserved milk and other milk products	Basic heading
1101143	Cheese and curd	Basic heading
1101144	Eggs and egg-based products	Basic heading
1101150	Oils and fats	Class
1101151	Butter and margarine	Basic heading
1101153	Other edible oils and fats	Basic heading
1101160	Fruit	Class
1101161	Fresh or chilled fruit	Basic heading
1101162	Frozen, preserved, or processed fruit and fruit-based products	Basic heading

Table C.2 *(Continued)*

Code	Name	Expenditure level
1101170	Vegetables	Class
1101171	Fresh or chilled vegetables, other than potatoes and other tuber vegetables	Basic heading
1101172	Fresh or chilled potatoes and other tuber vegetables	Basic heading
1101173	Frozen, preserved, or processed vegetables and vegetable-based products	Basic heading
1101180	Sugar, jam, honey, chocolate, and confectionery	Class
1101181	Sugar	Basic heading
1101182	Jams, marmalades, and honey	Basic heading
1101183	Confectionery, chocolate, and ice cream	Basic heading
1101190	Food products n.e.c.	Class
1101191	Food products n.e.c.	Basic heading
1101200	NONALCOHOLIC BEVERAGES	Group
1101210	Coffee, tea, and cocoa	Class
1101211	Coffee, tea, and cocoa	Basic heading
1101220	Mineral waters, soft drinks, and fruit and vegetable juices	Class
1101221	Mineral waters, soft drinks, and fruit and vegetable juices	Basic heading
1102000	ALCOHOLIC BEVERAGES, TOBACCO, AND NARCOTICS	Category
1102100	ALCOHOLIC BEVERAGES	Group
1102110	Spirits	Class
1102111	Spirits	Basic heading
1102120	Wine	Class
1102121	Wine	Basic heading
1102130	Beer	Class
1102131	Beer	Basic heading
1102200	TOBACCO	Group
1102210	Tobacco	Class
1102211	Tobacco	Basic heading
1102300	NARCOTICS	Group
1102310	Narcotics	Class
1102311	Narcotics	Basic heading
1103000	CLOTHING AND FOOTWEAR	Category
1103100	CLOTHING	Group
1103110	Clothing materials, other articles of clothing, and clothing accessories	Class
1103111	Clothing materials, other articles of clothing, and clothing accessories	Basic heading
1103120	Garments	Class
1103121	Garments	Basic heading
1103140	Cleaning, repair, and hire of clothing	Class
1103141	Cleaning, repair, and hire of clothing	Basic heading
1103200	FOOTWEAR	Group
1103210	Shoes and other footwear	Class
1103211	Shoes and other footwear	Basic heading

(continued)

Table C.2 *(Continued)*

Code	Name	Expenditure level
1103220	Repair and hire of footwear	Class
1103221	Repair and hire of footwear	Basic heading
1104000	HOUSING, WATER, ELECTRICITY, GAS, AND OTHER FUELS	Category
1104100	ACTUAL RENTALS FOR HOUSING	Group
1104110	Actual rentals for housing	Class
1104111	Actual rentals for housing *	Basic heading
1104200	IMPUTED RENTALS FOR HOUSING	Group
1104210	Imputed rentals for housing	Class
1104211	Imputed rentals for housing *	Basic heading
1104300	MAINTENANCE AND REPAIR OF THE DWELLING	Group
1104310	Maintenance and repair of the dwelling	Class
1104311	Maintenance and repair of the dwelling	Basic heading
1104400	WATER SUPPLY AND MISCELLANEOUS SERVICES RELATING TO THE DWELLING	Group
1104410	Water supply	Class
1104411	Water supply	Basic heading
1104420	Miscellaneous services relating to the dwelling	Class
1104421	Miscellaneous services relating to the dwelling	Basic heading
1104500	ELECTRICITY, GAS, AND OTHER FUELS	Group
1104510	Electricity	Class
1104511	Electricity	Basic heading
1104520	Gas	Class
1104521	Gas	Basic heading
1104530	Other fuels	Class
1104531	Other fuels	Basic heading
1105000	FURNISHINGS, HOUSEHOLD EQUIPMENT, AND ROUTINE HOUSEHOLD MAINTENANCE	Category
1105100	FURNITURE AND FURNISHINGS, CARPETS, AND OTHER FLOOR COVERINGS	Group
1105110	Furniture and furnishings	Class
1105111	Furniture and furnishings	Basic heading
1105120	Carpets and other floor coverings	Class
1105121	Carpets and other floor coverings	Basic heading
1105130	Repair of furniture, furnishings, and floor coverings	Class
1105131	Repair of furniture, furnishings, and floor coverings	Basic heading
1105200	HOUSEHOLD TEXTILES	Group
1105210	Household textiles	Class
1105211	Household textiles	Basic heading
1105300	HOUSEHOLD APPLIANCES	Group
1105310	Major household appliances whether electric or not	Class
1105311	Major household appliances whether electric or not	Basic heading
1105320	Small electric household appliances	Class
1105321	Small electric household appliances	Basic heading

Table C.2 *(Continued)*

Code	Name	Expenditure level
1105330	Repair of household appliances	Class
1105331	Repair of household appliances	Basic heading
1105400	GLASSWARE, TABLEWARE, AND HOUSEHOLD UTENSILS	Group
1105410	Glassware, tableware, and household utensils	Class
1105411	Glassware, tableware, and household utensils	Basic heading
1105500	TOOLS AND EQUIPMENT FOR HOUSE AND GARDEN	Group
1105510	Major tools and equipment	Class
1105511	Major tools and equipment	Basic heading
1105520	Small tools and miscellaneous accessories	Class
1105521	Small tools and miscellaneous accessories	Basic heading
1105600	GOODS AND SERVICES FOR ROUTINE HOUSEHOLD MAINTENANCE	Group
1105610	Nondurable household goods	Class
1105611	Nondurable household goods	Basic heading
1105620	Domestic services and household services	Class
1105621	Domestic services	Basic heading
1105622	Household services	Basic heading
1106000	HEALTH	Category
1106100	MEDICAL PRODUCTS, APPLIANCES, AND EQUIPMENT	Group
1106110	Pharmaceutical products	Class
1106111	Pharmaceutical products	Basic heading
1106120	Other medical products	Class
1106121	Other medical products	Basic heading
1106130	Therapeutic appliances and equipment	Class
1106131	Therapeutic appliances and equipment	Basic heading
1106200	OUTPATIENT SERVICES	Group
1106210	Medical services	Class
1106211	Medical services	Basic heading
1106220	Dental services	Class
1106221	Dental services	Basic heading
1106230	Paramedical services	Class
1106231	Paramedical services	Basic heading
1106300	HOSPITAL SERVICES	Group
1106310	Hospital services	Class
1106311	Hospital services	Basic heading
1107000	TRANSPORT	Category
1107100	PURCHASE OF VEHICLES	Group
1107110	Motor cars	Class
1107111	Motor cars	Basic heading
1107120	Motorcycles	Class
1107121	Motorcycles	Basic heading

(continued)

Table C.2 *(Continued)*

Code	Name	Expenditure level
1107130	Bicycles	Class
1107131	Bicycles	Basic heading
1107140	Animal-drawn vehicles	Class
1107141	Animal-drawn vehicles	Basic heading
1107200	OPERATION OF PERSONAL TRANSPORT EQUIPMENT	Group
1107220	Fuels and lubricants for personal transport equipment	Class
1107221	Fuels and lubricants for personal transport equipment	Basic heading
1107230	Maintenance and repair of personal transport equipment	Class
1107231	Maintenance and repair of personal transport equipment	Basic heading
1107240	Other services in respect of personal transport equipment	Class
1107241	Other services in respect of personal transport equipment	Basic heading
1107300	TRANSPORT SERVICES	Group
1107310	Passenger transport by railway	Class
1107311	Passenger transport by railway	Basic heading
1107320	Passenger transport by road	Class
1107321	Passenger transport by road	Basic heading
1107330	Passenger transport by air	Class
1107331	Passenger transport by air	Basic heading
1107340	Passenger transport by sea and inland waterway	Class
1107341	Passenger transport by sea and inland waterway	Basic heading
1107350	Combined passenger transport	Class
1107351	Combined passenger transport	Basic heading
1107360	Other purchased transport services	Class
1107361	Other purchased transport services	Basic heading
1108000	COMMUNICATION	Category
1108100	POSTAL SERVICES	Group
1108110	Postal services	Class
1108111	Postal services	Basic heading
1108200	TELEPHONE AND TELEFAX EQUIPMENT	Group
1108210	Telephone and telefax equipment	Class
1108211	Telephone and telefax equipment	Basic heading
1108300	TELEPHONE AND TELEFAX SERVICES	Group
1108310	Telephone and telefax services	Class
1108311	Telephone and telefax services	Basic heading
1109000	RECREATION AND CULTURE	Category
1109100	AUDIOVISUAL, PHOTOGRAPHIC, AND INFORMATION PROCESSING EQUIPMENT	Group
1109110	Audiovisual, photographic, and information processing equipment	Class
1109111	Audiovisual, photographic, and information processing equipment	Basic heading
1109140	Recording media	Class
1109141	Recording media	Basic heading

Table C.2 *(Continued)*

Code	Name	Expenditure level
1109150	Repair of audiovisual, photographic, and information processing equipment	Class
1109151	Repair of audiovisual, photographic, and information processing equipment	Basic heading
1109200	OTHER MAJOR DURABLES FOR RECREATION AND CULTURE	Group
1109210	Major durables for outdoor and indoor recreation	Class
1109211	Major durables for outdoor and indoor recreation	Basic heading
1109230	Maintenance and repair of other major durables for recreation and culture	Class
1109231	Maintenance and repair of other major durables for recreation and culture	Basic heading
1109300	OTHER RECREATIONAL ITEMS AND EQUIPMENT, GARDENS, AND PETS	Group
1109310	Other recreational items and equipment	Class
1109311	Other recreational items and equipment	Basic heading
1109330	Gardens and pets	Class
1109331	Gardens and pets	Basic heading
1109350	Veterinary and other services for pets	Class
1109351	Veterinary and other services for pets	Basic heading
1109400	RECREATIONAL AND CULTURAL SERVICES	Group
1109410	Recreational and sporting services	Class
1109411	Recreational and sporting services	Basic heading
1109420	Cultural services	Class
1109421	Cultural services	Basic heading
1109430	Games of chance	Class
1109431	Games of chance	Basic heading
1109500	NEWSPAPERS, BOOKS, AND STATIONERY	Group
1109510	Newspapers, books, and stationery	Class
1109511	Newspapers, books, and stationery	Basic heading
1109600	PACKAGE HOLIDAYS	Group
1109610	Package holidays	Class
1109611	Package holidays	Basic heading
1110000	EDUCATION	Category
1110100	EDUCATION	Group
1110110	Education	Class
1110111	Education	Basic heading
1111000	RESTAURANTS AND HOTELS	Category
1111100	CATERING SERVICES	Group
1111110	Catering services	Class
1111111	Catering services	Basic heading
1111200	ACCOMMODATION SERVICES	Group
1111210	Accommodation services	Class
1111211	Accommodation services	Basic heading

(continued)

Table C.2 *(Continued)*

Code	Name	Expenditure level
1112000	MISCELLANEOUS GOODS AND SERVICES	Category
1112100	PERSONAL CARE	Group
1112110	Hairdressing salons and personal grooming establishments	Class
1112111	Hairdressing salons and personal grooming establishments	Basic heading
1112120	Appliances, articles, and products for personal care	Class
1112121	Appliances, articles, and products for personal care	Basic heading
1112200	PROSTITUTION	Group
1112210	Prostitution	Class
1112211	Prostitution	Basic heading
1112300	PERSONAL EFFECTS N.E.C.	Group
1112310	Jewelry, clocks, and watches	Class
1112311	Jewelry, clocks, and watches	Basic heading
1112320	Other personal effects	Class
1112321	Other personal effects	Basic heading
1112400	SOCIAL PROTECTION	Group
1112410	Social protection	Class
1112411	Social protection	Basic heading
1112500	INSURANCE	Group
1112510	Insurance	Class
1112511	Insurance	Basic heading
1112600	FINANCIAL SERVICES N.E.C.	Group
1112610	Financial intermediation services indirectly measured (FISIM)	Class
1112611	Financial intermediation services indirectly measured (FISIM)	Basic heading
1112620	Other financial services n.e.c.	Class
1112621	Other financial services n.e.c.	Basic heading
1112700	OTHER SERVICES N.E.C.	Group
1112710	Other services n.e.c.	Class
1112711	Other services n.e.c.	Basic heading
1113000	NET PURCHASES ABROAD	Category
1113100	NET PURCHASES ABROAD	Group
1113110	Net purchases abroad	Class
1113111	Net purchases abroad *	Basic heading
1200000	**INDIVIDUAL CONSUMPTION EXPENDITURE BY NPISHs**	**Main aggregate**
1201000	HOUSING	Category
1201100	HOUSING	Group
1201110	Housing	Class
1201111	Housing *	Basic heading
1202000	HEALTH	Category
1202100	HEALTH	Group
1202110	Health	Class

Table C.2 *(Continued)*

Code	Name	Expenditure level
1202111	Health *	Basic heading
1203000	RECREATION AND CULTURE	Category
1203100	RECREATION AND CULTURE	Group
1203110	Recreation and culture	Class
1203111	Recreation and culture *	Basic heading
1204000	EDUCATION	Category
1204100	EDUCATION	Group
1204110	Education	Class
1204111	Education *	Basic heading
1205000	SOCIAL PROTECTION AND OTHER SERVICES	Category
1205100	SOCIAL PROTECTION AND OTHER SERVICES	Group
1205110	Social protection and other services	Class
1205111	Social protection and other services *	Basic heading
1300000	**INDIVIDUAL CONSUMPTION EXPENDITURE BY GOVERNMENT**	**Main aggregate**
1301000	HOUSING	Category
1301100	HOUSING	Group
1301110	Housing	Class
1301111	Housing	Basic heading
1302000	HEALTH	Category
1302100	HEALTH BENEFITS AND REIMBURSEMENTS	Group
1302110	Medical products, appliances, and equipment	Class
1302111	Pharmaceutical products	Basic heading
1302112	Other medical products	Basic heading
1302113	Therapeutic appliances and equipment	Basic heading
1302120	Health services	Class
1302121	Outpatient medical services	Basic heading
1302122	Outpatient dental services	Basic heading
1302123	Outpatient paramedical services	Basic heading
1302124	Hospital services	Basic heading
1302200	PRODUCTION OF HEALTH SERVICES	Group
1302210	Compensation of employees	Class
1302211	Compensation of employees	Basic heading
1302220	Intermediate consumption	Class
1302221	Intermediate consumption	Basic heading
1302230	Gross operating surplus	Class
1302231	Gross operating surplus	Basic heading
1302240	Net taxes on production	Class
1302241	Net taxes on production	Basic heading

(continued)

Table C.2 *(Continued)*

Code	Name	Expenditure level
1302250	Receipts from sales	Class
1302251	Receipts from sales	Basic heading
1303000	RECREATION AND CULTURE	Category
1303100	RECREATION AND CULTURE	Group
1303110	Recreation and culture	Class
1303111	Recreation and culture	Basic heading
1304000	EDUCATION	Category
1304100	EDUCATION BENEFITS AND REIMBURSEMENTS	Group
1304110	Education benefits and reimbursements	Class
1304111	Education benefits and reimbursements	Basic heading
1304200	PRODUCTION OF EDUCATION SERVICES	Group
1304210	Compensation of employees	Class
1304211	Compensation of employees	Basic heading
1304220	Intermediate consumption	Class
1304221	Intermediate consumption	Basic heading
1304230	Gross operating surplus	Class
1304231	Gross operating surplus	Basic heading
1304240	Net taxes on production	Class
1304241	Net taxes on production	Basic heading
1304250	Receipts from sales	Class
1304251	Receipt from sales	Basic heading
1305000	SOCIAL PROTECTION	Category
1305100	SOCIAL PROTECTION	Group
1305110	Social protection	Class
1305111	Social protection	Basic heading
1400000	**COLLECTIVE CONSUMPTION EXPENDITURE BY GOVERNMENT**	**Main aggregate**
1401000	COLLECTIVE SERVICES	Category
1401100	COLLECTIVE SERVICES	Group
1401110	Compensation of employees	Class
1401111	Compensation of employees	Basic heading
1401120	Intermediate consumption	Class
1401121	Intermediate consumption	Basic heading
1401130	Gross operating surplus	Class
1401131	Gross operating surplus	Basic heading
1401140	Net taxes on production	Class
1401141	Net taxes on production	Basic heading
1401150	Receipts from sales	Class
1401151	Receipts from sales	Basic heading

Table C.2 *(Continued)*

Code	Name	Expenditure level
1500000	**GROSS CAPITAL FORMATION**	**Main aggregate**
1501000	GROSS FIXED CAPITAL FORMATION	Category
1501100	MACHINERY AND EQUIPMENT	Group
1501110	Metal products and equipment	Class
1501111	Fabricated metal products, except machinery and equipment	Basic heading
1501112	Electrical and optical equipment	Basic heading
1501115	General purpose machinery	Basic heading
1501116	Special purpose machinery	Basic heading
1501120	Transport equipment	Class
1501121	Road transport equipment	Basic heading
1501122	Other transport equipment	Basic heading
1501200	CONSTRUCTION	Group
1501210	Residential buildings	Class
1501211	Residential buildings	Basic heading
1501220	Nonresidential buildings	Class
1501221	Nonresidential buildings	Basic heading
1501230	Civil engineering works	Class
1501231	Civil engineering works	Basic heading
1501300	OTHER PRODUCTS	Group
1501310	Other products	Class
1501311	Other products	Basic heading
1502000	CHANGES IN INVENTORIES	Category
1502100	CHANGES IN INVENTORIES	Group
1502110	Changes in inventories	Class
1502111	Changes in inventories *	Basic heading
1503000	ACQUISITIONS LESS DISPOSALS OF VALUABLES	Category
1503100	ACQUISITIONS LESS DISPOSALS OF VALUABLES	Group
1503110	Acquisitions less disposals of valuables	Class
1503111	Acquisitions less disposals of valuables *	Basic heading
1600000	**BALANCE OF EXPORTS AND IMPORTS**	**Main aggregate**
1601000	BALANCE OF EXPORTS AND IMPORTS	Category
1601100	BALANCE OF EXPORTS AND IMPORTS	Group
1601110	Balance of exports and imports	Class
1601111	Exports of goods and services	Basic heading
1601112	Imports of goods and services	Basic heading

Source: ICP.

Note: n.e.c. = not elsewhere classified. * = newly introduced basic headings.

APPENDIX D

Reference PPPs used in ICP 2017

The gross domestic product (GDP) expenditures used for the 2017 International Comparison Program (ICP) were classified into 155 basic headings. However, prices for 55 basic headings were not collected in some ICP regions. For some of these basic headings, it was too difficult to specify comparable items that could be priced across economies; for others, it was too expensive and time-consuming to collect prices. The basic headings for which prices were not collected in some ICP regions are listed in table D.1. Some examples are narcotics (1102311), prostitution (1112211), financial intermediation services indirectly measured (FISIM) (1112611), and changes in inventories (1502111).

Without prices for those basic headings, aggregation at higher aggregate levels is not possible because it is necessary to have a complete matrix of basic-heading purchasing power parities (PPPs). For that reason, reference PPPs were used in ICP 2017 as proxies for PPPs of the basic headings for which no prices were collected. The use of reference PPPs has been standard practice in all ICP comparisons, and this appendix sets out the reference PPPs used in the ICP 2017 cycle. Further information is available on the ICP website.

In calculating reference PPPs, the weighted Gini-Éltető-Köves-Szulc (GEKS) method was used. The weights were the expenditures on the basic headings whose PPPs were being averaged. In applying this procedure, basic headings with reference PPPs were not used to generate reference PPPs for other basic headings for which no prices were collected.

The reference PPPs proposed for use in ICP 2017 in all regions and the basic headings to which they apply are listed in table D.1. In most cases, reference PPPs were based on the PPPs of only a few basic headings considered similar to the basic headings for which no prices were collected. For example, the reference PPP for hospital services (1106311) is based on the aggregation of the PPP for medical services (1106211), the PPP for dental services (1106221), and the PPP for paramedical services (1106231), where the weights used in the aggregation are the expenditures on the constituent basic headings. In a few cases, reference PPPs are based on the PPPs of a large group of basic headings, the objective being to ensure that the use of a reference PPP does not change the PPP of the larger group to which the basic heading with a missing PPP belongs. For example, the PPP for individual consumption expenditure by households is used as the reference PPP for the basic-heading FISIM (1112611), among others.

The number of reference PPPs by ICP main aggregate is the following: 21 under individual consumption expenditure by households, 5 under individual consumption expenditure by nonprofit institutions serving households

(NPISHs), 19 under individual consumption expenditure by government, 4 under collective consumption expenditure by government, 4 under gross capital formation, and 2 under the balance of exports and imports. Finally, while regions were advised to apply the reference PPPs listed in table D.1, it was ultimately up to each region to decide the basic heading to which a reference PPP corresponds and what basic headings make up a given reference PPP.

Table D.1 ICP 2017 Reference PPPs

ICP main aggregate	Basic heading		Reference PPPs
Individual consumption expenditure by households	1102311	Narcotics	PPP(s) for tobacco (1102211), pharmaceutical products (1106111)
	1104211	Imputed rentals for housing	PPP(s) for actual rentals for housing (1104111)
	1104421	Miscellaneous services relating to the dwelling	PPP(s) for maintenance and repair of the dwelling (1104311), water supply (1104411)
	1105131	Repair of furniture, furnishings, and floor coverings	PPP(s) for maintenance and repair of the dwelling (1104311)
	1105331	Repair of household appliances	PPP(s) for maintenance and repair of the dwelling (1104311)
	1106311	Hospital services	PPP(s) for medical services (1106211), dental services (1106221), paramedical services (1106231)
	1107141	Animal-drawn vehicles	PPP(s) for bicycles (1107131)
	1107341	Passenger transport by sea and inland waterway	PPP(s) for passenger transport by railway (1107311), passenger transport by road (1107321), passenger transport by air (1107331)
	1107351	Combined passenger transport	PPP(s) for passenger transport by railway (1107311), passenger transport by road (1107321)
	1107361	Other purchased transport services	PPP(s) for passenger transport by railway (1107311), passenger transport by road (1107321)
	1109211	Major durables for outdoor and indoor recreation	PPP(s) for furniture and furnishings (1105111), carpets and other floor coverings (1105121), major household appliances whether electric or not (1105311), major tools and equipment (1105511), therapeutic appliances and equipment (1106131), motor cars (1107111), motor cycles (1107121), bicycles (1107131), telephone and telefax equipment (1108211), audiovisual, photographic, and information processing equipment (1109111), jewelry, clocks, and watches (1112311)
	1109231	Maintenance and repair of other major durables for recreation and culture	PPP(s) for maintenance and repair of personal transport equipment (1107231), repair of audiovisual, photographic, and information processing equipment (1109151)
	1109431	Games of chance	PPP(s) for recreational and sporting services (1109411)
	1109611	Package holidays	PPP(s) for passenger transport by railway (1107311), passenger transport by road (1107321), passenger transport by air (1107331), catering services (1111111), accommodation services (1111211)
	1112211	Prostitution	PPP(s) for individual consumption expenditure by households (110000), excluding health and education basic headings and basic headings with reference PPPs
	1112411	Social protection—individual consumption expenditure by households	PPP(s) for compensation of employees—individual health government (1302211), intermediate consumption—individual health government (1302221), gross operating surplus—individual health government (1302231), compensation of employees—individual education government (1304211), intermediate consumption—individual education government (1304221), gross operating surplus—individual education government (1304231)
	1112511	Insurance	PPP(s) for individual consumption expenditure by households (110000), excluding health and education basic headings and basic headings with reference PPPs

Table D.1 *(Continued)*

ICP main aggregate		Basic heading	Reference PPPs
	1112611	Financial intermediation services indirectly measured (FISIM)	PPP(s) for individual consumption expenditure by households (110000), excluding health and education basic headings and basic headings with reference PPPs
	1112621	Other financial services n.e.c.	PPP(s) for individual consumption expenditure by households (110000), excluding health and education basic headings and basic headings with reference PPPs
	1112711	Other services n.e.c.	PPP(s) for individual consumption expenditure by households (110000), excluding health and education basic headings and basic headings with reference PPPs
	1113111	Net purchases abroad	Market exchange rates
Individual consumption expenditure by nonprofit institutions serving households (NPISHs)	1201111	Housing—NPISHs	PPP(s) for actual rentals for housing (1104111)
	1202111	Health—NPISHs	PPP(s) for compensation of employees—individual health government (1302211), intermediate consumption—individual health government (1302221), gross operating surplus—individual health government (1302231)
	1203111	Recreation and culture—NPISHs	PPP(s) for recreational and sporting services (1109411), cultural services (1109421)
	1204111	Education—NPISHs	PPP(s) for compensation of employees—individual education government (1304211), intermediate consumption—individual education government (1304221), gross operating surplus—individual education government (1304231)
	1205111	Social protection and other services—NPISHs	PPP(s) for compensation of employees—individual health government (1302211), intermediate consumption—individual health government (1302221), gross operating surplus—individual health government (1302231), compensation of employees—individual education government (1304211), intermediate consumption—individual education government (1304221), gross operating surplus—individual education government (1304231)
Individual consumption expenditure by government	1301111	Housing	PPP(s) for actual rentals for housing (1104111)
	1302111	Pharmaceutical products	PPP(s) for pharmaceutical products (1106111)
	1302112	Other medical products	PPP(s) for other medical products (1106121)
	1302113	Therapeutic appliances and equipment	PPP(s) for therapeutic appliances and equipment (1106131)
	1302121	Outpatient medical services	PPP(s) for medical services (1106211)
	1302122	Outpatient dental services	PPP(s) for dental services (1106221)
	1302123	Outpatient paramedical services	PPP(s) for paramedical services (1106231)
	1302124	Hospital services	PPP(s) for hospital services (1106311)
	1302221	Intermediate consumption	PPP(s) for individual consumption expenditure by households (110000), excluding health and education basic headings and basic headings with reference PPPs
	1302231	Gross operating surplus	PPP(s) for fabricated metal products, except machinery and equipment (1501111), electrical and optical equipment (1501112), general-purpose machinery (1501115), special-purpose machinery (1501116), road transport equipment (1501121), residential buildings (1501211), nonresidential buildings (1501221), civil engineering works (1501231)
	1302241	Net taxes on production—individual health government	PPP(s) for compensation of employees—individual health government (1302211), intermediate consumption—individual health government (1302221), gross operating surplus—individual health government (1302231)
	1302251	Receipts from sales—individual health government	PPP(s) for compensation of employees—individual health government (1302211), intermediate consumption—individual health government (1302221), gross operating surplus—individual health government (1302231)

(continued)

Table D.1 *(Continued)*

ICP main aggregate		Basic heading	Reference PPPs
	1303111	Recreation and culture	PPP(s) for recreational and sporting services (1109411), cultural services (1109421)
	1304111	Education benefits and reimbursements	PPP(s) for education (1110111)
	1304221	Intermediate consumption—individual education government	PPP(s) for individual consumption expenditure by households (110000), excluding health and education basic headings and basic headings with reference PPPs
	1304231	Gross operating surplus—individual education government	PPP(s) for fabricated metal products, except machinery and equipment (1501111), electrical and optical equipment (1501112), general-purpose machinery (1501115), special-purpose machinery (1501116), road transport equipment (1501121), residential buildings (1501211), nonresidential buildings (1501221), civil engineering works (1501231)
	1304241	Net taxes on production—individual education government	PPP(s) for compensation of employees—individual education government (1304211), intermediate consumption—individual education government (1304221), gross operating surplus—individual education government (1304231)
	1304251	Receipt from sales—individual education government	PPP(s) for compensation of employees—individual education government (1304211), intermediate consumption—individual education government (1304221), gross operating surplus—individual education government (1304231)
	1305111	Social protection—individual consumption expenditure by government	PPP(s) for compensation of employees—individual health government (1302211), intermediate consumption—individual health government (1302221), gross operating surplus—individual health government (1302231), compensation of employees—individual education government (1304211), intermediate consumption—individual education government (1304221), gross operating surplus—individual education government (1304231)
Collective consumption expenditure by government	1401121	Intermediate consumption—collective government	PPP(s) for individual consumption expenditure by households (110000), excluding health and education basic headings and basic headings with reference PPPs
	1401131	Gross operating surplus—collective government	PPP(s) for fabricated metal products, except machinery and equipment (1501111), electrical and optical equipment (1501112), general-purpose machinery (1501115), special-purpose machinery (1501116), road transport equipment (1501121), residential buildings (1501211), nonresidential buildings (1501221), civil engineering works (1501231)
	1401141	Net taxes on production—collective government	PPP(s) for compensation of employees—collective government (1401111), intermediate consumption—collective government (1401121), gross operating surplus—collective government (1401131)
	1401151	Receipts from sales—collective government	PPP(s) for compensation of employees—collective government (1401111), intermediate consumption—collective government (1401121), gross operating surplus—collective government (1401131)
Gross capital formation	1501122	Other transport equipment	PPP(s) for road transport equipment (1501121)
	1501311	Other products	PPP(s) for fabricated metal products, except machinery and equipment (1501111), electrical and optical equipment (1501112), general-purpose machinery (1501115), special-purpose machinery (1501116), road transport equipment (1501121)
	1502111	Changes in inventories	PPP(s) for all basic headings classified as containing predominantly goods (rather than goods and services), excluding basic headings with reference PPPs
	1503111	Acquisitions less disposals of valuables	Market exchange rates
Balance of exports and imports	1601111	Exports of goods and services	Market exchange rates
	1601112	Imports of goods and services	Market exchange rates

Note: ICP = International Comparison Program; PPP = purchasing power parity; n.e.c. = not elsewhere classified.

APPENDIX E

Revised 2011 results and comparisons with original ICP 2011 results

This appendix provides revised 2011 results for the International Comparison Program (ICP) and compares them with the original 2011 results published in 2014.

Tables E.1 to E.6 present revised global 2011 results using updated 2011 expenditures, regional purchasing power parities (PPPs), population, and market exchange rate data. Subsequently, all related indicators were revised. More detailed data sets are available through online databases, which are accessible through the ICP website[1] and through the World Bank's Databank[2] and Data Catalog.[3]

In addition, users may acquire access to unpublished ICP data sets, as detailed in the ICP data access and archive policy (World Bank 2019a).

Results presented in these tables are produced by the ICP Global Office and regional implementing agencies, based on data supplied by participating economies, and in accordance with the methodology recommended by the ICP Technical Advisory Group and approved by the ICP Governing Board. As such, these results are not produced by participating economies as part of their national official statistics.

This appendix provides the main set of results for the following headings:

- Table E.1 Gross domestic product (GDP)
- Table E.2 Actual individual consumption (AIC)
- Table E.3 Individual consumption expenditure by households
- Table E.4 Consumption expenditure by government
- Table E.5 Gross fixed capital formation (GFCF)
- Table E.6 Domestic absorption.

The table structure follows that of the 2017 results (see chapter 2 for the details).

In addition, supplementary table E.7 provides a limited set of results for selected economies that did not participate in the 2011 cycle. The approach for imputing the PPPs for these economies is described in chapter 5.

Tables E.8 and E.9 compare revised 2011 PPPs with original 2011 PPPs, as well as expenditures in current local currency units for both data sets for the following headings:

- Table E.8 Gross domestic product (GDP)
- Table E.9 Individual consumption expenditure by households.

The comparison tables cover the following indicators for each heading:

- *Column (00).* Name of the economy and its International Organization for Standardization (ISO) code
- *Column (01).* Revised 2011 PPPs with the US dollar equal to 1
- *Column (02).* Original 2011 PPPs with the US dollar equal to 1
- *Column (03).* Percentage difference between columns (01) and (02)
- *Column (04).* Revised 2011 expenditures in local currency units
- *Column (05).* Original 2011 expenditures in local currency units
- *Column (06).* Percentage difference between columns (04) and (05).

Notes

1. See icp.worldbank.org/programs/icp#5.
2. See data.worldbank.org.
3. See datacatalog.worldbank.org.

Table E.1 Gross domestic product (GDP): Revised ICP 2011 results

GROSS DOMESTIC PRODUCT		Expenditure (billion US$)		Expenditure per capita (US$)		Price level index (world = 100.0)[a]	Expenditure per capita indexes[b]				Share (world = 100%)[b]			PPPs[c] (US$ = 1.000)	Reference data		
							World = 100.0		United States = 100.0		Expenditure				Market exchange rates[c] (US$ = 1.000)	Expenditure (billion LCU)	Population (millions)
Economy		Based on PPPs	Based on XRs	Based on PPPs	Based on XRs		Based on PPPs	Based on XRs	Based on PPPs	Based on XRs	Based on PPPs	Based on XRs	Population				
(00)		(01)	(02)	(03)	(04)	(05)	(06)	(07)	(08)	(09)	(10)	(11)	(12)	(13)	(14)	(15)	(16)
East Asia and Pacific																	
Australia	AUS	971.2	1,513.8	43,474	67,761	201.1	312.3	628.1	87.3	136.0	1.0	2.1	0.3	1.511	0.969	1,467.6	22.34
Brunei Darussalam	BRN	33.0	18.5	84,005	47,095	72.3	603.5	436.5	168.6	94.5	0.0	0.0	0.0	0.705	1.258	23.3	0.39
Cambodia	KHM	38.0	12.8	2,654	897	43.6	19.1	8.3	5.3	1.8	0.0	0.0	0.2	1,371.235	4,058.500	52,068.7	14.31
China	CHN	13,883.0	7,572.6	10,329	5,634	70.4	74.2	52.2	20.7	11.3	14.8	10.4	20.0	3.524	6.461	48,930.1	1,344.13
Fiji	FJI	7.7	4.1	9,047	4,786	68.3	65.0	44.4	18.2	9.6	0.0	0.0	0.0	0.949	1.793	7.3	0.85
Hong Kong SAR, China	HKG	369.7	248.5	52,277	35,142	86.7	375.5	325.7	105.0	70.6	0.4	0.3	0.1	5.233	7.784	1,934.4	7.07
Indonesia	IDN	2,229.5	893.0	9,213	3,690	51.7	66.2	34.2	18.5	7.4	2.4	1.2	3.6	3,512.754	8,770.433	7,831,726.0	241.99
Japan	JPN	4,573.2	6,157.5	35,775	48,169	173.7	257.0	446.5	71.8	96.7	4.9	8.5	1.9	107.454	79.807	491,408.5	127.83
Korea, Rep.	KOR	1,625.3	1,253.2	32,547	25,096	99.5	233.8	232.6	65.3	50.4	1.7	1.7	0.7	854.586	1,108.292	1,388,937.3	49.94
Lao PDR	LAO	26.8	8.9	4,386	1,456	42.8	31.5	13.5	8.8	2.9	0.0	0.0	0.1	2,666.535	8,030.055	71,543.6	6.12
Macao SAR, China[d]	MAC	66.3	36.7	120,358	66,644	71.4	864.6	617.7	241.6	133.8	0.1	0.1	0.0	4.440	8.018	294.3	0.55
Malaysia	MYS	621.9	298.0	21,398	10,252	61.8	153.7	95.0	43.0	20.6	0.7	0.4	0.4	1.466	3.060	911.7	29.06
Mongolia	MNG	24.7	10.4	8,862	3,736	54.4	63.7	34.6	17.8	7.5	0.0	0.0	0.0	533.527	1,265.516	13,173.8	2.79
Myanmar	MMR	167.7	53.7	3,377	1,081	41.3	24.3	10.0	6.8	2.2	0.2	0.1	0.7	261.784	817.917	43,900.0	49.66
New Zealand	NZL	142.2	166.9	32,370	37,999	151.5	232.5	352.2	65.0	76.3	0.2	0.2	0.1	1.486	1.266	211.3	4.39
Philippines	PHL	536.4	224.1	5,696	2,380	53.9	40.9	22.1	11.4	4.8	0.6	0.3	1.4	18.098	43.313	9,708.3	94.18
Singapore	SGP	415.0	279.4	80,052	53,891	86.9	575.1	499.5	160.7	108.2	0.4	0.4	0.1	0.847	1.258	351.4	5.18
Taiwan, China	TWN	944.7	485.7	40,736	20,943	66.3	292.6	194.1	81.8	42.0	1.0	0.7	0.3	15.151	29.469	14,312.2	23.19
Thailand	THA	912.8	370.8	13,785	5,600	52.4	99.0	51.9	27.7	11.2	1.0	0.5	1.0	12.387	30.492	11,306.9	66.21
Vietnam	VNM	402.0	135.5	4,562	1,538	43.5	32.8	14.3	9.2	3.1	0.4	0.2	1.3	6,915.335	20,509.750	2,779,880.2	88.11
Total (20)	**EAB**	**27,991.0**	**19,744.1**	**12,850**	**9,064**	**91.0**	**92.3**	**84.0**	**25.8**	**18.2**	**29.9**	**27.2**	**32.3**	**n.a.**	**n.a**	**n.a.**	**2,178.31**
Europe and Central Asia																	
Albania	ALB	29.7	12.9	10,208	4,441	56.1	73.3	41.2	20.5	8.9	0.0	0.0	0.0	43.858	100.812	1,300.6	2.91
Armenia	ARM	23.1	10.1	7,624	3,350	56.7	54.8	31.0	15.3	6.7	0.0	0.0	0.0	163.650	372.500	3,777.9	3.03
Austria	AUT	373.0	431.7	44,469	51,463	149.3	319.5	477.0	89.3	103.3	0.4	0.6	0.1	0.831	0.718	310.1	8.39
Azerbaijan	AZE	135.8	65.9	15,001	7,282	62.6	107.8	67.5	30.1	14.6	0.1	0.1	0.1	0.384	0.790	52.1	9.05
Belarus	BLR	156.7	54.8	16,543	5,786	45.1	118.8	53.6	33.2	11.6	0.2	0.1	0.1	0.196	0.561	30.7	9.47
Belgium	BEL	451.9	523.3	40,942	47,412	149.4	294.1	439.4	82.2	95.2	0.5	0.7	0.2	0.832	0.718	376.0	11.04
Bosnia and Herzegovina	BIH	36.5	18.7	9,976	5,099	65.9	71.7	47.3	20.0	10.2	0.0	0.0	0.1	0.718	1.405	26.2	3.66
Bulgaria	BGR	115.1	57.4	15,661	7,815	64.4	112.5	72.4	31.4	15.7	0.1	0.1	0.1	0.701	1.405	80.7	7.35
Croatia	HRV	88.8	62.4	20,732	14,558	90.6	148.9	134.9	41.6	29.2	0.1	0.1	0.1	3.753	5.344	333.2	4.28
Cyprus	CYP	28.3	27.6	33,314	32,397	125.5	239.3	300.3	66.9	65.0	0.0	0.0	0.0	0.699	0.718	19.8	0.85
Czech Republic	CZE	302.3	228.3	28,796	21,754	97.5	206.9	201.6	57.8	43.7	0.3	0.3	0.2	13.345	17.665	4,033.8	10.50
Denmark	DNK	247.4	345.0	44,408	61,948	180.0	319.0	574.2	89.2	124.4	0.3	0.5	0.1	7.466	5.352	1,846.9	5.57
Estonia	EST	32.9	23.4	24,739	17,618	91.9	177.7	163.3	49.7	35.4	0.0	0.0	0.0	0.512	0.718	16.8	1.33
Finland	FIN	220.5	275.6	40,917	51,150	161.3	293.9	474.1	82.1	102.7	0.2	0.4	0.1	0.898	0.718	198.0	5.39

Table E.1 *(Continued)*

GROSS DOMESTIC PRODUCT		Expenditure (billion US$)		Expenditure per capita (US$)		Price level index	Expenditure per capita indexes[b]				Share (world = 100%)[b]				Reference data		
							World = 100.0		United States = 100.0		Expenditure				Market exchange rates[c]		
Economy		Based on PPPs	Based on XRs	Based on PPPs	Based on XRs	(world = 100.0)[a]	Based on PPPs	Based on XRs	Based on PPPs	Based on XRs	Based on PPPs	Based on XRs	Population	PPPs[c] (US$ = 1.000)	(US$ = 1.000)	Expenditure (billion LCU)	Population (millions)
(00)		(01)	(02)	(03)	(04)	(05)	(06)	(07)	(08)	(09)	(10)	(11)	(12)	(13)	(14)	(15)	(16)
France	FRA	2,446.5	2,865.2	37,448	43,858	151.1	269.0	406.5	75.2	88.0	2.6	3.9	1.0	0.841	0.718	2,058.4	65.33
Georgia	GEO	31.4	15.1	8,360	4,022	62.1	60.1	37.3	16.8	8.1	0.0	0.0	0.1	0.811	1.686	25.5	3.76
Germany	DEU	3,415.0	3,749.4	42,542	46,707	141.7	305.6	432.9	85.4	93.8	3.6	5.2	1.2	0.789	0.718	2,693.6	80.28
Greece	GRC	290.3	288.2	26,141	25,951	128.1	187.8	240.5	52.5	52.1	0.3	0.4	0.2	0.713	0.718	207.0	11.11
Hungary	HUN	228.3	141.4	22,894	14,176	79.9	164.5	131.4	46.0	28.5	0.2	0.2	0.1	124.272	200.697	28,370.8	9.97
Iceland	ISL	13.0	15.2	40,769	47,515	150.4	292.9	440.4	81.8	95.4	0.0	0.0	0.0	135.152	115.963	1,757.7	0.32
Ireland	IRL	205.4	237.8	44,870	51,936	149.3	322.3	481.4	90.1	104.3	0.2	0.3	0.1	0.832	0.718	170.8	4.58
Italy	ITA	2,173.2	2,295.1	36,183	38,213	136.3	259.9	354.2	72.6	76.7	2.3	3.2	0.9	0.759	0.718	1,648.8	60.06
Kazakhstan	KAZ	344.0	192.6	20,779	11,634	72.2	149.3	107.8	41.7	23.4	0.4	0.3	0.2	82.090	146.620	28,243.1	16.56
Kyrgyz Republic	KGZ	18.2	6.2	3,457	1,178	44.0	24.8	10.9	6.9	2.4	0.0	0.0	0.1	15.728	46.144	286.0	5.26
Latvia	LVA	40.6	28.1	19,700	13,670	89.5	141.5	126.7	39.5	27.4	0.0	0.0	0.0	0.499	0.718	20.2	2.06
Lithuania	LTU	69.1	43.5	22,824	14,358	81.2	164.0	133.1	45.8	28.8	0.1	0.1	0.0	0.452	0.718	31.2	3.03
Luxembourg	LUX	47.7	60.1	91,813	115,675	162.6	659.6	1,072.1	184.3	232.2	0.1	0.1	0.0	0.905	0.718	43.2	0.52
Moldova	MDA	19.8	8.4	5,554	2,366	55.0	39.9	21.9	11.2	4.8	0.0	0.0	0.1	4.996	11.726	98.8	3.56
Montenegro	MNE	9.0	4.5	14,473	7,329	65.3	104.0	67.9	29.1	14.7	0.0	0.0	0.0	0.364	0.718	3.3	0.62
Netherlands	NLD	777.9	905.3	46,599	54,232	150.2	334.8	502.7	93.6	108.9	0.8	1.2	0.2	0.836	0.718	650.4	16.69
North Macedonia	MKD	24.1	10.5	11,690	5,101	56.3	84.0	47.3	23.5	10.2	0.0	0.0	0.0	19.290	44.202	464.2	2.06
Norway	NOR	307.5	498.8	62,078	100,708	209.3	445.9	933.4	124.6	202.2	0.3	0.7	0.1	9.083	5.599	2,792.7	4.95
Poland	POL	869.8	529.3	22,576	13,739	78.5	162.2	127.3	45.3	27.6	0.9	0.7	0.6	1.801	2.960	1,566.8	38.53
Portugal	PRT	282.6	245.1	26,769	23,218	111.9	192.3	215.2	53.7	46.6	0.3	0.3	0.2	0.623	0.718	176.1	10.56
Romania	ROU	360.8	183.6	17,908	9,115	65.7	128.6	84.5	36.0	18.3	0.4	0.3	0.3	1.550	3.045	559.2	20.15
Russian Federation	RUS	3,268.5	2,051.7	22,863	14,351	81.0	164.2	133.0	45.9	28.8	3.5	2.8	2.1	18.444	29.382	60,282.5	142.96
Serbia	SRB	99.4	49.3	13,742	6,816	64.0	98.7	63.2	27.6	13.7	0.1	0.1	0.1	36.324	73.240	3,612.3	7.24
Slovak Republic	SVK	140.6	99.1	26,051	18,364	91.0	187.1	170.2	52.3	36.9	0.1	0.1	0.1	0.506	0.718	71.2	5.40
Slovenia	SVN	59.4	51.6	28,931	25,129	112.1	207.8	232.9	58.1	50.4	0.1	0.1	0.0	0.624	0.718	37.1	2.05
Spain	ESP	1,486.4	1,477.6	31,803	31,615	128.3	228.5	293.0	63.8	63.5	1.6	2.0	0.7	0.714	0.718	1,061.5	46.74
Sweden	SWE	420.5	573.3	44,504	60,675	175.9	319.7	562.4	89.3	121.8	0.4	0.8	0.1	8.844	6.487	3,719.1	9.45
Switzerland	CHE	444.5	701.6	56,184	88,671	203.6	403.6	821.9	112.8	178.0	0.5	1.0	0.1	1.397	0.885	621.3	7.91
Tajikistan	TJK	19.2	6.5	2,491	846	43.8	17.9	7.8	5.0	1.7	0.0	0.0	0.1	1.565	4.610	30.1	7.71
Turkey	TUR	1,443.3	832.5	19,445	11,217	74.4	139.7	104.0	39.0	22.5	1.5	1.1	1.1	0.966	1.675	1,394.5	74.22
Ukraine[d]	UKR	422.6	169.3	9,247	3,705	51.7	66.4	34.3	18.6	7.4	0.5	0.2	0.7	3.192	7.968	1,349.2	45.71
United Kingdom	GBR	2,350.8	2,662.1	37,146	42,066	146.1	266.8	389.9	74.6	84.5	2.5	3.7	0.9	0.706	0.623	1,659.8	63.29
Total (46)	**ECB**	**24,371.3**	**23,135.5**	**28,490**	**27,046**	**122.5**	**204.7**	**250.7**	**57.2**	**54.3**	**26.0**	**31.8**	**12.7**	**n.a.**	**n.a**	**n.a.**	**855.42**
Latin America and the Caribbean																	
Anguilla	AIA	0.4	0.3	28,940	21,336	95.1	207.9	197.8	58.1	42.8	0.0	0.0	0.0	1.990	2.700	0.8	0.01
Antigua and Barbuda	ATG	1.8	1.1	20,426	12,796	80.8	146.7	118.6	41.0	25.7	0.0	0.0	0.0	1.691	2.700	3.1	0.09
Aruba	ABW	3.6	2.6	34,794	25,326	93.9	249.9	234.7	69.9	50.8	0.0	0.0	0.0	1.303	1.790	4.6	0.10

(continued)

Table E.1 *(Continued)*

GROSS DOMESTIC PRODUCT		Expenditure (billion US$)		Expenditure per capita (US$)		Price level index (world = 100.0)[a]	Expenditure per capita indexes[b]				Share (world = 100%)[b]			PPPs[c] (US$ = 1.000)	Reference data		
							World = 100.0		United States = 100.0		Expenditure				Market exchange rates[c] (US$ = 1.000)	Expenditure (billion LCU)	Population (millions)
Economy		Based on PPPs	Based on XRs	Based on PPPs	Based on XRs		Based on PPPs	Based on XRs	Based on PPPs	Based on XRs	Based on PPPs	Based on XRs	Population				
(00)		(01)	(02)	(03)	(04)	(05)	(06)	(07)	(08)	(09)	(10)	(11)	(12)	(13)	(14)	(15)	(16)
Bahamas, The	BHS	11.2	10.1	31,168	28,006	115.9	223.9	259.6	62.6	56.2	0.0	0.0	0.0	0.899	1.000	10.1	0.36
Barbados	BRB	4.6	4.7	16,316	16,470	130.2	117.2	152.7	32.8	33.1	0.0	0.0	0.0	2.019	2.000	9.3	0.28
Belize	BLZ	2.6	1.5	7,821	4,502	74.3	56.2	41.7	15.7	9.0	0.0	0.0	0.0	1.151	2.000	3.0	0.33
Bolivia	BOL	55.8	23.8	5,460	2,331	55.1	39.2	21.6	11.0	4.7	0.1	0.0	0.2	2.981	6.982	166.2	10.21
Bonaire[e]	BON	...	...	...	...	...	...	...	...	...	...	...	...	...	1.000	...	0.02
Brazil	BRA	2,970.6	2,616.2	15,040	13,245	113.6	108.0	122.8	30.2	26.6	3.2	3.6	2.9	1.473	1.673	4,376.4	197.51
Cayman Islands	CYM	3.7	4.2	64,014	72,326	145.8	459.9	670.4	128.5	145.2	0.0	0.0	0.0	0.942	0.833	3.5	0.06
Chile	CHL	350.6	252.3	20,303	14,609	92.8	145.8	135.4	40.8	29.3	0.4	0.3	0.3	348.017	483.668	122,006.1	17.27
Colombia	COL	529.1	334.5	11,491	7,264	81.6	82.5	67.3	23.1	14.6	0.6	0.5	0.7	1,168.243	1,848.139	618,117.7	46.04
Costa Rica	CRI	62.0	42.3	13,514	9,208	87.9	97.1	85.3	27.1	18.5	0.1	0.1	0.1	344.546	505.664	21,370.7	4.59
Curaçao	CUW	4.1	3.0	26,959	19,950	95.5	193.7	184.9	54.1	40.1	0.0	0.0	0.0	1.325	1.790	5.4	0.15
Dominica	DMA	0.7	0.5	10,199	7,065	89.4	73.3	65.5	20.5	14.2	0.0	0.0	0.0	1.870	2.700	1.4	0.07
Dominican Republic	DOM	116.5	58.0	11,869	5,912	64.3	85.3	54.8	23.8	11.9	0.1	0.1	0.1	18.976	38.099	2,210.2	9.81
Ecuador	ECU	150.3	79.3	9,858	5,201	68.1	70.8	48.2	19.8	10.4	0.2	0.1	0.2	0.528	1.000	79.3	15.24
El Salvador	SLV	40.2	20.3	6,466	3,266	65.2	46.4	30.3	13.0	6.6	0.0	0.0	0.1	0.505	1.000	20.3	6.21
Grenada	GRD	1.2	0.8	11,116	7,291	84.6	79.9	67.6	22.3	14.6	0.0	0.0	0.0	1.771	2.700	2.1	0.11
Guatemala[d]	GTM	102.0	47.5	6,825	3,179	60.1	49.0	29.5	13.7	6.4	0.1	0.1	0.2	3.637	7.807	371.0	14.95
Haiti	HTI	17.1	7.7	1,694	764	58.2	12.2	7.1	3.4	1.5	0.0	0.0	0.1	18.495	40.977	316.4	10.10
Honduras	HND	33.3	17.6	3,928	2,074	68.1	28.2	19.2	7.9	4.2	0.0	0.0	0.1	10.057	19.048	335.0	8.48
Jamaica	JAM	23.1	14.4	8,160	5,110	80.8	58.6	47.4	16.4	10.3	0.0	0.0	0.0	53.805	85.911	1,240.7	2.83
Mexico	MEX	1,911.3	1,180.5	16,547	10,220	79.7	118.9	94.7	33.2	20.5	2.0	1.6	1.7	7.673	12.423	14,665.6	115.51
Montserrat	MSR	0.1	0.1	20,405	12,915	81.7	146.6	119.7	41.0	25.9	0.0	0.0	0.0	1.709	2.700	0.2	0.00
Nicaragua	NIC	25.2	9.8	4,263	1,656	50.1	30.6	15.3	8.6	3.3	0.0	0.0	0.1	8.710	22.424	219.2	5.90
Panama	PAN	62.7	34.7	16,924	9,358	71.3	121.6	86.7	34.0	18.8	0.1	0.0	0.1	0.553	1.000	34.7	3.71
Paraguay	PRY	66.4	33.8	10,491	5,334	65.6	75.4	49.4	21.1	10.7	0.1	0.0	0.1	2,126.670	4,183.127	141,315.8	6.33
Peru	PER	306.6	171.8	10,477	5,869	72.3	75.3	54.4	21.0	11.8	0.3	0.2	0.4	1.543	2.754	473.0	29.26
Sint Maarten	SXM	1.2	0.9	35,510	26,701	97.0	255.1	247.5	71.3	53.6	0.0	0.0	0.0	1.346	1.790	1.7	0.04
St. Kitts and Nevis	KNA	1.1	0.8	22,768	16,538	93.7	163.6	153.3	45.7	33.2	0.0	0.0	0.0	1.961	2.700	2.2	0.05
St. Lucia	LCA	2.1	1.4	12,141	8,227	87.4	87.2	76.3	24.4	16.5	0.0	0.0	0.0	1.830	2.700	3.9	0.18
St. Vincent and the Grenadines	VCT	1.2	0.7	10,634	6,443	78.2	76.4	59.7	21.3	12.9	0.0	0.0	0.0	1.636	2.700	1.9	0.11
Suriname	SUR	7.7	4.3	14,445	8,044	71.9	103.8	74.6	29.0	16.2	0.0	0.0	0.0	1.866	3.350	14.4	0.54
Trinidad and Tobago	TTO	41.9	25.7	31,321	19,250	79.3	225.0	178.4	62.9	38.6	0.0	0.0	0.0	3.950	6.426	165.3	1.34
Turks and Caicos Islands	TCA	0.7	0.7	21,232	21,835	132.7	152.5	202.4	42.6	43.8	0.0	0.0	0.0	1.028	1.000	0.7	0.03
Uruguay	URY	60.7	48.0	18,003	14,237	102.0	129.3	132.0	36.1	28.6	0.1	0.1	0.1	15.274	19.314	926.4	3.37
Venezuela, RB[d]	VEN	506.3	316.5	17,528	10,956	80.6	125.9	101.5	35.2	22.0	0.5	0.4	0.4	2.681	4.289	1,357.5	28.89
Virgin Islands, British	VGB	0.9	0.9	31,464	32,331	132.6	226.0	299.7	63.2	64.9	0.0	0.0	0.0	1.028	1.000	0.9	0.03
Total (39)	**LCB**	7,480.6	5,373.1	13,850	9,948	92.7	99.5	92.2	27.8	20.0	8.0	7.4	8.0	n.a.	n.a	n.a.	540.10

Table E.1 *(Continued)*

GROSS DOMESTIC PRODUCT		Expenditure (billion US$)		Expenditure per capita (US$)		Price level index (world = 100.0)[a]	Expenditure per capita indexes[b]				Share (world = 100%)[b]			PPPs[c] (US$ = 1.000)	Reference data		
							World = 100.0		United States = 100.0		Expenditure				Market exchange rates[c] (US$ = 1.000)	Expenditure (billion LCU)	Population (millions)
Economy		Based on PPPs	Based on XRs	Based on PPPs	Based on XRs		Based on PPPs	Based on XRs	Based on PPPs	Based on XRs	Based on PPPs	Based on XRs	Population				
(00)		(01)	(02)	(03)	(04)	(05)	(06)	(07)	(08)	(09)	(10)	(11)	(12)	(13)	(14)	(15)	(16)
Middle East and North Africa																	
Algeria	DZA	494.9	200.0	13,500	5,456	52.1	97.0	50.6	27.1	11.0	0.5	0.3	0.5	29.476	72.938	14,589.0	36.66
Bahrain	BHR	60.5	28.8	50,666	24,077	61.3	364.0	223.2	101.7	48.3	0.1	0.0	0.0	0.179	0.376	10.8	1.20
Djibouti	DJI	4.2	2.2	4,916	2,588	67.9	35.3	24.0	9.9	5.2	0.0	0.0	0.0	93.572	177.721	392.7	0.85
Egypt, Arab Rep.	EGY	905.5	255.0	11,245	3,166	36.3	80.8	29.3	22.6	6.4	1.0	0.4	1.2	1.675	5.947	1,516.4	80.53
Iran, Islamic Rep.	IRN	1,584.8	710.4	21,089	9,453	57.8	151.5	87.6	42.3	19.0	1.7	1.0	1.1	4,758.870	10,616.307	7,542,036.5	75.15
Iraq	IRQ	366.2	159.8	10,985	4,794	56.3	78.9	44.4	22.1	9.6	0.4	0.2	0.5	523.340	1,199.200	191,652.9	33.34
Israel	ISR	237.2	261.5	30,551	33,681	142.2	219.5	312.2	61.3	67.6	0.3	0.4	0.1	3.945	3.578	935.6	7.76
Jordan	JOR	70.5	29.0	10,077	4,141	53.0	72.4	38.4	20.2	8.3	0.1	0.0	0.1	0.291	0.708	20.5	6.99
Kuwait	KWT	247.6	151.8	80,758	49,526	79.1	580.1	459.0	162.1	99.4	0.3	0.2	0.0	0.172	0.280	42.5	3.07
Malta	MLT	11.9	9.5	28,586	22,846	103.1	205.4	211.8	57.4	45.9	0.0	0.0	0.0	0.574	0.718	6.8	0.42
Morocco	MAR	223.3	101.9	6,855	3,127	58.9	49.2	29.0	13.8	6.3	0.2	0.1	0.5	3.672	8.049	820.1	32.58
Oman	OMN	141.2	67.9	42,843	20,597	62.0	307.8	190.9	86.0	41.4	0.2	0.1	0.0	0.185	0.385	26.1	3.30
Qatar	QAT	283.7	167.3	163,740	96,563	76.1	1,176.3	895.0	328.7	193.9	0.3	0.2	0.0	2.153	3.650	610.7	1.73
Saudi Arabia	SAU	1,586.7	671.2	56,321	23,825	54.6	404.6	220.8	113.1	47.8	1.7	0.9	0.4	1.586	3.750	2,517.1	28.17
Tunisia	TUN	108.2	45.8	10,069	4,265	54.7	72.3	39.5	20.2	8.6	0.1	0.1	0.2	0.596	1.408	64.5	10.74
United Arab Emirates	ARE	605.6	350.7	69,831	40,437	74.7	501.6	374.8	140.2	81.2	0.6	0.5	0.1	2.127	3.673	1,287.8	8.67
West Bank and Gaza	PSE	15.6	10.5	4,015	2,698	86.7	28.8	25.0	8.1	5.4	0.0	0.0	0.1	2.405	3.578	37.4	3.88
Yemen, Rep.[d]	YEM	82.4	31.4	3,458	1,318	49.2	24.8	12.2	6.9	2.6	0.1	0.0	0.4	81.477	213.800	6,714.9	23.83
Total (17)	**MEB**	**7,030.1**	**3,254.7**	**19,589**	**9,069**	**59.7**	**140.7**	**84.1**	**39.3**	**18.2**	**7.5**	**4.5**	**5.3**	**n.a.**	**n.a**	**n.a.**	**358.87**
North America																	
Bermuda	BMU	4.0	5.6	61,692	86,171	180.2	443.2	798.7	123.9	173.0	0.0	0.0	0.0	1.397	1.000	5.6	0.07
Canada	CAN	1,430.8	1,792.8	41,663	52,204	161.7	299.3	483.9	83.6	104.8	1.5	2.5	0.5	1.240	0.990	1,774.1	34.34
United States	USA	15,542.6	15,542.6	49,811	49,811	129.0	357.8	461.7	100.0	100.0	16.6	21.4	4.6	1.000	1.000	15,542.6	312.03
Total (3)	**NAB**	**16,977.4**	**17,341.0**	**49,005**	**50,055**	**131.8**	**352.0**	**463.9**	**98.4**	**100.5**	**18.1**	**23.9**	**5.1**	**n.a.**	**n.a**	**n.a.**	**346.44**
South Asia																	
Bangladesh	BGD	421.0	132.9	2,812	888	40.7	20.2	8.2	5.6	1.8	0.4	0.2	2.2	23.410	74.152	9,855.2	149.70
Bhutan	BTN	5.2	1.8	7,625	2,679	45.3	54.8	24.8	15.3	5.4	0.0	0.0	0.0	16.397	46.670	85.0	0.68
India	IND	5,482.9	1,826.8	4,508	1,502	43.0	32.4	13.9	9.1	3.0	5.8	2.5	18.1	15.550	46.670	85,256.2	1,216.15
Maldives	MDV	5.2	2.8	12,681	6,827	69.5	91.1	63.3	25.5	13.7	0.0	0.0	0.0	7.862	14.602	40.5	0.41
Nepal	NPL	57.1	19.5	2,154	735	44.0	15.5	6.8	4.3	1.5	0.1	0.0	0.4	25.255	74.020	1,440.8	26.49
Pakistan	PAK	767.6	221.9	4,334	1,253	37.3	31.1	11.6	8.7	2.5	0.8	0.3	2.6	24.962	86.343	19,161.5	177.10
Sri Lanka	LKA	183.7	65.3	9,099	3,233	45.8	65.4	30.0	18.3	6.5	0.2	0.1	0.3	39.289	110.565	7,219.1	20.20
Total (7)	**SAB**	**6,922.6**	**2,270.9**	**4,352**	**1,428**	**42.3**	**31.3**	**13.2**	**8.7**	**2.9**	**7.4**	**3.1**	**23.6**	**n.a.**	**n.a**	**n.a.**	**1,590.72**
Sub-Saharan Africa																	
Angola	AGO	164.0	112.8	6,772	4,658	88.7	48.6	43.2	13.6	9.4	0.2	0.2	0.4	64.606	93.935	10,597.0	24.22
Benin	BEN	16.7	7.8	1,767	825	60.3	12.7	7.7	3.5	1.7	0.0	0.0	0.1	220.434	471.866	3,684.9	9.46
Botswana	BWA	28.7	15.4	14,253	7,617	69.0	102.4	70.6	28.6	15.3	0.0	0.0	0.0	3.655	6.838	105.0	2.02

(continued)

Table E.1 *(Continued)*

GROSS DOMESTIC PRODUCT Economy		Expenditure (billion US$) Based on PPPs	 Based on XRs	Expenditure per capita (US$) Based on PPPs	 Based on XRs	Price level index (world = 100.0)[a]	Expenditure per capita indexes[b] World = 100.0 Based on PPPs	 Based on XRs	 United States = 100.0 Based on PPPs	 Based on XRs	Share (world = 100%)[b] Expenditure Based on PPPs	 Based on XRs	 Population	PPPs[c] (US$ = 1.000)	Reference data Market exchange rates[c] (US$ = 1.000)	 Expenditure (billion LCU)	 Population (millions)
(00)		(01)	(02)	(03)	(04)	(05)	(06)	(07)	(08)	(09)	(10)	(11)	(12)	(13)	(14)	(15)	(16)
Burkina Faso	BFA	22.8	10.8	1,419	671	61.0	10.2	6.2	2.8	1.3	0.0	0.0	0.2	223.116	471.866	5,092.6	16.08
Burundi	BDI	6.1	2.3	686	251	47.2	4.9	2.3	1.4	0.5	0.0	0.0	0.1	461.509	1,261.073	2,837.7	8.96
Cabo Verde	CPV	3.0	1.9	5,966	3,738	80.8	42.9	34.6	12.0	7.5	0.0	0.0	0.0	49.695	79.323	147.9	0.50
Cameroon	CMR	58.0	29.3	2,774	1,403	65.3	19.9	13.0	5.6	2.8	0.1	0.0	0.3	238.707	471.866	13,843.1	20.91
Central African Republic	CAF	4.5	2.4	1,013	551	70.2	7.3	5.1	2.0	1.1	0.0	0.0	0.1	256.761	471.866	1,148.9	4.42
Chad	TCD	22.8	12.5	1,846	1,010	70.6	13.3	9.4	3.7	2.0	0.0	0.0	0.2	258.131	471.866	5,891.4	12.36
Comoros	COM	1.7	1.0	2,337	1,446	79.8	16.8	13.4	4.7	2.9	0.0	0.0	0.0	218.978	353.900	361.6	0.71
Congo, Dem. Rep.	COD	58.7	34.0	879	509	74.7	6.3	4.7	1.8	1.0	0.1	0.0	1.0	532.063	919.491	31,230.5	66.76
Congo, Rep.	COG	25.1	16.5	5,714	3,745	84.6	41.0	34.7	11.5	7.5	0.0	0.0	0.1	309.251	471.866	7,765.6	4.39
Côte d'Ivoire	CIV	51.1	25.7	2,431	1,221	64.8	17.5	11.3	4.9	2.5	0.1	0.0	0.3	236.911	471.866	12,112.7	21.03
Equatorial Guinea	GNQ	33.8	21.3	34,280	21,613	81.3	246.3	200.3	68.8	43.4	0.0	0.0	0.0	297.509	471.866	10,064.6	0.99
Eswatini	SWZ	8.5	4.7	7,889	4,403	72.0	56.7	40.8	15.8	8.8	0.0	0.0	0.0	4.052	7.261	34.3	1.07
Ethiopia	ETH	152.6	45.5	1,693	505	38.4	12.2	4.7	3.4	1.0	0.2	0.1	1.3	5.036	16.899	768.6	90.14
Gabon	GAB	27.9	19.3	16,562	11,433	89.1	119.0	106.0	33.2	23.0	0.0	0.0	0.0	325.733	471.866	9,088.2	1.68
Gambia, The	GMB	4.0	1.4	2,150	740	44.4	15.4	6.9	4.3	1.5	0.0	0.0	0.0	10.142	29.462	40.3	1.85
Ghana	GHA	85.8	39.6	3,379	1,558	59.5	24.3	14.4	6.8	3.1	0.1	0.1	0.4	0.697	1.512	59.8	25.39
Guinea	GIN	18.2	6.8	1,744	651	48.2	12.5	6.0	3.5	1.3	0.0	0.0	0.2	2,485.901	6,658.031	45,176.5	10.42
Guinea-Bissau	GNB	2.2	1.1	1,439	703	63.0	10.3	6.5	2.9	1.4	0.0	0.0	0.0	230.392	471.866	518.3	1.56
Kenya	KEN	105.3	42.0	2,439	972	51.4	17.5	9.0	4.9	2.0	0.1	0.1	0.6	35.396	88.811	3,727.4	43.18
Lesotho	LSO	4.8	2.7	2,386	1,341	72.5	17.1	12.4	4.8	2.7	0.0	0.0	0.0	4.081	7.261	19.5	2.00
Liberia	LBR	2.8	1.5	702	383	70.4	5.0	3.6	1.4	0.8	0.0	0.0	0.1	39.424	72.227	111.2	4.02
Madagascar	MDG	33.7	11.6	1,549	532	44.3	11.1	4.9	3.1	1.1	0.0	0.0	0.3	694.863	2,025.118	23,404.5	21.74
Malawi	MWI	15.9	8.0	1,063	535	64.9	7.6	5.0	2.1	1.1	0.0	0.0	0.2	78.769	156.515	1,253.2	14.96
Mali	MLI	28.3	13.0	1,827	837	59.1	13.1	7.8	3.7	1.7	0.0	0.0	0.2	216.090	471.866	6,123.9	15.51
Mauritania	MRT	12.1	5.2	3,372	1,436	54.9	24.2	13.3	6.8	2.9	0.0	0.0	0.1	119.682	281.118	1,452.4	3.60
Mauritius	MUS	25.1	13.9	20,102	11,102	71.3	144.4	102.9	40.4	22.3	0.0	0.0	0.0	15.853	28.706	398.7	1.25
Mozambique	MOZ	24.5	14.3	1,015	590	75.0	7.3	5.5	2.0	1.2	0.0	0.0	0.4	16.894	29.068	414.6	24.19
Namibia	NAM	19.1	12.4	8,859	5,772	84.1	63.6	53.5	17.8	11.6	0.0	0.0	0.0	4.732	7.261	90.4	2.16
Niger	NER	13.4	6.4	781	374	61.8	5.6	3.5	1.6	0.8	0.0	0.0	0.3	226.128	471.866	3,024.3	17.11
Nigeria	NGA	798.9	409.0	4,907	2,512	66.1	35.2	23.3	9.9	5.0	0.9	0.6	2.4	78.777	153.862	62,931.7	162.81
Rwanda	RWA	13.9	6.4	1,354	624	59.5	9.7	5.8	2.7	1.3	0.0	0.0	0.2	276.649	600.307	3,854.3	10.29
São Tomé and Príncipe	STP	0.6	0.3	3,259	1,374	54.4	23.4	12.7	6.5	2.8	0.0	0.0	0.0	7.431	17.623	4.5	0.18
Senegal	SEN	36.2	18.5	2,780	1,422	66.0	20.0	13.2	5.6	2.9	0.0	0.0	0.2	241.276	471.866	8,743.8	13.03
Seychelles	SYC	1.9	1.1	20,739	11,531	71.7	149.0	106.9	41.6	23.1	0.0	0.0	0.0	6.884	12.381	13.1	0.09
Sierra Leone	SLE	7.9	2.9	1,203	448	48.1	8.6	4.2	2.4	0.9	0.0	0.0	0.1	1,620.575	4,349.162	12,797.6	6.56
South Africa	ZAF	639.2	420.5	12,291	8,086	84.9	88.3	74.9	24.7	16.2	0.7	0.6	0.8	4.777	7.261	3,053.2	52.00
Sudan	SDN	147.9	50.2	4,354	1,477	43.8	31.3	13.7	8.7	3.0	0.2	0.1	0.5	1.231	3.630	182.2	33.98

Table E.1 *(Continued)*

GROSS DOMESTIC PRODUCT		Expenditure (billion US$)		Expenditure per capita (US$)		Price level index	Expenditure per capita indexes[b]				Share (world = 100%)[b]			PPPs[c] (US$ = 1.000)	Reference data		
							World = 100.0		United States = 100.0		Expenditure				Market exchange rates[c] (US$ = 1.000)	Expenditure (billion LCU)	Population (millions)
Economy		Based on PPPs	Based on XRs	Based on PPPs	Based on XRs	(world = 100.0)[a]	Based on PPPs	Based on XRs	Based on PPPs	Based on XRs	Based on PPPs	Based on XRs	Population				
(00)		(01)	(02)	(03)	(04)	(05)	(06)	(07)	(08)	(09)	(10)	(11)	(12)	(13)	(14)	(15)	(16)
Tanzania	TZA	101.6	35.3	2,224	773	44.8	16.0	7.2	4.5	1.6	0.1	0.0	0.7	546.073	1,572.116	55,469.0	45.67
Togo	TGO	8.0	3.9	1,218	590	62.5	8.8	5.5	2.4	1.2	0.0	0.0	0.1	228.625	471.866	1,837.1	6.60
Uganda	UGA	85.5	29.0	2,553	866	43.8	18.3	8.0	5.1	1.7	0.1	0.0	0.5	856.168	2,522.746	73,174.3	33.48
Zambia	ZMB	50.6	25.5	3,607	1,816	64.9	25.9	16.8	7.2	3.6	0.1	0.0	0.2	2.446	4.861	123.8	14.02
Zimbabwe	ZWE	23.3	12.1	1,803	938	67.1	13.0	8.7	3.6	1.9	0.0	0.0	0.2	0.520	1.000	12.1	12.89
Total (45)	**SSB**	**2,996.9**	**1,557.4**	**3,460**	**1,798**	**67.0**	**24.9**	**16.7**	**6.9**	**3.6**	**3.2**	**2.1**	**12.9**	**n.a.**	**n.a**	**n.a.**	**866.25**
World (178)	**WLD**	**93,769.9**	**72,676.7**	**13,920**	**10,789**	**100.0**	**100.0**	**100.0**	**27.9**	**21.7**	**100.0**	**100.0**	**100.0**	**n.a.**	**n.a.**	**n.a.**	**6,736.12**

Note: PPP = purchasing power parity; XR = market exchange rate; LCU = local currency unit; n.a. = not applicable; ... = data suppressed due to unavailability.

a. World totals used to calculate price level indexes (PLIs) in this table exclude nonparticipating economies.

b. Indexes and shares are rounded to one decimal place for presentation in this table.

c. PPPs and market exchange rates are rounded to three decimal places for presentation in this table.

d. National accounts expenditures for the revised ICP 2011 results are estimated by the ICP Global Office.

e. Bonaire's results are provided only for individual consumption expenditure by households. Therefore, to ensure consistency across tables, Bonaire is not included in either Latin America and the Caribbean or the world totals.

Table E.2 Actual individual consumption (AIC): Revised ICP 2011 results

ACTUAL INDIVIDUAL CONSUMPTION		Expenditure (billion US$)		Expenditure per capita (US$)		Price level index (world = 100.0)[a]	Expenditure per capita indexes[b]				Share (world = 100%)[b]			PPPs[c] (US$ = 1.000)	Reference data		
							World = 100.0		United States = 100.0		Expenditure				Market exchange rates[c] (US$ = 1.000)	Expenditure (billion LCU)	Population (millions)
Economy		Based on PPPs	Based on XRs	Based on PPPs	Based on XRs		Based on PPPs	Based on XRs	Based on PPPs	Based on XRs	Based on PPPs	Based on XRs	Population				
(00)		(01)	(02)	(03)	(04)	(05)	(06)	(07)	(08)	(09)	(10)	(11)	(12)	(13)	(14)	(15)	(16)
East Asia and Pacific																	
Australia	AUS	635.3	986.4	28,439	44,152	195.0	320.7	625.2	76.6	118.9	1.1	2.1	0.3	1.505	0.969	956.2	22.34
Brunei Darussalam	BRN	5.2	3.2	13,219	8,061	76.6	149.0	114.1	35.6	21.7	0.0	0.0	0.0	0.767	1.258	4.0	0.39
Cambodia	KHM	33.1	10.8	2,311	756	41.1	26.1	10.7	6.2	2.0	0.1	0.0	0.2	1,327.047	4,058.500	43,880.6	14.31
China	CHN	6,031.2	3,249.5	4,487	2,418	67.7	50.6	34.2	12.1	6.5	10.1	6.8	20.0	3.481	6.461	20,996.3	1,344.13
Fiji	FJI	5.7	3.0	6,725	3,560	66.5	75.8	50.4	18.1	9.6	0.0	0.0	0.0	0.949	1.793	5.5	0.85
Hong Kong SAR, China	HKG	241.7	165.7	34,177	23,426	86.1	385.3	331.7	92.0	63.1	0.4	0.3	0.1	5.335	7.784	1,289.5	7.07
Indonesia	IDN	1,316.2	525.1	5,439	2,170	50.1	61.3	30.7	14.6	5.8	2.2	1.1	3.6	3,499.323	8,770.433	4,605,767.6	241.99
Japan	JPN	3,154.7	4,312.6	24,678	33,737	171.7	278.3	477.7	66.4	90.8	5.3	9.1	1.9	109.100	79.807	344,176.3	127.83
Korea, Rep.	KOR	941.1	721.5	18,845	14,449	96.3	212.5	204.6	50.7	38.9	1.6	1.5	0.7	849.741	1,108.292	799,652.0	49.94
Lao PDR	LAO	16.5	5.6	2,698	912	42.4	30.4	12.9	7.3	2.5	0.0	0.0	0.1	2,713.182	8,030.055	44,775.1	6.12
Macao SAR, China[d]	MAC	14.4	8.7	26,210	15,883	76.1	295.5	224.9	70.6	42.8	0.0	0.0	0.0	4.859	8.018	70.2	0.55
Malaysia	MYS	339.5	162.3	11,682	5,586	60.1	131.7	79.1	31.4	15.0	0.6	0.3	0.4	1.463	3.060	496.8	29.06
Mongolia	MNG	15.1	5.9	5,423	2,131	49.4	61.2	30.2	14.6	5.7	0.0	0.0	0.0	497.347	1,265.516	7,515.7	2.79
Myanmar	MMR	108.1	32.9	2,177	663	38.3	24.5	9.4	5.9	1.8	0.2	0.1	0.7	249.138	817.917	26,938.9	49.66
New Zealand	NZL	100.1	116.8	22,784	26,582	146.5	256.9	376.4	61.3	71.6	0.2	0.2	0.1	1.477	1.266	147.8	4.39
Philippines	PHL	431.2	173.9	4,579	1,846	50.6	51.6	26.1	12.3	5.0	0.7	0.4	1.4	17.466	43.313	7,532.0	94.18
Singapore	SGP	137.6	111.5	26,554	21,512	101.7	299.4	304.6	71.5	57.9	0.2	0.2	0.1	1.019	1.258	140.3	5.18
Taiwan, China	TWN	588.2	301.7	25,366	13,010	64.4	286.0	184.2	68.3	35.0	1.0	0.6	0.3	15.114	29.469	8,891.0	23.19
Thailand	THA	593.9	229.8	8,970	3,470	48.6	101.1	49.1	24.1	9.3	1.0	0.5	1.0	11.797	30.492	7,006.7	66.21
Vietnam	VNM	264.2	86.0	2,998	975	40.9	33.8	13.8	8.1	2.6	0.4	0.2	1.3	6,673.613	20,509.750	1,762,838.5	88.11
Total (20)	**EAB**	**14,973.1**	**11,212.9**	**6,874**	**5,148**	**94.0**	**77.5**	**72.9**	**18.5**	**13.9**	**25.1**	**23.6**	**32.3**	**n.a.**	**n.a**	**n.a.**	**2,178.31**
Europe and Central Asia																	
Albania	ALB	23.7	10.8	8,174	3,711	57.0	92.2	52.5	22.0	10.0	0.0	0.0	0.0	45.770	100.812	1,086.9	2.91
Armenia	ARM	22.7	9.0	7,486	2,976	49.9	84.4	42.1	20.2	8.0	0.0	0.0	0.0	148.074	372.500	3,356.4	3.03
Austria	AUT	238.3	282.9	28,409	33,723	149.1	320.3	477.5	76.5	90.8	0.4	0.6	0.1	0.853	0.718	203.2	8.39
Azerbaijan	AZE	73.4	27.1	8,105	2,988	46.3	91.4	42.3	21.8	8.0	0.1	0.1	0.1	0.291	0.790	21.4	9.05
Belarus	BLR	108.8	31.3	11,483	3,300	36.1	129.5	46.7	30.9	8.9	0.2	0.1	0.1	0.161	0.561	17.5	9.47
Belgium	BEL	288.5	349.7	26,140	31,683	152.2	294.7	448.6	70.4	85.3	0.5	0.7	0.2	0.871	0.718	251.2	11.04
Bosnia and Herzegovina	BIH	32.7	17.9	8,941	4,877	68.5	100.8	69.1	24.1	13.1	0.1	0.0	0.1	0.766	1.405	25.1	3.66
Bulgaria	BGR	82.2	40.3	11,185	5,488	61.6	126.1	77.7	30.1	14.8	0.1	0.1	0.1	0.689	1.405	56.7	7.35
Croatia	HRV	60.7	44.6	14,182	10,415	92.2	159.9	147.5	38.2	28.0	0.1	0.1	0.1	3.925	5.344	238.4	4.28
Cyprus	CYP	19.8	20.4	23,254	24,020	129.7	262.2	340.1	62.6	64.7	0.0	0.0	0.0	0.742	0.718	14.7	0.85
Czech Republic	CZE	183.2	136.2	17,451	12,972	93.4	196.8	183.7	47.0	34.9	0.3	0.3	0.2	13.131	17.665	2,405.3	10.50
Denmark	DNK	152.3	229.6	27,336	41,228	189.4	308.2	583.8	73.6	111.0	0.3	0.5	0.1	8.073	5.352	1,229.1	5.57
Estonia	EST	19.6	14.2	14,706	10,662	91.1	165.8	151.0	39.6	28.7	0.0	0.0	0.0	0.521	0.718	10.2	1.33
Finland	FIN	143.9	188.6	26,701	35,007	164.6	301.1	495.7	71.9	94.2	0.2	0.4	0.1	0.942	0.718	135.5	5.39

Table E.2 *(Continued)*

ACTUAL INDIVIDUAL CONSUMPTION		Expenditure (billion US$)		Expenditure per capita (US$)		Price level index	Expenditure per capita indexes[b]				Share (world = 100%)[b]				Reference data		
							World = 100.0		United States = 100.0		Expenditure				Market exchange rates[c]		
Economy		Based on PPPs	Based on XRs	Based on PPPs	Based on XRs	(world = 100.0)[a]	Based on PPPs	Based on XRs	Based on PPPs	Based on XRs	Based on PPPs	Based on XRs	Population	PPPs[c] (US$ = 1.000)	(US$ = 1.000)	Expenditure (billion LCU)	Population (millions)
(00)		(01)	(02)	(03)	(04)	(05)	(06)	(07)	(08)	(09)	(10)	(11)	(12)	(13)	(14)	(15)	(16)
France	FRA	1,704.9	2,015.8	26,097	30,856	148.5	294.2	436.9	70.3	83.1	2.9	4.2	1.0	0.849	0.718	1,448.2	65.33
Georgia	GEO	29.2	13.0	7,781	3,469	56.0	87.7	49.1	20.9	9.3	0.0	0.0	0.1	0.752	1.686	22.0	3.76
Germany	DEU	2,260.3	2,491.8	28,157	31,041	138.4	317.5	439.5	75.8	83.6	3.8	5.2	1.2	0.792	0.718	1,790.1	80.28
Greece	GRC	227.5	232.8	20,483	20,960	128.5	230.9	296.8	55.1	56.4	0.4	0.5	0.2	0.735	0.718	167.2	11.11
Hungary	HUN	147.5	89.6	14,787	8,986	76.3	166.7	127.2	39.8	24.2	0.2	0.2	0.1	121.962	200.697	17,983.8	9.97
Iceland	ISL	8.6	10.2	27,020	31,925	148.4	304.7	452.0	72.7	85.9	0.0	0.0	0.0	137.011	115.963	1,181.0	0.32
Ireland	IRL	105.2	139.1	22,986	30,377	166.0	259.2	430.1	61.9	81.8	0.2	0.3	0.1	0.949	0.718	99.9	4.58
Italy	ITA	1,517.8	1,661.4	25,272	27,662	137.5	284.9	391.7	68.0	74.5	2.5	3.5	0.9	0.786	0.718	1,193.5	60.06
Kazakhstan	KAZ	189.6	90.7	11,452	5,475	60.0	129.1	77.5	30.8	14.7	0.3	0.2	0.2	70.097	146.620	13,291.4	16.56
Kyrgyz Republic	KGZ	18.8	5.8	3,568	1,103	38.8	40.2	15.6	9.6	3.0	0.0	0.0	0.1	14.269	46.144	267.8	5.26
Latvia	LVA	27.6	19.6	13,408	9,514	89.1	151.2	134.7	36.1	25.6	0.0	0.0	0.0	0.510	0.718	14.1	2.06
Lithuania	LTU	50.5	31.8	16,678	10,492	79.0	188.0	148.6	44.9	28.2	0.1	0.1	0.0	0.452	0.718	22.8	3.03
Luxembourg	LUX	16.9	24.8	32,593	47,805	184.2	367.5	676.9	87.7	128.7	0.0	0.1	0.0	1.054	0.718	17.8	0.52
Moldova	MDA	21.6	8.9	6,080	2,495	51.5	68.6	35.3	16.4	6.7	0.0	0.0	0.1	4.811	11.726	104.1	3.56
Montenegro	MNE	7.8	4.1	12,534	6,659	66.7	141.3	94.3	33.7	17.9	0.0	0.0	0.0	0.382	0.718	3.0	0.62
Netherlands	NLD	470.9	572.2	28,210	34,278	152.6	318.1	485.4	75.9	92.3	0.8	1.2	0.2	0.873	0.718	411.1	16.69
North Macedonia	MKD	18.7	8.6	9,087	4,184	57.8	102.5	59.2	24.5	11.3	0.0	0.0	0.0	20.350	44.202	380.7	2.06
Norway	NOR	152.4	271.6	30,765	54,841	223.9	346.9	776.5	82.8	147.6	0.3	0.6	0.1	9.980	5.599	1,520.8	4.95
Poland	POL	651.0	377.1	16,899	9,788	72.7	190.5	138.6	45.5	26.3	1.1	0.8	0.6	1.715	2.960	1,116.3	38.53
Portugal	PRT	203.8	187.3	19,300	17,743	115.5	217.6	251.2	52.0	47.8	0.3	0.4	0.2	0.660	0.718	134.6	10.56
Romania	ROU	251.1	129.1	12,465	6,407	64.6	140.5	90.7	33.6	17.2	0.4	0.3	0.3	1.565	3.045	393.1	20.15
Russian Federation	RUS	2,095.0	1,193.6	14,654	8,349	71.5	165.2	118.2	39.5	22.5	3.5	2.5	2.1	16.740	29.382	35,069.5	142.96
Serbia	SRB	81.9	42.4	11,319	5,863	65.0	127.6	83.0	30.5	15.8	0.1	0.1	0.1	37.935	73.240	3,107.3	7.24
Slovak Republic	SVK	93.0	63.6	17,221	11,782	85.9	194.2	166.8	46.4	31.7	0.2	0.1	0.1	0.491	0.718	45.7	5.40
Slovenia	SVN	39.3	35.5	19,148	17,282	113.3	215.9	244.7	51.5	46.5	0.1	0.1	0.0	0.648	0.718	25.5	2.05
Spain	ESP	979.2	1,040.3	20,952	22,258	133.4	236.2	315.2	56.4	59.9	1.6	2.2	0.7	0.763	0.718	747.3	46.74
Sweden	SWE	259.9	369.2	27,504	39,071	178.4	310.1	553.2	74.0	105.2	0.4	0.8	0.1	9.215	6.487	2,394.9	9.45
Switzerland	CHE	236.6	412.4	29,897	52,121	218.9	337.1	738.0	80.5	140.3	0.4	0.9	0.1	1.544	0.885	365.2	7.91
Tajikistan	TJK	22.5	7.5	2,922	973	41.8	32.9	13.8	7.9	2.6	0.0	0.0	0.1	1.535	4.610	34.6	7.71
Turkey	TUR	984.8	582.9	13,268	7,854	74.3	149.6	111.2	35.7	21.1	1.6	1.2	1.1	0.991	1.675	976.4	74.22
Ukraine[d]	UKR	372.8	134.0	8,156	2,932	45.2	92.0	41.5	22.0	7.9	0.6	0.3	0.7	2.865	7.968	1,067.9	45.71
United Kingdom	GBR	1,718.7	2,062.9	27,159	32,597	150.7	306.2	461.6	73.1	87.8	2.9	4.3	0.9	0.748	0.623	1,286.2	63.29
Total (46)	**ECB**	**16,415.3**	**15,732.2**	**19,190**	**18,391**	**120.4**	**216.4**	**260.4**	**51.7**	**49.5**	**27.5**	**33.1**	**12.7**	**n.a.**	**n.a**	**n.a.**	**855.42**
Latin America and the Caribbean																	
Anguilla	AIA	0.3	0.3	23,295	19,314	104.1	262.7	273.5	62.7	52.0	0.0	0.0	0.0	2.239	2.700	0.7	0.01
Antigua and Barbuda	ATG	1.1	0.8	12,426	8,822	89.2	140.1	124.9	33.5	23.8	0.0	0.0	0.0	1.917	2.700	2.1	0.09
Aruba	ABW	2.4	2.0	23,418	19,794	106.1	264.0	280.3	63.0	53.3	0.0	0.0	0.0	1.513	1.790	3.6	0.10

(continued)

Table E.2 *(Continued)*

ACTUAL INDIVIDUAL CONSUMPTION Economy		Expenditure (billion US$) Based on PPPs	Expenditure (billion US$) Based on XRs	Expenditure per capita (US$) Based on PPPs	Expenditure per capita (US$) Based on XRs	Price level index (world = 100.0)[a]	Expenditure per capita indexes[b] World = 100.0 Based on PPPs	Expenditure per capita indexes[b] World = 100.0 Based on XRs	Expenditure per capita indexes[b] United States = 100.0 Based on PPPs	Expenditure per capita indexes[b] United States = 100.0 Based on XRs	Share (world = 100%)[b] Expenditure Based on PPPs	Share (world = 100%)[b] Expenditure Based on XRs	Share (world = 100%)[b] Population	PPPs[c] (US$ = 1.000)	Reference data Market exchange rates[c] (US$ = 1.000)	Reference data Expenditure (billion LCU)	Reference data Population (millions)
(00)		(01)	(02)	(03)	(04)	(05)	(06)	(07)	(08)	(09)	(10)	(11)	(12)	(13)	(14)	(15)	(16)
Bahamas, The	BHS	6.9	7.1	19,257	19,769	128.9	217.1	279.9	51.8	53.2	0.0	0.0	0.0	1.027	1.000	7.1	0.36
Barbados	BRB	3.3	3.7	11,676	13,063	140.5	131.6	185.0	31.4	35.2	0.0	0.0	0.0	2.238	2.000	7.4	0.28
Belize	BLZ	2.0	1.1	6,200	3,364	68.1	69.9	47.6	16.7	9.1	0.0	0.0	0.0	1.085	2.000	2.2	0.33
Bolivia	BOL	37.8	14.8	3,700	1,454	49.3	41.7	20.6	10.0	3.9	0.1	0.0	0.2	2.743	6.982	103.6	10.21
Bonaire[e]	BON	...	...	...	...	...	...	...	...	...	...	...	...	...	1.000	...	0.02
Brazil	BRA	2,022.8	1,778.5	10,241	9,005	110.4	115.5	127.5	27.6	24.2	3.4	3.7	2.9	1.471	1.673	2,975.2	197.51
Cayman Islands	CYM	1.9	2.4	32,643	41,039	157.9	368.1	581.1	87.9	110.5	0.0	0.0	0.0	1.048	0.833	2.0	0.06
Chile	CHL	233.6	170.6	13,528	9,881	91.7	152.5	139.9	36.4	26.6	0.4	0.4	0.3	353.270	483.668	82,521.1	17.27
Colombia	COL	377.1	231.6	8,189	5,030	77.1	92.3	71.2	22.0	13.5	0.6	0.5	0.7	1,135.228	1,848.139	428,058.2	46.04
Costa Rica	CRI	49.7	33.1	10,827	7,211	83.6	122.1	102.1	29.1	19.4	0.1	0.1	0.1	336.767	505.664	16,734.4	4.59
Curaçao	CUW	3.0	2.3	19,915	14,921	94.1	224.5	211.3	53.6	40.2	0.0	0.0	0.0	1.341	1.790	4.1	0.15
Dominica	DMA	0.7	0.5	9,200	6,463	88.2	103.7	91.5	24.8	17.4	0.0	0.0	0.0	1.897	2.700	1.2	0.07
Dominican Republic	DOM	94.3	46.2	9,613	4,712	61.6	108.4	66.7	25.9	12.7	0.2	0.1	0.1	18.676	38.099	1,761.8	9.81
Ecuador	ECU	105.2	53.5	6,899	3,511	63.9	77.8	49.7	18.6	9.5	0.2	0.1	0.2	0.509	1.000	53.5	15.24
El Salvador	SLV	38.8	19.1	6,242	3,079	61.9	70.4	43.6	16.8	8.3	0.1	0.0	0.1	0.493	1.000	19.1	6.21
Grenada	GRD	1.1	0.8	10,078	7,132	88.9	113.6	101.0	27.1	19.2	0.0	0.0	0.0	1.911	2.700	2.1	0.11
Guatemala[d]	GTM	92.6	42.8	6,193	2,863	58.1	69.8	40.5	16.7	7.7	0.2	0.1	0.2	3.609	7.807	334.1	14.95
Haiti	HTI	18.8	8.8	1,866	872	58.7	21.0	12.3	5.0	2.3	0.0	0.0	0.1	19.149	40.977	360.8	10.10
Honduras	HND	29.4	15.1	3,463	1,782	64.6	39.1	25.2	9.3	4.8	0.0	0.0	0.1	9.803	19.048	287.9	8.48
Jamaica	JAM	20.3	13.5	7,173	4,761	83.3	80.9	67.4	19.3	12.8	0.0	0.0	0.0	57.018	85.911	1,155.8	2.83
Mexico	MEX	1,354.7	838.8	11,728	7,262	77.8	132.2	102.8	31.6	19.5	2.3	1.8	1.7	7.692	12.423	10,420.9	115.51
Montserrat	MSR	0.1	0.1	15,549	11,289	91.2	175.3	159.9	41.9	30.4	0.0	0.0	0.0	1.960	2.700	0.1	0.00
Nicaragua	NIC	21.9	8.1	3,703	1,380	46.8	41.7	19.5	10.0	3.7	0.0	0.0	0.1	8.359	22.424	182.7	5.90
Panama	PAN	41.1	21.1	11,087	5,685	64.4	125.0	80.5	29.8	15.3	0.1	0.0	0.1	0.513	1.000	21.1	3.71
Paraguay	PRY	47.2	23.0	7,449	3,629	61.2	84.0	51.4	20.1	9.8	0.1	0.0	0.1	2,037.699	4,183.127	96,145.6	6.33
Peru	PER	208.4	110.3	7,122	3,768	66.4	80.3	53.4	19.2	10.1	0.3	0.2	0.4	1.457	2.754	303.7	29.26
Sint Maarten	SXM	0.8	0.7	23,633	19,035	101.2	266.5	269.5	63.6	51.2	0.0	0.0	0.0	1.442	1.790	1.2	0.04
St. Kitts and Nevis	KNA	0.8	0.6	16,678	12,381	93.2	188.0	175.3	44.9	33.3	0.0	0.0	0.0	2.004	2.700	1.7	0.05
St. Lucia	LCA	1.7	1.2	9,807	6,921	88.6	110.6	98.0	26.4	18.6	0.0	0.0	0.0	1.905	2.700	3.3	0.18
St. Vincent and the Grenadines	VCT	1.0	0.6	8,936	5,917	83.1	100.8	83.8	24.1	15.9	0.0	0.0	0.0	1.788	2.700	1.7	0.11
Suriname	SUR	3.2	1.6	6,047	3,073	63.8	68.2	43.5	16.3	8.3	0.0	0.0	0.0	1.703	3.350	5.5	0.54
Trinidad and Tobago	TTO	21.7	13.9	16,264	10,394	80.3	183.4	147.2	43.8	28.0	0.0	0.0	0.0	4.107	6.426	89.2	1.34
Turks and Caicos Islands	TCA	0.3	0.3	8,147	9,366	144.4	91.9	132.6	21.9	25.2	0.0	0.0	0.0	1.150	1.000	0.3	0.03
Uruguay	URY	44.4	35.5	13,178	10,551	100.5	148.6	149.4	35.5	28.4	0.1	0.1	0.1	15.463	19.314	686.5	3.37
Venezuela, RB[d]	VEN	309.0	192.1	10,695	6,649	78.1	120.6	94.1	28.8	17.9	0.5	0.4	0.4	2.666	4.289	823.8	28.89
Virgin Islands, British	VGB	0.3	0.3	10,736	12,000	140.4	121.0	169.9	28.9	32.3	0.0	0.0	0.0	1.118	1.000	0.3	0.03
Total (39)	**LCB**	**5,199.6**	**3,696.9**	**9,627**	**6,845**	**89.3**	**108.5**	**96.9**	**25.9**	**18.4**	**8.7**	**7.8**	**8.0**	**n.a.**	**n.a**	**n.a.**	**540.10**

Table E.2 *(Continued)*

ACTUAL INDIVIDUAL CONSUMPTION Economy		Expenditure (billion US$)		Expenditure per capita (US$)		Price level index (world = 100.0)[a]	Expenditure per capita indexes[b]				Share (world = 100%)[b]			PPPs[c] (US$ = 1.000)	Reference data		
							World = 100.0		United States = 100.0		Expenditure				Market exchange rates[c] (US$ = 1.000)	Expenditure (billion LCU)	Popula-tion (millions)
		Based on PPPs	Based on XRs	Based on PPPs	Based on XRs		Based on PPPs	Based on XRs	Based on PPPs	Based on XRs	Based on PPPs	Based on XRs	Popula-tion				
(00)		(01)	(02)	(03)	(04)	(05)	(06)	(07)	(08)	(09)	(10)	(11)	(12)	(13)	(14)	(15)	(16)
Middle East and North Africa																	
Algeria	DZA	235.4	86.5	6,422	2,361	46.2	72.4	33.4	17.3	6.4	0.4	0.2	0.5	26.814	72.938	6,312.7	36.66
Bahrain	BHR	28.2	12.8	23,585	10,750	57.2	265.9	152.2	63.5	28.9	0.0	0.0	0.0	0.171	0.376	4.8	1.20
Djibouti	DJI	2.7	1.4	3,135	1,650	66.1	35.3	23.4	8.4	4.4	0.0	0.0	0.0	93.533	177.721	250.3	0.85
Egypt, Arab Rep.	EGY	807.1	212.2	10,023	2,636	33.0	113.0	37.3	27.0	7.1	1.4	0.4	1.2	1.564	5.947	1,262.2	80.53
Iran, Islamic Rep.	IRN	918.9	393.4	12,227	5,235	53.8	137.9	74.1	32.9	14.1	1.5	0.8	1.1	4,545.742	10,616.307	4,176,900.0	75.15
Iraq	IRQ	197.7	75.2	5,929	2,255	47.8	66.9	31.9	16.0	6.1	0.3	0.2	0.5	456.052	1,199.200	90,152.8	33.34
Israel	ISR	158.8	179.3	20,460	23,092	141.7	230.7	327.0	55.1	62.2	0.3	0.4	0.1	4.038	3.578	641.4	7.76
Jordan	JOR	59.3	24.9	8,483	3,562	52.7	95.6	50.4	22.8	9.6	0.1	0.1	0.1	0.297	0.708	17.6	6.99
Kuwait	KWT	71.7	47.3	23,379	15,444	83.0	263.6	218.7	62.9	41.6	0.1	0.1	0.0	0.185	0.280	13.3	3.07
Malta	MLT	7.8	6.6	18,822	15,822	105.6	212.2	224.0	50.7	42.6	0.0	0.0	0.0	0.604	0.718	4.7	0.42
Morocco	MAR	146.1	68.9	4,485	2,116	59.2	50.6	30.0	12.1	5.7	0.2	0.1	0.5	3.797	8.049	554.8	32.58
Oman	OMN	50.1	25.2	15,188	7,638	63.2	171.3	108.1	40.9	20.6	0.1	0.1	0.0	0.193	0.385	9.7	3.30
Qatar	QAT	36.7	28.2	21,189	16,260	96.4	238.9	230.2	57.0	43.8	0.1	0.1	0.0	2.801	3.650	102.8	1.73
Saudi Arabia	SAU	622.0	245.9	22,078	8,730	49.7	248.9	123.6	59.4	23.5	1.0	0.5	0.4	1.483	3.750	922.3	28.17
Tunisia	TUN	77.2	34.1	7,184	3,174	55.5	81.0	44.9	19.3	8.5	0.1	0.1	0.2	0.622	1.408	48.0	10.74
United Arab Emirates	ARE	249.1	159.3	28,728	18,367	80.3	323.9	260.1	77.3	49.4	0.4	0.3	0.1	2.348	3.673	584.9	8.67
West Bank and Gaza	PSE	16.2	10.3	4,176	2,648	79.6	47.1	37.5	11.2	7.1	0.0	0.0	0.1	2.269	3.578	36.7	3.88
Yemen, Rep.[d]	YEM	67.2	22.9	2,822	963	42.8	31.8	13.6	7.6	2.6	0.1	0.0	0.4	72.934	213.800	4,904.7	23.83
Total (17)	**MEB**	**3,752.2**	**1,634.6**	**10,456**	**4,555**	**54.7**	**117.9**	**64.5**	**28.1**	**12.3**	**6.3**	**3.4**	**5.3**	**n.a.**	**n.a**	**n.a.**	**358.87**
North America																	
Bermuda	BMU	2.1	3.6	32,682	54,995	211.3	368.5	778.7	88.0	148.0	0.0	0.0	0.0	1.683	1.000	3.6	0.07
Canada	CAN	952.1	1,223.3	27,723	35,622	161.4	312.6	504.4	74.6	95.9	1.6	2.6	0.5	1.271	0.990	1,210.5	34.34
United States	USA	11,590.9	11,590.9	37,146	37,146	125.6	418.8	526.0	100.0	100.0	19.4	24.4	4.6	1.000	1.000	11,590.9	312.03
Total (3)	**NAB**	**12,545.1**	**12,817.8**	**36,211**	**36,998**	**128.3**	**408.3**	**523.9**	**97.5**	**99.6**	**21.0**	**26.9**	**5.1**	**n.a.**	**n.a**	**n.a.**	**346.44**
South Asia																	
Bangladesh	BGD	330.2	100.2	2,206	670	38.1	24.9	9.5	5.9	1.8	0.6	0.2	2.2	22.508	74.152	7,432.8	149.70
Bhutan	BTN	2.7	0.9	4,021	1,326	41.4	45.3	18.8	10.8	3.6	0.0	0.0	0.0	15.388	46.670	42.0	0.68
India	IND	3,546.3	1,078.2	2,916	887	38.2	32.9	12.6	7.9	2.4	5.9	2.3	18.1	14.190	46.670	50,322.0	1,216.15
Maldives	MDV	1.9	1.0	4,651	2,555	69.0	52.4	36.2	12.5	6.9	0.0	0.0	0.0	8.021	14.602	15.2	0.41
Nepal	NPL	48.5	15.5	1,832	586	40.2	20.7	8.3	4.9	1.6	0.1	0.0	0.4	23.676	74.020	1,148.8	26.49
Pakistan	PAK	694.5	188.4	3,921	1,064	34.1	44.2	15.1	10.6	2.9	1.2	0.4	2.6	23.419	86.343	16,264.1	177.10
Sri Lanka	LKA	145.3	49.1	7,196	2,433	42.5	81.1	34.5	19.4	6.6	0.2	0.1	0.3	37.384	110.565	5,433.1	20.20
Total (7)	**SAB**	**4,769.5**	**1,433.4**	**2,998**	**901**	**37.7**	**33.8**	**12.8**	**8.1**	**2.4**	**8.0**	**3.0**	**23.6**	**n.a.**	**n.a**	**n.a.**	**1,590.72**
Sub-Saharan Africa																	
Angola	AGO	58.0	45.9	2,393	1,895	99.4	27.0	26.8	6.4	5.1	0.1	0.1	0.4	74.381	93.935	4,311.0	24.22
Benin	BEN	13.9	6.1	1,465	648	55.6	16.5	9.2	3.9	1.7	0.0	0.0	0.1	208.779	471.866	2,893.2	9.46
Botswana	BWA	14.5	8.2	7,185	4,051	70.8	81.0	57.4	19.3	10.9	0.0	0.0	0.0	3.855	6.838	55.8	2.02

(continued)

Table E.2 *(Continued)*

ACTUAL INDIVIDUAL CONSUMPTION		Expenditure (billion US$)		Expenditure per capita (US$)		Price level index (world = 100.0)[a]	Expenditure per capita indexes[b]				Share (world = 100%)[b]			PPPs[c] (US$ = 1.000)	Reference data		
							World = 100.0		United States = 100.0		Expenditure				Market exchange rates[c] (US$ = 1.000)	Expenditure (billion LCU)	Population (millions)
Economy		Based on PPPs	Based on XRs	Based on PPPs	Based on XRs		Based on PPPs	Based on XRs	Based on PPPs	Based on XRs	Based on PPPs	Based on XRs	Population				
(00)		(01)	(02)	(03)	(04)	(05)	(06)	(07)	(08)	(09)	(10)	(11)	(12)	(13)	(14)	(15)	(16)
Burkina Faso	BFA	16.1	7.0	1,004	438	54.8	11.3	6.2	2.7	1.2	0.0	0.0	0.2	205.922	471.866	3,325.4	16.08
Burundi	BDI	6.1	2.2	683	244	44.9	7.7	3.5	1.8	0.7	0.0	0.0	0.1	450.615	1,261.073	2,757.3	8.96
Cabo Verde	CPV	2.4	1.3	4,734	2,657	70.5	53.4	37.6	12.7	7.2	0.0	0.0	0.0	44.526	79.323	105.1	0.50
Cameroon	CMR	44.6	21.0	2,131	1,005	59.2	24.0	14.2	5.7	2.7	0.1	0.0	0.3	222.431	471.866	9,910.4	20.91
Central African Republic	CAF	4.1	2.1	937	477	64.0	10.6	6.8	2.5	1.3	0.0	0.0	0.1	240.351	471.866	995.0	4.42
Chad	TCD	15.5	7.6	1,253	611	61.2	14.1	8.6	3.4	1.6	0.0	0.0	0.2	230.002	471.866	3,562.8	12.36
Comoros	COM	1.6	1.0	2,312	1,393	75.6	26.1	19.7	6.2	3.7	0.0	0.0	0.0	213.162	353.900	348.2	0.71
Congo, Dem. Rep.	COD	38.9	20.7	582	310	66.8	6.6	4.4	1.6	0.8	0.1	0.0	1.0	489.288	919.491	19,021.3	66.76
Congo, Rep.	COG	7.9	4.7	1,786	1,059	74.4	20.1	15.0	4.8	2.9	0.0	0.0	0.1	279.715	471.866	2,196.1	4.39
Côte d'Ivoire	CIV	38.6	18.5	1,838	880	60.1	20.7	12.5	4.9	2.4	0.1	0.0	0.3	225.960	471.866	8,732.4	21.03
Equatorial Guinea	GNQ	8.2	5.3	8,311	5,380	81.3	93.7	76.2	22.4	14.5	0.0	0.0	0.0	305.437	471.866	2,505.2	0.99
Eswatini	SWZ	7.7	4.1	7,170	3,861	67.6	80.8	54.7	19.3	10.4	0.0	0.0	0.0	3.911	7.261	30.1	1.07
Ethiopia	ETH	114.3	33.4	1,268	371	36.7	14.3	5.3	3.4	1.0	0.2	0.1	1.3	4.942	16.899	565.0	90.14
Gabon	GAB	8.3	5.8	4,911	3,468	88.7	55.4	49.1	13.2	9.3	0.0	0.0	0.0	333.273	471.866	2,757.0	1.68
Gambia, The	GMB	3.6	1.2	1,971	663	42.2	22.2	9.4	5.3	1.8	0.0	0.0	0.0	9.910	29.462	36.1	1.85
Ghana	GHA	72.0	33.5	2,835	1,321	58.5	32.0	18.7	7.6	3.6	0.1	0.1	0.4	0.704	1.512	50.7	25.39
Guinea	GIN	16.2	5.7	1,559	546	44.0	17.6	7.7	4.2	1.5	0.0	0.0	0.2	2,331.030	6,658.031	37,870.5	10.42
Guinea-Bissau	GNB	2.0	1.0	1,255	608	60.9	14.1	8.6	3.4	1.6	0.0	0.0	0.0	228.728	471.866	448.5	1.56
Kenya	KEN	98.4	37.2	2,280	862	47.5	25.7	12.2	6.1	2.3	0.2	0.1	0.6	33.562	88.811	3,303.9	43.18
Lesotho	LSO	5.5	2.8	2,736	1,399	64.2	30.9	19.8	7.4	3.8	0.0	0.0	0.0	3.712	7.261	20.4	2.00
Liberia	LBR	2.6	1.4	635	345	68.2	7.2	4.9	1.7	0.9	0.0	0.0	0.1	39.202	72.227	100.0	4.02
Madagascar	MDG	28.2	8.9	1,298	408	39.5	14.6	5.8	3.5	1.1	0.0	0.0	0.3	637.466	2,025.118	17,986.0	21.74
Malawi	MWI	15.0	7.1	1,001	472	59.2	11.3	6.7	2.7	1.3	0.0	0.0	0.2	73.830	156.515	1,105.5	14.96
Mali	MLI	22.6	9.8	1,454	632	54.6	16.4	8.9	3.9	1.7	0.0	0.0	0.2	204.987	471.866	4,624.7	15.51
Mauritania	MRT	7.1	2.6	1,961	729	46.7	22.1	10.3	5.3	2.0	0.0	0.0	0.1	104.505	281.118	737.3	3.60
Mauritius	MUS	15.1	8.9	12,052	7,116	74.2	135.9	100.8	32.4	19.2	0.0	0.0	0.0	16.950	28.706	255.6	1.25
Mozambique	MOZ	21.3	11.2	879	462	66.0	9.9	6.5	2.4	1.2	0.0	0.0	0.4	15.272	29.068	324.7	24.19
Namibia	NAM	14.0	9.2	6,506	4,286	82.7	73.4	60.7	17.5	11.5	0.0	0.0	0.0	4.783	7.261	67.1	2.16
Niger	NER	11.0	4.9	642	287	56.2	7.2	4.1	1.7	0.8	0.0	0.0	0.3	211.097	471.866	2,318.0	17.11
Nigeria	NGA	552.2	274.5	3,392	1,686	62.4	38.2	23.9	9.1	4.5	0.9	0.6	2.4	76.499	153.862	42,241.1	162.81
Rwanda	RWA	13.3	5.3	1,288	516	50.3	14.5	7.3	3.5	1.4	0.0	0.0	0.2	240.593	600.307	3,188.5	10.29
São Tomé and Príncipe	STP	0.5	0.2	2,719	1,307	60.4	30.7	18.5	7.3	3.5	0.0	0.0	0.0	8.471	17.623	4.3	0.18
Senegal	SEN	31.7	15.5	2,436	1,187	61.2	27.5	16.8	6.6	3.2	0.1	0.0	0.2	230.011	471.866	7,302.7	13.03
Seychelles	SYC	1.1	0.6	12,234	7,074	72.6	137.9	100.2	32.9	19.0	0.0	0.0	0.0	7.159	12.381	8.0	0.09
Sierra Leone	SLE	7.6	2.9	1,156	441	47.9	13.0	6.2	3.1	1.2	0.0	0.0	0.1	1,657.769	4,349.162	12,580.1	6.56
South Africa	ZAF	446.6	292.0	8,588	5,615	82.1	96.8	79.5	23.1	15.1	0.7	0.6	0.8	4.748	7.261	2,120.4	52.00
Sudan	SDN	99.4	36.1	2,927	1,062	45.6	33.0	15.0	7.9	2.9	0.2	0.1	0.5	1.318	3.630	131.0	33.98

Table E.2 *(Continued)*

ACTUAL INDIVIDUAL CONSUMPTION		Expenditure (billion US$)		Expenditure per capita (US$)		Price level index (world = 100.0)[a]	Expenditure per capita indexes[b]				Share (world = 100%)[b]				Reference data		
							World = 100.0		United States = 100.0		Expenditure				Market exchange rates[c]		
Economy		Based on PPPs	Based on XRs	Based on PPPs	Based on XRs		Based on PPPs	Based on XRs	Based on PPPs	Based on XRs	Based on PPPs	Based on XRs	Population	PPPs[c] (US$ = 1.000)	(US$ = 1.000)	Expenditure (billion LCU)	Population (millions)
(00)		(01)	(02)	(03)	(04)	(05)	(06)	(07)	(08)	(09)	(10)	(11)	(12)	(13)	(14)	(15)	(16)
Tanzania	TZA	76.7	26.4	1,680	578	43.2	18.9	8.2	4.5	1.6	0.1	0.1	0.7	540.694	1,572.116	41,486.7	45.67
Togo	TGO	7.2	3.2	1,086	492	56.9	12.2	7.0	2.9	1.3	0.0	0.0	0.1	213.798	471.866	1,531.7	6.60
Uganda	UGA	67.0	22.9	2,001	684	42.9	22.6	9.7	5.4	1.8	0.1	0.0	0.5	861.869	2,522.746	57,732.7	33.48
Zambia	ZMB	27.7	13.8	1,975	988	62.8	22.3	14.0	5.3	2.7	0.0	0.0	0.2	2.431	4.861	67.3	14.02
Zimbabwe	ZWE	22.2	11.0	1,723	852	62.1	19.4	12.1	4.6	2.3	0.0	0.0	0.2	0.495	1.000	11.0	12.89
Total (45)	**SSB**	**2,088.3**	**1,044.9**	**2,411**	**1,206**	**62.8**	**27.2**	**17.1**	**6.5**	**3.2**	**3.5**	**2.2**	**12.9**	**n.a.**	**n.a**	**n.a.**	**866.25**
World (178)	**WLD**	**59,743.2**	**47,572.8**	**8,869**	**7,062**	**100.0**	**100.0**	**100.0**	**23.9**	**19.0**	**100.0**	**100.0**	**100.0**	**n.a.**	**n.a.**	**n.a.**	**6,736.12**

Note: PPP = purchasing power parity; XR = market exchange rate; LCU = local currency unit; n.a. = not applicable; ... = data suppressed due to unavailability.

a. World totals used to calculate price level indexes (PLIs) in this table exclude nonparticipating economies.

b. Indexes and shares are rounded to one decimal place for presentation in this table.

c. PPPs and market exchange rates are rounded to three decimal places for presentation in this table.

d. National accounts expenditures for the revised ICP 2011 results are estimated by the ICP Global Office.

e. Bonaire's results are provided only for individual consumption expenditure by households. Therefore, to ensure consistency across tables, Bonaire is not included in either Latin America and the Caribbean or the world totals.

Table E.3 Individual consumption expenditure by households: Revised ICP 2011 results

INDIVIDUAL CONSUMPTION EXPENDITURE BY HOUSEHOLDS		Expenditure (billion US$)		Expenditure per capita (US$)		Price level index (world = 100.0)[a]	Expenditure per capita indexes[b]: World = 100.0		Expenditure per capita indexes[b]: United States = 100.0		Share (world = 100%)[b]: Expenditure			PPPs[c] (US$ = 1.000)	Reference data: Market exchange rates[c] (US$ = 1.000)	Reference data: Expenditure (billion LCU)	Reference data: Population (millions)
Economy		Based on PPPs	Based on XRs	Based on PPPs	Based on XRs		Based on PPPs	Based on XRs	Based on PPPs	Based on XRs	Based on PPPs	Based on XRs	Population				
(00)		(01)	(02)	(03)	(04)	(05)	(06)	(07)	(08)	(09)	(10)	(11)	(12)	(13)	(14)	(15)	(16)
East Asia and Pacific																	
Australia	AUS	522.8	822.8	23,402	36,832	189.0	319.4	603.9	68.6	108.0	1.1	2.0	0.3	1.526	0.969	797.7	22.34
Brunei Darussalam	BRN	3.6	2.4	9,101	6,019	79.4	124.2	98.7	26.7	17.6	0.0	0.0	0.0	0.832	1.258	3.0	0.39
Cambodia	KHM	27.7	10.2	1,939	714	44.2	26.5	11.7	5.7	2.1	0.1	0.0	0.2	1,493.254	4,058.500	41,431.0	14.31
China	CHN	4,546.6	2,601.8	3,383	1,936	68.7	46.2	31.7	9.9	5.7	9.2	6.3	20.0	3.698	6.461	16,811.1	1,344.13
Fiji	FJI	4.9	2.8	5,782	3,277	68.1	78.9	53.7	17.0	9.6	0.0	0.0	0.0	1.016	1.793	5.0	0.85
Hong Kong SAR, China	HKG	216.8	157.3	30,661	22,244	87.1	418.5	364.7	89.9	65.2	0.4	0.4	0.1	5.647	7.784	1,224.4	7.07
Indonesia	IDN	1,115.2	494.9	4,608	2,045	53.3	62.9	33.5	13.5	6.0	2.3	1.2	3.6	3,892.218	8,770.433	4,340,605.4	241.99
Japan	JPN	2,485.3	3,586.8	19,442	28,059	173.3	265.4	460.0	57.0	82.3	5.0	8.7	1.9	115.178	79.807	286,254.9	127.83
Korea, Rep.	KOR	787.3	641.6	15,765	12,849	97.9	215.2	210.7	46.2	37.7	1.6	1.6	0.7	903.294	1,108.292	711,118.8	49.94
Lao PDR	LAO	13.9	5.4	2,280	887	46.7	31.1	14.5	6.7	2.6	0.0	0.0	0.1	3,124.075	8,030.055	43,566.6	6.12
Macao SAR, China[d]	MAC	12.0	7.7	21,788	14,032	77.4	297.4	230.1	63.9	41.1	0.0	0.0	0.0	5.164	8.018	62.0	0.55
Malaysia	MYS	275.7	142.9	9,486	4,918	62.3	129.5	80.6	27.8	14.4	0.6	0.3	0.4	1.586	3.060	437.3	29.06
Mongolia	MNG	11.7	5.4	4,192	1,924	55.1	57.2	31.5	12.3	5.6	0.0	0.0	0.0	580.638	1,265.516	6,782.7	2.79
Myanmar	MMR	95.3	32.4	1,919	653	40.9	26.2	10.7	5.6	1.9	0.2	0.1	0.7	278.394	817.917	26,528.1	49.66
New Zealand	NZL	78.1	97.4	17,770	22,161	149.8	242.6	363.3	52.1	65.0	0.2	0.2	0.1	1.579	1.266	123.2	4.39
Philippines	PHL	380.0	164.7	4,034	1,748	52.1	55.1	28.7	11.8	5.1	0.8	0.4	1.4	18.772	43.313	7,132.6	94.18
Singapore	SGP	117.7	102.2	22,699	19,713	104.3	309.9	323.2	66.6	57.8	0.2	0.2	0.1	1.092	1.258	128.5	5.18
Taiwan, China	TWN	483.3	264.7	20,842	11,412	65.8	284.5	187.1	61.1	33.5	1.0	0.6	0.3	16.136	29.469	7,799.0	23.19
Thailand	THA	479.5	200.6	7,241	3,030	50.3	98.8	49.7	21.2	8.9	1.0	0.5	1.0	12.759	30.492	6,117.6	66.21
Vietnam	VNM	217.6	79.9	2,470	907	44.1	33.7	14.9	7.2	2.7	0.4	0.2	1.3	7,528.385	20,509.750	1,638,345.5	88.11
Total (20)	**EAB**	**11,875.0**	**9,423.9**	**5,451**	**4,326**	**95.3**	**74.4**	**70.9**	**16.0**	**12.7**	**24.1**	**22.9**	**32.3**	**n.a.**	**n.a**	**n.a.**	**2,178.31**
Europe and Central Asia																	
Albania	ALB	18.6	10.1	6,414	3,477	65.1	87.6	57.0	18.8	10.2	0.0	0.0	0.0	54.653	100.812	1,018.4	2.91
Armenia	ARM	19.1	8.5	6,303	2,803	53.4	86.0	45.9	18.5	8.2	0.0	0.0	0.0	165.629	372.500	3,161.0	3.03
Austria	AUT	194.4	230.4	23,178	27,471	142.4	316.4	450.4	68.0	80.6	0.4	0.6	0.1	0.851	0.718	165.5	8.39
Azerbaijan	AZE	60.0	24.6	6,627	2,713	49.2	90.5	44.5	19.4	8.0	0.1	0.1	0.1	0.323	0.790	19.4	9.05
Belarus	BLR	80.8	26.7	8,527	2,818	39.7	116.4	46.2	25.0	8.3	0.2	0.1	0.1	0.185	0.561	15.0	9.47
Belgium	BEL	220.8	269.7	20,001	24,437	146.8	273.0	400.7	58.6	71.7	0.4	0.7	0.2	0.878	0.718	193.8	11.04
Bosnia and Herzegovina	BIH	25.9	15.7	7,066	4,297	73.0	96.5	70.5	20.7	12.6	0.1	0.0	0.1	0.854	1.405	22.1	3.66
Bulgaria	BGR	63.2	35.7	8,604	4,861	67.9	117.4	79.7	25.2	14.3	0.1	0.1	0.1	0.794	1.405	50.2	7.35
Croatia	HRV	48.3	38.2	11,273	8,912	95.0	153.9	146.1	33.1	26.1	0.1	0.1	0.1	4.225	5.344	204.0	4.28
Cyprus	CYP	17.2	18.1	20,186	21,321	126.9	275.5	349.6	59.2	62.5	0.0	0.0	0.0	0.759	0.718	13.0	0.85
Czech Republic	CZE	137.0	112.0	13,056	10,671	98.2	178.2	175.0	38.3	31.3	0.3	0.3	0.2	14.439	17.665	1,978.7	10.50
Denmark	DNK	106.1	165.3	19,054	29,682	187.1	260.1	486.6	55.9	87.0	0.2	0.4	0.1	8.338	5.352	884.9	5.57
Estonia	EST	14.5	11.7	10,922	8,819	97.0	149.1	144.6	32.0	25.9	0.0	0.0	0.0	0.580	0.718	8.4	1.33
Finland	FIN	108.2	146.5	20,079	27,193	162.7	274.1	445.8	58.9	79.7	0.2	0.4	0.1	0.973	0.718	105.3	5.39

Table E.3 *(Continued)*

INDIVIDUAL CONSUMPTION EXPENDITURE BY HOUSEHOLDS Economy		Expenditure (billion US$) Based on PPPs	Expenditure (billion US$) Based on XRs	Expenditure per capita (US$) Based on PPPs	Expenditure per capita (US$) Based on XRs	Price level index (world = 100.0)[a]	Expenditure per capita indexes[b] World = 100.0 Based on PPPs	Expenditure per capita indexes[b] World = 100.0 Based on XRs	Expenditure per capita indexes[b] United States = 100.0 Based on PPPs	Expenditure per capita indexes[b] United States = 100.0 Based on XRs	Share (world = 100%)[b] Expenditure Based on PPPs	Share (world = 100%)[b] Expenditure Based on XRs	Share (world = 100%)[b] Population	PPPs[c] (US$ = 1.000)	Reference data Market exchange rates[c] (US$ = 1.000)	Reference data Expenditure (billion LCU)	Reference data Population (millions)
(00)		(01)	(02)	(03)	(04)	(05)	(06)	(07)	(08)	(09)	(10)	(11)	(12)	(13)	(14)	(15)	(16)
France	FRA	1,286.4	1,575.4	19,690	24,114	147.1	268.8	395.4	57.7	70.7	2.6	3.8	1.0	0.880	0.718	1,131.7	65.33
Georgia	GEO	25.1	12.4	6,679	3,308	59.5	91.2	54.2	19.6	9.7	0.1	0.0	0.1	0.835	1.686	21.0	3.76
Germany	DEU	1,771.2	2,039.2	22,065	25,403	138.3	301.2	416.5	64.7	74.5	3.6	5.0	1.2	0.827	0.718	1,464.9	80.28
Greece	GRC	188.4	201.4	16,962	18,135	128.4	231.5	297.3	49.7	53.2	0.4	0.5	0.2	0.768	0.718	144.7	11.11
Hungary	HUN	109.2	74.6	10,946	7,482	82.1	149.4	122.7	32.1	21.9	0.2	0.2	0.1	137.179	200.697	14,973.8	9.97
Iceland	ISL	6.5	7.9	20,408	24,781	145.8	278.6	406.3	59.8	72.7	0.0	0.0	0.0	140.808	115.963	916.7	0.32
Ireland	IRL	82.7	110.3	18,072	24,095	160.1	246.7	395.0	53.0	70.7	0.2	0.3	0.1	0.958	0.718	79.3	4.58
Italy	ITA	1,236.8	1,402.7	20,592	23,354	136.2	281.1	382.9	60.4	68.5	2.5	3.4	0.9	0.815	0.718	1,007.7	60.06
Kazakhstan	KAZ	150.4	81.3	9,085	4,909	64.9	124.0	80.5	26.6	14.4	0.3	0.2	0.2	79.222	146.620	11,916.1	16.56
Kyrgyz Republic	KGZ	14.6	5.2	2,783	983	42.4	38.0	16.1	8.2	2.9	0.0	0.0	0.1	16.296	46.144	238.5	5.26
Latvia	LVA	21.9	17.3	10,630	8,387	94.8	145.1	137.5	31.2	24.6	0.0	0.0	0.0	0.567	0.718	12.4	2.06
Lithuania	LTU	38.2	27.1	12,603	8,959	85.4	172.0	146.9	37.0	26.3	0.1	0.1	0.0	0.511	0.718	19.5	3.03
Luxembourg	LUX	13.8	18.8	26,580	36,245	163.8	362.8	594.2	77.9	106.3	0.0	0.0	0.0	0.980	0.718	13.5	0.52
Moldova	MDA	17.0	7.8	4,766	2,199	55.4	65.1	36.0	14.0	6.4	0.0	0.0	0.1	5.410	11.726	91.8	3.56
Montenegro	MNE	6.0	3.7	9,736	5,978	73.8	132.9	98.0	28.5	17.5	0.0	0.0	0.0	0.441	0.718	2.7	0.62
Netherlands	NLD	339.3	413.2	20,326	24,751	146.3	277.5	405.8	59.6	72.6	0.7	1.0	0.2	0.875	0.718	296.8	16.69
North Macedonia	MKD	14.5	7.8	7,060	3,770	64.1	96.4	61.8	20.7	11.1	0.0	0.0	0.0	23.608	44.202	343.1	2.06
Norway	NOR	114.6	201.0	23,143	40,576	210.6	315.9	665.3	67.9	119.0	0.2	0.5	0.1	9.816	5.599	1,125.2	4.95
Poland	POL	508.3	325.3	13,194	8,445	76.9	180.1	138.5	38.7	24.8	1.0	0.8	0.6	1.895	2.960	963.1	38.53
Portugal	PRT	168.1	161.5	15,919	15,298	115.4	217.3	250.8	46.7	44.9	0.3	0.4	0.2	0.690	0.718	116.0	10.56
Romania	ROU	196.0	116.5	9,726	5,782	71.4	132.8	94.8	28.5	17.0	0.4	0.3	0.3	1.810	3.045	354.8	20.15
Russian Federation	RUS	1,617.0	1,026.6	11,311	7,181	76.3	154.4	117.7	33.2	21.1	3.3	2.5	2.1	18.655	29.382	30,164.8	142.96
Serbia	SRB	62.5	37.3	8,642	5,148	71.5	118.0	84.4	25.3	15.1	0.1	0.1	0.1	43.629	73.240	2,728.5	7.24
Slovak Republic	SVK	71.4	55.2	13,226	10,231	92.9	180.5	167.7	38.8	30.0	0.1	0.1	0.1	0.556	0.718	39.7	5.40
Slovenia	SVN	30.9	29.2	15,063	14,206	113.3	205.6	232.9	44.2	41.7	0.1	0.1	0.0	0.677	0.718	20.9	2.05
Spain	ESP	789.2	865.9	16,886	18,528	131.8	230.5	303.8	49.5	54.3	1.6	2.1	0.7	0.788	0.718	622.1	46.74
Sweden	SWE	191.5	266.4	20,270	28,188	167.0	276.7	462.1	59.4	82.7	0.4	0.6	0.1	9.021	6.487	1,727.8	9.45
Switzerland	CHE	214.5	372.9	27,103	47,127	208.8	370.0	772.7	79.5	138.2	0.4	0.9	0.1	1.540	0.885	330.2	7.91
Tajikistan	TJK	18.0	7.0	2,332	904	46.5	31.8	14.8	6.8	2.7	0.0	0.0	0.1	1.786	4.610	32.1	7.71
Turkey	TUR	776.3	525.9	10,459	7,085	81.4	142.8	116.2	30.7	20.8	1.6	1.3	1.1	1.135	1.675	880.9	74.22
Ukraine[d]	UKR	285.1	113.9	6,239	2,491	48.0	85.2	40.8	18.3	7.3	0.6	0.3	0.7	3.182	7.968	907.2	45.71
United Kingdom	GBR	1,374.3	1,711.2	21,716	27,040	149.6	296.4	443.3	63.7	79.3	2.8	4.2	0.9	0.776	0.623	1,066.9	63.29
Total (46)	**ECB**	**12,853.8**	**12,935.1**	**15,026**	**15,121**	**120.9**	**205.1**	**247.9**	**44.1**	**44.3**	**26.0**	**31.5**	**12.7**	**n.a.**	**n.a**	**n.a.**	**855.42**
Latin America and the Caribbean																	
Anguilla	AIA	0.3	0.2	19,569	18,133	111.3	267.1	297.3	57.4	53.2	0.0	0.0	0.0	2.502	2.700	0.7	0.01
Antigua and Barbuda	ATG	0.9	0.7	9,742	7,945	98.0	133.0	130.3	28.6	23.3	0.0	0.0	0.0	2.202	2.700	1.9	0.09
Aruba	ABW	1.8	1.6	17,177	15,716	109.9	234.5	257.7	50.4	46.1	0.0	0.0	0.0	1.638	1.790	2.9	0.10

(continued)

Table E.3 *(Continued)*

INDIVIDUAL CONSUMPTION EXPENDITURE BY HOUSEHOLDS		Expenditure (billion US$)		Expenditure per capita (US$)		Price level index	Expenditure per capita indexes[b]				Share (world = 100%)[b]				Reference data		
							World = 100.0		United States = 100.0		Expenditure						
Economy		Based on PPPs	Based on XRs	Based on PPPs	Based on XRs	(world = 100.0)[a]	Based on PPPs	Based on XRs	Based on PPPs	Based on XRs	Based on PPPs	Based on XRs	Population	PPPs[c] (US$ = 1.000)	Market exchange rates[c] (US$ = 1.000)	Expenditure (billion LCU)	Population (millions)
(00)		(01)	(02)	(03)	(04)	(05)	(06)	(07)	(08)	(09)	(10)	(11)	(12)	(13)	(14)	(15)	(16)
Bahamas, The	BHS	5.6	6.3	15,574	17,525	135.2	212.6	287.3	45.7	51.4	0.0	0.0	0.0	1.125	1.000	6.3	0.36
Barbados	BRB	2.8	3.3	9,832	11,764	143.7	134.2	192.9	28.8	34.5	0.0	0.0	0.0	2.393	2.000	6.7	0.28
Belize	BLZ	1.8	1.0	5,394	3,167	70.5	73.6	51.9	15.8	9.3	0.0	0.0	0.0	1.174	2.000	2.1	0.33
Bolivia	BOL	34.9	14.5	3,418	1,415	49.7	46.7	23.2	10.0	4.1	0.1	0.0	0.2	2.891	6.982	100.9	10.21
Bonaire[e]	BON	0.2	0.2	8,735	8,015	110.0	119.8	131.7	25.6	23.5	0.0	0.0	0.0	0.918	1.000	0.2	0.02
Brazil	BRA	1,597.5	1,576.9	8,088	7,984	118.6	110.4	130.9	23.7	23.4	3.2	3.8	2.9	1.651	1.673	2,637.8	197.51
Cayman Islands	CYM	1.7	2.3	28,808	39,060	162.9	393.2	640.4	84.5	114.5	0.0	0.0	0.0	1.130	0.833	1.9	0.06
Chile	CHL	189.6	151.7	10,983	8,784	96.1	149.9	144.0	32.2	25.8	0.4	0.4	0.3	386.817	483.668	73,356.8	17.27
Colombia	COL	333.4	218.5	7,241	4,745	78.7	98.8	77.8	21.2	13.9	0.7	0.5	0.7	1,210.993	1,848.139	403,766.7	46.04
Costa Rica	CRI	40.8	28.2	8,887	6,140	83.0	121.3	100.7	26.1	18.0	0.1	0.1	0.1	349.407	505.664	14,250.9	4.59
Curaçao	CUW	2.5	2.0	16,419	13,412	98.1	224.1	219.9	48.1	39.3	0.0	0.0	0.0	1.462	1.790	3.7	0.15
Dominica	DMA	0.6	0.4	7,975	6,012	90.5	108.9	98.6	23.4	17.6	0.0	0.0	0.0	2.035	2.700	1.2	0.07
Dominican Republic	DOM	81.2	44.2	8,272	4,509	65.5	112.9	73.9	24.3	13.2	0.2	0.1	0.1	20.765	38.099	1,685.7	9.81
Ecuador	ECU	88.8	48.7	5,827	3,192	65.8	79.5	52.3	17.1	9.4	0.2	0.1	0.2	0.548	1.000	48.7	15.24
El Salvador	SLV	33.1	17.8	5,336	2,866	64.5	72.8	47.0	15.6	8.4	0.1	0.0	0.1	0.537	1.000	17.8	6.21
Grenada	GRD	0.9	0.7	8,455	6,595	93.7	115.4	108.1	24.8	19.3	0.0	0.0	0.0	2.106	2.700	1.9	0.11
Guatemala[d]	GTM	81.3	40.5	5,440	2,712	59.9	74.3	44.5	16.0	8.0	0.2	0.1	0.2	3.892	7.807	316.5	14.95
Haiti	HTI	16.0	8.1	1,587	807	61.1	21.7	13.2	4.7	2.4	0.0	0.0	0.1	20.833	40.977	333.9	10.10
Honduras	HND	25.3	13.7	2,988	1,610	64.7	40.8	26.4	8.8	4.7	0.1	0.0	0.1	10.264	19.048	260.1	8.48
Jamaica	JAM	16.9	12.4	5,994	4,387	87.9	81.8	71.9	17.6	12.9	0.0	0.0	0.0	62.876	85.911	1,065.1	2.83
Mexico	MEX	1,069.6	765.0	9,259	6,623	85.9	126.4	108.6	27.2	19.4	2.2	1.9	1.7	8.886	12.423	9,504.3	115.51
Montserrat	MSR	0.1	0.0	11,606	9,566	99.0	158.4	156.8	34.0	28.1	0.0	0.0	0.0	2.225	2.700	0.1	0.00
Nicaragua	NIC	18.3	7.5	3,099	1,278	49.5	42.3	21.0	9.1	3.7	0.0	0.0	0.1	9.251	22.424	169.2	5.90
Panama	PAN	34.8	19.3	9,392	5,196	66.4	128.2	85.2	27.5	15.2	0.1	0.0	0.1	0.553	1.000	19.3	3.71
Paraguay	PRY	40.1	21.5	6,333	3,394	64.4	86.4	55.6	18.6	10.0	0.1	0.1	0.1	2,242.096	4,183.127	89,930.6	6.33
Peru	PER	181.0	103.8	6,185	3,546	68.9	84.4	58.1	18.1	10.4	0.4	0.3	0.4	1.579	2.754	285.8	29.26
Sint Maarten	SXM	0.7	0.6	19,678	17,923	109.4	268.6	293.9	57.7	52.6	0.0	0.0	0.0	1.630	1.790	1.1	0.04
St. Kitts and Nevis	KNA	0.7	0.6	13,690	11,322	99.3	186.9	185.6	40.1	33.2	0.0	0.0	0.0	2.233	2.700	1.5	0.05
St. Lucia	LCA	1.5	1.1	8,435	6,511	92.7	115.1	106.7	24.7	19.1	0.0	0.0	0.0	2.084	2.700	3.1	0.18
St. Vincent and the Grenadines	VCT	0.8	0.6	7,089	5,246	88.9	96.8	86.0	20.8	15.4	0.0	0.0	0.0	1.998	2.700	1.5	0.11
Suriname	SUR	2.7	1.5	5,101	2,893	68.1	69.6	47.4	15.0	8.5	0.0	0.0	0.0	1.900	3.350	5.2	0.54
Trinidad and Tobago	TTO	16.8	11.8	12,583	8,852	84.5	171.8	145.1	36.9	26.0	0.0	0.0	0.0	4.520	6.426	76.0	1.34
Turks and Caicos Islands	TCA	0.2	0.3	6,823	8,596	151.3	93.1	140.9	20.0	25.2	0.0	0.0	0.0	1.260	1.000	0.3	0.03
Uruguay	URY	37.2	32.0	11,053	9,504	103.3	150.9	155.8	32.4	27.9	0.1	0.1	0.1	16.608	19.314	618.4	3.37
Venezuela, RB[d]	VEN	254.4	174.6	8,806	6,043	82.4	120.2	99.1	25.8	17.7	0.5	0.4	0.4	2.944	4.289	748.8	28.89
Virgin Islands, British	VGB	0.3	0.3	9,429	11,349	144.6	128.7	186.1	27.6	33.3	0.0	0.0	0.0	1.204	1.000	0.3	0.03
Total (39)	**LCB**	**4,216.8**	**3,334.4**	**7,807**	**6,174**	**95.0**	**106.6**	**101.2**	**22.9**	**18.1**	**8.5**	**8.1**	**8.0**	**n.a.**	**n.a**	**n.a.**	**540.10**

Table E.3 *(Continued)*

INDIVIDUAL CONSUMPTION EXPENDITURE BY HOUSEHOLDS		Expenditure (billion US$)		Expenditure per capita (US$)		Price level index	Expenditure per capita indexes[b]				Share (world = 100%)[b]				Reference data		
							World = 100.0		United States = 100.0		Expenditure						
Economy		Based on PPPs	Based on XRs	Based on PPPs	Based on XRs	(world = 100.0)[a]	Based on PPPs	Based on XRs	Based on PPPs	Based on XRs	Based on PPPs	Based on XRs	Population	PPPs[c] (US$ = 1.000)	Market exchange rates[c] (US$ = 1.000)	Expenditure (billion LCU)	Population (millions)
(00)		(01)	(02)	(03)	(04)	(05)	(06)	(07)	(08)	(09)	(10)	(11)	(12)	(13)	(14)	(15)	(16)
Middle East and North Africa																	
Algeria	DZA	145.1	62.7	3,957	1,710	51.9	54.0	28.0	11.6	5.0	0.3	0.2	0.5	31.518	72.938	4,571.9	36.66
Bahrain	BHR	23.7	11.2	19,805	9,409	57.1	270.3	154.3	58.1	27.6	0.0	0.0	0.0	0.179	0.376	4.2	1.20
Djibouti	DJI	2.3	1.3	2,731	1,546	68.0	37.3	25.3	8.0	4.5	0.0	0.0	0.0	100.624	177.721	234.6	0.85
Egypt, Arab Rep.	EGY	700.2	201.9	8,695	2,507	34.6	118.7	41.1	25.5	7.4	1.4	0.5	1.2	1.715	5.947	1,200.6	80.53
Iran, Islamic Rep.	IRN	763.7	382.9	10,162	5,096	60.2	138.7	83.5	29.8	14.9	1.5	0.9	1.1	5,323.442	10,616.307	4,065,433.1	75.15
Iraq	IRQ	159.7	63.6	4,790	1,907	47.8	65.4	31.3	14.0	5.6	0.3	0.2	0.5	477.559	1,199.200	76,260.3	33.34
Israel	ISR	124.6	148.1	16,046	19,076	142.8	219.0	312.8	47.1	55.9	0.3	0.4	0.1	4.254	3.578	529.9	7.76
Jordan	JOR	51.1	23.5	7,308	3,355	55.1	99.8	55.0	21.4	9.8	0.1	0.1	0.1	0.325	0.708	16.6	6.99
Kuwait	KWT	57.9	36.8	18,872	12,008	76.4	257.6	196.9	55.3	35.2	0.1	0.1	0.0	0.178	0.280	10.3	3.07
Malta	MLT	6.3	5.6	15,215	13,405	105.8	207.7	219.8	44.6	39.3	0.0	0.0	0.0	0.633	0.718	4.0	0.42
Morocco	MAR	118.4	60.7	3,634	1,862	61.6	49.6	30.5	10.7	5.5	0.2	0.1	0.5	4.125	8.049	488.3	32.58
Oman	OMN	39.3	20.9	11,932	6,355	64.0	162.9	104.2	35.0	18.6	0.1	0.1	0.0	0.205	0.385	8.1	3.30
Qatar	QAT	27.4	22.4	15,798	12,950	98.5	215.6	212.3	46.3	38.0	0.1	0.1	0.0	2.992	3.650	81.9	1.73
Saudi Arabia	SAU	451.1	183.5	16,011	6,512	48.8	218.6	106.8	46.9	19.1	0.9	0.4	0.4	1.525	3.750	687.9	28.17
Tunisia	TUN	61.4	30.4	5,717	2,830	59.5	78.0	46.4	16.8	8.3	0.1	0.1	0.2	0.697	1.408	42.8	10.74
United Arab Emirates	ARE	206.2	134.5	23,775	15,515	78.4	324.5	254.4	69.7	45.5	0.4	0.3	0.1	2.397	3.673	494.1	8.67
West Bank and Gaza	PSE	14.1	9.6	3,646	2,484	81.8	49.8	40.7	10.7	7.3	0.0	0.0	0.1	2.438	3.578	34.5	3.88
Yemen, Rep.[d]	YEM	59.6	21.4	2,500	898	43.1	34.1	14.7	7.3	2.6	0.1	0.1	0.4	76.766	213.800	4,573.2	23.83
Total (17)	**MEB**	**3,011.9**	**1,421.1**	**8,393**	**3,960**	**56.7**	**114.6**	**64.9**	**24.6**	**11.6**	**6.1**	**3.5**	**5.3**	**n.a.**	**n.a**	**n.a.**	**358.87**
North America																	
Bermuda	BMU	1.7	3.1	26,123	47,706	219.3	356.6	782.2	76.6	139.9	0.0	0.0	0.0	1.826	1.000	3.1	0.07
Canada	CAN	773.4	1,002.2	22,520	29,183	155.7	307.4	478.5	66.0	85.6	1.6	2.4	0.5	1.282	0.990	991.8	34.34
United States	USA	10,641.1	10,641.1	34,103	34,103	120.1	465.5	559.1	100.0	100.0	21.6	25.9	4.6	1.000	1.000	10,641.1	312.03
Total (3)	**NAB**	**11,416.2**	**11,646.5**	**32,953**	**33,617**	**122.5**	**449.8**	**551.2**	**96.6**	**98.6**	**23.1**	**28.3**	**5.1**	**n.a.**	**n.a**	**n.a.**	**346.44**
South Asia																	
Bangladesh	BGD	294.8	98.3	1,969	657	40.1	26.9	10.8	5.8	1.9	0.6	0.2	2.2	24.732	74.152	7,291.8	149.70
Bhutan	BTN	2.1	0.8	3,049	1,113	43.9	41.6	18.3	8.9	3.3	0.0	0.0	0.0	17.044	46.670	35.3	0.68
India	IND	3,112.4	1,019.2	2,559	838	39.3	34.9	13.7	7.5	2.5	6.3	2.5	18.1	15.283	46.670	47,565.7	1,216.15
Maldives	MDV	1.5	0.9	3,737	2,254	72.5	51.0	37.0	11.0	6.6	0.0	0.0	0.0	8.810	14.602	13.4	0.41
Nepal	NPL	42.8	14.9	1,615	562	41.8	22.1	9.2	4.7	1.6	0.1	0.0	0.4	25.743	74.020	1,101.6	26.49
Pakistan	PAK	615.0	181.6	3,473	1,025	35.5	47.4	16.8	10.2	3.0	1.2	0.4	2.6	25.496	86.343	15,679.6	177.10
Sri Lanka	LKA	119.7	46.5	5,925	2,304	46.7	80.9	37.8	17.4	6.8	0.2	0.1	0.3	42.988	110.565	5,143.7	20.20
Total (7)	**SAB**	**4,188.2**	**1,362.2**	**2,633**	**856**	**39.1**	**35.9**	**14.0**	**7.7**	**2.5**	**8.5**	**3.3**	**23.6**	**n.a.**	**n.a**	**n.a.**	**1,590.72**
Sub-Saharan Africa																	
Angola	AGO	45.3	39.0	1,869	1,611	103.5	25.5	26.4	5.5	4.7	0.1	0.1	0.4	80.932	93.935	3,664.5	24.22
Benin	BEN	11.8	5.6	1,250	597	57.4	17.1	9.8	3.7	1.8	0.0	0.0	0.1	225.412	471.866	2,665.7	9.46
Botswana	BWA	11.4	7.1	5,661	3,528	74.9	77.3	57.9	16.6	10.3	0.0	0.0	0.0	4.262	6.838	48.6	2.02

(continued)

Table E.3 *(Continued)*

INDIVIDUAL CONSUMPTION EXPENDITURE BY HOUSEHOLDS		Expenditure (billion US$)		Expenditure per capita (US$)		Price level index (world = 100.0)[a]	Expenditure per capita indexes[b]				Share (world = 100%)[b]			PPPs[c] (US$ = 1.000)	Reference data		
							World = 100.0		United States = 100.0		Expenditure				Market exchange rates[c] (US$ = 1.000)	Expenditure (billion LCU)	Population (millions)
Economy		Based on PPPs	Based on XRs	Based on PPPs	Based on XRs		Based on PPPs	Based on XRs	Based on PPPs	Based on XRs	Based on PPPs	Based on XRs	Population				
(00)		(01)	(02)	(03)	(04)	(05)	(06)	(07)	(08)	(09)	(10)	(11)	(12)	(13)	(14)	(15)	(16)
Burkina Faso	BFA	13.6	6.4	847	400	56.8	11.6	6.6	2.5	1.2	0.0	0.0	0.2	223.073	471.866	3,037.2	16.08
Burundi	BDI	5.2	2.0	579	228	47.3	7.9	3.7	1.7	0.7	0.0	0.0	0.1	496.117	1,261.073	2,573.5	8.96
Cabo Verde	CPV	1.9	1.2	3,873	2,346	72.8	52.9	38.5	11.4	6.9	0.0	0.0	0.0	48.057	79.323	92.8	0.50
Cameroon	CMR	39.3	20.2	1,878	966	61.8	25.6	15.8	5.5	2.8	0.1	0.0	0.3	242.678	471.866	9,526.5	20.91
Central African Republic	CAF	3.6	2.0	823	463	67.6	11.2	7.6	2.4	1.4	0.0	0.0	0.1	265.661	471.866	965.9	4.42
Chad	TCD	13.3	7.1	1,076	571	63.7	14.7	9.4	3.2	1.7	0.0	0.0	0.2	250.251	471.866	3,328.6	12.36
Comoros	COM	1.4	1.0	2,025	1,348	80.0	27.6	22.1	5.9	4.0	0.0	0.0	0.0	235.604	353.900	337.1	0.71
Congo, Dem. Rep.	COD	33.5	19.9	501	298	71.4	6.8	4.9	1.5	0.9	0.1	0.0	1.0	546.732	919.491	18,298.8	66.76
Congo, Rep.	COG	6.6	4.3	1,506	969	77.3	20.6	15.9	4.4	2.8	0.0	0.0	0.1	303.724	471.866	2,009.9	4.39
Côte d'Ivoire	CIV	34.1	17.6	1,621	836	62.0	22.1	13.7	4.8	2.5	0.1	0.0	0.3	243.461	471.866	8,298.4	21.03
Equatorial Guinea	GNQ	6.2	4.3	6,328	4,400	83.5	86.4	72.1	18.6	12.9	0.0	0.0	0.0	328.091	471.866	2,048.8	0.99
Eswatini	SWZ	6.6	3.8	6,187	3,504	68.0	84.5	57.4	18.1	10.3	0.0	0.0	0.0	4.112	7.261	27.3	1.07
Ethiopia	ETH	97.0	32.0	1,076	355	39.6	14.7	5.8	3.2	1.0	0.2	0.1	1.3	5.575	16.899	540.5	90.14
Gabon	GAB	7.0	5.3	4,168	3,174	91.5	56.9	52.0	12.2	9.3	0.0	0.0	0.0	359.344	471.866	2,523.1	1.68
Gambia, The	GMB	3.2	1.2	1,717	636	44.5	23.4	10.4	5.0	1.9	0.0	0.0	0.0	10.912	29.462	34.6	1.85
Ghana	GHA	62.0	31.9	2,442	1,258	61.9	33.3	20.6	7.2	3.7	0.1	0.1	0.4	0.779	1.512	48.3	25.39
Guinea	GIN	14.2	5.5	1,363	532	46.9	18.6	8.7	4.0	1.6	0.0	0.0	0.2	2,599.891	6,658.031	36,919.5	10.42
Guinea-Bissau	GNB	1.7	0.9	1,072	587	65.8	14.6	9.6	3.1	1.7	0.0	0.0	0.0	258.323	471.866	432.9	1.56
Kenya	KEN	84.2	33.8	1,949	782	48.2	26.6	12.8	5.7	2.3	0.2	0.1	0.6	35.621	88.811	2,997.9	43.18
Lesotho	LSO	4.6	2.5	2,293	1,239	64.9	31.3	20.3	6.7	3.6	0.0	0.0	0.0	3.926	7.261	18.0	2.00
Liberia	LBR	2.0	1.2	507	303	71.9	6.9	5.0	1.5	0.9	0.0	0.0	0.1	43.207	72.227	88.0	4.02
Madagascar	MDG	24.7	8.6	1,138	393	41.5	15.5	6.4	3.3	1.2	0.1	0.0	0.3	700.228	2,025.118	17,322.0	21.74
Malawi	MWI	13.4	6.7	895	450	60.4	12.2	7.4	2.6	1.3	0.0	0.0	0.2	78.703	156.515	1,053.6	14.96
Mali	MLI	19.6	9.3	1,262	600	57.1	17.2	9.8	3.7	1.8	0.0	0.0	0.2	224.357	471.866	4,394.5	15.51
Mauritania	MRT	5.8	2.3	1,603	643	48.2	21.9	10.5	4.7	1.9	0.0	0.0	0.1	112.849	281.118	650.8	3.60
Mauritius	MUS	12.9	8.3	10,315	6,668	77.6	140.8	109.3	30.2	19.6	0.0	0.0	0.0	18.555	28.706	239.5	1.25
Mozambique	MOZ	18.3	10.0	756	412	65.4	10.3	6.8	2.2	1.2	0.0	0.0	0.4	15.826	29.068	289.6	24.19
Namibia	NAM	11.4	8.2	5,289	3,820	86.7	72.2	62.6	15.5	11.2	0.0	0.0	0.0	5.244	7.261	59.8	2.16
Niger	NER	9.5	4.6	556	272	58.7	7.6	4.5	1.6	0.8	0.0	0.0	0.3	230.417	471.866	2,192.8	17.11
Nigeria	NGA	489.4	265.9	3,006	1,633	65.2	41.0	26.8	8.8	4.8	1.0	0.6	2.4	83.583	153.862	40,904.9	162.81
Rwanda	RWA	12.1	5.1	1,174	492	50.3	16.0	8.1	3.4	1.4	0.0	0.0	0.2	251.305	600.307	3,038.1	10.29
São Tomé and Príncipe	STP	0.4	0.2	1,934	1,151	71.5	26.4	18.9	5.7	3.4	0.0	0.0	0.0	10.487	17.623	3.7	0.18
Senegal	SEN	27.1	14.3	2,080	1,099	63.5	28.4	18.0	6.1	3.2	0.1	0.0	0.2	249.278	471.866	6,756.4	13.03
Seychelles	SYC	0.9	0.6	9,277	6,169	79.9	126.6	101.1	27.2	18.1	0.0	0.0	0.0	8.233	12.381	7.0	0.09
Sierra Leone	SLE	6.7	2.8	1,026	431	50.4	14.0	7.1	3.0	1.3	0.0	0.0	0.1	1,825.528	4,349.162	12,295.1	6.56
South Africa	ZAF	364.1	252.3	7,001	4,851	83.2	95.6	79.5	20.5	14.2	0.7	0.6	0.8	5.031	7.261	1,831.8	52.00
Sudan	SDN	86.8	35.0	2,556	1,031	48.5	34.9	16.9	7.5	3.0	0.2	0.1	0.5	1.465	3.630	127.2	33.98

Table E.3 *(Continued)*

INDIVIDUAL CONSUMPTION EXPENDITURE BY HOUSEHOLDS Economy		Expenditure (billion US$)		Expenditure per capita (US$)		Price level index	Expenditure per capita indexes[b]				Share (world = 100%)[b]			PPPs[c] (US$ = 1.000)	Reference data		
							World = 100.0		United States = 100.0		Expenditure				Market exchange rates[c] (US$ = 1.000)	Expenditure (billion LCU)	Population (millions)
		Based on PPPs	Based on XRs	Based on PPPs	Based on XRs	(world = 100.0)[a]	Based on PPPs	Based on XRs	Based on PPPs	Based on XRs	Based on PPPs	Based on XRs	Population				
(00)		(01)	(02)	(03)	(04)	(05)	(06)	(07)	(08)	(09)	(10)	(11)	(12)	(13)	(14)	(15)	(16)
Tanzania	TZA	66.3	24.8	1,452	544	45.0	19.8	8.9	4.3	1.6	0.1	0.1	0.7	588.785	1,572.116	39,059.9	45.67
Togo	TGO	6.0	3.0	912	457	60.2	12.4	7.5	2.7	1.3	0.0	0.0	0.1	236.587	471.866	1,422.5	6.60
Uganda	UGA	57.5	21.5	1,717	643	45.0	23.4	10.5	5.0	1.9	0.1	0.1	0.5	944.256	2,522.746	54,266.8	33.48
Zambia	ZMB	24.3	13.1	1,736	933	64.5	23.7	15.3	5.1	2.7	0.0	0.0	0.2	2.611	4.861	63.6	14.02
Zimbabwe	ZWE	18.3	9.8	1,419	760	64.3	19.4	12.5	4.2	2.2	0.0	0.0	0.2	0.535	1.000	9.8	12.89
Total (45)	**SSB**	**1,785.3**	**962.4**	**2,061**	**1,111**	**64.7**	**28.1**	**18.2**	**6.0**	**3.3**	**3.6**	**2.3**	**12.9**	**n.a.**	**n.a**	**n.a.**	**866.25**
World (178)	**WLD**	**49,347.2**	**41,085.5**	**7,326**	**6,099**	**100.0**	**100.0**	**100.0**	**21.5**	**17.9**	**100.0**	**100.0**	**100.0**	**n.a.**	**n.a.**	**n.a.**	**6,736.12**

Note: PPP = purchasing power parity; XR = market exchange rate; LCU = local currency unit; n.a. = not applicable; ... = data suppressed due to unavailability.

a. World totals used to calculate price level indexes (PLIs) in this table exclude nonparticipating economies.

b. Indexes and shares are rounded to one decimal place for presentation in this table.

c. PPPs and market exchange rates are rounded to three decimal places for presentation in this table.

d. National accounts expenditures for the revised ICP 2011 results are estimated by the ICP Global Office.

e. Bonaire's results are provided only for individual consumption expenditure by households. Therefore, to ensure consistency across tables, Bonaire is not included in either Latin America and the Caribbean or the world totals.

Table E.4 Consumption expenditure by government: Revised ICP 2011 results

CONSUMPTION EXPENDITURE BY GOVERNMENT		Expenditure (billion US$)		Expenditure per capita (US$)		Price level index	Expenditure per capita indexes[b]				Share (world = 100%)[b]			PPPs[c]	Reference data		
							World = 100.0		United States = 100.0		Expenditure				Market exchange rates[c]		
Economy		Based on PPPs	Based on XRs	Based on PPPs	Based on XRs	(world = 100.0)[a]	Based on PPPs	Based on XRs	Based on PPPs	Based on XRs	Based on PPPs	Based on XRs	Population	(US$ = 1.000)	(US$ = 1.000)	Expenditure (billion LCU)	Population (millions)
(00)		(01)	(02)	(03)	(04)	(05)	(06)	(07)	(08)	(09)	(10)	(11)	(12)	(13)	(14)	(15)	(16)
East Asia and Pacific																	
Australia	AUS	199.0	271.6	8,907	12,155	217.8	300.4	654.3	110.6	151.0	1.0	2.2	0.3	1.323	0.969	263.3	22.34
Brunei Darussalam	BRN	10.8	3.5	27,483	8,820	51.2	926.9	474.8	341.4	109.6	0.1	0.0	0.0	0.404	1.258	4.4	0.39
Cambodia	KHM	6.1	1.1	429	75	28.1	14.5	4.1	5.3	0.9	0.0	0.0	0.2	713.781	4,058.500	4,380.9	14.31
China	CHN	2,645.5	1,121.2	1,968	834	67.6	66.4	44.9	24.5	10.4	13.2	9.0	20.0	2.738	6.461	7,244.8	1,344.13
Fiji	FJI	1.6	0.7	1,917	765	63.7	64.6	41.2	23.8	9.5	0.0	0.0	0.0	0.716	1.793	1.2	0.85
Hong Kong SAR, China	HKG	37.3	21.6	5,280	3,061	92.6	178.1	164.8	65.6	38.0	0.2	0.2	0.1	4.513	7.784	168.5	7.07
Indonesia	IDN	352.6	80.9	1,457	334	36.6	49.1	18.0	18.1	4.2	1.8	0.6	3.6	2,011.816	8,770.433	709,450.8	241.99
Japan	JPN	1,204.2	1,243.1	9,421	9,724	164.8	317.7	523.5	117.0	120.8	6.0	9.9	1.9	82.380	79.807	99,204.5	127.83
Korea, Rep.	KOR	315.3	180.1	6,315	3,607	91.2	213.0	194.2	78.4	44.8	1.6	1.4	0.7	633.057	1,108.292	199,627.2	49.94
Lao PDR	LAO	6.2	0.8	1,019	127	19.9	34.4	6.9	12.7	1.6	0.0	0.0	0.1	1,003.569	8,030.055	6,258.4	6.12
Macao SAR, China[d]	MAC	5.3	2.6	9,682	4,743	78.2	326.5	255.3	120.3	58.9	0.0	0.0	0.0	3.928	8.018	21.0	0.55
Malaysia	MYS	121.1	39.5	4,168	1,361	52.1	140.6	73.2	51.8	16.9	0.6	0.3	0.4	0.999	3.060	121.0	29.06
Mongolia	MNG	7.4	1.3	2,667	458	27.4	89.9	24.6	33.1	5.7	0.0	0.0	0.0	217.279	1,265.516	1,614.5	2.79
Myanmar	MMR	37.8	6.4	761	130	27.2	25.7	7.0	9.5	1.6	0.2	0.1	0.7	139.197	817.917	5,262.1	49.66
New Zealand	NZL	38.5	32.8	8,768	7,470	136.0	295.7	402.1	108.9	92.8	0.2	0.3	0.1	1.079	1.266	41.5	4.39
Philippines	PHL	61.3	21.7	651	231	56.6	21.9	12.4	8.1	2.9	0.3	0.2	1.4	15.367	43.313	941.8	94.18
Singapore	SGP	47.0	25.8	9,076	4,973	87.5	306.1	267.7	112.8	61.8	0.2	0.2	0.1	0.689	1.258	32.4	5.18
Taiwan, China	TWN	191.7	73.6	8,264	3,172	61.3	278.7	170.7	102.7	39.4	1.0	0.6	0.3	11.310	29.469	2,167.6	23.19
Thailand	THA	205.4	61.1	3,102	924	47.5	104.6	49.7	38.5	11.5	1.0	0.5	1.0	9.077	30.492	1,864.6	66.21
Vietnam	VNM	86.4	14.1	981	160	26.0	33.1	8.6	12.2	2.0	0.4	0.1	1.3	3,341.661	20,509.750	288,815.9	88.11
Total (20)	**EAB**	**5,580.9**	**3,203.5**	**2,562**	**1,471**	**91.6**	**86.4**	**79.2**	**31.8**	**18.3**	**27.9**	**25.6**	**32.3**	**n.a.**	**n.a**	**n.a.**	**2,178.31**
Europe and Central Asia																	
Albania	ALB	8.3	1.4	2,845	487	27.3	95.9	26.2	35.3	6.1	0.0	0.0	0.0	17.270	100.812	142.7	2.91
Armenia	ARM	6.7	1.3	2,204	433	31.4	74.3	23.3	27.4	5.4	0.0	0.0	0.0	73.177	372.500	488.4	3.03
Austria	AUT	78.4	85.9	9,344	10,239	174.9	315.1	551.2	116.1	127.2	0.4	0.7	0.1	0.787	0.718	61.7	8.39
Azerbaijan	AZE	32.0	6.7	3,538	738	33.3	119.3	39.7	44.0	9.2	0.2	0.1	0.1	0.165	0.790	5.3	9.05
Belarus	BLR	50.3	7.4	5,308	778	23.4	179.0	41.9	65.9	9.7	0.3	0.1	0.1	0.082	0.561	4.1	9.47
Belgium	BEL	114.2	125.9	10,348	11,402	175.9	349.0	613.8	128.6	141.6	0.6	1.0	0.2	0.792	0.718	90.4	11.04
Bosnia and Herzegovina	BIH	13.7	4.3	3,738	1,177	50.3	126.1	63.4	46.4	14.6	0.1	0.0	0.1	0.443	1.405	6.1	3.66
Bulgaria	BGR	37.8	9.2	5,148	1,245	38.6	173.6	67.0	64.0	15.5	0.2	0.1	0.1	0.340	1.405	12.9	7.35
Croatia	HRV	28.1	12.9	6,570	3,008	73.1	221.6	161.9	81.6	37.4	0.1	0.1	0.1	2.447	5.344	68.9	4.28
Cyprus	CYP	6.2	5.3	7,285	6,184	135.5	245.7	332.9	90.5	76.8	0.0	0.0	0.0	0.610	0.718	3.8	0.85
Czech Republic	CZE	96.4	46.0	9,184	4,385	76.2	309.7	236.1	114.1	54.5	0.5	0.4	0.2	8.435	17.665	813.2	10.50
Denmark	DNK	74.9	91.7	13,449	16,456	195.3	453.6	885.9	167.1	204.4	0.4	0.7	0.1	6.549	5.352	490.6	5.57
Estonia	EST	10.4	4.4	7,811	3,301	67.4	263.4	177.7	97.0	41.0	0.1	0.0	0.0	0.304	0.718	3.2	1.33
Finland	FIN	61.7	64.4	11,445	11,949	166.6	386.0	643.2	142.2	148.4	0.3	0.5	0.1	0.750	0.718	46.3	5.39

Table E.4 *(Continued)*

CONSUMPTION EXPENDITURE BY GOVERNMENT		Expenditure (billion US$)		Expenditure per capita (US$)		Price level index	Expenditure per capita indexes[b]				Share (world = 100%)[b]				Reference data		
							World = 100.0		United States = 100.0		Expenditure				Market exchange rates[c]		
Economy		Based on PPPs	Based on XRs	Based on PPPs	Based on XRs	(world = 100.0)[a]	Based on PPPs	Based on XRs	Based on PPPs	Based on XRs	Based on PPPs	Based on XRs	Population	PPPs[c] (US$ = 1.000)	(US$ = 1.000)	Expenditure (billion LCU)	Population (millions)
(00)		(01)	(02)	(03)	(04)	(05)	(06)	(07)	(08)	(09)	(10)	(11)	(12)	(13)	(14)	(15)	(16)
France	FRA	686.2	680.3	10,503	10,414	158.3	354.2	560.6	130.5	129.4	3.4	5.4	1.0	0.712	0.718	488.8	65.33
Georgia	GEO	8.8	2.1	2,347	552	37.5	79.1	29.7	29.2	6.9	0.0	0.0	0.1	0.397	1.686	3.5	3.76
Germany	DEU	797.9	715.0	9,939	8,907	143.0	335.2	479.5	123.5	110.7	4.0	5.7	1.2	0.644	0.718	513.7	80.28
Greece	GRC	84.2	62.8	7,580	5,654	119.0	255.6	304.3	94.2	70.2	0.4	0.5	0.2	0.536	0.718	45.1	11.11
Hungary	HUN	82.0	29.3	8,223	2,937	57.0	277.3	158.1	102.1	36.5	0.4	0.2	0.1	71.690	200.697	5,878.1	9.97
Iceland	ISL	4.1	3.7	12,774	11,717	146.4	430.8	630.7	158.7	145.6	0.0	0.0	0.0	106.365	115.963	433.4	0.32
Ireland	IRL	39.5	43.6	8,625	9,524	176.2	290.9	512.7	107.1	118.3	0.2	0.3	0.1	0.793	0.718	31.3	4.58
Italy	ITA	490.6	454.8	8,168	7,572	148.0	275.5	407.6	101.5	94.1	2.5	3.6	0.9	0.666	0.718	326.7	60.06
Kazakhstan	KAZ	80.6	20.2	4,869	1,219	40.0	164.2	65.6	60.5	15.1	0.4	0.2	0.2	36.699	146.620	2,958.7	16.56
Kyrgyzstan	KGZ	7.6	1.1	1,453	215	23.6	49.0	11.6	18.1	2.7	0.0	0.0	0.1	6.819	46.144	52.1	5.26
Latvia	LVA	13.4	5.1	6,509	2,493	61.1	219.5	134.2	80.9	31.0	0.1	0.0	0.0	0.275	0.718	3.7	2.06
Lithuania	LTU	23.4	8.0	7,725	2,637	54.5	260.5	142.0	96.0	32.8	0.1	0.1	0.0	0.245	0.718	5.7	3.03
Luxembourg	LUX	6.6	10.0	12,728	19,308	242.1	429.2	1,039.3	158.1	239.9	0.0	0.1	0.0	1.090	0.718	7.2	0.52
Moldova	MDA	7.4	1.4	2,084	392	30.0	70.3	21.1	25.9	4.9	0.0	0.0	0.1	2.204	11.726	16.4	3.56
Montenegro	MNE	3.9	1.0	6,219	1,544	39.6	209.7	83.1	77.3	19.2	0.0	0.0	0.0	0.178	0.718	0.7	0.62
Netherlands	NLD	221.8	233.4	13,284	13,985	168.0	448.0	752.8	165.0	173.7	1.1	1.9	0.2	0.756	0.718	167.7	16.69
North Macedonia	MKD	9.1	1.9	4,401	924	33.5	148.4	49.8	54.7	11.5	0.0	0.0	0.0	9.284	44.202	84.1	2.06
Norway	NOR	63.9	104.3	12,896	21,067	260.8	434.9	1,134.1	160.2	261.7	0.3	0.8	0.1	9.146	5.599	584.2	4.95
Poland	POL	265.3	95.5	6,886	2,480	57.5	232.2	133.5	85.5	30.8	1.3	0.8	0.6	1.066	2.960	282.8	38.53
Portugal	PRT	69.5	48.3	6,586	4,575	110.9	222.1	246.3	81.8	56.8	0.3	0.4	0.2	0.499	0.718	34.7	10.56
Romania	ROU	108.9	26.2	5,404	1,300	38.4	182.3	70.0	67.1	16.1	0.5	0.2	0.3	0.732	3.045	79.7	20.15
Russian Federation	RUS	1,087.5	358.3	7,607	2,506	52.6	256.6	134.9	94.5	31.1	5.4	2.9	2.1	9.680	29.382	10,527.4	142.96
Serbia	SRB	38.0	9.3	5,252	1,291	39.2	177.1	69.5	65.2	16.0	0.2	0.1	0.1	18.004	73.240	684.2	7.24
Slovak Republic	SVK	47.3	18.2	8,754	3,367	61.4	295.2	181.3	108.8	41.8	0.2	0.1	0.1	0.276	0.718	13.1	5.40
Slovenia	SVN	16.1	10.6	7,849	5,167	105.1	264.7	278.2	97.5	64.2	0.1	0.1	0.0	0.473	0.718	7.6	2.05
Spain	ESP	373.0	306.1	7,980	6,549	131.0	269.1	352.6	99.1	81.4	1.9	2.4	0.7	0.590	0.718	219.9	46.74
Sweden	SWE	115.1	143.3	12,179	15,166	198.8	410.8	816.4	151.3	188.4	0.6	1.1	0.1	8.078	6.487	929.6	9.45
Switzerland	CHE	49.4	82.0	6,250	10,358	264.5	210.8	557.6	77.6	128.7	0.2	0.7	0.1	1.468	0.885	72.6	7.91
Tajikistan	TJK	7.2	0.9	937	113	19.3	31.6	6.1	11.6	1.4	0.0	0.0	0.1	0.558	4.610	4.0	7.71
Turkey	TUR	372.6	114.1	5,020	1,537	48.9	169.3	82.7	62.4	19.1	1.9	0.9	1.1	0.513	1.675	191.1	74.22
Ukraine[d]	UKR	156.9	30.9	3,432	676	31.4	115.8	36.4	42.6	8.4	0.8	0.2	0.7	1.568	7.968	246.0	45.71
United Kingdom	GBR	600.8	558.2	9,494	8,821	148.3	320.2	474.8	117.9	109.6	3.0	4.5	0.9	0.579	0.623	348.0	63.29
Total (46)	**ECB**	**6,557.5**	**4,646.6**	**7,666**	**5,432**	**113.1**	**258.5**	**292.4**	**95.2**	**67.5**	**32.8**	**37.1**	**12.7**	**n.a.**	**n.a**	**n.a.**	**855.42**
Latin America and the Caribbean																	
Anguilla	AIA	0.1	0.1	9,189	3,708	64.4	309.9	199.6	114.2	46.1	0.0	0.0	0.0	1.090	2.700	0.1	0.01
Antigua and Barbuda	ATG	1.0	0.3	10,805	3,193	47.2	364.4	171.9	134.2	39.7	0.0	0.0	0.0	0.798	2.700	0.8	0.09
Aruba	ABW	1.4	0.7	13,481	6,490	76.8	454.7	349.4	167.5	80.6	0.0	0.0	0.0	0.862	1.790	1.2	0.10

(continued)

Table E.4 *(Continued)*

CONSUMPTION EXPENDITURE BY GOVERNMENT		Expenditure (billion US$)		Expenditure per capita (US$)		Price level index (world = 100.0)[a]	Expenditure per capita indexes[b]				Share (world = 100%)[b]			PPPs[c] (US$ = 1.000)	Reference data		
							World = 100.0		United States = 100.0		Expenditure				Market exchange rates[c] (US$ = 1.000)	Expenditure (billion LCU)	Population (millions)
Economy		Based on PPPs	Based on XRs	Based on PPPs	Based on XRs		Based on PPPs	Based on XRs	Based on PPPs	Based on XRs	Based on PPPs	Based on XRs	Population				
(00)		(01)	(02)	(03)	(04)	(05)	(06)	(07)	(08)	(09)	(10)	(11)	(12)	(13)	(14)	(15)	(16)
Bahamas, The	BHS	4.3	2.1	12,073	5,815	76.9	407.2	313.0	150.0	72.2	0.0	0.0	0.0	0.482	1.000	2.1	0.36
Barbados	BRB	1.4	0.9	4,945	3,114	100.5	166.8	167.7	61.4	38.7	0.0	0.0	0.0	1.260	2.000	1.8	0.28
Belize	BLZ	0.6	0.2	1,793	695	61.8	60.5	37.4	22.3	8.6	0.0	0.0	0.0	0.775	2.000	0.5	0.33
Bolivia	BOL	7.4	3.3	728	321	70.4	24.6	17.3	9.0	4.0	0.0	0.0	0.2	3.080	6.982	22.9	10.21
Bonaire[e]	BON	...	...	...	...	...	...	...	...	...	...	...	...	...	1.000	...	0.02
Brazil	BRA	732.3	488.4	3,708	2,473	106.4	125.0	133.1	46.1	30.7	3.7	3.9	2.9	1.116	1.673	817.0	197.51
Cayman Islands	CYM	0.4	0.4	7,372	6,733	145.8	248.6	362.4	91.6	83.6	0.0	0.0	0.0	0.761	0.833	0.3	0.06
Chile	CHL	68.8	30.1	3,983	1,740	69.7	134.3	93.7	49.5	21.6	0.3	0.2	0.3	211.358	483.668	14,535.2	17.27
Colombia	COL	92.8	44.7	2,015	971	76.9	67.9	52.3	25.0	12.1	0.5	0.4	0.7	890.769	1,848.139	82,635.0	46.04
Costa Rica	CRI	12.3	7.3	2,688	1,581	93.9	90.6	85.1	33.4	19.6	0.1	0.1	0.1	297.366	505.664	3,668.1	4.59
Curaçao	CUW	1.0	0.5	6,297	2,960	75.0	212.4	159.3	78.2	36.8	0.0	0.0	0.0	0.841	1.790	0.8	0.15
Dominica	DMA	0.2	0.1	2,310	1,227	84.8	77.9	66.0	28.7	15.2	0.0	0.0	0.0	1.434	2.700	0.2	0.07
Dominican Republic	DOM	21.9	5.4	2,230	551	39.4	75.2	29.7	27.7	6.8	0.1	0.0	0.1	9.415	38.099	206.0	9.81
Ecuador	ECU	24.4	10.1	1,599	662	66.1	53.9	35.6	19.9	8.2	0.1	0.1	0.2	0.414	1.000	10.1	15.24
El Salvador	SLV	9.3	3.2	1,504	515	54.6	50.7	27.7	18.7	6.4	0.0	0.0	0.1	0.342	1.000	3.2	6.21
Grenada	GRD	0.3	0.1	2,958	1,156	62.4	99.8	62.2	36.8	14.4	0.0	0.0	0.0	1.055	2.700	0.3	0.11
Guatemala[d]	GTM	13.4	4.8	900	324	57.5	30.3	17.4	11.2	4.0	0.1	0.0	0.2	2.811	7.807	37.8	14.95
Haiti	HTI	2.2	0.7	217	71	52.5	7.3	3.8	2.7	0.9	0.0	0.0	0.1	13.483	40.977	29.6	10.10
Honduras	HND	5.8	2.8	680	333	78.2	22.9	17.9	8.5	4.1	0.0	0.0	0.1	9.327	19.048	53.8	8.48
Jamaica	JAM	6.1	2.3	2,148	808	60.0	72.4	43.5	26.7	10.0	0.0	0.0	0.0	32.308	85.911	196.1	2.83
Mexico	MEX	458.3	139.0	3,967	1,204	48.4	133.8	64.8	49.3	15.0	2.3	1.1	1.7	3.769	12.423	1,727.2	115.51
Montserrat	MSR	0.1	0.0	17,239	5,640	52.2	581.4	303.6	214.2	70.1	0.0	0.0	0.0	0.883	2.700	0.1	0.00
Nicaragua	NIC	6.0	1.3	1,009	225	35.6	34.0	12.1	12.5	2.8	0.0	0.0	0.1	5.006	22.424	29.8	5.90
Panama	PAN	10.7	4.1	2,893	1,110	61.3	97.6	59.8	35.9	13.8	0.1	0.0	0.1	0.384	1.000	4.1	3.71
Paraguay	PRY	10.1	3.3	1,595	523	52.4	53.8	28.2	19.8	6.5	0.1	0.0	0.1	1,372.133	4,183.127	13,860.5	6.33
Peru	PER	41.5	17.8	1,417	608	68.5	47.8	32.7	17.6	7.6	0.2	0.1	0.4	1.182	2.754	49.0	29.26
Sint Maarten	SXM	0.4	0.2	12,208	4,887	63.9	411.7	263.0	151.7	60.7	0.0	0.0	0.0	0.717	1.790	0.3	0.04
St. Kitts and Nevis	KNA	0.4	0.1	7,210	2,835	62.8	243.2	152.6	89.6	35.2	0.0	0.0	0.0	1.062	2.700	0.4	0.05
St. Lucia	LCA	0.4	0.2	2,500	1,034	66.0	84.3	55.7	31.1	12.8	0.0	0.0	0.0	1.117	2.700	0.5	0.18
St. Vincent and the Grenadines	VCT	0.5	0.1	4,208	1,358	51.5	141.9	73.1	52.3	16.9	0.0	0.0	0.0	0.871	2.700	0.4	0.11
Suriname	SUR	1.8	0.6	3,365	1,098	52.1	113.5	59.1	41.8	13.6	0.0	0.0	0.0	1.093	3.350	2.0	0.54
Trinidad and Tobago	TTO	7.0	2.3	5,239	1,749	53.3	176.7	94.1	65.1	21.7	0.0	0.0	0.0	2.145	6.426	15.0	1.34
Turks and Caicos Islands	TCA	0.3	0.2	9,587	4,878	81.2	323.3	262.6	119.1	60.6	0.0	0.0	0.0	0.509	1.000	0.2	0.03
Uruguay	URY	10.2	6.1	3,028	1,817	95.7	102.1	97.8	37.6	22.6	0.1	0.0	0.1	11.586	19.314	118.2	3.37
Venezuela, RB[d]	VEN	103.2	36.5	3,572	1,262	56.4	120.5	67.9	44.4	15.7	0.5	0.3	0.4	1.515	4.289	156.4	28.89
Virgin Islands, British	VGB	0.1	0.1	4,926	2,742	88.8	166.1	147.6	61.2	34.1	0.0	0.0	0.0	0.557	1.000	0.1	0.03
Total (39)	**LCB**	**1,658.3**	**820.3**	**3,070**	**1,519**	**79.0**	**103.6**	**81.8**	**38.1**	**18.9**	**8.3**	**6.6**	**8.0**	**n.a.**	**n.a**	**n.a.**	**540.10**

Table E.4 *(Continued)*

CONSUMPTION EXPENDITURE BY GOVERNMENT Economy		Expenditure (billion US$) Based on PPPs	Expenditure (billion US$) Based on XRs	Expenditure per capita (US$) Based on PPPs	Expenditure per capita (US$) Based on XRs	Price level index (world = 100.0)[a]	Expenditure per capita indexes[b] World = 100.0 Based on PPPs	Expenditure per capita indexes[b] World = 100.0 Based on XRs	Expenditure per capita indexes[b] United States = 100.0 Based on PPPs	Expenditure per capita indexes[b] United States = 100.0 Based on XRs	Share (world = 100%)[b] Expenditure Based on PPPs	Share (world = 100%)[b] Expenditure Based on XRs	Share (world = 100%)[b] Population	PPPs[c] (US$ = 1.000)	Reference data Market exchange rates[c] (US$ = 1.000)	Reference data Expenditure (billion LCU)	Reference data Population (millions)
(00)		(01)	(02)	(03)	(04)	(05)	(06)	(07)	(08)	(09)	(10)	(11)	(12)	(13)	(14)	(15)	(16)
Middle East and North Africa																	
Algeria	DZA	225.3	41.0	6,145	1,119	29.1	207.2	60.2	76.3	13.9	1.1	0.3	0.5	13.280	72.938	2,991.5	36.66
Bahrain	BHR	10.9	4.0	9,108	3,330	58.4	307.2	179.3	113.1	41.4	0.1	0.0	0.0	0.137	0.376	1.5	1.20
Djibouti	DJI	0.5	0.2	610	239	62.5	20.6	12.9	7.6	3.0	0.0	0.0	0.0	69.637	177.721	36.3	0.85
Egypt, Arab Rep.	EGY	187.9	27.7	2,333	344	23.5	78.7	18.5	29.0	4.3	0.9	0.2	1.2	0.876	5.947	164.6	80.53
Iran, Islamic Rep.	IRN	410.1	64.6	5,457	860	25.2	184.0	46.3	67.8	10.7	2.1	0.5	1.1	1,673.585	10,616.307	686,332.2	75.15
Iraq	IRQ	115.4	35.7	3,460	1,069	49.3	116.7	57.6	43.0	13.3	0.6	0.3	0.5	370.620	1,199.200	42,754.8	33.34
Israel	ISR	70.7	58.7	9,110	7,566	132.6	307.2	407.3	113.2	94.0	0.4	0.5	0.1	2.972	3.578	210.2	7.76
Jordan	JOR	21.7	5.3	3,098	754	38.9	104.5	40.6	38.5	9.4	0.1	0.0	0.1	0.172	0.708	3.7	6.99
Kuwait	KWT	33.9	22.6	11,066	7,371	106.3	373.2	396.8	137.5	91.6	0.2	0.2	0.0	0.186	0.280	6.3	3.07
Malta	MLT	3.3	1.9	7,990	4,497	89.8	269.5	242.1	99.3	55.9	0.0	0.0	0.0	0.404	0.718	1.3	0.42
Morocco	MAR	57.2	19.1	1,756	585	53.2	59.2	31.5	21.8	7.3	0.3	0.2	0.5	2.681	8.049	153.4	32.58
Oman	OMN	34.1	12.3	10,336	3,720	57.4	348.6	200.3	128.4	46.2	0.2	0.1	0.0	0.138	0.385	4.7	3.30
Qatar	QAT	35.6	18.5	20,548	10,660	82.8	693.0	573.8	255.3	132.4	0.2	0.1	0.0	1.894	3.650	67.4	1.73
Saudi Arabia	SAU	428.8	128.5	15,221	4,561	47.8	513.3	245.5	189.1	56.7	2.1	1.0	0.4	1.124	3.750	481.9	28.17
Tunisia	TUN	34.9	8.3	3,252	769	37.7	109.7	41.4	40.4	9.6	0.2	0.1	0.2	0.333	1.408	11.6	10.74
United Arab Emirates	ARE	64.4	34.9	7,424	4,025	86.5	250.4	216.7	92.2	50.0	0.3	0.3	0.1	1.991	3.673	128.2	8.67
West Bank and Gaza	PSE	5.9	2.9	1,528	746	77.9	51.5	40.1	19.0	9.3	0.0	0.0	0.1	1.747	3.578	10.3	3.88
Yemen, Rep.[d]	YEM	15.3	4.4	641	186	46.2	21.6	10.0	8.0	2.3	0.1	0.0	0.4	61.864	213.800	945.5	23.83
Total (17)	**MEB**	**1,755.8**	**490.4**	**4,893**	**1,367**	**44.6**	**165.0**	**73.6**	**60.8**	**17.0**	**8.8**	**3.9**	**5.3**	**n.a.**	**n.a**	**n.a.**	**358.87**
North America																	
Bermuda	BMU	0.8	0.8	12,193	12,584	164.7	411.2	677.4	151.5	156.3	0.0	0.0	0.0	1.032	1.000	0.8	0.07
Canada	CAN	333.7	379.1	9,718	11,039	181.3	327.7	594.2	120.7	137.1	1.7	3.0	0.5	1.124	0.990	375.1	34.34
United States	USA	2,511.8	2,511.8	8,050	8,050	159.6	271.5	433.3	100.0	100.0	12.6	20.1	4.6	1.000	1.000	2,511.8	312.03
Total (3)	**NAB**	**2,846.3**	**2,891.7**	**8,216**	**8,347**	**162.2**	**277.1**	**449.3**	**102.1**	**103.7**	**14.3**	**23.1**	**5.1**	**n.a.**	**n.a**	**n.a.**	**346.44**
South Asia																	
Bangladesh	BGD	33.2	6.7	222	45	32.4	7.5	2.4	2.8	0.6	0.2	0.1	2.2	15.053	74.152	499.3	149.70
Bhutan	BTN	2.1	0.4	3,110	538	27.6	104.9	28.9	38.6	6.7	0.0	0.0	0.0	8.066	46.670	17.0	0.68
India	IND	792.5	202.8	652	167	40.8	22.0	9.0	8.1	2.1	4.0	1.6	18.1	11.944	46.670	9,465.4	1,216.15
Maldives	MDV	1.9	0.6	4,598	1,462	50.7	155.1	78.7	57.1	18.2	0.0	0.0	0.0	4.642	14.602	8.7	0.41
Nepal	NPL	6.8	1.9	255	70	44.0	8.6	3.8	3.2	0.9	0.0	0.0	0.4	20.417	74.020	138.0	26.49
Pakistan	PAK	117.0	22.5	661	127	30.7	22.3	6.8	8.2	1.6	0.6	0.2	2.6	16.583	86.343	1,941.0	177.10
Sri Lanka	LKA	39.2	5.6	1,941	277	22.7	65.5	14.9	24.1	3.4	0.2	0.0	0.3	15.754	110.565	617.7	20.20
Total (7)	**SAB**	**992.6**	**240.4**	**624**	**151**	**38.7**	**21.0**	**8.1**	**7.8**	**1.9**	**5.0**	**1.9**	**23.6**	**n.a.**	**n.a**	**n.a.**	**1,590.72**
Sub-Saharan Africa																	
Angola	AGO	40.1	20.4	1,656	842	81.1	55.8	45.3	20.6	10.5	0.2	0.2	0.4	47.756	93.935	1,914.9	24.22
Benin	BEN	4.3	1.3	458	136	47.3	15.4	7.3	5.7	1.7	0.0	0.0	0.1	139.916	471.866	605.9	9.46
Botswana	BWA	8.3	2.8	4,118	1,408	54.6	138.9	75.8	51.2	17.5	0.0	0.0	0.0	2.339	6.838	19.4	2.02

(continued)

Table E.4 *(Continued)*

CONSUMPTION EXPENDITURE BY GOVERNMENT		Expenditure (billion US$)		Expenditure per capita (US$)		Price level index (world = 100.0)[a]	Expenditure per capita indexes[b]				Share (world = 100%)[b]			PPPs[c] (US$ = 1.000)	Reference data		
							World = 100.0		United States = 100.0		Expenditure				Market exchange rates[c] (US$ = 1.000)	Expenditure (billion LCU)	Population (millions)
Economy		Based on PPPs	Based on XRs	Based on PPPs	Based on XRs		Based on PPPs	Based on XRs	Based on PPPs	Based on XRs	Based on PPPs	Based on XRs	Population				
(00)		(01)	(02)	(03)	(04)	(05)	(06)	(07)	(08)	(09)	(10)	(11)	(12)	(13)	(14)	(15)	(16)
Burkina Faso	BFA	6.6	2.2	407	139	54.3	13.7	7.5	5.1	1.7	0.0	0.0	0.2	160.599	471.866	1,052.4	16.08
Burundi	BDI	1.8	0.4	199	46	37.0	6.7	2.5	2.5	0.6	0.0	0.0	0.1	292.235	1,261.073	521.1	8.96
Cabo Verde	CPV	0.8	0.3	1,647	692	67.1	55.6	37.3	20.5	8.6	0.0	0.0	0.0	33.346	79.323	27.4	0.50
Cameroon	CMR	10.6	3.6	507	170	53.5	17.1	9.1	6.3	2.1	0.1	0.0	0.3	158.288	471.866	1,676.6	20.91
Central African Republic	CAF	0.8	0.3	170	57	54.1	5.7	3.1	2.1	0.7	0.0	0.0	0.1	159.791	471.866	119.9	4.42
Chad	TCD	4.0	1.5	328	122	59.4	11.0	6.6	4.1	1.5	0.0	0.0	0.2	175.462	471.866	710.4	12.36
Comoros	COM	0.3	0.1	420	154	58.6	14.2	8.3	5.2	1.9	0.0	0.0	0.0	129.901	353.900	38.5	0.71
Congo, Dem. Rep.	COD	11.6	3.7	173	55	51.1	5.8	3.0	2.2	0.7	0.1	0.0	1.0	294.368	919.491	3,405.6	66.76
Congo, Rep.	COG	4.4	2.2	1,009	495	78.3	34.0	26.6	12.5	6.1	0.0	0.0	0.1	231.502	471.866	1,026.3	4.39
Côte d'Ivoire	CIV	7.8	2.9	370	136	58.5	12.5	7.3	4.6	1.7	0.0	0.0	0.3	172.992	471.866	1,346.9	21.03
Equatorial Guinea	GNQ	4.7	2.7	4,797	2,749	91.5	161.8	148.0	59.6	34.2	0.0	0.0	0.0	270.399	471.866	1,280.1	0.99
Eswatini	SWZ	1.9	1.0	1,804	887	78.5	60.8	47.7	22.4	11.0	0.0	0.0	0.0	3.570	7.261	6.9	1.07
Ethiopia	ETH	21.2	3.2	235	36	24.5	7.9	1.9	2.9	0.4	0.1	0.0	1.3	2.590	16.899	54.9	90.14
Gabon	GAB	6.2	2.8	3,674	1,655	71.9	123.9	89.1	45.6	20.6	0.0	0.0	0.0	212.527	471.866	1,315.3	1.68
Gambia, The	GMB	0.8	0.1	412	79	30.5	13.9	4.2	5.1	1.0	0.0	0.0	0.0	5.629	29.462	4.3	1.85
Ghana	GHA	25.6	7.4	1,009	292	46.2	34.0	15.7	12.5	3.6	0.1	0.1	0.4	0.437	1.512	11.2	25.39
Guinea	GIN	5.1	1.0	490	98	31.8	16.5	5.2	6.1	1.2	0.0	0.0	0.2	1,325.512	6,658.031	6,765.0	10.42
Guinea-Bissau	GNB	0.8	0.2	522	130	39.8	17.6	7.0	6.5	1.6	0.0	0.0	0.0	117.740	471.866	96.0	1.56
Kenya	KEN	17.5	5.9	404	136	53.6	13.6	7.3	5.0	1.7	0.1	0.0	0.6	29.839	88.811	520.9	43.18
Lesotho	LSO	2.2	1.0	1,083	486	71.6	36.5	26.1	13.5	6.0	0.0	0.0	0.0	3.255	7.261	7.1	2.00
Liberia	LBR	1.1	0.4	272	93	54.6	9.2	5.0	3.4	1.2	0.0	0.0	0.1	24.721	72.227	27.0	4.02
Madagascar	MDG	6.6	1.6	302	73	38.5	10.2	3.9	3.7	0.9	0.0	0.0	0.3	488.473	2,025.118	3,203.3	21.74
Malawi	MWI	1.8	0.7	122	50	64.7	4.1	2.7	1.5	0.6	0.0	0.0	0.2	63.489	156.515	116.1	14.96
Mali	MLI	7.4	2.2	476	142	47.6	16.1	7.6	5.9	1.8	0.0	0.0	0.2	140.672	471.866	1,039.7	15.51
Mauritania	MRT	3.3	0.9	912	260	45.5	30.7	14.0	11.3	3.2	0.0	0.0	0.1	80.207	281.118	263.1	3.60
Mauritius	MUS	4.1	1.3	3,295	1,040	50.4	111.1	56.0	40.9	12.9	0.0	0.0	0.0	9.058	28.706	37.3	1.25
Mozambique	MOZ	4.9	2.6	204	108	84.7	6.9	5.8	2.5	1.3	0.0	0.0	0.4	15.419	29.068	76.1	24.19
Namibia	NAM	6.7	2.9	3,093	1,334	68.9	104.3	71.8	38.4	16.6	0.0	0.0	0.0	3.132	7.261	20.9	2.16
Niger	NER	2.9	1.0	168	59	55.5	5.7	3.2	2.1	0.7	0.0	0.0	0.3	164.022	471.866	473.0	17.11
Nigeria	NGA	109.1	35.2	670	216	51.4	22.6	11.6	8.3	2.7	0.5	0.3	2.4	49.595	153.862	5,412.0	162.81
Rwanda	RWA	1.8	0.9	177	85	76.7	6.0	4.6	2.2	1.1	0.0	0.0	0.2	288.376	600.307	524.2	10.29
São Tomé and Príncipe	STP	0.4	0.1	2,175	445	32.6	73.3	23.9	27.0	5.5	0.0	0.0	0.0	3.605	17.623	1.4	0.18
Senegal	SEN	7.6	2.6	586	203	55.3	19.8	10.9	7.3	2.5	0.0	0.0	0.2	163.400	471.866	1,247.5	13.03
Seychelles	SYC	1.1	0.3	12,479	3,171	40.6	420.9	170.7	155.0	39.4	0.0	0.0	0.0	3.146	12.381	3.6	0.09
Sierra Leone	SLE	1.3	0.3	201	45	35.9	6.8	2.4	2.5	0.6	0.0	0.0	0.1	978.764	4,349.162	1,289.1	6.56
South Africa	ZAF	160.1	82.7	3,079	1,590	82.5	103.8	85.6	38.2	19.8	0.8	0.7	0.8	3.751	7.261	600.6	52.00
Sudan	SDN	24.9	3.6	733	106	23.1	24.7	5.7	9.1	1.3	0.1	0.0	0.5	0.525	3.630	13.1	33.98

Table E.4 *(Continued)*

CONSUMPTION EXPENDITURE BY GOVERNMENT		Expenditure (billion US$)		Expenditure per capita (US$)		Price level index (world = 100.0)[a]	Expenditure per capita indexes[b]				Share (world = 100%)[b]			PPPs[c] (US$ = 1.000)	Reference data		
							World = 100.0		United States = 100.0		Expenditure				Market exchange rates[c] (US$ = 1.000)	Expenditure (billion LCU)	Population (millions)
Economy		Based on PPPs	Based on XRs	Based on PPPs	Based on XRs		Based on PPPs	Based on XRs	Based on PPPs	Based on XRs	Based on PPPs	Based on XRs	Population				
(00)		(01)	(02)	(03)	(04)	(05)	(06)	(07)	(08)	(09)	(10)	(11)	(12)	(13)	(14)	(15)	(16)
Tanzania	TZA	16.2	4.6	355	102	45.6	12.0	5.5	4.4	1.3	0.1	0.0	0.7	449.517	1,572.116	7,294.0	45.67
Togo	TGO	2.1	0.7	326	101	49.4	11.0	5.4	4.0	1.3	0.0	0.0	0.1	146.117	471.866	313.9	6.60
Uganda	UGA	16.6	3.8	495	113	36.3	16.7	6.1	6.2	1.4	0.1	0.0	0.5	573.563	2,522.746	9,506.1	33.48
Zambia	ZMB	6.7	2.6	477	184	61.4	16.1	9.9	5.9	2.3	0.0	0.0	0.2	1.869	4.861	12.5	14.02
Zimbabwe	ZWE	7.6	2.6	586	205	55.9	19.8	11.1	7.3	2.6	0.0	0.0	0.2	0.350	1.000	2.6	12.89
Total (45)	**SSB**	**581.7**	**220.6**	**672**	**255**	**60.5**	**22.6**	**13.7**	**8.3**	**3.2**	**2.9**	**1.8**	**12.9**	**n.a.**	**n.a**	**n.a.**	**866.25**
World (178)	**WLD**	**19,973.3**	**12,513.5**	**2,965**	**1,858**	**100.0**	**100.0**	**100.0**	**36.8**	**23.1**	**100.0**	**100.0**	**100.0**	**n.a.**	**n.a.**	**n.a.**	**6,736.12**

Note: PPP = purchasing power parity; XR = market exchange rate; LCU = local currency unit; n.a. = not applicable; ... = data suppressed due to unavailability.

a. World totals used to calculate price level indexes (PLIs) in this table exclude nonparticipating economies.

b. Indexes and shares are rounded to one decimal place for presentation in this table.

c. PPPs and market exchange rates are rounded to three decimal places for presentation in this table.

d. National accounts expenditures for the revised ICP 2011 results are estimated by the ICP Global Office.

e. Bonaire's results are provided only for individual consumption expenditure by households. Therefore, to ensure consistency across tables, Bonaire is not included in either Latin America and the Caribbean or the world totals.

Table E.5 Gross fixed capital formation (GFCF): Revised ICP 2011 results

GROSS FIXED CAPITAL FORMATION Economy		Expenditure (billion US$)		Expenditure per capita (US$)		Price level index	Expenditure per capita indexes[b]				Share (world = 100%)[b]				Reference data		
							World = 100.0		United States = 100.0		Expenditure						
		Based on PPPs	Based on XRs	Based on PPPs	Based on XRs	(world = 100.0)[a]	Based on PPPs	Based on XRs	Based on PPPs	Based on XRs	Based on PPPs	Based on XRs	Population	PPPs[c] (US$ = 1.000)	Market exchange rates[c] (US$ = 1.000)	Expenditure (billion LCU)	Population (millions)
(00)		(01)	(02)	(03)	(04)	(05)	(06)	(07)	(08)	(09)	(10)	(11)	(12)	(13)	(14)	(15)	(16)
East Asia and Pacific																	
Australia	AUS	228.8	400.5	10,241	17,927	223.4	310.3	693.1	109.3	191.4	1.0	2.3	0.3	1.697	0.969	388.3	22.34
Brunei Darussalam	BRN	8.3	5.7	21,157	14,364	86.6	641.0	555.4	225.9	153.3	0.0	0.0	0.0	0.854	1.258	7.1	0.39
Cambodia	KHM	3.6	1.5	255	104	52.0	7.7	4.0	2.7	1.1	0.0	0.0	0.2	1,654.904	4,058.500	6,035.3	14.31
China	CHN	5,766.0	3,452.3	4,290	2,568	76.4	130.0	99.3	45.8	27.4	25.9	19.8	20.0	3.869	6.461	22,306.6	1,344.13
Fiji	FJI	1.4	0.7	1,595	876	70.1	48.3	33.9	17.0	9.4	0.0	0.0	0.0	0.985	1.793	1.3	0.85
Hong Kong SAR, China	HKG	82.3	58.5	11,640	8,271	90.7	352.7	319.8	124.3	88.3	0.4	0.3	0.1	5.531	7.784	455.3	7.07
Indonesia	IDN	636.7	279.6	2,631	1,155	56.0	79.7	44.7	28.1	12.3	2.9	1.6	3.6	3,850.688	8,770.433	2,451,914.0	241.99
Japan	JPN	975.1	1,348.7	7,628	10,551	176.5	231.1	407.9	81.4	112.6	4.4	7.7	1.9	110.387	79.807	107,637.5	127.83
Korea, Rep.	KOR	468.8	377.9	9,388	7,568	102.9	284.4	292.6	100.2	80.8	2.1	2.2	0.7	893.384	1,108.292	418,824.8	49.94
Lao PDR	LAO	7.4	2.9	1,203	470	49.9	36.4	18.2	12.8	5.0	0.0	0.0	0.1	3,140.557	8,030.055	23,103.7	6.12
Macao SAR, China[d]	MAC	7.2	4.6	13,116	8,315	80.9	397.4	321.5	140.0	88.8	0.0	0.0	0.0	5.083	8.018	36.7	0.55
Malaysia	MYS	122.6	65.8	4,218	2,264	68.5	127.8	87.5	45.0	24.2	0.6	0.4	0.4	1.642	3.060	201.3	29.06
Mongolia	MNG	9.2	5.0	3,285	1,809	70.3	99.5	69.9	35.1	19.3	0.0	0.0	0.0	696.773	1,265.516	6,377.7	2.79
Myanmar	MMR	41.7	16.8	840	337	51.2	25.5	13.0	9.0	3.6	0.2	0.1	0.7	328.456	817.917	13,705.0	49.66
New Zealand	NZL	24.6	32.9	5,603	7,486	170.5	169.7	289.4	59.8	79.9	0.1	0.2	0.1	1.691	1.266	41.6	4.39
Philippines	PHL	89.5	42.0	950	446	59.9	28.8	17.2	10.1	4.8	0.4	0.2	1.4	20.331	43.313	1,819.3	94.18
Singapore	SGP	109.9	70.5	21,204	13,602	81.9	642.4	525.9	226.4	145.2	0.5	0.4	0.1	0.807	1.258	88.7	5.18
Taiwan, China	TWN	202.5	113.6	8,734	4,898	71.6	264.6	189.4	93.2	52.3	0.9	0.7	0.3	16.525	29.469	3,346.9	23.19
Thailand	THA	210.8	97.8	3,184	1,477	59.2	96.5	57.1	34.0	15.8	0.9	0.6	1.0	14.146	30.492	2,982.1	66.21
Vietnam	VNM	95.7	40.3	1,086	458	53.8	32.9	17.7	11.6	4.9	0.4	0.2	1.3	8,642.484	20,509.750	827,032.2	88.11
Total (20)	**EAB**	**9,092.2**	**6,417.4**	**4,174**	**2,946**	**90.1**	**126.5**	**113.9**	**44.6**	**31.5**	**40.9**	**36.8**	**32.3**	**n.a.**	**n.a**	**n.a.**	**2,178.31**
Europe and Central Asia																	
Albania	ALB	6.8	3.8	2,354	1,304	70.7	71.3	50.4	25.1	13.9	0.0	0.0	0.0	55.843	100.812	381.9	2.91
Armenia	ARM	2.5	2.6	827	871	134.5	25.1	33.7	8.8	9.3	0.0	0.0	0.0	392.534	372.500	982.7	3.03
Austria	AUT	87.4	97.0	10,419	11,565	141.7	315.7	447.1	111.2	123.5	0.4	0.6	0.1	0.797	0.718	69.7	8.39
Azerbaijan	AZE	13.5	13.3	1,490	1,469	125.8	45.2	56.8	15.9	15.7	0.1	0.1	0.1	0.779	0.790	10.5	9.05
Belarus	BLR	28.5	20.5	3,004	2,163	91.9	91.0	83.6	32.1	23.1	0.1	0.1	0.1	0.404	0.561	11.5	9.47
Belgium	BEL	121.3	120.4	10,991	10,910	126.7	333.0	421.8	117.3	116.5	0.5	0.7	0.2	0.713	0.718	86.5	11.04
Bosnia and Herzegovina	BIH	6.0	3.5	1,630	944	73.9	49.4	36.5	17.4	10.1	0.0	0.0	0.1	0.814	1.405	4.9	3.66
Bulgaria	BGR	19.0	12.0	2,588	1,637	80.7	78.4	63.3	27.6	17.5	0.1	0.1	0.1	0.889	1.405	16.9	7.35
Croatia	HRV	18.0	12.6	4,191	2,948	89.8	127.0	114.0	44.7	31.5	0.1	0.1	0.1	3.759	5.344	67.5	4.28
Cyprus	CYP	6.2	5.2	7,312	6,167	107.6	221.5	238.5	78.1	65.8	0.0	0.0	0.0	0.606	0.718	3.8	0.85
Czech Republic	CZE	70.1	60.4	6,676	5,754	110.0	202.3	222.5	71.3	61.4	0.3	0.3	0.2	15.227	17.665	1,067.0	10.50
Denmark	DNK	51.6	62.7	9,267	11,249	154.9	280.8	434.9	98.9	120.1	0.2	0.4	0.1	6.497	5.352	335.4	5.57
Estonia	EST	8.1	6.1	6,061	4,619	97.3	183.6	178.6	64.7	49.3	0.0	0.0	0.0	0.547	0.718	4.4	1.33
Finland	FIN	54.6	62.3	10,140	11,568	145.6	307.2	447.3	108.2	123.5	0.2	0.4	0.1	0.820	0.718	44.8	5.39

Table E.5 *(Continued)*

GROSS FIXED CAPITAL FORMATION Economy		Expenditure (billion US$) Based on PPPs	Expenditure (billion US$) Based on XRs	Expenditure per capita (US$) Based on PPPs	Expenditure per capita (US$) Based on XRs	Price level index (world = 100.0)[a]	Expenditure per capita indexes[b] World = 100.0 Based on PPPs	Expenditure per capita indexes[b] World = 100.0 Based on XRs	Expenditure per capita indexes[b] United States = 100.0 Based on PPPs	Expenditure per capita indexes[b] United States = 100.0 Based on XRs	Share (world = 100%)[b] Expenditure Based on PPPs	Share (world = 100%)[b] Expenditure Based on XRs	Share (world = 100%)[b] Population	PPPs[c] (US$ = 1.000)	Reference data Market exchange rates[c] (US$ = 1.000)	Reference data Expenditure (billion LCU)	Reference data Population (millions)
(00)		(01)	(02)	(03)	(04)	(05)	(06)	(07)	(08)	(09)	(10)	(11)	(12)	(13)	(14)	(15)	(16)
France	FRA	562.9	642.5	8,616	9,835	145.7	261.0	380.3	92.0	105.0	2.5	3.7	1.0	0.820	0.718	461.6	65.33
Georgia	GEO	3.2	3.1	854	817	122.0	25.9	31.6	9.1	8.7	0.0	0.0	0.1	1.613	1.686	5.2	3.76
Germany	DEU	660.2	763.8	8,224	9,515	147.7	249.2	367.9	87.8	101.6	3.0	4.4	1.2	0.831	0.718	548.7	80.28
Greece	GRC	43.5	44.0	3,920	3,962	129.0	118.8	153.2	41.9	42.3	0.2	0.3	0.2	0.726	0.718	31.6	11.11
Hungary	HUN	38.5	27.8	3,865	2,786	92.0	117.1	107.7	41.3	29.7	0.2	0.2	0.1	144.665	200.697	5,575.6	9.97
Iceland	ISL	1.7	2.3	5,463	7,316	170.9	165.5	282.9	58.3	78.1	0.0	0.0	0.0	155.307	115.963	270.7	0.32
Ireland	IRL	45.1	39.5	9,848	8,622	111.7	298.4	333.4	105.1	92.0	0.2	0.2	0.1	0.629	0.718	28.4	4.58
Italy	ITA	487.2	452.4	8,111	7,533	118.5	245.8	291.3	86.6	80.4	2.2	2.6	0.9	0.667	0.718	325.0	60.06
Kazakhstan	KAZ	43.8	41.3	2,647	2,497	120.4	80.2	96.6	28.3	26.7	0.2	0.2	0.2	138.299	146.620	6,062.3	16.56
Kyrgyz Republic	KGZ	1.5	1.5	285	279	124.8	8.6	10.8	3.0	3.0	0.0	0.0	0.1	45.132	46.144	67.8	5.26
Latvia	LVA	7.8	6.2	3,790	3,009	101.3	114.8	116.4	40.5	32.1	0.0	0.0	0.0	0.570	0.718	4.5	2.06
Lithuania	LTU	10.6	8.0	3,493	2,658	97.1	105.8	102.8	37.3	28.4	0.0	0.0	0.0	0.547	0.718	5.8	3.03
Luxembourg	LUX	11.4	11.5	22,036	22,185	128.5	667.6	857.8	235.2	236.8	0.1	0.1	0.0	0.723	0.718	8.3	0.52
Moldova	MDA	2.0	2.0	554	548	126.3	16.8	21.2	5.9	5.9	0.0	0.0	0.1	11.602	11.726	22.9	3.56
Montenegro	MNE	1.3	0.9	2,073	1,430	88.0	62.8	55.3	22.1	15.3	0.0	0.0	0.0	0.495	0.718	0.6	0.62
Netherlands	NLD	164.4	182.3	9,849	10,921	141.5	298.4	422.3	105.1	116.6	0.7	1.0	0.2	0.797	0.718	131.0	16.69
North Macedonia	MKD	4.5	2.5	2,207	1,200	69.4	66.9	46.4	23.6	12.8	0.0	0.0	0.0	24.041	44.202	109.2	2.06
Norway	NOR	67.5	107.3	13,637	21,666	202.8	413.2	837.7	145.6	231.3	0.3	0.6	0.1	8.895	5.599	600.8	4.95
Poland	POL	133.3	109.5	3,461	2,842	104.8	104.9	109.9	37.0	30.3	0.6	0.6	0.6	2.430	2.960	324.1	38.53
Portugal	PRT	59.6	45.2	5,643	4,277	96.7	171.0	165.4	60.2	45.7	0.3	0.3	0.2	0.544	0.718	32.4	10.56
Romania	ROU	81.0	50.0	4,018	2,482	78.8	121.7	96.0	42.9	26.5	0.4	0.3	0.3	1.881	3.045	152.3	20.15
Russian Federation	RUS	445.0	424.4	3,112	2,969	121.7	94.3	114.8	33.2	31.7	2.0	2.4	2.1	28.027	29.382	12,470.7	142.96
Serbia	SRB	13.8	8.6	1,912	1,193	79.6	57.9	46.1	20.4	12.7	0.1	0.0	0.1	45.697	73.240	632.4	7.24
Slovak Republic	SVK	25.5	23.1	4,730	4,279	115.4	143.3	165.4	50.5	45.7	0.1	0.1	0.1	0.650	0.718	16.6	5.40
Slovenia	SVN	12.0	10.3	5,857	5,012	109.2	177.4	193.8	62.5	53.5	0.1	0.1	0.0	0.615	0.718	7.4	2.05
Spain	ESP	341.1	296.5	7,299	6,344	110.9	221.1	245.3	77.9	67.7	1.5	1.7	0.7	0.624	0.718	213.0	46.74
Sweden	SWE	95.3	132.9	10,083	14,064	178.0	305.5	543.8	107.6	150.1	0.4	0.8	0.1	9.048	6.487	862.1	9.45
Switzerland	CHE	113.1	164.2	14,294	20,755	185.3	433.1	802.5	152.6	221.6	0.5	0.9	0.1	1.286	0.885	145.4	7.91
Tajikistan	TJK	2.2	2.1	284	274	123.2	8.6	10.6	3.0	2.9	0.0	0.0	0.1	4.449	4.610	9.7	7.71
Turkey	TUR	364.2	233.7	4,906	3,148	81.9	148.6	121.7	52.4	33.6	1.6	1.3	1.1	1.075	1.675	391.4	74.22
Ukraine[d]	UKR	36.4	31.4	797	688	110.1	24.2	26.6	8.5	7.3	0.2	0.2	0.7	6.876	7.968	250.5	45.71
United Kingdom	GBR	414.9	410.3	6,556	6,484	126.2	198.6	250.7	70.0	69.2	1.9	2.4	0.9	0.617	0.623	255.8	63.29
Total (46)	**ECB**	**4,788.2**	**4,763.7**	**5,597**	**5,569**	**127.0**	**169.6**	**215.3**	**59.8**	**59.4**	**21.5**	**27.3**	**12.7**	**n.a.**	**n.a**	**n.a.**	**855.42**
Latin America and the Caribbean																	
Anguilla	AIA	0.1	0.0	5,337	3,308	79.1	161.7	127.9	57.0	35.3	0.0	0.0	0.0	1.674	2.700	0.1	0.01
Antigua and Barbuda	ATG	0.4	0.2	4,310	2,662	78.8	130.6	102.9	46.0	28.4	0.0	0.0	0.0	1.667	2.700	0.6	0.09
Aruba	ABW	1.2	0.7	12,073	6,685	70.7	365.8	258.5	128.9	71.4	0.0	0.0	0.0	0.991	1.790	1.2	0.10

(continued)

Table E.5 *(Continued)*

GROSS FIXED CAPITAL FORMATION		Expenditure (billion US$)		Expenditure per capita (US$)		Price level index	Expenditure per capita indexes[b]				Share (world = 100%)[b]				Reference data		
							World = 100.0		United States = 100.0		Expenditure						
Economy		Based on PPPs	Based on XRs	Based on PPPs	Based on XRs	(world = 100.0)[a]	Based on PPPs	Based on XRs	Based on PPPs	Based on XRs	Based on PPPs	Based on XRs	Population	PPPs[c] (US$ = 1.000)	Market exchange rates[c] (US$ = 1.000)	Expenditure (billion LCU)	Population (millions)
(00)		(01)	(02)	(03)	(04)	(05)	(06)	(07)	(08)	(09)	(10)	(11)	(12)	(13)	(14)	(15)	(16)
Bahamas, The	BHS	3.6	2.9	10,066	7,928	100.5	305.0	306.6	107.5	84.6	0.0	0.0	0.0	0.788	1.000	2.9	0.36
Barbados	BRB	0.9	0.8	3,276	2,762	107.6	99.2	106.8	35.0	29.5	0.0	0.0	0.0	1.686	2.000	1.6	0.28
Belize	BLZ	0.2	0.2	708	686	123.7	21.4	26.5	7.6	7.3	0.0	0.0	0.0	1.938	2.000	0.5	0.33
Bolivia	BOL	8.5	4.5	830	442	68.0	25.2	17.1	8.9	4.7	0.0	0.0	0.2	3.718	6.982	31.5	10.21
Bonaire[e]	BON	...	...	...	...	...	...	...	...	...	...	...	...	...	1.000	...	0.02
Brazil	BRA	682.0	539.2	3,453	2,730	100.9	104.6	105.5	36.9	29.1	3.1	3.1	2.9	1.322	1.673	901.9	197.51
Cayman Islands	CYM	0.6	0.6	9,675	9,892	130.5	293.1	382.5	103.3	105.6	0.0	0.0	0.0	0.852	0.833	0.5	0.06
Chile	CHL	75.8	58.3	4,390	3,377	98.2	133.0	130.6	46.9	36.1	0.3	0.3	0.3	372.146	483.668	28,207.4	17.27
Colombia	COL	95.1	71.5	2,065	1,552	95.9	62.6	60.0	22.0	16.6	0.4	0.4	0.7	1,389.490	1,848.139	132,090.0	46.04
Costa Rica	CRI	10.7	8.3	2,335	1,811	99.0	70.7	70.0	24.9	19.3	0.0	0.0	0.1	392.116	505.664	4,201.9	4.59
Curaçao	CUW	0.9	0.8	5,968	5,182	110.8	180.8	200.4	63.7	55.3	0.0	0.0	0.0	1.554	1.790	1.4	0.15
Dominica	DMA	0.1	0.1	1,468	1,172	101.9	44.5	45.3	15.7	12.5	0.0	0.0	0.0	2.155	2.700	0.2	0.07
Dominican Republic	DOM	21.5	14.4	2,193	1,463	85.1	66.4	56.5	23.4	15.6	0.1	0.1	0.1	25.412	38.099	546.8	9.81
Ecuador	ECU	32.8	20.5	2,150	1,343	79.7	65.1	51.9	22.9	14.3	0.1	0.1	0.2	0.625	1.000	20.5	15.24
El Salvador	SLV	5.0	3.3	806	532	84.2	24.4	20.6	8.6	5.7	0.0	0.0	0.1	0.660	1.000	3.3	6.21
Grenada	GRD	0.2	0.2	2,088	1,457	89.1	63.3	56.3	22.3	15.6	0.0	0.0	0.0	1.884	2.700	0.4	0.11
Guatemala[d]	GTM	12.9	7.0	866	471	69.3	26.2	18.2	9.2	5.0	0.1	0.0	0.2	4.241	7.807	54.9	14.95
Haiti	HTI	3.8	2.0	375	194	65.9	11.4	7.5	4.0	2.1	0.0	0.0	0.1	21.146	40.977	80.1	10.10
Honduras	HND	6.9	4.3	811	507	79.7	24.6	19.6	8.7	5.4	0.0	0.0	0.1	11.899	19.048	81.9	8.48
Jamaica	JAM	4.2	3.0	1,484	1,070	92.0	45.0	41.4	15.8	11.4	0.0	0.0	0.0	61.956	85.911	259.8	2.83
Mexico	MEX	351.6	262.9	3,044	2,276	95.4	92.2	88.0	32.5	24.3	1.6	1.5	1.7	9.290	12.423	3,266.6	115.51
Montserrat	MSR	0.0	0.0	5,016	3,410	86.8	152.0	131.8	53.5	36.4	0.0	0.0	0.0	1.836	2.700	0.0	0.00
Nicaragua	NIC	3.9	2.4	658	408	79.1	19.9	15.8	7.0	4.4	0.0	0.0	0.1	13.895	22.424	53.9	5.90
Panama	PAN	14.2	10.8	3,828	2,914	97.1	116.0	112.7	40.9	31.1	0.1	0.1	0.1	0.761	1.000	10.8	3.71
Paraguay	PRY	11.0	7.1	1,742	1,119	82.0	52.8	43.3	18.6	11.9	0.0	0.0	0.1	2,686.447	4,183.127	29,638.3	6.33
Peru	PER	57.1	40.1	1,950	1,370	89.7	59.1	53.0	20.8	14.6	0.3	0.2	0.4	1.935	2.754	110.5	29.26
Sint Maarten	SXM	0.1	0.1	3,157	2,204	89.1	95.6	85.2	33.7	23.5	0.0	0.0	0.0	1.250	1.790	0.1	0.04
St. Kitts and Nevis	KNA	0.3	0.3	5,879	5,114	111.0	178.1	197.7	62.8	54.6	0.0	0.0	0.0	2.349	2.700	0.7	0.05
St. Lucia	LCA	0.5	0.4	2,614	2,069	101.0	79.2	80.0	27.9	22.1	0.0	0.0	0.0	2.138	2.700	1.0	0.18
St. Vincent and the Grenadines	VCT	0.2	0.2	2,307	1,588	87.8	69.9	61.4	24.6	16.9	0.0	0.0	0.0	1.858	2.700	0.5	0.11
Suriname	SUR	2.3	1.6	4,335	2,982	87.8	131.3	115.3	46.3	31.8	0.0	0.0	0.0	2.305	3.350	5.3	0.54
Trinidad and Tobago	TTO	6.8	3.9	5,061	2,919	73.6	153.3	112.9	54.0	31.2	0.0	0.0	0.0	3.706	6.426	25.1	1.34
Turks and Caicos Islands	TCA	0.1	0.1	2,530	3,132	158.0	76.6	121.1	27.0	33.4	0.0	0.0	0.0	1.238	1.000	0.1	0.03
Uruguay	URY	11.6	9.2	3,450	2,722	100.7	104.5	105.2	36.8	29.1	0.1	0.1	0.1	15.236	19.314	177.1	3.37
Venezuela, RB[d]	VEN	83.6	56.1	2,894	1,942	85.7	87.7	75.1	30.9	20.7	0.4	0.3	0.4	2.879	4.289	240.7	28.89
Virgin Islands, British	VGB	0.2	0.2	6,484	7,730	152.2	196.4	298.9	69.2	82.5	0.0	0.0	0.0	1.192	1.000	0.2	0.03
Total (39)	**LCB**	**1,510.9**	**1,138.0**	**2,797**	**2,107**	**96.1**	**84.8**	**81.5**	**29.9**	**22.5**	**6.8**	**6.5**	**8.0**	**n.a.**	**n.a**	**n.a.**	**540.10**

Table E.5 *(Continued)*

GROSS FIXED CAPITAL FORMATION — Economy		Expenditure (billion US$): Based on PPPs	Expenditure (billion US$): Based on XRs	Expenditure per capita (US$): Based on PPPs	Expenditure per capita (US$): Based on XRs	Price level index (world = 100.0)[a]	Expenditure per capita indexes[b]: World = 100.0: Based on PPPs	Expenditure per capita indexes[b]: World = 100.0: Based on XRs	Expenditure per capita indexes[b]: United States = 100.0: Based on PPPs	Expenditure per capita indexes[b]: United States = 100.0: Based on XRs	Share (world = 100%)[b]: Expenditure: Based on PPPs	Share (world = 100%)[b]: Expenditure: Based on XRs	Share (world = 100%)[b]: Population	PPPs[c] (US$ = 1.000)	Reference data: Market exchange rates[c] (US$ = 1.000)	Reference data: Expenditure (billion LCU)	Reference data: Population (millions)
(00)		(01)	(02)	(03)	(04)	(05)	(06)	(07)	(08)	(09)	(10)	(11)	(12)	(13)	(14)	(15)	(16)
Middle East and North Africa																	
Algeria	DZA	107.9	63.3	2,943	1,728	74.9	89.2	66.8	31.4	18.4	0.5	0.4	0.5	42.825	72.938	4,620.3	36.66
Bahrain	BHR	12.1	6.1	10,101	5,073	64.1	306.0	196.1	107.8	54.2	0.1	0.0	0.0	0.189	0.376	2.3	1.20
Djibouti	DJI	1.7	0.9	1,955	1,084	70.8	59.2	41.9	20.9	11.6	0.0	0.0	0.0	98.556	177.721	164.5	0.85
Egypt, Arab Rep.	EGY	80.4	38.0	999	472	60.3	30.3	18.2	10.7	5.0	0.4	0.2	1.2	2.808	5.947	225.9	80.53
Iran, Islamic Rep.	IRN	255.3	161.3	3,398	2,146	80.6	102.9	83.0	36.3	22.9	1.1	0.9	1.1	6,705.487	10,616.307	1,712,186.3	75.15
Iraq	IRQ	52.7	31.1	1,581	932	75.2	47.9	36.0	16.9	9.9	0.2	0.2	0.5	706.775	1,199.200	37,255.3	33.34
Israel	ISR	47.9	53.3	6,173	6,870	142.0	187.0	265.6	65.9	73.3	0.2	0.3	0.1	3.982	3.578	190.8	7.76
Jordan	JOR	15.9	7.3	2,272	1,050	59.0	68.8	40.6	24.3	11.2	0.1	0.0	0.1	0.327	0.708	5.2	6.99
Kuwait	KWT	31.7	19.6	10,338	6,402	79.0	313.2	247.5	110.4	68.3	0.1	0.1	0.0	0.173	0.280	5.5	3.07
Malta	MLT	2.1	1.7	5,098	4,098	102.6	154.5	158.5	54.4	43.8	0.0	0.0	0.0	0.578	0.718	1.2	0.42
Morocco	MAR	71.9	32.1	2,207	985	57.0	66.9	38.1	23.6	10.5	0.3	0.2	0.5	3.592	8.049	258.3	32.58
Oman	OMN	36.4	15.8	11,058	4,793	55.3	335.0	185.3	118.0	51.2	0.2	0.1	0.0	0.167	0.385	6.1	3.30
Qatar	QAT	103.7	48.6	59,871	28,034	59.8	1,813.9	1,083.9	639.1	299.3	0.5	0.3	0.0	1.709	3.650	177.3	1.73
Saudi Arabia	SAU	346.0	151.7	12,280	5,384	55.9	372.1	208.2	131.1	57.5	1.6	0.9	0.4	1.644	3.750	568.8	28.17
Tunisia	TUN	22.4	10.0	2,082	932	57.1	63.1	36.0	22.2	10.0	0.1	0.1	0.2	0.630	1.408	14.1	10.74
United Arab Emirates	ARE	142.1	75.3	16,391	8,680	67.6	496.6	335.6	175.0	92.7	0.6	0.4	0.1	1.945	3.673	276.4	8.67
West Bank and Gaza	PSE	3.5	2.4	892	608	87.0	27.0	23.5	9.5	6.5	0.0	0.0	0.1	2.439	3.578	8.4	3.88
Yemen, Rep.[d]	YEM	7.9	4.1	330	174	67.4	10.0	6.7	3.5	1.9	0.0	0.0	0.4	112.837	213.800	886.4	23.83
Total (17)	**MEB**	**1,341.6**	**722.6**	**3,738**	**2,014**	**68.7**	**113.3**	**77.9**	**39.9**	**21.5**	**6.0**	**4.1**	**5.3**	**n.a.**	**n.a**	**n.a.**	**358.87**
North America																	
Bermuda	BMU	0.7	0.7	10,588	10,792	130.1	320.8	417.3	113.0	115.2	0.0	0.0	0.0	1.019	1.000	0.7	0.07
Canada	CAN	349.9	421.5	10,188	12,273	153.7	308.7	474.5	108.8	131.0	1.6	2.4	0.5	1.192	0.990	417.1	34.34
United States	USA	2,922.9	2,922.9	9,367	9,367	127.6	283.8	362.2	100.0	100.0	13.1	16.8	4.6	1.000	1.000	2,922.9	312.03
Total (3)	**NAB**	**3,273.5**	**3,345.1**	**9,449**	**9,656**	**130.4**	**286.3**	**373.3**	**100.9**	**103.1**	**14.7**	**19.2**	**5.1**	**n.a.**	**n.a**	**n.a.**	**346.44**
South Asia																	
Bangladesh	BGD	95.7	37.0	639	247	49.4	19.4	9.6	6.8	2.6	0.4	0.2	2.2	28.711	74.152	2,746.8	149.70
Bhutan	BTN	2.5	1.2	3,733	1,820	62.2	113.1	70.4	39.9	19.4	0.0	0.0	0.0	22.746	46.670	57.7	0.68
India	IND	1,425.0	604.9	1,172	497	54.2	35.5	19.2	12.5	5.3	6.4	3.5	18.1	19.811	46.670	28,230.8	1,216.15
Maldives	MDV	1.5	0.9	3,674	2,289	79.5	111.3	88.5	39.2	24.4	0.0	0.0	0.0	9.099	14.602	13.6	0.41
Nepal	NPL	9.2	4.2	346	157	58.1	10.5	6.1	3.7	1.7	0.0	0.0	0.4	33.706	74.020	308.5	26.49
Pakistan	PAK	70.4	28.9	398	163	52.4	12.0	6.3	4.2	1.7	0.3	0.2	2.6	35.439	86.343	2,494.9	177.10
Sri Lanka	LKA	34.8	17.2	1,725	850	62.9	52.3	32.9	18.4	9.1	0.2	0.1	0.3	54.471	110.565	1,897.7	20.20
Total (7)	**SAB**	**1,639.1**	**694.3**	**1,030**	**436**	**54.1**	**31.2**	**16.9**	**11.0**	**4.7**	**7.4**	**4.0**	**23.6**	**n.a.**	**n.a**	**n.a.**	**1,590.72**
Sub-Saharan Africa																	
Angola	AGO	70.8	44.2	2,922	1,825	79.7	88.5	70.6	31.2	19.5	0.3	0.3	0.4	58.671	93.935	4,151.7	24.22
Benin	BEN	2.8	1.9	301	196	83.0	9.1	7.6	3.2	2.1	0.0	0.0	0.1	306.835	471.866	873.3	9.46
Botswana	BWA	9.9	4.9	4,904	2,441	63.5	148.6	94.4	52.4	26.1	0.0	0.0	0.0	3.404	6.838	33.6	2.02

(continued)

Table E.5 *(Continued)*

GROSS FIXED CAPITAL FORMATION		Expenditure (billion US$)		Expenditure per capita (US$)		Price level index (world = 100.0)[a]	Expenditure per capita indexes[b]				Share (world = 100%)[b]			PPPs[c] (US$ = 1.000)	Reference data		
							World = 100.0		United States = 100.0		Expenditure				Market exchange rates[c] (US$ = 1.000)	Expenditure (billion LCU)	Population (millions)
Economy		Based on PPPs	Based on XRs	Based on PPPs	Based on XRs		Based on PPPs	Based on XRs	Based on PPPs	Based on XRs	Based on PPPs	Based on XRs	Population				
(00)		(01)	(02)	(03)	(04)	(05)	(06)	(07)	(08)	(09)	(10)	(11)	(12)	(13)	(14)	(15)	(16)
Burkina Faso	BFA	4.6	2.8	288	176	78.1	8.7	6.8	3.1	1.9	0.0	0.0	0.2	288.820	471.866	1,336.6	16.08
Burundi	BDI	0.6	0.3	68	39	71.8	2.1	1.5	0.7	0.4	0.0	0.0	0.1	709.607	1,261.073	435.1	8.96
Cabo Verde	CPV	1.2	0.9	2,309	1,747	96.5	70.0	67.5	24.7	18.6	0.0	0.0	0.0	60.010	79.323	69.1	0.50
Cameroon	CMR	10.8	7.1	516	339	83.9	15.6	13.1	5.5	3.6	0.0	0.0	0.3	310.323	471.866	3,348.4	20.91
Central African Republic	CAF	0.5	0.3	103	74	91.6	3.1	2.9	1.1	0.8	0.0	0.0	0.1	338.650	471.866	154.2	4.42
Chad	TCD	4.6	3.4	371	278	95.7	11.2	10.8	4.0	3.0	0.0	0.0	0.2	353.817	471.866	1,622.9	12.36
Comoros	COM	0.3	0.2	491	327	84.8	14.9	12.6	5.2	3.5	0.0	0.0	0.0	235.215	353.900	81.7	0.71
Congo, Dem. Rep.	COD	15.8	12.0	237	179	96.4	7.2	6.9	2.5	1.9	0.1	0.1	1.0	694.904	919.491	10,992.8	66.76
Congo, Rep.	COG	7.1	6.0	1,615	1,362	107.6	48.9	52.7	17.2	14.5	0.0	0.0	0.1	397.846	471.866	2,824.0	4.39
Côte d'Ivoire	CIV	2.8	1.7	131	81	78.7	4.0	3.1	1.4	0.9	0.0	0.0	0.3	291.121	471.866	803.6	21.03
Equatorial Guinea	GNQ	13.6	8.1	13,748	8,248	76.6	416.5	318.9	146.8	88.0	0.1	0.0	0.0	283.083	471.866	3,840.7	0.99
Eswatini	SWZ	0.9	0.5	874	455	66.4	26.5	17.6	9.3	4.9	0.0	0.0	0.0	3.780	7.261	3.5	1.07
Ethiopia	ETH	33.4	13.8	371	153	52.6	11.2	5.9	4.0	1.6	0.2	0.1	1.3	6.964	16.899	232.8	90.14
Gabon	GAB	6.9	5.6	4,098	3,312	103.1	124.1	128.0	43.7	35.4	0.0	0.0	0.0	381.355	471.866	2,632.4	1.68
Gambia, The	GMB	0.6	0.3	346	188	69.2	10.5	7.3	3.7	2.0	0.0	0.0	0.0	15.968	29.462	10.2	1.85
Ghana	GHA	14.0	6.9	550	271	62.9	16.7	10.5	5.9	2.9	0.1	0.0	0.4	0.745	1.512	10.4	25.39
Guinea	GIN	2.9	1.8	276	173	80.1	8.4	6.7	2.9	1.8	0.0	0.0	0.2	4,179.494	6,658.031	12,012.5	10.42
Guinea-Bissau	GNB	0.1	0.1	77	47	78.8	2.3	1.8	0.8	0.5	0.0	0.0	0.0	291.289	471.866	35.0	1.56
Kenya	KEN	16.3	8.5	378	197	66.3	11.5	7.6	4.0	2.1	0.1	0.0	0.6	46.153	88.811	754.2	43.18
Lesotho	LSO	1.1	0.7	554	350	80.6	16.8	13.5	5.9	3.7	0.0	0.0	0.0	4.587	7.261	5.1	2.00
Liberia	LBR	1.0	0.6	250	142	72.3	7.6	5.5	2.7	1.5	0.0	0.0	0.1	40.943	72.227	41.2	4.02
Madagascar	MDG	5.4	2.9	247	131	67.9	7.5	5.1	2.6	1.4	0.0	0.0	0.3	1,076.806	2,025.118	5,775.0	21.74
Malawi	MWI	1.6	1.0	110	68	78.8	3.3	2.6	1.2	0.7	0.0	0.0	0.2	96.643	156.515	158.5	14.96
Mali	MLI	4.0	2.4	258	156	77.1	7.8	6.0	2.8	1.7	0.0	0.0	0.2	285.083	471.866	1,142.5	15.51
Mauritania	MRT	3.1	2.0	865	542	80.0	26.2	21.0	9.2	5.8	0.0	0.0	0.1	176.184	281.118	548.3	3.60
Mauritius	MUS	10.4	5.7	8,301	4,581	70.4	251.5	177.1	88.6	48.9	0.0	0.0	0.0	15.841	28.706	164.5	1.25
Mozambique	MOZ	4.5	3.1	185	126	87.1	5.6	4.9	2.0	1.3	0.0	0.0	0.4	19.844	29.068	88.8	24.19
Namibia	NAM	4.8	2.8	2,219	1,306	75.1	67.2	50.5	23.7	13.9	0.0	0.0	0.0	4.273	7.261	20.5	2.16
Niger	NER	4.1	2.5	241	145	76.8	7.3	5.6	2.6	1.5	0.0	0.0	0.3	284.069	471.866	1,169.5	17.11
Nigeria	NGA	104.9	64.3	644	395	78.3	19.5	15.3	6.9	4.2	0.5	0.4	2.4	94.366	153.862	9,897.2	162.81
Rwanda	RWA	2.3	1.5	227	142	80.0	6.9	5.5	2.4	1.5	0.0	0.0	0.2	376.454	600.307	879.1	10.29
São Tomé and Príncipe	STP	0.1	0.1	805	410	65.0	24.4	15.8	8.6	4.4	0.0	0.0	0.0	8.976	17.623	1.3	0.18
Senegal	SEN	5.9	3.7	455	287	80.4	13.8	11.1	4.9	3.1	0.0	0.0	0.2	297.359	471.866	1,764.3	13.03
Seychelles	SYC	0.6	0.4	6,688	4,653	88.8	202.6	179.9	71.4	49.7	0.0	0.0	0.0	8.614	12.381	5.3	0.09
Sierra Leone	SLE	2.5	1.2	375	186	63.4	11.4	7.2	4.0	2.0	0.0	0.0	0.1	2,158.937	4,349.162	5,315.9	6.56
South Africa	ZAF	116.9	75.4	2,247	1,450	82.4	68.1	56.1	24.0	15.5	0.5	0.4	0.8	4.686	7.261	547.6	52.00
Sudan	SDN	33.9	12.2	998	359	45.9	30.2	13.9	10.7	3.8	0.2	0.1	0.5	1.305	3.630	44.2	33.98

Table E.5 *(Continued)*

GROSS FIXED CAPITAL FORMATION		Expenditure (billion US$)		Expenditure per capita (US$)		Price level index (world = 100.0)[a]	Expenditure per capita indexes[b]				Share (world = 100%)[b]			PPPs[c] (US$ = 1.000)	Reference data		
							World = 100.0		United States = 100.0		Expenditure				Market exchange rates[c] (US$ = 1.000)	Expenditure (billion LCU)	Population (millions)
Economy		Based on PPPs	Based on XRs	Based on PPPs	Based on XRs		Based on PPPs	Based on XRs	Based on PPPs	Based on XRs	Based on PPPs	Based on XRs	Population				
(00)		(01)	(02)	(03)	(04)	(05)	(06)	(07)	(08)	(09)	(10)	(11)	(12)	(13)	(14)	(15)	(16)
Tanzania	TZA	26.6	10.2	582	224	49.1	17.6	8.7	6.2	2.4	0.1	0.1	0.7	605.344	1,572.116	16,078.2	45.67
Togo	TGO	1.7	1.1	263	167	80.9	8.0	6.5	2.8	1.8	0.0	0.0	0.1	299.272	471.866	519.3	6.60
Uganda	UGA	15.8	6.6	472	197	53.2	14.3	7.6	5.0	2.1	0.1	0.0	0.5	1,051.369	2,522.746	16,621.3	33.48
Zambia	ZMB	12.5	6.6	888	468	67.3	26.9	18.1	9.5	5.0	0.1	0.0	0.2	2.562	4.861	31.9	14.02
Zimbabwe	ZWE	3.7	2.4	287	189	84.2	8.7	7.3	3.1	2.0	0.0	0.0	0.2	0.660	1.000	2.4	12.89
Total (45)	**SSB**	**587.9**	**340.7**	**679**	**393**	**74.0**	**20.6**	**15.2**	**7.2**	**4.2**	**2.6**	**2.0**	**12.9**	**n.a.**	**n.a**	**n.a.**	**866.25**
World (178)	**WLD**	**22,233.5**	**17,421.8**	**3,301**	**2,586**	**100.0**	**100.0**	**100.0**	**35.2**	**27.6**	**100.0**	**100.0**	**100.0**	**n.a.**	**n.a.**	**n.a.**	**6,736.12**

Note: PPP = purchasing power parity; XR = market exchange rate; LCU = local currency unit; n.a. = not applicable; ... = data suppressed due to unavailability.

a. World totals used to calculate price level indexes (PLIs) in this table exclude nonparticipating economies.

b. Indexes and shares are rounded to one decimal place for presentation in this table.

c. PPPs and market exchange rates are rounded to three decimal places for presentation in this table.

d. National accounts expenditures for the revised ICP 2011 results are estimated by the ICP Global Office.

e. Bonaire's results are provided only for individual consumption expenditure by households. Therefore, to ensure consistency across tables, Bonaire is not included in either Latin America and the Caribbean or the world totals.

Table E.6 Domestic absorption: Revised ICP 2011 results

DOMESTIC ABSORPTION Economy		Expenditure (billion US$)		Expenditure per capita (US$)		Price level index (world = 100.0)[a]	Expenditure per capita indexes[b]				Share (world = 100%)[b]			PPPs[c] (US$ = 1.000)	Reference data		
							World = 100.0		United States = 100.0		Expenditure				Market exchange rates[c] (US$ = 1.000)	Expenditure (billion LCU)	Population (millions)
		Based on PPPs	Based on XRs	Based on PPPs	Based on XRs		Based on PPPs	Based on XRs	Based on PPPs	Based on XRs	Based on PPPs	Based on XRs	Population				
(00)		(01)	(02)	(03)	(04)	(05)	(06)	(07)	(08)	(09)	(10)	(11)	(12)	(13)	(14)	(15)	(16)
East Asia and Pacific																	
Australia	AUS	954.3	1,502.4	42,715	67,253	202.7	310.4	629.1	82.7	130.2	1.0	2.1	0.3	1.526	0.969	1,456.6	22.34
Brunei Darussalam	BRN	19.0	11.2	48,371	28,505	75.9	351.5	266.6	93.6	55.2	0.0	0.0	0.0	0.741	1.258	14.1	0.39
Cambodia	KHM	38.2	12.8	2,673	898	43.2	19.4	8.4	5.2	1.7	0.0	0.0	0.2	1,362.864	4,058.500	52,125.2	14.31
China	CHN	13,449.7	7,377.9	10,006	5,489	70.6	72.7	51.3	19.4	10.6	14.5	10.2	20.0	3.544	6.461	47,672.1	1,344.13
Fiji	FJI	8.2	4.3	9,573	5,048	67.9	69.6	47.2	18.5	9.8	0.0	0.0	0.0	0.946	1.793	7.7	0.85
Hong Kong SAR, China	HKG	349.9	238.9	49,485	33,789	87.9	359.5	316.1	95.8	65.4	0.4	0.3	0.1	5.315	7.784	1,860.0	7.07
Indonesia	IDN	2,189.5	870.9	9,048	3,599	51.2	65.7	33.7	17.5	7.0	2.4	1.2	3.6	3,488.424	8,770.433	7,637,914.8	241.99
Japan	JPN	4,619.5	6,190.9	36,137	48,430	172.5	262.6	453.0	69.9	93.7	5.0	8.6	1.9	106.955	79.807	494,076.9	127.83
Korea, Rep.	KOR	1,629.2	1,239.3	32,625	24,818	97.9	237.0	232.1	63.1	48.0	1.8	1.7	0.7	843.079	1,108.292	1,373,531.9	49.94
Lao PDR	LAO	27.8	9.2	4,547	1,504	42.6	33.0	14.1	8.8	2.9	0.0	0.0	0.1	2,656.649	8,030.055	73,889.7	6.12
Macao SAR, China[d]	MAC	25.2	15.4	45,818	27,988	78.6	332.9	261.8	88.7	54.2	0.0	0.0	0.0	4.898	8.018	123.6	0.55
Malaysia	MYS	521.7	251.6	17,952	8,656	62.1	130.4	81.0	34.7	16.8	0.6	0.3	0.4	1.475	3.060	769.7	29.06
Mongolia	MNG	29.9	12.7	10,720	4,554	54.7	77.9	42.6	20.7	8.8	0.0	0.0	0.0	537.603	1,265.516	16,057.8	2.79
Myanmar	MMR	174.6	55.7	3,515	1,121	41.1	25.5	10.5	6.8	2.2	0.2	0.1	0.7	260.897	817.917	45,541.9	49.66
New Zealand	NZL	139.2	163.5	31,693	37,211	151.1	230.3	348.1	61.3	72.0	0.2	0.2	0.1	1.486	1.266	206.9	4.39
Philippines	PHL	556.7	232.3	5,911	2,466	53.7	42.9	23.1	11.4	4.8	0.6	0.3	1.4	18.072	43.313	10,061.3	94.18
Singapore	SGP	279.4	202.5	53,898	39,056	93.3	391.6	365.3	104.3	75.6	0.3	0.3	0.1	0.911	1.258	254.6	5.18
Taiwan, China	TWN	876.8	453.0	37,811	19,534	66.5	274.7	182.7	73.2	37.8	0.9	0.6	0.3	15.225	29.469	13,349.4	23.19
Thailand	THA	898.1	363.3	13,564	5,486	52.1	98.6	51.3	26.3	10.6	1.0	0.5	1.0	12.333	30.492	11,076.9	66.21
Vietnam	VNM	419.0	141.1	4,756	1,602	43.4	34.6	15.0	9.2	3.1	0.5	0.2	1.3	6,908.460	20,509.750	2,894,767.7	88.11
Total (20)	**EAB**	**27,206.0**	**19,348.9**	**12,490**	**8,883**	**91.6**	**90.7**	**83.1**	**24.2**	**17.2**	**29.3**	**26.9**	**32.3**	**n.a.**	**n.a**	**n.a.**	**2,178.31**
Europe and Central Asia																	
Albania	ALB	34.8	15.8	11,986	5,450	58.5	87.1	51.0	23.2	10.5	0.0	0.0	0.0	45.844	100.812	1,596.3	2.91
Armenia	ARM	27.5	12.5	9,074	4,140	58.7	65.9	38.7	17.6	8.0	0.0	0.0	0.0	169.943	372.500	4,669.4	3.03
Austria	AUT	362.5	419.6	43,218	50,025	149.0	314.0	467.9	83.6	96.8	0.4	0.6	0.1	0.832	0.718	301.5	8.39
Azerbaijan	AZE	100.9	44.6	11,140	4,927	56.9	80.9	46.1	21.6	9.5	0.1	0.1	0.1	0.349	0.790	35.2	9.05
Belarus	BLR	159.6	55.4	16,843	5,846	44.7	122.4	54.7	32.6	11.3	0.2	0.1	0.1	0.195	0.561	31.0	9.47
Belgium	BEL	453.4	523.9	41,074	47,459	148.7	298.4	443.9	79.5	91.9	0.5	0.7	0.2	0.830	0.718	376.3	11.04
Bosnia and Herzegovina	BIH	43.7	23.1	11,943	6,311	68.0	86.8	59.0	23.1	12.2	0.0	0.0	0.1	0.742	1.405	32.5	3.66
Bulgaria	BGR	116.2	57.2	15,815	7,785	63.4	114.9	72.8	30.6	15.1	0.1	0.1	0.1	0.692	1.405	80.4	7.35
Croatia	HRV	91.8	63.6	21,444	14,850	89.1	155.8	138.9	41.5	28.7	0.1	0.1	0.1	3.701	5.344	339.9	4.28
Cyprus	CYP	29.6	28.6	34,827	33,637	124.3	253.0	314.6	67.4	65.1	0.0	0.0	0.0	0.694	0.718	20.6	0.85
Czech Republic	CZE	293.8	219.6	27,994	20,921	96.2	203.4	195.7	54.2	40.5	0.3	0.3	0.2	13.202	17.665	3,879.3	10.50
Denmark	DNK	227.3	323.0	40,808	57,986	182.9	296.5	542.4	79.0	112.2	0.2	0.4	0.1	7.606	5.352	1,728.8	5.57
Estonia	EST	31.5	22.1	23,691	16,602	90.2	172.1	155.3	45.9	32.1	0.0	0.0	0.0	0.503	0.718	15.9	1.33
Finland	FIN	223.0	277.8	41,395	51,549	160.3	300.8	482.2	80.1	99.8	0.2	0.4	0.1	0.895	0.718	199.5	5.39

Table E.6 *(Continued)*

DOMESTIC ABSORPTION		Expenditure (billion US$)		Expenditure per capita (US$)		Price level index (world = 100.0)[a]	Expenditure per capita indexes[b]				Share (world = 100%)[b]			PPPs[c] (US$ = 1.000)	Reference data		
							World = 100.0		United States = 100.0		Expenditure				Market exchange rates[c] (US$ = 1.000)	Expenditure (billion LCU)	Population (millions)
Economy		Based on PPPs	Based on XRs	Based on PPPs	Based on XRs		Based on PPPs	Based on XRs	Based on PPPs	Based on XRs	Based on PPPs	Based on XRs	Population				
(00)		(01)	(02)	(03)	(04)	(05)	(06)	(07)	(08)	(09)	(10)	(11)	(12)	(13)	(14)	(15)	(16)
France	FRA	2,508.5	2,921.1	38,397	44,712	149.9	279.0	418.2	74.3	86.5	2.7	4.1	1.0	0.837	0.718	2,098.5	65.33
Georgia	GEO	36.3	17.9	9,664	4,753	63.3	70.2	44.5	18.7	9.2	0.0	0.0	0.1	0.829	1.686	30.1	3.76
Germany	DEU	3,241.7	3,565.4	40,383	44,415	141.6	293.4	415.4	78.2	86.0	3.5	5.0	1.2	0.790	0.718	2,561.4	80.28
Greece	GRC	312.6	307.7	28,150	27,709	126.7	204.5	259.2	54.5	53.6	0.3	0.4	0.2	0.707	0.718	221.1	11.11
Hungary	HUN	219.0	132.7	21,960	13,309	78.0	159.6	124.5	42.5	25.8	0.2	0.2	0.1	121.633	200.697	26,635.3	9.97
Iceland	ISL	11.9	14.0	37,285	43,855	151.4	270.9	410.2	72.2	84.9	0.0	0.0	0.0	136.395	115.963	1,622.3	0.32
Ireland	IRL	163.1	193.0	35,622	42,158	152.4	258.8	394.3	68.9	81.6	0.2	0.3	0.1	0.850	0.718	138.7	4.58
Italy	ITA	2,214.5	2,327.2	36,871	38,748	135.3	267.9	362.4	71.4	75.0	2.4	3.2	0.9	0.755	0.718	1,671.8	60.06
Kazakhstan	KAZ	289.2	154.5	17,465	9,329	68.8	126.9	87.3	33.8	18.1	0.3	0.2	0.2	78.318	146.620	22,647.7	16.56
Kyrgyz Republic	KGZ	21.7	7.9	4,125	1,498	46.7	30.0	14.0	8.0	2.9	0.0	0.0	0.1	16.754	46.144	363.5	5.26
Latvia	LVA	43.0	29.5	20,863	14,350	88.5	151.6	134.2	40.4	27.8	0.0	0.0	0.0	0.494	0.718	21.2	2.06
Lithuania	LTU	71.5	44.6	23,615	14,744	80.4	171.6	137.9	45.7	28.5	0.1	0.1	0.0	0.449	0.718	32.1	3.03
Luxembourg	LUX	30.6	40.5	58,973	78,047	170.4	428.5	730.0	114.1	151.1	0.0	0.1	0.0	0.951	0.718	29.1	0.52
Moldova	MDA	25.0	11.2	7,013	3,160	58.0	51.0	29.6	13.6	6.1	0.0	0.0	0.1	5.283	11.726	131.9	3.56
Montenegro	MNE	10.6	5.5	17,093	8,939	67.3	124.2	83.6	33.1	17.3	0.0	0.0	0.0	0.376	0.718	4.0	0.62
Netherlands	NLD	704.4	828.0	42,195	49,604	151.3	306.6	464.0	81.7	96.0	0.8	1.1	0.2	0.845	0.718	594.9	16.69
North Macedonia	MKD	27.7	12.5	13,456	6,068	58.1	97.8	56.8	26.0	11.7	0.0	0.0	0.0	19.933	44.202	552.1	2.06
Norway	NOR	254.4	434.6	51,355	87,743	219.9	373.1	820.7	99.4	169.8	0.3	0.6	0.1	9.566	5.599	2,433.1	4.95
Poland	POL	894.4	539.7	23,216	14,007	77.7	168.7	131.0	44.9	27.1	1.0	0.7	0.6	1.786	2.960	1,597.5	38.53
Portugal	PRT	296.4	255.4	28,073	24,191	110.9	204.0	226.3	54.3	46.8	0.3	0.4	0.2	0.619	0.718	183.5	10.56
Romania	ROU	380.2	194.3	18,873	9,644	65.8	137.1	90.2	36.5	18.7	0.4	0.3	0.3	1.556	3.045	591.7	20.15
Russian Federation	RUS	3,081.8	1,886.4	21,557	13,196	78.8	156.6	123.4	41.7	25.5	3.3	2.6	2.1	17.986	29.382	55,428.1	142.96
Serbia	SRB	110.3	55.6	15,244	7,688	64.9	110.8	71.9	29.5	14.9	0.1	0.1	0.1	36.940	73.240	4,074.8	7.24
Slovak Republic	SVK	140.7	98.4	26,068	18,234	90.0	189.4	170.6	50.5	35.3	0.2	0.1	0.1	0.503	0.718	70.7	5.40
Slovenia	SVN	59.1	51.0	28,803	24,823	110.9	209.3	232.2	55.7	48.0	0.1	0.1	0.0	0.619	0.718	36.6	2.05
Spain	ESP	1,489.3	1,473.5	31,866	31,527	127.4	231.5	294.9	61.7	61.0	1.6	2.0	0.7	0.711	0.718	1,058.5	46.74
Sweden	SWE	397.9	548.0	42,104	57,990	177.3	305.9	542.4	81.5	112.2	0.4	0.8	0.1	8.934	6.487	3,554.6	9.45
Switzerland	CHE	396.7	642.4	50,142	81,191	208.5	364.3	759.4	97.0	157.1	0.4	0.9	0.1	1.434	0.885	568.9	7.91
Tajikistan	TJK	26.5	10.2	3,442	1,322	49.5	25.0	12.4	6.7	2.6	0.0	0.0	0.1	1.771	4.610	47.0	7.71
Turkey	TUR	1,545.3	900.3	20,820	12,129	75.0	151.3	113.5	40.3	23.5	1.7	1.3	1.1	0.976	1.675	1,508.0	74.22
Ukraine[d]	UKR	447.3	179.9	9,787	3,935	51.8	71.1	36.8	18.9	7.6	0.5	0.2	0.7	3.203	7.968	1,433.1	45.71
United Kingdom	GBR	2,382.3	2,686.2	37,644	42,447	145.2	273.5	397.0	72.9	82.2	2.6	3.7	0.9	0.703	0.623	1,674.8	63.29
Total (46)	**ECB**	**24,029.7**	**22,656.0**	**28,091**	**26,485**	**121.4**	**204.1**	**247.7**	**54.4**	**51.3**	**25.9**	**31.5**	**12.7**	**n.a.**	**n.a**	**n.a.**	**855.42**
Latin America and the Caribbean																	
Anguilla	AIA	0.5	0.3	33,536	24,788	95.2	243.7	231.9	64.9	48.0	0.0	0.0	0.0	1.996	2.700	0.9	0.01
Antigua and Barbuda	ATG	2.0	1.2	22,001	13,932	81.5	159.9	130.3	42.6	27.0	0.0	0.0	0.0	1.710	2.700	3.4	0.09
Aruba	ABW	4.1	3.0	40,142	29,294	93.9	291.7	274.0	77.7	56.7	0.0	0.0	0.0	1.306	1.790	5.4	0.10

(continued)

Table E.6 *(Continued)*

DOMESTIC ABSORPTION Economy		Expenditure (billion US$) Based on PPPs	Expenditure (billion US$) Based on XRs	Expenditure per capita (US$) Based on PPPs	Expenditure per capita (US$) Based on XRs	Price level index (world = 100.0)[a]	Expenditure per capita indexes[b] World = 100.0 Based on PPPs	Expenditure per capita indexes[b] World = 100.0 Based on XRs	Expenditure per capita indexes[b] United States = 100.0 Based on PPPs	Expenditure per capita indexes[b] United States = 100.0 Based on XRs	Share (world = 100%)[b] Expenditure Based on PPPs	Share (world = 100%)[b] Expenditure Based on XRs	Share (world = 100%)[b] Population	PPPs[c] (US$ = 1.000)	Reference data Market exchange rates[c] (US$ = 1.000)	Reference data Expenditure (billion LCU)	Reference data Population (millions)
(00)		(01)	(02)	(03)	(04)	(05)	(06)	(07)	(08)	(09)	(10)	(11)	(12)	(13)	(14)	(15)	(16)
Bahamas, The	BHS	12.9	11.4	35,887	31,777	114.0	260.7	297.2	69.5	61.5	0.0	0.0	0.0	0.885	1.000	11.4	0.36
Barbados	BRB	5.2	5.2	18,546	18,236	126.6	134.8	170.6	35.9	35.3	0.0	0.0	0.0	1.967	2.000	10.3	0.28
Belize	BLZ	2.6	1.5	7,930	4,577	74.3	57.6	42.8	15.3	8.9	0.0	0.0	0.0	1.154	2.000	3.0	0.33
Bolivia	BOL	52.3	22.5	5,117	2,198	55.3	37.2	20.6	9.9	4.3	0.1	0.0	0.2	2.999	6.982	156.8	10.21
Bonaire[e]	BON	. . .	. . .	. . .	. . .	. . .	. . .	. . .	. . .	. . .	. . .	. . .	. . .	. . .	1.000	. . .	0.02
Brazil	BRA	3,014.0	2,636.3	15,260	13,347	112.6	110.9	124.8	29.5	25.8	3.3	3.7	2.9	1.463	1.673	4,410.1	197.51
Cayman Islands	CYM	2.7	3.2	47,389	55,748	151.4	344.3	521.5	91.7	107.9	0.0	0.0	0.0	0.980	0.833	2.7	0.06
Chile	CHL	343.7	243.9	19,905	14,124	91.3	144.6	132.1	38.5	27.3	0.4	0.3	0.3	343.188	483.668	117,957.6	17.27
Colombia	COL	533.2	337.5	11,580	7,330	81.5	84.1	68.6	22.4	14.2	0.6	0.5	0.7	1,169.914	1,848.139	623,796.8	46.04
Costa Rica	CRI	64.6	43.8	14,066	9,552	87.4	102.2	89.4	27.2	18.5	0.1	0.1	0.1	343.394	505.664	22,169.5	4.59
Curaçao	CUW	5.1	3.8	33,598	24,996	95.8	244.1	233.8	65.0	48.4	0.0	0.0	0.0	1.332	1.790	6.8	0.15
Dominica	DMA	0.8	0.6	11,634	8,115	89.8	84.5	75.9	22.5	15.7	0.0	0.0	0.0	1.883	2.700	1.6	0.07
Dominican Republic	DOM	126.9	64.2	12,931	6,539	65.1	94.0	61.2	25.0	12.7	0.1	0.1	0.1	19.267	38.099	2,444.8	9.81
Ecuador	ECU	152.6	81.1	10,009	5,317	68.4	72.7	49.7	19.4	10.3	0.2	0.1	0.2	0.531	1.000	81.1	15.24
El Salvador	SLV	47.8	24.6	7,699	3,962	66.3	55.9	37.1	14.9	7.7	0.1	0.0	0.1	0.515	1.000	24.6	6.21
Grenada	GRD	1.5	1.0	13,680	9,157	86.2	99.4	85.7	26.5	17.7	0.0	0.0	0.0	1.807	2.700	2.6	0.11
Guatemala[d]	GTM	110.8	52.6	7,411	3,520	61.2	53.8	32.9	14.3	6.8	0.1	0.1	0.2	3.709	7.807	410.8	14.95
Haiti	HTI	22.8	10.8	2,260	1,072	61.1	16.4	10.0	4.4	2.1	0.0	0.0	0.1	19.436	40.977	443.7	10.10
Honduras	HND	39.3	21.1	4,634	2,483	69.0	33.7	23.2	9.0	4.8	0.0	0.0	0.1	10.204	19.048	401.0	8.48
Jamaica	JAM	27.8	17.8	9,834	6,290	82.3	71.5	58.8	19.0	12.2	0.0	0.0	0.0	54.952	85.911	1,527.1	2.83
Mexico	MEX	1,938.8	1,197.0	16,784	10,362	79.5	122.0	96.9	32.5	20.1	2.1	1.7	1.7	7.670	12.423	14,870.3	115.51
Montserrat	MSR	0.1	0.1	28,258	18,616	84.8	205.3	174.1	54.7	36.0	0.0	0.0	0.0	1.779	2.700	0.2	0.00
Nicaragua	NIC	29.2	11.9	4,947	2,017	52.5	35.9	18.9	9.6	3.9	0.0	0.0	0.1	9.142	22.424	266.9	5.90
Panama	PAN	66.1	36.8	17,835	9,922	71.6	129.6	92.8	34.5	19.2	0.1	0.1	0.1	0.556	1.000	36.8	3.71
Paraguay	PRY	64.7	33.1	10,215	5,228	65.9	74.2	48.9	19.8	10.1	0.1	0.0	0.1	2,140.926	4,183.127	138,522.3	6.33
Peru	PER	289.8	163.1	9,904	5,575	72.5	72.0	52.1	19.2	10.8	0.3	0.2	0.4	1.550	2.754	449.3	29.26
Sint Maarten	SXM	1.2	0.9	33,498	25,014	96.1	243.4	234.0	64.8	48.4	0.0	0.0	0.0	1.337	1.790	1.6	0.04
St. Kitts and Nevis	KNA	1.3	1.0	26,419	19,274	93.9	192.0	180.3	51.1	37.3	0.0	0.0	0.0	1.970	2.700	2.6	0.05
St. Lucia	LCA	2.5	1.7	14,056	9,614	88.1	102.1	89.9	27.2	18.6	0.0	0.0	0.0	1.847	2.700	4.6	0.18
St. Vincent and the Grenadines	VCT	1.4	0.9	13,135	8,207	80.4	95.4	76.8	25.4	15.9	0.0	0.0	0.0	1.687	2.700	2.4	0.11
Suriname	SUR	7.3	4.0	13,584	7,534	71.4	98.7	70.5	26.3	14.6	0.0	0.0	0.0	1.858	3.350	13.5	0.54
Trinidad and Tobago	TTO	31.6	18.6	23,650	13,927	75.8	171.8	130.3	45.8	27.0	0.0	0.0	0.0	3.784	6.426	119.6	1.34
Turks and Caicos Islands	TCA	0.5	0.6	15,907	16,639	134.7	115.6	155.6	30.8	32.2	0.0	0.0	0.0	1.046	1.000	0.6	0.03
Uruguay	URY	61.1	48.2	18,144	14,294	101.4	131.8	133.7	35.1	27.7	0.1	0.1	0.1	15.216	19.314	930.1	3.37
Venezuela, RB[d]	VEN	456.8	284.0	15,812	9,833	80.1	114.9	92.0	30.6	19.0	0.5	0.4	0.4	2.667	4.289	1,218.4	28.89
Virgin Islands, British	VGB	0.6	0.6	20,116	21,198	135.7	146.2	198.3	38.9	41.0	0.0	0.0	0.0	1.054	1.000	0.6	0.03
Total (39)	**LCB**	**7,526.1**	**5,389.8**	**13,935**	**9,979**	**92.2**	**101.2**	**93.3**	**27.0**	**19.3**	**8.1**	**7.5**	**8.0**	**n.a.**	**n.a**	**n.a.**	**540.10**

Table E.6 *(Continued)*

DOMESTIC ABSORPTION		Expenditure (billion US$)		Expenditure per capita (US$)		Price level index (world = 100.0)[a]	Expenditure per capita indexes[b]				Share (world = 100%)[b]			Reference data			
							World = 100.0		United States = 100.0		Expenditure			PPPs[c] (US$ = 1.000)	Market exchange rates[c] (US$ = 1.000)	Expenditure (billion LCU)	Population (millions)
Economy		Based on PPPs	Based on XRs	Based on PPPs	Based on XRs		Based on PPPs	Based on XRs	Based on PPPs	Based on XRs	Based on PPPs	Based on XRs	Population				
(00)		(01)	(02)	(03)	(04)	(05)	(06)	(07)	(08)	(09)	(10)	(11)	(12)	(13)	(14)	(15)	(16)
Middle East and North Africa																	
Algeria	DZA	450.2	179.8	12,280	4,905	51.4	89.2	45.9	23.8	9.5	0.5	0.2	0.5	29.131	72.938	13,115.2	36.66
Bahrain	BHR	47.2	21.7	39,496	18,134	59.1	287.0	169.6	76.4	35.1	0.1	0.0	0.0	0.173	0.376	8.1	1.20
Djibouti	DJI	4.7	2.4	5,486	2,864	67.2	39.9	26.8	10.6	5.5	0.0	0.0	0.0	92.781	177.721	434.5	0.85
Egypt, Arab Rep.	EGY	952.5	269.6	11,828	3,348	36.4	85.9	31.3	22.9	6.5	1.0	0.4	1.2	1.684	5.947	1,603.6	80.53
Iran, Islamic Rep.	IRN	1,464.3	661.8	19,485	8,806	58.2	141.6	82.4	37.7	17.0	1.6	0.9	1.1	4,797.945	10,616.307	7,025,557.5	75.15
Iraq	IRQ	308.0	129.6	9,239	3,888	54.2	67.1	36.4	17.9	7.5	0.3	0.2	0.5	504.623	1,199.200	155,438.1	33.34
Israel	ISR	239.4	262.0	30,834	33,748	140.9	224.0	315.7	59.7	65.3	0.3	0.4	0.1	3.916	3.578	937.4	7.76
Jordan	JOR	89.2	36.5	12,758	5,224	52.7	92.7	48.9	24.7	10.1	0.1	0.1	0.1	0.290	0.708	25.9	6.99
Kuwait	KWT	123.9	80.0	40,417	26,090	83.1	293.7	244.0	78.2	50.5	0.1	0.1	0.0	0.181	0.280	22.4	3.07
Malta	MLT	11.7	9.3	28,207	22,332	101.9	204.9	208.9	54.6	43.2	0.0	0.0	0.0	0.569	0.718	6.7	0.42
Morocco	MAR	253.5	116.2	7,781	3,566	59.0	56.5	33.4	15.1	6.9	0.3	0.2	0.5	3.689	8.049	935.1	32.58
Oman	OMN	102.0	47.7	30,968	14,472	60.2	225.0	135.4	59.9	28.0	0.1	0.1	0.0	0.180	0.385	18.3	3.30
Qatar	QAT	147.7	89.5	85,219	51,644	78.0	619.2	483.1	164.9	100.0	0.2	0.1	0.0	2.212	3.650	326.6	1.73
Saudi Arabia	SAU	1,237.8	493.0	43,935	17,499	51.3	319.2	163.7	85.0	33.9	1.3	0.7	0.4	1.494	3.750	1,848.7	28.17
Tunisia	TUN	115.6	49.2	10,761	4,584	54.8	78.2	42.9	20.8	8.9	0.1	0.1	0.2	0.600	1.408	69.3	10.74
United Arab Emirates	ARE	427.2	250.8	49,258	28,917	75.6	357.9	270.5	95.3	56.0	0.5	0.3	0.1	2.156	3.673	921.0	8.67
West Bank and Gaza	PSE	22.7	14.4	5,853	3,710	81.6	42.5	34.7	11.3	7.2	0.0	0.0	0.1	2.268	3.578	51.5	3.88
Yemen, Rep.[d]	YEM	85.5	31.7	3,590	1,331	47.8	26.1	12.5	6.9	2.6	0.1	0.0	0.4	79.303	213.800	6,784.1	23.83
Total (17)	**MEB**	**6,083.2**	**2,745.2**	**16,951**	**7,650**	**58.1**	**123.2**	**71.6**	**32.8**	**14.8**	**6.6**	**3.8**	**5.3**	**n.a.**	**n.a**	**n.a.**	**358.87**
North America																	
Bermuda	BMU	3.0	4.4	46,166	68,210	190.2	335.4	638.0	89.4	132.0	0.0	0.0	0.0	1.478	1.000	4.4	0.07
Canada	CAN	1,453.3	1,813.3	42,316	52,800	160.6	307.5	493.9	81.9	102.2	1.6	2.5	0.5	1.235	0.990	1,794.3	34.34
United States	USA	16,122.0	16,122.0	51,668	51,668	128.7	375.4	483.3	100.0	100.0	17.4	22.4	4.6	1.000	1.000	16,122.0	312.03
Total (3)	**NAB**	**17,578.3**	**17,939.8**	**50,740**	**51,783**	**131.4**	**368.7**	**484.4**	**98.2**	**100.2**	**19.0**	**24.9**	**5.1**	**n.a.**	**n.a**	**n.a.**	**346.44**
South Asia																	
Bangladesh	BGD	451.0	143.1	3,013	956	40.9	21.9	8.9	5.8	1.9	0.5	0.2	2.2	23.530	74.152	10,613.0	149.70
Bhutan	BTN	6.6	2.4	9,649	3,463	46.2	70.1	32.4	18.7	6.7	0.0	0.0	0.0	16.750	46.670	109.8	0.68
India	IND	5,764.7	1,928.0	4,740	1,585	43.1	34.4	14.8	9.2	3.1	6.2	2.7	18.1	15.609	46.670	89,983.0	1,216.15
Maldives	MDV	4.5	2.5	11,063	6,040	70.3	80.4	56.5	21.4	11.7	0.0	0.0	0.0	7.972	14.602	35.8	0.41
Nepal	NPL	69.1	24.1	2,608	911	45.0	19.0	8.5	5.0	1.8	0.1	0.0	0.4	25.860	74.020	1,786.9	26.49
Pakistan	PAK	814.0	236.5	4,596	1,336	37.4	33.4	12.5	8.9	2.6	0.9	0.3	2.6	25.087	86.343	20,422.1	177.10
Sri Lanka	LKA	206.3	73.9	10,214	3,660	46.1	74.2	34.2	19.8	7.1	0.2	0.1	0.3	39.615	110.565	8,171.4	20.20
Total (7)	**SAB**	**7,316.2**	**2,410.5**	**4,599**	**1,515**	**42.4**	**33.4**	**14.2**	**8.9**	**2.9**	**7.9**	**3.3**	**23.6**	**n.a.**	**n.a**	**n.a.**	**1,590.72**
Sub-Saharan Africa																	
Angola	AGO	127.8	88.9	5,276	3,672	89.6	38.3	34.3	10.2	7.1	0.1	0.1	0.4	65.376	93.935	8,354.3	24.22
Benin	BEN	18.8	8.8	1,986	931	60.4	14.4	8.7	3.8	1.8	0.0	0.0	0.1	221.291	471.866	4,157.4	9.46
Botswana	BWA	30.1	15.9	14,934	7,895	68.1	108.5	73.8	28.9	15.3	0.0	0.0	0.0	3.615	6.838	108.8	2.02

(continued)

Table E.6 *(Continued)*

DOMESTIC ABSORPTION Economy		Expenditure (billion US$) Based on PPPs	Expenditure (billion US$) Based on XRs	Expenditure per capita (US$) Based on PPPs	Expenditure per capita (US$) Based on XRs	Price level index (world = 100.0)[a]	Expenditure per capita indexes[b] World = 100.0 Based on PPPs	Expenditure per capita indexes[b] World = 100.0 Based on XRs	Expenditure per capita indexes[b] United States = 100.0 Based on PPPs	Expenditure per capita indexes[b] United States = 100.0 Based on XRs	Share (world = 100%)[b] Expenditure Based on PPPs	Share (world = 100%)[b] Expenditure Based on XRs	Share (world = 100%)[b] Population	PPPs[c] (US$ = 1.000)	Reference data Market exchange rates[c] (US$ = 1.000)	Reference data Expenditure (billion LCU)	Reference data Population (millions)
(00)		(01)	(02)	(03)	(04)	(05)	(06)	(07)	(08)	(09)	(10)	(11)	(12)	(13)	(14)	(15)	(16)
Burkina Faso	BFA	24.6	11.7	1,531	725	61.0	11.1	6.8	3.0	1.4	0.0	0.0	0.2	223.551	471.866	5,504.8	16.08
Burundi	BDI	7.4	2.8	823	315	49.2	6.0	2.9	1.6	0.6	0.0	0.0	0.1	481.961	1,261.073	3,555.2	8.96
Cabo Verde	CPV	4.0	2.4	7,998	4,815	77.5	58.1	45.0	15.5	9.3	0.0	0.0	0.0	47.751	79.323	190.5	0.50
Cameroon	CMR	61.2	30.8	2,926	1,474	64.9	21.3	13.8	5.7	2.9	0.1	0.0	0.3	237.811	471.866	14,545.3	20.91
Central African Republic	CAF	4.9	2.6	1,106	596	69.4	8.0	5.6	2.1	1.2	0.0	0.0	0.1	254.507	471.866	1,243.3	4.42
Chad	TCD	24.4	13.2	1,972	1,070	69.8	14.3	10.0	3.8	2.1	0.0	0.0	0.2	255.978	471.866	6,238.1	12.36
Comoros	COM	2.1	1.2	2,903	1,744	77.4	21.1	16.3	5.6	3.4	0.0	0.0	0.0	212.659	353.900	436.1	0.71
Congo, Dem. Rep.	COD	62.2	35.6	931	533	73.6	6.8	5.0	1.8	1.0	0.1	0.0	1.0	525.931	919.491	32,695.5	66.76
Congo, Rep.	COG	19.3	12.9	4,381	2,940	86.4	31.8	27.5	8.5	5.7	0.0	0.0	0.1	316.579	471.866	6,096.0	4.39
Côte d'Ivoire	CIV	43.1	21.5	2,049	1,021	64.2	14.9	9.6	4.0	2.0	0.0	0.0	0.3	235.239	471.866	10,134.6	21.03
Equatorial Guinea	GNQ	21.6	13.7	21,899	13,873	81.6	159.1	129.8	42.4	26.9	0.0	0.0	0.0	298.922	471.866	6,460.1	0.99
Eswatini	SWZ	9.7	5.3	9,055	4,974	70.7	65.8	46.5	17.5	9.6	0.0	0.0	0.0	3.989	7.261	38.7	1.07
Ethiopia	ETH	160.6	50.0	1,782	555	40.1	12.9	5.2	3.4	1.1	0.2	0.1	1.3	5.261	16.899	845.1	90.14
Gabon	GAB	19.8	14.1	11,782	8,352	91.3	85.6	78.1	22.8	16.2	0.0	0.0	0.0	334.469	471.866	6,638.9	1.68
Gambia, The	GMB	4.6	1.7	2,503	902	46.4	18.2	8.4	4.8	1.7	0.0	0.0	0.0	10.622	29.462	49.1	1.85
Ghana	GHA	100.8	46.7	3,969	1,838	59.6	28.8	17.2	7.7	3.6	0.1	0.1	0.4	0.700	1.512	70.5	25.39
Guinea	GIN	21.2	8.2	2,031	786	49.8	14.8	7.4	3.9	1.5	0.0	0.0	0.2	2,578.046	6,658.031	54,550.5	10.42
Guinea-Bissau	GNB	2.4	1.2	1,515	738	62.7	11.0	6.9	2.9	1.4	0.0	0.0	0.0	229.778	471.866	544.1	1.56
Kenya	KEN	119.5	48.7	2,768	1,127	52.4	20.1	10.5	5.4	2.2	0.1	0.1	0.6	36.157	88.811	4,321.9	43.18
Lesotho	LSO	7.5	4.1	3,751	2,040	70.0	27.3	19.1	7.3	3.9	0.0	0.0	0.0	3.950	7.261	29.7	2.00
Liberia	LBR	4.0	2.2	1,003	538	69.0	7.3	5.0	1.9	1.0	0.0	0.0	0.1	38.731	72.227	156.1	4.02
Madagascar	MDG	36.2	12.8	1,664	590	45.7	12.1	5.5	3.2	1.1	0.0	0.0	0.3	718.131	2,025.118	25,988.0	21.74
Malawi	MWI	18.5	9.3	1,237	620	64.6	9.0	5.8	2.4	1.2	0.0	0.0	0.2	78.498	156.515	1,452.8	14.96
Mali	MLI	30.6	14.1	1,973	907	59.2	14.3	8.5	3.8	1.8	0.0	0.0	0.2	217.017	471.866	6,642.1	15.51
Mauritania	MRT	12.8	5.5	3,551	1,527	55.3	25.8	14.3	6.9	3.0	0.0	0.0	0.1	120.867	281.118	1,544.6	3.60
Mauritius	MUS	28.1	15.3	22,493	12,267	70.2	163.4	114.7	43.5	23.7	0.0	0.0	0.0	15.655	28.706	440.5	1.25
Mozambique	MOZ	30.0	17.1	1,239	706	73.4	9.0	6.6	2.4	1.4	0.0	0.0	0.4	16.577	29.068	496.6	24.19
Namibia	NAM	22.0	13.9	10,204	6,460	81.5	74.1	60.4	19.7	12.5	0.0	0.0	0.0	4.597	7.261	101.2	2.16
Niger	NER	16.8	8.1	984	475	62.1	7.2	4.4	1.9	0.9	0.0	0.0	0.3	227.749	471.866	3,837.3	17.11
Nigeria	NGA	721.4	368.2	4,431	2,261	65.7	32.2	21.2	8.6	4.4	0.8	0.5	2.4	78.519	153.862	56,646.1	162.81
Rwanda	RWA	16.0	7.4	1,555	723	59.8	11.3	6.8	3.0	1.4	0.0	0.0	0.2	279.059	600.307	4,467.7	10.29
São Tomé and Príncipe	STP	0.9	0.4	4,610	2,020	56.4	33.5	18.9	8.9	3.9	0.0	0.0	0.0	7.721	17.623	6.6	0.18
Senegal	SEN	41.6	21.2	3,192	1,624	65.5	23.2	15.2	6.2	3.1	0.0	0.0	0.2	240.031	471.866	9,986.0	13.03
Seychelles	SYC	2.3	1.3	25,314	13,925	70.8	183.9	130.2	49.0	27.0	0.0	0.0	0.0	6.811	12.381	15.8	0.09
Sierra Leone	SLE	11.1	4.4	1,684	664	50.8	12.2	6.2	3.3	1.3	0.0	0.0	0.1	1,715.919	4,349.162	18,964.0	6.56
South Africa	ZAF	643.1	417.1	12,366	8,021	83.5	89.8	75.0	23.9	15.5	0.7	0.6	0.8	4.710	7.261	3,028.7	52.00
Sudan	SDN	152.5	51.7	4,489	1,520	43.6	32.6	14.2	8.7	2.9	0.2	0.1	0.5	1.229	3.630	187.5	33.98

Table E.6 *(Continued)*

DOMESTIC ABSORPTION		Expenditure (billion US$)		Expenditure per capita (US$)		Price level index (world = 100.0)[a]	Expenditure per capita indexes[b]				Share (world = 100%)[b]			PPPs[c] (US$ = 1.000)	Reference data		
							World = 100.0		United States = 100.0		Expenditure				Market exchange rates[c] (US$ = 1.000)	Expenditure (billion LCU)	Population (millions)
Economy		Based on PPPs	Based on XRs	Based on PPPs	Based on XRs		Based on PPPs	Based on XRs	Based on PPPs	Based on XRs	Based on PPPs	Based on XRs	Population				
(00)		(01)	(02)	(03)	(04)	(05)	(06)	(07)	(08)	(09)	(10)	(11)	(12)	(13)	(14)	(15)	(16)
Tanzania	TZA	105.1	37.3	2,302	817	45.7	16.7	7.6	4.5	1.6	0.1	0.1	0.7	557.688	1,572.116	58,631.0	45.67
Togo	TGO	9.7	4.7	1,468	712	62.5	10.7	6.7	2.8	1.4	0.0	0.0	0.1	228.944	471.866	2,217.3	6.60
Uganda	UGA	94.1	33.1	2,812	988	45.2	20.4	9.2	5.4	1.9	0.1	0.0	0.5	886.618	2,522.746	83,454.3	33.48
Zambia	ZMB	47.1	23.5	3,360	1,679	64.3	24.4	15.7	6.5	3.3	0.1	0.0	0.2	2.429	4.861	114.5	14.02
Zimbabwe	ZWE	28.8	14.9	2,235	1,156	66.6	16.2	10.8	4.3	2.2	0.0	0.0	0.2	0.517	1.000	14.9	12.89
Total (45)	**SSB**	**2,970.2**	**1,525.4**	**3,429**	**1,761**	**66.1**	**24.9**	**16.5**	**6.6**	**3.4**	**3.2**	**2.1**	**12.9**	**n.a.**	**n.a**	**n.a.**	**866.25**
World (178)	**WLD**	**92,709.8**	**72,015.6**	**13,763**	**10,691**	**100.0**	**100.0**	**100.0**	**26.6**	**20.7**	**100.0**	**100.0**	**100.0**	**n.a.**	**n.a.**	**n.a.**	**6,736.12**

Note: PPP = purchasing power parity; XR = market exchange rate; LCU = local currency unit; n.a. = not applicable; ... = data suppressed due to unavailability.

a. World totals used to calculate price level indexes (PLIs) in this table exclude nonparticipating economies.

b. Indexes and shares are rounded to one decimal place for presentation in this table.

c. PPPs and market exchange rates are rounded to three decimal places for presentation in this table.

d. National accounts expenditures for the revised ICP 2011 results are estimated by the ICP Global Office.

e. Bonaire's results are provided only for individual consumption expenditure by households. Therefore, to ensure consistency across tables, Bonaire is not included in either Latin America and the Caribbean or the world totals.

Table E.7 Gross domestic product (GDP) and individual consumption expenditure for nonparticipating economies: Revised ICP 2011 results

Economy		GROSS DOMESTIC PRODUCT						Reference data			INDIVIDUAL CONSUMPTION EXPENDITURE BY HOUSEHOLDS
		Expenditure (billion US$)		Expenditure per capita (US$)		Price level index[a] (world = 100.0)	PPPs[b] (US$ = 1.000)	Market exchange rates[b] (US$ = 1.000)	Expenditure, gross domestic product (billion LCU)	Population (millions)	PPPs[b] (US$ = 1.000)
		Based on PPPs	Based on XRs	Based on PPPs	Based on XRs						
(00)		(01)	(02)	(03)	(04)	(05)	(13)	(14)	(15)	(16)	(13)
Nonparticipating economies											
Afghanistan	AFG	51.2	18.2	1,699	604	46.0	16.613	46.747	850.3	30.12	16.788
Argentina[c]	ARG	797.3	528.0	19,295	12,779	85.7	2.733	4.127	2,179.0	41.32	3.161
Eritrea	ERI	6.6	2.6	1,475	583	51.2	6.077	15.375	40.1	4.47	6.440
Guyana[c]	GUY	5.2	2.6	6,971	3,426	63.6	100.269	204.018	525.7	0.75	120.832
Lebanon	LBN	76.6	40.1	14,723	7,703	67.7	788.752	1,507.500	60,414.1	5.20	830.624
Libya	LBY	71.7	34.7	11,582	5,603	62.6	0.592	1.224	42.5	6.19	0.622
Puerto Rico	PRI	117.1	100.4	31,824	27,279	111.0	0.857	1.000	100.4	3.68	0.962
South Sudan	SSD	32.4	17.3	3,296	1,757	69.0	1.593	2.989	51.6	9.83	1.624
Timor-Leste	TLS	2.3	1.1	2,085	948	58.8	0.455	1.000	5.7	1.11	0.502
Turkmenistan	TKM	58.4	29.2	11,295	5,650	64.7	1.426	2.850	83.3	5.17	1.462
Uzbekistan	UZB	161.0	56.5	5,489	1,926	45.4	601.998	1,715.430	96,949.6	29.34	630.993

Note: PPP = purchasing power parity; XR = market exchange rate; LCU = local currency unit; n.a. = not applicable.

a. World totals used to calculate price level indexes (PLIs) in this table include nonparticipating economies.

b. PPPs and market exchange rates are rounded to three decimal places for presentation in this table.

c. GDP and individual consumption expenditure by households PPPs for Argentina and Guyana are based on a time-series estimation approach.

Table E.8 Gross domestic product: Comparison of revised ICP 2011 results with original ICP 2011 results

GROSS DOMESTIC PRODUCT		PPP (US$ = 1.000)			Expenditure in local currency unit (billions)		
Economy		Revised 2011	Original 2011	Percentage difference	Revised 2011	Original 2011	Percentage difference
(00)		(01)	(02)[a]	(03)[b]	(04)	(05)[a]	(06)[c]
East Asia and Pacific							
Australia	AUS	1.511	1.511	0.0	1,467.6	1,444.5	1.6
Brunei Darussalam	BRN	0.705	0.717	−1.7	23.3	21.0	11.0
Cambodia	KHM	1,371.235	1,347.115	1.8	52,068.7	52,068.7	0.0
China	CHN	3.524	3.506	0.5	48,930.1	47,310.4	3.4
Fiji	FJI	0.949	1.042	−9.0	7.3	6.7	8.9
Hong Kong SAR, China	HKG	5.233	5.462	−4.2	1,934.4	1,936.1	−0.1
Indonesia	IDN	3,512.754	3,606.566	−2.6	7,831,726.0	7,422,781.2	5.5
Japan	JPN	107.454	107.454	0.0	491,408.5	470,623.2	4.4
Korea, Rep.	KOR	854.586	854.586	0.0	1,388,937.3	1,235,160.5	12.4
Lao PDR	LAO	2,666.535	2,467.753	8.1	71,543.6	64,727.1	10.5
Macao SAR, China	MAC	4.440	4.589	−3.2	294.3	295.0	−0.2
Malaysia	MYS	1.466	1.459	0.5	911.7	884.5	3.1
Mongolia	MNG	533.527	537.127	−0.7	13,173.8	12,546.8	5.0
Myanmar	MMR	261.784	234.974	11.4	43,900.0	45,128.0	−2.7
New Zealand	NZL	1.486	1.486	0.0	211.3	204.5	3.3
Philippines	PHL	18.098	17.854	1.4	9,708.3	9,706.3	0.0
Singapore	SGP	0.847	0.891	−5.0	351.4	334.1	5.2
Taiwan, China	TWN	15.151	15.112	0.3	14,312.2	13,709.1	4.4
Thailand	THA	12.387	12.370	0.1	11,306.9	11,120.5	1.7
Vietnam	VNM	6,915.335	6,709.192	3.1	2,779,880.2	2,779,880.2	0.0
Total (20)	**EAB**	**n.a.**	**n.a.**	**0.2**	**n.a.**	**n.a.**	**4.1**
Europe and Central Asia							
Albania	ALB	43.858	45.452	−3.5	1,300.6	1,282.3	1.4
Armenia	ARM	163.650	187.095	−12.5	3,777.9	3,777.9	0.0
Austria	AUT	0.831	0.830	0.2	310.1	299.2	3.6
Azerbaijan	AZE	0.384	0.360	6.4	52.1	52.1	0.0
Belarus[e]	BLR	0.196	0.189	3.8	30.7	29.7	3.4
Belgium	BEL	0.832	0.839	−0.8	376.0	369.3	1.8
Bosnia and Herzegovina	BIH	0.718	0.724	−0.8	26.2	26.8	−2.0
Bulgaria	BGR	0.701	0.660	6.2	80.7	75.3	7.1
Croatia	HRV	3.753	3.802	−1.3	333.2	330.2	0.9
Cyprus	CYP	0.699	0.673	3.8	19.8	17.9	10.8
Czech Republic	CZE	13.345	13.468	−0.9	4,033.8	3,823.4	5.5
Denmark	DNK	7.466	7.689	−2.9	1,846.9	1,791.8	3.1
Estonia	EST	0.512	0.524	−2.4	16.8	16.2	3.8
Finland	FIN	0.898	0.907	−1.0	198.0	188.7	4.9
France	FRA	0.841	0.845	−0.4	2,058.4	2,001.4	2.8
Georgia	GEO	0.811	0.859	−5.5	25.5	24.3	4.7
Germany	DEU	0.789	0.779	1.3	2,693.6	2,609.9	3.2
Greece	GRC	0.713	0.693	2.9	207.0	208.5	−0.7

(continued)

Table E.8 *(Continued)*

GROSS DOMESTIC PRODUCT Economy		PPP (US$ = 1.000) Revised 2011	Original 2011	Percentage difference	Expenditure in local currency unit (billions) Revised 2011	Original 2011	Percentage difference
(00)		(01)	(02)[a]	(03)[b]	(04)	(05)[a]	(06)[c]
Hungary	HUN	124.272	123.650	0.5	28,370.8	27,635.4	2.7
Iceland	ISL	135.152	133.563	1.2	1,757.7	1,628.7	7.9
Ireland	IRL	0.832	0.827	0.5	170.8	162.6	5.1
Italy	ITA	0.759	0.768	−1.3	1,648.8	1,580.4	4.3
Kazakhstan	KAZ	82.090	80.171	2.4	28,243.1	27,571.9	2.4
Kyrgyz Republic	KGZ	15.728	17.757	−11.4	286.0	286.0	0.0
Latvia[e]	LVA	0.499	0.491	1.4	20.2	20.2	0.0
Lithuania[e]	LTU	0.452	0.454	−0.4	31.2	31.0	0.9
Luxembourg	LUX	0.905	0.906	−0.1	43.2	41.7	3.4
Moldova	MDA	4.996	5.535	−9.7	98.8	82.3	19.9
Montenegro	MNE	0.364	0.369	−1.4	3.3	3.2	1.0
Netherlands	NLD	0.836	0.832	0.5	650.4	599.0	8.6
North Macedonia	MKD	19.290	18.680	3.3	464.2	459.8	1.0
Norway	NOR	9.083	8.973	1.2	2,792.7	2,750.0	1.6
Poland	POL	1.801	1.823	−1.2	1,566.8	1,528.1	2.5
Portugal	PRT	0.623	0.628	−0.7	176.1	171.1	2.9
Romania	ROU	1.550	1.615	−4.0	559.2	556.7	0.5
Russian Federation	RUS	18.444	17.346	6.3	60,282.5	55,799.6	8.0
Serbia	SRB	36.324	37.288	−2.6	3,612.3	3,208.6	12.6
Slovakia	SVK	0.506	0.508	−0.4	71.2	69.0	3.2
Slovak Republc	SVN	0.624	0.625	−0.2	37.1	36.1	2.5
Spain	ESP	0.714	0.705	1.2	1,061.5	1,046.3	1.4
Sweden	SWE	8.844	8.820	0.3	3,719.1	3,480.5	6.9
Switzerland	CHE	1.397	1.441	−3.0	621.3	585.1	6.2
Tajikistan	TJK	1.565	1.740	−10.0	30.1	30.1	0.0
Turkey	TUR	0.966	0.987	−2.1	1,394.5	1,297.7	7.5
Ukraine	UKR	3.192	3.434	−7.0	1,349.2	1,302.1	3.6
United Kingdom	GBR	0.706	0.698	1.1	1,659.8	1,536.9	8.0
Total (46)	**ECB**	**n.a.**	**n.a.**	**0.6**	**n.a.**	**n.a.**	**4.5**
Latin America and the Caribbean							
Anguilla	AIA	1.990	2.077	−4.2	0.8	0.8	−0.8
Antigua and Barbuda	ATG	1.691	1.731	−2.3	3.1	3.0	1.3
Aruba	ABW	1.303	1.260	3.4	4.6	4.6	0.0
Bahamas, The	BHS	0.899	0.949	−5.3	10.1	7.9	27.9
Barbados	BRB	2.019	2.017	0.1	9.3	8.7	6.8
Belize	BLZ	1.151	1.150	0.1	3.0	3.0	−0.4
Bolivia	BOL	2.981	2.946	1.2	166.2	166.1	0.1
Bonaire[d]	BON	...	...	...	...	...	...
Brazil	BRA	1.473	1.471	0.1	4,376.4	4,143.0	5.6
Cayman Islands	CYM	0.942	0.959	−1.8	3.5	2.7	29.4
Chile	CHL	348.017	348.017	0.0	122,006.1	121,492.7	0.4
Colombia	COL	1,168.243	1,161.910	0.5	618,117.7	621,615.0	−0.6

Table E.8 *(Continued)*

GROSS DOMESTIC PRODUCT Economy		PPP (US$ = 1.000)			Expenditure in local currency unit (billions)		
		Revised 2011	Original 2011	Percentage difference	Revised 2011	Original 2011	Percentage difference
(00)		(01)	(02)[a]	(03)[b]	(04)	(05)[a]	(06)[c]
Costa Rica	CRI	344.546	346.738	–0.6	21,370.7	20,748.0	3.0
Curaçao	CUW	1.325	1.292	2.5	5.4	5.4	0.0
Dominica	DMA	1.870	1.861	0.5	1.4	1.3	2.0
Dominican Republic	DOM	18.976	19.449	–2.4	2,210.2	2,119.3	4.3
Ecuador	ECU	0.528	0.526	0.3	79.3	79.8	–0.6
El Salvador	SLV	0.505	0.503	0.4	20.3	23.1	–12.3
Grenada	GRD	1.771	1.783	–0.7	2.1	2.1	0.0
Guatemala	GTM	3.637	3.626	0.3	371.0	371.3	–0.1
Haiti	HTI	18.495	19.108	–3.2	316.4	297.7	6.3
Honduras	HND	10.057	9.915	1.4	335.0	335.0	0.0
Jamaica	JAM	53.805	54.122	–0.6	1,240.7	1,241.8	–0.1
Mexico	MEX	7.673	7.673	0.0	14,665.6	14,536.9	0.9
Montserrat	MSR	1.709	1.943	–12.0	0.2	0.2	8.9
Nicaragua	NIC	8.710	8.919	–2.3	219.2	216.1	1.4
Panama	PAN	0.553	0.547	1.0	34.7	31.3	10.7
Paraguay	PRY	2,126.670	2,227.340	–4.5	141,315.8	105,203.2	34.3
Peru	PER	1.543	1.521	1.4	473.0	497.8	–5.0
Sint Maarten	SXM	1.346	1.379	–2.4	1.7	1.7	–1.5
St. Kitts and Nevis	KNA	1.961	1.803	8.8	2.2	2.0	12.3
St. Lucia	LCA	1.830	1.844	–0.8	3.9	3.3	19.3
St. Vincent and the Grenadines	VCT	1.636	1.691	–3.3	1.9	1.8	3.1
Suriname	SUR	1.866	1.826	2.2	14.4	14.3	1.1
Trinidad and Tobago	TTO	3.950	3.938	0.3	165.3	150.9	9.5
Turks and Caicos Islands	TCA	1.028	1.100	–6.5	0.7	0.7	0.0
Uruguay	URY	15.274	15.282	–0.1	926.4	896.8	3.3
Venezuela, RB	VEN	2.681	2.713	–1.2	1,357.5	1,357.5	0.0
Virgin Islands, British	VGB	1.028	1.076	–4.5	0.9	0.9	0.0
Total (39)	**LCB**	**n.a.**	**n.a.**	**0.5**	**n.a.**	**n.a.**	**3.1**
Middle East and North Africa							
Algeria	DZA	29.476	30.502	–3.4	14,589.0	14,481.0	0.7
Bahrain	BHR	0.179	0.211	–15.2	10.8	10.9	–0.9
Djibouti	DJI	93.572	94.003	–0.5	392.7	205.3	91.3
Egypt, Arab Rep.	EGY	1.675	1.625	3.1	1,516.4	1,371.1	10.6
Iran, Islamic Rep.	IRN	4,758.870	4,657.463	2.2	7,542,036.5	6,121,004.0	23.2
Iraq	IRQ	523.340	516.521	1.3	191,652.9	191,652.9	0.0
Israel	ISR	3.945	3.945	0.0	935.6	923.9	1.3
Jordan	JOR	0.291	0.293	–0.8	20.5	20.5	0.1
Kuwait	KWT	0.172	0.172	–0.2	42.5	44.3	–4.1
Malta	MLT	0.574	0.558	2.8	6.8	6.6	3.1
Morocco	MAR	3.672	3.677	–0.1	820.1	802.6	2.2
Oman	OMN	0.185	0.192	–3.5	26.1	26.9	–3.0
Qatar	QAT	2.153	2.419	–11.0	610.7	624.2	–2.2

(continued)

Table E.8 *(Continued)*

GROSS DOMESTIC PRODUCT Economy		PPP (US$ = 1.000) Revised 2011	Original 2011	Percentage difference	Expenditure in local currency unit (billions) Revised 2011	Original 2011	Percentage difference
(00)		(01)	(02)[a]	(03)[b]	(04)	(05)[a]	(06)[c]
Saudi Arabia	SAU	1.586	1.837	−13.6	2,517.1	2,510.6	0.3
Tunisia	TUN	0.596	0.592	0.7	64.5	64.7	−0.4
United Arab Emirates	ARE	2.127	2.544	−16.4	1,287.8	1,280.2	0.6
West Bank and Gaza	PSE	2.405	2.189	9.9	37.4	35.0	7.1
Yemen, Rep.	YEM	81.477	75.818	7.5	6,714.9	6,714.9	0.0
Total (18)	**MEB**	**n.a.**	**n.a.**	**−5.3**	**n.a.**	**n.a.**	**5.1**
North America							
Bermuda	BMU	1.397	1.564	−10.7	5.6	5.6	0.9
Canada	CAN	1.240	1.243	−0.2	1,774.1	1,759.7	0.8
United States	USA	1.000	1.000	0.0	15,542.6	15,533.8	0.1
Total (3)	**NAB**	**n.a.**	**n.a.**	**0.0**	**n.a.**	**n.a.**	**0.1**
South Asia							
Bangladesh	BGD	23.410	23.145	1.1	9,855.2	9,702.9	1.6
Bhutan	BTN	16.397	16.856	−2.7	85.0	85.9	−1.2
India	IND	15.550	15.109	2.9	85,256.2	86,993.1	−2.0
Maldives	MDV	7.862	8.527	−7.8	40.5	31.6	28.3
Nepal	NPL	25.255	24.628	2.5	1,440.8	1,449.5	−0.6
Pakistan	PAK	24.962	24.346	2.5	19,161.5	19,187.9	−0.1
Sri Lanka	LKA	39.289	38.654	1.6	7,219.1	6,542.7	10.3
Total (7)	**SAB**	**n.a.**	**n.a.**	**2.7**	**n.a.**	**n.a.**	**−1.3**
Sub-Saharan Africa							
Angola	AGO	64.606	68.315	−5.4	10,597.0	9,767.6	8.5
Benin	BEN	220.434	214.035	3.0	3,684.9	3,439.8	7.1
Botswana	BWA	3.655	3.764	−2.9	105.0	102.5	2.4
Burkina Faso	BFA	223.116	213.659	4.4	5,092.6	4,868.5	4.6
Burundi	BDI	461.509	425.768	8.4	2,837.7	2,599.9	9.1
Cabo Verde	CPV	49.695	48.592	2.3	147.9	149.0	−0.7
Cameroon	CMR	238.707	227.212	5.1	13,843.1	12,545.7	10.3
Central African Republic	CAF	256.761	255.862	0.4	1,148.9	1,029.7	11.6
Chad	TCD	258.131	250.443	3.1	5,891.4	5,725.3	2.9
Comoros	COM	218.978	207.584	5.5	361.6	95.4	278.9
Congo, Dem. Rep.	COD	532.063	521.870	2.0	31,230.5	23,146.1	34.9
Congo, Rep.	COG	309.251	289.299	6.9	7,765.6	6,982.5	11.2
Côte d'Ivoire	CIV	236.911	228.228	3.8	12,112.7	12,275.5	−1.3
Equatorial Guinea	GNQ	297.509	294.572	1.0	10,064.6	8,367.3	20.3
Eswatini	SWZ	4.052	3.900	3.9	34.3	29.7	15.4
Ethiopia	ETH	5.036	4.919	2.4	768.6	506.1	51.9
Gabon	GAB	325.733	318.156	2.4	9,088.2	8,046.1	13.0
Gambia, The	GMB	10.142	9.939	2.0	40.3	26.6	51.5
Ghana	GHA	0.697	0.699	−0.3	59.8	59.8	0.0
Guinea	GIN	2,485.901	2,518.386	−1.3	45,176.5	33,128.3	36.4
Guinea-Bissau	GNB	230.392	220.085	4.7	518.3	464.7	11.5

Table E.8 *(Continued)*

GROSS DOMESTIC PRODUCT Economy		PPP (US$ = 1.000) Revised 2011	Original 2011	Percentage difference	Expenditure in local currency unit (billions) Revised 2011	Original 2011	Percentage difference
(00)		(01)	(02)[a]	(03)[b]	(04)	(05)[a]	(06)[c]
Kenya	KEN	35.396	34.298	3.2	3,727.4	3,048.9	22.3
Lesotho	LSO	4.081	3.923	4.0	19.5	18.3	6.4
Liberia[e]	LBR	39.424	37.345	5.6	111.2	82.9	34.1
Madagascar	MDG	694.863	673.730	3.1	23,404.5	20,276.4	15.4
Malawi	MWI	78.769	76.259	3.3	1,253.2	1,140.8	9.8
Mali	MLI	216.090	210.193	2.8	6,123.9	5,024.5	21.9
Mauritania	MRT	119.682	115.855	3.3	1,452.4	1,309.4	10.9
Mauritius	MUS	15.853	15.941	−0.5	398.7	323.0	23.5
Mozambique	MOZ	16.894	16.030	5.4	414.6	364.7	13.7
Namibia	NAM	4.732	4.663	1.5	90.4	90.6	−0.2
Niger	NER	226.128	221.087	2.3	3,024.3	3,025.5	0.0
Nigeria	NGA	78.777	74.378	5.9	62,931.7	38,017.0	65.5
Rwanda	RWA	276.649	260.751	6.1	3,854.3	3,814.4	1.0
São Tomé and Príncipe[e]	STP	7.431	8.527	−12.9	4.5	4.4	2.1
Senegal	SEN	241.276	236.287	2.1	8,743.8	6,766.8	29.2
Seychelles	SYC	6.884	6.690	2.9	13.1	13.1	0.0
Sierra Leone	SLE	1,620.575	1,553.139	4.3	12,797.6	12,754.9	0.3
South Africa	ZAF	4.777	4.774	0.1	3,053.2	2,917.5	4.6
Sudan	SDN	1.231	1.224	0.6	182.2	186.6	−2.4
Tanzania	TZA	546.073	522.483	4.5	55,469.0	37,533.0	47.8
Togo	TGO	228.625	215.060	6.3	1,837.1	1,739.2	5.6
Uganda	UGA	856.168	833.540	2.7	73,174.3	45,944.1	59.3
Zambia[e]	ZMB	2.446	2.378	2.9	123.8	101.1	22.4
Zimbabwe	ZWE	0.520	0.504	3.2	12.1	8.9	36.5
Total (45)	**SSB**	**n.a.**	**n.a.**	**0.4**	**n.a.**	**n.a.**	**22.0**
World (178)	**WLD**	**n.a.**	**n.a.**	**−0.1**	**n.a.**	**n.a.**	**3.4**

Note: PPP = purchasing power parity; LCU = local currency unit; n.a. = not applicable; ... = data suppressed due to unavailability.

a. Data source: ICP 2011.

b. Totals for the regions and the world show average percentage change of PPPs, weighted by the size of expenditures converted by PPPs.

c. Totals for the regions and the world show average percentage change of expenditures, weighted by the size of expenditures converted by market exchange rate.

d. Bonaire's results are provided only for individual consumption expenditure by households.

e. Original ICP 2011 data were released in a different currency unit and were converted to the same currency as ICP 2017 in this table for comparison purposes.

Table E.9 Individual consumption expenditure by households: Comparison of revised ICP 2011 results with original ICP 2011 results

INDIVIDUAL CONSUMPTION EXPENDITURE BY HOUSEHOLDS Economy		PPP (US$ = 1.000) Revised 2011	Original 2011	Percentage difference	Expenditure in local currency units (billions) Revised 2011	Original 2011	Percentage difference
(00)		(01)	(02)[a]	(03)[b]	(04)	(05)[a]	(06)[c]
East Asia and Pacific							
Australia	AUS	1.526	1.527	−0.1	797.7	774.5	3.0
Brunei Darussalam	BRN	0.832	0.853	−2.4	3.0	4.1	−27.2
Cambodia	KHM	1,493.254	1,527.558	−2.2	41,431.0	41,431.0	0.0
China	CHN	3.698	3.696	0.0	16,811.1	16,254.7	3.4
Fiji	FJI	1.016	1.217	−16.5	5.0	4.8	4.8
Hong Kong SAR, China	HKG	5.647	5.753	−1.9	1,224.4	1,224.8	0.0
Indonesia	IDN	3,892.218	4,091.939	−4.9	4,340,605.4	4,053,363.6	7.1
Japan	JPN	115.178	116.103	−0.8	286,254.9	284,784.3	0.5
Korea, Rep.	KOR	903.294	912.021	−1.0	711,118.8	655,386.6	8.5
Lao PDR	LAO	3,124.075	2,914.847	7.2	43,566.6	36,750.1	18.5
Macao SAR, China	MAC	5.164	5.462	−5.5	62.0	60.5	2.4
Malaysia	MYS	1.586	1.586	0.0	437.3	418.3	4.6
Mongolia	MNG	580.638	590.330	−1.6	6,782.7	6,885.5	−1.5
Myanmar	MMR	278.394	275.828	0.9	26,528.1	28,760.0	−7.8
New Zealand	NZL	1.579	1.589	−0.7	123.2	122.2	0.8
Philippines	PHL	18.772	18.873	−0.5	7,132.6	7,132.6	0.0
Singapore	SGP	1.092	1.171	−6.7	128.5	130.2	−1.3
Taiwan, China	TWN	16.136	15.995	0.9	7,799.0	8,235.4	−5.3
Thailand	THA	12.759	12.844	−0.7	6,117.6	6,076.1	0.7
Vietnam	VNM	7,528.385	7,624.973	−1.3	1,638,345.5	1,638,345.5	0.0
Total (20)	**EAB**	**n.a.**	**n.a.**	**−1.1**	**n.a.**	**n.a.**	**2.2**
Europe and Central Asia							
Albania	ALB	54.653	58.168	−6.0	1,018.4	1,029.6	−1.1
Armenia	ARM	165.629	183.780	−9.9	3,161.0	3,161.0	0.0
Austria	AUT	0.851	0.848	0.5	165.5	163.9	1.0
Azerbaijan	AZE	0.323	0.329	−1.8	19.4	19.4	0.0
Belarus[d]	BLR	0.185	0.183	1.1	15.0	14.2	5.6
Belgium	BEL	0.878	0.879	−0.1	193.8	194.7	−0.5
Bosnia and Herzegovina	BIH	0.854	0.867	−1.4	22.1	22.2	−0.4
Bulgaria	BGR	0.794	0.765	3.8	50.2	47.0	6.8
Croatia	HRV	4.225	4.359	−3.1	204.0	197.8	3.1
Cyprus	CYP	0.759	0.712	6.6	13.0	12.1	7.6
Czech Republic	CZE	14.439	14.901	−3.1	1,978.7	1,935.2	2.2
Denmark	DNK	8.338	8.524	−2.2	884.9	872.4	1.4
Estonia	EST	0.580	0.609	−4.7	8.4	8.2	2.8
Finland	FIN	0.973	0.980	−0.7	105.3	105.2	0.1
France	FRA	0.880	0.880	0.0	1,131.7	1,155.3	−2.0
Georgia	GEO	0.835	0.842	−0.8	21.0	18.0	16.3
Germany	DEU	0.827	0.818	1.1	1,464.9	1,498.4	−2.2
Greece	GRC	0.768	0.758	1.3	144.7	155.6	−7.0

Table E.9 *(Continued)*

INDIVIDUAL CONSUMPTION EXPENDITURE BY HOUSEHOLDS Economy		PPP (US$ = 1.000) Revised 2011	Original 2011	Percentage difference	Expenditure in local currency units (billions) Revised 2011	Original 2011	Percentage difference
(00)		(01)	(02)[a]	(03)[b]	(04)	(05)[a]	(06)[c]
Hungary	HUN	137.179	137.883	–0.5	14,973.8	14,725.9	1.7
Iceland	ISL	140.808	138.895	1.4	916.7	844.8	8.5
Ireland	IRL	0.958	0.952	0.6	79.3	78.2	1.4
Italy	ITA	0.815	0.825	–1.3	1,007.7	967.9	4.1
Kazakhstan	KAZ	79.222	83.612	–5.3	11,916.1	11,791.9	1.1
Kyrgyz Republic	KGZ	16.296	17.538	–7.1	238.5	238.5	0.0
Latvia[d]	LVA	0.567	0.571	–0.7	12.4	12.6	–1.3
Lithuania[d]	LTU	0.511	0.517	–1.3	19.5	19.4	0.2
Luxembourg	LUX	0.980	0.989	–1.0	13.5	13.3	2.0
Moldova	MDA	5.410	5.451	–0.8	91.8	79.5	15.4
Montenegro	MNE	0.441	0.449	–1.8	2.7	2.7	–0.2
Netherlands	NLD	0.875	0.869	0.7	296.8	271.8	9.2
North Macedonia	MKD	23.608	22.936	2.9	343.1	345.3	–0.6
Norway	NOR	9.816	9.797	0.2	1,125.2	1,131.7	–0.6
Poland	POL	1.895	1.936	–2.2	963.1	933.9	3.1
Portugal	PRT	0.690	0.704	–1.9	116.0	113.0	2.7
Romania	ROU	1.810	2.001	–9.5	354.8	353.5	0.4
Russian Federation	RUS	18.655	16.769	11.2	30,164.8	27,398.6	10.1
Serbia	SRB	43.629	45.370	–3.8	2,728.5	2,469.4	10.5
Slovak Republic	SVK	0.556	0.567	–2.0	39.7	39.7	–0.1
Slovenia	SVN	0.677	0.681	–0.6	20.9	20.8	0.8
Spain	ESP	0.788	0.777	1.5	622.1	612.8	1.5
Sweden	SWE	9.021	9.105	–0.9	1,727.8	1,671.2	3.4
Switzerland	CHE	1.540	1.613	–4.6	330.2	335.4	–1.6
Tajikistan	TJK	1.786	1.883	–5.1	32.1	32.1	0.0
Turkey	TUR	1.135	1.164	–2.5	880.9	923.8	–4.7
Ukraine	UKR	3.182	3.311	–3.9	907.2	875.6	3.6
United Kingdom	GBR	0.776	0.756	2.6	1,066.9	992.3	7.5
Total (46)	**ECB**	**n.a.**	**n.a.**	**0.6**	**n.a.**	**n.a.**	**1.9**
Latin America and the Caribbean							
Anguilla	AIA	2.502	2.591	–3.4	0.7	0.7	0.1
Antigua and Barbuda	ATG	2.202	2.200	0.1	1.9	1.8	4.8
Aruba	ABW	1.638	1.653	–0.9	2.9	2.9	0.0
Bahamas, The	BHS	1.125	1.151	–2.2	6.3	5.6	12.8
Barbados	BRB	2.393	2.413	–0.8	6.7	7.1	–6.3
Belize	BLZ	1.174	1.183	–0.7	2.1	2.1	–2.2
Bolivia	BOL	2.891	2.906	–0.5	100.9	101.3	–0.4
Bonaire	BON	0.918	0.919	0.0	0.2	0.2	0.0
Brazil	BRA	1.651	1.659	–0.5	2,637.8	2,499.5	5.5
Cayman Islands	CYM	1.130	1.136	–0.5	1.9	1.9	–0.6
Chile	CHL	386.817	391.644	–1.2	73,356.8	74,405.2	–1.4
Colombia	COL	1,210.993	1,196.955	1.2	403,766.7	381,323.0	5.9

(continued)

Table E.9 *(Continued)*

INDIVIDUAL CONSUMPTION EXPENDITURE BY HOUSEHOLDS		PPP (US$ = 1.000)			Expenditure in local currency units (billions)		
Economy		Revised 2011	Original 2011	Percentage difference	Revised 2011	Original 2011	Percentage difference
(00)		(01)	(02)[a]	(03)[b]	(04)	(05)[a]	(06)[c]
Costa Rica	CRI	349.407	343.786	1.6	14,250.9	13,555.4	5.1
Curaçao	CUW	1.462	1.429	2.3	3.7	3.8	−2.7
Dominica	DMA	2.035	2.069	−1.6	1.2	1.1	6.1
Dominican Republic	DOM	20.765	20.741	0.1	1,685.7	1,833.7	−8.1
Ecuador	ECU	0.548	0.547	0.1	48.7	48.7	−0.1
El Salvador	SLV	0.537	0.531	1.2	17.8	21.6	−17.5
Grenada	GRD	2.106	2.092	0.7	1.9	1.9	0.6
Guatemala	GTM	3.892	3.873	0.5	316.5	316.6	0.0
Haiti	HTI	20.833	20.706	0.6	333.9	334.0	0.0
Honduras	HND	10.264	10.080	1.8	260.1	260.1	0.0
Jamaica	JAM	62.876	63.354	−0.8	1,065.1	1,063.5	0.1
Mexico	MEX	8.886	8.940	−0.6	9,504.3	9,640.8	−1.4
Montserrat	MSR	2.225	2.336	−4.7	0.1	0.1	−0.1
Nicaragua	NIC	9.251	9.160	1.0	169.2	168.1	0.7
Panama	PAN	0.553	0.553	0.0	19.3	18.9	2.1
Paraguay	PRY	2,242.096	2,309.430	−2.9	89,930.6	73,739.5	22.0
Peru	PER	1.579	1.569	0.7	285.8	296.0	−3.4
Sint Maarten	SXM	1.630	1.678	−2.8	1.1	1.0	9.4
St. Kitts and Nevis	KNA	2.233	2.221	0.6	1.5	1.3	12.3
St. Lucia	LCA	2.084	2.139	−2.6	3.1	2.4	27.7
St. Vincent and the Grenadines	VCT	1.998	2.039	−2.0	1.5	1.5	2.3
Suriname	SUR	1.900	1.885	0.8	5.2	5.3	−2.7
Trinidad and Tobago	TTO	4.520	4.619	−2.1	76.0	69.1	10.0
Turks and Caicos Islands	TCA	1.260	1.282	−1.8	0.3	0.3	9.8
Uruguay	URY	16.608	16.424	1.1	618.4	609.2	1.5
Venezuela, RB	VEN	2.944	2.915	1.0	748.8	748.8	0.0
Virgin Islands, British	VGB	1.204	1.250	−3.7	0.3	0.3	0.0
Total (39)	**LCB**	**n.a.**	**n.a.**	**0.4**	**n.a.**	**n.a.**	**2.4**
Middle East and North Africa							
Algeria	DZA	31.518	31.772	−0.8	4,571.9	4,552.7	0.4
Bahrain	BHR	0.179	0.215	−17.1	4.2	4.2	0.0
Djibouti	DJI	100.624	101.481	−0.8	234.6	136.2	72.3
Egypt, Arab Rep.	EGY	1.715	1.803	−4.9	1,200.6	1,036.1	15.9
Iran, Islamic Rep.	IRN	5,323.442	5,001.363	6.4	4,065,433.1	2,557,440.1	59.0
Iraq	IRQ	477.559	573.418	−16.7	76,260.3	76,260.3	0.0
Israel	ISR	4.254	4.270	−0.4	529.9	529.2	0.1
Jordan	JOR	0.325	0.319	1.8	16.6	14.6	13.6
Kuwait	KWT	0.178	0.180	−1.3	10.3	10.3	−0.1
Malta	MLT	0.633	0.629	0.7	4.0	4.0	−0.5
Morocco	MAR	4.125	4.193	−1.6	488.3	472.9	3.3
Oman	OMN	0.205	0.200	2.4	8.1	8.1	−0.3
Qatar	QAT	2.992	2.640	13.3	81.9	79.7	2.8

Table E.9 *(Continued)*

INDIVIDUAL CONSUMPTION EXPENDITURE BY HOUSEHOLDS Economy		PPP (US$ = 1.000) Revised 2011	Original 2011	Percentage difference	Expenditure in local currency units (billions) Revised 2011	Original 2011	Percentage difference
(00)		(01)	(02)[a]	(03)[b]	(04)	(05)[a]	(06)[c]
Saudi Arabia	SAU	1.525	1.785	−14.6	687.9	681.8	0.9
Tunisia	TUN	0.697	0.697	0.0	42.8	42.5	0.7
United Arab Emirates	ARE	2.397	2.718	−11.8	494.1	661.8	−25.3
West Bank and Gaza	PSE	2.438	2.523	−3.4	34.5	33.7	2.1
Yemen, Rep.	YEM	76.766	82.094	−6.5	4,573.2	4,573.2	0.0
Total (18)	**MEB**	**n.a.**	**n.a.**	**−6.4**	**n.a.**	**n.a.**	**10.3**
North America							
Bermuda	BMU	1.826	1.900	−3.9	3.1	3.7	−16.8
Canada	CAN	1.282	1.285	−0.2	991.8	980.1	1.2
United States	USA	1.000	1.000	0.0	10,641.1	10,711.8	−0.7
Total (3)	**NAB**	**n.a.**	**n.a.**	**0.0**	**n.a.**	**n.a.**	**−0.5**
South Asia							
Bangladesh	BGD	24.732	24.849	−0.5	7,291.8	7,154.3	1.9
Bhutan	BTN	17.044	16.963	0.5	35.3	37.6	−6.0
India	IND	15.283	14.975	2.1	47,565.7	48,648.2	−2.2
Maldives	MDV	8.810	10.676	−17.5	13.4	10.2	31.3
Nepal	NPL	25.743	25.759	−0.1	1,101.6	1,114.6	−1.2
Pakistan	PAK	25.496	25.414	0.3	15,679.6	15,712.2	−0.2
Sri Lanka	LKA	42.988	42.219	1.8	5,143.7	4,568.4	12.6
Total (7)	**SAB**	**n.a.**	**n.a.**	**1.7**	**n.a.**	**n.a.**	**−1.2**
Sub-Saharan Africa							
Angola	AGO	80.932	73.833	9.6	3,664.5	4,957.5	−26.1
Benin	BEN	225.412	224.917	0.2	2,665.7	2,631.4	1.3
Botswana	BWA	4.262	4.438	−4.0	48.6	48.6	0.0
Burkina Faso	BFA	223.073	222.242	0.4	3,037.2	3,169.0	−4.2
Burundi	BDI	496.117	487.327	1.8	2,573.5	2,244.6	14.7
Cabo Verde	CPV	48.057	47.565	1.0	92.8	93.0	−0.2
Cameroon	CMR	242.678	230.375	5.3	9,526.5	9,519.1	0.1
Central African Republic	CAF	265.661	267.869	−0.8	965.9	925.6	4.4
Chad	TCD	250.251	251.296	−0.4	3,328.6	3,811.5	−12.7
Comoros	COM	235.604	220.572	6.8	337.1	93.6	260.1
Congo, Dem. Rep.	COD	546.732	537.732	1.7	18,298.8	14,337.3	27.6
Congo, Rep.	COG	303.724	296.500	2.4	2,009.9	1,552.7	29.4
Côte d'Ivoire	CIV	243.461	235.688	3.3	8,298.4	8,294.8	0.0
Equatorial Guinea	GNQ	328.091	321.354	2.1	2,048.8	1,004.4	104.0
Eswatini	SWZ	4.112	4.049	1.6	27.3	25.1	8.6
Ethiopia	ETH	5.575	5.439	2.5	540.5	397.6	35.9
Gabon	GAB	359.344	359.219	0.0	2,523.1	2,813.0	−10.3
Gambia, The	GMB	10.912	10.826	0.8	34.6	20.2	71.4
Ghana	GHA	0.779	0.788	−1.2	48.3	36.8	31.4
Guinea	GIN	2,599.891	2,572.343	1.1	36,919.5	18,424.7	100.4
Guinea-Bissau	GNB	258.323	248.236	4.1	432.9	311.0	39.2

(continued)

Table E.9 *(Continued)*

INDIVIDUAL CONSUMPTION EXPENDITURE BY HOUSEHOLDS Economy		PPP (US$ = 1.000) Revised 2011	Original 2011	Percentage difference	Expenditure in local currency units (billions) Revised 2011	Original 2011	Percentage difference
(00)		(01)	(02)[a]	(03)[b]	(04)	(05)[a]	(06)[c]
Kenya	KEN	35.621	35.430	0.5	2,997.9	2,304.9	30.1
Lesotho	LSO	3.926	3.864	1.6	18.0	17.8	1.4
Liberia[d]	LBR	43.207	41.005	5.4	88.0	93.3	–5.7
Madagascar	MDG	700.228	704.913	–0.7	17,322.0	17,830.7	–2.9
Malawi	MWI	78.703	78.017	0.9	1,053.6	1,062.3	–0.8
Mali	MLI	224.357	221.868	1.1	4,394.5	3,180.8	38.2
Mauritania	MRT	112.849	112.807	0.0	650.8	678.7	–4.1
Mauritius	MUS	18.555	18.285	1.5	239.5	237.2	1.0
Mozambique	MOZ	15.826	15.527	1.9	289.6	290.6	–0.4
Namibia	NAM	5.244	5.131	2.2	59.8	55.9	7.0
Niger	NER	230.417	228.753	0.7	2,192.8	2,342.3	–6.4
Nigeria	NGA	83.583	79.531	5.1	40,904.9	22,840.8	79.1
Rwanda	RWA	251.305	246.834	1.8	3,038.1	3,181.4	–4.5
São Tomé and Príncipe[d]	STP	10.487	10.195	2.9	3.7	4.9	–23.9
Senegal	SEN	249.278	246.107	1.3	6,756.4	5,312.1	27.2
Seychelles	SYC	8.233	7.895	4.3	7.0	6.9	1.3
Sierra Leone	SLE	1,825.528	1,767.190	3.3	12,295.1	11,163.1	10.1
South Africa	ZAF	5.031	5.068	–0.7	1,831.8	1,731.7	5.8
Sudan	SDN	1.465	1.486	–1.4	127.2	129.9	–2.1
Tanzania	TZA	588.785	585.520	0.6	39,059.9	24,815.7	57.4
Togo	TGO	236.587	232.215	1.9	1,422.5	1,474.2	–3.5
Uganda	UGA	944.256	946.890	–0.3	54,266.8	37,758.9	43.7
Zambia[d]	ZMB	2.611	2.505	4.2	63.6	52.5	21.2
Zimbabwe	ZWE	0.535	0.536	–0.1	9.8	7.8	26.4
Total (45)	**SSB**	**n.a.**	**n.a.**	**–0.4**	**n.a.**	**n.a.**	**22.4**
World (178)	**WLD**	**n.a.**	**n.a.**	**–0.7**	**n.a.**	**n.a.**	**1.9**

Note: PPP = purchasing power parity; LCU = local currency unit; n.a. = not applicable; ... = data suppressed due to unavailability.

a. Data source: ICP 2011.

b. Totals for the regions and the world show average percentage change of PPPs, weighted by the size of expenditures converted by PPPs.

c. Totals for the regions and the world show average percentage change of expenditures, weighted by the size of expenditures converted by market exchange rate.

d. Original ICP 2011 data were released in a different currency unit and were converted to the same currency as ICP 2017 in this table for comparison purposes.

APPENDIX F

Comparison of ICP 2017 results with World Development Indicators data

This appendix compares the purchasing power parities (PPPs) produced by the International Comparison Program (ICP) 2017 cycle with PPP estimates published in the World Bank's World Development Indicators (WDI) database based on extrapolations from the original 2011 ICP PPPs. It also compares the expenditures used in ICP 2017 with WDI 2017 expenditures.

These extrapolated 2017 PPPs were published in the WDI database released in February 2020, prior to the release of the ICP 2017 results. To extrapolate to a given year, the WDI takes the difference between the rate of inflation observed in each economy over each period from or to 2011 and the rate of inflation in the United States (the base economy for PPPs) over the same period and applies it to the 2011 PPP to estimate the economy's PPP for a given year. Extrapolation for the gross domestic product (GDP) PPPs uses the change in the GDP implicit deflator, while extrapolation for the individual consumption expenditure by households PPPs uses the change in the consumer price index. For the economies participating in the Statistical Office of the European Union (Eurostat)–Organisation for Economic Co-operation and Development (OECD) PPP Programme, WDI obtained annual PPP estimates by Eurostat-OECD, and thus the data for those economies are not based on the WDI extrapolation method.

Tables F.1 and F.2 compare ICP 2017 PPPs with WDI's 2017 PPPs extrapolated from ICP 2011 PPPs, and compare ICP 2017 expenditures in current local currency units with WDI 2017 expenditures, for the following headings:

- Table F.1 Gross domestic product (GDP)
- Table F.2 Individual consumption expenditure by households.

The comparison tables cover the following indicators for each heading:

- *Column (00).* Name of the economy and its International Organization for Standardization (ISO) code
- *Column (01).* ICP 2017 PPPs with the US dollar equal to 1
- *Column (02).* WDI 2017 PPPs (as of February 2020) with the US dollar equal to 1, extrapolated from ICP 2011 PPPs
- *Column (03).* Percentage difference between columns (01) and (02)
- *Column (04).* ICP 2017 expenditures in local currency units
- *Column (05).* WDI 2017 expenditures in local currency units (as of February 2020)
- *Column (06).* Percentage difference between columns (04) and (05).

Table F.1 Gross domestic product (GDP): Comparison of ICP 2017 results with data in World Development Indicators

GROSS DOMESTIC PRODUCT		PPP (US$ = 1.000)			Expenditure in local currency unit (billions)		
Economy		2017	2017 (WDI extrapolation)	Percentage difference	2017	2017 (WDI)	Percentage difference
(00)		(01)	(02)[a, b]	(03)[c]	(04)	(05)[a, b]	(06)[c]
East Asia and Pacific							
Australia[g]	AUS	1.466	1.444	1.5	1,808.6	1,763.6	2.6
Brunei Darussalam	BRN	0.647	0.494	30.8	16.7	16.7	0.0
Cambodia	KHM	1,428.354	1,395.909	2.3	89,830.5	89,830.5	0.0
China	CHN	4.184	3.528	18.6	82,075.4	82,075.4	0.0
Fiji	FJI	0.939	1.221	−23.1	11.1	11.1	0.0
Hong Kong SAR, China	HKG	6.011	5.837	3.0	2,662.8	2,662.8	0.0
Indonesia	IDN	4,695.659	4,181.150	12.3	13,587,212.6	13,587,212.6	0.0
Japan	JPN	105.379	102.470	2.8	545,121.9	545,121.9	0.0
Korea, Rep.	KOR	871.696	866.009	0.7	1,835,698.2	1,730,398.5	6.1
Lao PDR	LAO	2,789.109	2,915.892	−4.3	140,697.7	140,749.0	0.0
Malaysia	MYS	1.655	1.469	12.7	1,353.4	1,371.6	−1.3
Mongolia	MNG	791.436	699.879	13.1	27,876.3	27,876.3	0.0
Myanmar[g]	MMR	366.713	274.511	33.6	85,980.8	90,450.9	−4.9
New Zealand	NZL	1.453	1.471	−1.2	282.7	285.1	−0.8
Philippines	PHL	19.385	18.021	7.6	15,807.6	15,807.6	0.0
Singapore	SGP	0.886	0.862	2.7	467.3	467.3	0.0
Taiwan, China	TWN	15.730	...	...	17,501.2	...	...
Thailand	THA	12.845	12.461	3.1	15,452.0	15,452.0	0.0
Vietnam	VNM	7,395.338	7,716.431	−4.2	5,005,975.5	5,005,975.0	0.0
Total (19)	**EAB**	**n.a.**	**n.a.**	**n.a.**	**n.a.**	**n.a.**	**n.a.**
Europe and Central Asia							
Albania	ALB	41.231	41.753	−1.2	1,551.3	1,551.3	0.0
Armenia	ARM	155.971	196.407	−20.6	5,564.5	5,564.5	0.0
Austria	AUT	0.770	0.780	−1.3	370.3	370.3	0.0
Azerbaijan	AZE	0.505	0.407	24.1	70.3	70.3	0.0
Belarus	BLR	0.609	0.589	3.5	105.7	105.7	0.0
Belgium	BEL	0.773	0.781	−1.1	446.4	446.4	0.0
Bosnia and Herzegovina	BIH	0.676	0.682	−0.8	31.4	31.4	0.0
Bulgaria	BGR	0.674	0.682	−1.1	102.3	101.0	1.3
Croatia	HRV	3.327	3.371	−1.3	366.4	366.4	0.0
Cyprus	CYP	0.615	0.632	−2.7	20.0	20.0	0.0
Czech Republic	CZE	12.378	12.531	−1.2	5,047.3	5,047.3	0.0
Denmark	DNK	6.852	6.951	−1.4	2,175.1	2,175.1	0.0
Estonia	EST	0.534	0.536	−0.4	23.8	23.8	0.0
Finland	FIN	0.863	0.877	−1.5	225.8	225.8	0.0
France	FRA	0.766	0.776	−1.2	2,295.1	2,295.1	0.0
Georgia	GEO	0.805	0.977	−17.6	40.8	40.8	0.0
Germany	DEU	0.741	0.754	−1.8	3,245.0	3,245.0	0.0
Greece	GRC	0.576	0.586	−1.8	180.2	180.2	0.0
Hungary	HUN	134.363	136.069	−1.3	38,835.2	38,835.2	0.0

Table F.1 *(Continued)*

GROSS DOMESTIC PRODUCT Economy		PPP (US$ = 1.000) 2017	2017 (WDI extrapolation)	Percentage difference	Expenditure in local currency unit (billions) 2017	2017 (WDI)	Percentage difference
(00)		(01)	(02)[a, b]	(03)[c]	(04)	(05)[a, b]	(06)[c]
Iceland	ISL	137.122	137.725	−0.4	2,613.0	2,616.4	−0.1
Ireland	IRL	0.791	0.797	−0.7	297.1	297.1	0.0
Italy	ITA	0.687	0.696	−1.4	1,736.6	1,736.6	0.0
Kazakhstan	KAZ	121.253	113.802	6.5	54,378.9	54,378.9	0.0
Kyrgyz Republic	KGZ	16.959	22.923	−26.0	530.5	530.5	0.0
Latvia	LVA	0.484	0.491	−1.3	26.8	26.8	0.0
Lithuania	LTU	0.442	0.449	−1.5	42.3	42.3	0.0
Luxembourg	LUX	0.844	0.861	−2.0	56.8	56.8	0.0
Moldova	MDA	5.572	7.348	−24.2	178.9	178.9	0.0
Montenegro	MNE	0.351	0.357	−1.8	4.3	4.3	0.0
Netherlands	NLD	0.778	0.791	−1.5	738.1	738.1	0.0
North Macedonia	MKD	19.043	19.358	−1.6	618.1	616.6	0.2
Norway	NOR	9.922	10.070	−1.5	3,295.4	3,295.4	0.0
Poland	POL	1.737	1.750	−0.7	1,989.4	1,988.7	0.0
Portugal	PRT	0.575	0.580	−0.9	195.9	195.9	0.0
Romania	ROU	1.604	1.645	−2.4	857.9	857.9	0.0
Russian Federation	RUS	24.050	24.342	−1.2	92,101.3	92,101.3	0.0
Serbia	SRB	40.795	41.207	−1.0	4,754.4	4,754.4	0.0
Slovak Republic	SVK	0.503	0.482	4.3	84.5	84.5	0.0
Slovenia	SVN	0.568	0.576	−1.4	43.0	43.0	0.0
Spain	ESP	0.630	0.641	−1.7	1,161.9	1,161.9	0.0
Sweden	SWE	8.719	8.856	−1.5	4,621.0	4,621.0	0.0
Switzerland	CHE	1.180	1.193	−1.1	669.5	669.5	0.0
Tajikistan	TJK	2.231	2.142	4.1	61.2	61.2	0.0
Turkey	TUR	1.373	1.374	−0.1	3,110.7	3,110.7	0.0
Ukraine	UKR	5.916	8.079	−26.8	2,983.9	2,983.9	0.0
United Kingdom	GBR	0.682	0.691	−1.3	2,071.7	2,071.7	0.0
Total (46)	**ECB**	**n.a.**	**n.a.**	**n.a.**	**n.a.**	**n.a.**	**n.a.**
Latin America and the Caribbean							
Anguilla	AIA	2.295	...	...	0.8	...	...
Antigua and Barbuda	ATG	2.094	1.685	24.2	4.1	4.0	3.3
Argentina[e]	ARG	10.257	11.595	−11.5	10,644.8	10,644.8	0.0
Aruba	ABW	1.351	1.163	16.2	5.5	4.8	...
Bahamas, The	BHS	0.901	1.022	−11.8	12.2	12.2	0.0
Barbados	BRB	2.203	1.912	15.2	9.4	10.0	−5.6
Belize	BLZ	1.375	1.170	17.5	3.7	3.7	1.4
Bolivia	BOL	2.749	3.096	−11.2	259.2	259.2	0.0
Bonaire[d]	BON	...	...	...	...	...	...
Brazil	BRA	2.182	2.013	8.4	6,583.3	6,553.8	0.4
Cayman Islands	CYM	0.974	0.931	4.6	4.3	4.3	0.0
Chile	CHL	411.264	402.359	2.2	180,211.3	180,211.3	0.0
Colombia	COL	1,314.787	1,297.107	1.4	920,194.0	920,194.0	0.0

(continued)

Table F.1 *(Continued)*

GROSS DOMESTIC PRODUCT Economy		PPP (US$ = 1.000) 2017	2017 (WDI extrapolation)	Percentage difference	Expenditure in local currency unit (billions) 2017	2017 (WDI)	Percentage difference
(00)		(01)	(02)[a, b]	(03)[c]	(04)	(05)[a, b]	(06)[c]
Costa Rica	CRI	350.817	392.887	−10.7	34,386.7	33,014.8	4.2
Curaçao	CUW	1.367	1.261	8.4	5.6	5.6	0.0
Dominica	DMA	1.738	1.844	−5.8	1.4	1.4	0.0
Dominican Republic	DOM	21.613	22.094	−2.2	3,802.7	3,802.7	0.0
Ecuador	ECU	0.535	0.540	−1.0	104.3	104.3	0.0
El Salvador	SLV	0.463	0.489	−5.5	24.9	24.9	0.0
Grenada	GRD	1.690	1.873	−9.7	3.0	3.0	0.0
Guyana[e]	GUY	105.353	116.305	−9.4	734.2	734.2	0.0
Haiti[g]	HTI	28.498	27.637	3.1	587.5	552.0	6.4
Honduras	HND	10.362	11.703	−11.5	543.4	542.6	0.2
Jamaica	JAM	67.582	72.281	−6.5	1,898.8	1,894.7	0.2
Mexico	MEX	8.871	9.041	−1.9	21,911.9	21,911.9	0.0
Montserrat	MSR	1.790	...	...	0.2	...	...
Nicaragua	NIC	10.807	11.457	−5.7	416.0	416.0	0.0
Panama	PAN	0.497	0.620	−19.7	62.3	62.3	0.0
Paraguay	PRY	2,534.377	2,460.652	3.0	219,188.4	219,188.4	0.0
Peru	PER	1.749	1.589	10.1	688.0	688.0	0.0
Sint Maarten	SXM	1.387	1.408	−1.5	1.8	1.8	...
St. Kitts and Nevis	KNA	2.040	1.791	13.9	2.5	2.7	−5.5
St. Lucia	LCA	1.996	2.007	−0.6	4.6	4.9	−6.2
St. Vincent and the Grenadines	VCT	1.590	1.653	−3.8	2.3	2.1	6.8
Suriname	SUR	2.578	2.685	−4.0	24.0	23.0	4.6
Trinidad and Tobago	TTO	4.162	3.499	19.0	154.4	152.4	1.4
Turks and Caicos Islands	TCA	1.018	1.086	−6.3	1.0	1.0	2.0
Uruguay	URY	23.294	21.856	6.6	1,707.1	1,707.1	0.0
Virgin Islands, British	VGB	1.069	...	...	1.3	...	...
Total (39)	**LCB**	**n.a.**	**n.a.**	**n.a.**	**n.a.**	**n.a.**	**n.a.**
Middle East and North Africa							
Algeria	DZA	38.856	29.513	31.7	18,591.7	18,575.8	0.1
Bahrain	BHR	0.187	0.187	0.0	13.3	13.3	−0.4
Djibouti	DJI	106.023	...	...	520.2	491.7	5.8
Egypt, Arab Rep.[g]	EGY	3.267	3.064	6.6	4,127.1	3,470.0	18.9
Iran, Islamic Rep.[g]	IRN	13,061.295	9,035.962	44.5	16,954,811.5	15,316,530.0	10.7
Iraq	IRQ	560.761	351.198	59.7	206,530.1	231,049.1	−10.6
Israel	ISR	3.745	3.755	−0.3	1,271.6	1,271.6	0.0
Jordan	JOR	0.300	0.320	−6.1	29.0	28.9	0.4
Kuwait	KWT	0.177	0.126	41.0	35.5	36.6	−3.2
Malta	MLT	0.578	0.582	−0.7	11.3	11.3	0.0
Morocco	MAR	4.023	3.560	13.0	1,063.4	1,063.4	0.0
Oman	OMN	0.200	0.140	42.9	27.1	27.1	0.0
Qatar	QAT	2.346	1.790	31.1	607.6	607.6	0.0
Saudi Arabia	SAU	1.649	1.453	13.5	2,582.2	2,582.2	0.0

Table F.1 *(Continued)*

GROSS DOMESTIC PRODUCT Economy		PPP (US$ = 1.000) 2017	2017 (WDI extrapolation)	Percentage difference	Expenditure in local currency unit (billions) 2017	2017 (WDI)	Percentage difference
(00)		(01)	(02)[a, b]	(03)[c]	(04)	(05)[a, b]	(06)[c]
Tunisia	TUN	0.794	0.699	13.6	96.6	96.3	0.3
United Arab Emirates	ARE	2.222	1.999	11.1	1,387.1	1,387.1	0.0
West Bank and Gaza	PSE	2.036	2.289	−11.1	52.2	...	...
Total (17)	**MEB**	**n.a.**	**n.a.**	**n.a.**	**n.a.**	**n.a.**	**n.a.**
North America							
Bermuda	BMU	1.366	...	...	6.2	...	...
Canada	CAN	1.205	1.252	−3.8	2,142.0	2,137.5	0.2
United States	USA	1.000	1.000	0.0	19,519.4	19,485.4	0.2
Total (3)	**NAB**	**n.a.**	**n.a.**	**n.a.**	**n.a.**	**n.a.**	**n.a.**
South Asia							
Bangladesh[g]	BGD	29.738	30.948	−3.9	21,131.5	19,758.2	7.0
Bhutan	BTN	19.208	21.705	−11.5	164.6	159.6	3.2
India[g]	IND	20.648	17.813	15.9	166,225.6	170,950.0	−2.8
Maldives	MDV	8.161	10.108	−19.3	74.9	72.9	2.7
Nepal[g]	NPL	31.235	33.672	−7.2	2,611.2	2,674.5	−2.4
Pakistan[g]	PAK	33.589	29.292	14.7	33,270.4	31,922.3	4.2
Sri Lanka	LKA	49.390	48.587	1.7	13,317.3	13,418.3	−0.8
Total (7)	**SAB**	**n.a.**	**n.a.**	**n.a.**	**n.a.**	**n.a.**	**n.a.**
Sub-Saharan Africa							
Angola	AGO	92.952	102.181	−9.0	20,365.4	20,262.3	0.5
Benin	BEN	216.774	211.563	2.5	5,450.9	5,382.5	1.3
Botswana	BWA	4.734	4.592	3.1	180.3	180.1	0.1
Burkina Faso	BFA	208.757	200.349	4.2	7,263.3	7,177.4	1.2
Burundi	BDI	654.896	686.482	−4.6	5,562.4	5,485.1	1.4
Cabo Verde	CPV	48.477	45.967	5.5	172.4	173.1	−0.4
Cameroon	CMR	232.801	227.035	2.5	20,277.0	20,328.4	−0.3
Central African Republic	CAF	286.829	318.818	−10.0	1,235.2	1,203.3	2.7
Chad	TCD	243.655	200.411	21.6	5,936.3	5,806.8	2.2
Comoros	COM	190.126	205.015	−7.3	479.8	469.2	2.3
Congo, Dem. Rep.	COD	645.391	769.674	−16.1	72,390.1	55,676.1	30.0
Congo, Rep.	COG	297.674	176.521	68.6	7,827.5	5,065.0	54.5
Côte d'Ivoire	CIV	253.746	231.131	9.8	22,150.8	22,150.8	0.0
Equatorial Guinea	GNQ	248.934	231.055	7.7	7,153.6	7,153.6	0.0
Eswatini	SWZ	6.206	5.143	20.7	60.8	59.3	2.6
Ethiopia[g]	ETH	8.521	9.078	−6.1	1,466.0	1,832.6	−20.0
Gabon	GAB	279.766	236.363	18.4	7,296.5	8,668.9	−15.8
Gambia, The	GMB	15.286	12.854	18.9	66.7	70.1	−4.9
Ghana	GHA	1.764	1.977	−10.8	256.7	256.7	0.0
Guinea	GIN	3,216.035	3,281.563	−2.0	110,474.2	93,833.9	17.7
Guinea-Bissau	GNB	222.749	247.213	−9.9	784.0	784.0	0.0
Kenya	KEN	40.185	49.773	−19.3	8,196.7	8,144.4	0.6
Lesotho	LSO	5.506	5.247	4.9	34.5	34.4	0.4

(continued)

Table F.1 *(Continued)*

GROSS DOMESTIC PRODUCT Economy		PPP (US$ = 1.000) 2017	2017 (WDI extrapolation)	Percentage difference	Expenditure in local currency unit (billions) 2017	2017 (WDI)	Percentage difference
(00)		(01)	(02)[a, b]	(03)[c]	(04)	(05)[a, b]	(06)[c]
Liberia[f]	LBR	51.957	60.884	−14.7	311.4	370.3	−15.9
Madagascar	MDG	1,013.435	885.412	14.5	40,445.3	41,058.8	−1.5
Malawi	MWI	251.074	205.176	22.4	4,635.6	4,603.1	0.7
Mali	MLI	214.509	217.068	−1.2	8,931.3	8,928.0	0.0
Mauritania[f]	MRT	111.258	101.928	9.2	1,760.7	1,756.3	0.2
Mauritius	MUS	16.882	16.172	4.4	534.8	457.2	17.0
Mozambique	MOZ	22.856	20.683	10.5	804.5	840.5	−4.3
Namibia	NAM	7.021	6.769	3.7	179.0	180.6	−0.9
Niger	NER	258.460	216.014	19.6	4,727.1	4,726.4	0.0
Nigeria	NGA	115.978	102.243	13.4	102,593.5	114,899.2	−10.7
Rwanda	RWA	325.126	305.275	6.5	7,025.7	7,600.4	−7.6
São Tomé and Príncipe	STP	10.055	11.885	−15.4	6.8	8.2	−16.9
Senegal	SEN	246.787	223.796	10.3	12,158.0	12,271.5	−0.9
Seychelles	SYC	7.969	7.365	8.2	21.4	20.5	4.1
Sierra Leone	SLE	2,244.995	2,387.706	−6.0	27,610.8	27,614.7	0.0
South Africa	ZAF	6.427	6.075	5.8	4,715.2	4,653.6	1.3
Sudan	SDN	4.619	4.129	11.9	815.9	822.4	−0.8
Tanzania	TZA	885.083	724.689	22.1	110,651.1	118,844.1	−6.9
Togo	TGO	239.722	214.920	11.5	2,689.4	2,798.7	−3.9
Uganda[g]	UGA	1,270.608	1,145.394	10.9	116,251.5	91,718.3	26.7
Zambia	ZMB	4.193	3.572	17.4	237.0	246.3	−3.8
Zimbabwe	ZWE	0.511	0.567	−9.8	18.6	22.8	−18.3
Total (45)	**SSB**	**n.a.**	**n.a.**	**n.a.**	**n.a.**	**n.a.**	**n.a.**
World (176)	**WLD**	**n.a.**	**n.a.**	**n.a.**	**n.a.**	**n.a.**	**n.a.**

Note: PPP = purchasing power parity; WDI = World Development Indicators; n.a. = not applicable; ... = data suppressed due to unavailability.

a. Data source: WDI (World Bank) [data as of February 2020].

b. WDI obtains PPP data from the Eurostat-Organisation for the Economic Co-operation and Development (OECD) PPP programme directly. Hence, data for economies participating in that programme are not based on the WDI extrapolation method.

c. Totals for the regions and the world are not provided due to differences in the availability of data for economies between the ICP and WDI.

d. Bonaire's results are provided only for individual consumption expenditure by households.

e. Argentina and Guyana did not participate in ICP 2011. WDI's extrapolation is based on imputed PPPs for 2011.

f. WDI data were released in a different currency unit and were converted to the same currency unit as ICP 2017 in this table for comparison purposes.

g. For WDI the economy reports national accounts data for its fiscal year.

Table F.2 Individual consumption expenditure by households: Comparison of ICP 2017 results with data in World Development Indicators

INDIVIDUAL CONSUMPTION EXPENDITURE BY HOUSEHOLS Economy		PPP (US$ = 1.000) 2017	2017 (WDI extrapolation)	Percentage difference	Expenditure in local currency unit (billions) 2017	2017 (WDI)	Percentage difference
(00)		(01)	(02)[a, b]	(03)[c]	(04)	(05)[a, b]	(06)[c]
East Asia and Pacific							
Australia[f]	AUS	1.529	1.538	−0.6	1,020.8	1,000.2	2.1
Brunei Darussalam	BRN	0.697	0.769	−9.4	3.4	3.4	0.0
Cambodia	KHM	1,488.798	1,655.539	−10.1	72,193.8	65,927.9	9.5
China	CHN	4.147	3.827	8.4	30,964.1	31,796.4	−2.6
Fiji	FJI	0.986	1.300	−24.1	7.5	...	...
Hong Kong SAR, China	HKG	6.242	6.408	−2.6	1,785.5	1,785.5	0.0
Indonesia	IDN	5,089.686	5,067.604	0.4	7,788,168.4	7,788,168.4	0.0
Japan	JPN	113.023	108.572	4.1	302,490.5	302,490.5	0.0
Korea, Rep.	KOR	974.206	962.003	1.3	872,791.4	832,234.7	4.9
Lao PDR	LAO	3,133.812	3,204.507	−2.2	76,447.5	...	...
Malaysia	MYS	1.727	1.687	2.4	748.9	759.7	−1.4
Mongolia	MNG	873.542	853.487	2.3	14,922.2	14,922.2	0.0
Myanmar[f]	MMR	389.843	348.525	11.9	48,963.3	...	...
New Zealand	NZL	1.573	1.605	−2.0	162.7	164.1	−0.9
Philippines	PHL	19.393	19.882	−2.5	11,614.1	11,614.1	0.0
Singapore	SGP	1.080	1.156	−6.6	167.8	166.5	0.8
Taiwan, China	TWN	16.598	...	...	9,265.1	...	...
Thailand	THA	13.287	12.636	5.2	7,378.1	7,529.4	−2.0
Vietnam	VNM	7,807.612	9,186.042	−15.0	2,957,279.8	3,405,750.0	−13.2
Total (19)	**EAB**	**n.a.**	**n.a.**	**n.a.**	**n.a.**	**n.a.**	**n.a.**
Europe and Central Asia							
Albania	ALB	50.357	51.847	−2.9	1,237.1	1,237.1	0.0
Armenia	ARM	167.312	194.589	−14.0	4,453.3	4,453.3	0.0
Austria	AUT	0.831	0.840	−1.1	193.3	193.3	0.0
Azerbaijan	AZE	0.487	0.419	16.2	40.5	40.5	0.0
Belarus	BLR	0.617	0.504	22.4	57.6	57.6	0.0
Belgium	BEL	0.845	0.857	−1.4	229.5	229.5	0.0
Bosnia and Herzegovina	BIH	0.782	0.789	−0.9	24.7	24.5	0.8
Bulgaria	BGR	0.735	0.752	−2.2	61.5	61.5	0.0
Croatia	HRV	3.815	3.902	−2.2	212.8	212.8	0.0
Cyprus	CYP	0.668	0.694	−3.7	13.1	13.1	0.0
Czech Republic	CZE	13.651	13.892	−1.7	2,393.2	2,393.2	0.0
Denmark	DNK	7.891	7.990	−1.2	1,012.1	1,012.1	0.0
Estonia	EST	0.596	0.604	−1.3	12.0	12.0	0.0
Finland	FIN	0.933	0.947	−1.4	120.2	120.2	0.0
France	FRA	0.835	0.847	−1.3	1,239.5	1,239.5	0.0
Georgia	GEO	0.925	0.884	4.6	28.5	28.5	0.0
Germany	DEU	0.787	0.805	−2.2	1,697.0	1,697.0	0.0
Greece	GRC	0.646	0.661	−2.2	123.8	123.8	0.0
Hungary	HUN	147.377	150.736	−2.2	19,232.5	19,232.5	0.0

(continued)

Table F.2 *(Continued)*

INDIVIDUAL CONSUMPTION EXPENDITURE BY HOUSEHOLS Economy		PPP (US$ = 1.000)			Expenditure in local currency unit (billions)		
		2017	2017 (WDI extrapolation)	Percentage difference	2017	2017 (WDI)	Percentage difference
(00)		(01)	(02)[a, b]	(03)[c]	(04)	(05)[a, b]	(06)[c]
Iceland	ISL	155.648	154.881	0.5	1,317.5	1,317.5	0.0
Ireland	IRL	0.971	0.984	−1.3	95.6	95.6	0.0
Italy	ITA	0.767	0.780	−1.7	1,046.8	1,046.8	0.0
Kazakhstan	KAZ	125.263	119.764	4.6	28,596.7	27,584.3	3.7
Kyrgyz Republic	KGZ	19.373	20.917	−7.4	435.4	435.4	0.0
Latvia	LVA	0.554	0.564	−1.9	16.0	16.0	0.0
Lithuania	LTU	0.488	0.500	−2.4	26.3	26.3	0.0
Luxembourg	LUX	0.966	0.974	−0.8	16.9	16.9	0.0
Moldova	MDA	6.383	7.147	−10.7	153.2	153.2	0.0
Montenegro	MNE	0.419	0.431	−2.9	3.2	3.2	0.0
Netherlands	NLD	0.850	0.867	−2.0	327.3	327.3	0.0
North Macedonia	MKD	22.167	22.861	−3.0	412.0	406.3	1.4
Norway	NOR	10.743	10.784	−0.4	1,471.7	1,471.7	0.0
Poland	POL	1.842	1.866	−1.2	1,160.2	1,160.2	0.0
Portugal	PRT	0.657	0.665	−1.1	126.5	126.5	0.0
Romania	ROU	1.805	1.864	−3.2	540.4	540.4	0.0
Russian Federation	RUS	25.218	26.183	−3.7	48,516.2	48,516.3	0.0
Serbia	SRB	47.992	48.851	−1.8	3,367.5	3,367.5	0.0
Slovak Republic	SVK	0.579	0.540	7.3	47.2	47.2	0.0
Slovenia	SVN	0.639	0.648	−1.4	22.6	22.6	0.0
Spain	ESP	0.703	0.715	−1.7	678.2	678.2	0.0
Sweden	SWE	9.223	9.353	−1.4	2,077.2	2,077.2	0.0
Switzerland	CHE	1.359	1.375	−1.2	359.6	359.6	0.0
Tajikistan	TJK	2.595	...	...	47.5	50.4	−5.8
Turkey	TUR	1.647	1.681	−2.0	1,836.2	1,836.2	0.0
Ukraine	UKR	7.006	6.623	5.8	2,001.5	2,001.5	0.0
United Kingdom	GBR	0.780	0.789	−1.2	1,346.9	1,346.9	0.0
Total (46)	**ECB**	**n.a.**	**n.a.**	**n.a.**	**n.a.**	**n.a.**	**n.a.**
Latin America and the Caribbean							
Anguilla	AIA	2.595	...	...	0.6	...	...
Antigua and Barbuda	ATG	2.468	2.194	12.5	1.7	...	...
Argentina[e]	ARG	10.808	...	...	7,295.3	7,059.0	3.3
Aruba	ABW	1.480	1.483	−0.2	3.3	2.7	...
Bahamas, The	BHS	1.103	1.135	−2.8	7.7	8.2	−6.1
Barbados	BRB	2.371	2.514	−5.7	6.7	6.3	7.5
Belize	BLZ	1.477	...	...	2.6	2.6	1.2
Bolivia	BOL	2.612	3.456	−24.4	175.3	175.3	0.0
Bonaire	BON	0.812	...	...	0.2	...	...
Brazil	BRA	2.327	2.222	4.7	4,245.1	4,193.9	1.2
Cayman Islands	CYM	1.150	...	...	2.3	...	...
Chile	CHL	478.996	461.246	3.8	113,565.7	113,565.7	0.0
Colombia	COL	1,419.374	1,400.684	1.3	630,818.0	630,818.0	0.0

Table F.2 *(Continued)*

INDIVIDUAL CONSUMPTION EXPENDITURE BY HOUSEHOLS Economy		PPP (US$ = 1.000) 2017	2017 (WDI extrapolation)	Percentage difference	Expenditure in local currency unit (billions) 2017	2017 (WDI)	Percentage difference
(00)		(01)	(02)[a, b]	(03)[c]	(04)	(05)[a, b]	(06)[c]
Costa Rica	CRI	372.669	371.372	0.3	22,319.8	21,079.1	5.9
Curaçao	CUW	1.483	1.407	5.4	3.5	...	...
Dominica	DMA	1.876	1.931	−2.8	1.2	...	...
Dominican Republic	DOM	24.391	22.552	8.2	2,641.0	2,641.0	0.0
Ecuador	ECU	0.575	0.596	−3.7	62.5	62.5	0.0
El Salvador	SLV	0.515	0.509	1.1	20.8	20.8	0.0
Grenada	GRD	1.800	1.985	−9.4	2.7	...	...
Guyana[d]	GUY	115.626	130.906	−11.7	469.7	498.5	−5.8
Haiti[f]	HTI	31.103	28.483	9.2	561.6	526.9	6.6
Honduras	HND	10.839	11.962	−9.4	417.4	416.0	0.3
Jamaica	JAM	70.392	81.506	−13.6	1,490.0	1,483.5	0.4
Mexico	MEX	9.861	10.172	−3.0	14,301.2	14,301.2	0.0
Montserrat	MSR	2.118	...	...	0.1	...	...
Nicaragua	NIC	11.528	11.445	0.7	294.9	294.9	0.0
Panama	PAN	0.508	0.583	−12.9	31.3	31.3	0.0
Paraguay	PRY	2,539.985	2,635.282	−3.6	140,077.6	140,077.6	0.0
Peru	PER	1.894	1.747	8.4	441.3	441.3	0.0
Sint Maarten	SXM	1.488	1.717	−13.3	1.3	...	...
St. Kitts and Nevis	KNA	2.547	2.034	25.2	1.7	...	...
St. Lucia	LCA	2.079	2.064	0.8	1.6	...	...
St. Vincent and the Grenadines	VCT	1.807	1.944	−7.0	1.7	1.7	0.0
Suriname	SUR	2.934	3.879	−24.3	12.4	...	...
Trinidad and Tobago	TTO	4.212	5.659	−25.6	98.1	...	...
Turks and Caicos Islands	TCA	1.246	...	...	0.4	...	...
Uruguay	URY	24.854	24.373	2.0	1,147.3	1,147.3	0.0
Virgin Islands, British	VGB	1.096	...	...	0.5	...	...
Total (39)	**LCB**	**n.a.**	**n.a.**	**n.a.**	**n.a.**	**n.a.**	**n.a.**
Middle East and North Africa							
Algeria	DZA	38.210	39.717	−3.8	8,071.9	8,034.2	0.5
Bahrain	BHR	0.204	0.229	−10.7	5.6	5.6	0.0
Djibouti	DJI	104.737	103.006	1.7	334.8	306.3	9.3
Egypt, Arab Rep.[f]	EGY	3.408	3.474	−1.9	3,623.5	3,057.9	18.5
Iran, Islamic Rep.[f]	IRN	13,944.904	12,800.390	8.9	8,104,686.7	7,294,401.0	11.1
Iraq	IRQ	555.391	593.934	−6.5	114,058.4	136,377.3	−16.4
Israel	ISR	4.207	4.237	−0.7	695.0	695.0	0.0
Jordan	JOR	0.329	0.336	−1.9	24.9	25.0	−0.4
Kuwait	KWT	0.187	0.197	−4.7	15.0	15.9	−5.7
Malta	MLT	0.628	0.633	−0.8	5.0	5.0	0.0
Morocco	MAR	4.291	4.148	3.4	615.9	615.9	0.0
Oman	OMN	0.212	0.198	6.7	11.3	11.9	−5.1
Qatar	QAT	2.893	2.776	4.2	149.4	149.5	−0.1
Saudi Arabia	SAU	1.724	1.827	−5.7	1,070.8	1,063.6	0.7

(continued)

Table F.2 *(Continued)*

INDIVIDUAL CONSUMPTION EXPENDITURE BY HOUSEHOLS Economy		PPP (US$ = 1.000) 2017	2017 (WDI extrapolation)	Percentage difference	Expenditure in local currency unit (billions) 2017	2017 (WDI)	Percentage difference
(00)		(01)	(02)[a, b]	(03)[c]	(04)	(05)[a, b]	(06)[c]
Tunisia	TUN	0.742	0.840	−11.6	69.6	69.5	0.1
United Arab Emirates	ARE	2.835	2.802	1.2	513.4	513.4	0.0
West Bank and Gaza	PSE	2.066	2.497	−17.3	45.9	...	...
Total (17)	**MEB**	n.a.	n.a.	n.a.	n.a.	n.a.	n.a.
North America							
Bermuda	BMU	1.576	...	...	3.3	...	...
Canada	CAN	1.287	1.340	−4.0	1,221.6	1,240.4	−1.5
United States	USA	1.000	1.000	0.0	13,312.1	13,312.1	0.0
Total (3)	**NAB**	**n.a.**	**n.a.**	**n.a.**	**n.a.**	**n.a.**	**n.a.**
South Asia							
Bangladesh[f]	BGD	29.514	33.004	−10.6	14,751.8	13,568.9	8.7
Bhutan	BTN	20.474	22.657	−9.6	86.9	86.0	1.0
India[f]	IND	19.469	20.177	−3.5	97,813.2	100,831.2	−3.0
Maldives	MDV	9.794	12.013	−18.5	29.8	...	...
Nepal[f]	NPL	30.513	...	...	2,002.9	2,015.4	−0.6
Pakistan[f]	PAK	33.251	32.698	1.7	27,355.3	26,148.6	4.6
Sri Lanka	LKA	55.501	53.400	3.9	8,262.7	9,382.5	−11.9
Total (7)	**SAB**	**n.a.**	**n.a.**	**n.a.**	**n.a.**	**n.a.**	**n.a.**
Sub-Saharan Africa							
Angola	AGO	107.270	167.629	−36.0	11,898.4	11,586.5	2.7
Benin	BEN	219.476	218.948	0.2	3,964.4	4,096.3	−3.2
Botswana	BWA	5.009	5.300	−5.5	88.8	88.7	0.1
Burkina Faso	BFA	199.741	214.588	−6.9	4,173.7	3,952.8	5.6
Burundi	BDI	654.422	769.945	−15.0	4,781.8	4,184.8	14.3
Cabo Verde	CPV	47.612	45.095	5.6	109.2	112.9	−3.3
Cameroon	CMR	236.912	235.321	0.7	14,169.0	14,220.3	−0.4
Central African Republic	CAF	306.808	...	...	1,113.8	998.2	11.6
Chad	TCD	237.656	...	...	4,484.7	4,654.9	−3.7
Comoros	COM	213.518	...	...	434.7	432.2	0.6
Congo, Dem. Rep.	COD	630.606	...	...	46,322.8	40,491.2	14.4
Congo, Rep.	COG	285.969	322.619	−11.4	3,022.7	1,870.9	61.6
Côte d'Ivoire	CIV	247.134	231.827	6.6	14,550.6	14,550.6	0.0
Equatorial Guinea	GNQ	304.287	340.998	−10.8	3,326.9	3,326.9	0.0
Eswatini	SWZ	6.118	5.432	12.6	46.3	38.8	19.2
Ethiopia[f]	ETH	8.496	9.330	−8.9	1,058.1	1,219.4	−13.2
Gabon	GAB	319.160	371.897	−14.2	3,211.8	3,464.9	−7.3
Gambia, The	GMB	15.114	14.352	5.3	60.0	61.4	−2.3
Ghana	GHA	1.751	1.545	13.4	186.6	180.2	3.6
Guinea	GIN	3,213.984	4,254.455	−24.5	82,442.7	69,410.5	18.8
Guinea-Bissau	GNB	232.199	242.123	−4.1	654.9	682.1	−4.0
Kenya	KEN	41.635	49.167	−15.3	6,196.5	6,645.2	−6.8
Lesotho	LSO	5.244	4.819	8.8	28.0	27.1	3.0

Table F.2 *(Continued)*

INDIVIDUAL CONSUMPTION EXPENDITURE BY HOUSEHOLS Economy		PPP (US$ = 1.000) 2017	2017 (WDI extrapolation)	Percentage difference	Expenditure in local currency unit (billions) 2017	2017 (WDI)	Percentage difference
(00)		(01)	(02)[a, b]	(03)[c]	(04)	(05)[a, b]	(06)[c]
Liberia[e]	LBR	47.996	97.738	−14.7	192.1	510.0	−15.9
Madagascar	MDG	962.960	949.475	1.4	28,886.2	29,401.9	−1.8
Malawi	MWI	241.931	226.339	6.9	3,989.0	3,687.7	8.2
Mali	MLI	205.273	217.986	−5.8	6,986.4	6,666.1	4.8
Mauritania[e]	MRT	124.453	125.430	−0.8	988.6	1,035.1	−4.5
Mauritius	MUS	18.009	19.747	−8.8	349.2	342.1	2.0
Mozambique	MOZ	21.988	...	...	572.3	544.0	5.2
Namibia	NAM	6.898	6.548	5.4	124.4	124.4	0.0
Niger	NER	245.160	222.036	10.4	3,129.6	3,158.5	−0.9
Nigeria	NGA	112.098	141.063	−20.5	79,505.3	92,065.1	−13.6
Rwanda	RWA	293.705	322.184	−8.8	5,195.5	5,737.3	−9.4
São Tomé and Príncipe	STP	10.757	14.041	−23.4	6.7	...	...
Senegal	SEN	238.578	233.419	2.2	8,550.5	8,843.2	−3.3
Seychelles	SYC	9.027	8.696	3.8	12.0	12.0	0.0
Sierra Leone	SLE	2,128.519	2,669.458	−20.3	27,172.5	25,703.9	5.7
South Africa	ZAF	6.549	6.467	1.3	2,812.5	2,756.5	2.0
Sudan	SDN	5.377	...	...	715.4	603.0	18.6
Tanzania	TZA	754.621	834.588	−9.6	71,675.1	70,646.7	1.5
Togo	TGO	246.596	229.434	7.5	1,929.5	1,904.7	1.3
Uganda[f]	UGA	1,221.088	1,243.113	−1.8	82,956.1	68,364.0	21.3
Zambia	ZMB	4.224	3.909	8.1	115.7	...	...
Zimbabwe	ZWE	0.485	0.502	−3.3	14.1	17.5	−19.4
Total (45)	**SSB**	**n.a.**	**n.a.**	**n.a.**	**n.a.**	**n.a.**	**n.a.**
World (176)	**WLD**	**n.a.**	**n.a.**	**n.a.**	**n.a.**	**n.a.**	**n.a.**

Note: PPP = purchasing power parity; WDI = World Development Indicators; n.a. = not applicable; ... = data suppressed due to unavailability.

a. Data source: WDI (World Bank) [data as of February 2020].

b. WDI obtains PPP data from the Eurostat-Organisation for the Economic Co-operation and Development (OECD) PPP programme directly. Hence, data for economies participating in that programme are not based on the WDI extrapolation method.

c. Totals for the regions and the world are not provided due to differences in the availability of data for economies between the ICP and WDI.

d. Argentina and Guyana did not participate in ICP 2011. WDI's extrapolation is based on imputed PPPs for 2011.

e. WDI data were released in a different currency unit and were converted to the same currency unit as ICP 2017 in this table for comparison purposes.

f. For WDI the economy reports national accounts data for its fiscal year.

APPENDIX G

ICP research agenda

Over the last 50 years, the International Comparison Program (ICP) has recorded many significant achievements, including establishing an effective partnership and an efficient governance structure for the ICP; designing survey instruments for price collection; developing methods dealing with comparison-resistant services, such as housing, health, and education; and identifying multilateral index number methods suitable for international comparisons of prices and real expenditures. Notwithstanding the impressive progress made, the ICP continues to strive for improvement and refinements in its approach, with the goal of providing reliable and timely estimates of purchasing power parities (PPPs) and real expenditures.

This appendix lists the main components of the ICP research agenda (World Bank 2017) which was proposed by the ICP's Technical Advisory Group (TAG) in May 2017 and subsequently adopted by the ICP's Governing Board in September 2017. The agenda comprises 13 research items and focuses on improving the methodology and approaches underlying the ICP:

1. Compilation of annual PPPs and the rolling survey approach

   Component 1: Moving toward rolling price surveys

   Component 2: Linking interim regional updates into a global comparison

   Component 3: Compiling annual PPPs for the interim period

2. PPPs and real expenditures for dwelling services
3. Productivity adjustment for government and construction labor
4. Fine-tuning global linking procedures
5. Quality and reliability of PPPs

   Component 1: Quality of data

   Component 2: Reliability measures for PPPs

6. Uses of PPPs for national and international policy making
7. Consumer price index (CPI)–ICP synergies and subnational PPPs
8. PPPs for exports and imports
9. PPPs for construction
10. PPPs for health and education
11. ICP PPPs and global poverty measurement
12. Exploring innovations in technology and data sources for PPP measurement
13. Accounting for item quality differences in PPP measurement.

Throughout the ICP 2017 cycle, research has been carried out on moving toward the use of rolling price surveys; linking interim regional updates into a global comparison; compiling annual PPPs for the interim period; constructing PPPs and real expenditures for dwelling services; addressing productivity adjustment for government and construction labor; fine-tuning global linking procedures; assessing the quality of data and results; and providing guidance on CPI-ICP synergies and subnational PPPs.

Further research in the immediate future will continue to examine global linking procedures as well as PPPs and real expenditures for dwelling services. Experts will also investigate and make recommendations on the use of PPPs in global poverty measurement and, more broadly, in national and international policy making. Other research agenda items, such as PPPs for exports and imports and exploring innovations in technology and data sources for PPP measurement, will be taken forward starting in ICP 2021.

APPENDIX H

ICP data access and archive policy

This appendix outlines the objectives, guiding principles, and procedures for accessing and archiving International Comparison Program (ICP) data. The enhanced ICP data access and archive policy (World Bank 2019a) was endorsed by the ICP Governing Board in December 2019 and provides full details of the data and metadata covered by this policy and the relevant access and archive processes.

Background

The ICP entails a large price data collection and detailed national accounts expenditure data compilation for participating economies. Its main outputs are indicators on purchasing power parities (PPPs), price level indexes (PLIs), and real and per capita real expenditures in international dollars for various headings under the ICP classification of final expenditure on gross domestic product (GDP).[1]

The published data for the ICP 2005 cycle[2] was restricted to main aggregates and categories, with some additional aggregates—a total of 24 headings. The 2005 ICP data access and archive policy (World Bank 2008b) strongly limited access to unpublished detailed price and expenditure data: users were able to access basic-heading level data and a limited set of national average prices at the item level for the 18 economies that participated in the global linking exercise. By the end of the 2005 cycle, it was clear that the user community was pressing for greater access to more detailed data in subsequent ICP cycles.

A total of 26 headings were published for the ICP 2011 cycle.[3] In response to mounting user demands for more detailed data, the ICP Executive Board endorsed the 2011 ICP data access and archive policy (World Bank 2012), which improved access to include national average prices at the item level for all participating economies, while respecting confidentiality constraints and data-quality limitations. To improve the quality and increase the utility of the data collected, the ICP 2011 cycle also focused on collecting, archiving, and providing access to metadata. Moreover, throughout the course of the ICP 2011 cycle, calls for greater government transparency and accountability through the open-data movement gained traction. These open-data initiatives aimed to improve the availability and reuse of data.

Furthermore, the Statistical Office of the European Union (Eurostat)[4] and the Organisation for Economic Co-operation and Development (OECD)[5] publish their respective results at a finer level of detail than the ICP, covering 61 and 50 headings, respectively. The Commonwealth of Independent States (CIS)[6] has published its 2014 results at a similar level of detail as the OECD.

Recognizing that inadequate access to underlying ICP data inhibits research and policy development and restricts feedback about quality, the United Nations Statistical Commission Friends of the Chair (FOC) evaluation of the 2011 ICP (ECOSOC 2016) noted the need "to reach out and demonstrate the value of ICP data to policy makers and other important users and donors, in particular showcasing to donors that the ICP generally responds to user needs and strives for further openness with regard to access to data and metadata." The evaluation concluded by recommending that "the Governing Board establish policies that improve openness with regard to access to ICP data and metadata."

Data access objectives

The long-standing objective of the ICP data access and archive policy is as follows: *Data derived from the ICP should be utilized to the maximum extent possible for statistical, research, and analytical purposes*. To enhance data access per the FOC's recommendation, the current policy has two overall objectives:

- *Objective 1.* To provide users with more detailed results beyond what was published through the 2005 and 2011 ICP, the number of published headings such as groups and classes will be increased where feasible to a level agreed-on by the ICP Global Office and regional implementing agencies, as delegated by the ICP Governing Board, taking into consideration the quality, availability, and confidentiality of data.[7]
- *Objective 2.* To enable in-depth policy analyses on specific fields of studies, user access to unpublished data at a finer level of detail will be expanded, where feasible. To this latter point, national implementing agencies may voluntarily provide access to subnational average prices and individual price observations, where applicable and permitted by national law.

The policy also has five detailed objectives, reflecting enhanced publication and access:

1. PPPs, PLIs, and expenditure data for all economies are disseminated in ICP publications and through an ICP-dedicated online database at the agreed-on publication level, with supporting metadata.
2. PPPs, PLIs, and expenditure data at various levels of detail below the publication level for all economies, with supporting metadata, are available to users through a formal application.
3. National average price data at the item level for items on the global core lists for all economies, with supporting metadata and measures of quality, are available to users through a formal application, except when the confidentiality of respondents is jeopardized.
4. National average price data at the item level for regional items not on the global core lists for all economies, with supporting metadata and measures of quality, are available to users through a formal application, except when the confidentiality of respondents is jeopardized.
5. Individual price observations and subnational[8] average prices with supporting metadata are available to users where permitted by the laws of individual economies, as long as the confidentiality of respondents is protected.[9]

Guiding principles

The following principles guide the management of ICP data and support the objective of enhancing data access:

1. *Appropriate use.* ICP data should be made available for analytical, research, and statistical purposes. Users should not misuse the data by attempting to deduce underlying confidential data.
2. *Equality of access.* ICP data are global public goods and should be made available on an equal basis to anyone who wants to use them, in the same way that most national statistical offices make data available to users.
3. *Preservation of respondent confidentiality.* Provision of ICP data should be consistent with legal and other necessary arrangements that ensure the confidentiality of respondents.
4. *Transparency.* The principles and procedures for access to ICP data, as well as the applications of these data, should be transparent and publicly available.

5. *Consistency.* The principles and procedures for data access should strive to be consistent across all regions and economies to promote equality in the treatment of all economies.
6. *Reciprocity.* Reciprocity between participating economies should be established to the maximum extent possible. All ICP national implementing agencies are automatically considered approved users of ICP data. Nonparticipating economies are not considered approved users of ICP data but may apply for access to these data following the procedures stipulated later in this appendix.
7. *Reliability.* Releases of ICP data should be accompanied by appropriate metadata, including metadata describing the quality limitations of the data.
8. *Quality limitations.* Users of ICP data should be informed of the data's quality limitations, and they should agree that the data are still useful for their purposes.
9. *Serviceability.* The ICP data should be archived to ensure that they can be used to service future approved requests for access to data, that they are available for possible use in future ICP comparisons, and that they are available as a backup in case these data are lost through disaster or other reasons by a region or an economy.
10. *Disclosure limitations.* Users accessing unpublished ICP data should not disseminate these data.
11. *Promotion of uses.* To promote the use of ICP data, users are required to share their research findings with the ICP Global Office, consistent with the disclosure limitations in this policy. The ICP Global Office will, in turn, share these research findings with ICP stakeholders.
12. *Limitations on users' findings.* Indicators computed by users based on ICP data are not considered part of the official results of the ICP.
13. *Ease of access.* Data access procedures should ensure a simple and expedited process for accessing ICP data, while safeguarding the confidentiality of unpublished data.

Procedures for archiving data

This section describes the procedures for archiving ICP data and metadata.

1. *PPPs, PLIs, and expenditure data for all economies are disseminated at the agreed-on publication level,* with supporting metadata. They are archived by the ICP Global Office and by the relevant regional implementing agencies.
2. *PPPs, PLIs, and expenditure data at various levels of detail below the publication level* for all economies, with supporting metadata, are archived by the ICP Global Office and by the relevant regional implementing agencies.
3. *National and subnational average price data at the item level for items on the global core lists* for all economies, with supporting metadata and measures of quality, are archived by the ICP Global Office and by the relevant regional implementing agencies.
4. *National and subnational average price data at the item level for regional items not on the global core lists* for all economies, with supporting metadata and measures of quality, are archived by the ICP Global Office and by the relevant regional implementing agencies.
5. *Individual price observations and subnational average price data,* with supporting metadata, are archived by national implementing agencies. However, some national implementing agencies may request that the ICP Global Office or relevant regional implementing agency archive the individual price observations and subnational average price because they do not have their own facilities to archive these data. If an economy asks the ICP Global Office or relevant regional implementing agency to archive these data, the economy in question can choose to have the data encrypted and hold the encryption key.

The unpublished data archived by the ICP Global Office will be treated with confidentiality. The data will be archived in a secure database with limited access rights and administered by a designated data custodian. Access to the data (or any portions of the data) will be subject to the procedures specified next.

Procedures for accessing data

This section describes the procedures for accessing ICP data and metadata:

1. *PPPs, PLIs, and expenditure data for all economies at the agreed-on publication level,* with supporting metadata, will be disseminated in ICP publications and through an ICP-dedicated online database.
2. *PPPs, PLIs, and expenditure data at various levels of detail below the publication level* for all economies, with supporting metadata, can be accessed by users through a formal online application addressed to the ICP Global Office.
3. *National average price data at the item level for items on the global core lists* for all economies, with supporting metadata and measures of quality, can be accessed by users through a formal application addressed to the ICP Global Office, consistent with the confidentiality laws and processes of participating economies. National implementing agencies should inform the relevant regional implementing agencies, which, in turn, will inform the ICP Global Office, which information is considered confidential and hence cannot be shared. Item brands and models will be anonymized before sharing with users.
4. *National average price data at the item level for regional items not on the global core lists* for all economies, with supporting metadata and measures of quality, can be accessed by users through a formal application addressed to the ICP Global Office, consistent with the confidentiality laws and processes of participating economies. National implementing agencies should inform the relevant regional implementing agencies, which, in turn, will inform the ICP Global Office, which information is considered confidential and hence cannot be shared. Item brands and models will be anonymized before sharing with users.
5. *Individual price observations and subnational average price data,* with supporting metadata, are available to users where permitted by the laws of individual economies, as long as the confidentiality of respondents is protected. Users may submit a formal application of access to these data to the national implementing agency, either directly or through the ICP Global Office or relevant regional implementing agency.

Users apply for access to the ICP data sets by submitting a formal application and a signed declaration of use addressed to the ICP Global Office.[10] The ICP Global Office decides whether to approve requests, in line with the access policy approved by the ICP Governing Board and outlined in this document. Once the ICP Global Office approves the formal data access request, it notifies the requesting user(s) and grants secure online access to a custom confidential data set containing the data requested. Such access requires two-factor authentication, an approach that provides an additional layer of security.

Alternatively, users may approach relevant regional implementing agencies for access to regional data sets or relevant national implementing agencies for access to national data sets. In these cases, regional and national implementing agencies will follow the access policy agreed by the ICP Governing Board. Access to regional and national data sets does not require clearance from the ICP Global Office.

Notes

1. See icp.worldbank.org/programs/icp#6.
2. See icp.worldbank.org/en/programs/icp#5.
3. See icp.worldbank.org/en/programs/icp#5.
4. See https://ec.europa.eu/eurostat/web/purchasing-power-parities/data/database.
5. See http://www.oecd.org/sdd/prices-ppp/.
6. See http://www.cisstat.org/icp/.
7. The headings included in each published ICP data set will be listed on the ICP website.
8. Capital city or first-level administrative divisions within an economy (for example, states, provinces).
9. For example, through data anonymization techniques.
10. See Annex 4 of World Bank (2019a).

APPENDIX I

ICP revision policy

This appendix describes the International Comparison Program (ICP) revision policy (World Bank 2019b) endorsed by the ICP Governing Board in December 2019. It sets out the triggers and procedures for revising previously published and unpublished results from the ICP to ensure that the program's outputs reflect the latest available information and methodologies, are of the highest quality, and remain relevant to users. It describes the timing of revisions and the steps to be taken to communicate these revisions to users.

Background

The ICP's main outputs are indicators on purchasing power parities (PPPs), price level indexes (PLIs), and real and per capita real expenditures in international dollars for various headings under the ICP classification of final expenditure on gross domestic product (GDP).[1]

The ICP publishes full data sets for reference years, such as 2011 and 2017. Annual PPPs for nonreference years are estimated through retropolation, interpolation, and extrapolation using consumer price index (CPI) and national accounts deflator time series. The ICP classification level at which these results are published is determined by the ICP data access and archive policy, described in appendix H.

ICP-published results are available through various portals, including the ICP website[2] and the World Bank's Databank[3] and Data Catalog;[4] indicators using ICP data are included in World Development Indicators.[5] Additional unpublished results and data are available to users upon application to the ICP Global Office.[6]

Triggers for revising ICP indicators

The triggers prompting revisions of ICP data include revisions or changes in input data and changes in methodology.

Revisions and changes in input data

- Revisions in the GDP estimate trigger a revision of real and per capita real expenditures and nominal and per capita nominal expenditures.
- Revisions in the national accounts expenditure components (that is, national accounts structure) trigger a revision of real and per capita real expenditures and nominal and per capita nominal expenditures. They may also trigger a revision of PPPs and PLIs.
- Revisions in population figures trigger a revision of per capita real expenditures and per capita nominal expenditures.
- Revisions to CPI and national accounts deflator time series trigger a revision of annual PPPs and PLIs and of real and per capita real expenditures.

- Changes in economies' currency units trigger a revision of real and per capita real expenditures, PPPs, PLIs, and nominal and per capita nominal expenditures.
- Correction of errors in source data or results may trigger a revision of PPPs and PLIs, real and per capita real expenditures, and nominal and per capita nominal expenditures.

New methodology

- Significantly improved PPP computation and aggregation methods trigger a revision of real and per capita real expenditures, PPPs, and PLIs.
- A significantly improved global linking approach triggers a revision of real and per capita real expenditures, PPPs, and PLIs.
- A significantly improved retropolation, interpolation, and extrapolation method triggers a revision of annual PPPs and PLIs and real and per capita real expenditures.
- A revision to the System of National Accounts (SNA) or the Classification of Individual Consumption According to Purpose (COICOP) may trigger a change in the ICP Classification of final expenditure on GDP.

This appendix summarizes these triggers and subsequent revisions.

Guidelines for revising ICP indicators

Revisions of ICP results should be made infrequently and should adhere to the following guidelines.

Historical revisions

- Revisions to historical input data from economies may trigger a revision to ICP results. These revisions will be limited to the period of revisions to the input data. For example, retrospective revisions of an economy's GDP from 2012 to 2019 would trigger a revision of the real and per capita real expenditures for that period only; 2011 results would not be revised.
- Historical revisions based on new methodologies are subject to the feasibility of introducing the new methodology retrospectively, based on the availability and limitations of input data.

Geographic scope

- Revisions of regional data should precede revisions of global data in order to preserve the consistency between regional and global data sets.
- Regional implementing agencies are responsible for revising reference-year indicators and associated interpolated annual indicators at the regional level, and the ICP Global Office is responsible for revising reference-year indicators and interpolated annual indicators at the global level (that is, denominated in the global numeraire).
- Revised global reference-year results should respect, to the extent possible, regional fixity—the convention whereby the price relativities established between economies in a regional comparison are retained when the economies are included in the global comparison.

Categories of indicators

- *PPPs and PLIs* may be revised depending on the level of detail of the revisions of the national accounts expenditure structure or a change in the ICP classification of final expenditure on GDP. When economies revise their expenditure data for major components, categories, groups, classes, or basic headings, then PPPs (and resulting PLIs) may be revised at levels above the lowest level for which expenditures were revised. These revisions are introduced in conjunction with the release of new reference-year results and are limited to the PPPs and PLIs from the previous reference-year exercise only. These revisions will, in turn, trigger a revision in the time series of PPPs and PLIs for nonreference years. Annual PPPs and PLIs for nonreference years may also be revised if CPI and national accounts deflator time series are revised.

- *Real and per capita real expenditures* are revised when national accounts expenditure data or population data are revised. These revisions are introduced on an annual basis.
- *Nominal and per capita nominal expenditures* are revised when national accounts expenditure data or population data are revised. These revisions are introduced on an annual basis.

Quality review

- Revised ICP data will be subject to an expert review before they are published, to ensure data quality.

Publication of revised results

- Revised ICP indicators will be published once they have been compiled and undergone the quality review process.
- Revised ICP indicators will be released at the publication level of the reference-year results, as established by the ICP data access and archive policy.
- The ICP Global Office will archive the various vintages of the data.

Consistency between published and unpublished data sets

- The ICP Global Office can make available to researchers a detailed data set, as stipulated in the ICP data access and archive policy. This data set includes real and per capita real expenditures, PPPs and PLIs, and nominal and per capita nominal expenditures at all classification levels, as well as average prices. When revising published ICP indicators, this unpublished detailed data set may need to be revised to maintain consistency between the published and unpublished data sets.

Timing and communication of revisions

- Revisions to real and per capita real expenditures and nominal and per capita nominal expenditures, triggered by revisions of national accounts expenditure and population data, will be introduced on an annual basis. Revisions to PPPs and PLIs will be introduced in conjunction with the release of new reference-year results and be limited to the PPPs and PLIs from the previous reference-year exercise and interpolated annual PPPs and PLIs for nonreference years.
- The schedule of revisions will be announced to stakeholders and users well in advance.
- When methodology is improved, the new methods will be communicated to users well in advance.
- Results will be made publicly available on the ICP website, the World Bank's Databank and Data Catalog, World Development Indicators, and other relevant websites.

Notes

1. See icp.worldbank.org/programs/#6.
2. See icp.worldbank.org/programs/icp#5.
3. See databank.worldbank.org.
4. See datacatalog.worldbank.org.
5. See http://datatopics.worldbank.org/world-development-indicators/.
6. See Annex 4 of World Bank (2019a).

APPENDIX J

Classification of the world's economies

The World Bank classifies its member countries and 28 other economies with populations of more than 30,000 by geographic region and income group. The four current income groups are defined using gross national income (GNI) per capita, in US dollars, converted from local currency using the World Bank Atlas method. For the 2020 fiscal year, low-income economies are defined as those with a GNI per capita of $1,025 or less in 2018; lower-middle income economies are those with GNI per capita between $1,026 and $3,995; upper-middle income economies are those with GNI per capita between $3,996 and $12,375; and high-income economies are those with GNI per capita of $12,376 or more. More information is available from the World Bank's Data Help Desk.[1]

Three ICP participating economies (Anguilla, Bonaire, and Monserrat) are not classified by income group because their populations are below the 30,000 threshold. While the World Bank does not assign them to a region for this same reason, they are included in the Latin America and the Caribbean region in this report.

Note

1. See https://datahelpdesk.worldbank.org/knowledgebase/articles/906519-world-bank-country-and-lending-groups.

Table J.1 Economies in East Asia and Pacific, classified by ICP 2017 administrative region and World Bank fiscal year 2020 income group

Economy	ICP 2017 administrative region	World Bank fiscal year 2020 income group
American Samoa	Nonparticipating	Upper middle income
Australia	Eurostat-OECD	High income
Brunei Darussalam	Asia and the Pacific	High income
Cambodia	Asia and the Pacific	Lower middle income
China	Asia and the Pacific	Upper middle income
Cook Islands	Nonparticipating	Not classified
Fiji	Asia and the Pacific	Upper middle income
French Polynesia	Nonparticipating	High income
Guam	Nonparticipating	High income
Hong Kong SAR, China	Asia and the Pacific	High income
Indonesia	Asia and the Pacific	Lower middle income
Japan	Eurostat-OECD	High income
Kiribati	Nonparticipating	Lower middle income
Korea, Rep.	Eurostat-OECD	High income
Lao PDR	Asia and the Pacific	Lower middle income
Macao SAR, China	Nonparticipating	High income
Malaysia	Asia and the Pacific	Upper middle income
Marshall Islands	Nonparticipating	Upper middle income
Micronesia, Fed. Sts.	Nonparticipating	Lower middle income
Mongolia	Asia and the Pacific	Lower middle income
Myanmar	Asia and the Pacific	Lower middle income
Nauru	Nonparticipating	Upper middle income
New Caledonia	Nonparticipating	High income
New Zealand	Eurostat-OECD	High income
Niue	Nonparticipating	Not classified
Northern Mariana Islands	Nonparticipating	High income
Palau	Nonparticipating	High income
Papua New Guinea	Nonparticipating	Lower middle income
Philippines	Asia and the Pacific	Lower middle income
Samoa	Nonparticipating	Upper middle income
Singapore	Asia and the Pacific	High income
Solomon Islands	Nonparticipating	Lower middle income
Taiwan, China	Asia and the Pacific	High income
Thailand	Asia and the Pacific	Upper middle income
Timor-Leste	Nonparticipating	Lower middle income
Tokelau	Nonparticipating	Not classified
Tonga	Nonparticipating	Upper middle income
Tuvalu	Nonparticipating	Upper middle income
Vanuatu	Nonparticipating	Lower middle income
Vietnam	Asia and the Pacific	Lower middle income
Wallis and Futuna	Nonparticipating	Not classified

Note: ICP = International Comparison Program; OECD = Organisation for Economic Co-operation and Development.

Table J.2 Economies in Europe and Central Asia, classified by ICP 2017 administrative region and World Bank fiscal year 2020 income group

Economy	ICP 2017 administrative region	World Bank fiscal year 2020 income group
Albania	Eurostat-OECD	Upper middle income
Armenia	CIS	Upper middle income
Austria	Eurostat-OECD	High income
Azerbaijan	CIS	Upper middle income
Belarus	CIS	Upper middle income
Belgium	Eurostat-OECD	High income
Bosnia and Herzegovina	Eurostat-OECD	Upper middle income
Bulgaria	Eurostat-OECD	Upper middle income
Croatia	Eurostat-OECD	High income
Cyprus	Eurostat-OECD	High income
Czech Republic	Eurostat-OECD	High income
Denmark	Eurostat-OECD	High income
Estonia	Eurostat-OECD	High income
Finland	Eurostat-OECD	High income
France	Eurostat-OECD	High income
Georgia	Special participation	Upper middle income
Germany	Eurostat-OECD	High income
Greece	Eurostat-OECD	High income
Hungary	Eurostat-OECD	High income
Iceland	Eurostat-OECD	High income
Ireland	Eurostat-OECD	High income
Italy	Eurostat-OECD	High income
Kazakhstan	CIS	Upper middle income
Kosovo	Nonparticipating	Upper middle income
Kyrgyz Republic	CIS	Lower middle income
Latvia	Eurostat-OECD	High income
Lithuania	Eurostat-OECD	High income
Luxembourg	Eurostat-OECD	High income
Moldova	CIS	Lower middle income
Montenegro	Eurostat-OECD	Upper middle income
Netherlands	Eurostat-OECD	High income
North Macedonia	Eurostat-OECD	Upper middle income
Norway	Eurostat-OECD	High income
Poland	Eurostat-OECD	High income
Portugal	Eurostat-OECD	High income
Romania	Eurostat-OECD	Upper middle income
Russian Federation[a]	CIS/Eurostat-OECD	Upper middle income
San Marino	Nonparticipating	High income
Serbia	Eurostat-OECD	Upper middle income
Slovak Republic	Eurostat-OECD	High income
Slovenia	Eurostat-OECD	High income
Spain	Eurostat-OECD	High income
Sweden	Eurostat-OECD	High income
Switzerland	Eurostat-OECD	High income
Tajikistan	CIS	Low income
Turkey	Eurostat-OECD	Upper middle income
Turkmenistan	Nonparticipating	Upper middle income
Ukraine	Special participation	Lower middle income
United Kingdom	Eurostat-OECD	High income
Uzbekistan	Experimental participation	Lower middle income

Note: CIS = Commonwealth of Independent States; ICP = International Comparison Program; OECD = Organisation for Economic Co-operation and Development.

a. Indicates a dual-participation economy in ICP 2017.

Table J.3 Economies in Latin America and the Caribbean, classified by ICP 2017 administrative region and World Bank fiscal year 2020 income group

Economy	ICP 2017 administrative region	World Bank fiscal year 2020 income group
Anguilla	Caribbean	Not classified
Antigua and Barbuda	Caribbean	High income
Argentina	Latin America	Upper middle income
Aruba	Caribbean	High income
Bahamas, The	Caribbean	High income
Barbados	Caribbean	High income
Belize	Caribbean	Upper middle income
Bolivia	Latin America	Lower middle income
Bonaire	Caribbean	Not classified
Brazil	Latin America	Upper middle income
Cayman Islands	Caribbean	High income
Chile	Eurostat-OECD	High income
Colombia	Eurostat-OECD	Upper middle income
Costa Rica	Eurostat-OECD	Upper middle income
Cuba	Nonparticipating	Upper middle income
Curaçao	Caribbean	High income
Dominica	Caribbean	Upper middle income
Dominican Republic	Latin America	Upper middle income
Ecuador	Latin America	Upper middle income
El Salvador	Latin America	Lower middle income
Grenada	Caribbean	Upper middle income
Guatemala	Nonparticipating	Upper middle income
Guyana	Caribbean	Upper middle income
Haiti	Latin America	Low income
Honduras	Latin America	Lower middle income
Jamaica	Caribbean	Upper middle income
Mexico	Eurostat-OECD	Upper middle income
Montserrat	Caribbean	Not classified
Nicaragua	Latin America	Lower middle income
Panama	Latin America	High income
Paraguay	Latin America	Upper middle income
Peru	Latin America	Upper middle income
Puerto Rico	Nonparticipating	High income
Sint Maarten	Caribbean	High income
St. Kitts and Nevis	Caribbean	High income
St. Lucia	Caribbean	Upper middle income
St. Vincent and the Grenadines	Caribbean	Upper middle income
Suriname	Caribbean	Upper middle income
Trinidad and Tobago	Caribbean	High income
Turks and Caicos Islands	Caribbean	High income
Uruguay	Latin America	High income
Venezuela, RB	Nonparticipating	Upper middle income
Virgin Islands, British	Caribbean	High income

Note: ICP = International Comparison Program; OECD = Organisation for Economic Co-operation and Development.

Table J.4 Economies in Middle East and North Africa, classified by ICP 2017 administrative region and World Bank fiscal year 2020 income group

Economy	ICP 2017 administrative region	World Bank fiscal year 2020 income group
Algeria	Africa	Upper middle income
Bahrain	Western Asia	High income
Djibouti	Africa	Lower middle income
Egypt, Arab Rep.[a]	Africa/Western Asia	Lower middle income
Iran, Islamic Rep.	Special participation	Upper middle income
Iraq	Western Asia	Upper middle income
Israel	Eurostat-OECD	High income
Jordan	Western Asia	Upper middle income
Kuwait	Western Asia	High income
Lebanon	Nonparticipating	Upper middle income
Libya	Nonparticipating	Upper middle income
Malta	Eurostat-OECD	High income
Morocco[a]	Africa/Western Asia	Lower middle income
Oman	Western Asia	High income
Qatar	Western Asia	High income
Saudi Arabia	Western Asia	High income
Syrian Arab Republic	Nonparticipating	Low income
Tunisia	Africa	Lower middle income
United Arab Emirates	Western Asia	High income
West Bank and Gaza	Western Asia	Lower middle income
Yemen, Rep.	Nonparticipating	Low income

Note: ICP = International Comparison Program; OECD = Organisation for Economic Co-operation and Development.
a. Indicates a dual-participation economy in ICP 2017.

Table J.5 Economies in North America, classified by ICP 2017 administrative region and World Bank fiscal year 2020 income group

Economy	ICP 2017 administrative region	World Bank fiscal year 2020 income group
Bermuda	Caribbean	High income
Canada	Eurostat-OECD	High income
United States	Eurostat-OECD	High income

Note: ICP = International Comparison Program; OECD = Organisation for Economic Co-operation and Development.

Table J.6 Economies in South Asia, classified by ICP 2017 administrative region and World Bank fiscal year 2020 income group

Economy	ICP 2017 administrative region	World Bank fiscal year 2020 income group
Afghanistan	Nonparticipating	Low income
Bangladesh	Asia and the Pacific	Lower middle income
Bhutan	Asia and the Pacific	Lower middle income
India	Asia and the Pacific	Lower middle income
Maldives	Asia and the Pacific	Upper middle income
Nepal	Asia and the Pacific	Low income
Pakistan	Asia and the Pacific	Lower middle income
Sri Lanka	Asia and the Pacific	Upper middle income

Note: ICP = International Comparison Program.

Table J.7 Economies in Sub-Saharan Africa, classified by ICP 2017 administrative region and World Bank fiscal year 2020 income group

Economy	ICP 2017 administrative region	World Bank fiscal year 2020 income group
Angola	Africa	Lower middle income
Benin	Africa	Low income
Botswana	Africa	Upper middle income
Burkina Faso	Africa	Low income
Burundi	Africa	Low income
Cabo Verde	Africa	Lower middle income
Cameroon	Africa	Lower middle income
Central African Republic	Africa	Low income
Chad	Africa	Low income
Comoros	Africa	Lower middle income
Congo, Dem. Rep.	Africa	Low income
Congo, Rep.	Africa	Lower middle income
Côte d'Ivoire	Africa	Lower middle income
Equatorial Guinea	Africa	Upper middle income
Eritrea	Nonparticipating	Low income
Eswatini	Africa	Lower middle income
Ethiopia	Africa	Low income
Gabon	Africa	Upper middle income
Gambia, The	Africa	Low income
Ghana	Africa	Lower middle income
Guinea	Africa	Low income
Guinea-Bissau	Africa	Low income
Kenya	Africa	Lower middle income
Lesotho	Africa	Lower middle income
Liberia	Africa	Low income
Madagascar	Africa	Low income
Malawi	Africa	Low income
Mali	Africa	Low income
Mauritania	Africa	Lower middle income
Mauritius	Africa	Upper middle income
Mozambique	Africa	Low income
Namibia	Africa	Upper middle income
Niger	Africa	Low income
Nigeria	Africa	Lower middle income
Rwanda	Africa	Low income
São Tomé and Príncipe	Africa	Lower middle income
Senegal	Africa	Lower middle income
Seychelles	Africa	High income
Sierra Leone	Africa	Low income
Somalia	Nonparticipating	Low income
South Africa	Africa	Upper middle income
South Sudan	Nonparticipating	Low income
Sudan[a]	Africa/Western Asia	Lower middle income
Tanzania	Africa	Low income
Togo	Africa	Low income
Uganda	Africa	Low income
Zambia	Africa	Lower middle income
Zimbabwe	Africa	Lower middle income

Note: ICP = International Comparison Program.

a. Indicates a dual-participation economy in ICP 2017.

Glossary

accounting period. The period to which estimates of GDP refer, usually a calendar year or a quarter. For ICP comparisons of GDP, the accounting period is a calendar year.

actual individual consumption. The total value of the individual consumption expenditures of households, of nonprofit institutions serving households, and of government. It is a measure of the individual goods and services that households actually consume as opposed to what they actually purchase.

additive. A method that, for each economy being compared, provides real expenditures for aggregates that are equal to the sum of the real expenditures of their constituent basic headings. An additive aggregation method provides real expenditures that satisfy the average test for volumes but are subject to the Gerschenkron effect.

aggregation. The process of weighting and averaging basic-heading PPPs to obtain PPPs for each level of aggregation up to GDP.

analytical categories. GDP, main aggregates, expenditure categories, expenditure groups, and expenditure classes for which the results of a comparison are published. This categorization is not necessarily the same as those of the hierarchical classification used for PPP calculations.

base country invariance. The property whereby the relativities between the PPPs, price level indexes, and volume indexes of economies are not affected by either the choice of local currency as numéraire or the choice of reference economy.

base economy. The economy, or group of economies, for which the value of the PPP is set at 1.00 and the value of the price level index and of the volume index is set at 100.

basic heading. The lowest aggregation level in the ICP expenditure classification. In theory, a basic heading is defined as a group of similar well-defined goods or services. In practice, it is defined by the lowest level of final expenditure for which explicit expenditure weights can be estimated. Thus an actual basic heading can cover a broader range of items than is theoretically desirable and include both goods and services. It is at the level of the basic heading that expenditures are defined and estimated, items are selected for pricing, prices are collected and validated, and PPPs are first calculated and averaged.

basic price. The amount received by the producer from the purchaser for a unit of good or service produced as output. It includes subsidies on products and other taxes on production. It excludes taxes on products, other subsidies on production, the supplier's retail and wholesale margins, and separately invoiced transport and insurance charges.

Basic prices are the prices most relevant for decision making by suppliers (producers).

bilateral or binary comparison. A price or volume comparison between two economies that draws on data only for those two economies.

bilateral or binary PPP. A PPP between two economies calculated using only the prices and weights for those two economies.

changes in inventories. The acquisition less disposals of stocks of raw materials, semifinished goods, and finished goods that are held by producer units prior to being processed further or sold or otherwise used. Semifinished goods cover work in progress (partially completed products whose production process will be continued by the same producer in a subsequent accounting period), including the natural growth of agricultural crops prior to harvest and the natural growth in livestock raised for slaughter. Inventories also cover all raw materials and goods stored by government as strategic reserves.

characteristics. The technical parameters and price-determining properties of an item listed in an item specification.

Classification of the Functions of Government (COFOG). Classification of transactions by government, including outlays on final consumption expenditure, intermediate consumption, gross fixed capital formation, and capital and current transfers, by function or purpose. A major use of COFOG is to identify which final consumption expenditures of government benefit households individually and which benefit households collectively.

Classification of Individual Consumption According to Purpose (COICOP). Classification of the individual consumption expenditures of three institutional sectors—households, nonprofit institutions serving households, and government—by the ends that they wish to achieve through these expenditures. Individual consumption expenditures are those that are made for the benefit of individual households. All final consumption expenditures by households and NPISHs are defined as individual, but only the final consumption expenditures by government on individual services are treated as individual.

collective consumption expenditure by government. The final consumption expenditure of government on collective services. It is a measure of the services that government provides to the community as a whole and that households consume collectively.

collective services. Services provided by government that benefit the community as a whole: general public services, defense, public order and safety, economic affairs, environmental protection, and housing and community amenities. They also include the overall policy-making, planning, budgetary, and coordinating responsibilities of government ministries overseeing individual services and government research and development for individual services. These activities cannot be identified with specific individual households and are considered to benefit households collectively.

comparability. The requirement that economies price items that are identical or, if not identical, equivalent. Items are said to be comparable if they have identical or equivalent technical parameters and price-determining properties. Equivalent means that they meet the same needs with equal efficiency so that purchasers are indifferent between them and are not prepared to pay more for one than for the other. The pricing of comparable items ensures that the differences in prices between economies for an item reflect actual price differences and are not affected by differences in quality. If differences in quality are not avoided or corrected, they can be mistaken for apparent price differences, leading to an underestimation or overestimation of price levels and an overestimation or underestimation of volume levels.

comparison-resistant. A term first used to describe nonmarket services that are difficult to compare across economies because they have no economically significant prices with which to value outputs, their units of output cannot be otherwise defined and measured, the institutional arrangements for their provision and the conditions of payment differ from economy to economy, and their quality varies between economies but the differences cannot be identified and quantified. The term is used, for example, to describe construction and the rental of housing, whose complexity, variation, and economy specificity can make it difficult to price them comparably across economies.

compensation of employees. All payments in cash and in kind made by employers to employees in return for work carried out during the accounting period. These payments comprise gross wages and salaries in cash and in kind, employers' actual social contributions, and imputed social contributions.

component. A subset of goods or services or both that make up some defined aggregate.

consumption expenditure by government. The actual and imputed final consumption expenditure incurred by government on individual goods and services and collective services. It is the total value of the individual consumption expenditure and collective consumption expenditure by government.

consumption of fixed capital. The reduction in the value of the fixed assets used in production during the accounting period resulting from physical deterioration, normal obsolescence, or normal accidental damage.

country aggregation with redistribution (CAR) procedure. A means of obtaining aggregate global volumes and PPPs for economies within each region that retain the relativities established between the economies in the regional comparison. In other words, each region's results for the aggregate remain fixed when linked with the results of other regions. The procedure is as follows. The global basic-heading PPPs for all economies in the comparison are aggregated to the level of the aggregate. The global PPPs for the aggregate are used to calculate global real expenditures for each economy, with which the total global real expenditure on the aggregate for each region can be determined. The total global real expenditure of each region is redistributed across the economies in the region in line with the distribution of real expenditures in the regional comparison. Global PPPs for economies are calculated indirectly with the redistributed global real expenditure.

country product dummy (CPD) method. The multilateral method used to obtain transitive PPPs at the basic-heading level through regression analysis. It treats the calculation of PPPs as a matter of statistical inference—that is, an estimation problem rather than an index number problem. The underlying hypothesis is that, apart from random disturbance, the PPPs for individual items within a basic heading are all constant between any given pair of economies. In other words, it is assumed that the pattern of the relative prices of different items within a given basic heading is the same in all economies. It is also assumed that each economy has its own overall price level for the basic heading and that this overall price level fixes the levels of absolute prices of the items in the basic heading for the economy. By treating the prices observed in the economies for the basic heading as random samples, the PPPs between each pair of economies and the common pattern of relative prices can be estimated using classical least square methods. The method allows the estimation of sampling errors for the PPPs.

country product dummy-weighted (CPD-W) method. A variant of the CPD method in which important items receive a higher weight in the calculation than less important items. The choice of weights is arbitrary, as it is in the Gini-Éltetö-Köves-Szulc* (GEKS*) method. However, the weight of 1 for an important item and 0 for a less important item used in the GEKS* method cannot be used in a weighted CPD because assigning a weight of 0 to the prices of less important items will remove them from the calculation. In ICP 2011 and ICP 2017, important items were given a weight of 3 and less important items a weight of 1.

deflation. The division of the current value of an aggregate by a price index—the deflator—in order to value its volumes at the prices of the price reference period.

economically significant price. A price that has a significant influence on the amounts that producers are willing to supply and the amounts that purchasers wish to buy. This is the basic price for producers and the purchase price for purchasers.

economic territory. The geographic territory of an economy plus any territorial enclaves in the rest of the world. By convention, it includes embassies, military bases, and ships and aircraft abroad. The economic territory does not include extraterritorial enclaves—that is, the parts of the economy's own geographic territory used by government agencies of other economies or by international organizations under international treaties or agreements between states.

editing. The first step of validation, which entails scrutinizing data for errors. It is the process of checking survey prices for nonsampling errors by identifying those prices that have extreme values—that is, prices whose value is determined to be either too high or too low vis-à-vis the average according to certain criteria. The price may score a value for a given test that exceeds a predetermined critical value, or its value may fall outside some prespecified range of acceptable values. Both are standard ways of detecting errors in survey data, and both are employed by the ICP. Prices with extreme values are not necessarily wrong. But the fact that their values are considered extreme suggests that they could be wrong. They are possible errors, and as such they need to be investigated to establish whether they are actual errors.

employers' actual social contributions. Payments actually made by employers to social security funds, insurance enterprises, or autonomous pension funds for the benefit of their employees.

error. The difference between the observed value of a PPP or volume index and its correct value. Errors may be random or systematic. Random errors are generally called errors; systematic errors are called biases.

expenditure weight. The share of nominal expenditure of a basic heading in GDP.

final consumption expenditure. The expenditure on goods and services consumed by individual households or the community to satisfy their individual or collective needs or wants.

financial intermediation services indirectly measured (FISIM). An indirect measure of the value of the financial intermediation services that financial institutions provide clients but for which they do not charge explicitly.

Fisher-type PPP. The PPP for an aggregate between two economies that is defined as the geometric mean of the Laspeyres-type PPP and the Paasche-type PPP for the aggregate.

fixity. The convention whereby the relativities between a group of economies that were established in a comparison covering just that group of economies remain unchanged, or fixed, when the economies of the group are included in comparisons with a wider group of economies. For example, the price and volume relativities of the ICP regions and Eurostat–OECD remain unchanged in the global comparison. If fixity were not observed, there would be two sets of relativities for the participating economies that would not necessarily be in agreement because the relativities and ranking of economies can change as the composition of the group of economies being compared changes. Fixity ensures that participating economies have only one set of results to explain to users.

Gerschenkron effect. An effect applicable only to aggregation methods that use either a reference price structure, whereby each economy's quantities are valued by a uniform set of prices to obtain volumes, or a reference volume structure, whereby each economy's prices are used to value a uniform set of quantities to obtain PPPs. For methods employing a reference price structure, an economy's share of total GDP—that is, the total for the group of economies being compared—will rise as the reference price structure becomes less characteristic of its own price structure. For methods employing a reference volume structure, an economy's share of total GDP will fall as the reference volume structure becomes less characteristic of its own volume structure. The Gerschenkron effect arises because of the negative correlation between prices and volumes.

Gini-Éltető-Köves-Szulc (GEKS) method. A method used to calculate PPPs for basic headings or to aggregate basic-heading PPPs to obtain PPPs for each level of aggregation up to GDP. There are two versions of the GEKS at the basic-heading level: one that takes account of the importance of the items priced and one that does not. The version that takes the importance of items into account is referred to as GEKS* in the literature.

Strictly speaking, the GEKS is a procedure whereby any set of intransitive binary index numbers are made transitive and multilateral while respecting characteristicity (the property in which the resulting multilateral indexes differ as little as possible from the original binary indexes). The procedure is independent of the method used to calculate the intransitive binary indexes. But as used in the current literature, GEKS covers both the way in which the intransitive binary PPPs are calculated and the procedure used to make them transitive and multilateral.

The intransitive binary PPPs for a basic heading or an aggregate are obtained by calculating first a matrix of Laspeyres-type PPPs and a matrix of Paasche-type PPPs and then taking the geometric mean of the two, a matrix of Fisher-type PPPs. The Fisher-type PPPs are made transitive and multilateral by applying the GEKS procedure, which involves replacing the Fisher-type PPP between each pair of economies by the geometric mean of itself squared and all the corresponding indirect Fisher-type PPPs between the pair obtained using the other economies as bridges. The resulting GEKS PPPs provide real expenditures that are not subject to the Gerschenkron effect and are not additive. GEKS results are considered better suited to comparisons across economies of the price and volume levels of individual basic headings or aggregates. See Laspeyres-type PPP and Paasche-type PPP (their formulation depends on whether they are being used to calculate basic-heading PPPs or to aggregate basic-heading PPPs).

global core item. An item priced for the specific purpose of providing a link or overlap between regional comparisons at the basic-heading level in order to combine them in a single world comparison. For ICP 2017, lists of global core items were compiled for consumer goods and services, government services, and capital goods by the Global Office in consultation with the regions, participating economies, and subject matter experts. Regions selected items from the global core item lists and added them to their regional item lists in line with each item's availability and importance in their region. The global core items priced by the regions were included in the regional comparisons as well as the world comparison.

goods. Physical objects for which a demand exists, over which ownership rights can be established, and whose ownership can be transferred from one institutional unit to another by engaging in transactions on the market. They are in demand because they may be used to satisfy the needs or wants of households or the community or used to produce other goods or services.

government. General government, which is the institutional sector that consists of federal, central, regional, state, and local government units together with the social security funds imposed and controlled by those units. It includes nonprofit institutions engaged in nonmarket production that are controlled and financed mainly by government units or social security funds.

gross capital formation. The total value of gross fixed capital formation, changes in inventories, and acquisitions less disposals of valuables.

gross domestic product (GDP). When estimated from the expenditure side, the total value of the final consumption expenditures of households, nonprofit institutions serving households, and government plus gross capital formation plus the balance of exports and imports.

gross fixed capital formation. The total value of acquisitions less disposals of fixed assets by resident institutional units during the accounting period, plus the additions to the value of nonproduced assets realized by the productive activity of resident institutional units.

gross operating surplus. The surplus or deficit accruing from production before taking into account (1) consumption of fixed capital by the enterprise; (2) any interest, rent, or similar charges payable on financial or tangible nonproduced assets borrowed or rented by the enterprise; or (3) any interest, rent, or similar charges receivable on financial or tangible nonproduced assets owned by the enterprise.

gross wages and salaries. The wages and salaries in cash and in kind paid by enterprises to employees before the deduction of taxes and social contributions payable by employees.

household. A small group of persons who share the same living accommodation, who pool some or all of their income and wealth, and who consume certain types of goods and services collectively, mainly food and housing. A household can consist of only one person.

importance. A concept that is defined in terms of a specific economy within a basic heading. An item is either important or less important in the economy for the given basic heading. An important item is one that accounts for a significant share of the expenditure on the basic heading in the economy in question. Weighted PPP estimation methods use importance as an indication of weight.

imputed rent. The imputations that have to be made when owners occupy a dwelling to produce housing services for themselves. In effect, owner-occupiers are renting the dwelling to themselves, and the value of the rent has to be imputed. The imputed rent should be valued at the estimated rent a tenant pays for a dwelling of the same size and quality in a comparable location with similar neighborhood amenities. When markets for rented accommodations are virtually nonexistent or unrepresentative, the value of the imputed rent has to be derived by some other objective procedure, such as the user cost method.

imputed social contributions. The imputations that have to be made when employers provide social benefits directly to their employees, former employees, or dependents out of their own resources without involving an insurance enterprise or autonomous pension fund and without creating a special fund or segregated reserve for the purpose.

indirect binary comparison. A price or volume comparison between two economies made through a third economy. For example, for economies A, B, and C, the PPP between A and C is obtained by dividing the PPP between A and B by the PPP between C and B, so that $PPP_{A/C} = PPP_{A/B} / PPP_{C/B}$.

individual consumption expenditure by government. The actual and imputed final consumption expenditure incurred by government on individual goods and services.

individual consumption expenditure by households. The actual and imputed final consumption expenditure incurred by resident households on individual goods and services. Includes expenditures on individual goods and services sold at prices that are not economically significant. By definition, all final consumption expenditures of households are for the benefit of individual households and are individual.

individual consumption expenditure by nonprofit institutions serving households (NPISHs). The actual and imputed final consumption expenditure incurred by NPISHs on individual goods and services. Because most final consumption expenditures of NPISHs are individual, all final consumption expenditures of NPISHs are treated by convention as individual.

individual good or service. A consumption good or service acquired by a household and used to satisfy the needs and wants of members of that household.

individual services. A term used to describe the services (and goods) provided to individual households by nonprofit institutions serving households and government. Such services include housing, health care, recreation and culture, education, and social protection. They do not include the overall policy-making, planning, budgetary, and coordinating responsibilities of the government ministries overseeing individual services. Nor do they include government research and development for individual services. These activities are considered to benefit households collectively and are therefore classified under collective services.

input price approach. The approach used to obtain PPPs for nonmarket services. Because there are no economically significant prices with which to value the outputs of these services, national accountants follow the convention of estimating the expenditures on nonmarket services by summing the costs of the inputs required to produce them. PPPs for nonmarket services are calculated using input prices because these prices are consistent with the prices underlying the estimated expenditures. In practice, prices are only collected for labor, which is by far the largest and most important input.

institutional sector. The five sectors identified by the System of National Accounts: nonfinancial corporations, financial corporations, government, households, and nonprofit institutions serving households.

intercountry validation. The validation that takes place after participating economies have completed their intracountry validation and submitted their survey prices to the regional coordinator. It is an iterative process consisting of several rounds of questions and answers between the regional coordinator and participating economies. It involves editing and verifying the average survey prices reported by participating economies for a basic heading and assessing the reliability of the PPPs they produce for the basic heading. The objective is to establish that the average survey prices are for comparable items, that the items have been priced accurately, and that the allocation of important indicators is correct. In other words, it seeks to ascertain whether economies have interpreted the item specifications in the same way and whether their price collectors have priced them without error. The Quaranta and Dikhanov editing procedures are employed for this purpose. Both procedures entail detecting outliers among the average survey prices by identifying outliers among the corresponding price ratios. Economies verify the outliers found in order to ascertain whether they are valid observations. If they are not, the economy either corrects or suppresses them.

intermediate consumption. The value of the goods and services, other than fixed assets, that are used or consumed as inputs by a process of production.

intracountry validation. The validation that precedes intercountry validation. It is undertaken by participating economies prior to submitting their survey prices to the regional coordinator. Each economy edits and verifies its own prices without reference to the price data of other economies. Validation is carried out at the item level. The objective is to establish that price collectors within the economy have priced items that match the item specifications and that the prices they have reported are accurate. This entails an economy searching for outliers first among the individual prices that have been collected for each item it has chosen to survey and then among the average prices for these items. Subsequently, the economy verifies the outliers found in order to ascertain whether they are valid observations. If they are not, the economy either corrects or suppresses them.

item. A good or service that is the result of production. Items are exchanged and used for various purposes—as inputs in the production of other goods and services, for final consumption, or for investment.

item list. The common list of well-defined goods and services from which economies participating in a comparison make a selection of items to price for the purpose of compiling PPPs.

item specification. A list of the physical and economic characteristics that can be used to identify an item selected for pricing, thereby ensuring that economies price comparable items. An item specification can be either brand and model specific (that is, a specification in which a particular brand and model is stipulated) or generic (that is, a specification in which only the relevant price-determining and technical characteristics are given and no brand is designated).

Jevons index. An elementary price index that is defined as the unweighted geometric average of the current to base period price relatives.

Laspeyres-type PPP. A PPP for an aggregate between two economies, economy B and economy A, where the reference economy is economy A and the weights are those of economy A. The PPP is defined as the weighted arithmetic average of the PPPs between economy B and economy A for the basic headings covered by the aggregate. The expenditure shares of economy A are used as weights.

market price. The amount of money a willing buyer pays to acquire a good or service from a willing seller—that is, the actual price for a transaction agreed to by the transactors. It is the net price inclusive of all discounts, surcharges, and rebates applied to the transaction. Also called the transaction price.

multilateral comparison. A price or volume comparison of more than two economies simultaneously that is made with price and expenditure data from all economies covered and that produces consistent relations among all pairs of participating economies—that is, one that satisfies the transitivity requirement, among other requirements.

national annual average price. A price that has been averaged both over all localities of an economy in order to take into account the regional variations in prices and over the whole of the reference year in order to allow for seasonal variations in prices as well as general inflation and changes in price structures.

net taxes on production. Taxes less subsidies on production.

nominal expenditure. An expenditure that is valued at national price levels. It can be expressed in local currencies or in a common currency to which it has been converted with market exchange rates. It reflects both volume and price differences between economies.

nonmarket service. A service that is provided to households free or at a price that is not economically significant by nonprofit institutions serving households or by government.

nonprofit institution serving households (NPISHs). A nonprofit institution that is not predominantly financed and controlled by government, that provides goods or services to households free or at prices that are not economically significant, and whose main resources are voluntary contributions by households.

numéraire currency. The currency unit selected to be the common currency in which PPPs and real and nominal expenditures are expressed.

observation. An individual price, or one of a number of individual prices, collected for an item at an outlet.

outlet. A shop, market, service establishment, Internet site, mail order service, or other place from where goods or services can be purchased and from where the purchasers' or list prices of the items sold can be obtained.

outlier. A term generally used to describe any extreme value in a set of survey data. Extreme values are not necessarily wrong, but the fact that they are considered extreme suggests that they could be wrong. They are possible errors, and as such they need to be investigated to establish whether they are actual errors.

Paasche-type PPP. A PPP for an aggregate between two economies, economy B and economy A, where the reference economy is economy A and the weights are those of economy B. The PPP is defined as the weighted harmonic average of the PPPs between economy B and economy A for the basic headings covered by the aggregate. The expenditure shares of economy B are used as weights.

Penn effect. The overstatement of the economic size of high-income economies with high price levels and the understatement of the economic size of low-income economies with low price levels that result when market exchange rate–converted GDP is used to establish the relative sizes of economies. It arises because market exchange rates do not take into account price level differences between economies when used to convert their GDP to a common currency.

price approach. The approach whereby the price comparison between two or more economies is made by comparing the prices for a representative sample of comparable items. PPPs are generally derived using the price approach.

price level index (PLI). The ratio of PPP to an market exchange rate. PLIs provide a measure of the differences in price levels between economies by indicating for a given aggregation level the number of units of the common currency needed to buy the same volume of the aggregation level in each economy. At the level of GDP, they provide a measure of the differences in the general price levels of economies.

price measure. PPPs and the price level indexes to which they give rise.

price relative. The ratio of the price of an individual item in one economy to the price of the same item in some other economy. It shows how many units of currency A must be spent in economy A to obtain the same quantity and quality—that is, the same volume—of the item that X units of currency B purchase in economy B.

product error. An error that occurs when price collectors price items that do not match the item specification and neglect to report having done so. They may not have been aware of the mismatch, such as when the item specification is too loose, or they may have priced a substitute item as required by the pricing guidelines but failed to mention that they had done so on the price reporting form.

productivity adjustment. An adjustment made to the prices paid by nonmarket producers for labor, capital, and intermediate inputs so that they correspond to a common level of multifactor productivity. In practice, it is an adjustment made to the prices (compensation of employees) paid by nonmarket producers for labor so that they represent the same level of labor productivity.

purchaser's price. The amount paid by the purchaser in order to take delivery of a unit of a good or service at the time and place required by the purchaser. It excludes any value added tax (or similar deductible tax on products) that purchasers can deduct from their own VAT liability with respect to the VAT invoiced to their customers. It includes suppliers' retail and wholesale margins, separately invoiced transport and insurance charges, and any VAT (or similar deductible tax on products) that purchasers cannot deduct from their own VAT liability. For equipment goods, it also includes the installation costs, if applicable. The purchaser's price is the price most relevant for decision making by buyers.

purchasing power parity (PPP). Spatial price deflators and currency converters that eliminate the effects of the differences in price levels between economies, thereby allowing volume comparisons of GDP and its components.

quantity approach. The approach whereby a volume comparison between two or more economies is made by comparing the volumes of a representative sample of comparable items. Volume comparisons are usually made not directly but indirectly, by dividing the expenditure ratios between economies by their corresponding price ratios.

real expenditure. An expenditure that has been converted to a common currency and valued at a uniform price level with PPPs. It reflects only volume differences between economies.

reference PPP. The PPP used for a basic heading for which no prices are collected and no PPP is calculated. It is based on prices collected for other basic headings and serves as a proxy for the missing PPP.

reference quantity. The quantity to which the prices collected for an item must be rebased to ensure that they refer to the same quantity being compared.

reference year. The calendar year to which the results of the comparison refer.

resident population. The number of people present in the economic territory at a given point in time.

services. Outputs that are produced to order and that cannot be traded separately from their production. Ownership rights cannot be established over services, and by the time their production is completed, they must have been provided to consumers. An exception to this rule is a group of industries, generally classified as service industries, some of whose outputs have the characteristics of goods. These industries are those concerned with the provision, storage, communication, and dissemination of information, advice, and entertainment in the broadest sense of those terms. The products of these industries, where ownership rights can be established, may be classified as either goods or services, depending on the medium by which these outputs are supplied.

social transfers in kind. Individual goods and services provided as transfers in kind to individual households by government units (including social security funds) and nonprofit institutions serving households. The goods and services can be purchased on the market or produced as nonmarket output by government units or nonprofit institutions serving households.

subsidies on production. Subsidies on goods and services produced as outputs by resident enterprises that become payable as a result of the production of these goods or services (that is, subsidies payable per unit of good or service produced) as well as subsidies that resident enterprises may receive as a consequence of engaging in production (for example, subsidies to reduce pollution or to increase employment). The former are called subsidies on products; the latter are called other subsidies on production.

System of National Accounts (SNA). The internationally agreed-on standard set of recommendations on how to compile measures of economic activity. The SNA describes a coherent, consistent, and integrated set of macroeconomic accounts in the context of a set of internationally agreed-on concepts, definitions, classifications, and accounting rules.

taxes on production. Taxes on the goods and services produced as outputs by resident enterprises that become payable as a result of the production of these goods or services (that is, taxes payable per unit of good or service produced, such as excise duties and a nondeductible value added tax) as well as taxes that resident enterprises may pay as a consequence of engaging in production (for example, payroll taxes and taxes on motor vehicles). The former are called taxes on products; the latter are called other taxes on production.

transitivity. The property whereby the direct PPP between any two economies yields the same result as an indirect comparison via any other economy. For example, for economies A, B, and C, the ratio of the PPP between A and B and the PPP between C and B is equal to the PPP between A and C, so that $PPP_{A/C} = PPP_{A/B} / PPP_{C/B}$.

user cost method. The method of estimating the value of imputed rentals for owner-occupiers by summing the relevant cost items: intermediate consumption (current maintenance and repairs, insurance), consumption of fixed capital, other taxes on production, and net operating surplus (nominal rate of return on the capital invested in the dwelling and land).

value added tax (VAT). A tax on products collected in stages by enterprises. This wide-ranging tax is usually designed to cover most or all goods and services. Producers are obliged to pay the government only the difference between the VAT on their sales and the VAT on their purchases for intermediate consumption or capital formation. The VAT is not usually levied on exports.

verification. The second step of validation, which entails investigating the possible errors detected during the editing of survey prices to establish whether they are actual errors and, if they are actual errors, correcting or suppressing them. In many cases, verification will require revisiting the outlets where the prices were collected to determine whether what was priced matches the item description and whether the correct price and quantity were recorded. Price observations found to be incorrect should be either eliminated or replaced by the correct observation.

volume index. A weighted average of the relative levels in the quantities of a specified set of goods and services between two economies. The quantities have to be homogeneous, and the relative levels for the different goods and services must be weighted by their economic importance as measured by their values in one or other or both economies.

volume measure. Volume measures are the real expenditures, the real expenditures per capita, and the volume indexes to which they give rise.

References

Clark, Colin. 1940. *The Conditions of Economic Progress.* London: Macmillan.

Clark, Colin. 1951. *The Conditions of Economic Progress, 2nd edition.* London: Macmillan.

Clark, Colin. 1957. *The Conditions of Economic Progress, 3rd edition.* London: Macmillan.

ECOSOC (United Nations Economic and Social Council). 1999. "Evaluation of the International Comparison Programme." ECOSOC, New York.

ECOSOC (United Nations Economic and Social Council). 2008. "Friends of the Chair: Review of the International Comparison Programme, 2005 Round." ECOSOC, New York.

ECOSOC (United Nations Economic and Social Council). 2016. "Final Report of the Friends of the Chair Group on the Evaluation of the 2011 Round of the International Comparison Programme." ECOSOC, New York.

Eurostat. 2008. *Statistical Classification of Products by Activity in the European Economic Community 2008.* Luxembourg: Publications Office of the European Union.

Gilbert, M., and Associates. 1958. *Comparative National Products and Price Levels: A Study of Western Europe and the United States.* Paris: Organisation for Economic Co-operation and Development.

Gilbert, M., and I. Kravis. 1954. *An International Comparison of National Products and the Purchasing Power of Currencies: A Study of the United States, the United Kingdom, France, Germany, and Italy.* Paris: Organisation for Economic Co-operation and Development.

Inklaar, Robert, and Prasada Rao. 2020. "ICP PPP Time Series Implementation." World Bank, Washington, DC.

Kravis, Irving B., Alan Heston, and Robert Summers. 1978. *International Comparisons of Real Product and Purchasing Power*. Baltimore: Johns Hopkins University Press.

Kravis, Irving B., Alan Heston, Robert Summers, and Irving Kravis. 1982. *World Product and Income: International Comparisons of Real Gross Product.* Baltimore: Johns Hopkins University Press.

Kravis, Irving B., Zoltan Kenessey, Alan Wiley Heston, and Robert Summers. 1975. *A System of International Comparisons of Gross Product and Purchasing Power.* Washington, DC: World Bank.

UNSC (United Nations Statistical Commission). 1993. *System of National Accounts 1993.* New York: UNSC.

UNSC (United Nations Statistics Commission). 2009. *System of National Accounts 2008.* New York: UNSC.

UNSD (United Nations Statistics Division). 2000a. *Classification of Individual Consumption According to Purpose (COICOP).* Classification of Expenditure According to Purpose. New York: United Nations.

UNSD (United Nations Statistics Division). 2000b. *Classification of the Purposes of Non-Profit Institutions Serving Households (COPNI).* Classification of Expenditure According to Purpose. New York: United Nations.

UNSD (United Nations Statistics Division). 2000c. "Classification of Expenditure According to Purpose." In *Classification of the Functions of Government (COFOG).* New York: United Nations.

World Bank. 2008a. *Global Purchasing Power Parities and Real Expenditures: 2005 International Comparison Program.* Washington, DC: World Bank.

World Bank. 2008b. "International Comparison Program Archiving and Accessing ICP 2005 Results." World Bank, Washington, DC.

World Bank. 2012. "2011 ICP Data Access and Archiving Policy: Guiding Principles and Procedures for Data Access." World Bank, Washington, DC.

World Bank. 2013. *Measuring the Real Size of the World Economy: The Framework, Methodology, and Results of the International Comparison Program—ICP.* Washington, DC: World Bank.

World Bank. 2014. *Purchasing Power Parities and Real Expenditures of World Economics: A Comprehensive Report of the 2011 International Comparison Program.* Washington, DC: World Bank.

World Bank. 2015. *Operational Guidelines and Procedures for Measuring the Real Size of the World Economy.* Washington, DC: World Bank.

World Bank. 2016a. "International Comparison Program Classification of Final Expenditure on GDP." World Bank, Washington, DC.

World Bank. 2016b. "International Comparison Program Governance Framework." World Bank, Washington, DC.

World Bank. 2017. "International Comparison Program Research Agenda for the 2017 Cycle and Beyond." World Bank, Washington, DC.

World Bank. 2019a. "International Comparison Program Data Access and Archive Policy." World Bank, Washington, DC.

World Bank. 2019b. "International Comparison Program Revision Policy." World Bank, Washington, DC.

www.ingramcontent.com/pod-product-compliance
Lightning Source LLC
LaVergne TN
LVHW080047210926
848481LV00011B/3293